THE CAMBRIDGE HISTORY OF LAW IN AMERICA

VOLUME I

Early America (1580–1815)

Law stands at the center of modern American life. Since the 1950s, American historians have produced an extraordinarily rich and diverse literature that has vastly expanded our knowledge of this familiar and vital yet complex and multifaceted phenomenon. But few attempts have been made to take full account of law's American history. *The Cambridge History of Law in America* has been designed for just this purpose. In three volumes we put on display all the intellectual vitality and variety of contemporary American legal history. We present as comprehensive and authoritative an account as possible of the present understanding and range of interpretation of the history of American law. We suggest where future research may lead.

American legal history has long treated the era of the founding of the republic and the early nineteenth century as its proper point of departure. Volume I of this *History* disputes that tendency, beginning our account of law in America with the very first moments of English colonization and settlement of the North American landmass. It follows those processes across 200 years to the eventual creation and stabilization of the American republic. Colonization, the fate of the seaboard's indigenous peoples, the creation of structures of jurisdiction and governance, patterns of imperial communication, the migration (voluntary and involuntary) of peoples and the disciplines to which they were subject, the construction of essential social categories and institutions (families, labor forces, plantations, slavery), economic and commercial activity, religion, the strains and ruptures of empire, revolutionary and constitutional politics: these are the material and imaginative worlds of early American law. All this is encompassed in our first volume.

The Cambridge History of Law in America has been made possible by the generous support of the American Bar Foundation. Volumes II and III cover the history of law, respectively, from the foundation of the republic until the immediate aftermath of World War I and from the 1920s until the early twenty-first century.

Michael Grossberg is the Sally M. Reahard Professor of History and a Professor of Law at Indiana University. His research focuses on the relationship between law and social change, particularly the intersection of law and the family.

Christopher Tomlins is Senior Research Fellow at the American Bar Foundation in Chicago. His research encompasses the relationship among labor, colonization, and law in early America; the conceptual history of police in Anglo-American law and politics; and the place of historical materialism in legal theory.

THE CAMBRIDGE HISTORY OF LAW IN AMERICA

VOLUME I

Early America (1580–1815)

Edited by

MICHAEL GROSSBERG

Indiana University

CHRISTOPHER TOMLINS

The American Bar Foundation, Chicago

CAMBRIDGE
UNIVERSITY PRESS

CAMBRIDGE UNIVERSITY PRESS
Cambridge, New York, Melbourne, Madrid, Cape Town, Singapore, São Paulo, Delhi

Cambridge University Press
32 Avenue of the Americas, New York, NY 10013-2473, USA

www.cambridge.org
Information on this title: www.cambridge.org/9780521803052

First published 2008

Printed in the United States of America

A catalog record for this publication is available from the British Library.

Library of Congress Cataloging in Publication Data

The Cambridge history of law in America / edited by Michael Grossberg,
Christopher Tomlins.
p. cm.
Includes bibliographical references and index.
ISBN 978-0-521-80305-2 (hardback)
1. Law – United States – History. I. Grossberg, Michael, 1950– II. Tomlins,
Christopher L., 1951– III. Title.
KF352.C36 2007
349.73 – dc22 2007017606

ISBN 978-0-521-80305-2 hardback

CONTENTS

EDITORS' PREFACE

In February 1776, declaiming against the oppressive and absolute rule of "the Royal Brute of Britain," the revolutionary pamphleteer Tom Paine announced to the world that "so far as we approve of monarchy . . . in America THE LAW IS KING"! Paine's declaration of Americans' "common sense" of the matter turned out to be an accurate forecast of the authority the legal order would amass in the revolutionary republic. Indeed, Paine's own fiery call to action was one of the stimuli that would help his prediction come true. We know ourselves that what he claimed for law then mostly remains true now. Yet, we should note, Paine's claim was not simply prophecy; it made sense in good part because of foundations already laid. Long before 1776, law and legal institutions had gained a place of some prominence in the British American colonies. The power and position of law, in other words, are apparent throughout American history, from its earliest moments. The three volumes of *The Cambridge History of Law in America* explain why Paine's synoptic insight should be understood as both an eloquent foretelling of what would be and an accurate summation of what already was.

The Cambridge History of Law in America belongs to a long and proud scholarly tradition. In March 1896, at the instigation of Frederick William Maitland, Downing Professor of the Laws of England at Cambridge University, and of Henry Jackson, tutor in Greek at Trinity College, the syndics of Cambridge University Press invited the University's Regius Professor of Modern History, Lord John Dalberg Acton, to undertake "the general direction of a History of the World." Six months later Acton returned with a plan for a (somewhat) more restrained endeavor, an account of Europe and the United States from *The Renaissance* to *The Latest Age*. Thus was born *The Cambridge Modern History*.

Acton's plan described a collaborative, collectively written multi-volume history. Under general editorial guidance, each volume would be divided among "specially qualified writers" primed to present extensive and authoritative accounts of their subjects.[1] They were to imagine themselves writing less for other professional historians than for a more general audience of "students of history" – anyone, that is, who sought an authoritative, thoughtful, and sophisticated assessment of a particular historical subject or issue. Acton envisioned a history largely clean of the professional apparatus of reference and citation – texts that would demonstrate the "highest pitch of knowledge without the display," reliant for their authority on the expertise of the authors chosen to write them. And although it was intended that the *History* be the most complete general statement of historical knowledge available, and to that extent definitive, Acton was not interested in simply reproducing (and thus by implication freezing) what was known. He desired that his authors approach the task critically, strive for originality in their research, and take it on themselves to revise and improve the knowledge they encountered.[2]

Acton did not live to see even the first volume in print, but between 1902 and 1911 *The Cambridge Modern History* appeared in twelve substantial volumes under the editorial direction of Adolphus Ward and Stanley Leathes. The *History* quickly found a broad audience – the first volume, *The Renaissance*, sold out in a month. Other Cambridge histories soon followed: *The Cambridge History of English Literature*, which began to appear under Ward's editorship in 1907; *The Cambridge Medieval History* (1911–36); *The Cambridge History of American Literature* (1917–21); *The Cambridge Ancient History* (1923–39); *The Cambridge History of the British Empire* (1929–67); *The Cambridge History of India* (1922–60), and more. All told, close to a hundred Cambridge histories have been published. More than fifty are currently in print. Cambridge histories have justly become famous. They are to be found in the collections of libraries and individuals throughout the world.

Acton's plan for *The Cambridge Modern History* invoked certain essentials – an ideal of collective authorship and a commitment to make expertise accessible to a wider audience than simply other specialists. To these he added grander, programmatic touches. The *History* would be "an epic," a "great argument" conveying "forward progress . . . upward growth." And it would provide "chart and compass for the coming century." Such ambitions are

[1] When, early on, Acton ran into difficulties in recruiting authors for his intimidating project, Maitland gently suggested that "his omniscient lordship" simply write the whole thing himself. Acton (we note with some relief) demurred. There is humor here, but also principle. Collective authorship is a practice ingrained in the Cambridge histories from the beginning.

[2] Our account of Acton's plan and its realization gratefully relies throughout on Josef L. Altholz, "Lord Acton and the Plan of the *Cambridge Modern History*," *The Historical Journal*, 39, no. 3 (September 1996), 723–36.

characteristic of Acton's moment – the later nineteenth century – when in Britain and Continental Europe history still claimed an educative mantle "of practical utility," the means rather than science (or law) to equip both elites and ordinary citizens "to deal with the problems of their time." It was a moment, also, when history's practitioners could still imagine filling historical time with a consistent, standardized account – the product, to be sure, of many minds, but minds that thought enough alike to agree on an essential common purpose: "men acting together for no other object than the increase of accurate knowledge." Here was history (accurate knowledge) as "the teacher and the guide that regulates public life," the means by which "the recent past" would yield up "the key to present time." Here as well, lest we too quickly dismiss the vision as naïve or worse, was the shouldering of a certain responsibility. "We have to describe the ruling currents, to interpret the sovereign forces, that still govern and divide the world. There are, I suppose, at least a score of them, in politics, economics, philosophy and religion. . . . But if we carry history down to the last syllable of recorded time, and leave the reader at the point where study passes into action, we must explain to him the cause, and the growth, and the power of every great intellectual movement, and equip him for many encounters of life."

Acton's model – a standard general history, a guiding light produced by and for an intellectually confident elite – could not survive the shattering effects of two world wars. It could not survive the democratization of higher education, the proliferation of historical scholarship, the constant emergence of new fields and subdisciplines, the eventual decentering of Europe and "the West." When, amid the rubble and rationing of a hastily de-colonizing post–World War II Britain, Cambridge University Press's syndics decided a revised version was required – a *New Cambridge Modern History* for a new day – their decision acknowledged how much the world had changed. The revised version bore them out. Gone was Acton's deep faith in history's authority and grandeur. The general editor, G. N. Clark, wrote, "Historians in our self-critical age are aware that there will not be general agreement with their conclusions, nor even with some of the premises which they regard as self-evident. They must be content to set out their own thought without reserve and to respect the differences which they cannot eradicate" – including, he might have added (but perhaps there was no need) the many fundamental differences that existed among historians themselves. Cambridge histories no longer aspired to create standardized accounts of the way things had been nor to use the past to pick the lock on the future. The differences in perspective and purpose that a less confident, more self-critical age had spawned were now the larger part of the picture.

Yet the genre Acton helped found has now entered its second century. It still bears, in some fashion, his imprint. The reason it has survived, indeed prospered, has less to do with some sense of overall common purpose than the more modest but nevertheless essential precept of continued adherence to certain core principles of design simply because they have worked: individual scholars charged to synthesize the broad sweep of current knowledge of a particular topic, but also free to present an original interpretation aimed at encouraging both reflection and further scholarship, and an overall architecture that encourages new understandings of an entire subject or area of historical scholarship. Neither encyclopedias nor compilations, textbooks nor works of reference, Cambridge histories have become something quite unique – each an avowedly collective endeavor that offers the single best point of entry to the wide range of an historical subject, topic, or field; each in overall conceptual design and substance intent not simply on defining its field's development to date but on pushing it forward with new ideas. Critique and originality, revision and improvement of knowledge – all remain germane.

Readers will find that *The Cambridge History of Law in America* adheres to these core goals. Of course, like other editors we have our own particular ambitions. And so the three volumes of this Cambridge history have been designed to present to full advantage the intellectual vitality and variety of contemporary American legal history. Necessarily then – and inevitably – *The Cambridge History of Law in America* dwells on areas of concern and interpretive debates that preoccupy the current generation of legal historians. We do not ignore our predecessors.[3] Nor, however, do we attempt in the body of the *History* to chart the development of the field over their time and ours in any great detail. Readers will find a more substantial accounting of that development in the bibliographic essays that accompany each chapter, but as editors we have conceived our job to be to facilitate the presentation of as comprehensive and authoritative a rendition of the present understanding of the history of American law as possible and to suggest where future research may lead.

Cambridge histories always define their audiences widely; ours is no exception. One part of our intended audience is scholarly, but hardly confined to other legal historians; they are already the best equipped to know something of what is retailed here. So to an important extent we try to look past legal historians to historians at large. We also look beyond history to scholars across the broad sweep of law, the humanities, and the social sciences – indeed to any scholar who may find a turn to law's history useful (or simply diverting) in answering questions about law and society in America.

[3] See, for example, the graceful retrieval and reexamination of themes from the "imperial school" of American colonial historians undertaken by Mary Sarah Bilder in Volume I, Chapter 3.

A second part of our audience is the legal profession. Lawyers and judges experience in their professional lives something of a practical encounter with the past, although the encounter may not be one they would recognize as "historical." As John Reid has written, "The lawyer and the historian have in common the fact that they go to the past for evidence, but there the similarity largely ends." Here lawyers and judges can discover for themselves what historians do with evidence. In the process, they will also discover that not inconsiderable attention has been paid to their own lives and experiences. Legal historians have always known how important legal thought and legal education are in the formation of the professional world of the law, and both feature prominently in this *History*. Here the profession encounters the history of its activities and of the medium it inhabits from a standpoint outside itself.

The third segment of our intended audience is the general public. Our purposes in this encounter are not Acton's. We do not present this *History* as the means to educate a citizenry to deal with the problems of the moment. (Indeed, it is worth noting that in America law appropriated that role to itself from the earliest days of the republic.) Like G. N. Clark, today's historians live in self-critical times and have lower expectations than Lord Acton of what historical practice might achieve. That said, readers will find that this *History* touches on many past attempts to use law to "deal with" many past problems: in the America where law is king, it has been law's fate to be so employed. And if their accounts leave some of our authors critical in their analysis of outcomes or simply rueful in recounting the hubris (or worse) of the attempts, that in itself can be counted an education of sorts. Moreover, as Volume III's chapters show repeatedly, Americans continue to turn to law as their key medium of private problem solving and public policy formation and implementation, and on an expanding – global – stage. In that light, there is perhaps something for us to learn from Acton's acknowledgment that the scholar-expert should not abandon the reader "at the point where study passes into action." We can at the very least offer some reflection on what an encounter with the past might bring by way of advice to the "many encounters of life" lying ahead.

In reaching all three of our intended audiences, we are greatly assisted by the pronounced tendency to "demystify" and diversify its subject that has characterized American legal history for a half-century. To some, the field's very title – "legal history" – will conjure merely an arcane preoccupation with obscure terminologies and baffling texts, the doctrines and practices of old (hence defunct) law, of no obvious utility to the outsider whether historian or social scientist or practicing lawyer or just plain citizen. No doubt, legal history has at times given grounds to suppose that such a view of the discipline is generally warranted. But what is interesting in American legal history as currently practiced is just how inappropriate that characterization seems.

To read the encomia that have accumulated over the years, one might suppose that the demise of legal history's obscurity was the single-handed achievement of one man, James Willard Hurst, who on his death in 1997 was described in the *New York Times* as "the dean of American legal historians." Indeed, Hurst himself occasionally suggested the same thing; it was he who came up with the aphorism "snakes in Ireland" to describe legal history in America at the time he began working in the field in the 1930s. Though not an immodest man, it seems clear whom he cast as St. Patrick. Yet the *Times'* description was merited. Hurst's lifework – the unpacking of the changing roles of American law, market, and state from the early nineteenth to the early twentieth centuries – set the agenda of American legal historians from the 1950s well into the 1980s. That agenda was a liberation from narrower and more formalistic preoccupations, largely with the remote origins of contemporary legal doctrine or with the foundations of American constitutionalism, that had characterized the field, such as it was, earlier in the century. Most important, Hurst's work displayed some recognition of the multidimensionality of law in society – as instrument, the hallmark with which he is most associated, but also as value and as power. Hurst, in short, brought legal history into a continuing dialogue with modernity, capitalism, and the liberal state, a dialogue whose rich dividends are obvious in this *History*.

Lawyers have sometimes asked aggressively anachronistic questions of history, like – to use an apocryphal example of Robert Gordon's – "Did the framers of the Constitution confer on the federal government the power to construct an interstate highway system?" Hurstian legal history did not indulge such questions. But Hurstians did demonstrate a gentler anachronism in their restriction of the scope of the subject and their interpretation of it. Famously, for Hurst, American legal history did not begin until the nineteenth century. And when it did begin it showed a certain consistency in cause and effect. As Kermit Hall summarized the view in 1989, "Our legal history reflects back to us generations of pragmatic decision making rather than a quest for ideological purity and consistency. Personal and group interests have always ordered the course of legal development; instrumentalism has been the way of the law."[4] The Hurstian determination to demystify law occasionally reduced it to transparency – a dependent variable of society and economy (particularly economy) tied functionally to social and economic change.

[4] Kermit L. Hall, *The Magic Mirror: Law in American History* (New York, 1989), 335.

As a paradigm for the field, Hurstian legal history long since surrendered its dominance. What has replaced it? In two words, astonishing variety. Legal historians are aware that one cannot talk or write about economic or social or political or intellectual history, or indeed much of any kind of history, without immediately entering into realms of definition, prohibition, understanding, practice, and behavior that must imply law to have meaning. Try talking about property in any of those contexts, for example, without implying law. Today's legal historians are deeply engaged across the full range of historical investigation in demonstrating the inextricable salience of law in human affairs. As important, the interests of American historians at large have never been more overtly legal in their implications than now. To take just four popular areas of inquiry in American history – citizenship and civic personality, identity, spatiality, and the etiology of social hierarchy and subordination – it is simply impossible to imagine how one could approach any of these areas historically without engaging with law, legal ideology, legal institutions, legal practices, and legal discourse. Legal historians have been and remain deeply engaged with and influenced by social history, and as that field has drifted closer and closer to cultural history and the historical construction of identity so legal history has moved with it. The interpretive salience of race and ethnicity, of gender and class is as strong in contemporary legal historical practice as in any other realm of history. Add to that the growing influence of legal pluralism in legal history – the migration of the field from a focus on "the law" to a focus on the conditions of existence of "legality" and the competition of many alternative "legalities" – and one finds oneself at work in a field of immense opportunity and few dogmas.

"Astonishing variety" demonstrates vitality, but also suggests the benefits of a judicious collective effort at authoritative summation. The field has developed at an extraordinary rate since the early 1970s, but offers no work that could claim to approach the full range of our understanding of the American legal past.[5] *The Cambridge History of Law in America* addresses both

[5] The field has two valuable single-author surveys: Lawrence M. Friedman's *A History of American Law* (New York, 1973; 3rd ed. 2005) and Kermit Hall's *The Magic Mirror*. Neither approaches the range of what is on display here. The field also boasts volumes of cases and commentary, prepared according to the law teaching "case book" model, such as Stephen B. Presser and Jamil S. Zainaldin, *Law and Jurisprudence in American History: Cases and Materials* (St. Paul, MN, 1980; 6th ed. 2006) and Kermit Hall, et al., *American Legal History, Cases and Materials* (New York, 3rd ed., 2003). There also exist edited volumes of commentary and materials that focus on broad subject areas within the discipline of legal history; a preponderance deal with constitutional law, such as Lawrence M. Friedman and Harry N. Scheiber, eds., *American Law and the Constitutional Order: Historical Perspectives* (Cambridge, MA, 1978; enlarged ed. 1988). Valuable in

the vitality of variety and its organizational challenge. Individually, each chapter in each volume is a comprehensive interrogation of a key issue in a particular period of American legal history. Each is intended to extend the substantive and interpretative boundaries of our knowledge of that issue. The topics they broach range widely – from the design of British colonizing to the design of the successor republic and of its successive nineteenth- and twentieth-century reincarnations; from legal communications within empires to communications among nation-states within international law to a sociology of the "legalization" that enwraps contemporary globalism; from changes in legal doctrine to litigation trend assessments; from clashes over law and religion to the intersection of law and popular culture; from the movement of peoples to the production of subalternship among people (the indigenous, slaves, dependents of all kinds); and from the discourse of law to the discourse of rights. Chapters also deal with developments in specific areas of law and of the legal system – crime and criminal justice, economic and commercial regulation, immigration and citizenship, technology and environment, military law, family law, welfare law, public health and medicine, and antitrust.[6]

Individual chapters illustrate the dynamism and immense breadth of American legal history. Collectively, they neither exhaust its substance nor impose a new interpretive regimen on the field. Quite the contrary, *The Cambridge History of Law in America* intentionally calls forth the broad array of methods and arguments that legal historians have developed. The contents of each volume demonstrate not just that expansion of subject and method is common to every period of American legal history but also that as the long-ascendant socio-legal perspective has given way to an increasing diversity of analytical approaches, new interpretive opportunities are rife everywhere. Note the influence of regionalism in Volume I and of institutionalism in Volume II. Note the attention paid in Volume III not only to race and gender but also to sexuality. The *History* shows how legal history

their own right, such volumes are intended as specific-purpose teaching tools and do not purport to be comprehensive. Finally, there are, of course, particular monographic works that have proven widely influential for their conceptual acuity, or their capacity to set a completely new tone in the way the field at large is interpreted. The most influential have been such studies as James Willard Hurst, *Law and the Conditions of Freedom in the Nineteenth-Century United States* (Madison, WI, 1956), and Morton J. Horwitz, *The Transformation of American Law, 1780–1860* (Cambridge, MA, 1977).

[6] Following the tradition of Cambridge histories, each chapter includes only such footnotes as the author deems necessary to document essential (largely primary) sources. In place of the dense display of citations beloved of scholarly discourse that Acton's aesthetic discouraged, each author has written a bibliographic essay that provides a summary of his or her sources and a guide to scholarly work on the subject.

has entered dialogue with the full array of "histories" pursued within the academy – political, intellectual, social, cultural, economic, business, diplomatic, and military – and with their techniques.

The Cambridge History of Law in America is more than the sum of its parts. The *History*'s conceptual design challenges existing understandings of the field. We divide the American legal past into three distinct eras and devote a complete volume to each one: first *Early America*, then *The Long Nineteenth Century*, and last *The Twentieth Century and After*. The first volume, *Early America*, examines the era from the late sixteenth century through the early nineteenth – from the beginnings of European settlement through the creation and stabilization of the American republic. The second volume, *The Long Nineteenth Century*, begins with the appearance of the United States in the constituted form of a nation-state in 1789; it ends in 1920, in the immediate aftermath of World War I, with the world poised on the edge of the "American Century." The final volume, *The Twentieth Century and After*, concentrates on that American century both at home and abroad and peers into the murk of the twenty-first century. Within each of these broad chronological divisions occurs a much more detailed subdivision that combines an appreciation of chronology with the necessities of topical specialization.

Where appropriate, topics are revisited in successive volumes (crime and criminal justice, domestic relations law, legal thought, and legal education are all examples). Discussion of economic growth and change is ubiquitous, but we accord it no determinative priority. To facilitate comparisons and contrasts within and between eras, sequences of subjects have been arranged in similar order in each volume. Specific topics have been chosen with an eye to their historical significance and their social, institutional, and cultural coherence. They cannot be walled off from each other, so readers will notice substantive overlaps when more than one author fastens on the same issues, often to create distinct interpretations of them. History long since ceased to speak with one voice. In this *History*, readers are invited into a conversation.

Readers will notice that our chronology creates overlaps at the margins of each era. They will also notice that some chapters focus on only particular decades within a specific era[7] or span more than one era.[8] All this is

[7] Chronologically specific topics – the American Revolution and the creation of the republic in Volume I, the Civil War in Volume II, the New Deal era in Volume III – are treated as such. Chapters on the legal profession in Volumes II and III divide its development at the Civil War, as do those, in Volume II, on the state and on industrial organization.

[8] Volume II's chapter on the military deals with both the nineteenth and twentieth centuries, as do Volume III's chapters on agriculture and the state and on law and the environment. The latter chapter, indeed, also gestures toward the colonial period.

intentional. Historians construct history by placing subjects in relation to each other within the continuum of historical time. Historians manipulate time by creating periods to organize the placement of subjects. Thus, when historians say that a subject has been "historicized," they mean it has been located in what they consider its appropriate historical-temporal context or period. Slicing and dicing time in this fashion is crucial to the historian's objective of rendering past action coherent and comprehensible, but necessarily it has a certain arbitrariness. No matter how familiar – the colonial period, the Gilded Age, the Progressive period, and so forth – no historical period is a natural division: all are constructs. Hence we construct three "eras" in the interests of organizational coherence, but our overlaps and the distinct chronologies chosen by certain of our authors allow us to recognize different temporalities at work.

That said, the tripartite division of these volumes is intended to provide a new overall conceptual schema for American legal history, one that is broad and accommodating but that locates legal history in the contours of American history at large. Maitland never forgot that, at bottom, just as religious history is history not theology, legal history is history not law. Notwithstanding law's normative and prescriptive authority in "our" culture, it is a phenomenon for historical inquiry, not the source of an agenda. And so we take our cue, broadly, from American history. If it is anything, American history is the history of the colonization and settlement of the North American mainland, it is the history of the creation and expansion of an American nation-state, and it is the history of that state's place in and influence on the world at large. The contents and the organization of *The Cambridge History of Law in America* speak to how law became king in this America and of the multitudinous empire of people and possibilities over which that king reigned. Thus we address ourselves to the endless ramifications, across more than four centuries, of the meaning of Tom Paine's exclamation in 1776.

The Cambridge History of Law in America could not have been produced without the support and commitment of the American Bar Foundation, Cambridge University Press, and our cadre of authors. We thank them all.

The American Bar Foundation housed the project and, together with the Press, funded it. The Foundation was there at the creation: it helped initiate the project by sponsoring a two-day meeting of an ad hoc editorial consulting group in January 2000. Members of that group (Laura Edwards, Tony Freyer, Robert Gordon, Bruce H. Mann, William Novak, Stephen Siegel, Barbara Young Welke, and Victoria Saker Woeste) patiently debated the editors' initial thoughts on the conceptual and intellectual direction that the *History* should follow and helped identify potential contributors. Since then, the project has benefited from the support of two ABF directors, Bryant Garth and his successor Robert Nelson, and the sustained and enthusiastic interest of the Foundation's Board of Directors during the tenure of four Board presidents: Jacqueline Allee, M. Peter Moser, the late Robert Hetlage, and David Tang. We owe a particular debt of gratitude to Robert MacCrate for his early support and encouragement. As all this suggests, the American Bar Foundation's role in the production of *The Cambridge History of Law in America* has been of decisive importance. The part the Foundation has played underlines its standing as the preeminent research center for the study of law and society in the United States and its long tradition of support for the development of American legal history.

Cambridge University Press has, of course, been central to the project throughout. We are grateful to the syndics for their encouragement and to Frank Smith and his staff in New York for their assistance and support. Frank first suggested the project in 1996. He continued to suggest it for three years until we finally succumbed. During the years the *History* has been in development, Frank has accumulated one responsibility after another at the Press. Once we rubbed shoulders with the Executive Editor for Social Sciences. Now we address our pleas to the Editorial Director for Academic Books. But Frank will always be a history editor at heart, and he has maintained a strong interest in this *History*, always available with sage advice as the project rolled relentlessly onward. He helped the editors understand the intellectual ambitions of a Cambridge history. Those who have had the privilege of working with Frank Smith will know how important his advice and friendship have been to us throughout.

Finally, the editors want to thank the authors of the chapters in these volumes. A project like this is not to every author's taste – some took to it more easily than others. But together the sixty authors who joined us to write the *History* have done a magnificent job, and we are deeply grateful to every one. From the beginning our goal was not only to recruit as participants those whom all would identify as leading figures of our field but also to include those who, we were confident, would be leading figures of its next generation. We are delighted that so many of each were willing. We acknowledge also those who were unable for one reason or another to see an initial commitment through to the end: their efforts, too, helped us define and establish the project. And obviously, we owe a particular debt to those others who came later to take the places of the fallen.

To oversee a project in which so many people have at one time or another been involved has seemed on occasion like being the mayors of a village. People arrive and (much less frequently, thank goodness) depart. Those who settle in for the duration become a community of friends and neighbors. Over time, one learns much from one's friends and neighbors about the joys and vicissitudes of life. One learns who (and whose family) may be ailing, and who is well. One learns of hurts and difficulties; one revels in successes. And one may learn, as we did so sadly in August 2006, of an untimely death. Notwithstanding the demands of his immensely successful career in academic administration, our colleague Kermit Hall never laid down his historian's pen and was an enthusiastic participant in this project. He died suddenly and unexpectedly. His contributions to the field have been great, and he is greatly missed.

Throughout, the many authors in this project have responded courteously to our editorial advice. They have reacted with grace and occasional humor to our endless demands that they meet their deadlines. Sometimes they even sent their manuscripts too. Most important, they have striven to achieve what we asked of them – the general goals of a Cambridge history and the specific goals of *this* history, as we have described them in this preface. Their achievements are evident in the pages of each volume. In an individualistic intellectual culture, the scholarship on display here demonstrates the possibilities inherent in a collective intellectual enterprise. In the end, of course, the editors, not the authors, are responsible for the contents of these volumes. Yet, it is the authors who have given the *History* its meaning and significance.

Michael Grossberg
Christopher Tomlins

1

LAW, COLONIZATION, LEGITIMATION, AND THE EUROPEAN BACKGROUND

ANTHONY PAGDEN

The conquest, occupation, and settlement of the Americas was the first large-scale European colonizing venture since the fall of the Roman Empire. Like the Roman Empire, various occupying powers acquired overseas possessions in territories in which they had no clear and obvious authority. Their actions demanded an extensive reexamination, and sometimes reworking, of whole areas of the legal systems of early modern Europe, just as they threw into question earlier assumptions about the nature of sovereignty, utterly transformed international relations, and were ultimately responsible for the evolution of what would eventually come to be called "international law."

Broadly understood, the legal questions raised by this new phase in European history can be broken down into three general categories: the legitimacy of the occupation of territories that, prima facie at least, were already occupied; the authority, if any, that the colonizers might acquire over the inhabitants of those territories; and – ultimately the most pressing question of all – the nature of the legal relationship between metropolitan authority and the society that the colonists themselves would establish.

Of the five major European powers to establish large-scale and enduring settlements on the American mainland – Spain, Portugal, Holland, France, and England – the English were relative latecomers. Although there are more similarities between them and the other European colonial powers than has sometimes been supposed, in many respects both the legal character and the administration of their colonies were unusual. The overseas possessions of the Spanish, despite early incorporation into the Crown of Castile, were legally identified as separate kingdoms – the *reinos de Indias* – governed by a separate body of legislation (codified in 1680) and administered by a royal council whose functions were similar to those of the councils that administered the European regions of the empire: Italy, Flanders, and Castile itself. The Spanish possessions were thus a separate but legally incorporated part of a single imperium, embodied in the person of the monarch – what has often be referred to as a "composite monarchy." The Portuguese overseas dependencies were, with the exception of Brazil, trading stations (*feitorias*) not dissimilar to the factories the English later established in Asia and were under the direct control of the crown. The French kings looked on New France – what would later become Canada – as part of the royal demesne. However, unlike their English neighbors, the French settlers were governed according to a body of local administrative law called the *Coutume de Paris*, a situation that would determine the ideological shape of the empire until the collapse of the monarchy itself. The Dutch Republic's possessions in America, both in the New Netherlands and, while it lasted, New Holland (a part of Portuguese Brazil that the Dutch held between 1630 and 1654), were held by the Dutch West Indian Company, which had a monopoly on all land and trading concessions. The governors appointed to the regions by the Dutch Republic were officers in the Company's employ. The laws they administered were those of the Dutch Republic, and Dutch settlers in the Americas never thought of themselves as anything other than Dutchmen overseas.

By contrast, each of the thirteen colonies that were eventually to make up the United States, from Puritan New England to Catholic Avalon, had a different foundation, a different form of administration, and represented different demographic and cultural aspects of the of the British Isles. The legal status of the English colonies was also both more varied and much less precisely defined than that of their Spanish, Portuguese, French, or Dutch (or even later their Swedish, Russian, and German) counterparts. Some colonies were proprietary, like Maryland; some were corporate, in which the King had granted powers of self-government to a company or to a body of settlers, like Massachusetts. Virginia (after 1624) and New York were administered directly by the Crown (as was Maryland between 1689 and 1715). As Edmund and William Burke noted in 1757, "There is scarce any form of government known, that does not prevail in some of our plantations."[1]

The same applied to the various legal systems employed throughout the colonies. As one anonymous settler in Virginia complained in the early eighteenth century, "No one can tell what is law and what is not in the Plantations."[2] The English common law, unlike the law in Spain and France during the sixteenth century, was uncodified. The absence of any accepted body of legislation made the resulting conflict between the Parliament,

[1] Edmund and William Burke, *An Account of the European Settlements in America*, 2 vols. (London, 1757), II: 288–9.

[2] Quoted in Craig Yirush, *From the Perspective of Empire: the Common Law, Natural Rights and the Formation of American Political Theory, 1689–1775*. Unpublished PhD diss., Johns Hopkins University, 2004, Chapter 2.

the Crown, and the various colonies and overseas dependencies difficult to resolve. It was this lack of any single constitutional definition of empire that led the historian Sir Robert Seeley in 1883 to make his famous remark that it seemed as if England had "conquered and peopled half the world in a fit of absence of mind." And it would remain a defining feature of the British Empire until its final demise in the twentieth century.

There was a further difference between the English and their European rivals. From the beginning of their colonizing ventures, the English seem to have taken a far more detached view of the possible relations between the mother country and its colonies than their continental neighbors. Spain, quite obviously, and France, less certainly, represented themselves as the true heirs to Rome. Britain, which at least until the eighteenth century had a very weak sense of itself as an empire – a word that, as John Adams said later, belonged "not to the language of the common law, but the language of newspapers and political pamphlets" – held to a far stricter distinction between a "colony," on the one hand, and a separate, if distinct kingdom within a "composite monarchy," on the other.[3] But if there was, in effect, no true British Empire before Disraeli created one for Queen Victoria in 1878, and if the American colonies were not, as those of both Spain and France were, united to the mother country by a shared *ius publicum* embodied in the legal person of the King, what was their relationship to the metropolis? On the answer to this question hinged the entire nature of their legal identity.

To understand just how the English colonies in America acquired their distinctive legal character, we have to begin where the colonists themselves had a fortiori to begin: with the question of legitimacy. From the early sixteenth century until well into the eighteenth, Spain, France, and Britain waged a moral, theological, and legal battle over the legitimacy of the conquest and settlement of the Americas. This struggle has often been presented as a concern with the justice of the treatment of indigenous peoples. In large part this was indeed the case. What is frequently overlooked, however, is that the question of justice was also a question about the juridical status of the European settlements, both under what we would now term "international law" – then called the "law of nations" (*ius gentium*) – and under the civil law of the European states from which the settlers had come. And because it involved questions of juridical status no less than of humanity, the struggle over legitimacy had far-reaching consequences both for the legal history of the English colonies themselves and for the eventual United States.

[3] Charles Francis Adams, ed., *Works*, 10 vols. (Boston, 1850–56), IV: 37.

I. GROUNDS FOR POSSESSION

Like their European rivals the English could make no a priori claims to rights of any kind in the Americas. "[We] shall be put to defend our title," the Virginia Company early recognized, "not yet publicly quarreled, not only comparatively to be as good as the Spaniards, but absolutely to be good against the Natural people." Claims to both sovereignty and property in the American had thus to be sustained on two fronts: first against prior claims by another European power – in this case Spain, which by the Treaty of Tordesillas with Portugal in 1494 had stated its rights to all territory in the western hemisphere – and then against all those others, the "Natural people," whose rights would seem to be antecedent to those of any European. Because no argument from English civil law could be applied anywhere outside the jurisdiction of the English courts, the English, like their European rivals, had to find some argument that would be considered valid in either natural law (*ius naturae*) or the law of nations (*ius gentium*), laws that were believed to be binding on all humankind no matter what their civil constitution might be. The complex and extended attempts to find this argument rumbled on well into the nineteenth century and are still being rehearsed in Canada and Australia to this day.

All the European empires faced the same dilemma. However, whereas the Spanish, the French, and to some degree the Portuguese were troubled primarily by their political (and ethical) relationship with the indigenous populations whom they sought, at one level or another, to assimilate into the new colonial order, the English were prompted far more by concerns over the consequences that the grounds for occupation might have for the rights and liberties of the colonists themselves vis à vis the Crown. Both the Spanish and the French, in their different ways, had attempted to establish not colonies but overseas dependencies and had tried to incorporate the indigenous peoples into new multi-ethnic societies. The Native Americans were peasants, serfs, and sometimes allies. A few could even be landowners with European servants, and at least in the early years in Spanish America they could occupy semi-bureaucratic positions in the new overseas dependencies. Under a law of 1664, all native inhabitants of New France who had converted to Christianity were held to be "denizens and French natives, and as such entitled for all rights of succession, goods laws and other dispositions, without being obliged to obtain any letter of naturalization."[4] For the English, by contrast, the indigenes were always only of secondary

[4] "Etablissement de la Compagnie des Indes Occidentales," *Édits, ordonnances royaux, declarations et arrêts du conseil d'état du Roi concernant le Canada*, 3 vols. (Quebec, 1854–6) I: 46.

importance, persons who were to be displaced, not incorporated –"savages," in the terms of Charles II's charter to settle Carolina – who belonged in the same general category with "other enemies pirates and robbers."[5] It was the manner of their displacement which was crucial since it raised substantial legal questions about the status of those who were engaged in – and benefiting from – the displacing.

Unlike the Spanish, furthermore, and to some degree the French, the English lacked any initial founding charter issued by an international authority because the only such authority that existed at the time was the papacy. Henry VII's letters patent to John Cabot of 1496 were to some degree an attempt to replicate the language of papal legislation, as were the grants made by Elizabeth I to Sir Walter Raleigh in March 1584. But for all their assumed authority neither Henry nor Elizabeth were pontiffs; neither could make the least claim to excise jurisdiction beyond their realms. In the end, possession or sovereignty in the Americas could only be made legitimate on three distinct grounds: by right of conquest; by "discovery," which crucially, as we see, implied that the territory being "discovered" was also unoccupied; or by purchase from, or voluntary concession by, the native and legitimate owners or rulers.

II. CONQUEST

Of these grounds for legitimacy, the most contentious was indisputably conquest because no conquest could be legitimate unless it were the consequence of a just war, and there were no immediate or obvious reasons for considering the European invasions of America as in any sense just. In general, conquest as prior grounds for claims of property rights or sovereignty was looked on with mistrust throughout the entire history of the European overseas empires.[6] "The Sea," as the Scottish political theorist and soldier of fortune, Andrew Fletcher, declared in 1698, "is the only Empire which can naturally belong to us. Conquest is not our Interest."[7] The Portuguese spoke of "conquering" the seas, but rarely the land, and even the Spanish, whose American empire was so obviously and in the early years so proudly based on conquest, banned all official use of the term in 1680. In England,

[5] "The Second Charter Granted by Charles II to the Proprietors of Carolina," in *Historical Collection of South Carolina; embracing many rare and valuable pamphlets and other documents relating to the State from its first discovery until its independence in the year* 1776, 2 vols. (New York, 1836), II: 44.

[6] *Second Treatise* 2.175 in *Locke's Two Treatises of Government*, 2nd ed. (Cambridge, 1967), 403.

[7] "A Discourse on Government with Relation to Militias" in *The Political Works of Andrew Fletcher* (London, 1737), 66.

furthermore, there existed a long-standing distrust of conquest – to which I shall return – that originated in the Norman occupation after 1066 and resulted in the "continuity theory" of constitutional law in which the legal and political institutions of the conquered are deemed to survive a conquest.

Yet, at least during the first phase of the colonization of America, from the moment of Raleigh's short-lived settlement at Roanoke, the English Crown and its agents maintained consistently that the American colonies were "lands of conquest," no matter what the realities of their actual occupation. Virginia, New York, and Jamaica, for instance, were consistently referred to as conquests. The "Emperor" of Virginia, Powhatan, was even crowned by Christopher Newport in an attempt to create the image of a North American Atahualpa. (The Privy Council, however, sent a copper crown for the ceremony rather than gold, thus carefully indicating the inferior status of James I's new tributary ruler.) As late as 1744, in the negotiations which led to the treaty of Lancaster with the Iroquois, the Virginia delegation declared that "the King holds Virginia by right of conquest, and the bounds of that conquest to the westward is the great sea." The Virginia colony, that is, reached all the way to the Pacific.

Virginia was the clearest instance of a land of conquest, but it was by no means the only one. The early charters and letters patent are all liberally scattered with references to conquests and occupations, which for some jurists at least, seem to have been taken to be the same thing. Occupation, declared the most influential of them, Sir Edward Coke, "signifieth a putting out of a man's freehold in time of warre . . . *occupare* is sometimes taken to conquer."[8]

The initial claim that America was a land of conquest, was not, however, made in isolation. It was but one, of which the annexation of India by the British Crown in 1858 was to be perhaps the last, of a long series of "conquests," some more obviously so than others: the conquest of Wales, completed in 1536; the conquest, or at least the seizure, of the Channel Islands (although this was not completed until 1953); the conquest of the Isle of Man in 1406; the prolonged conquests of Ireland between 1175 and 1603; and the initial attempt at union with Scotland or of the subordination of Scotland to an English Parliament, which was to become one of the issues at stake in the Civil War, in 1603. For more than two centuries before the first colonies were established on the eastern seaboard of North America, England had been in a state of constant and determined expansion. It was to remain more or less uninterruptedly in this state until World War I.

In all previous cases, and in the protracted English attempts to seize parts of northern France, conquest had been justified on grounds of dynastic

[8] *First Institute of the laws of England* (Philadelphia, 1826–7), II: 249b.

inheritance: a claim, that is, based on civil law. In America, however, this claim obviously could not be used. There would seem, therefore, to be no prima facie justification for "conquering" the Indians since they had clearly not given the English grounds for waging war against them.

Like the other European powers, therefore, the English turned to rights in natural law, or – more troubling – to justifications based on theology. The Indians were infidels, "barbarians," and English Protestants no less than Spanish Catholics had a duty before God to bring them into the fold and, in the process, to "civilize" them. The First Charter of the Virginia Company (1606) proclaimed that its purpose was to serve in "propagating of Christian religion to such people, {who} as yet live in darkness and miserable ignorance of the true knowledge and worship of God, and may in time bring the infidels and salvages living in these parts to humane civility and to a settled and quiet government." In performing this valuable and godly service, the English colonists were replicating what their Roman ancestors had once done for the ancient Britons. The American settlers, argued William Strachey in 1612, were like Roman generals in that they, too, had "reduced the conquered parts of our barbarous Island into provinces and established in them colonies of old soldiers building castles and towns in every corner, teaching us even to know the powerful discourse of divine reason."[9]

In exchange for these acts of civility, the conqueror acquired some measure of sovereignty over the conquered peoples and, by way of compensation for the trouble to which he had been put in conquering them, was also entitled to a substantial share of the infidels' goods. Empire was always conceived to be a matter of reciprocity at some level, and as Edward Winslow nicely phrased it in 1624, America was clearly a place where "religion and profit jump together." For the more extreme Calvinists, such as Sir Edward Coke who seems to have believed that all infidels, together presumably with all Catholics, lay so far from God's grace that no amount of civilizing would be sufficient to save them, such peoples might legitimately be conquered; in Coke's dramatic phrasing, because "A perpetual enemy (though there be no wars by fire and sword between them) cannot maintain any action or get any thing within this Realm. All infidels are in law *perpetui inimici*, perpetual enemies, (for the law presumes not that they will be converted, that being *remota potentia*, a remote possibility) for between them, as with devils, whose subjects they be, and the Christians, there is perpetual hostility and can be no peace."

[9] *The Historie of Travell into Virginia Britania*, ed. Louis B. Wright and Virginia Freund (London, 1953), 24. I am grateful to David Armitage for drawing my attention to this text.

Like all Calvinists, Coke adhered to the view that as infidels the Native Americans could have no share in God's grace, and because authority and rights derived from grace, not nature, they could have no standing under the law. Their properties and even their persons were therefore forfeit to the first "godly" person with the capacity to subdue them. "If a Christian King," he wrote, "should conquer a kingdom of an infidel, and bring them [sic] under his subjection, there *ipso facto* the laws of the infidel are abrogated, for that they be not only against Christianity, but against the law of God and nature contained in the Decalogue."[10] Grounded as this idea was not only in the writings of Calvin himself but also in those of the fourteenth-century English theologian John Wycliffe, it enjoyed considerable support among the early colonists. As the dissenting dean of Gloucester, Josiah Tucker, wrote indignantly to Edmund Burke in 1775, "Our Emigrants to *North-America*, were mostly Enthusiasts of a particular Stamp. They were that set of Republicans, who believed, or pretended to believe, that *Dominion was founded in Grace*. Hence they conceived, that they had the best Right in the World, both to *tax* and to *persecute* the *Ungodly*. And they did both, as soon as they got power into their Hands, in the most open and atrocious Manner."[11]

By the end of the seventeenth century, however, this essentially eschatological argument had generally been dropped. If anything it was now the "papists" (because the canon lawyers shared much the same views as the Calvinists on the binding nature of grace) who were thought to derive rights of conquest from the supposed ungodliness of non-Christians. The colonists themselves, particularly when they came in the second half of the eighteenth century to raid the older discussions over the legitimacy of the colonies in search of arguments for cessation, had no wish to be associated with an argument that depended upon their standing before God. For this reason, if for no other, it was, as James Otis noted in 1764, a "madness" which, at least by his day, had been "pretty generally exploded and hissed off the stage."[12]

Otis, however, had another more immediate reason for dismissing this account of the sources of sovereign authority. For if America had been conquered, it followed that the colonies, like all other lands of conquest, were a part not of the King's realm but of the royal demesne. This would have made them the personal territory of the monarch, to be governed at the King's "pleasure," instead of being subject to English law and to the English Parliament. It was this claim that sustained the fiction that "New England

[10] *The Reports of Sir Edward Coke*, Book VII (London, 1658), 601–2.

[11] *A Letter to Edmund Burke, Esq., A Member of Parliament for the City of Bristol . . . in Answer to his Printed Speech* (Gloucester, 1775), 18–20.

[12] "The Rights of the British colonies asserted and proved" [Boston, 1764], in Bernard Bailyn, ed., *Pamphlets of the American Revolution. I 1750–1765* (Cambridge. MA, 1965), 422.

lies within England," which would govern the Crown's legal association with its colonies until the very end of the empire itself. As late as 1913, for instance, Justice Isaac Isaacs of the Australian High Court could be found declaring that, at the time Governor Arthur Phillip received his commission in 1786, Australia had, rightly or wrongly, been conquered, and that "The whole of the lands of Australia were already in law the *property* of the King of England," a fact that made any dispute over its legality a matter of civil rather than international law.

It was precisely because all conquered territories were a part of the royal demesne that the monarch was able to grant charters to the colonies in the first place. For however empty those charters might have been considered by some, they were indisputably concessions made by the Crown. Charters, wrote Thomas Hobbes, "are Donations of the Soveraign; and not Lawes but exemptions from Law. The phrase of a Law is *Jubeo, Injugo, I Command* and *Enjoyn*; the phrase of a Charter is *Dedi, Concessi, I have Given I have Granted.*"[13] If this were so, and Hobbes is here stating a legal commonplace, then in one quite specific sense the English colonies had feudal foundations. Most of the lands in America had originally been granted in "free and common socage" as of the manor of East Greenwich in Kent. This formula allowed for what were, in effect, allodial grants, which derived from a contract between the Crown and the landowner but at the same time avoided the duties of feudal tenure – such as the need to provide *auxilium et consilium*, in effect military assistance to the sovereign. In this way the colonies were both free and unencumbered while at the same time remaining legally part of the royal demesne, and every part of the *terra regis* had to form a constitutive part of a royal manor in England. Land in Ireland, for instance, was held as of Carregrotian, or of Trim or of Limerick or of the Castle of Dublin, and when Charles II made over Bombay to the East India Company this land too was granted in "free and common socage" of the manor of East Greenwich. In the proprietorial colonies, by contrast, a large area of land was granted to a single individual, who then allocated lands more or less as he pleased. But even here the Crown still maintained that it possessed the ultimate rights of ownership and that it could therefore dispose of the territory in question as it wished. (The Spanish Crown, by contrast, although often represented as the most despotic and centralizing of the European monarchies, only ever made claims to exercise property rights in several limited areas which were described as being under "the King's head," or *cabeza del rey*.)

The English King's persistent belief that the overseas dependencies remained his personal property, despite the charters that the monarchy itself had granted to each of its parts, led to some strain in the relationship between King and Parliament. When, in 1660, Charles II acquired

[13] *Leviathan*, ed. Richard Tuck (Cambridge, 1991), 200.

Jamaica, together with Dunkirk and Tangier, he immediately moved that these territories were also part of the royal demesne and thus his to dispose of as he willed. As a preemptive move, on September 11, 1660, the House of Commons passed a bill "for annexing Dukirke . . . and the Island of Jamaica in America to the Crown of England." Charles rejected this law, and on October 17, 1662 sold Dunkirk to Louis XIV for £5 million. Selling off what Parliament held to be parts of the realm was an extreme measure, but there was little Parliament could do about it at the time. What was at stake here was the status of private rights as against the sovereign rights of the monarchy. The royal claim created obvious difficulties when, after the end of the Seven Year's War, Parliament attempted to tighten its hold over the fiscal and commercial activities of the colonies.

The exceptions to the rule were those areas, Maryland and the Carolinas, which had been created as palatinates, "as of any Bishop of Durham, within the Bishopric, or County Palatinate of Durham."[14] Although much reduced in power since 1535, Durham itself remained a palatinate until 1836. The bishop had, in effect, powers very similar to those of the Spanish viceroys. The charter of Maryland also offered its proprietor, Lord Calvert, "free and common socage." In exchange for a nominal rent of two Indian arrows and one-fifth of all gold and silver ore payable annually to the Crown, the proprietor was given the right to grant or lease any portion of the territory in fee simple or fee tail. Among other privileges he could also erect manors with courts baron and courts leet.

Both approaches, however, still preserved lands as part of the royal patrimony, albeit at one remove; consequently, both denied inhabitants any right of appeal against their immediate proprietor. For as both the bishop and the proprietor were, in effect, delegates of the Crown, the colonists could make no claim to constitute an independent sovereign body. This resulted in some very strained interpretations of the historical facts of conquest. In 1694 the inhabitants of Barbados argued before the House of Lords that they were entitled to rights under English law as "their birthright" because Barbados had been, quite literally, uninhabited when they arrived. They were told that, notwithstanding the facts of the matter, Barbados was nevertheless held to be a "conquered territory." Any protection the settlers might have under English law was therefore at the discretion of the monarch. As Coke put it, "If a king come to a Christian kingdom by conquest, seeing that he hath *vitae et necis potestatem*, he may at his pleasure alter and change the laws of that kingdom" – a statement which, of course, was a direct contradiction of the continuity theory of conquest.[15] If Coke were right then the same

[14] Fundamental Constitutions of Carolina, in *John Locke: Political Essays*, ed. Mark Goldie (Cambridge, 1997), 161–2.

[15] *The Reports of Sir Edward Coke*, Book VII, 601–2.

would apply to the Americas, even if there was, in effect, no prior recognizable system of legislation. Indeed, in Coke's view it would apply with even greater force in a country of "Infidels" such as America, because the laws of such peoples had no basis in right at all.

Here the long-standing suspicion of conquest, which originated in the Norman Conquest of Britain, could be turned to the Crown's advantage. If America had been conquered, its laws could only be made by royal decree, and its inhabitants would be bound by those laws. Further, because those laws were royal decrees they would not be subject to the provisions of Magna Carta or any of the subsequent constraints that Parliament had succeeded in imposing on the monarchy. This did not much appeal either to the settlers or to Parliament, which took the view that, although such laws might have been made by the monarch acting very much as, to use the Roman term, "unfettered by law" (*legibus solutus*), once they had been enacted they became, in effect, laws passed by Parliament. In Coke's view, for instance, although King John had introduced the laws of England into Ireland without Parliamentary consent, "no succeeding king could alter the same without parliament." It was for this reason that Sir William Blackstone, in what has become perhaps the most celebrated statement on the subject, declared that "our American plantations" had been "obtained in the last century either by right of conquest and driving out the natives (with what natural justice I shall not at present inquire) or by treaties. And therefore the common law of England, as such, has no allowance or authority there, they being no part of the mother country, but distinct though dependent dominions. They are subject, however, to the control of Parliament."[16]

On occasion the same was also said of Ireland, which although indisputably a land of conquest was nevertheless frequently described as a "dominion separate and divided from England."[17] "Of all the objections raised against us," complained William Molyneux in 1698 of attempts to classify Ireland as a colony and thereby to remove it from the legal jurisdiction of Parliament, "I take this to be the most extravagant: it seems not to have the least foundation or colour from reason or record. . . . Do not the Kings of England bear the Stile of Ireland amongst the rest of their Kingdoms? Is this Agreeable to the nature of a Colony? Do they use the title of Kings of Virginia, New England or Maryland?"[18] The same was true of the Isle of Man, which, although governed by its own laws, could be bound to Westminster any time Parliament chose because it had originally been acquired under Henry IV "by conquest."

[16] Sir William Blackstone, *Commentaries on the Laws of England*, ed. Stanley Katz (Chicago, 1979), I: 105.
[17] Howell, *State Trials*, II: 648.
[18] *The Case of Ireland's being bound by Acts of Parliament* (London, 1698), 148.

What Blackstone's claim implied, of course, was that in the case of both conquest and treaty (for a treaty could only be entered into by a sovereign state) New England was not "within England." Nor was it the case that English law – English common law at least – followed Englishmen wherever they went, as was so often stated. Paradoxically, the consequence of such a view was that whereas the colonies were themselves nothing other than extensions of the royal demesne, the laws by which they were ruled were, in the terms of the various charters by which they had been established, the creation of the colonists themselves. It was this situation that led Andrew Fletcher in 1704 to compare the British *overseas* empire to the leagues of the Greek city-states, a semi-federal structure in which each community was responsible for its own internal affairs, and consequently its own legislative order, while being dependent or semi-dependent on a central power for its external regulation.[19] It would become a popular model that would be applied later by James Madison and James Wilson to their proposals for a federal structure for the United States. This quasi-independent status, both political and legal, with respect to the metropolis did not make the American colonies distinct from other colonial settlements within the British Empire, despite repeated attempts by American historians in pursuit of the origins of American exceptionalism to demonstrate that it did. Similar patterns would later be repeated in India, Africa, and Australia. However, it did distinguish them from the colonial settlements of other European powers in the Americas.

Their freedom had, however, been conceded to the settlers either directly by the Crown or by those to whom the Crown had made grants or charters. And because they were not a part of what Francis Bacon had called "one imperial crown" they could not enjoy the benefits of the English common law. The position involved, of course, a great deal of incoherence, which was captured nicely by Benjamin Franklin when he demanded to know, "What have these inhabitants of East Greenwich in Kent done, that they, more than any other inhabitants of Kent, should be curbed in their manufactures and commerce?"[20] For if the colonists were virtual residents of East Greenwich then they should have enjoyed *all* the rights enjoyed by the English, just as any laborer on the East Greenwich estate would necessarily have done. The argument that because the colonies were the personal property of the

[19] "An account of a Conversation concerning the Regulation of Governments for the Common Good of Mankind" in Andrew Fletcher, *The Political Works of Andrew Fletcher* (London, 1737), 436.

[20] "On the tenure of the Manor of East Greenwich" [January 11, 1766] in Benjamin Franklin, *The Papers of Benjamin Franklin*, ed. William B. Wilcox (New Haven, 1959–1993), 13, 21.

monarch their inhabitants could be denied the rights and freedoms enjoyed by those of other places within the British monarchy was also perceived by many to be a short road to the establishment of the kind of unfettered legislative powers which the British constitution had struggled so hard for so long to prevent. It was one of the reasons why Edmund Burke upheld the rights of self-determination claimed by the American revolutionaries. "In order to prove that the Americans have no right to their liberties," he wrote in 1776, "we are every day endeavoring to subvert the maxims which preserve the whole Spirit of our own."

No matter what the legal status of the colonies was thought to be in England, in America de facto self-government in most of the settlements resulted in a great deal of autonomous legislation. It also led, inexorably, to a political climate in which, in Burke's words, the colonists tended to "augur misgovernment at a distance and snuff the approach of tyranny in every tainted breeze." The conflict over the status of the relationship between the Crown and its overseas subjects first came to a head in the years after the Restoration in 1660 when an attempt was made to transform the scattered American colonies into something resembling the Spanish empire, with a centralized structure. Between 1651 and 1696, a series of Navigation Acts were passed whose purpose was to restrict trade between the colonies and the mother country and to exclude the Scots from what was, in effect, an English mercantile system. A new authority of the Privy Council called the Lords of Trade and Plantations was also established to administer the colonies, and although the name of this body still indicated the degree to which the Crown looked upon its overseas possessions in Baconian terms, it remained the case that this was far closer to the Spanish Council of the Indies than anything that had existed previously. More significantly, the royal charters of the corporate colonies were revoked by royal decree. The Crown had already resumed the charter of the Virginia Company in 1624, and between then and the 1680s various, although frequently inconsistent, attempts were made to establish Crown sovereignty over all the remaining settlements.

From the late seventeenth century until the eve of the Revolution, the Crown or its more legal-minded officials had looked with envy at the degree of administrative and judicial authority the Spanish exercised in their colonies. In the opening years of the eighteenth century, the English political and economic theorist Charles Davenant, although one of the fiercest critics of what he saw as Spanish cruelty and Spanish popery, nevertheless recommended that "a constitution something like what we call the Council of the Indies in Spain" should be established in Britain. "Whoever considers the laws and political institutions of *Spain*," he went on, "will find them as well formed, and contrived with as much skill and wisdom, as in any country perhaps in the world."[21] In accordance with this sentiment, by the 1670s the Crown had begun to put into operation a plan to divide the thirteen colonies into four separate viceroyalties.

In the end, however, only one viceroyalty was ever established, the Dominion of New England, which combined the former colonies of New England – Massachusetts, Plymouth, Maine, New Hampshire, Rhode Island, and Connecticut – with New Jersey and New York. Like the Spanish viceroyalties, the Dominion was ruled by a single individual appointed by the Crown, who governed with a council but without a locally elected assembly, and who exercised certain legislative and executive powers. After the Glorious Revolution of 1688 and the demise of the Stuart monarchy, the colonists threw the governor and the members of his advisory council into jail, and the Dominion ceased to be. Nevertheless, by 1776 only three of the thirteen mainland colonies – Massachusetts, Rhode Island, and Connecticut – still had charters. Two others – Maryland and Pennsylvania – had proprietors. All the rest, mainland and Caribbean, had become royal territories.

In the eyes of the Crown, then, the American colonies were in all legal respects lands of conquest. They were so not because any actual conquests had occurred, but because the definition enabled the Crown to assert unlimited rights to grant concessions, or, if it so wished, to repeal them without consultation, just as, when the time came, it would assert an unlimited right to raise exceptional taxes without consent. The claim of the American revolutionaries that taxation without representation in Westminster was illegal amounted to a denial of the status that the Crown had conferred on them since the beginning. Their denial was predicated on an alternative narrative of the legal foundations of the settlements which had begun to emerge during the eighteenth century, one which would have a powerful and enduring hold on the legal history of the revolution and indeed of the fledgling United States.

III. DISCOVERY

In 1804, in the first volume of his misleadingly titled *Life of Washington*, Chief Justice John Marshall stated categorically: "There is not a single grant from the British Crown from the earliest of Elizabeth down to the latest of George II that affects to look at any title except that founded on discovery. Conquest or cession is not once alluded to." Conquest, in Marshall's view, only became grounds for possession in the eighteenth century when the

[21] "On the Plantation Trade," in *The Political and Commercial Works of that Celebrated Writer, Charles D'Avenant LL.D.*, 5 vols. (London, 1771), II: 30–1.

thirteen colonies that would make up the new United States had already been securely established and most of their remaining indigenous populations effectively dispossessed. The claim that the earliest, and crucial phase of colonization was based solely on discovery provided the historical basis for Marshall's celebrated ruling in *Johnson v. M'Intosh* (1823). It became an accepted commonplace and was repeated frequently by the United States with regard to its own internal colonization.[22] It seems to have been based very largely on Marshall's reading of Henry VII's letters patent to John Cabot of 1496, which had echoed exactly the terms of the bulls by which Pope Alexander VI had granted to the Catholic Monarchs of Spain, Ferdinand and Isabella, dominion over all territories in the western hemisphere not already occupied by another Christian prince. In Marshall's understanding the right to occupation derived not from the conquest of such territories (although Cabot is explicitly charged with conquest) but from the absence of occupation by any power that the English were prepared to recognize as sovereign.

Even if such an interpretation of Henry VII's letters is warranted, it is difficult to see how a man of Marshall's learning could have insisted that "discovery" had continued to be the *sole* justification employed by the English Crown in view of all the subsequent evidence. But Marshall was certainly not the first to make this claim. In 1754, faced with the prospect of a French invasion, the delegates to the Albany Congress agreed "[t]hat his Majesty's title to the northern continent of America appears founded on the discovery thereof first made, and the possession thereof first taken, in 1497 under a commission from Henry VII of England to Sebastian Cabot." In 1774, James Abercromby, as influential a jurist as Marshall in his own day, stated, "The point of Territorial Right in America at first turned totally, on the priority of Discovery." These statements show that from the moment that the colonists began to distance themselves from the Crown, until well after independence, there existed a movement to redefine the question of legitimacy in such a way as to remove the notion that America had ever been, de facto or de iure, a land of conquest.[23]

Proponents had good reason for wishing to do so. Marshall clearly shared with his near contemporary, Joseph Story, and with John Adams

[22] U.S. (8 Wheaton) 543.

[23] "Representation of the Present State of the Colonies," in Benjamin Franklin, *The Papers of Benjamin Franklin*, ed. William B. Wilcox (New Haven, 1959–1993), V, 368; *Magna Charta for America*: James Abercromby's "An Examination of the Acts of Parliament Relative to the Trade and the Government of our American Colonies" (1752) and "*De Jure et Gubernatione Coloniarum*, or An Inquiry in the Nature, and the Rights of Colonies, Ancient, and Modern" (1774), ed. Jack P. Greene, Charles F. Mullett, and Edward C. Papenfuse, Jr. (Philadelphia, 1986), 200.

the widespread unease that the United States might have been created on lands that had been seized illicitly from their original occupants, who might therefore at any time attempt to claim them back again.[24] In view of recent developments in Canada, and the ruling of the Australian High Court in *Mabo v. The State of Queensland* (1992) conceding that the land of the Meriam peoples of the Murray Islands in the Torres Straits had been unjustly taken from them, he had some grounds for anxiety.[25] For all that he is represented as one of the earliest defenders of aboriginal rights, Marshall, like most of his contemporaries, looked upon Indians as what he called "domestic dependent nations,"[26] who might possess the "right to retain possession of it [the land] and to use it according to their own discretion," but nevertheless enjoyed greatly diminished "rights to complete sovereignty, as independent nations."[27] To make good this claim, their lands had to have been acquired by any means other than force.

Abercromby, Story, Adams, and Marshall all knew that, of all the claims to sovereignty made by the European powers in America, discovery had, in what by Marshall's day had become known as international law, been the one discredited most easily. As English jurists of the seventeenth century were quick to point out, even the Spanish had been reluctant to base assertions of either sovereignty or possession on anything so flimsy. "Discovery," observed the great Spanish theologian Francisco de Vitoria, "of itself provides no support for possession of these lands, any more than it would if they had discovered us."[28] But flimsy or not, discovery had the advantage not only of securing rights of occupation "in nature" but also of distancing the history of the English settlements in America from those of the Spanish, which successive generations of English jurists had maintained were, in fact, little more than usurpations. It was for precisely these reason that the settlers in Barbados had argued that their lands, genuinely unoccupied, could not possibly be counted as conquests.

Both Marshall and, more immediately, Abercromby were also the beneficiaries of an Enlightenment attempt to detach the legacy of the crumbling

[24] "The European power which had first discovered the country and set up marks of possession was deemed to have gained the right, though it had not yet formed a regular colony there." *Commentaries on the Constitution of the United States*, 2 vols. (Boston, 1891), 2 vols. [first published 1833], I: 106.

[25] This is the celebrated Mabo case. *Commonwealth Law Reports* (Australia) 175 (1991–1992), *Commonwealth Law Reports* (Aus) 175 (1991–1992). In this case, however, the High Court was disputing the British government's original claim to land rights in Australia under *terra nullius*, which for Marshall was an entirely legitimate means of acquiring lands.

[26] *Cherokee Nation* v. *Georgia*, 30 U.S. (5 Peters) 17 (1831).

[27] *Johnson v. M'Intosh*, 23 U.S. (8 Wheaton) 591–2.

[28] *Political Writings*, ed. Anthony Pagden and Jeremy Lawrance (Cambridge, 1992), 264–5.

Spanish empire from that of the more robust and prosperous British and French settlements. By the middle of the eighteenth century it was widely assumed across Europe – even by the Spanish themselves – that it had been precisely the Spanish obsession with conquest that had reduced Spain by the 1740s to little more than a dependency on its own colonies. In his *Spirit of the Laws* (1748), which would become one of the most influential legal treatises in the American colonies, Montesquieu had argued that because the English and the French were "more refined" than the Spanish (he does not mention the Portuguese) they had sought in the New World not "the foundation of a town or of a new empire," but instead "objects of commerce and, as such, [had] directed their attention to them."[29]

In the very denial of empire, Montesquieu was himself picking up on James Harrington's definition of Britain as a state that exercised not *imperium* over its various dependencies but *patrocinium* (protectorate). This, too, was how Marshall and Abercromby wished to see it. But if the British Empire – as it was coming to be named – was now what Edmund Burke called "an empire of liberty," it could hardly be founded on the same legal grounds as the Spanish, in British eyes the most despised tyranny of them all. The claim of discovery thus had two distinct advantages. It distanced the English settlers from their Spanish, Catholic, and consequently despotic neighbors. And it was one of two grounds – contract or purchase being the other – that settlers could plausibly cite to deny usurpation in either natural law or the law of nations.

The trouble with discovery as a title to possession, however, lay not only in its lack of credibility. Even if it were accepted as a legitimate claim in the way Marshall insisted it had been, it could never amount to more than something like a right to first refusal. For behind Marshall's attempts to resuscitate the argument from discovery lay another legal debate, one that would prove the most contentious and most widely discussed of all European assertions to rights in overseas colonies, from Africa to Australia: the debate over "vacant lands" or *terra nullius*.

In 1608 the Dutch humanist Hugo Grotius published what was to become one of the foundational texts of modern international law, *Mare liberum* (*The Freedom of the Seas*). Grotius's objective was to refute the Portuguese claim to *dominium* over the Indian Ocean and, by implication, the possibility of any claim to property rights in the world's oceans. In a world of rapidly expanding trading empires which came increasingly in conflict with one another, the topic of property rights was of considerable legal and political importance. Debate spread throughout Europe. In 1636 it prompted John Selden to respond to Grotius with what became one of the

[29] *De l'esprit des lois*, Bk. XXI. cap. 21.

most widely read legal texts of the seventeenth century, *Mare clausum*, a defense of England's right to close the North Sea to foreign shipping.

Grotius's argument had centered on the question of whether discovery could be grounds for *dominium* –that is sovereignty – and furthermore what act, or acts, would count as a discovery. To the first of these questions he answered that discovery could only provide a right of possession if what had been discovered was genuinely unknown and unoccupied – what was known as *res* or *terra nullius*. To the second he replied that the Latin term *invenire* implied not merely seeing for the first time but also possession. Discovery, therefore, "is not merely to seize with the eyes (*occulis usurpare*) but to apprehend."[30] Since it would be absurd to say that anyone could "apprehend" a body of water, the Portuguese claim to have "discovered" the Indian Ocean was evidently invalid. But what applied to the ocean applied also to the land. To claim, as the Portuguese had done, that their mere presence in Indian territorial waters granted them the sole right to trade there was the same as arguing that any Japanese fleet cruising in the Atlantic could claim *dominium* over the kingdom of Portugal. In both cases the premises were as evidently absurd as the conclusion.

On March 15, 1613, Grotius went to England as a member of a Dutch delegation sent to work out an agreement between England and Holland over their respective commercial interests in the East Indies. According to the Dutch account of this visit, James I is said to have remarked, "Where neither was in possession neither should impede the other's free commerce." In order, that is, to constitute *rights*, both possession and sovereignty (*dominium iurisdictionis*) have to be exercised, a view that the Grotius of *Mare liberum* would have shared. More than a century later, the English radical dissenter, Richard Price would make the same point in exactly the same language. "If sailing along a coast can give a right to a country," he wrote in 1776, "then might the people of Japan become, as soon as they please, the proprietors of Britain."[31] This, as Price also pointed out, was the real theoretical weakness of the arguments set out in the Spanish Bulls of Donation. For "it is not a donation that grants *dominium* but consequent delivery of that thing and the subsequent possession thereof." "Nothing but possession by a colony, a settlement or a fortress," Arthur Young had written a few years earlier, "is now allowed to give a right from discovery."[32] Clearly the setting up

[30] *Mare liberum. The Freedom of the Seas, or the right which belongs to the Dutch to take part in the East India Trade*, trans. with a revision of the Latin text of 1633 by Ralph van Deman Magoffin (Oxford,1916), 11–12.

[31] "Observations on the Nature of Civil Liberty, the Principles of Government, and the Justice and Policy of the War with America" in *Political Writings*, ed. D. O. Thomas (Cambridge, 1991), 40.

[32] Arthur Young, *Political Essays Concerning the Present State of the British Empire* (London, 1772), 472.

of stone crosses, planting flags, burying bottles and other such devices to which generations of Europeans had resorted were quaint and wholly insubstantial as legally recognizable claims to possession. "To pass by and eye," as the French King Francois I once icily informed the Spanish ambassador, "is no title of possession."

Before the English could claim that discovery had made them legitimate masters of America, therefore, they had not only to have been there first but they had also to have exercised some kind of actual sovereignty. Yet, in a great many of the areas to which they laid claim, their presence was merely proclamatory or cartographic. At a time when the only English presence consisted of a handful of settlers in the malarial swamps along the banks of the St. James River, the Virginia Company's charter declared it exercised jurisdiction over all "territories in America either appertaining unto us, or which are not now actually possessed by any Christian prince or people, situate, lying and being all along the sea coasts between four and thirty degrees of northerly latitude from the equinoctial line and five and forty degrees of the same latitude, and in the main land between the same four and thirty and five and forty degrees, and the islands thereunto adjacent or within one hundred miles of the coast thereof." In fact, the English knew little about either the real extent of these territories or the nature of their inhabitants. The charter's outlandish territorial claims belong rather to the language of international diplomacy and were intended to establish primacy over any other European power in the region, in particular the French. As the drafters of the charter would have known, no right of discovery could ever be made undisputedly against any prior occupant. Sovereignty, that is, required not only discovery and a real presence. It also required that the territories being occupied should be truly vacant or *terra nullius*. "I like a plantation in a pure soil," Francis Bacon had written in 1625, "that is, where people are not displaced to the end to plant in others. For else it is rather an extirpation than a plantation."[33]

Terra nullius is a principle which has been much discussed and remains a topic for debate in both Australian and Canadian disputes over the rights of indigenous peoples. It therefore requires some clarification. The term itself, although widely used by historians to describe claims made in the early modern period, does not in fact appear before the mid-nineteenth century.[34] It has its origins, however, in Justinian's *Digest* XLI. 1 and the law *Ferae bestiae*, of the *Institutes* (II. 1. 2), which simply states, "Natural reason admits the title of the first occupant to that which previously had no owner." It is also significant that the idea of vacancy, of being "of no-one," is a concept in

[33] *On Plantations*, in *The Works of Francis Bacon*, ed. James Spedding, 14 vols. (London, 1857–74), VI: 457.

[34] I am grateful to David Armitage for pointing this out to me.

natural law that, along with many such general claims, Justinian's lawyers had absorbed into the Roman civil law. No such process was available, however, in English law in which all land occupied by Englishmen was ultimately the property of the Crown and had been acquired either though descent or, as was claimed of America, through conquest. Precisely because it was in origin a *natural* right, whose only codification is Justinian's brief entries, the principle of *terra* or *res nullius* is expressed in several different and sometimes frankly contradictory ways. This has led some modern historians to argue that, as a legal claim to possession in America, *terra nullius* was devised ex post facto – as indeed Marshall seems to have done. But although Marshall was clearly, for good political reasons, overstating the case, some version of *terra nullius* had been in use since at least the early seventeenth century.

Determining what constituted a *terra nullius*, however, posed considerable legal difficulties and had far-reaching political and ethical implications. What did it mean for a land to belong to "no-one?" In Roman law any territory that had not been formally enclosed in some manner and could not be defended, or had once been occupied, but was now abandoned, was held to be vacant. "In the Law of Nature and of Nations," John Donne told the members of the Virginia Company in 1622, "a land never inhabited by any, or utterly derelicted and immemorially abandoned by the former inhabitants, becomes theirs that will possess it."[35] In the American context, however, such an account would have left very little space for European occupation. Most, if not quite all, of the eastern seaboard of North America was clearly neither uninhabited nor "utterly derelicted" nor "immemorially abandoned," no matter what the Virginia Company might think.

This argument also raised other difficulties. As its opponents frequently pointed out, even in Europe there existed large tracts of land – the most contentious being the royal forests – which although they were essentially vacant, did not thus become the property of anyone who chose to settle on and cultivate them. "That which lies in common and has never been replenished or subdued," wrote John Winthrop in his *Reasons for the Plantation in New England* (c. 1628), "is free to any that will possess and improve it." The same general argument was also applied to the territories within the Ottoman Empire, which were widely believed to be effectively "unused" and thus might similarly be claimed as *terrae nullius* by Europeans. But even the great sixteenth-century jurist, Alberico Gentili, although a firm proponent of the claim that "God did not create the world to be empty" and who was generally prepared to concede extensive rights to Europeans

[35] *A Sermon Preached to the Honourable Company of the Virginia Plantation 13 nov. 1622* (London, 1623), 26.

over non-Europeans on the grounds of their greater technical capacities, was certain that although the occupation of lands formally under the jurisdiction of the Ottoman state would be licit the settlers would nevertheless be bound to accept the sovereignty of the Sultan.[36] The same general point was also made in the following century by Hugo Grotius.

A more demanding criterion had therefore to be found. This was based on what came to be called "improvement." The obligation on any holder of land deemed to be *terra nullius* to improve it was applied literally by both the English and the French. In 1648, for instance, the General Court of Massachusetts decreed that anyone who received a grant of land by what the court termed *vacuum domicilium* but did not build on or "improve" it within a space of three years would lose it.[37]

The concept of improvement also had its origins in natural law. Since antiquity, it had been assumed that one of the features of humankind was the uniquely human ability to transform nature, or, in conventional Aristotelian terms, to make actual what was otherwise only potential. This was the root meaning of technology. Possession and sovereignty were consequently acts that established relationships between persons and their external and social worlds. Because those who failed to develop nature's potentiality could not be counted as true persons, they could not possibly establish such relationships. "God and his Reason," wrote John Locke in what was to become the most influential formulation of this supposition, "commanded him to subdue the Earth, *i.e.* improve it for the benefit of Life, and therein lay something upon it that was his own, his labour. He that in his Obedience to this Command of God, subdued, tilled and sowed any part of it, thereby annexed to it something that was his *Property*, which another had no Title to, nor could without injury take from him."[38]

Locke's celebrated theory of property is, in effect, a development of *Ferae bestiae*, and clearly it evolved in the context of the debates over the rights of the American Indians in the years preceding the Glorious Revolution. But what Locke had done, and which no previous writer on the topic had attempted, was to associate the claims to possession with those of sovereignty, because now what was being claimed was that only persons who lived in civil society could possibly exercise property rights. What this implied in the American context was far reaching. Nothing short of agricultural exploitation and a recognizable civil society could provide grounds for legitimate political control. The Native Americans, by general

[36] *De Iure belli*, trans R. C. Rolfe (Oxford, 1933), I, XVII, para 131.

[37] *Records of the Governor and Company of the Massachusetts Bay*, ed. Nathaniel Shurtleff (Boston, 1853–4), II: 245.

[38] *Locke's Two Treatises of Government*, 309: *Second Treatise* 32.

consent, lacked the capacity to employ culture in this manner. They might live on the land, but because, in Robert Cushman's words, "they run over the grass as do also the foxes and wild beasts," they could not be said to possess it.[39] And since they did not possess it, any attempt on their part to prevent the Europeans from putting it to its proper natural, and in the terms employed by Locke, also God-ordained use, constituted a violation of the natural law. As such they could, in Locke's celebrated denunciation, "be destroyed as a *Lion* or a *Tiger*, one of those wild Savage beasts, with whom Men can have no Society nor Security." Furthermore, under the terms of the *ius ad bellum* (the law, that is, which governs the condition under which a war may be waged) the would-be settlers might make war on such peoples "to seek reparation upon any injury received from them."[40] In other words, the seizure of the lands from "those wild Savage beasts" might indeed, involve conquest, but now it was wholly legitimate under natural law, rather than a status established under English civil law.

Despite the considerable difficulties it presented and for all that it involved a necessarily slippery distinction between possession and sovereignty, *terra nullius* became perhaps the most enduring of the natural rights arguments for overseas occupation. The colonists who through the seventeenth and well into the eighteenth century had maintained that their rights depended upon purchase from legitimate indigenous landowners (to which I shall return) gradually began to turn to one or another version of the "agriculturalist" argument – as it has come to be called – to support what were, in effect claims to both legal and political independence from the Crown. As the New Jersey jurist, Robert Hunter Morris, put it in the mid-eighteenth century, "If the people settling . . . the British Dominions in America can derive property in soil or powers of government from any source other than the Crown which by the laws of England is the fountain of powers and property then they are as much independent of the Crown & Nation of Britain as any people whatever." In one form or another, *terra nullius* became the argument of final appeal in most of the American colonies. As we have seen, it would later be considered final by John Marshall. It also became the basis for the British occupation of Australia and, when any justification at all was offered, of much of southern Africa. It was still being invoked in the 1990s.

Terra nullius was part of the same essentially existential juridical argument as an equally enduring Roman conception, namely prescription. This allowed for long-term de facto occupation *(preascriptio longi temporis)* to be

[39] *Reasons and Considerations Touching the Lawfullness of Removing out of England into Parts of America* (London, 1622), f.2v.

[40] *Locke's Two Treatises of Government, Second Treatise* 12, 292.

recognized de iure as conferring retrospective rights of property and of jurisdiction. Despite its Roman origins, prescription was entirely in keeping with most English constitutional thinking and with the process of the English common law. "Our Constitution is a prescriptive Constitution" declared Edmund Burke:

> it is a Constitution, whose sole authority is that it has existed time out of mind . . . Prescription is the most solid of all titles, not only to property, but, which is more to secure that property to Government. . . . It is a better presumption even of the choice of a nation, far better than any sudden or temporary arrangement by actual election. Because a nation is not an idea only of local extent and individual momentary aggregation, but it is an idea of continuity, which extends in time as well as in numbers, and in space.[41]

The legitimacy of a state or condition, that is, depended on its continual and successful existence. Crucially, because prescription relied upon objective conditions, it was able to transform natural into legal rights, and in the end, in America, it was always legal rights that were under discussion.

Prescription, however, also presented considerable difficulties of interpretation, particularly in the American context. One of the most obvious was the length of time required to establish title. The English, claimed Robert Johnson in 1609, had been in Virginia "long since without any interruption or invasion either of the Savages (the natives of the country) or any other Prince or people," which conferred upon James I the right to grant "rule or Dominion" over all "those English and Indian people." In fact, "long since" amounted to little more than two years' continuous presence. It is unlikely that any jurist, however zealous, could have accepted two years as sufficient. (In English common law the minimum period was generally held to be twelve years.) There was also the broader and more telling point, which Grotius had made, that because prescription was indeed a truly existential argument, it could only be a matter of civil law rather than part of the law of nations, in which case it clearly could not apply to contracts between "kings or between free peoples."[42]

All this notwithstanding, prescription, like *terra nullius*, was generally accepted by a large number of English jurists. Like *terra nullius*, it has had a long life in the subsequent history of international law. And since, *pace* Grotius, it was also widely held to be a part of the Law of Nations, it applied to all peoples everywhere. Robert Ferguson, one of the champions of the abortive scheme to create a settlement of Scotsmen in the Isthmus

[41] Edmund Burke, "Speech on the State of Representation of Commons in Parliament," in *Writings and Speeches* ed J. F. Taylor (New York, 1901), 7: 94–5.

[42] *Nova Britannia, offring most excellent fruites by planting in Virginia* (London, 1609), 47.

of Darien in 1699, acknowledged that the only rights which the Spaniards might have in America derived exclusively from their "claim and upon the foot of prescription thro' their having inhabited, occupied and inherited them for 200 years without interruption, disseizure or dispossession."[43] This implied that Ferguson's own attempts to supplant them would be invalid in law, unless, as he hoped would happen, the indigenous people turned out to welcome the Scots as saviors from Spanish tyranny – which, unsurprisingly perhaps, they failed to do.

IV. PURCHASE AND CONCESSION

The other argument, which John Marshall claimed was "not once alluded to" in any "single grant from the British Crown" until the eighteenth century, is cessation. British colonists, like their French and Dutch and later Swedish and other European counterparts, made wide and varied use of land purchases and of several kinds of land grants arrived at through treaty. Indeed, for most colonists, purchase, gift, or treaty was the most usual way in which individual colonists had acquired their land and had been so from the beginning.[44] Whether in the Chesapeake or in Massachusetts, the earliest settlers purchased land whenever controversies over occupancy threatened. As with all such claims, the Crown's right to grant a patent in the first place was not in question. Sovereignty, however, did not provide rights to property. Even after independence when much of the semi-independent status granted to the Indians by the Crown had been swept away, the new United States claimed only the right to preempt attempts by other nations to take possession. In their recognition of aboriginal title, as in so much else, the British were following French and most immediately Dutch examples, in particular after the Anglo-Dutch conflicts in the Connecticut valley in the 1630s. The Dutch West India Company, eager as always to distance itself from the behavior of the Spanish, "less we call down the wrath of God upon our unrighteousness beginning," insisted that all land had to be "righteously" acquired without "craft or fraud," so that, in the words of the colony's governor, Willem Verhulst, in 1625, none of the Algonquin inhabitants of the Delaware and Hudson rivers should be "driven away by force or threats, but by good words be persuaded to leave, or be given something therefore for their satisfaction." In accordance with this general principle, the following year Verhulst's successor, Pieter Minuit, purchased Manhattan Island for sixty guilders.

[43] *A Just and Modest Vindication of the Scots Design, for Having Established a Colony at Darien.* (N.P, 1699), 72–3.

[44] Stuart Banner, *How the Indians Lost Their Land: Law and Power on the Frontier* (Cambridge, MA, 2005), 10–48.

The Dutch may have preferred the idea of cessation because of religious scruples and because their presence in America was always over-stretched. The British had similar motives for denying their own official status as conquerors. But they were also aware that a conqueror in the service of a monarch could only ever be a subject and, at least by feudal contract, a vassal. If, in contrast, the settlers had purchased their lands, they might claim some measure of independence from the Crown or, where this applied, from the proprietary holder of the colony. Understanding this concept, Maryland's proprietor declared all lands purchased from the Indians subject to forfeiture.

Furthermore, if the colonists had purchased their lands or acquired them through treaty, it followed that the indigenous peoples had been in legitimate possession of them; otherwise the lands would not have been theirs to sell. The English, insisted Edward Rawson in *The Revolution in New England Justified* (1689), had "purchased from the Natives their right to the soil in that part of the world, not withstanding what right they had by virtue of their charter from the kings of England." Rawson was a supporter of the revolt against the Dominion of New England – to which the title of his pamphlet refers. In the eyes of the colonists, one of the more heinous crimes of the late governor, Edmund Andros, had been precisely to dissolve all land claims based on what he called "pretended purchases from the Indians" on the grounds that "from the Indians no title can be Derived." If that action were allowed to stand, a group of prominent Bostonians protested, "no Man was owner of a Foot of Land in all the Colony." As Rawson stressed elsewhere, any attempt by the Crown to limit the rights to self-determination that the English had acquired by "venturing their lives overseas to enlarge the King's Dominions" made them a conquered people, "deprived of their English liberties and in the same condition with the slaves in France or Turkey." In 1721, Jeremiah Dummer reiterated the same point. There could exist "no other right than that in which the honest New-England planters rely on having purchased it with their money. The Indian title, therefore, as much as it is decry'd and undervalued here, seems the only fair and just one."[45]

If, however, America were a land of conquest and thus a part of the royal demesne, any contract to dispose of any part of it between parties who were both subjects of the Crown was necessarily invalid. In addition, even if such purchases were considered to be merely private agreements they were, as many subsequent historians have pointed out, generally fraudulent. At least by implication, this was the point made by the Royal Proclamation of 1763, which set out the principles of government for the lands acquired by the British by the Treaty of Paris at the end of the Seven Years War.

[45] Jeremiah. Dummer, *A Defence of the New-England Charters* (London, 1721), 14.

The purpose of the Proclamation was to bind the former New France much more tightly to the Crown than the original English settlements in North America. To achieve this objective the Crown was compelled to limit the damage that might be inflicted upon Native American interests by colonists' intrusions on their lands. Hence the Proclamation conferred on what came to be called the "Aboriginal Peoples of America" a form of ill-defined de iure nationhood that ceded a large measure of autonomy to "the several Nations or Tribes of Indians." The Proclamation accepted that the Indians had use – but not true possession – of "such Parts of our Dominions and Territories as, not having been ceded to or purchased by Us, are reserved to them, or any of them, as their Hunting Grounds." The Proclamation also defined all the lands west of the Appalachians as "under our Sovereign Protection and Dominion for the use of the said Indians," and it forbade any future settlement there.[46] This last injunction reinforced the Treaty of Easton of 1758, which had prohibited any settlement west of the Alleghenies. The bans were unworkable in practice, not least because the Iroquois, the Cherokee, and the Creek all had ancestral lands to the east of the line, while by 1763 there were already settlements from Virginia to the west. The Proclamation line would become one of the principal grievances leveled against the Crown by the colonists.

The Proclamation was not, however, merely an attempt to limit the colonists' powers of acquisition. Nor was it an isolated case. In many ways it can be seen as the final resolution to a legal dispute dating from the 1690s between the Mohegan nation and the government of Connecticut, to which John Bulkley's *An Inquiry into the right of the aboriginal natives to land in America* had been a contribution. The Mohegans had argued that they were a sovereign nation and, as such, could not be deprived of their lands by the claim that they "lack such thing as a civil Polity, nor [do they possess] hardly any one of the circumstances essential to the existence of a state."[47] On August 24, 1705, the Privy Council had decided in favor of the Mohegans. Despite fierce lobbying from the colonists it reaffirmed the decision the following year. Not until 1763, however, was the matter decided by a formal royal decree intended to be irrevocable. The Proclamation has also had a long subsequent history. It was incorporated into the British North America Act of 1867 (now renamed the Constitution Act, 1867) and still forms the basis for much of the dealing between the Canadian federal government and Canada's Aboriginal Peoples. As recently as 1982, Lord Denning declared that the Proclamation was as binding today "as if there had been included in

[46] W. P. M. Kennedy, ed. *Documents of the Canadian Constitution* (Toronto, 1918), 20.

[47] J. H. Smith, *Appeals to the Privy Council from the American Plantations* (New York, 1950), 434.

the statute a sentence: 'The aboriginal peoples of Canada shall continue to have all their rights and freedoms as recognized by the Royal Proclamation of 1763'."[48]

The Proclamation clearly intended to grant a measure of legal autonomy to the Native Americans, as successive interpreters have supposed. But the repeated references in the document to the "sovereignty," "protection," and "dominion" that the British Crown exercised across the whole of America, north of New Spain, Florida, and California make it clear that this autonomy was intended to be severely limited. The Indian "nations" may have been self-governing communities with rights over their own ancestral lands. but they certainly could make no claims to independence from His Majesty. Indian rights did comprise the king's seisin fee – legal ownership. The Indians were perpetual tenants. They exercised, in effect, only what Marshall later deemed, in *Johnson v. M'Intosh*, a "right of occupancy" – use, rather than full property rights – because they lacked, in Marshall's words, the "ultimate dominion" that had been granted to the "nations of Europe . . . a power to convey the soil, while yet in possession of the natives."[49] Similarly, their political status was severely restricted by the presence of an "ultimate" form of jurisdiction that, in the Romanized formulation in which these distinctions were made, was also conceived as a form of property – *dominium jurisdictionis*. They were, in Bruce Clark's words, "sovereign in the same way that the colonial government was sovereign – that is vested with a delimited jurisdiction independent of all other governments except as against the imperial government." It was only by assuming that the United States had acquired the imperial authority formerly exercised by the Crown that Marshall was able to make his famous and still authoritative ruling that the Native American peoples constituted nations.

Although the Proclamation does not explicitly restate the rights of the Crown through conquest, it does insist that, because "great frauds and abuses have been committed in purchasing lands of the Indians, to the great prejudice of our interest, and to the great dissatisfaction of the said Indians," all further purchases had to be made "for Us in our name at some public meeting or assembly of the said Indians."[50] They had therefore to be a matter of public law, rather than private contract.

[48] *R. v. Secretary of State for Foreign & Commonwealth Affairs* [1982] Law Rep. Q.B. 892, 914.

[49] *Johnson v. M'Intosh*, U.S. (8 Wheaton), 574. Although the concept of a "right of occupancy" exists in Roman law, Stuart Banner argues that it only came into use in America after independence and only gained currency with American lawyers in the early nineteenth century. *How the Indians Lost Their Land: Law and Power on the Frontier*, 150–90.

[50] The text of the Proclamation is printed in W. P. M. Kennedy, ed. *Documents of the Canadian Constitution*, 20–1.

But the argument from purchase was too powerful to be disposed of so easily. For, as Richard Price argued in 1776, if the lands of the settlers had indeed been purchased and developed – and he was in no doubt that they had – then, "It is, therefore now on a double account their property, and no power on earth can have any right to disturb them in the possession of it, or to take from them, without their consent, any part of its produce."[51] Price was a staunch defender of the cause of the American colonists during the War of Independence. His arguments, like Dummer's before him, were intended not only to clear the original settlers of the charge, which so many English writers leveled against the Spanish, of illicit occupation on the basis of conquest; they were also meant to give greater weight to the argument that the colonies had been original and thus effectively independent foundations, over which, in Dummer's words, "the English king could give . . . nothing more than a bare *right of preemption*."[52] For the argument from purchase or concession, backed by the claim to have "improved" the land, also gave added force to the colonists' resistance to a government that had denied them the right of representation in Parliament.

There was further advantage to any claim based on free sale or concession. For if the colonists had acquired their lands through purchase or concession from legitimate indigenous holders, they might also thereby evade the monarch's right to limit the movement of his subjects – the right of *ne exeat regno* – which the monarch held under common law (and, many would argue, under natural law). Later opponents of colonial rule, like Richard Bland, whom Jefferson described as a "most learned and logical man, profound in constitutional law," would argue that in fact the colonies had been Lockean foundations created like the first human societies, quite literally out of the state of nature. "When subjects are deprived of their civil rights, or are dissatisfied with the place they hold in the community", he wrote in 1766:

> they have a natural right to quit the society of which they are members, and to retire into another country. Now when men exercise this right of withdrawing themselves from their country, they recover their natural freedom and independence; the jurisdiction and sovereignty of the states they have quitted ceases; and if they unite, and by common consent take possession of a new country and form themselves into a political society, they become a sovereign state, independent of the state from which they separated.[53]

[51] "Observations on the Nature of Civil Liberty, the Principles of Government, and the Justice and Policy of the War with America," in Richard Price, *Political Writings*, ed. D. O. Thomas (Cambridge, 1991), 40.

[52] Jeremiah Dummer, *A Defence of the New-England Charters*, 13.

[53] *An Enquiry into the Rights of the British Colonies* (London, 1769), 12.

Once established in their new country, their rights – which could only of course, be natural rights – could be based only on *terra nullius* or purchase or a combination of both. Only then would the settler population be in a position to demand the same kind of sovereign rights that the Crown was claiming to exercise on their behalf.

CONCLUSION

In the end, the prolonged dispute over the legality of the occupation of America resolved itself into a dispute over the sources of sovereign authority. Who, in other words, had the right to make the law, and on behalf of whom?

In 1776, Adam Smith complained that the rulers of Great Britain "have for more than a century past, amused the people with the imagination that they possessed a great empire on the west side of the Atlantic. This empire, however, has hitherto existed in imagination only. It has hitherto been not an empire but the project of an empire."[54] As Smith had seen, the de facto situation in the colonies, where every individual settlement enjoyed its own peculiar rights, laws were made at a local level, and separate constitutions and even separate semi-feudal hierarchies (think of the Carolinas with its Caribbean Caciques, and Hanoverian Landgraves) might be established, could hardly be an "empire" as the term was currently employed. This "project of an empire" had been brought into being largely because, unlike the French or the Spanish, the English Crown had never had any clear conception of what were the grounds for the occupation of the Americas. As we have seen, the Crown had generally insisted that its colonies overseas were lands of conquest, even though very few acts of conquest had actually taken place. Under English common law, conquest made them integral parts of the royal demesne and subject directly to royal command, not Parliament. Logically the colonists were not, as was later claimed, represented "virtually" in Parliament; they were represented literally, just not in person but by the "King in Parliament." Yet, its general jurisdictional claim put to one side, the Crown not only made grants of lands to its subjects but it also permitted those subjects to make their own laws – something that none of the other European monarchies, all of whose colonies were governed by codes issued in the metropolis, ever did. What this meant was that in practice, if never in law, the Crown shared sovereignty with its settler populations. Much later this would be transformed into a recognized principal of imperial law. After centuries of struggle, sovereignty in Europe had become indivisible. But

[54] *An Inquiry into the Nature and Causes of the Wealth of Nations*, ed. R. H. Campbell and A. S. Skinner, *The Glasgow Edition of the Works and Correspondence of Adam Smith* 2 vols. (Oxford, 1976), II: 946–7.

beyond the frontiers of Europe – as Henry Sumner Maine, sometime Regius Professor of Civil Law at Cambridge and Member of the Viceroy of India's Council, would declare in 1887 – "sovereignty has always been regarded as divisible."[55] As Maine recognized, although the problem had never been formulated as such, up until the end of the Seven Years War, this had effectively been the practice in British North America. As an anonymous contributor to the *Pennsylvania Journal* in March 1766 expressed it, "In a confederacy of States independent of each other yet united under one head, such as I conceive the British empire at present to be, all the power of legislation may subsist full and complete in each part, and the respective legislatures be absolutely independent of each other."

After 1763 when faced with a government determined to regain full sovereignty over all its domains, both within the British Isles and overseas, the American colonists turned to those arguments that, in natural rather than civil law, could help them secure the survival of their de facto rights. This demanded that they reexamine, and very substantially rewrite, the early history of the original settlements. For questions as to how and by what authority indigenous peoples had been deprived of what in natural law was usually conceded to be their *dominium* would in the end determine not so much the status of whatever remained of *those* peoples as the future legal status of the English colonies and their inhabitants and, more important, the status of what the successors to those colonies might be. For most of the jurists who attempted to construct a convincing legal argument for independence from the Crown, and for the early legislators of the new republic, the task was to set aside the long-standing English argument that America had been a land of conquest. To do this they turned to those two other claims, discovery (as in *terra nullius*) and purchase or concession, which had always appealed to the early colonists precisely because they might provide rights in natural law, but had never, for that very same reason, figured in the official legal languages of the metropolis. American law was and is based upon English common law. But it should never be forgotten that the early history of American law was marked by a struggle for emancipation that also demanded a reconstruction of the relationship between the Europeans and the Native Americans.

The English waited until the early eighteenth century before they began to contemplate the awful possibility of separation from the mother country. But the forms of government and the legal system in effect in the colonies had from the beginning established a de facto independence that no other

[55] *International Law. A series of lectures delivered before the University of Cambridge 1887* (London: John Murray, 1888), 55–7.

European monarchy had permitted its settler populations. The entire subsequent history of law in the United States, the fact that much of it remains to this day closer to its English common law origins than the legal systems of any of the other former European colonies in the Americas resemble theirs, has its origins in their experience of *de facto* independence.

2

THE LAW OF NATIVE AMERICANS, TO 1815

KATHERINE A. HERMES

At the time of European contact with North America in the early sixteenth century, Native Americans across the continent lived in a diversity of groups characterized by highly varied governmental and family structures. Geography, language, and economy affected the way in which these societies understood law and formed legal institutions. It is not easy to cover in one essay the many legalities and legal practices of Native American peoples before their eventual designation as "domestic dependent nations" of the United States in 1831, but it is possible – and perhaps more important – to show how their jurispractice changed as European colonization began to alter their law.

No historian has ever attempted a narrative of indigenous American jurisprudence. Indeed, until the 1970s it was difficult to find historians who would even admit that Native Americans had something that was identifiable as "law" in the way that Europeans use the term. By then, discovery narratives had begun to give way to neo-conquest analyses that stressed the brutality of European behavior and the often fatal biological consequences of European occupation of the Americas after 1492. However, until the cross-cultural encounter narratives of the 1990s began to appear it was difficult to find anything in the historical literature that seriously suggested that pre-contact American Indians possessed laws, much less had structures and systems. Even though legal anthropology had begun to have significant effects on legal history by the 1980s, the historical narrative of Native American jurispractices for the centuries prior to Chief Justice John Marshall's "Indian" trilogy seemed more or less immune from its influence.[1]

It is safe to say that before the mid-eighteenth century there was no Native American jurisprudence, either in a pan-Indian sense or among the tribes,

[1] *Johnson v. M'Intosh*, 21 U.S. 543 (1823); *Cherokee Nation v. Georgia*, 30 U.S. 1 (1830); *Worcester v. Georgia*, 31 U.S. 515 (1832).

nations, and confederacies that made up the various governments of indigenous people. But if jurisprudence is the philosophy of law, and if law itself is interwoven, sometimes inextricably, with morality, custom, or other means to force people to act in ways they would not otherwise choose, American Indians certainly possessed law. They may have had no way in which to disperse and debate philosophical principles, but they shared certain concepts that created a legal mentalité – what I here call "jurispractice" – that evolved as an indigenous way of acting legally, both within indigenous societies and among them, and that could, after European settlement, be communicated to colonial authorities whose systems were different. Indigenous jurispractices were founded on expectations of people that were not subject to arbitrariness or to change without formal discussion. They encompassed mechanisms for resolving disputes that were time-honored and consistent. They remedied wrongs, through restitution or punishment, in ways that were bound by rule. Deviation from these rules evoked objections from those who considered them unalterable.

Some colonists understood that Indians had law. Others did not. Most European colonial regimes, however, gave some measure of acknowledgment to Indian expectations that seemed to them "legal," or as custom that had to be enforced. What historians know of Native American law before 1750 comes filtered largely through European sources. The Spanish in the southwest developed a system of imposing court days and elections on the Indians they conquered, but southwestern Indians dispensed justice in a way that combined Spanish process with Indian substance. They may have been forced to use the trappings of Spanish procedure to hold their courts, but the justice provided within was probably traditional. Modification would follow as Spanish law became known and understood. In New France, Jesuit missionaries frequently analogized Indian law to the old Germanic or Salic law, referring to Indian payments of wampumpeag for restitution as *wergeld*. But the Jesuits understood that they could not deduce Indian law by these means. Puritan authorities in the English colonies, meanwhile, held Indian law to resemble that of their primitive ancestors or as related to their own understandings of justice.

Whether or not Europeans were interested in Indian jurispractice did not matter to Native Americans, who tried to make known their own expectations, even in colonial courts. By the eighteenth century some Indians, usually Christians, had become literate enough to produce works that detailed their own peoples' customs, but often these writers did not use the language of law or of legal systems as much as that of custom and government. Whether this was an outgrowth of a Europeanized view that they had adopted or a matter of deliberate choice is hard to say.

Overall, what emerges from all these sources is an imperfect picture of Native American jurispractice, but one that is nevertheless quite recognizable as law.

Tracing the evolution of jurispractice during the period after contact with Europeans requires recognition of several fundamental realities. First, there were many levels of contact. The 500 or more Native American tribes and nations that existed at the time of contact were not homogeneous. All had laws particular to their cultures that may or may not have been shared with others, even nearby native communities. Second, several layers of European and colonial government came first to interact with and then to overlie the heterogeneous sovereign entities of the tribes themselves. By 1815, the native peoples residing in the area of the modern United States had been subjected to the law of Spain, of France, and of England; to the law of the colonies and subsequently states that formed around them; to the law of the United States under the Articles of Confederation; and lastly to the law of the United States under the Constitution of 1787. As if these many entities, each claiming sovereignty or at least some degree of dominion over the native peoples in their territories, were not enough, the process of colonization itself created a divide between types of Indians that affected which law applied to them. Native peoples who maintained themselves in autonomous Indian communities retained a measure of self-government; in theory this distinguished them from individual Indians who lived in colonial towns and who therefore were under some form of colonial law.

To understand the effect of contact on Indian jurispractice through the early nineteenth century – arguably one of the most complex legal periods of American and U.S. history – one must recognize three premises that acted both alternately and, occasionally, simultaneously on Native American law. The first was the belief held by Indians that their law was in their control. This premise was entirely true for the pre-contact period and often true thereafter. The second was the belief held by colonists, and later by federal and state officials, that Indians had only partial control of their law because Anglo-European law always trumped native law whenever they met. The third was an ideal on the part of Anglo-Europeans, shared as a belief by Indians, that justice should be accorded to Native Americans in the same way it was to whites. Despite the apparent accord on the matter, this third premise was problematic because so often native perceptions of justice were simply not the same as those of the colonists or the later federal government. Most native ideas of justice entailed some sort of reciprocity, which often took the form of a gift exchange, so that neither side would be bitter at the result.

Some differences that arose in the contact period between colonists and Indians could be resolved out of court, but most – for example, disputes over boundary lines, fencing, and animal trespass – could not. Communities in which mediation was a familiar legal mechanism for resolving disputes could implement the native idea of justice as reciprocity. Mostly, however, disputes were resolved antagonistically. The adversarial system of British law in particular resulted in great dissatisfaction for the Indians. Where law failed to be the mediating factor, trade became the sole "middle ground" between Europeans and Indians. Indians who violated European legal norms in the post-contact period were frequently viewed by colonists as military enemies.

In the North Atlantic colonial world, Native Americans and European colonists negotiated the terms of the law that would exist in the space they co-inhabited. Each had their own laws that they followed in the spaces they did not share.[2] There were, consequently, multiple legalities in the colonized North Atlantic world. But most overlapped, for the different peoples could not inhabit entirely separate spheres.[3] Most of these coexisting legalities were found among native peoples, although not exclusively, because European regimes also differed among themselves, not only by national origin but by the particular colonial objectives of the settlers. The interpenetration of jurispractice among Native Americans was, however, complicated by circumstances that did not particularly confront Europeans – namely, the repeated ethnogenesis that tribes were forced to undergo as they attempted to make new social entities from what remained after disease, warfare, poverty, and trauma had all taken their toll. Rents and repairs in the social fabric supporting jurispractice were not the sole factor in the erosion of negotiated legal power sharing after contact. Cultural fusion or cultural hybridization, both forms of ethnogenesis, created new political identities necessary for the groups' survival. In tribes whose composition changed, laws had to be renegotiated and legal customs altered.

Over time, the possibility of maintaining some form of mutual creolized law in North America disintegrated. Although it is easy to attribute this disintegration largely to sheer power imbalances that favored the Europeans, the answer is not that simple. The mere existence of power imbalances did not mean that domination would necessarily result. Several cultural factors

[2] I refer to "space" and not territory, because the concept of territorial jurisdiction is problematic for Native Americans, as discussed below.

[3] "Legality [refers to] meanings, sources of authority, and cultural practices that are commonly recognized as legal, regardless of who employs them or for what ends. We conceive of legality as an emergent structure of social life that manifests itself in diverse places, including but not limited to formal institutional settings. Legality operates as both an interpretative framework and a set of resources with which and through which the social world is constituted." Patricia Ewick and Susan Silbey. *The Common Place of Law: Stories from Everyday Life* (Chicago, 1998), 22–3.

in the European world had a bearing on the shift. First, even as the number of Indians decreased, settlers' fear of them grew. The legal culture of the English settlements, meanwhile, became generally less hospitable to Native Americans as it became more "English"; as the common law ascended, English legalities became more adversarial, more formal, and less equitable. In addition, changes among the Indian population altered their participation in the system they helped create. Some Native Americans became increasingly hostile to Europeans and rejected cooperation altogether. Other Native Americans opted for accommodation or assimilation and began using the colonial court systems without the protections, demands, or special processes they had once reserved for themselves. Among those who adapted to European ways there were gendered divisions in the use of laws and legal procedures. Women, perhaps because they tended to become domestic servants if they lived among colonists, sometimes saw European legal practices as expeditious, such as the writing of wills to transfer property and ensure inheritance. Men, in contrast, especially as time went on, became suspicious of European legal instruments that had so often proved deceptive, such as land deeds.

Europeans, meanwhile, used their opportunities to dominate in ways that were not merely oppressive but might be described as casually abusive. The rules shifted from one town to the next and across colony lines. They were insisted on at some times, but not at others. Overall, European legalities were simply unpredictable. It became impossible for Native Americans to guess which protocols and processes might be required in colonial courts or when they had to resort to them, making it very difficult to maintain standing or to operate at all effectively within two separate yet overlapping spheres of jurispractice.

One final factor must be mentioned before embarking on the story of Native American law and of how a negotiated realm of jurispractice arose and fell in North America as divergent legal ideas vied for space. It is crucial to touch on the effect of this evolutionary process on Anglo-American or U.S. law. The idea that Native Americans contributed anything to Anglo-American or U.S. law is hotly contested among scholars. Although it is a truism that in cross-cultural encounters neither side remains unchanged by the other, this does not mean that every aspect of one culture will be influenced by the other. Nevertheless, there are legal practices that historians and anthropologists, and even eighteenth-century contemporaries, suggest might have come to the present from the indigenous past in America. When Sarah Kemble Knight, a female traveler who in 1704 wondered in her journal whether the New England Indian custom of casually casting away one's spouse might be responsible for the high rate of divorce among couples in Connecticut, she was not without grounds for her speculations.

When modern historians suggest that the Iroquois Confederacy might have contributed to the conception of a U.S. federal government, they should not be taken lightly. No conclusive proof of direct adoption from Native law to European law exists at the present time, but among scholars the inquiry has only just begun in earnest.

I. FROM THE BEGINNING: THE LANGUAGE, STRUCTURES, AND PRINCIPLES OF NATIVE AMERICAN LAW

In separating certain periods from others, pre-contact from contact, colonial from post-Constitutional, one must bear in mind that at no time was the law of Native America institutionally stagnant. When one looks at pre-contact law and considers native traditions and how they were changed by contact, it is imperative to recognize that these legal systems would have changed in any case. Most native legal systems in North America were quite flexible. Like many systems that use custom to judge present cases, and this included Anglo-American legal systems, the good of the community as it stands weighed on the minds of those judging the case at hand. Throughout native North America, whether the system was based on the use of councils who adjudicated disputes or dependent on a paramount chief who decided matters in consultation with his advisors, law was personal. In face-to-face communities, no judgment was distanced from the people who wanted a resolution.

Before 1815, the Native Americans who lived within what would become the borders of the United States – east of the Mississippi River, south into Florida and Louisiana, north to the Canadian line, and along the Atlantic seaboard – were mainly of five general linguistic groups: Algonquian, Iroquois, Sioux, Inuit, and Muskhogean. These linguistic groups were not determinative of culture per se. Those who lived in the eastern woodlands, whether Algonquian or Siouan, had more in common than those who lived in the interior, in the Great Lakes region, or in the southeastern area below the Chesapeake. Nevertheless, language and law are intertwined, for language gives life to legal concepts. Social groupings also affect jurisdiction; that is, the right to claim power over territory, persons, or certain objects or subjects. Where the usual social grouping was the clan, owing some allegiance to a chief but living apart from a central chiefdom, law was institutionally less structured than in societies that had constructed confederacies of many tribal nations. Several such confederacies existed in North America in the period just before contact with Europeans. The most notable were the Powhatan Confederacy of the Chesapeake, the Iroquois Confederacy of the Great Lakes region, the Appalachian Confederacy, and the Cherokee Confederation of the Southeast.

The first visitors from Europe reported almost universally that they had found a people without laws. Visitors friendly to the natives accorded them a knowledge of the law of nature, but no system; for example, the Jesuit missionary Jean de Brébeuf described the Huron as "not without laws" and left a description of their system of punishment, which noted that they punished murderers according to a four-step ritual, with a specific incantation for each step. Skeptics believed them to be completely lawless. Another Jesuit, Paul Le Jeune, held that loyalty to a chief was the only reason the Montaignes were constrained from killing one another. "[T]he Indians have neither civil regulation, nor administrative offices, nor dignitaries, nor any positions of command," he wrote.[4]

A few reformers guessed that there had once been a legal system among natives, but that it had been destroyed. In a 1553 letter to Charles V, Louis de León Romano, an administrator of the viceroyalty of New Spain, described native society as "without order and governance whatever." Yet, Romano insisted this was "because the system of government has been turned so much to the opposite of what it once was. For the sort of people they are, their former system of government was the best that ever [a] nation had, except for the salvation of their souls." Indeed, the indigenous people in North America did have laws and legal systems, just as they had religious beliefs and practices that were also invisible to many European observers.

Some systems were more complex than others. Their languages demonstrate some of the legal concepts Native Americans held, though one cannot infer too much from the existence of a word if there is no evidence as to what natives really understood it to mean. (Frequently, that evidence is missing.) The Algonquians had certain words that signified the practice of law. The root "tepa" or "tipa" combined with "wa," "wew," or "kew" meant judging or measuring something; it could even mean to control. That this word for judge probably had some legal meaning can be inferred from the words that surround it: in Cree, an Algonquian language, the expression "tipeyeimew" meant "he rules over him." In Nahuatl there were words to express such technical and complex ideas as land and water rights, as well as words for many types of rulers. The Nahuatl word "altepetl" expressed the idea of "city-state." The Muskhogean tribes include, among others, the Choctaw, Creeks, Chickasaws, Seminoles, and Apalachi. The Cherokee, who would be recognized by Europeans as one of the "Five Civilized Tribes," spoke an Iroquois dialect. Whether the Cherokee linguistic difference had any enabling effect on their later development of an alphabet and a constitution is a matter for speculation, but the Iroquois language and culture seem to have facilitated certain political associations.

[4] Brébeuf, *Jesuit Relations*, 10: 210–35; Le Jeune, *Jesuit Relations*, 6:228–35.

The Confederacies make up an important part of the legal landscape for native North America. At first viewed by historians primarily as political entities, the confederacies are currently seen as economic and military alliances. They were also entities that maintained legal structures and enforced legal customs among their members. Among the eastern tribal nations such alliances were common, both as a means of protection and a system of tribute. The first alliance encountered by Europeans was the Iroquois Confederacy, formed about 1390, which consisted of five nations: the Seneca, Oneida, Mohawk, Cayuga, and Onondaga. The Iroquois Confederacy spread across the Ohio Valley, up toward the Great Lakes, and into the St. Lawrence River Valley around present-day Quebec. In 1715, the Tuscaroras of Virginia moved northward and joined the Iroquois Confederacy when English settlement across the Blue Ridge Mountains made it too difficult to remain in that region.

The Iroquois Confederacy had a very distinct system of law when compared with other eastern cultures. The confederacy itself was a diplomatic and military bond, which later evolved into an economic unit as well. The Iroquois depended on frequent meetings, spending considerable time in council. Groupings for council were determined by locality, sex, age, and the specific question at hand. Each had its own protocol and devices for gaining consensus.

The Hurons, like most northern Indians, also made decisions by council. In some villages the council met daily. There were a set of elders who garnered respect at these meetings, but the forums were open. Huron councils exerted little control over individuals, beyond what was necessary to keep social order. The councils had a formal protocol, and even the oratory was procedural, with each speaker summarizing the issue and arguments of the previous speaker. In a non-literate society, this method could have been a means to ensure that everyone understood the issues and arguments; listening was an essential quality. Brébeuf admired the practice, which he thought gave clarity to the proceedings and made it easy for a stranger to understand what was going on.

Whatever structure of legal decision making was in place, the most important legal concept among Native Americans was the principle of reciprocity. Reciprocity was first recognized as a principle common among native peoples by early twentieth- century anthropologists, although somewhat anachronistically and without any historical particularism. In fact, the principle had important variations among Native Americans in the colonial period. Moreover, although it is true that the principle of reciprocity was used in other areas of society, from religion to economics, its use as a legal principle was particularly distinctive among the several tribes, nations, and confederacies.

For the native peoples, the practice of give-and-take transcended legal boundaries and existed as an economic and social value. In the legal realm, however, it meant that reparation could be made for wrongdoing. It also meant that, when a wrong occurred, all parties took away something so that, in most cases, no one bore the entire burden of the legal infraction. Europeans found Indian legal customs unfathomable when they observed such processes at work, but they also accepted that the core value of reciprocity corresponded to their own systems of law. For Puritans and legal reformers in New England, the value in reciprocity was that it allowed the law to be a mediator between parties rather than an adversarial tool. For the French and the Dutch, both of which had civil law rather than common law systems, justice was less about moral absolutes and more about fairness. Thus, in the period of contact, from about 1600 to 1675, all four interacting legal systems were operating on an assumption that justice could be and should be equal between all parties.

An example of reciprocity in native jurispractice was the concept of restitution for harm. In the current Anglo-American system of law, tort law and criminal law present two different types of legal redress for dealing with harm. We now think of the state as the complaining party in criminal cases, though even in England in the seventeenth century, individuals could bring private criminal prosecutions. In Indian North America few tribal nations had a concept that distinguished between criminal and civil offenses as precisely as English law, but most had a system that involved the group in seeking redress for the individual and determining whether both the individual and the group needed compensation for the harm. The concept of harm to the group, even for an action against an individual, was commonplace. The means of settling the matter between the offending parties, also defined according to complex norms involving ideas about who was responsible – chief and tribe or individual – differed from region to region. At the core, however, was a strong belief common to most societies that harm to an individual member was harm to all and that the individual should not have to face his victimization alone. Leaders offered communal protection.

Embodying the principle of reciprocity, in most Indian communities a designated person served as peacemaker, a type of mediator who was well versed in community norms and knew how to restore harmony. The role of the peacemaker was critical to the community. In the Iroquois nations, peacemakers were part of the formal judicial system. In the southwest, they tended to have less formal roles, being chosen by the parties rather than as part of the formal process.

The Iroquois believed in a system of law that the Jesuits who first encountered them described, as we have seen, as analogous to *wergeld*, the ancient

German law that exacted material goods for wrongs. To modern eyes, the distinction between tort law and criminal law seems blurred by the Iroquois, and it is easy to assume that they had no distinction between a crime against the state, as it were, and a personal injury. In fact that was not the case. The payments that could be demanded depended very much on whether the transgression was against an individual or the tribe as a community. The homicide of a sachem brought warfare and sanctions against the people from whom the killer came, whether a clan within the same tribe or another nation. If another nation was involved, captives taken from the wrongdoer's people were either tortured and killed or adopted into the avenging tribe. This practice, known as the mourning war, became more prevalent as time went on, compensating the tribe that had been victimized not only for murder but also for losses from disease, warfare, or hardship once the Europeans settled in North America.

Other wrongs, such as the killing of a person by accident or negligence, or a theft of a valuable item, were punished by demanding payment of some kind in relation to the level of harm done. Furs and other goods such as wampum belts from the coast compensated victims. Usually a council set the payment, and if there was any dispute between the parties as to the justice of the demanded amount, it would become the subject of negotiation.

Yet, the Iroquois legal system was not *wergeld* in any strict sense. That was merely the closest European analogy the Jesuits could think of. Priests and travelers described a system of rules that carried specific penalties for specific wrongs. Elaborate rules governed behavior, but the principle that dictated most judgments was reciprocity. Justice was usually satisfied by putting the world back in balance. Yet, the Iroquois went further than many eastern woodland tribes in their scale of punishments. They included torture as a legitimate punishment, something most Algonquian tribes did not.

Jean de Brébeuf's 1636 *Relation* gives us perhaps the fullest account of the government of the Hurons. Brébeuf was familiar with the laws of many civilizations, including the Chinese and Japanese, with whom the Jesuits had missions, and so he had a basis for comparison outside European law. He thought the Huron primitive, but not without civilization. The system he described eschewed private vengeance but punished wrongdoers. Vengeance, he remarked, was the "blackest" crime, even worse than murder. The rule of law could never be thwarted without incurring terrible punishments. Brébeuf commented that the Indians of his time were not as strict against murderers as in former times, suggesting that the death penalty was once exacted on murderers. The relative of a murdered person brought the prosecution to the village of the alleged killer. The family was paid in gifts, sixty to be precise. Each series of presents had meaning and was apparently stipulated by law. The ritual was designed to restore peace to the country, an exchange that required the "guilty" party to give back, in a sense, what was taken from the group that lost a member, thereby eliminating the need to exact vengeance. If Brébeuf was correct, what modern lawyers would now call the penalty or sentencing phase of a trial was more important than the proof of a person's guilt or innocence. In earlier, harsher times, the murderer was forced to stand beneath the body of the slain person, where he had to endure the experience of having the corpse release its fluids onto him and into his food. This practice seems to have faded by 1636. Even as late as the nineteenth century, the prohibition against vengeance still functioned, particularly if the murderer was within the kin group of the victim.

In their encounters with the Indians, the Jesuits did not perceive that the ritualized system of restitution in lieu of vengeance corresponded with any pressing need to curb deviant behavior; they actually found very little crime among the Indians, as Europeans defined it. The principle was an overarching one, applying not only to transgressions within the Huron tribe but also to their relations with other tribes. The Huron had rules for intertribal relations that covered such matters as trade routes. Their rules also extended to intertribal transgressions. If one tribe or a person under the tribe's jurisdiction committed a wrong against a person in another tribe and would not make restitution, this constituted grounds for war. During war, according to Brébeuf, both torture and ritual cannibalism were permissible.[5]

The power to restore balance in a complex society riven at times by transgressions against individuals or groups is but one of the powers we may recognize as inherent in the right to govern. In all societies with any kind of ruling power, there is a way in which that power asserts its right to govern. The claim may be the right to exercise authority over territory, persons, or certain subject matters, but having jurisdiction, whether formally used as a concept or not, means the right to impose rule over some place, some one, or something, and occasionally all of these. Although jurisdiction and tribute were not the same phenomenon, one finds hierarchical power expressed in native North America through the system of tribute.

Tribute was a form of payment by one tribe or clan to a higher political authority. It was a way of recognizing superior authority, whether that was an authority won by conquest or as a means of mutual diplomacy. The tribute system predated contact, but Native Americans adapted it to meet the changing post-contact world. In pre-contact native societies the system of tribute affected many people, from the highly organized and militarily powerful system established by the Aztec Empire to the smaller systems

[5] Brébeuf, *Jesuit Relations*, 10: 210–261.

of control among tribal nations elsewhere. When the Pequot controlled the wampum trade, the small tribes along the Connecticut River paid them tribute. After the ruinous war of 1637, the Pequot paid tribute to the Mohegan sachem, Uncas, or to the Connecticut colonial government, depending on who offered protection. Tribute might be paid in gold and precious metal in the southwest or, depending on where one lived, in maize, wampum, or skins.

The system of tribute and jurisdiction could go hand in hand; that is, a person who exacted tribute might at times claim jurisdiction over that people, but at other times not. Just as often, nations exacting tribute left governance and jurisdiction to the local chief or leader. At the time of contact in North America, the primary eastern groups that would encounter the European colonists, such as the Powhatan Confederacy of Tsenacommacah (now Virginia), were organized as tribute systems. The Powhatans, under their paramount chief by the same name, controlled Algonquian-, Siouan-, and Iroquoian-speaking peoples in the Chesapeake region as far as the Appalachians. In the Powhatan system tribute and jurisdiction were intertwined but not inseparable. For example, Powhatan claimed to the English that he did not have the authority to punish wrongdoers from his tributaries. If the English had problems with members of a confederate tribe, they had to take it up with the tribe's werowance, or chief.

Just as Native American personal jurisdiction mystified Europeans, territorial jurisdiction appeared to colonists as nonexistent outside of confederacies. Historians frequently blame this problem on the different understandings held by Indians and Europeans regarding possession of the land. We must also distinguish between Indians' views of jurisdiction and their view of property. Territorial boundaries were well known among the tribes, nations, and confederacies and sometimes were contested. There was no unfettered movement between lands, and chiefs had some sense of control over territory. If a problem occurred within their territory, chiefs were more likely to hand over the transgressors to their own tribal leaders. Yet, there was no property ownership, as Europeans understood it, among most Native American peoples of North America. Typically, before colonization and in the period immediately following it, most Indians followed a law of usufruct that enabled them to use land for various purposes, such as farming, hunting, and maintaining a dwelling.

Alden Vaughan, sometimes viewed as an apologist for the Puritans in their interactions with Native Americans, argues that Algonquians resented colonial rules and colonial courts from the beginning, but he identifies this claim with the Indians' resentment of land acquisitions. It is necessary to differentiate between the early willingness of Algonquians to try to reach understandings with the colonists on matters of law and their later realization of the damage done by the colonists' insatiable hunger for land. The majority of Algonquians who faced the colonists' Christianizing efforts from 1650 to 1750 adopted the same line of resistance: they preferred to live as their fathers and grandfathers had lived. Land was at the heart of this conflict, not law. The Algonquian tribes before 1675 had shown a willingness to compromise on legal procedures to facilitate good relations with the colonists, and their willingness had been reciprocated by various colonial governments. As Yasuhide Kawashima has shown, King Philip's War in 1675, in part the violent reaction to a legal decision in a murder trial that resulted in the hanging deaths of three Wampanoags for the death of a Christianized Indian, marked the end of attempts at mutual accommodation. The war was a turning point in legal relations, as in all other interactions in southeastern New England.

II. RECIPROCITY AND TRADE AS LEGAL MEDIATORS IN THE COLONIAL WORLD

When the Pilgrims landed at Plymouth Rock in the winter of 1620, they were greeted by an English-speaking Native American whose name they rendered as "Samoset." He in turn brought them another Indian whose command of English was even better. Tisquantum, otherwise known as Squanto, had been to England, taken there by men who had been fishing and trading in the Northern Atlantic regions of North America long before there was any colony at Plymouth. Tisquantum introduced the Pilgrims to the powerful Wampanoag sachem, Massasoit, who shortly thereafter signed a treaty with them. Thus began the legal history of native and English contact, the interplay of jurisdiction and jurispractice on both sides, and the resultant creation of a new and fragile legal space – a kind of international law and domestic law all at once, in which dramatically different cultures struggled for fairness and justice. These goals often eluded them, but not always. Indeed, it is worth remarking on those instances where the law was both formed and followed, for there is something almost incredible about this part of the story – not often told and even less frequently believed. The history of violence almost always obscures the history of mediation through law. Indeed, historians most often see law as a means to do violence – a tool of oppression rather than a forum to reach common ground. Colonization was an inherently violent process, but it was ameliorated by the nature of legal compromise and creation that took place over two centuries.

In the period of contact, from about 1600 to 1675, interactions between indigenous and European legal systems operated on the assumption that justice could be and should be equal between all parties. The compromise and creation that occurred in the shared legal landscape after contact can best be illustrated with an analysis of jurisdiction in New England. Of the three types of jurisdiction recognized by English law – territorial, personal, and subject matter – the Algonquian tribes of the region subscribed to practices akin only to the second and third. The chiefs of the various tribes, whether they were called sachems, sagamores, or werowances, exercised a varying degree of personal jurisdiction over members of their tribes. Depending on their alliances with other tribes, the chiefs might also have certain responsibilities to decide particular issues. In their interaction with Europeans, Indians almost never accorded jurisdiction over their persons to colonial governments. Intra-indigenous disputes could not be settled in English courts just as intra-colonial disputes could not be settled by native authorities. This rule was observed more or less rigorously.

The eastern Algonquians, such as the Wampanoags, actively shaped the nature of personal jurisdiction exercised over tribal members by Indian and colonial governments in the first decades of colonization of New England. They decided by protocol, agreement, or individual volition whether to appear in colonial courts. For example, the agreement signed by Massasoit provided that any Wampanoag who harmed the English would appear in a colonial court. This agreement would have fatal consequences half a century after it was made. Only in cases of murder of a colonist would a colonial court "fetch" an Indian without consent, and then only after his sachem was unable to persuade the accused to appear. Sometimes individual Indians appear to have acquiesced to pressure from tribal councils to confess to a crime against the colonists, because they were convinced that it was in the best interests of the tribe. In the Algonquian worldview, trading one man's life for peace with the colonists was the ultimate act of reciprocity. The exercise of Indian jurisdiction over the persons of colonists is less clear. It may be argued that the use by some New England colonial courts of mixed juries composed of Indians and colonists in certain intra-group homicide cases constituted a cession of personal jurisdiction. Indians did not keep records, and although there are stories that Indians subjected Europeans to native processes for transgressions within their own tribal lands, it is doubtful that this was a common practice.

In negotiating the legal space we now call "subject matter jurisdiction" the Algonquian position was very clear. They insisted that Europeans take jurisdiction over the troubles they brought with them, namely, alcohol, guns, and livestock. What historians have often mistaken as colonial usurpation of power over the persons of Native Americans was actually the demand by tribes that colonists fix the problems that they created. The appearance of Native Americans in colonial courts before 1675 did not signify a loss of autonomy; it was, in fact, the opposite. They came with explicit requests for justice.

The year 1675 is a well-recognized watershed in relations between Indians and Europeans because it marks the start of King Philip's War, a conflict between the tribes of southern New England and the English that spread as far as the borders of New France. It is no coincidence that it was a legal spark that ignited the war, one that included issues of trial methods, punishment, and jurisdiction. The war shattered the relative stability of the negotiated legal sphere. After 1675, Algonquian jurisdictional autonomy as it had developed over the decades ended abruptly. Algonquians were reduced to exercising jurisdiction over themselves at English sufferance, on reservation lands set aside for them.

This seventeenth-century jurisdictional picture is complicated by the conversion of Indians to Christianity and the creation of segregated "praying towns" in New England. Both the French and the English established separate towns for Indians who converted to Christianity, suggesting that Indians and Europeans each had reasons for preferring segregation between traditionalists and converts. Yet, New England convert towns took on a character quite distinct from those of the French, and there has been debate about whether English "praying towns," as they were known, were actually the first reservations. Praying Indians of New England developed hybrid laws and governmental structures that reflected colonial values, but in distinctly Algonquian ways. They held their own courts, which in the seventeenth century were presided over most frequently by Indian magistrates. Men such as Waban at Natick, Massachusetts, sat as magistrates in judgment of their fellow Christian Indians. The praying Indians voted for their selectmen, usually by holding up their hands, at town meetings. Fraudulent elections of selectmen sometimes occurred when white settlers hoodwinked Indian inhabitants by using paper ballots, but the paternalism of the colonial governments and the overseers often resulted in the overturning of such results. Natick Indians learned to keep written records in a transliterated version of their language. Eventually, after King Philip's War instilled fear of all Indians into the colonists, colonial authorities began to replace Indian magistrates with colonial overseers.

Throughout the eighteenth century the personal jurisdiction that had been crucial to Algonquians before King Philip's War eroded even further. Deeply in debt to colonists, the praying Indians petitioned colonial governments to give them "the rights of Englishmen," which amounted to the right to sell off common lands to pay what they owed. In this respect, the praying Indians ended up in much the same position as their non-Christian brethren. Although colonial governments' general desire was to protect the Indian inhabitants of the praying towns, the substance of that protection was frequently questionable in its benefits, for the governments also responded to pressure from their own constituents. Native peoples were caught in an unhappy middle, heavily indebted to European neighbors and in some cases signing away land to avoid going to jail for debt after being sued in colonial courts. This cession of territory sealed their jurisdictional fate in the minds of the colonial government, which equated territory with governing power.

The mediated jurisdictional space of early colonial New England, built on shared principles of reciprocity and justice, had been destroyed by war. Its history nevertheless offers a slightly different picture than that which emerges from the Chesapeake area, where trade networks rather than principles of fairness were the legal mediators. In that space, acts of war had a different role.

In general, the Chesapeake colonies rarely brought Indians to court except to have their ages confirmed as servants or slaves or to punish those already in bondage for running away. Few instances of violent crime were treated as individual crimes. What might have been called murder in New England was usually an act of war or petit treason in the Chesapeake. Thus, the jurispractice of Indians eroded much more quickly in the Chesapeake, where it was given much less chance of creating a hybrid colonial legal space. After the early wars of 1622–5 and 1644, Indians either lived on the periphery of Chesapeake society, and outside of its court system, or in bondage within it. Yet, Native Americans fared better than the other subjected culture in the Chesapeake, the Africans. The tripartite racial community of the Chesapeake created a hierarchy of races in which Indians occupied a precarious middle station.

Although the courts in the Chesapeake tended to treat unfree Indians much as they would unfree Africans, free Indians received better treatment by the courts than free Africans. All of the major remaining tribes in Virginia, for example, were able to assert successful claims for reservation lands during the seventeenth and eighteenth centuries. Indians also went to the county courts for redress when colonists assaulted them or stole from them. Indians could prevail in these cases, and frequently reparations were ordered paid to Indian victims. Nonetheless, there were clearly differences in the treatment of white men and Indians in the courts. When, for example, an Indian from a Virginia Indian town was killed by a group of servants belonging to an Englishman, the master of the servants was ordered to pay money to the Indian town, and the servants had their time on indentures extended. The payment of money was not necessarily an insult to the Indians, who traditionally had compensated victims of homicide in just such a way, but the colonists did not view it as following any principle of reciprocity. It was merely a way to keep peace.

Trade networks rather than the courts were the usual venues of settling disputes between the majority of Indians and settlers in the Chesapeake.

Indians in Virginia tended to live in Indian towns within the colony, which were not like the praying towns of New England but more like reservations with semi-autonomous government. Others lived on the frontier itself in their own societal configurations. With each succeeding generation, they moved further westward. Dispute resolution was usually part of a treaty-making process if it was peaceful or a battle if it was not.

Even when traders tried to take Indians to court for such matters as bad debts, the Virginia legislature stepped in to forbid it. Traders were expected to treat the Indians well, but it was the economy itself that colonial governments in the Chesapeake expected would regulate human behavior and establish new customs. Bacon's Rebellion in 1676 was fought in part over the privileges given to Indian fur traders by the Virginia ruling class, at least as Nathaniel Bacon and his followers saw it. The Governor of Virginia had alliances with Indians that were crucial to the colony, and Indians accepted these trade relations as establishing quasi-legal norms of behavior.

Settlers in the Chesapeake did not want Indians in their midst. Those Indians who did live among them were usually servants or slaves, and there was a steady amalgamation of Indian and African peoples. Nevertheless the slave narratives of the Works Progress Administration suggest there were still "full-blooded" Indians in the Chesapeake during the nineteenth century, and many of the former slaves claimed a full Indian ancestry. Indians who were not amalgamated into the general population of servants or placed on reservations became in effect enemy combatants, people to be dealt with by the military rather than by the courts when trading went awry.

Trading relationships in the north were also fraught with tension, but provided, as Richard White has called it, a "middle ground," where natives and colonists could meet without hostility. A nascent fur trade arose in the seventeenth century and burgeoned in the eighteenth and early nineteenth centuries. Trade along the Great Lakes region forced movement among the Indians, introducing economic competition into the native communal norm. The trading areas were largely free of formal legal institutions, and Native Americans could insist, in the early period, on using native practices to negotiate the terms of exchange. As trading became a larger industry, however, both the British and the French Crowns attempted to regulate its conditions.

The introduction of liquor often affected the contracts made between native fur traders and colonial or crown purchasers of furs. Alcohol complicated the resolution of differences, usually by making it impossible to wait for a legal decision and settling matters by violence. Indian traders often did not understand the English and French law of contract and debt obligations. When courts did decide cases that involved payments or debts owed, they often resorted to the concept of *quantum meruit*, an obligation based on "reasonableness and justice," rather than on the consent of the parties. This should have worked in favor of the Indians to some extent, but by the time the fur trade had been established in the mid-eighteenth century, the once common idea that Indian alcohol abuse was the fault of Europeans had faded, and Indians were held to individual accountability. With alcohol often the cause of misunderstandings if not outright deliberate deception on the part of colonial traders, Indians lost their cases because courts assumed they were "reasonable" when they made their trades or ought to have been. The lack of legal protection in areas of trade, whether because disputes were settled on the ground, as it were, or because Indians lost when in court, turned the middle ground into a dangerous place. It created a situation that perpetuated Indian indebtedness, forcing them to continue to hunt further away from home and to leave their families for extended periods. It also forced the sale of Indian lands to repay debts incurred while trapping.

Whether New England courts or Chesapeake commercial relationships were the venue for early colonial dispute resolution, by the eighteenth century Indian resort or subjection to the power of Anglo-European courts was the common denominator throughout the colonies, as it would be later in the United States. The dominance of the Anglo-European legal system did not, however, completely obliterate Indian jurispractice.

III. ANGLO-EUROPEAN LAW ABOUT NATIVE AMERICANS AFTER CONTACT, 1730–1815

Assimilated Indians, or those living within the borders of Anglo-European towns, began using the colonial court system almost exclusively by the 1730s. Indian use of Anglo-European courts to settle disputes began earlier, as we have seen, but it was not the only forum for settling differences in the seventeenth century. By the eighteenth century, however, Indians who had managed to survive among colonists adopted many of their legal practices – though not without leaving an Indian imprint.

In the Chesapeake, Indian heritage contributed to the retention of certain practices involving property. Despite the preference for primogeniture in Anglo-Virginia, at least one Anglo-Indian man, who had a large estate, made his daughter the executrix of his will and left her his land, making gifts of money and chattel to his sons. Whether this was a legacy of Algonquian matrilineal customs or simply a preference for his daughter over his sons is not certain, but there is other evidence that Indian heritage played a role in their use of the colonial law.[6]

[6] Kathleen M. Brown, *Good Wives, Nasty Wenches and Anxious Patriarchs: Gender, Race and Power in Colonial Virginia* (Chapel Hill, 1996), 242–43.

More frequently, Indians found themselves being used by colonial law. The rise of a distant royal voice of authority among the colonists, along with increasing royal pronouncements about treatment of the Indians and the presumption by royal agents that Indians were either wards or quasi-subjects in need of protection, took from the Indians much of the autonomy they had managed to preserve. The European wars of the eighteenth century that were fought on North American terrain led to a new era of Anglo-Native American conflict in which territorial jurisdiction and national sovereignty were the dominant themes.

British Imperial Law and Native Americans

Michael Leroy Oberg has argued persuasively that two principles governed the British interaction with Native Americans in the seventeenth century: dominion and civility. These dual principles extended well into the eighteenth century when the Indians were British allies. As long as the British could dominate, they expected to maintain civil relationships with the tribes. Domination and civility required face-to-face relationships and even friendships of a sort between the individual parties representing each side. The British agent or superintendent became the counterpart to the chief. Although Native Americans had frequently insisted on the presence of councils at meetings, or the use of female interpreters, these practices faded as men sent by Britain to regulate Indian affairs insisted on dealing with one chief. An artificial system of designating one male chief became cemented in eighteenth-century diplomacy.

Colonial governors appointed by the crown often had a very different perspective on the legal rights of Native Americans than colonists and their elected officials. Governor Berkeley of Virginia tried to secure a Crown-Indian relationship that left Indians dependent on England but not on the colonists per se. He co-opted Indian assistance by treaties that, for example, made them accomplices in hunting down non-friendly Indians who murdered colonists. Likewise, the Indians favored Governor Andros, who ruled over New York and later the short-lived Dominion of New England (1686–9) and who alienated the colonists of New England by his attempts to challenge land titles obtained from Indians. His protection of their rights even against those of his countrymen was worth the price of submission and loyalty for many Indian nations.

In the eighteenth century, the charters and governments of many colonies were remade to a more uniform standard. Their legal systems were altered to be more consistent procedurally with one another, and the Crown appointed royal governors for all but the proprietary colonies, Pennsylvania and Maryland. The royal governors tended to take an imperial rather than local view of Indian relations, one that increasingly diverged from the desires of the colonists. In war after war begun in Europe but played out on American soil, European monarchies and their Indian allies fought for control of North America. By the time of the French and Indian War (1754–63), or the Great War for Empire as it is also known in North America and the Seven Years War as it is known in Europe (1756–63), America had long ceased to be a sideshow on the stage of European rivalries. What many Native Americans had been requesting for years – that is, meetings with true representatives of the Crown – came to fruition, not, however, because of Indian efforts but in the service of metropolitan imperial ambition.

After more than 150 years of colonization, the wars of the mid-eighteenth century gave the English control of all of eastern North America. With rapidly growing populations, the English colonies now turned inward away from the sea to a larger destiny. The Great War for Empire in the 1750s and 1760s had resulted in the expulsion of the French political and military presence from the interior. The powerful Native American nations of the interior no longer had European allies to assist them against English settlers' incursions. At the same time, the need to coordinate British power in America in the face of the French threat had already led, in 1755, to the appointment of a superintendent of Native American affairs for the northern department, an office to which Sir William Johnson was appointed. In 1756 a similar superintendency for the southern colonies was established, with Sir Edmond Atkin as superintendent. The superintendents reported directly to the commander-in-chief of British forces in America. Although not taking the conduct of Native American relations entirely out of the hands of the colonial governors and assemblies, the existence of these new colonial officers marked a significant reduction of the powers inherited and assumed by the individual English colonies.

With the end of the French and Indian War, the English government established further controls on colonial freedom to act, particularly in restricting western settlement within the chartered limits of the colonies. By the Proclamation of 1763, the lands beyond the Appalachian mountain chain were declared off-limits to settlers, albeit that the Atlantic colonies claimed their borders ran all the way to the Pacific. The lands over which the British Crown reasserted its sovereignty were reserved for the Indians, though less by formal means than by understanding. There were, of course, important treaties that guaranteed preservation of land and rights to Indians. The anger of the colonists who itched to move westward was tempered only by the knowledge that the ban was not necessarily permanent.

The status of the Native American nations of the interior is not easy to describe, because each entity entertained different perceptions. The Indian nations attributed to themselves an independent status, which they felt able to maintain by force of arms. The English government, on the other hand, asserted ultimate sovereignty over Native American lands by virtue of the ancient charters that former kings of England had granted to those undertaking to plant colonies in the New World. Though speculative in origin and based on ignorance of the geography of the New World and of the power of the Native American nations in the interior, the charters were brought forth in legal arguments whenever their full realization seemed possible. Law in the form of treaties began to replace negotiated jurispractice with colonial governments at the cost, in some cases, of individualized justice.

In their dealings with the Native American nations, the English authorities used the treaty form of negotiation, in which solemn covenants were entered into as between equals. The Iroquois analogized English forms to their own "Covenant Chain," the name given by them to an intricate network of parties who treated with one another. The idea of the chain harkened back to the pre-contact history of the Iroquois in which their own confederacy, the Haudenosaunee, became a chain. They linked arms with their treaty partners to signify the human chain they were creating by their entry into treaties. In 1763 the Indian nations of the southeast signed the Treaty of Augusta with Great Britain, giving the Crown, and not the colonists, control over Indian relations. Indian territory was then carefully plotted out. Native peoples adjusted their jurispractice to incorporate a concept of territorial jurisdiction that never sat easily among their other legal principles.

During the period from 1763 to 1775, a series of boundaries between the colonists and the Native Americans of the interior were created from Lake Ontario to Florida, confirming in the minds of Native Americans (and many colonists) the belief that the Native American country was closed to speculation and settlement by the increasingly aggressive colonists. Except for South Carolina, where there were few violent land disputes after 1763 until the Revolutionary War, colonists continued to usurp the powers of the crown extra-legally by buying Indian lands and entering into unenforceable treaties. Until the dawn of the American Revolution, colonists had to find ways of negotiating with Indians without contravening English law's assertion of royal sovereignty and exclusive right to treat with Indians as foreign nations.

Lord Dunmore's War of 1774 began to erode the arrangements by which the seaboard colonies and the Native American nations of the interior were to be divided. Dunmore, the royal governor of Virginia, wanted to acquire Fort Pitt, abandoned by the French but not the Indians during the French and Indian War, in support of Virginia's charter claims. Dunmore's move into the trans-Allegheny areas of western Pennsylvania (Virginia's charter claims were to the west and northwest) led to war with the Delaware and Shawnee. The war initiated a response from the Iroquois to the north, who stood in the relation of elder brothers to the Shawnee and Delaware. Perhaps the most prominent guarantor of the relationship was William Johnson. A patriarchal figure with a Mohawk second family who inspired trust with the Iroquois Confederacy, Johnson was a man who mediated the interests of King, colonies, and Indians. As an agent for the King, Johnson often acted outside his legal authority to ensure Indian rights. As Superintendent of Native American Affairs, Johnson worked diligently to keep the Iroquois out of war. He pointed out that the Six Nations that comprised the Iroquois Confederacy had renewed and confirmed the Covenant Chain that existed between them at the Treaty of Fort Stanwix, entered into on October 26, 1768.

The Iroquois demanded to know why Anglo-Europeans were not honoring the former treaties and boundary lines and were moving beyond the mountains into the Ohio River valley. In 1774, while arguing in council to prevent Iroquois participation in Dunmore's War, William Johnson died. His successor met with the Iroquois representatives in a series of conferences culminating in a great meeting at Onondaga. The Iroquois ultimately endorsed the pledge to remain at peace with the English and persuaded the Shawnee to settle their differences with the Virginians. Joseph Brant, a Mohawk graduate of Eleazar Wheelock's Native American School at Lebanon, Connecticut (later Dartmouth in Hanover, New Hampshire), was particularly influential in these conferences. What had once been a unitary system of law that incorporated diplomacy with other jurispractices was replaced by a dual legal system of local justice and international diplomatic relations. This dual legal system in turn divided native leaders and created new legal roles in tribal communities.

To keep colonists and Indians apart, the British government continued to enforce the Proclamation of 1763. The Quebec Act, which replaced and changed the Proclamation, precluded colonial expansion into the lands that colonies claimed by their charters. It extended the province of Quebec as far south as the Ohio River and placed management in the hands of a royal governor with a standing army under his command to support him. As Francis Jennings has pointed out, the significance of the Quebec Act was that it halted the rampant land speculation of the seaboard colonists. It placed issues of sovereignty and control of the areas of likely expansion in the hands of Parliament rather than of colonial legislatures. It acknowledged that Indian nations and tribes would remain on the lands that were either traditionally theirs or, in the case of tribes already pushed westward, that were now through custom or treaty established as theirs.

British restrictions on colonial freedom of action in this as in other fields helped convince the colonists that violent reaction might be the preferable alternative. Revolutionary action soon arrived on the horizon. During the period in which colonists began to form structures of governance, the British imperial model for treating with the Indians was followed in form, though not in substance. In July 1775, the Continental Congress proposed a plan similar to the superintendencies created by the Crown for managing Native American affairs except that it created three rather than two geographical departments, with Commissioners appointed for each. At this point the role of the Commissioners was to urge neutrality on Indian nations, but they were largely unsuccessful.

During the ensuing Revolutionary War, most Native Americans chose to side with the British. The involvement of many Indian tribes in the war on the side of the British had legal repercussions after the war. The fact that four of the six nations of the Iroquois Confederacy had fought on behalf of the Crown and two had fought with the rebelling colonists, along with the continued division among the Six Nations, enabled the United States to argue in 1783 at the war's end that no Iroquois Confederation continued to exist, thus calling into question any sovereignty the Confederacy's members claimed for their union.

In addition to the upheaval the American Revolution caused at the level of diplomatic and military relations, it also disrupted other institutions, particularly in the South. Enslaved people who claimed Indian ancestry, particularly on the maternal side, sued for freedom in Southern courts or ran away, expecting that their Indian descent would serve as a protection from reenslavement. In *Robin v. Hardaway*, a Virginia case in 1772, the plaintiffs argued that Indians brought into Virginia after 1705 could not be enslaved; any descendants must therefore be set free. In the post-war period, especially in eastern Virginia, slaves who could demonstrate Indian ancestry frequently won their freedom in court. This trend continued into the early republic. Although the legal status of Indian nations reached a nadir in terms of hardship, individual Indians were again finding it possible to enter local Anglo-American courts to claim justice.

U.S. Federal Law and Native Americans

The failure of the British negotiators to include provisions protecting Britain's Indian allies in the Preliminary Articles of Peace of 1783 astounded Indians and Europeans alike. No Indian tribes were present at the signing of the treaty, despite their participation in the war. England could have inserted a clause to protect the Indian allies' rights to land tenure. The Spanish representative at the Paris negotiations, the Conde de Aranda, asserted that the territory west of the Appalachians to the Mississippi, which England handed over to the Americans without pause, belonged to free and independent nations of Indians to which Europeans had no right. But the American negotiators rejected this claim on behalf of the Native Americans and asserted the rightful authority of the colonies to govern the lands west to the Mississippi.

In their negotiations with the Native Americans back in North America, the former colonists tried to persuade the Indians that by siding with the British in the Revolutionary War their tribes had lost all rights. The new federal government asserted that the Native Americans were a conquered people. The governor of New York was advised not to enter into any treaty with the Iroquois Confederacy as an equal party, because its former independence and even the Six Nations as separate sovereigns had ceased to exist.

The relations between the Five Civilized Tribes and the various European powers had been perhaps the best on the North American continent. By the mid-eighteenth century, the southeastern tribes lived in ways that were recognizably "civilized" to most Europeans. The American Revolution, however, abruptly ended all prior friendships, particularly when the United States came into sole possession of the southeast and the former colonists began to colonize the southern Indian nations. Beginning in 1785 with the Treaty of Hopewell between the Commissioners Plenipotentiary of the United States of America and the Head-Men and Warriors of all the Cherokees, the United States started to establish quasi-jurisdiction over the Five Civilized Tribes. A second treaty in 1786 was the first attempt by the United States to establish hegemony over the Choctaw. It required the return of escaped slaves, the extradition of any Choctaw who had been convicted of crimes by the United States, and the return of any property that had been captured during the Revolutionary War. Until 1798, Spain still claimed sovereignty over the territory occupied by the Choctaw. As soon as Spain ceded the region, the United States began enforcing the harsh provisions of the Treaty of Hopewell.

Neither the Iroquois, nor the Indians of the Old Northwest, nor those of the South meekly accepted colonial claims of sovereignty by right of conquest. The treaties the Indians were compelled to sign acknowledging this late version of colonial history were instruments of power that the Indians could not have anticipated. Such claims of conquest would have sounded strange a century before to most of the tribal nations that now were signatories to treaties, because previously they had existed as recognized nations on a par with the English. The conquered tribes had been those of the first wave of colonization, the Powhatans and the Pequots. The Iroquois and the Cherokee did not view their own situations as remotely similar to those tribal histories. Although the majority of Indian nations responsible for stemming the tide of colonial expansion had sided with the English in the Revolutionary War, they still possessed land and power only partially diminished by the war. The British government, shamed by Indian remonstrances, continued to occupy the forts of the Old Northwest, providing trade goods to their former allies. Nevertheless, they refused military aid for a renewed attack against the Americans.

Unsuccessful attempts by the United States to impose its will on the Native Americans confirmed that the Indians had not been vanquished by the Americans during the Revolutionary War. In numerous expeditions undertaken by American generals in the 1790s, Native Americans defeated U.S. attempts to gain physical control of their lands. In 1794, General Anthony Wayne finally managed to defeat the northwest Indians at Fallen Timbers. Yet, the resistance and strength of the natives refuted the notion that conquest could simply be asserted rather than won. Tribes refused to yield sovereignty and jurisdiction to the United States.

With the formation of the Constitution and the establishment of a new government, Secretary of War Henry Knox, Secretary of State Thomas Jefferson, and President George Washington articulated a formal policy of honor and good will toward the Native Americans. As expressed in the Northwest Ordinance, the policy claimed, "The utmost good faith shall always be observed towards the Indians; their land and property shall never be taken from them without their consent; and in their property, rights, and liberty, they shall never be invaded or disturbed, unless in just and lawful wars authorized by Congress; but laws founded in justice and humanity shall from time to time be made, for preventing wrongs being done to them, and for preserving peace and friendship with them." This was not the policy, though, that the U.S. government followed. Indeed, it is fair to say that there were two policies, one stated and one hidden. Under the Federalists and Jefferson, the Indians were to be semi-segregated from the English population but assimilated to Anglo-American culture, an approach evidenced in agriculture, trade, and law. Despite Jefferson's repeated desires to have a native American race into which was bred the best of the English and the Indians, real Indians had to stay away from white Americans as much as possible. It was thus one of the great ironies of history that the Cherokee, who accepted this plan more than any other nation of Indians and who assimilated, farmed with the use of slave labor, traded, and created laws in the form of a written constitution, became the first to come under attack and were ultimately removed in the Trail of Tears.

Writers in the early federal period were still affected by ideas of the noble savage on the one hand, and the Indian frontier presence on the other. Travel writers, the past generation of whom had compared Indian government to monarchies, now saw the Indians possessed of republican forms of government. Some Indian nations were receptive to republican ideas, notably the Cherokee. The Iroquois too had long lived under a confederation that loosely resembled the first U.S. government under the Articles of Confederation. Many Native Americans had, even before contact with Europeans, practiced forms of government compatible with a democratic republic even if not conceived in that way. The idea that the people should have a voice through learned councilors was typical of many native legal and political systems. Yet, the United States continued to view the Indians as anathema to principles of democracy and republican government. They needed civilizing, according to almost every Anglo-American commentator, if they were to survive. Those who wished them ill believed they could not be civilized and therefore would vanish. Others had hope. The Indians themselves continually expressed confusion that Americans did not understand that they were sovereign and governed themselves on just principles.

When Thomas Jefferson became president he announced policy objectives for the Indians that included peace, land cessions, and civilization. Hidden in the agenda was removal, if it became necessary, and the extermination of resistant tribes if that proved unavoidable. That Jefferson never acted on these feared inevitabilities does not mean they had no lasting effect, for by positing resistance, removal, and annihilation as foregone conclusions, much as he had the demise of slavery at some time in the future, he propelled succeeding generations to ponder the message and, in a sense, rigged the future. Jefferson saw the Indians as savage, even if noble. He did not acknowledge that they had either legal systems or self-governance that was rational. Jeffersonian theory essentially misunderstood the nature of tribal culture and how it could be reformed.

Many Americans thought only in terms of how Indians should be reformed, without realizing that Native American culture and law was evolving right alongside them. The good intentions of missionaries to the Indians and their advocates in Congress were in themselves an assault on Indian society and sovereignty. The missionaries thought of themselves as genuine friends of the Indians. Nevertheless, their intent was to destroy the Indians' world. Jeffersonian policy was naïve and confused. In wanting what was best for these noble savages, reformers ultimately desired the elimination of the tribal order. Like their predecessors, they rarely recognized native legal or religious institutions. If they did acknowledge Indian jurispractices, they often tried to suppress them.

The Jeffersonian Indian policy of coexistence and gradualism – a steady if slow accommodation of Indians to the Anglo-American lifestyle through the transforming process of civilization, culminating in absorption into the dominant Anglo-American society through intermarriage – was an ideal that Jefferson himself never accepted fully as a real possibility. As in the matter of slavery, Jefferson compartmentalized his philosophical beliefs and his day-to-day actions. Jefferson wrote of his hopes of bringing civilization to the Indians and constantly urged tribal leaders to change their lifestyle in order to require less land for their people. He directed governors of the Northwest Territory, Michigan Territory, and Indiana Territory to "promote energetically" the national government's plan for civilizing Indians and authorized the assignment of blacksmiths and other artisans to cooperative Indian tribes to maintain plows and other implements for Indian apprentices. He encouraged missionaries to take part in the Indian civilization process. In 1803 he directed the Cherokee agent to erect a schoolhouse for Gideon Blackburn, a Presbyterian missionary, to enable him to instruct Cherokee children. The number of tribal schools increased until, in 1824, twenty-one schools with nearly 1,000 Indian students were functioning. But the plan did not include, as the Spanish, English, and French had all acknowledged to some extent at the beginning of colonization, any institutionalized Indian court of justice.

Jeffersonian Indian policy fitted well with the growing land needs of Anglo-American pioneers. It accepted the inevitability of their advance across the frontier, with the national government maintaining firm though regularly changing boundaries through an orderly, managed progression of settlements, made possible by periodic land openings. It held that new settlement zones would be created from new cessions by Native American proprietors.

Yet, despite Jefferson's strong commitment to Indian civilization, the program was never successful because at no time was it ever sufficiently supported, fiscally or politically, by Congress and officials in the government. Cynical politicians regarded the nation's "Indian problem" as solvable through the steady advance of hardy American pioneers; in due time extermination rather than assimilation would rid the nation of this vexing complication to its expansion, growth, and development. Native American tribal authorities often experienced rifts in their councils, as they tried to determine their level of cooperation with the civilization program. Men of European and Indian heritage tended to be more willing to do what the United States demanded than those with only Indian ancestry. In some tribal communities there emerged strata of class and race that had not been present in the past. The effect on law was palpable, as tribes fought over whether or not to adopt Anglicized legal systems.

The lack of evidence of noticeable progress in Indian civilization during his tenure as the nation's chief executive led Jefferson to consider alternatives for protecting Indian interests and making tribal land available for settlement by Anglo-American pioneers. Jefferson preferred that the eastern Indians remain on their progressively diminished tribal territories and support themselves by agriculture. After the United States acquired the Louisiana territory, he considered relocating certain eastern Indians there.

In each Indian nation Jefferson found that there were factions who seemingly could not cope with the relentless advance of the settler tide across established boundaries onto tribal territories that the national government had pledged to protect from trespass. Jefferson urged tribes to consider exchanging eastern lands for wilderness tracts. Thus for eastern Indians removal appeared to be an alternative to life on a compressed tribal estate attempting to coexist with Anglo-American neighbors.

Portions of Jefferson's Indian policy persisted after he left the presidency. The policy of his immediate successors – James Madison, James Monroe, and John Quincy Adams – continued in varying degrees the Jeffersonian style for managing the Indian tribes. Gradually, though, removal and segregation by exile into the trans-Mississippi wilderness eclipsed his semi-segregated assimilationism as cornerstones of federal management of the eastern tribes. As native peoples began to understand more fully the democratic discourse spread by so many Anglo-Americans, they began to change their laws, adopt some Anglo-American principles, and apply these principles to everyone within their jurisdiction. This bold assertion of legal authority may itself have initiated the reprisals that resulted in the segregation of the native people. At any rate, the years after 1815 saw drastic change for the Indians as U.S. Supreme Court decisions limited their sovereignty and federal and state governments pressed for their removal. Lynn Hudson Parsons, who has examined the federal Indian policy of John Quincy Adams and Andrew Jackson, finds that each in fact embraced similar policies toward the Indians, whether as presidents or policymakers. Adams would change his mind about the Indians as he grew older, but the policies of the new Democratic-Republicans were arguably genocidal in the cultural sense and possibly in the physical sense. They were intent on wiping out native language and traditions, and certainly native law, even the laws that some tribal nations had taken great care to prepare as semi-assimilated peoples sharing the North American landmass.

As early as 1675 when King Philip went to war in large part because of his anger over the trial and execution of Indians of his nation, the colonists had punished native peoples by placing them on reservations. The idea that Indians had a right, even if it was a lesser right, to the land had been eroding ever since. By 1800 there were few white Americans who thought of Indians as "civilized" and entitled to legal protection, despite the growing familiarity that all eastern Indians had with Anglo-American law and principles.

The reservation system that existed in the years between 1675 and 1800 was undeveloped and confined. It was largely under the control of the states until the federal government claimed the right to oversee it in 1787. Federal power was weak, though, and for the most part states did as they pleased. Reservation Indians, more than others, were placed in a legal limbo, where they could never be sure of the extent of the power they were allowed to exercise. Many continued to act as they had before the federal government claimed any power over them. The Pamunkeys of Virginia, for example, continued to pay tribute to the governor of the state as their sovereign conqueror in compliance with a seventeenth-century treaty. In fact, the continuance of the use of the treaty as the instrument to negotiate legal norms remained a contentious issue throughout the nineteenth century, even after the questions of federal legal primacy and tribal sovereign status within the American polity had been settled by Chief Justice Marshall in *Worcester v. Georgia* (1832). Whether on reservations or off them, tribal nations faced multiple layers of legal norms, but without the choice of forum that had characterized the colonial period.

CONCLUSION

In thinking about law and Native Americans in the pre- and post-contact periods in North America, the term "jurispractice" captures most precisely the reality of that world. Though they did not lack principles, the legal and moral ideas that informed the people of North America, Indian and colonist alike, by necessity manifested a higher degree of expediency than principle. The balance was simply tipped toward the perception of reality from each group's standpoint. Law, the rules that govern society's conduct, presumed by societies to be immutable at least until an authoritative change occurs, is embedded in the fabric of the societies it governs. It is distinguished from custom by its articulated permanence.

In the current anthropological literature and historiography, where law is just one of many elements subsumed under the rubric of culture – no different from architecture or fashion – it is perhaps old-fashioned to claim it is imbued with some higher supracultural significance. Yet, although the European colonists of New England may have criticized rude Algonquian wigwams and their forms of "savage" dress, they did not even realize that Algonquians had "law." That invisibility distinguishes law from other subsets of culture. Structures of wood are recognizable, and sometimes even structures of governance are dimly recognized as something akin to what the observer knows: a werowance is like a prince, the mamanatowick like a king or an emperor. Law, though, is something one can only know by the deepest understanding of a society. Even law's ritual practices, or legal procedures, can be better understood sooner than the law itself. The historical understanding of pre-literate legal culture is essentially the attempt to understand its jurispractice, its recognizable expression of legal ideas through the ways in which they are practiced by a society. Jurispractice is, indeed, all we can know about the law of the Native Americans who lived in the pre-contact and contact periods. We can infer from that practice that they may have had a philosophy of law as well as a body of laws, but we will never possess it in the way we can possess a copy of jurisprudential treatises by Samuel Pufendorf or even the ever-practical Blackstone's *Commentaries*.

Understanding the evolution of jurispractice after contact requires recognition of multiple realities as well as legalities. Initial colonial impressions of Native jurispractice reflected colonizers' own expectations, models, and familiarity with law, derived from the particular European societies and legal systems with which the colonial observers were conversant. As Indians began to exercise and communicate their own expectations within colonial legal realms, the picture of their jurispractice reflected in treaties, court records, and other documents generated in those realms became more precise, more particular, and more problematic. Heterogeneous tribes, both those that were indigenous and those that were formed by post-contact ethnogenesis, with their concomitant multiplicities of jurispractice, operated in separate but overlapping spheres of power with several layers of European and colonial law and government.

During this period the operative premises were a mutual belief in equal application of justice to Indian and non-Indian alike, negotiation of the terms of engagement in the shared legal space, and autonomy of jurispractice in separate spheres of sovereignty. Indians and Europeans operated under different beliefs as to the limits placed on Indian legal autonomy by Anglo-European law and, most essentially, as to what constituted "justice." Despite the tensions arising from differing beliefs and differing approaches of jurispractice, such as mediation and adversarial contest, both Indians and colonists managed for a time to operate successfully in an arena of shifting legalities.

This change in jurispractice reflecting a period of shared power and interaction in a negotiated legal space broke down under the pressures of change on both sides. Increased hostility on the part of both Indians and colonists made cooperation less tenable and less desirable. The increased formality of English legal systems operating in the colonial period made it more difficult to maintain equitable cross-cultural arrangements. Increased assimilation on the part of individual Indians put more and more natives beyond the pale of shared legal power and within the pale of colonial court systems, without the protections, demands, and special processes previously negotiated. The increasing unpredictability of processes and protocols negotiated by colonial governments at all levels made it very difficult for Indians to operate within separate yet overlapping spheres of jurispractice. Two sets of rules may be viable; multiple sets that may or may not apply lead to chaos.

The breakdown of the fragile balance of power between sovereign legal actors was long completed by the time of the American Revolution, which marked a significant change in the position of Indian tribes within the larger legal system of a new federal republic. The new federal government initially asserted that Native Americans were conquered peoples without any sovereignty. In 1787 this gave way to a stated policy that seemed to recognize tribal autonomy. Such stated deference to the "rights" of Native Americans was belied by subsequent actions on the part of both federal and state governments. Although tribes still operated on the premise that their law was in their control, during the Early Republic federal and state officials acted as if native control of their law was defeasible.

From contact through the Early Republic, significant changes occurred in Native American jurispractice in response to the pressures of European-American legalities. In looking at the rise and fall of a negotiated realm of Anglo-Native jurispractice in North America the challenge before scholars at present is to explore the ways in which sustained interaction with native jurispractice affected the jurispractice and structures of governance in the emerging polity that would come to be called the United States of America.

3

ENGLISH SETTLEMENT AND LOCAL GOVERNANCE

MARY SARAH BILDER

In late 1584, as Sir Walter Raleigh began to organize an effort to send settlers to Roanoke Island, an anonymous author asked, "What manner of geouernement is to be vsed and what offics to geouerne?"[1] The mysterious end to the Roanoke settlement offers no answer. Yet, as the vast record of charters, letters patent, and correspondence about governance testifies, the manner of government preoccupied settlers, investors, and Crown officials. The question of governance also intrigued past generations of historians. Simply put, when English settlement began in the 1570s, not one of the institutions that symbolized American representative government was in existence; by the 1720s, colonial American institutional development was largely complete.

For the casual reader, institutional histories of early America often revel in overly obscure details of colonial and English political organization. The current tendency to reject the entire venture, however, goes too far the other way. As we shall see, institutional history is important for two reasons. First, it helps us understand the development of authority – in this case, the roots of American federalism and representative democracy. Second, it helps us put British North America in its transatlantic context as part of English politics, the expanding English empire, and the Atlantic world.

For much of the past century, with notable exceptions, early American historians have shied away from institutional history. We can attribute this shift in part to the quantity and quality of work written in the first half of the twentieth century by the "imperial school" of colonial historians. Their detailed accounts of colonial American institutional development in an English world, crowned by Charles McClean Andrews' magnificent four-volume *The Colonial Period of American History* (1934–8), seemed definitive. The foundations apparently set, succeeding generations of historians

[1] "Anonymous Notes for the Guidance of Raleigh and Cavendish" (1584–1585) in David Beers Quinn, ed., *The Roanoke Voyages* (London,1955), 1: 136.

turned to different concerns. In part, too, for the imperial school historians – mostly born in the nineteenth century and raised in a nation whose governing structure had been torn apart and remade and which had then embarked on its own imperial expansion – the colonial period encouraged institutional explanations for contemporary questions, such as regional differences, discussions of legitimate and illegitimate colonial and imperial policies, and theories of American democratic identity. Later historians, raised in a nation with an apparently unalterable governmental structure but torn by social tensions, looked to the colonial period for insights into different matters – the problems of the modern "United States": economics and class, politics and ideology, social relations, race, gender, sexuality, and cultural practices.

Although historians turned away from writing institutional history, the questions relating to it have never disappeared. The arrangement of power and authority that developed over the first century of English colonization remains a central, inescapable theme in American history. Yet, our approach to these questions has necessarily changed. Interpretations and theories about historical development become dated; the insights that produce interpretive originality carry intentional or unconscious oversights. In its way this chapter is no exception, for the reader will find that I advance here my own argument about a certain "American manner of government." But in fact my main concern is not to construct a particular, new interpretive approach. Rather, I hope to suggest the ways in which old questions about governance retain their vitality and interest.

To this end, the chapter retraces the classic institutional narrative, focusing on moments where a reexamination disrupts conventional expectations. The theme is simple. Institutions of government are not preordained. Governance practices are contingent and embedded in particular contexts, and institutional labels and meanings change over time. A revitalized institutional history hence should focus on offices, officers, and the "manner of government" of the early colonial period. So pursued, institutional history reveals law as an instrument of governance and a rhetoric of authority – a discourse about legitimating and also contesting power.

In focusing on governance and authority, I suggest that we should reverse our traditional understanding. We have recognized that both in England and in the North American settlements concerns about the location of authority lay at the center of seventeenth-century English institutional development. But we have approached debates over authority as if there could be only one authority. What is striking about the early colonial period, however, is the centrality of the practice (and hence the problem) of the delegation of authority and the recurrence of developments that created dual authorities and then embraced their inherent tensions. To put it simply, for the first century and a half, English governance in America was *imperium in imperio*.

Two final preliminaries. First, I focus here on the mainland settlements that eventually become the United States. Additional coverage of Canadian and Caribbean English settlements – the Newfoundland fishing communities, the proprietary colony of Barbados, the long-lived corporation colony of Bermuda, the royal colony of Jamaica, all of which remained longer within the British empire and British imperial governance practices –would reinforce the argument that dual authorities were not inherently unmanageable. Second, I have chosen the agenda for this chapter recognizing how influential the tendency to frame discussions by current institutional assumptions remains. Conventional approaches usually discuss colonial institutions under an executive-legislative-judicial model – that is, starting from the premise that powers can and need be separated. The courts, however, were not a separate branch, and the controversy was whether courts were to be controlled by the legislature or the Crown through the governor. In fact, for most of the colonial period, the "third branch" was the English Crown and Privy Council. To emphasize these understandings, the Privy Council appears as part of governance and the courts as part of the culture of law.

I. SETTLING COLONIES

Discoursing on patterns of colonial settlement often precedes discussion of governance. However, because the Crown began to delegate governmental authority long before any settlements arose, governance is an inescapable foundation for settlement. Yet, English settlement in North America did not proceed according to any preconceived master plan established by the Crown, or private individuals, or groups of investors. Discovery, trade, and military outposts, not settlement, were the initial goals in exploring North America. Ireland, not North America, was the first site for English colonization and plantation. Nonetheless, all the initial English efforts at exploration required a delegation of the Crown's governmental authority.

Early delegations occurred in letters patent, grants under seal by which the Crown gave privileges and authority but did not necessarily constitute any particular political entity. *Patent* referred to the open or public nature of the grant. Letters patent usually began with the words, "To all to whom these presents shall come, greeting." In 1496, Henry VII gave John Cabot (Giovanni Caboto) the first English letters patent over land in North America. The Latin words of the document implicitly delegated governance in that Cabot and his sons were enabled to conquer, "occupy and possess" lands as "vassals and governors lieutenants and deputies."[2] Soon after, letters patent given to Bristol merchants in 1501 and 1502 contained explicit delegations of governance authority, but did not address the specific structure of government. The patentees received authority to govern and to establish laws, ordinances, statutes, and proclamations for good and peaceful government.

Historians tend to use *charter* as a generic term to refer to the Crown's grants for mainland settlements. In fact, most of these documents were letters patent and referred to themselves as such. Technically and traditionally, letters patent and charters are somewhat different documents. A charter was a grant of privileges in perpetuity; it was more formal, with more witnesses, written in Latin and, until the early sixteenth century, filed in the Charter Rolls. The first documents of North American settlement that explicitly referred to themselves as charters came not as we might expect with the early corporate colonies, but with the first proprietary colonies, followed by the 1644 Parliamentary charter to Rhode Island. Before 1660, contemporaries usually talked not of charters but of patents and of their holders as patentees. Indeed, the etymology of *patent* as a term referring to land conferred by letters patent can be traced to this specific North American context. Only after 1660 did colonists and English officials begin to refer consistently to foundational documents as charters.

In discussions of the substance of the letters patents and charters, the temptation has been to identify the charters as proto-democratic constitutions. Most gave inhabitants the right to the liberties, franchises, immunities, and privileges of free denizens and natural subjects as if born in England. Several provided for land to be held relatively free of feudal obligations. In legal terms, land was to be granted in a technical form: as of the Manor at East Greenwich in the County of Kent in free and common socage and not *in capite* nor in knights service. Free and common socage meant that the land was to be held in fee simple with limited payments (for example, one-fifth of the gold or a certain number of beaver skins).

Many proprietary charters, however, did not envision a settlement of freeholding inhabitants. Although by the early seventeenth century, English landholders largely held land directly from the Crown, these charters permitted land to be held with feudal services and rents owed to a lord. Such grants contradicted the statute Quia Emptores Terrarum (1290), which had initiated the decline of English feudalism by permitting the sale of land without penalty, and in fact, these charters explicitly rejected application of

[2] All quotations from charters and patents unless otherwise noted are from Francis Newton Thorpe, ed., *The Federal and State Constitutions, Colonial Charters, and other Organic Laws . . .*, (1909; reprint, Buffalo, 1993).

the statute. The proprietary charters thus affected to resurrect feudal landholding practices. Letters patent and charters were compatible with both feudal and freeholding practices.

The Corporation Colony

In narratives of English settlement, the corporate form is a crucial component of the American institutional story. The corporation's role, however, was not necessarily that which has been emphasized. Certainly, the corporation provided a mechanism for delegating governance authority to private individuals. Ironically, however, the corporation's failings as a delegated authority and its reinvention as an independent authority would be its lasting contributions to American colonial governance.

Discussions of the corporation as a vehicle for settlement often have implied that the corporation and corporate governance were stable legal forms. The corporate form, however, was itself developing as settlement began. Corporations were created by means of letters patent granting the privilege of incorporation. By the mid-sixteenth century, incorporation signaled a particular set of privileges: the capacity to sue and be sued, possession of a seal, perpetual succession, the power to hold lands, and the power to pass bylaws. The use of this form for overseas trade remained haphazard. The first joint-stock trading company was the Muscovy Company, created in 1555, with governors, assistants, and a collective fellowship empowered to pass statutes, acts, and ordinances. Other joint-stock trading companies developed slowly in the late sixteenth century: the Merchant Adventurers, the Eastland (Baltic) Company, the Levant or Turkey Company, and the East India Company. But it was not until John Wheeler's account of the Merchant Adventurers, *A Treatise of Commerce* (1601), that the structure of corporate governance began to acquire a stable cultural definition as a governor, deputy governor, and twenty-four assistants with "politike gouernement, lawes, and orders."[3]

Incorporation did not require this particular form of governance. Boroughs, for example, were also incorporated entities. As England shifted from a feudal society to one in which increasingly power came directly from the Crown, boroughs repeatedly requested new Crown charters. But the restructuring these bodies politic sought was not uniform. Not until the 1660s did corporate boroughs begin to possess relatively similar municipal governmental charters. Instead, borough corporations retained their older municipal offices (such as mayor, high steward, bailiff, and recorder) and governance practices. After the Corporation Act (1661) restricted

[3] John Wheeler, *A Treatise of Commerce* (London, 1601), 24.

corporate offices to those who were willing to participate in the Anglican Communion, borough corporations came to symbolize sectarianism in English governance. In neither respect, then, were seventeenth-century English models of corporate governance for local government necessarily "democratic."

The first attempt to use the legal form of the corporation for purposes of colonization reveals the delegated authority underlying corporate governance. In the 1560s, Sir Humphrey Gilbert became interested in English settlement in Ireland. In 1568–9, Gilbert requested privileges to make "a Corporat Towne" in Munster. Gilbert's interest lay in self-governance: the power "to make Sutch statutes and lawes as shall seeme good to their discrecions, for the better ordring of them selves, and their people, those being agreeable to the lawes of this Realme." The "chieften of this company" was to have power to make "laws and ordinances, not contrary to the laws of Ireland."[4] The Crown granted Gilbert letters patent with lawmaking authority limited by the laws of England. By the late sixteenth century, corporations in general were understood to be similarly bound.

Gilbert kept alive the idea of lawmaking authority limited by the laws of England while aspiring to create a more feudal-style settlement in Newfoundland where English fisheries for catching and drying salt cod existed. In 1578, he obtained letters patent that gave him "full and meere power and authoritie to correct, punish, pardon, governe and rule" with laws "for the better governement of the said people," but "as neere as conveniently may, agreeable to the forme of the lawes & pollicy of England." Gilbert claimed the area for the Crown in 1583, but his death on the voyage home ended his scheme.

We can conceptualize this formula of lawmaking authority bounded by the laws of England as a constitutionally limited delegation of governance. The formula appeared in letters patent and charters, as well as in royal instructions, commissions, internal delegations of authority, gubernatorial correspondence, colonial laws, court proceedings, and appeals to the Privy Council. The precise language varied, as did the various types of colonial lawmaking that were contemplated: laws, statutes, ordinances, constitutions, acts, orders, bylaws, rules, methods, directions, instructions, as well as court proceedings, procedures, and penalties. Common variations included "not contrary," "be as near as conveniently may, agreeable," and "not repugnant." Many versions included a repugnancy principle (colonial laws could

[4] Requests of Sir Warham St. Leger . . . Humphrey Gilbert, et al., *The Voyages and Colonising Enterprises of Sir Humphrey Gilbert*, ed. David Beers Quinn (Hakluyt Society, 1940; reprint, Nendeln, 1967), 1: 122–124; Petition to the Privy Council (1569) and "A brief of thinges allowable . . . (1569), 493–6.

not be repugnant to the laws of England), as well as an explicit or implicit divergence principle (the laws could diverge for local circumstances). Similar variations on the "laws of England" appeared. The phrase included "laws and statutes," but "government," "customs," "policy," "proceedings," and "rights" also might appear. Eventually the formula was understood to bind even self-authorized settlements: the 1641 Piscataqua River settlers gave their freemen lawmaking authority "not repugnant to the laws of England."

Although the corporate form offered the capacity to raise funds, adapting the corporate governance of the trading companies to transatlantic settlements was a different story, as Gilbert's half-brother, Sir Walter Ralegh (Raleigh), discovered in attempting to use the corporation to govern a settlement. Raleigh's first attempt in 1585 to settle Roanoke Island failed within a year. The letters patent had granted constitutionally limited lawmaking authority, but had made no provision for specific forms of governance. In his second attempt, Raleigh delegated his authority to a "Bodye pollitique & Corporate," the governor and assistants of the City of Raleigh in Virginia.[5] Reflecting the settlement's intended future social hierarchy, the governor, John White, and the twelve assistants were each given a coat of arms. Corporate governance was divided, with three assistants remaining in England while the others and approximately 100 men, women, and children sailed to Roanoke. The need for additional supplies brought White back to England in 1587, but the fragmented corporate structure and the following year's fight against the Armada foiled fundraising efforts. A new company was created to raise funds for a relief effort in 1590, but by then the settlement had vanished. Whatever the fate of the settlers, Raleigh's colleague Thomas Hariot pointed out that there was "noe especiall example" of a corporation for planting that had "proued well."[6]

Difficulties with the corporate form continued. In 1606, James I granted letters patent for two companies (the Virginia Company of London and the Virginia Company of Plymouth) and two colonies. The Plymouth Company undertook only one venture. In 1607, Sir Ferdinando Gorges and George Popham organized 120 settlers to land in Sagadahoc (Maine). The corporate structure remained in England. Difficulties with supplies, bad weather, and, perhaps most important, the governor's return to England ended the colony a year later. Another small corporation, the London and Bristol Company, fared no better. Its settlement under John Guy at Cuper's Cove, Newfoundland, in 1610 declined after Guy returned to England several years later. By 1620, disenchantment with the corporate form led the Plymouth arm of

[5] *The Roanoke Voyages*, 2: 508.

[6] "Thomas Hariot's Notes on Corporations for Trade and Plantations" (n.d.) in *The Roanoke Voyages*, 1: 389.

the Virginia Company to reorganize as the Council for New England with authority transferred to a small group of titled lords.

Even when a settlement survived, governing it through a London-based corporation proved difficult. The Virginia Company of London encountered repeated governance problems. The initial letters patent created a multi-layered delegation of authority: a Crown-appointed London council, a resident council, and a requirement that the council's laws be signed by the Crown. In 1607, 104 men set forth to found Jamestown. In barely enough time for the news to travel to England and back, never mind any laws to be approved, disease and starvation reduced the colony by two-thirds. In 1609, the company reincorporated with a single London council that held constitutionally limited lawmaking authority and was to delegate this authority to an appointed governor. Under a strict martial code, the 1611 *Lawes Divine, Morall and Martiall, &c.*, Governors Sir Thomas Gates and Sir Thomas Dale stabilized the settlement. But their discretionary authority seemed contrary to the corporate form, so in 1612, new letters patent returned lawmaking authority to the London corporation's general court. Now, the Virginia settlers were left with insufficient discretion. In 1618, the Company issued a "greate Charter or commission of privileges, orders, and laws," delegating its authority to a subsidiary political corporation with a council and assembly of elected representatives.[7] The first assembly met at Jamestown in July 1619. According to the 1621 ordinance, laws were to be ratified and confirmed in England and the assembly required "to imitate and follow the Policy of the Form of Government, Laws, Customs, and Manner of Trial, and other Administration of Justice, used in the Realm of *England*, as near as may be, even as ourselves, by his Majesty's Letters Patent, are required."

This corporation-within-a-corporation was, theoretically, a coherent model for London-based governance, but the only settlement actually governed that way was Bermuda. In 1612, a subsidiary venture of the Virginia Company settled Bermuda and incorporated in 1615 as the London-based Governor and Company of the Somer Islands (the Bermuda Company). In 1619, Bermuda followed Virginia in encouraging settlement with company instructions to establish an assembly for local governance with the power to make laws not "repugnant to the laws of England," the governor's instructions, or any company laws and subject to confirmation by the company. The assembly convened in 1620, and until 1684 Bermuda was governed as a corporation-within-a-corporation.

No other London-based corporation governed a settlement successfully. The Virginia Company's financial difficulties were a constant liability for

[7] Susan Myra Kingsbury, *The Records of the Virginia Company of London* (Washington, 1906), 3: 158.

the settlement, and in 1624 the Crown repealed its letters patent by writ of *quo warranto*, a procedure used to revoke borough corporate charters. *Quo warranto* ("by what authority") accused the corporation of acting outside its charter. In 1625, the new King, Charles I, proclaimed that the government of Virginia would "depend upon Our Selfe."[8] The governor became a Crown appointee bound by Crown instructions. Yet, although the corporation no longer existed and the assembly's legal status was in some doubt, corporate practices continued. In 1629, answers to a set of propositions seemed to confirm authorization of a "grand assembly to ordain laws."[9] In 1639, Crown instructions at last specifically acknowledged that the governor and assembly held lawmaking authority so long as its laws were as near as may be to the laws of England. Virginia became a royal colony after 1676, when that designation came to signify a new institutional form that would become dominant in the English settlements. Before then, Virginia looked more like a corporate colony in which the Crown had simply substituted itself for the London corporation.

Virginia was not the only settlement in which the maintenance of corporate governance practices – not necessarily the legal corporate entity – was understood to confer self-governing authority. The English separatists in Leyden, the Pilgrims, were not a corporation as such. London-based investors met as a company with a president and treasurer while the planters sailed off with a governor. Nonetheless, the settlers asserted self-governing authority analogous to corporate authority in a combination (later known as the Mayflower Compact) signed after the *Mayflower* landed outside any authorizing letters patent. The Plymouth leaders in 1629 obtained a patent from the Council of New England that allowed them to "incorporate by some usual or fitt name" and make orders, ordinances, and constitutions, "not repugnante to the lawes of Englande," and the 1636 laws referred to Plymouth as a corporation. A governor and assistants were to be elected at a general court, and laws passed. By 1640, Bradford surrendered all authority under the patent to the "Freeman of this Corporacon of New Plymouth."

Plymouth's experience suggested that corporate lawmaking authority could be acquired by self-governance practices. The same desire for self-governance without regard to formal corporate status appears also in Massachusetts Bay. In 1629, a company was incorporated as the Governour and Company of the Massachusetts Bay, a "Bodie politique and corporate" with letters patent based on the defunct 1612 Virginia document but emphasizing local government. A governor, deputy governor, and eighteen assistants

[8] Clarence S. Brigham, ed., *British Royal Proclamations Relating to America, 1603–1783* (Worcester, 1911), 53.

[9] *Calendar of State Papers, Colonial Series, America and West Indies, 1574–1660*, ed. W. Noel Sainsbury (1860; reprint, Vaduz, 1964), 1: 100.

elected by the freemen would take care of the plantation and "Government of the People there," with constitutionally limited lawmaking authority.

The location of government worried Massachusetts Bay leaders. From the outset, the corporate form made the settlement vulnerable to dissenting shareholders and the Crown. As conditions in England worsened for Puritans, a minority of shareholders successfully voted to transfer the government of the settlement to the inhabitants in New England. This transfer alleviated the need for a corporation-within-a-corporation and placed the physical distance of the Atlantic between settlement governance and the Crown. Without such a transfer, a similar settlement in Providence Island (near Nicaragua) under a similar letters patent failed by 1641.

The sectarian leaders of Massachusetts Bay clung to a belief in corporate self-governance while treating English laws governing corporations as avoidable technicalities. Repeatedly, Crown officials and some colonists challenged the colony's authority. A year into settlement, Massachusetts Bay leaders restricted participation in corporate governance by requiring that freemen be male members of an approved colony church. Between 1635 and 1637, the Crown conducted *quo warranto* proceedings to revoke the letters patent; however, the writ was not served. Meanwhile, to bolster sectarian governance, the government tried and banished recalcitrants: Roger Williams, Anne Hutchinson, and John Wheelwright. In 1638, the corporation was told to send the patent to the Crown, but Governor John Winthrop refused to do so.

Meanwhile, events in England lessened the threat from the Crown, but raised new challenges. In 1646, Robert Child argued that as all corporations were subject to the laws of England, English laws now favorable to Presbyterians should be followed; this argument was unsuccessful. When Puritan sympathizers took over the English government, the colony's governance practices were left alone. In 1648, the colony's first published law code, *The Book of the General Lawes and Libertyes*, proclaimed the general court's authority over its inhabitants. By the 1660s, the colony coined money, executed Quakers, denied appeals to the Crown, required oaths of fidelity, and ignored English trade laws. Over three decades, the colony's sectarian corporate governance practices and lawmaking authority surpassed the legal limits of the corporate form.

The perception that corporate governance practices created lawmaking authority – in essence, a government – appears also in Connecticut. In the late 1630s, Puritans similar to those in Massachusetts Bay founded the towns of Connecticut. At first, settlers struggled over the precise terminology for the self-authorized governments. In 1639, Connecticut referred to itself both as a "Publike State or Commonwelth" and a "Combination and Confederation." That same year, New Haven – founded by settlers of a particular political-religious bent – chose a "civil government, according to God" under a "plantation covenant." Soon, however, both adopted the governance practices of Massachusetts Bay, and in 1643 Connecticut, New Haven, Massachusetts Bay, and Plymouth united under "Articles of Confederation in a "firm and perpetual league of friendship" as the United Colonies of New England.

The sectarian tendencies of these corporate-type governments have not always been appreciated. Yet, many dissenters who fled the Massachusetts Bay colony initially chose other political forms of self-governance. Providence, for example, followed a "government by way of Arbitration" and insisted on "liberty of Conscience." When Portsmouth and Newport later adopted the corporate practices of a governor, deputy governor, and freemen, they insisted on the absence of religious limitation, declaring "the Government which this Bodie Politick doth attend . . . is a DEMOCRACIE, or Popular Government." The "Body of Freemen orderly assembled" had the power "to make or constitute Just Lawes." The governmental authority of the corporation was separated from particular governance practices in Rhode Island's "free Charter of Civil Incorporation and Government," the first to incorporate a preexisting, self-governed settlement. The Parliamentary commissioners granting the 1644 charter gave the towns the "full Power and Authority to rule themselves" by "voluntary consent of all, or the greater Part of them" as was "most suitable to their Estate and Condition." The towns chose to elect a president, four assistants, and deputies. In 1647, the assembly emphasized the nonsectarian nature of its government as "DEMOCRATICALL . . . a Government held by the free and voluntarie consent of all, or the greater parte of the free Inhabitants."[10]

By the 1660s, corporate governance practices and a corporate charter or letters patent had come to symbolize constitutionally limited self-governance. This understanding led to the incorporation of Connecticut and Rhode Island. With the Restoration of Charles II, both colonies grew concerned about their political authority. Connecticut had no authorizing document and, in 1662, quickly obtained letters patent from Charles II. The towns became the "Body Corporate and politique" of the "Governor and Company of the English colony of Connecticut." Rhode Island thought it advisable to replace its Parliamentary charter with new letters patent – referred to by Rhode Islanders as a "charter" – with "full libertie in religious concernements." Like Connecticut, the colony was incorporated as a Governor and Company (governor, deputy governor, and assistants chosen by the freemen) with constitutionally limited lawmaking authority. The

[10] John Russell Bartlett, ed., *Records of the Colony of Rhode Island* (Providence, 1856) [hereinafter *R.I. Colony Recs.*], 1: 156.

charter affirmed the colony's "livlie experiment" in religious liberty. Rhode Island was now "Company, Corporation and Collony."[11]

The incorporation of Rhode Island and Connecticut meant formal recognition of the institution of the corporation colony: a political document, explicitly called a charter, incorporated the government (the Governor and Company), corporate officers (governor and assistants) were elected by freemen, and the assembly held lawmaking authority limited by the laws of England. In theory, incorporation placed the settlements under English law, limited their lawmaking authority, and made them vulnerable to *quo warranto* proceedings. In reality, as Edward Randolph criticized, incorporation made the New England colonies "Independent Governm[en]ts."[12] Self-governing corporate authority on the far side of the Atlantic circumvented English corporate laws and English Crown control. After 1663, no more corporation colonies were created.

Seeds of American institutions can be found in this story of corporate governance – but not necessarily the expected ones. Corporate authority theoretically required prior delegation of authority from the Crown, but the repeated failure of corporations for settlement and the development instead of self-authorized settlements with corporate governance practices created the perception that a government based on corporate practices could validate itself. Recognizing the corporation's association with self-governing authority establishes that the desire for this governance, not simply fundraising, led to the adoption of the corporation for settlement activity. Corporate governance practices had created *imperium in imperio*. An emphasis on these governance practices, rather than on the legal corporation, helps explain why colonies without corporate charters nonetheless adopted the governance structure of governors, councils, and assemblies. Long before the Revolution, these offices and practices lost their association with the corporate form and became instead symbols of self-governing authority and the foundation of American institutions. With the seventeenth-century corporate charters no longer representing Crown delegation of authority but independent self-government, Connecticut and Rhode Island would later retain them as new state constitutions.

The Proprietary Colony

Because post-Revolutionary American government resembled the practices of the corporation colonies, proprietary governments often have been

[11] *R.I. Colony Recs.*, 2: 24 (Mar. 1, 1664).

[12] Petition of Edward Randolph (Aug. 9, 1687) in Robert Noxon Toppan, ed., *Edward Randolph; including his letters and official papers...* (Boston, 1899), 4: 166.

neglected. Yet, the proprietary form represented an equally plausible approach to delegating governance authority. Englishmen interested in the settlements viewed the invention of the proprietary form as an improvement over the corporation colony; proprietaries achieved real settlement success. Nova Scotia (1621), Avalon (1623), Maryland (1632), and Maine (1639), as well as Carolina (1663), New York and New Jersey (1664), Pennsylvania (1681), and East Jersey (1682), all followed the proprietary form. The coexistence of settlements with authority delegated through corporate governance practices and those with authority delegated to individual feudal proprietors indicates the absence of preconceived notions about the appropriate manner of government for colonies.

Although we tend to think of the charter as emblematic of democratic constitutionalism, the term *charter* first appeared in the early proprietary grants. The proprietary form involved governing practices under which an inheritable proprietorship was given by the Crown to a nobleman, a cohort of titled lords served as councilors, and a dependent assembly assented to legislation. The proprietor acquired social status as the highest lord and the economic privilege of collecting quitrents (in essence, rents or taxes on land). His political authority was similar to the English palatinates of Durham and Chester; the social aspiration came from idealized English manorial society.

The impetus for proprietary charters seems to have arisen both from frustration with the corporation and the feudalistic aspirations of a few noblemen. The oft-forgotten Sir Ferdinando Gorges played an important role. Since 1607, Gorges had been involved in the failed colonial ventures of the Plymouth Company. In 1620, he abandoned the corporation approach and had the Company restructured as the "Council . . . for the planting, ruling, ordering, and governing of New-England" (the Council for New England). The Council was in form a board of proprietors, made up of noblemen and gentlemen. It held constitutionally limited lawmaking authority and granted land to Gorges, Council members, and friends. Some grants were never used and reverted; others did not prove particularly successful.

Although the Council's grants did not prosper, others adopted the idea of proprietary settlements. In 1621, a Scottish nobleman, Sir William Alexander, obtained a charter from James I and the Scottish Privy Council naming him hereditary Lieutenant General over Nova Scotia (New Scotland). The charter, the first so described, gave Alexander extensive powers so long as the laws were "as consistent as possible" with those of Scotland. Alexander's was a feudal vision: he established a Scottish-style feudal order, planned to raise money by creating hereditary Knights-Baronet, and obtained a coat of arms. By contemporary standards, Nova Scotia was successful, surviving until the early 1630s when the settlement was evacuated pursuant to a French agreement.

The proprietary approach was of interest to men who were rising in the ranks of the nobility through service to the King. In 1623, James granted letters patent for the Province of Avalon (Newfoundland) to his Secretary of State, Sir George Calvert – later to become Lord Baltimore and a Catholic convert. Calvert had already been involved in the Virginia Company and the Council of New England. The Avalon patent granted him the most extensive governance authority residing in any individual in England other than the Crown by granting him the powers of the Bishop of Durham. Avalon failed when Calvert found the weather too cold. The proprietary grant over the Caribbee (Barbados, the Leeward Islands, and others) obtained by James Hay, recently elevated to Earl of Carlisle, in the late 1620s was initially more successful, prevailing over the corporate scheme of Courteen and Associates.

During the 1630s, proprietary grants continued to vest broad government authority in a proprietor. In 1632, Calvert's son Cecilius acquired a Latin "charter" granting Maryland "forever," responding in part to his desire to found a settlement for Catholics. The charter established a palatine province in which the proprietor controlled the courts and possessed lawmaking authority limited only by the "Advice, Assent, and Approbation" of the freemen and the familiar repugnancy provision. In 1634, Catholic and Protestant settlers landing in Maryland laid out manors, parishes, and hundreds, with quitrents paid to the proprietor. In 1639, Gorges acquired similar letters patent for the Province of Maine. Gorges's narrative described the patent as a "Royal Charter," implicitly distinguishing the direct Crown delegation from the Council of New England's subsidiary "patents." Gorges envisioned an idealized England and began to settle Maine with borough towns and cathedral cities. His death in 1647, however, ended the proprietary.[13]

For the first half-century of settlement, the corporation and proprietary coexisted as different approaches to the problem of delegating governance and authority. In the 1640s, English political developments led Parliament to reject the chartered proprietary with its cultural associations of lords, dependent assemblies, and noble titles. Parliament's sole new charter was given to Rhode Island as an incorporated political body. This shift toward legislative authority and Protestantism left the Maryland proprietary and its charter vulnerable to charges of religious intolerance. In 1649, the assembly

[13] Ferdinando Gorges, "A Brief Narration of the Originall Undertakings of the Advancement of Plantations . . . " (posthumously published 1658), in *Sir Ferdinando Gorges and His Province of Maine* (Boston, 1890), 2: 65.

and the newly appointed Protestant governor, William Stone, assented to, and in 1650 the proprietor confirmed, an act permitting a certain degree of "conscience in matters of Religion." Despite the act, in 1652, the family lost control of the proprietary to Parliamentary commissioners.

Parliament had been quick to reject the proprietary form, but the restored Crown did not perceive it as an affront to Crown authority. Hence the Restoration revived proprietary grants and returned Maryland to the Calverts. Nor did the Crown bring an immediate end to corporate self-governance. Between 1662 and 1664, Charles II incorporated Rhode Island and Connecticut while also granting proprietary charters for two huge provinces, Carolina (stretching from Virginia to Florida) and an unnamed territory (including New York, New Jersey, parts of Maine, Martha's Vineyard, and Nantucket). Because Charles would make no additional grants until the 1680s, these 1660s charters left governance by both proprietary and corporation once again apparently legitimate.

The Restoration grants confirmed the Crown's willingness to give extensive governing authority to proprietors. The 1663 Carolina charter was given to eight lords. The multiplicity of proprietors made nonsensical the grant of Bishop of Durham powers, but the proprietors were given constitutionally limited lawmaking power on the assent of the assembly, authority to grant titles and incorporate boroughs and leet manors, and the ability to collect feudal quitrents. As in Maryland, the proprietors' vision included a degree of religious toleration. In the 1664 letters patent for territory later known as New York, Charles did not technically name James, Duke of York, as lord proprietor, but conveyed similar authority: "full and absolute power and authority" to govern, limited only in that the laws be agreeable and the Crown have the right to hear appeals. James's own 1664 grant of New Jersey to Carolina proprietors John Lord Berkeley and Sir George Carteret, for the nominal yearly rent of a peppercorn and, if demanded, twenty nobles (an old coin), reveals the same understanding of the proprietary. The two men established proprietary governance, planned to collect quitrents, and extended liberty of conscience to the province (declaring it the one principle that the assembly could not alter). Proprietary practices involved lawmaking authority in the proprietor, feudal rent collection, and some degree of religious tolerance.

Initially, proprietors controlled lawmaking. In New York the "Duke's Laws" (1665) were likely prepared by Governor Richard Nicolls and legally trained Matthias Nicolls. In Carolina, proprietor Anthony Ashley Cooper and John Locke produced the "Fundamental Constitutions" (1670), outlining an elaborate feudal society, which legalized slavery and provided liberty of conscience for believers in the public worship of God. Proprietorial authority was diminished, however, by the growing cultural assumption of the legitimacy of assembly authority. In Carolina, the proprietors failed to persuade the Carolina assembly to assent to the Fundamental Constitutions and they never became colony law. In New Jersey representatives of one town rejected the proprietary altogether as "soe obscure to us that at present we are ignorant what it is" and refused even to pay quitrents.[14] The New Jersey proprietary's political difficulties only increased in the 1680s after Berkeley's share had passed into the hands of a group of Quakers and Carteret's share became held by twenty-four new proprietors. In 1683, even the Duke of York was compelled to permit an assembly with lawmaking power subject to governor and proprietor concurrence.

This late-seventeenth-century transformation of proprietary governance is reflected in the final proprietary, the province and seignory of Pennsylvania given to William Penn by Charles II in a "Royall Charter" in 1681. Like other proprietors, Penn, a Quaker, provided religious toleration of a sort (here for Quakers and other dissenting Protestants) and planned to collect quitrents. Penn's authority as lord proprietor, however, was bounded by Crown and assembly. Penn's charter did not include the broad powers of the Bishop of Durham. Penn, instead, was to send his laws to the Privy Council for confirmation or disallowance, permit appeals to the Crown, follow Crown colonial policies, and keep an agent in London to respond to Crown concerns. Although like earlier proprietors, Penn's 1682 "Charter of Liberties" and frame of government attempted to have the governor and council write legislation and the assembly simply accept or reject it, by 1696 this approach was deemed no longer appropriate to circumstance. The assembly took over lawmaking authority, proposing and passing legislation subject to the governor's veto and the Crown's disallowance.

What significance should we accord the proprietary form? From Canada to the Caribbean, proprietors settled and governed a far larger area than the corporation colonies. Landholding practices in the middle and southern colonies long continued to reflect the proprietary's feudal, manorial vision. The proprietary's ability to combine this vision of landholding with some degree of religious tolerance reminds us that our association of religious tolerance with democratic government is deeply contingent. Like the corporation, governance under the proprietary produced a version of *imperium in imperio* – but in this case the development of multiple authorities. This approach, however, failed. Initial proprietor ascendancy was eroded by the growth in the assembly's lawmaking authority and the Crown's desire for direct governance. Faced with these dual challenges, almost everywhere

[14] Middletown paper (1669), quoted in Charles M. Andrews, *The Colonial Period of American History* (New Haven, 1937), 3: 147.

the proprietor's authority collapsed. Two proprietaries, Maryland and Pennsylvania, survived at least in name because of the intense commitment of their founding families, but the proprietors per se came to hold little real authority.

The Royal Colony

By the Revolution, most colonies had become royal colonies held directly by the Crown. Conventional accounts often imply that the path to royal dependency was straight and that the Crown pursued a strategic course, limited only by colonial opposition. The institution of the royal colony, however, developed over a century in fits and starts. In 1625, the Crown proclaimed "there may be one uniforme course of Government, in, and through Our whole Monarchie, That the Government of the Colonie of Virginia shall immediately depend upon Our Selfe, and not be committed to any Company or Corporation, to whom it . . . cannot bee fit or safe to communicate the ordering of State-affaires."[15] But the Crown proved to be inconsistent in following this policy. Despite sporadic efforts aimed at Massachusetts Bay, not one other colony was reduced to dependency during the reign of Charles I. What a uniform course of government and, equally important, colonial dependence actually looked like remained unclear for a century.

Policy after the Restoration depended on the Crown's political advisor and his vision. Sir Edward Hyde, the Earl of Clarendon and Lord Chancellor, sought increased colonial control but used existing mechanisms: a Privy Council committee on the colonies was established in 1660, Virginia was given a seal proclaiming it the fifth royal dominion in 1663, and a Crown-appointed governor and council were placed in Jamaica (seized from Spain in 1655). New charters for Carolina (with Clarendon as a proprietor), Rhode Island, and Connecticut followed traditional delegations of authority. Crown commissioners attempted to end Massachusetts Bay's sectarian political practices and require conformity to English law, but the Crown did not pursue their recommendation to revoke the letters patent. After Clarendon fell from power in 1667, the Crown lost interest as it dealt with problems caused by the Great Fire of London and war with the Dutch.

In 1675, Sir Thomas Osborne, Earl of Danby and Lord Treasurer, resurrected the idea of a uniform course of colonial government predicated on Crown ascendancy. The new Committee on Trade and Plantations (the Lords of Trade) initiated changes in lawmaking to make colonial laws the

[15] Brigham, ed., *British Royal Proclamations*, 53.

enactment of the Crown instead of the assemblies. In 1676, the Crown rejected a proposed Virginia charter affirming assembly lawmaking power subject only to review by the Crown and instead issued new letters patent that placed Virginia in "immediate Dependance upon the Crowne of England" without mention of an assembly.[16] In Jamaica, the Lords attempted to impose Crown lawmaking modeled on English control over Ireland. In New England, Edward Randolph cited numerous grounds on which to revoke the corporate charters, including violations of the laws of England, refusals to take oaths or permit political participation of members of the Church of England, denial of appeals to the Crown, and the obstruction of trade laws.

Colonial opposition and Danby's fall from power meant that the Crown's attempt to take over colonial lawmaking went nowhere. Crown efforts to exert greater control turned instead to creating limits on colonial lawmaking authority by developing means to enforce the rhetoric of repugnancy and agreeableness to the laws of England, which avoided the difficulty and drama of *quo warranto* proceedings. Thus when, in 1679, the Crown established a royal province in New Hampshire with a Crown-appointed president and council, the assembly's power was constrained by requirements that the president and council approve laws and that the Privy Council have an opportunity for review. Bermuda was similarly restructured after *quo warranto* proceedings permitted a new colonial government under a royal governor in 1684 – a move initially welcomed by colonists tired of the company. The Massachusetts charter was vacated in somewhat similar fashion and Massachusetts and Maine placed in theoretical dependency on the Crown.

Charles's death in 1685 halted the process in some confusion, leaving Massachusetts without a charter and Rhode Island and Connecticut as the only remaining corporation colonies. The accession of James, Duke of York, again altered the Crown vision of colonial government and royal dependency. Consistent with James's policies in England, the colonies were envisaged as a small number of large dominions, with diminished assembly lawmaking authority. James's own proprietorial colony of New York was merged with East and West Jersey, Massachusetts (and Plymouth), New Hampshire, Maine, Rhode Island, and Connecticut into a new Dominion of New England to parallel the old southern dominion of Virginia and the huge Carolina proprietary. The governor-in-chief, Sir Edmund Andros, was

16 Grant from Charles II (Oct. 10, 1676) in John Burk, The *History of Virginia, from its settlement to the present day (Petersburg, 1804–1816)*, 2, Appendix, xl–xli; Virginia Colonial Records Project 578, § 2582, Virginia Center for Digital History, University of Virginia (www.virtualjamestown.org/virtjam6.html).

given constitutionally limited lawmaking authority and required to send laws to the Crown for approval. By 1688, Andros obtained the charters of the Jerseys and Rhode Island, although Connecticut's eluded him, hidden allegedly in an oak tree. Andros faced opposition throughout, however, and in 1689 the Dominion of New England collapsed amid local uprisings and the overthrow of James II.

Crown policy on the colonies changed yet again under William of Orange and his wife, Mary (James II's daughter). More accepting of Parliamentary authority, the Crown now confirmed colonial assembly power while maintaining Crown supervision. In 1691, Massachusetts Bay received a "Royall Charter" in which the Crown appointed the governor, and the freeholders elected the assembly and the twenty-eight assistants of the governor's council. Assembly control of the council limited the royal governor's legislative control, but the assembly was still required to send laws to the Crown for approval. Privy Council appeals could no longer be prevented, but jurisdiction was limited to personal actions, permitting the colony for decades to deny appeals over real property disputes. New York, meanwhile, was given a Crown-appointed governor and council, an assembly, and Privy Council review of legislation. The Jersey proprietaries, Connecticut, and Rhode Island had their charters returned. Pennsylvania was returned to William Penn after a brief period of Crown rule arising from Penn's political troubles. Maryland fared less well under a Protestant Crown unhappy with its Catholic proprietors. Although the proprietary technically remained, the Crown acquired the power to appoint and instruct the governor and the Privy Council gained the power to review legislation and hear appeals. The Crown's overall approach to supervisory authority was confirmed in 1696 with the creation of the Board of Trade.

The trend to uniformity in Crown policy created a perception that the proprietary and corporate charters made those colonies exceptional. In particular, the corporate governments appeared to make repugnant laws, refuse appeals, and flout the trade acts. They harbored pirates, coined money, competed with English goods, and did not take care of their own defense. In 1701, the Board of Trade recommended that the charters "be re-assumed to the Crown; and those colonies put into the same state and dependency."[17] Proprietors and corporation governments sought to reduce their charters' vulnerability by voluntarily responding to inhabitant and Crown concerns. Penn's "Charter of Privileges" (1701) affirmed legislative power in the unicameral assembly. Colonial lobbying and the death of William in 1702 put a stop to a pending revocation bill, but a new bill to create colonial uniformity

[17] State of Government under the Plantations (1701), *Proceedings and Debates of the British Parliaments respecting North America* (Washington, 1927), 2: 401.

through royal appointments and appeals appeared in 1705, during Queen Anne's reign. This bill failed too. Nevertheless, Rhode Island and Connecticut decided to permit appeals to the Privy Council and Connecticut even voluntarily sent occasional laws over for review.

The Crown did not reduce any additional colonies to dependency by direct policies after 1700. Nonetheless, disagreements ended proprietaries that had multiple proprietors. In 1702, the Jersey proprietors surrendered governance to the Crown while maintaining rights to the land. In Carolina, the proprietors' shares became embroiled in inheritance disputes, and residents petitioned the Crown to revoke the charter. In 1720 after a local revolution, the Crown appointed a royal governor in South Carolina and insisted on approving the governor for northern Carolina. In 1729 it repossessed the proprietary charter.

With the accession of George I, antagonism to the remaining charters quieted after another effort to recall them failed in 1715. That year, the Crown restored the Maryland proprietary to Charles Calvert, the Protestant great-grandson of Cecilius Calvert. In Pennsylvania, the Penns also retained their proprietary and even appointed governors (technically deputy governors) into the 1770s. In Rhode Island and Connecticut, the corporation governments remained intact even after the Revolution. Uniform government in the colonies was never completely achieved. Nevertheless, amid the variety a common denominator form emerged: a local assembly holding constitutionally limited lawmaking authority and overseen by either Privy Council appeal or review.

In 1732, the last charter granted by the Crown confirmed the emergence of this form of governance, in the process replaying the long history of settlement practices as if it were an institutional teleology. Initially, the Crown had delegated its governing authority to private individuals, as corporations or proprietors. The Georgia charter thus incorporated a group of trustees as a "body politic and corporate." The "corporation" of trustees, in turn, elected a council that appointed a governor, subject to Crown approval. After settlement, however, the Crown was to have supervisory governance returned to it. The Georgia corporation would therefore dissolve after twenty-one years, and the Crown would thereafter appoint the governor. The manner of government under the future royal governor did not have to be stated: he and the assembly would pass laws, and the Privy Council would review laws and appeals to ensure no repugnancies to the laws of England.

In 1701, the anonymous author of *An Essay upon the Government of the English Plantations* noted that if "any Alterations in the Government of the Plantations are necessary, they may be much more easily done now they are in their infancy, than hereafter when they grow more populous, and the Evils have taken deeper Root, and are more interwoven with the Laws and Constitutions of the several Colonies." Alterations in government were indeed done more easily in infancy. Unfortunately, by 1701, the government of the colonies was already well on the path to maturity. Every passing decade embedded common denominator governance practices more firmly and rooted colonial government into the colonial constitution. The failure to reduce the colonies to complete dependency before 1701 – indeed, the failure of the Crown even to develop a uniform idea of what constituted colonial dependency – would quietly become England's biggest problem. English efforts in the 1760s to impose dependency on this colonial constitution led toward revolution.

II. GOVERNING SETTLEMENTS

By the early eighteenth century local governance in the English colonies depended on relations among the governor and council, the assembly, and the Privy Council. Of course, more immediate authorities governed ordinary inhabitants' daily life. Local subdivisions – towns in New England, counties in the middle colonies, parishes in the Carolinas – governed the community by recording real estate and contract transactions, making probate determinations, imposing minor fines and penalties, dividing land, surveying highways, and policing poor and dependent individuals. Religious associations and institutions governed religious behavior. Male heads of households governed wives and children. White masters governed indentured servants and enslaved Africans, African Americans, and Indians. Compacts and treaties between English settlers and the Native American tribes, as well as intercolonial commissions and confederations, governed relations among the colonies and with their neighbors. Although all these forms of governance are important, here I focus on the transformation of settlement governance from its somewhat haphazard beginnings to a theoretically coherent, surprisingly effective, transatlantic colonial system.

The Governor and Council

We often assume the office of *governor* predated settlement. Although the origins of the office remain unclear, the word did not originally mean colony leader. At times, it referred descriptively to the one who governs, and at other times it signified a specific official, such as the governor-general of a garrison. The use of the term *governor* in the settlement context seems to reflect the early influence of the trading corporations that usually had a governor, deputy governor, and assistants, all elected by the assembled generality. But even among early corporate ventures the title given to the chief executive officer varied. Raleigh's 1589 venture referred to a governor but the 1606 Virginia letters patent had no such reference, whereas the 1607 Sagadahoc venture had a president. The term "governor" often seemed generic, as in the "Governor or principal Officer" of the 1609 Virginia letters patent. By the 1630s, however, governor was becoming the preferred term in corporate and proprietary colonies, and by the Restoration it was the dominant term. Almost all post-Restoration charters had a governor, and later Crown instructions named appointees as the Governor in Chief.

Historians' focus on the legislature has left the governor's importance often unstated. The governor symbolized the location of supreme authority in the settlement. In the colonies that followed corporate practices, the inhabitants selected the governor. In Plymouth, the men "chose, or rather confirmed, Mr. John Carver (a man godly and well approved amongst them) their Governor for that year."[18] In Massachusetts, Connecticut, and Rhode Island, the general assembly elected the governor. In proprietary colonies, the proprietor appointed the governor or held the position himself. The Crown's gradual attempt to acquire more authority over the colonies concentrated on controlling the governor. In the 1660s, Charles II unsuccessfully encouraged colonies to request new charters with Crown gubernatorial appointment. Later, James II made Edmund Andros Captain General and Governor in Chief of the Dominion of New England. Under William and Mary, the 1696 Navigation Act required that governors nominated by proprietors be approved by the Crown. By the 1720s, only Rhode Island, Connecticut, and, to a certain degree, Pennsylvania remained outside this system of royal governor appointment and control.

Selecting the governor symbolically demonstrated authority and reinforced loyalty to that authority. Into the eighteenth century, corporation colonies repeatedly elected the same few prominent local residents who had a vested interest in the success of the colony, often because of their large landholdings or extensive mercantile assets. In the proprietaries, appointments reflected varying theories of authority. Maryland favored Calvert family members. Pennsylvania chose English or Welsh officers and colonial administrators, though many switched loyalties and died in the colony. In Virginia, early Crown appointments favored local residents, but by the late 1670s Crown governors usually came from the English military and other colonies. Francis Nicholson, for example, had served in the English army and then in the Dominion of New England. Appointed lieutenant governor of Virginia (1690–2), Nicholson then became Governor of Maryland (1694–8), Virginia (1698–1705), and South Carolina (1721–5). Although New England governors' loyalties often remained in the colony, southern

[18] William Bradford, *Of Plymouth Plantation, 1620–1647*, ed. Samuel Eliot Morrison (New York, 1952), 76.

royal governors like Nicholson began to exemplify the emergence of career interests in the English colonial system and the development of aspirations for a uniform colonial policy.

Governors rarely acted alone, instead serving with a deputy and council. The office of deputy governor or lieutenant governor was ill defined, its duties ambiguous and varied across the colonies. The council's precursors lay in the broad array of English advisory institutions, ranging from borough councils to the trading company councils to the Privy Council. Certain New England settlements initially used the term *magistrate* for council members, but in corporation colonies the term *assistant* predominated. *Councilor*, with its English governmental associations, was preferred in the proprietaries. With the exception of Massachusetts, in colonies under Crown control, governors nominated councils of twelve inhabitants. Royal instructions required these members "be men of good life and well affected to our government and of good estates and abilities and not necessitous persons or much in debt." The council advised the governor, sat as a court, composed the upper house in bicameral assemblies, and consulted in certain colonies on judicial and other appointments.

The office of governor was all important. Early governors physically founded their settlements; their absence often doomed the settlement. The thirty-six instructions given to Virginia Governor Sir Thomas Gates in 1609 indicate the extensive expectations placed on governors. Gates was to sail the fleet to Jamestown; take control of public records; appoint, consult, and dismiss counselors; ensure worship of the Church of England; befriend and try to convert the native peoples; use martial law and chancery power; make laws; settle a principal seat, build a fort and additional towns; encourage trade; oversee employment; search out additional commodities; oversee meals; keep track of letters and instructions from England; listen to all opinions and objections; and keep secret sealed documents.

Instructions to later royal governors demonstrate the same breadth of authority and obligation. They held the power of appointment, oath, and oversight over other governmental branches. They were not to assent to laws that circumvented disallowance requirements, affected trade or shipping, or prejudiced the prerogative or property of subjects. They had discretionary powers ranging from the discouragement of drunkenness to the licensing of printing presses. They oversaw escheats, collected quitrents, and supervised the value of currency. In commerce, they assisted admiralty and customs officers, aided the royal navy (for example, by enforcing laws to preserve trees for masts), enforced the laws regarding the plantations trade, and encouraged the Royal African Company's monopoly over the slave trade. They were heads of the military, empowered to assist other colonies, but not to declare war except against "Indians upon emergencies." They promoted the established Church of England, encouraged the conversion of "Negroes and Indians to the Christian religion," and permitted religious liberty of various degrees (in some colonies without restriction; in others to all but "Papists").[19]

Governors became conduits for Crown authority and flows of information. They surveyed and transmitted maps. They wrote reports relating to population, colony affairs, and injuries to English subjects by other nations. They wrote accounts of judicial and other governmental functions, of finance, and of commercial imports and exports (including the numbers and prices of slaves imported). Although governors in royal colonies tried to follow the written commissions and instructions that specifically defined their powers and duties, governors in corporation colonies spent time trying politely and cleverly to refuse to comply with Crown requests.

Governors also supervised colonial law. The governor and council initially possessed significant lawmaking authority. In early settlements, particularly in the proprietaries and royal colonies, governors authored or helped draft legislation. Assembly lawmaking power and bicameralism would eventually reduce this direct power over legislation, whereupon governors resorted to the veto, used powers to summon and dissolve the assembly, and sent controversial laws to the Privy Council for disallowance. By the early eighteenth century, the governor, possessing only indirect control over lawmaking, appeared nevertheless to be a bar to legislation.

Into the eighteenth century, governors retained judicial authority through which they might try to control the interpretation of laws. In every colony, the governor and council initially sat as the central court. Over time, a growing caseload converted the governor and council to a court of appeal in many civil matters. The governor's judicial authority over equity was particularly controversial because that control was seen as symbolizing supreme authority. In royal colonies and certain proprietaries, the governor and council sat as a chancery court under the theory that equity fell within the Crown's prerogative power. Crown lawyers interpreted the Massachusetts royal charter as retaining equity courts under the Crown prerogative and therefore barring the legislature from appointing equity judges. In Pennsylvania, the assembly and governor fought over who held this equitable authority. The corporation colonies remained controversial exceptions by insisting that supreme equitable authority lay in their assemblies.

[19] For royal instructions, see Leonard Woods Labaree, *Royal Instructions to British Colonial Governors, 1670–1776* (New York, 1935), 2 vols.; for Gates's instructions, see David B. Quinn, ed., *The Extension of Settlement in Florida, Virginia, and the Spanish Southwest* (New York, 1979), 212–18.

The Assembly

We should not take the existence of the assembly for granted, for the idea that the governed should participate in governance was somewhat unusual. In English boroughs and palatines, the assembled governing body was usually referred to as a council. An *assembly* was a more representative gathering with self-governing authority. Early English trading corporations held assemblies (general courts) to enact bylaws; for example, the Presbyterian Church of Scotland had been organized by a general assembly. In 1619, the first colonial lawmaking gathering in Virginia adopted the term, referring to itself as a "General assembly." Specific local variants appeared (Virginia had a House of Burgesses and Massachusetts Bay had a General Court) but most colonies and Crown instructions referred to a *general assembly*. The term remained ambiguous, however, with *assembly* referring to the assembly of governor, assistants, and deputies, as well as only the lower branch of the legislature. Over the seventeenth century, the assembly in both senses established its existence by gaining lawmaking authority.

Once assemblies began to appear, they quickly became part of colonial government. In Virginia and Bermuda, the assemblies that convened in 1619 and 1620 likely brought some stability to local relationships. The Maryland proprietary charter provided for an assembly of freemen that would help frame laws; such an assembly met possibly as early as 1635. In 1639, the Crown officially recognized the Virginia assembly in royal instructions. Parliamentary control during the Interregnum strengthened colonial assemblies, and the Restoration did not have a significant adverse effect on them. James, Duke of York, did not include an assembly in his plans for New York, but one met in 1683. By then, Crown instructions generally assumed the presence of assemblies.

As representative institutions, assembly composition ran the theoretical gamut. The early freemen in Massachusetts Bay were also largely officers; the general court thus tended to duplicate the council. In Maryland, all freemen were initially summoned to the assembly. The need to make government work for the inhabitants altered both approaches. In Massachusetts, the complaints of ordinary landholders led to enlargement of the class of freemen electing deputies. In Maryland, freemen desiring to avoid attendance at the assembly developed an informal proxy system among themselves. Maryland would shrink participation to elected representatives. By the 1640s, representatives in most settlements were elected from towns or other defined localities. Inhabitants' concerns about governance also prompted a shift to bicameralism, which was dominant by the end of the seventeenth century. Representatives of towns, burgesses, or counties sat in the lower house; members of the governor's council sat in the upper house. Pennsylvania remained an exception with an explicitly unicameral structure. Regardless of structure, elections were seldom contested before the end of the seventeenth century.

The idea that assemblies should exercise lawmaking authority was also accepted rapidly. In corporation colonies, the assembly was recognized as the supreme lawmaking authority. In the proprietaries, the assemblies' authority over lawmaking was initially more limited, the Maryland charter simply requiring the "Advice, Assent, and Approbation of the Free-men" or "their Delegates or Deputies" to laws made by the proprietor. By the end of the seventeenth century, however, assemblies were generally exercising significant lawmaking authority. The Crown's failed attempt in the late 1670s at imposing lawmaking on Jamaica and Virginia only confirmed assembly authority over law.

The Privy Council

The role of the Privy Council (strictly, the King in Council) in colonial governance took a century to cohere. The first Virginia patent gave the Crown a brief direct role, but otherwise early letters patents provided no formal part, leaving the Crown to address issues through private petitions and complaints. During the mid-1630s, a permanent committee on trade and a commission on foreign plantations were created. The latter, under William Laud, theoretically enjoyed broad powers over the colonies – the power to make laws, hear cases, and revoke charters and patents – but it accomplished little. During the 1640s and 1650s, Parliamentary leaders passed the first Navigation Act regulating colonial trade, sent commissioners to the settlements, and began to review laws from the Barbados. Coherent governance, however, did not occur, and various standing committees went in and out of existence.

After the Restoration, the Privy Council turned to colonial matters, in particular, disputes over the array of patents, charters, grants and indentures doled out over the past eighty years. This role was explicitly acknowledged in the 1663 Rhode Island charter, which permitted appeals to the Crown in matters of public controversy. In private matters, for which discontented individuals in New England had long argued for a right to appeal under Crown prerogative or English corporate law, the Privy Council also began to consider a formal role. In 1664, letters patent to the Duke of York for the first time explicitly reserved to the Crown the hearing of private appeals. The same year the Privy Council sent an investigatory commission to New England. But the commission foundered and the Crown was distracted from its concern over colonial affairs by more pressing foreign policy matters.

Efforts to create a coherent and cohesive role for the Privy Council developed after 1676 with the creation of the twenty-one-member committee known as the Committee for Trade and Plantations (the Lords of Trade). At first the committee aspired to a direct role in colonial lawmaking. Since the 1660s, laws had been sent from Barbados, Jamaica, the Leeward Islands, and, on occasion, Virginia for sporadic review; the committee now proposed drafting laws for the Jamaican assembly itself. The effort failed and by 1680 the English attorney general had confirmed that Jamaica would be governed by laws made by its own assembly. The committee settled for a supervisory role. Instructions to the Caribbean and Virginia governors and to John Cutt, president of New Hampshire, required the transmission of laws so that the Privy Council could review them. By the 1680s, the committee was also hearing appeals from the colonies. In 1681, the Pennsylvania charter became the first both to require transmission of laws and to reserve explicitly the Crown's right to hear appeals. Between 1682 and 1692, such supervision spread by royal instruction and new charter to Virginia, the Dominion of New England, Massachusetts, New Hampshire, and Maryland.

At the turn of the century, the Privy Council began to decide in specific instances whether colonial laws and customs fell outside the bounds of an imperial conception of English law and customs. In 1696, it created a new advisory committee of the whole, the Committee for Hearing Appeals from the Plantations. The Crown established the separate Lords Commissioners for Trade and Plantations (the Board of Trade), composed of state officers (initially the chancellor, president, treasurer, high admiral, secretary of state, and chancellor of the exchequer) and eight appointed and paid commissioners, usually members of Parliament, to advise as to colonial laws among other duties. The approach proved effective and would remain largely in place through the eighteenth century.

Review of colonial legislation and appeals was an intriguing approach to supervising colonial law. The Crown could claim ultimate authority and ensure uniformity while still permitting local authorities to pass legislation, decide cases, and diverge from English law in the first instance. After 1690, more than 8,500 acts were submitted for review from the mainland colonies, with approximately 470 disallowed. Between 1670 and the Revolution, around 250 cases were appealed from the mainland American colonies, with Massachusetts, Rhode Island, and Virginia accounting for the largest number. Laws found repugnant to the laws of England or contrary to the royal prerogative touched on inheritance (diminishing primogeniture, limiting dower rights, treating jointly held property as tenancy in common); escheats to the Crown; relief of debtors; religious establishment and religious toleration (or the lack thereof); assembly authority and powers; regulation of attorneys; creation of courts (particularly equity, chancery, and admiralty courts), juries, and court procedures; trade and piracy regulation; and the creation of ports and regulation of custom officers. Yet, most colonial laws remained in force without any action from the Privy Council. Colonial legislatures nonetheless manipulated disallowance by passing temporary laws or reenacting substantially similar laws, notwithstanding Crown instructions intended to prevent such evasions.

Appeals of cases provided another avenue for Privy Council decision making as to whether a colony's law was repugnant to the laws of England or a permissible departure for local circumstances, although it was more costly and dependent on individual initiative. In theory the Privy Council heard appeals as a committee of the whole. In reality the appeal was usually assigned to a smaller group, including either the Chief Justice of King's Bench or Common Pleas. Colonists retained English solicitors and Crown law officers (often the Solicitor or Attorney General) to argue the appeal. Between 1696 and 1720, civil, criminal, probate, and vice-admiralty appeals were brought from Massachusetts, New York, Virginia, Connecticut, Rhode Island, Maryland, New Hampshire, South Carolina, New Jersey, and Pennsylvania.

Theoretically, Rhode Island and Connecticut stood outside this system. Their corporate charters did not authorize Privy Council review or appeals. Throughout the 1690s the Crown and various colonists repeatedly tried to bring the colonies under the review regime, only to receive messy manuscript copies of laws from Rhode Island and a twenty-year-old edition of Connecticut's statutes. Eventually, in 1715, the English Attorney General declared that the two colonies had no obligation under their charters to transmit laws. In the 1730s, however, Connecticut would do so voluntarily. The colonies were less successful at barring appeals, the Board of Trade proclaiming that appeals were an inherent right of the Crown. Despite local legislative efforts to discourage them, appeals were heard from Connecticut and Rhode Island. Appeals became particularly prevalent in Rhode Island as the only path for review of laws.

By the eighteenth century, the Privy Council had become the third branch of colonial government. Law – both its making and interpretation – involved the governor, legislature, and the Crown's Privy Council. Rather than an early example of separated powers, colonial government was thus the English theory of mixed powers – Crown intertwined with legislative authority, known as the King in Parliament – extended to the far side of the Atlantic.

III. THE CULTURE OF LAW IN THE SETTLEMENTS

The manner and offices of colonial government depended on a culture of law. The term *legal culture* has become ubiquitous in contemporary scholarship even as the concept itself remains elusive. Rather than attempt a definition,

I want instead to plumb a component of colonial legal culture – the world of courts, attorneys, and law – in the expectation that an understanding of the meanings that came to be attached to them can suggest avenues for the broader inquiry into legal culture in general

Courts

We often discuss early seventeenth-century colonial courts as if they were a separate branch of government. They were not. The institutional names of courts – the General Court or Quarter Court (Virginia), the Court of Assistants (Massachusetts and Connecticut), the General Court of Trials (Rhode Island), the General Court of Assizes (New York), and the Provincial Court (Maryland and Pennsylvania) – prove misleading. The composition of all these courts was the same: they were all made up of the governor and council. Some might dismiss these courts as "courts" because many of the judges had not trained as attorneys, but to do so is historically inappropriate. Procedurally, the jury usually made decisions, and judges decided issues raised on motion by attorneys. Traditional legal training was unnecessary for the entire bench. Questions were resolved according to colonial laws, legal records, or English instructions (to which judges as political officers had access). The job of attorneys – and likely any legally trained judges – was to explain any additional English laws. Should there be disagreement, by the end of the seventeenth century the Privy Council (also, as we have seen, comprised of political officers) heard appeals. Because many cases turned on whether a colonial law or practice was repugnant or agreeable to England, political acumen was as valuable as formal study in addressing the question, and political power and status were as potent as a degree in ensuring respect for the answer.

The courts arranged below and above these courts in the early settlements were not separate branches either. The diversity of early inferior courts paralleled local political structures: there were county courts (Massachusetts), town courts (Rhode Island), and manor courts (parts of New York and Maryland). After 1660, county courts became the common inferior court across the colonies. Justices of peace (in many places, the members of the governor's council) served as justices, as well as often handling immediate, local problems on an individual basis. Despite the possibility of an appeal, many matters never moved beyond these courts. Above the governor and council court, in several early colonies – Massachusetts, Virginia, Connecticut, Rhode Island, and even Maryland – was the assembly that heard cases and appeals as a court. The theory behind this jurisdiction was most apparent in the corporation colonies in which the legislature was seen as the supreme colonial authority.

The Crown's growing desire for control over law altered this system. In the 1680s, the Crown began to end where it could the assembly's jurisdiction as the highest court of appeal in favor of appeal to the Privy Council from the colony's court. New and recurring disputes over the existence and authority of other colonial courts with jurisdiction over probate, chancery, fines and recoveries, admiralty, and arbitration reflected this same fight for control between the Crown (usually in the guise of the royal governor) and the legislature.

This struggle produced the oft-claimed ancestor of modern supreme courts, the Superior Court of Judicature, comprised of an appointed chief justice and associate justices. This transformation should not be misconstrued as the separation of the judicial function from colony government; to the contrary, it was an effort to retain Crown control of the judiciary, as well as an acknowledgment of the time constraints placed on the governor and council by growth of the colonies. The new court structure appeared in the Dominion of New England in 1687 and in 1681 in Jamaican legislation. After 1691, Superior Courts of Judicature soon sat with judges appointed by the royal governor in New York (technically the Supreme Court of Judicature), Massachusetts, New Hampshire, and New Jersey. A Superior Court of Judicature heard appeals and had original jurisdiction in cases involving title to land or significant amounts of money. County sessions and inferior courts of common pleas heard smaller cases. This new terminology spread to Connecticut (1711) and Rhode Island (1729), although the legislature retained the power to appoint justices. Although Pennsylvania adopted a Supreme Court in 1722, most southern colonies retained the names of general or provincial courts and left power in the governor and council, either directly or by appeal.

The absence of published court opinions reinforced the perception that courts were not a separate branch. Most proceedings remained solely of local interest and included prosecutions for fornication, disputes over title to land, disagreements over inheritances, contested debts, and accusations of slander. Knowledge of the court was acquired by being in court, relying on the oral or written reports of others, and reading the manuscript records. When court proceedings appeared in print they reflected public interest in the substantive matter and a printer's hope for financial return. William Bradford printed the court proceedings in the West Jersey trial and execution of Thomas Lutherland for murder under the title *Blood Will Out* (1692), as well as legal materials relating to a controversy involving himself and Quaker George Keith. Other early printed legal materials include Cotton Mather's account of five of the Salem witch trials, accounts of Jacob Leisler's rebellion, Nicholas Bayard's trial for treason, and a significant number of piracy trials. Apparently unique was the printing in 1720 of copies of the briefs in a Massachusetts civil case, *Nathaniel Matson v. Nathaniel Thomas*, involving the question whether Massachusetts had to follow the English law of primogeniture and entail. Descriptions of courts nonetheless occurred in official correspondence and printed descriptions and discussions of the colonies. From a transatlantic perspective, what the courts governed seemed less important than who governed them.

Legal Practitioners

We have tended to assume that relatively few lawyers were to be found in the seventeenth-century colonies. Certainly most criminal defendants entered the court unrepresented, and many litigants in lower courts proceeded without attorneys. In 1705, Robert Beverley of Virginia wrote, "Every one that pleases, may plead his own Cause, or else his Friends for him, there being no restraint in that case, nor any licensed Practitioners in the Law." Yet, attorneys, legal practitioners, and other legal literates abounded in the colonies. Their presence necessitates reconsideration of the seventeenth-century colonies as a world of law without lawyers.

Throughout this period, *attorney* or *practitioner* of law was the preferred label; *lawyer* was the preferred epithet. In every colony, court records, statutes, letters, and other documents demonstrate that people labeled as "attorneys" appeared early and often. In England, the term *attorney* had become ubiquitous between 1550 and 1650. *Practitioner* referred to these attorneys, along with clerks and solicitors. Attorneys conducted routine matters in central, local, and chancery courts; composed pleadings; gave advice; prepared litigation; and served as clerks of the court. Early seventeenth-century law books were aimed at these legal practitioners. Over the course of the early seventeenth century, attorneys became differentiated from barristers. Barristers were more likely to be from elite social circles, instructed at one of the Inns of Court. Only barristers could argue issues of law before King's Bench or Common Pleas. Nonetheless, this distinction was still developing during the early decades of colonial settlement.

Legal practitioners abounded in the early colonies, both in number and variety. Some had English legal training. Before 1660, a significant number of attorneys practicing in the colonies had been trained as attorneys or barristers or had studied in the Inns of Court. Familiar with English law, such men played a crucial role in writing early colonial legal codes in Massachusetts, Connecticut, Rhode Island, and New York. English-trained practitioners also served as early critics of colonial divergences from English laws. A second group of legal practitioners was comprised of men who held political offices that involved the law: recorders and clerks, general attorneys, governors, and members of councils. In 1649, because people had asked magistrates (councilors) for advice in cases that later went to trial, Massachusetts prohibited such a practice. For similar reasons, after 1670, colonial acts prevented clerks, sheriffs, constables, deputies, and justices of the peace from practicing law. A third group of practitioners can be labeled simply as legally literate. Written literacy, combined with speaking skills and basic legal knowledge, permitted competent participation in the legal system despite the absence of formal training. Some legal literates acted as attorneys; others limited themselves to representing themselves, friends, associates, or dependents. Merchants comprised one category of legal literates because the skills needed for transatlantic business and law overlapped.

Women appeared as attorneys, representing themselves, their husbands, or other family members. Although these appointments have been described as "attorney-in-fact" appointments, the phrase was not used, and the distinction between attorneys-in-fact and those in-law seems a later development. Female attorneys may have often had the same knowledge and skill as male legal literates, although they could not serve in political office. The social response to female practice is unclear. In Maryland in the 1650s, Margaret Brent famously served as an attorney while a single woman. She litigated cases, served as executrix for the previous proprietor, and, in that capacity, unsuccessfully sought to vote in the assembly as the proprietor's attorney. In 1658, a Maryland proclamation barred wives from acting as attorneys for their husbands. The eventual spread of licensing procedures may have significantly limited the number of female attorneys. Women nonetheless continued to serve as executors, suing to collect debts, arranging property transfers, and defending estates against claims.

After 1660, a new generation of legal practitioners arose, many of whom acquired their legal training in the colonies. Law schools did not exist, and the colleges that had been established, like Harvard, did not train lawyers. Attorneys were, in essence, home-schooled: sons learned from fathers, aspiring practitioners served as clerks or studied with prominent attorneys, and practicing attorneys shared English law books and commonplace books of notes. Some practitioners continued to seek English legal training. Men from Massachusetts and Virginia on occasion traveled to England to spend time at the Inns of Court. Though the Inns no longer provided a comprehensive educational experience, attendance provided an opportunity to purchase English law books, observe at the courts, and learn about the law through available avenues. Barristers, members of the Inns of Court, attorneys, solicitors, and clerks could also be found among the waves of new English and Scottish migrants. Some started colonial practices; others served in the offices of the expanding royal governments, for example, as judges in the vice-admiralty courts.

Although the colonies never acquired the hardened barrister-solicitor distinction of English legal practice, colonial legal practice did have a hierarchy. By the late seventeenth and early eighteenth centuries, a small group of attorneys in each colony monopolized practice in the superior courts. In Maryland, five or six attorneys handled most legal matters, with several attorneys arguing 90 to 100 cases apiece. Perhaps to prevent litigants from literally monopolizing such attorneys, Rhode Island and New York had statutes attempting to limit parties from hiring more than two attorneys. Colonies set fees based on the court and the type of legal work. The superior court practice involved appeals and disputes over the application of the laws of England – and generated higher fees. In the early eighteenth century, prominent attorneys advocated for even higher fees for cases argued on appeal and with numerous pleadings on matters of law. These men also began to consider forming associations to seek fee and attorney regulation. In 1709, six prominent "practisers of the law" in the City of New York formed an association to lobby for fee alterations. The ability to acquire higher fees permitted some of these attorneys to earn their living from legal practice. [20]

Provisions barring attorneys were few. Of the laws that were passed, most focused on fees. In Massachusetts' *Body of Libertyes* (1641), number 26 stated that "Every man that findeth himselfe unfit to plead his owne cause in any Court shall have Libertie to imploy any man against whom the Court doth not except, to helpe him, Provided he give him noe fee or reward for his paines." The provision, however, was not included in the 1648 printed *Laws and Libertyes*. Carolina's *Constitutions* stated that "it shall be a base and vile thing to plead for money or reward," but the *Constitutions* were never adopted. In the 1640s and 1650s Virginia did bar attorneys from receiving fees – but it also repealed these laws and at times insisted that parties be permitted to have men plead their case when necessary. It is unclear, in short, whether fee prohibition had any real impact.

Instead of prohibiting attorneys, colonies began to regulate their behavior. Statutes sought to prevent misuse of the legal system. The Massachusetts *Laws and Libertyes* discouraged the "common barrater" who was "vexing others with unjust, frequent and endles sutes" and permitted treble damages against litigants who had "willingly & wittingly done wrong" to the defendant. Virginia and Maryland made early efforts to license attorneys; after 1670, several colonies required that attorneys be admitted by the governor or the courts. In 1666, attorneys in Maryland took the oath of attorney before admission to practice. In 1686, Massachusetts adopted a

[20] Paul Hamlin and Charles E. Baker, *Supreme Court of Judicature of the State of New York, 1691–1704* (New York, 1959), 1: 273 n. 27.

version of the fifteenth-century English attorney oath, and over the next three decades New Hampshire, New York, Pennsylvania, Delaware, Rhode Island, Connecticut, and South Carolina followed. The colonies also occasionally sought to regulate attorney argument. A 1682 Maryland statute insisted that attorneys should "speak distinctly to one Error first" before proceeding to the next. In 1736, Rhode Island attorneys tried to bar those from Massachusetts in part because they "tire the ears of the judges with their needless repetitions, and sometimes confound and perplex the juries with their circumlocutions and sophistry so as to obscure and darken the case more than if it had not been pleaded at all." In 1718 the colony had required that at least one retained attorney be a colony resident.[21]

Several colonies provided attorneys for defendants who appeared disadvantaged by self-representation. In 1647, Virginia permitted courts to appoint a man to plead a cause if the party might otherwise lose the case by his "weakeness."[22] That same year, Rhode Island allowed litigants to plead their own case or use the town attorney. Some statutes even required that an attorney take any case for which a fee was presented. Although English law barred defendants in felony cases from retaining attorneys, Rhode Island in 1669 and Pennsylvania in 1701 authorized indicted defendants to retain attorneys. Although colonial legislatures understood the problems with attorneys – excessive litigation, excessive fees, excessive talking – they also seem to have understood that attorneys could aid people in negotiating authority and protesting illegitimate governance.

Colonial Law

In 1701, the anonymous "American" author of *An Essay upon the Government of the English Plantations* noted, "It is a great Unhappiness, that no one can tell what is Law, and what is not, in the Plantations." The relationship between the laws of England and the laws of the colonies was uncertain. Some thought that the law of England was "chiefly to be respected." Some "are of Opinion, that the Laws of the Colonies are to take the first place." Others "contend for the Laws of the Colonies, in Conjunction with those that were in force in England" at the time of settlement and those where the "Reason of the Law" is applicable to the colonies. A final group held that no acts of Parliament

[21] *Archives of Maryland*: Proceedings and Acts of the General Assembly, October 1678–November 1683 (Baltimore, 1889), 7: 361; Mary Sarah Bilder, *The Transatlantic Constitution: Colonial Legal Culture and the Empire* (Cambridge, 2004), 118 (quoting 1736 Petition).

[22] *Colony Laws of Virginia*, ed. John D. Cushing (Wilmington, 1978), 2: 349.

bound the colonies unless particularly named. The author suggested that "some Rule be established, to know what Laws the Plantations are to be subject to" and how far Parliamentary acts not mentioning the colonies did "affect them." Until then, "we are left in the dark."

People had been in the dark about what was "law" in the colonies for a century. The existence of the question itself was proof of the ambiguity over the location of lawmaking authority. Non-English areas controlled by England certainly existed before settlement of the American colonies, but there was no uniform approach to when English laws governed. In Ireland, the English Crown essentially could write laws for Ireland. Under Poynings' law (1495), legislation was to be approved by the English Crown and Privy Council before being passed by the Irish Parliament. In Wales, an English statute in 1535 replaced Welsh laws with the laws of England and authorized the King and Council to reenact any necessary divergent Welsh customs. In the Channel Islands of Jersey and Guernsey, customary Norman law was followed, but the Privy Council had the right to hear appeals.

The requirement in the patents and charters that laws be "as near as conveniently they may be, agreeable" or not repugnant to the laws of England created a foundation for debate. What this constitutional limit meant in practice was unclear. Very early arguments over the application of English law in the New England colonies approached the question as one of corporate law and discussed the authority under the patent. There was little else to discuss. For most of the seventeenth century, English case law on what law governed the colonies was largely unhelpful. Two cases discussing the rights of Scots over land in England seemed to bear on the issue, but provided little if any guidance. In *Calvin's Case* (1608), Chief Justice Edward Coke established a set of categories (inherited versus conquered kingdoms), but did not explicitly discuss the question of the law in future American colonies. The awkward fit of these categories for the mainland colonies was apparent by 1624 when Coke and others considered the application of "conquest" to the New England patent.[23] Decades later, in *Craw v. Ramsey* (1670), Chief Justice John Vaughan referred to the now existent "plantations"; however, the case involved the ability of a dominion to alter English law in England, not the application of English law in the colonies. Through the 1660s, the focus of the colonial law question was whether a colony's passage of plausibly repugnant laws was sufficiently outside the colony's charter to justify *quo warranto* proceedings. In the 1670s, the Crown's effort to write colonial laws rendered the question almost moot.

[23] *Proceedings and Debates of the British Parliaments respecting North America*, ed. Leo Francis Stock (Washington, 1924), 1: 58–61.

In the early 1680s, the Crown's acceptance of colonial assembly lawmaking and the passage of new property laws in England shifted the focus to whether new English statutes applied in the colonies. Of particular importance in the colonies, the Statute of Frauds (1677) altered the requirement for a valid will from two to three witnesses. In the colonies where wills had long been made with two witnesses, the new English statute threatened to invalidate two-witness wills. The relationship of the requirement to the colonies would be litigated repeatedly. In 1683, a Virginia case addressed the issue of whether the Statute of Frauds applied. Virginia attorney William Fitzhugh argued for invalidation of a 1681 two-witness will because the "Laws of England are in force here, except where the Acts of Assembly have otherwise provided, by reason of the Constitution of the place & people."[24] In England, however, Attorney General William Jones reached a different conclusion, which was apparently shown "to all the then Judges of England, Who declared the same to be the Law." Jones stated that the colonies were only bound by new statutes if expressly named. Jones explained that Parliament could not have considered "the particular circumstances and conditions of the plantations, especially considering no Member" came from there to Parliament. Moreover, the Atlantic meant that colonists would not know of the law until after it took effect. In short, Parliament was not expected to include the colonies in ordinary legislation, and the colonial legislatures were the more appropriate lawmaking authorities.[25]

The common law was an even trickier matter. In the 1690s, cases involving English colonial officers in the Caribbean continued to debate when the laws of England applied. In King's Bench, *Blankard v. Galdy* involved the sale of the Provost Marshal of Jamaica's office for seven and a half years and whether a sixteenth-century English statute barring the practice applied in Jamaica. Chief Justice John Holt concluded that Jamaica had been conquered, and therefore the laws of England were not in force until so declared. Because Jamaica had been conquered from the Spanish, the case's application to the seemingly not conquered mainland colonies was unclear. The House of Lords appeal, *Dutton v. Howell*, involved a dispute between the governor of Barbados, Richard Dutton, and the executors of John Witham, his deputy governor, for Dutton's alleged false imprisonment of Witham. Among other arguments, Dutton claimed that the action could not lie because the laws might be different in Barbados. The executors responded that Barbados was a "colony or plantation" and that the common law must

[24] Richard Beale Davis, ed., *William Fitzhugh and His Chesapeake World, 1676–1701* (Chapel Hill, 1963), 107 (Fitzhugh to Ralph Wormerly, Feb. 26, 1681/1682).

[25] *Virginia Colonial Decisions: The Reports by Sir John Randolph and by Edward Barrandall . . .*, ed. R.T. Barton (Boston, 1909), 2: B1–2.

apply in a "new Settlement" of Englishmen. The executors lost, despite elaborate argument and without explanation. The cases did not provide an answer, but confirmed the contemporary difference of opinion.

Into the eighteenth century, as the anonymous author had complained, no one in the colonies or England could "tell what is Law, and what is not, in the Plantations." Given the lack of clarity, certain colonies sought their own rules as to when laws of England would apply. One approach is probably best referred to as an introduction statute, authorizing English law in appropriate circumstances. For example, in 1700, the Rhode Island assembly declared that, where the colony's laws or customs did not reach or comprehend a matter or cause, it was lawful to put into execution the laws of England. The introduction of English laws then could be made on a case-by-case basis by courts and officials depending on local conditions. A second approach adopted in South Carolina in 1712 and North Carolina in 1715 resembled later reception statutes. Here, the colony transferred various English statutes into its own law and thereby ensured that certain laws could be pleaded in the courts.

The idea that colonies might be more properly considered new settlements than conquered territories gathered support in the early eighteenth century. A new publication of *Blankard* in William Salkeld's *Reports* (1718) claimed that Holt had declared that in "an uninhabited Country newly found by our English Subjects," the laws in England were in force. A 1720 opinion by Richard West, counsel for the Board of Trade, agreed that the common law and statutes in affirmance prior to settlement were in force as well as later statutes that mentioned the colonies. A 1722 memorandum recounted a Privy Council determination of a colonial appeal apparently from Barbados that similarly distinguished conquered countries from uninhabited countries found out by English subjects who brought their laws with them.[26] Nonetheless, a report of *Smith v. Brown and Cooper*, a slavery case, contained a statement by Holt that "the laws of England do not extend to Virginia, being a conquered country." As debates between the proprietor and the Maryland assembly and the instructions from Connecticut to its agent in the 1720s demonstrate, people continued to disagree over the cases, the rules, and the factual history of the colonies – whether they were plantations in countries found out by English people or conquered lands.

[26] Mr. West's opinion on the admiralty jurisdiction, in the *plantations (1720)*, George Chalmers, *Opinions of Eminent Lawyers on Various Points of English Jurisprudence* (1814; New York, 1971), 2: 202; Memorandum (1722), Peere Williams, *Reports* (London, 1740), 2: 75–6.

In 1729, an opinion by the English Attorney General further complicated matters. Earlier comments had implied that a colony assembly had to enact post-settlement English law before it applied. The opinion concluded that a colony could introduce such an English statute by assembly act or receive it by "long uninterrupted usage or practice." Colonial custom and practice, in particular, the degree to which English laws had been followed, became an additional debatable issue.

These arguments about the application of the laws of England to the colonies, as well as the requirement that colonial lawmaking be not repugnant to the laws of England, depended on knowledge of the laws of England. Desirable English law books, therefore, were those that described the "laws of England." The phrase was broad and ambiguous, but seemed to include at its core the Magna Carta, English statutes, and the principles and terms of English common law. In selecting law books, colonial legal attorneys favored texts that provided comprehensive overviews of English law and were designed for general practitioners. Treatises, particularly on such subjects as property and inheritance, offered comprehensible discussions. Statute collections such as Pulton's *Sundry Statutes* or Keble's *Statutes at Large* provided convenient access to English statutes. Guides for justices of the peace and jurors succinctly described the court system. Form books such as the *Compleat Clerke* provided necessary models for legal documents, and law dictionaries explained vocabulary. More popular than case reports themselves were abridgments of reports; a unique interpretation of an English case had little value. More unusual books related to legal issues of particular interest in the colonies: for example, charters, oaths, the liberties of Englishmen, and divergent English customs. Early colonial publications emphasized these same areas and included a book on indictments brought against the Duke of York; a treatise on Parliamentary laws and customs; a book including Magna Carta and the charter to William Penn; and reprints of books on the right to juries, on inheritance, and guides for constables and sheriffs. In the early 1720s, Boston and Philadelphia printers both published *English Liberties; or, the Free-born Subject's Inheritance*, a volume including the Magna Carta, fundamental laws, and comments relating to the "Constitution of our English Government." As these books were bought, borrowed, and copied into commonplace books, a colonial vision of the laws of England spread.

Adding to the uncertainty over the nature of colonial law was ambiguity over the lawmaking authority present in the colonial legislatures. We tend to gloss over the words used in colonial lawmaking – acts, ordinances, laws, statutes – but they could convey subtle and important differences. The Massachusetts *Body of Liberties*, for example, noted that the laws were "expressed onely under the name and title of Liberties, and not in the exact forme of Laws or Statutes." However, it "intreate[d]" authorities to "consider them as laws." As the author of *An Essay upon the Government of the Plantations* pointed out, it was uncertain "how far the Legislature is in their Assemblies." Were the colonial assemblies little more than corporations or did they have the power of "Naturalization, Attainder of Heirs, cutting off Intails, settling Titles to Lands, and other things of that nature"? Colonial criminal laws seem to have been of particular concern, and a better understanding of this issue may help explain the tendency of New England assemblies to cite biblical sources for criminal laws. The author also wanted to know whether "they may make Laws disagreeable to the Laws of *England*, in such Cases, where the Circumstances of the Places are vastly different, as concerning Plantations, Waste, the Church, &c." Colonial assemblies accepted this justification. The South Carolina "Negro-Act" (1740) thus explained that crimes that gave a "Slave, Free-Negro, Mulatto, Indian or Mestizo" the death sentence were "peculiar to the Condition and Situation of this province, [and] could not fall within the Provision of the Laws of England."[27]

The form in which colonial laws appeared similarly reflected shifting uncertainties about authority. A printed collection of laws testified publicly and permanently as to the location of government and lawmaking authority. Although most colonies required laws to be read publicly or sent to towns and churches, a printed volume offered constant access for literate readers on both sides of the Atlantic. This accessibility thus also posed a danger – a printed law book could provide evidence that colonial laws were repugnant to the laws of England and bring about *quo warranto* proceedings. Before 1648, the only authoritative collection of printed colonial laws was *For the colony in Virginea Britannia. Lavves diuine, morall and martiall, &c.* (London, 1612), a collection written and imposed by the governors. Although John Cotton's *An Abstract or the Lawes of New England* (London, 1641) appeared with extensive biblical citations, the collection represented his own draft and was never adopted by the assembly. The code bearing a closer resemblance to the assembly's laws, Nathaniel Ward's *Body of Liberties* (1641), remained in manuscript and was never technically adopted.

The corporation colonies' growing confidence in their lawmaking authority resulted in printed law collections that testified to that authority. Massachusetts Bay was the first and only colony that domestically printed its laws before the 1670s. *The Book of the General Laws and Libertyes* (Cambridge, 1648) appeared the year before Charles I's execution as English

[27] "An Act for the better ordering and governing negroes and other slaves in this province," [Acts passed by the General Assembly of South-Carolina, May 10, 1740–July 10, 1742] [Charleston: Printed by Peter Timothy, 1740–1742], 3, 9 (Early American Imprints, Series I (Evans), nos. 40211, 40286).

politics shifted away from Crown authority. The volume emphasized the general court's authority. Yet, the edition had a short life, as by 1651 legislative changes left it judged "unvendible," largely turned to "wast pap'r" and burnt.[28] The assembly published a new version of the *Laws and Libertyes* in 1660 and continued to print later session laws. In 1672 and 1673, the corporate governments of Massachusetts, Plymouth, and Connecticut had Samuel Green of Cambridge print their laws with title pages that emphasized the "General Court," not the Crown or England, and opening pages that addressed the "Inhabitants" and "Freemen" of the colonies. In Virginia, the Crown-appointed governor used printed laws to promote a different authority. His collection for Crown officials, *The Lawes of Virginia Now in Force* (London, 1662), prominently displayed the King's name on the title page and proclaimed Crown as well as assembly authority. Amidst controversies over colonial authority, printed laws declared legislative authority to inhabitants and to England. Edward Randolph used the printed laws to demonstrate repugnancies to Crown officials, and the Connecticut edition was sent to London as evidence. To avoid such scrutiny, Rhode Island never printed its laws in the seventeenth century.

In the 1690s, colonial law printing began to flourish as the relationship between Crown and assembly became clarified. The Crown's requirement that colonies send laws to England for review and acceptance of assembly lawmaking authority combined to produce the laws of their "Majesties" provinces: New York (1694) New Hampshire (1699), and New Jersey (1709). As the threat to the charters receded, corporation and proprietary colonies also printed laws. Early editions of proprietary laws appeared in Maryland and Pennsylvania in 1700–1. Between 1714 and 1720, these two colonies, along with Massachusetts, Connecticut, New Hampshire, New York, New Jersey, and Rhode Island, published official versions. The Rhode Island, Connecticut, and Massachusetts editions carefully acknowledged both English and local authority. With the title pages declaring in small print his or her "Majesties Colony," the charter appeared as the first document. Rhode Island nonetheless remained wary and silently altered certain laws to conform to current English laws. The southern royal colonies were curiously slow in printing official collections: Virginia (1733), South Carolina (1736), and North Carolina (1751). Despite the growth in printed collections, as the author of *An Abridgement of the Laws in Force and Use in Her Majesty's Plantations* (London, 1704) noted, gentlemen concerned with the plantations had "great Difficulty" in procuring copies of the laws to compare "the Laws and Constitutions of each Country, or Province, one

[28] Petition of Richard Russell (1651), *The Laws and Liberties of Massachusetts* (Cambridge, 1929), viii (Max Farrand introduction).

with another." The question, what is law in the colonies, remained difficult as a theoretical and practical matter.

CONCLUSION

A century and a half after the question was asked, "What manner of government is to be used," the settlements had produced one answer. In the two corporation colonies, two proprietaries, and remaining royal colonies, a governor served as translator for Crown policies, an assembly held the lawmaking authority limited by the requirement of non-repugnancy to the laws of England, and the Crown through the Privy Council supervised the boundaries of colonial authority.

What manner of government was this system? English settlement practices had created a government of dual authorities, legitimizing both Crown and colonial legislative authority. Acceptance of these dual authorities permitted colonial governance to successfully negotiate the geographic problem of the Atlantic. Although these dual authorities were in tension, they were not perceived as incoherent. By the mid-eighteenth century, however, as William Blackstone demonstrated, English political thought had become rhetorically intolerant of dual authorities. He wrote that "there is and must be" in all governments "a supreme, irresistible, absolute, uncontrolled authority, in which the *jura summi imperii*, or the rights of sovereignty, reside." Blackstone placed this "sovereignty of the British Constitution" in Parliament – the King, the Lords, and the House of Commons.[29]

For colonial lawyers, this construction threw into confusion two hundred years of settlement governance. As James Wilson, in *Considerations on the Nature and the Extent of the Legislative Authority of the British Parliament* (1774), wrote, "Dependence of the Mother Country" – of allegiance to the Crown – was understood "by the first planters of the Colonies, and also by the most eminent Lawyers, at that time, in England." It was, however, a "dependence founded upon the principles of reason, of liberty, and of law"; not the "slavish and unaccountable" dependence and "unlimited authority" contended for by the Parliament. This understanding of dependence – dual authority created by supervised, constitutionally limited lawmaking – produced the Revolution and the commitment to federalism. Perhaps in this sense, institutional history helps us better understand an American manner of government.[30]

[29] William Blackstone, *Commentaries on the Laws of England* (1765–1769; reprint, Chicago,1979), 1: 49, 51.

[30] James Wilson, *Considerations on the Nature and the Extent of the Legislative Authority of the British Parliament* (Philadelphia, 1774), 29, 31, 34.

4

LEGAL COMMUNICATIONS AND IMPERIAL GOVERNANCE: BRITISH NORTH AMERICA AND SPANISH AMERICA COMPARED

RICHARD J. ROSS

Strategies and practices for the communication of law were vital to England's capacity to govern its North American colonies. A diverse array of mechanisms for exchange of legal information characterized the expanding English empire – Crown instructions to governors, Privy Council review of colonial legislation and appellate cases, petitioning, the stationing of colony agents in London and royal officials in America, the training or immigration of lawyers, the transmission of information through lobbying and interest groups, the discussion of law in congregations and universities, and publication by the linked media of print, manuscript, and speech. Here I use the protean concept of "legal communications" to bundle together several distinguishable practices both to achieve breadth and to demonstrate their interrelationships.

In what ways did legal communications in the seventeenth- and eighteenth-century Anglo-American world affect imperial governance? First, the strengthening of English oversight of the colonies after the Restoration required the cultivation of an assortment of legal communications techniques. We are already quite familiar with the general growth and functioning of imperial institutions and trans-Atlantic politics that this entailed. Here, I explore the variety of different roles that legal communications played in tying the empire together administratively and intellectually. This exploration provides the basis for the chapter's second and more extensive part, which advances the main argument. In that second part, we see that the empire's communications practices actually had a double nature. Although they facilitated greater imperial oversight, they also inadvertently shielded a significant measure of local control and diversity in the colonial legal systems themselves. An examination of the contrast between legal communications in the English and Spanish colonial empires makes this point clear. Comparison with Spanish America reveals the basic presuppositions and limitations of the English system. It also suggests why legal communications became an unreliable and inconsistent agent of imperial centralization in the Anglo-American case.

I. THE ROLE OF COMMUNICATIONS IN THE TIGHTENING OF IMPERIAL OVERSIGHT

Sheer distance and the slow, expensive, and fallible communications that went with it hindered effective English oversight of the early and middle seventeenth-century colonial legal systems. Four to twelve weeks were required to cross the Atlantic Ocean. Under such circumstances, episodic and inefficient supervision by central authorities could surprise no one. The Privy Council and national tribunals at Westminster could not supervise Massachusetts and Virginia as closely as they could Durham and Bristol. No assize system of traveling royal judges fanned out from London to hear disputes in the colonies. Settlers could not appeal cases to the King's courts at Westminster but only to the Privy Council, and these petitions were few and far between. Royally appointed commissions seldom appeared in the colonies. Geographic distance and slow, irregular communications encouraged the autonomy and interpretive leeway of local elites at the expense of their nominal superiors. Opportunities to organize colonial law and politics in ways that differed meaningfully from seventeenth-century England abounded. The result was far more variety among the early legal orders of New England, New York, and Carolina than, say, among those of Devon, Sussex, and York.

The "imperial school" of colonial historians has charted the movement away from this initial seventeenth-century starting point. Their work explains how and why, beginning in the last third of the century, the Crown tightened supervision of the colonies. It was during this period that institutions and governing practices coalesced to form the mature system of royal superintendence. First, to toughen enforcement of the Navigation Acts and enhance general supervisory capacities, the English government expanded the powers of the customs service and founded permanent vice-admiralty courts under Parliamentary sanction. The Lords of Trade (1675–96) followed by the Board of Trade (1696–1782) collected information and assembled reports on American conditions, drafted questionnaires and instructions for royal governors, and provided lists of candidates for colonial councils. The Board of Trade called on colonies to commission agents who lived in London. It advised the Privy Council when that body reviewed colonial legislation and heard appeals of judicial cases (mainly an eighteenth-century business). Second, to reduce the autonomy of the colonies, the Crown set out to transform proprietary and chartered colonies into royal colonies. It also regulated judicial and legislative process through governors' instructions and the disallowance of statutes and reorganized the legal system to favor Superior Courts of Judicature and the governor and his council at the expense of local tribunals.

A witness to these developments, the mid-eighteenth-century Massachusetts governor, Thomas Pownall, complained that the new regime of imperial governance lacked coordination in the collection and analysis of information.[1] Pownall's concerns informed the historians of the imperial school and their successors, and at times their work considers explicitly the strategies that the English government used to overcome distance and the obstacles of communication. At other points their work provides "raw material" that enables us to appreciate how the empire encouraged communications as a byproduct of institutions and policies established for other purposes. Such inadvertent prompts to information exchange, no less than the explicit strategies, were part of the empire's legal communications system.

Consider, first, the institutions directly charged with acquiring knowledge about the colonies' governance and legal systems. The Crown organized a series of Interregnum and Restoration commissions, and later the Lords of Trade and the Board of Trade, as *repositories and clearinghouses* of information. Their duty was to investigate the laws and government of the colonies. To that end, they collected records and reports and corresponded with governors and other officials, merchants, agents, ship captains, and visiting settlers. They called on the colonies to commission resident agents in London who would be available for consultation. The Lords of Trade and the Board of Trade dispatched questionnaires to governors and demanded periodic forwarding of important public papers and the journals of assemblies. They used the information they collected in preparing reports for the Crown, suggesting compromises of American disputes and recommending the approval or disallowance of colonial laws. They standardized and updated instructions to governors about judicature and traced how well those instructions worked in different colonies.

These efforts significantly improved the empire's capacity to gather and record information. Royal servants in the mid-seventeenth century had possessed limited and unsystematic knowledge of colonial affairs. The Lords of Trade and especially the Board of Trade acted more methodically and proactively, diversifying sources of information and establishing topics of inquiry. Their efforts required a small bureaucracy of long-serving clerks maintaining cross-referenced entry books. Nor were they alone. The Secretary of State for the Southern Department, the Treasury and Customs service, the Admiralty, and the Bishop of London all contributed to the Crown's

[1] Thomas Pownall, "The Administration of the Colonies, Wherein their Rights and Constitution are Discussed and Stated" (London, 1971 [4th ed. 1768]), 12–27.

growing capacity to acquire and organize information too, though what they learned remained split up among numerous, ill-coordinated agencies.

The Crown could demand that colonies send correspondence, reports, laws, and agents to London, but actually obtaining them was another matter. Royal officials complained that questionnaires and requests for public documents went unanswered, that laws and agents simply did not arrive. To encourage communications, the empire used *incentives and coercion*. If creating proactive clearinghouses and repositories for information was the Crown's first strategy for mitigating distance, its second was to support those institutions with inducements and punishments. Colonial charters, Board of Trade correspondence, and governors' instructions all contained threats. The Pennsylvania charter required that the proprietor keep an agent in London to answer complaints and pay damages, or face loss of the province. The Crown reprimanded governors who did not write frequently enough. It threatened to withhold salary from governors who did not transmit their colony's laws or to remove them from office if they failed to return questionnaires about colonial law and government.

Enticements to communicate about law were less obvious and require teasing out. They often arose indirectly as a byproduct of trans-Atlantic patronage and lobbying. Colonists who sent royal officials analyses of the shortcomings of customs inspections along with suggestions for reform might receive a position as an inspector. Those whose jobs depended on Crown patronage, such as royal governors, would keep leading English politicians informed about the state of colonial governance as a means of self-defense in local factional intrigues. Board of Trade investigations of unjust colonial laws and official misconduct would lead complainants, defendants, and their allies to provide considerable quantities of otherwise elusive facts and opinions, along with supporting documents. Colonial interest groups working through London contacts would supply the government with information to secure influence over policymaking.

The review of colonial statutes by the Board of Trade, as advisor to the Privy Council, provides a good example of the empire's incentives to legal communications. The Board and Council gained information by directly questioning a wide range of sources about the origins and effects of colonial laws. This much is obvious. Other effects were more subtle. First, burdened with many responsibilities, the Board and Council might ignore colonial laws for months or years at a time or be tempted to examine them superficially. Knowing this, English interest groups and lobbyists favoring disallowance or approval of laws provided the Board and Council with their own analyses of statutes and colonial conditions. They hoped to influence the outcome of the process and set the terms of the review, but also, more fundamentally, to engage the attention of distracted administrators.

Second, the Board might hold off recommending confirmation or rejection of statutes and allow them to "lie by probationary." This status, a form of administrative limbo, allowed for submission of critiques or defenses of colonial statutes as social and economic conditions changed. Should objections emerge, the Board could invite proponents to comment or ask the governor for his opinion. To establish priorities and provide context, the process for reviewing statutes not only welcomed commentary from interested parties but also depended on it, and even was structured to encourage it.

Royal administrators not only tried to attract legal information to England through the formation of boards to serve as clearinghouses and through incentives and threats. They also placed in the colonies *institutions and personnel loyal to the Crown*. This was the empire's third strategy. It projected metropolitan views of law into America by such means as establishing permanent vice-admiralty courts, dispatching resident customs inspectors, and appointing learned lawyers as the attorneys general and chief justices of royal colonies.

The *dissemination of English law books* was a fourth method of legal communications in the empire. Crown administrators sometimes sent to the colonies compilations of English law specially assembled for a particular purpose. Three times in the late seventeenth century they forwarded guidebooks of trade regulations to customs officials in the colonies. After 1689, they provided all new governors with printed copies of the Navigation Acts and, on occasion, sent "trade instructions" prepared by the Commissioners of the Customs. Governors trying to unravel legal tangles in their colonies might receive descriptions of English law along with an admonition to do justice.

Yet the distribution of English legal materials by Crown officials ran a distant second to the colonists' own importations, reprintings, and purchases of law books. The number and variety of English law books available in the colonies greatly expanded in the eighteenth century. Estate inventories and booksellers' records reveal that the most popular categories of law books were general overviews of the English legal system; guidebooks for local officers (such as the justice of the peace, court clerk, and constable); legal dictionaries and compilations of forms; reports of English cases and manuals on pleading; controversial works on natural law, jurisprudence, and constitutional law; and treatises on property, inheritance, commerce, criminal law, equity, and admiralty. Colonists acquired these works both to enhance their status by appearing informed and to pursue practical goals – to sell land and settle estates, discharge local offices, and improve skills in pleading and legal argument.

In the course of offering workaday knowledge, however, English law books began to reshape the colonial legal systems by disseminating the institutional and conceptual framework presupposed by English law. Books conveyed more than their primary content – doctrines and procedures on a given subject (for example, the duties of a justice of the peace). They also alluded to English constitutional arrangements, methods of legal interpretation, strategies for mediating among coordinate authorities and for supervising subordinate ones, and theories of jurisprudence (including ideas about the relations of different bodies of law). There was, of course, no uniform metropolitan view of these matters. English law books offered a range of opinions that could later be brought to bear on contested political, legal, and constitutional questions. They offered colonists jurisprudential tools, precedents, and a framework of assumptions for disputing with each other and with the English government. Used both as forensic resources and practical guides, English law books made metropolitan legal understandings more prominent in the eighteenth-century colonies.

II. LEGAL COMMUNICATIONS AND THE PROBLEM OF CENTRALIZATION

It is tempting to describe the growing presence of metropolitan law and the tighter imperial supervision of the colonies as a centralization of power in the English empire and to identify legal communications as an important tool in that process.[2] Indeed, historians have often spoken of centralization, but always with significant reservations. First, the eighteenth century saw not only improved royal control but also more sophisticated and coordinated resistance to metropolitan superintendence. Colonists became adept at defending their laws and legal institutions by lobbying and mobilizing interest groups in London and by wielding anti-prerogative Whig rhetoric. Second, centralization implies only a *relative* increase in the effectiveness of royal supervision of the colonies. Settlers remained effective at deflecting and evading unpalatable elements of Crown policy in the eighteenth century, as before.[3] Third, the term "centralization" obscures what Jack Greene

[2] Historians commonly point to several interrelated developments as evidence of centralization in the post-Restoration English empire: tighter administrative and judicial control of the colonies; growing regulation of overseas trade; better exchange of information through Crown boards and commissions, agents, lobbying, and interest group activity; and trans-Atlantic patronage politics.

[3] This theme, prominent among scholars of the English empire, finds echoes among comparative historians as well. Silvio Zavala has linked better eighteenth-century communications to centralization not only in British North America but also in the French, Portuguese, and Spanish empires. Zavala treats the "greater uniformity of administration" visible across the Americas as evidence of a "tendency" toward centralization – that is, as a movement in *relative* terms, not as a completed process. Silvio Zavala, *The Colonial Period in the History of the New World*, translation and abridgement by Max Savelle (Mexico City, 1962), 195.

has called the "negotiated" quality of the English empire – the way that governmental practices took hold not because of London's pronouncements, but through a process of bargaining that produced consent or acquiescence. Finally, the notion of centralization overstates the ambitions and constancy of English imperial authorities. They did not aim at centralization as an end in itself so much as a means to uphold prerogative and manage trade to the benefit of the mother country and her well-connected merchant groups. Even in this limited sense, centralizing initiatives proved inconsistent and hesitant, subject to postponements and alterations caused by turnover in imperial administrators and vicissitudes in English domestic politics.

However qualified, centralization did occur. Yet as it proceeded, the colonies' legal systems remained significantly diverse and subject to local (more than imperial) direction. Despite some measure of convergence, the legal cultures of eighteenth-century New England, the ethnically and religiously heterogeneous middle colonies of New York and Pennsylvania, and the slaveholding Chesapeake were noticeably more varied than English regions. One constant within this colonial diversity, though, was the salience of local control of legal institutions and decision making. As Stephen Botein observed some years ago, in the middle of the eighteenth century "the legal apparatus of empire still amounted to little more than an overlay on localized habits of colonial governance." Colonial law responded to local more than imperial direction for several reasons. County and town institutions staffed by notables from the vicinity provided the backbone of day-to-day governance. In conjunction with juries, they reflected and defended community custom, which guided enforcement priorities and the resolution of disputes. Even when appointed by royal governors, ground-level officials – constables, clerks, selectmen, justices of the peace, and sheriffs – undermined distasteful imperial policies through their control of investigation and enforcement or just through quiet inaction. Crown officials from the governor down to the sheriffs and justices of the peace could not exercise effective authority without the cooperation of local communities and their representatives in the assembly. Although the assembly might clash with towns and counties, for certainly colony-wide and truly "local" governments sometimes pursued conflicting interests, they worked together to resist spirited assertions of royal prerogative and to frustrate unwelcome imperial placemen and programs.

The persistence of a significant measure of local control and diversity in the colonies' legal systems in an era of imperial centralization calls for explanation. This study of Anglo-American legal communications suggests a way to approach the problem. The mechanisms of legal communication that evolved in the empire between the Restoration and the onset of the Revolution had a double nature. Although designed to foster imperial control – to centralize – they also shielded a measure of local control and diversity in the colonies' legal systems.

This point is not as easy to see from within the colonies as from outside – from a comparative perspective. I use the Spanish empire in the Americas to suggest how incomplete and uneven were English efforts to communicate and enforce metropolitan law, even after post-Restoration centralizing reforms. The Spanish-American experience serves as a counterpoint that highlights how distinctive features of the Anglo-American system of legal communications unwittingly lent support to local control and diversity.

My depictions of the Spanish and English empires resemble ideal types more than the messy, diverse, and evolving polities that they were, for I wish to compare the forms of imperial governance in Spanish and English America at their respective moments of maturity, rather than at the same chronological moment. My portrayal of the Spanish empire hence focuses on the period from c.1570–1710, after the solidification of Crown institutions but before the Bourbon monarchy appointed intendants in the Americas and slowly moved away from conciliar government at home. The full array of English imperial institutions and policies (including routine Privy Council appellate jurisdiction and review of colonial legislation, the agency system, permanent vice-admiralty courts, and an invigorated customs service) did not coalesce until the early eighteenth century. The mature English empire ran from c.1700 until 1763, when it underwent significant, fatal changes before the Revolution.

Comparing mature forms of imperial governance slights colonists' varying orientations to the empire and the hesitancies and contradictions of Crown policies. It also underplays historical development (more so in Spanish America than in the English empire, where the transition from seventeenth- to eighteenth-century governmental and communicative practices is a central concern of my analysis). Yet the method has signal advantages. Constructing ideal types of the legal communications systems of the English and Spanish empires facilitates comparison by drawing attention to their decisive features. An ideal type isolates and accentuates elements that were durable (rather than transitory), significant (rather than trivial), and widely shared (rather than local). In this sense, one can speak of the jury-rigged network of people and institutions that communicated law as a "system." Though the term overstates the predictability and conscious design of legal communications in the English and Spanish empires, it is a useful shorthand for the cluster of practices and assumptions that made the transmission of law work differently between Castile and New Spain, on one hand, and between London and Massachusetts, on the other hand.

I begin with a short description of Spain's bureaucratic and legal apparatus in the Americas before turning to the main work of comparison.

III. COMPARISON OF LEGAL COMMUNICATIONS SYSTEMS IN BRITISH AND SPANISH AMERICA

In the words of John Elliott, Spain maintained in America a "highly institutionalized empire, with an elaborate bureaucratic system dedicated to the vigorous assertion of the Crown's authority." This "intrusive (if not always effective) state" involved itself "in many different aspects of colonial life." By the middle seventeenth century, Spain had dispatched approximately 400,000 *cedulas* (royal decrees) to its New World communities and officials.[4] At the top of the system were the Spanish Crown and the Council of the Indies. The Council supervised and sanctioned officials, drafted laws, and served as an appellate court in civil cases. No significant expenditure of money or change in governmental policy could go forward in the Spanish empire without the approval of the Council or the Crown.[5]

In the Americas, two viceroys (one for New Spain and one for Peru) and several governors represented the Crown in executing law, overseeing civil and military affairs, and nominating the senior personnel of the church. A series of judicial-administrative tribunals, the *audiencias*, served as the backbone of the Spanish American bureaucracy. The *audiencia* heard civil and criminal cases. It also served as the court of appeals in its district, as an advisory panel for the viceroy or governor, and as a legislative body for making local regulations. Ten *audiencias* operated in Spain's sixteenth-century American empire; more were added later. University-trained civil and canon lawyers (*letrados*) supplied the *audiencia* judges and a substantial portion of the membership of the Council of the Indies. Alongside the viceroys and *audiencias* stood a fiscal hierarchy that enjoyed coordinate power in the business of overseeing royal revenue.

The ecclesiastical system further complicated the institutional structure of the Spanish empire. Bishops reported to the Crown in matters of administration and to the Pope in matters of faith. Though the viceroy or governor coordinated the government of his territory and nominated most of the lesser officeholders, *audiencia* judges and senior officials of the ecclesiastical

[4] Clarence Haring claims that the seventeenth-century statutory compilation, the *Recopilacion de leyes de los reynos de las Indias* (1681), distilled 400,000 royal *cedulas* down to 6,400 laws. Haring, *The Spanish Empire in America* (New York, 1963), 105. Prof. Mark Burkholder (in a communication to the author) has suggested that the figure of 400,000 *cedulas* may be high. Still, the Spanish empire sent many times more metropolitan decrees (laws, Crown orders, and administrative interventions) to its New World colonies than did the English empire.

[5] The Crown sometimes acted in the New World directly or through institutions other than the Council of the Indies – for instance, the Council of Castile.

and fiscal hierarchies received their appointments directly from the Crown and exercised substantial autonomous authority. Like the viceroys and governors, they enjoyed the right to correspond with and appeal to the Council in Spain. John Leddy Phelan observed a half-century ago that the Spanish Crown had created a "complex bureaucratic pyramid with multiple, partly independent and partly interdependent hierarchies."

The viceroys, governors, and *audiencias* oversaw smaller units of jurisdiction. *Corregidores* or *acaldes mayores*, appointed by the Crown or viceroy, governed towns and the surrounding countryside. These local officers exercised political, administrative, and to a lesser extent judicial authority within their districts. Within the towns, they worked with a municipal council (*cabildo*), which heard judicial cases, distributed land, supervised communally owned property and local infrastructure, and imposed taxes.

The Crown was suspicious of its distant officials in the Americas. A steady stream of royal orders, decrees, and regulations sought to direct their activities or, at least, lessen the boundaries of their discretion. The Crown also designed *residencia* and *visita* procedures to scrutinize and control officeholders by hearing complaints of malfeasance. At the end of a magistrate's term of office, an investigating judge collected and evaluated grievances against the departing official in a *residencia* process. All Crown appointees, from the viceroy down to the local *corregidor* and the municipal *cabildo*, went through a *residencia*. From time to time, in a *visita* procedure, a specially appointed judge heard evidence in secret in order to investigate the conduct of an official or tribunal. The *visita* served various purposes: it assessed the enforcement of particular laws, superintended troubled institutions or wayward officeholders, re-inspired obedience among officials identifying more with the local community than the Crown, and reported to the Council of the Indies on the administrative or political situation. The judges conducting the *residencia* or *visita* could advise, fine, suspend, or exile the officials under investigation, although the Council might alter or reverse sanctions recommended or imposed in the Americas. Through *visitas* and *residencias*; through judicial appeals, correspondence, and complaints; and through requests for adjustments in legislation and policy, the Council received considerable quantities of detailed, if self-serving, information.

This sketch of the Spanish bureaucracy in the Americas can help highlight distinctive features of English imperial governance and its system of communications. We can see immediately that, in comparison with Spain, England's review of colonial legislation, judicial decisions, and official conduct did not press down as deeply into the administrative structure and into society. In his descriptions of Tudor government, G. R. Elton looked for what he termed the "points of contact" between the Crown and the localities (e.g., the Privy Council, Parliament, the royal court). In this vein, consider the points of contact between the imperial center and the colonial periphery. England maintained communications channels with officials and institutions at the top of the colonial legal and political hierarchies. The Privy Council heard appeals only from the highest court in the colony (which might be the governor and his council). It would not accept an appeal from intermediate colonial appellate courts, let alone from town, county, probate, or orphans' tribunals or from justices of the peace. Nor would it second-guess jury verdicts.[6] The Privy Council reviewed legislation passed by assemblies, but not town ordinances, or local customs, or the bylaws of corporations. England sent instructions to and required reports from governors. No similar demands went out to assembly representatives, town selectmen, or justices of the peace.

To be sure, England assumed that by focusing communication and review at the highest points of the political and legal hierarchies, imperial priorities would influence colonial society indirectly. Assembly legislation might confirm or revise local ordinances and customs and, in so doing, bring them before the Privy Council. Judicial decisions in a colony's highest court, which could be appealed to the Council, would take note of and shape the activities of lower tribunals. The governor would serve as a point of contact between the metropolis and lesser executive and judicial officials that he or the Crown appointed (which, in some colonies, included the critical local figure, the justice of the peace). The governor could pass on sections of his instructions and collect information to forward to London.[7]

What stands out in this picture is how mediated and indirect communication about law was between London and colonial society. The Spanish empire, by contrast, encouraged direct communication between the Council and a wide variety of officeholders at the bottom as well as the top of its multiple bureaucratic hierarchies. By creating a variety of bureaucracies with ill-defined and overlapping jurisdictions, the Spanish Crown created conditions for rivalry. With rivalries came denunciations of opponents and appeals to Spain for redress and instructions. The Council of the Indies made sure that the viceroys and governors were not the primary conduit for communications – and hence a potential chokepoint. Spanish law guaranteed colonial officials below the viceroys and governors the *right* to

[6] In addition, the Privy Council would not hear a case in the first instance (through "original" rather than "appellate" jurisdiction). Joseph H. Smith, *Appeals to the Privy Council from the American Plantations* (New York, 1950), 202, 225, 408. On the Council's unwillingness to review jury verdicts, see its reaction to the New York case of *Forsey v. Cunningham*, in Smith, *Appeals*, 383–416.

[7] The English government expected instructions to be private, not public, documents. The Governor could pass on selected sections of his instructions to his Council and the public at his discretion.

communicate directly with the Council over the heads of their superiors.[8] *Audiencia* judges, treasury officials, cathedral chapters, and *corregidores* routinely availed themselves of this privilege. Some towns hired attorneys in Spain to represent their interests before the Council of the Indies. Indeed, the Council positively encouraged these institutions, interest groups, and officials to inform them about the state of government in their districts. On occasion, the Council sent secret instructions to *audiencia* judges to report on suspect viceroys. It also welcomed letters from "common" people who were not officeholders or representatives of organized interests. Thus, the Spanish empire anticipated, even tacitly encouraged, a struggle for influence among its American subjects that would generate a flow of information back to the metropolis.

The *residencia* and *visita* procedures also served to disseminate knowledge about law in both directions across the Atlantic. In Spanish America, not only the viceroy and *audiencia* but also the *corregidor* and his town council (*cabildo*) underwent a *residencia* at the end of their term. The judge conducting the *residencia* process – appointed by the Council of the Indies or the Crown's representative, the viceroy – learned much about a territory's customs, legal procedures, and habits of thought that he might pass on to the Council. Because his findings might lead to the discipline or suspension of officials, he served as a powerful mechanism for communicating imperial understandings of law and justice. The *visita*, although more irregular in timing, played a similar role. It swept up into its investigations officials as high as the viceroy and as modest as local clerks and parish priests. No English royal institutions carried imperial understandings of law as deeply and directly into colonial society.[9]

Spain's system of communications, like England's, emerged out of the peculiar challenges of governing across the Atlantic. Neither possessed the fiscal, military, and administrative resources to rule far-off colonies as though they were provinces of the mother country. Distance made political decentralization attractive. Both Crowns ceded unusually large authority (by metropolitan standards) to local authorities in the Americas, making it critical that both secure the consent of colonial leaders.

[8] The Council tried to protect subjects corresponding about the conduct of Crown officials in the Americas. It several times instructed viceroys, governors, and *audiencia* judges not to seize or open letters so that subjects could write without fear. *Recopilacion de Leyes de los Reynos de las Indias* (Madrid, 1943 [1681]), Book III, Title XVI, Laws 6–8.

[9] English royal commissions in America did not play the same role as the Spanish American *visita* and *residencia*. Royal commissions were irregular and typically focused on one important issue, for instance, a border dispute. Even the more broad-based and intrusive commissions, such as the one that arrived in Massachusetts in 1664, were supposed to leave the regular processes of government untouched as far as possible.

Yet, the English and Spanish empires negotiated consent and achieved decentralization in dissimilar ways. In Spanish America, the importance of consent can be obscured by features of the empire's emphasis on top-down direction: the heavy reliance on royally appointed bureaucracies, the absence of representative assemblies, the conversion of town councils into self-perpetuating oligarchies, and the eagerness of the Council of the Indies to legislate on so many minute aspects of colonial life. On closer inspection, though, Spain's governing apparatus and its communications system served as a device for mobilizing consent (or at least acquiescence) and assuaging dissatisfaction among Spaniards and creoles in America. Irritated colonists did not protest Crown policies through assemblies, because they had none. Rather, they sent petitions, letters, and agents to the Council of the Indies. Or they set one section of the bureaucracy against another or played the church off against the state. Or they pressed their opinions on administrators informally, sounding out their willingness to accept a new tax or enforce a proposed policy. Or when faced with troubling royal orders, they encouraged officeholders to invoke the formula, "I obey, but do not execute." Spanish law permitted officials to suspend temporarily enforcement of an unjust metropolitan order – unjust, perhaps, because the Crown did not foresee that it would cause disorder or unwelcome consequences. This power was not license to obstruct, however. After refusing to execute a directive, the official was bound to explain his reasons to the Council and suggest ways of reshaping the royal legislation to fit local conditions. It was one more way, in other words, to generate the steady flow of correspondence, questions, and suggestions that allowed for negotiation and compromise among the metropolis, officeholders, and colonial interest groups.

An empire so reliant on trans-Atlantic communications as a vehicle for securing consent and disciplining officials would not be content, as were the English, to connect the metropolis to the top of the legal and political hierarchies in the Americas. Instead, as we have seen, the Spanish empire forged a multiplicity of alternative communications links that penetrated directly and deeply into colonial society, down to parish priests, clerks, *corregidores* and *cabildos*, and the "common" people.

One can find surface analogies between the communications systems of the English and Spanish empires. Multiple arms of the English imperial government – the Board of Trade, the customs service, the Admiralty, the church of England, the agents in London – maintained separate communications channels to the colonies and reported on one another's doings. Unclear jurisdictional boundaries between the customs service, the vice-admiralty tribunals, the governors, and the colonial courts bred conflicts that led to pleas to England for redress. Colonial politicians and interest groups mobilized patrons and allies in the mother country and kept up a steady stream of correspondence to leading statesmen, the Board of Trade, and the Secretary of State for the southern department. There was even a dim echo of the Spanish doctrine of "I obey, but do not execute." In 1752, the Board of Trade demanded that governors not deviate from their instructions unless faced with an emergency. Should the governor lay aside his instructions, he must write to England and explain his reasons.

Yet on closer inspection, these apparent similarities mask critical differences between the English and Spanish systems. The English empire did not use royal bureaucracies as its primary device for negotiating consent in a decentralized empire. The Crown did not aspire to be the direct regulator of the settlers' day-to-day affairs. It left this work to the governors, assemblies, courts, and local officials, who collectively served as intermediaries between the colonists and the metropolis. The English empire focused on overseeing these intermediate authorities through such devices as gubernatorial instructions and review of legislation and judicial appeals. Although colonists did lobby in London, they principally expressed their consent or opposition to royal policies through the intermediary authorities that lay between the metropolis and themselves. In the English system of political decentralization, the empire fastened its lines of communication to these intermediary authorities, these points of contact. It connected to the governors through instructions and through the trans-Atlantic minuet of patronage. It connected to the assemblies through Privy Council review of legislation and through gubernatorial instructions demanding restraint of the legislatures. It connected to the courts through appeals to London, through royally determined appointments to the chief justiceship, and through assessment of colonial statutes establishing judicial organization and procedures.

The English empire did not try to circumvent these points of contact and create direct, vibrant communications routes downward into the counties and towns and outward into the wider society. It seldom deliberately established overlapping bureaucracies or provoked jurisdictional conflict as a way of generating a flow of information to London. Instead, it tried, with partial success, to route communications to and from the Crown through the colonial governors at the expense of lesser officials and assemblies. These policies sharply contrasted with Spanish insistence that officeholders beneath the viceroy, from *audiencia* judges and *corregidores* to cathedral chapters and town councils, enjoyed a legally protected "right" to correspond with the Council of the Indies over the head of their superiors. Unlike Spain, England did not build multiple, alternative channels of communications into the middle and bottom of legal, social, and political hierarchies.

The nature and limits of England's communications system emerged from the economic and political conditions of its empire. Unlike Spain, England did not require an extensive colonial state to organize the mining and transport of precious metals. Indeed, only as staple crop exports increased in value in the middle seventeenth century did England begin to establish its more modest imperial structures. Nor did England need to supervise the exploitation of the labor and tribute of indigenous peoples or try, in any serious sense, to protect and Christianize them. England expected to govern colonies of its own settlers who would engage, as they did at home, in self-government under loose royal supervision. Finally, although the Crown regulated and taxed overseas trade, it scarcely touched economic activity within the colonies themselves (in contrast to Spain's extensive system of internal taxes and commercial controls).

The communications practices to which these circumstances and assumptions gave rise were attended by important inadvertent effects. Seven particularly notable features of the English system helped preserve a significant measure of local control and diversity in the colonies' legal systems even amid tightening imperial oversight.[10]

Legal Regulation of Institutions Versus Individual Justice

The English empire displayed relatively little interest in providing justice to *individuals* injured by colonial institutions and officials. It viewed itself as a guarantor of justice in the New World, but it upheld justice in much the same indirect and mediated fashion as it conducted government – by providing oversight of colonial institutions through the review of legislation or through instructions to governors about proper judicial and legislative procedures. Two features of the imperial system appeared to offer justice to individual colonists: the Privy Council's appellate jurisdiction and the Board of Trade's power to investigate official misconduct. Although important, neither called into question the English empire's preference for superintending governing institutions, rather than assuring individual justice.

The Privy Council accepted judicial appeals from the colonies, but it imposed significant restrictions on what it was willing to hear. The Council did not offer original jurisdiction. It took only appeals and then only from the highest tribunal in a colony, which excluded cases brought from intermediate-level courts. It refused to reconsider felony convictions. It

[10] The great distances that the Atlantic Ocean created between colonies and metropoles provides (by itself) a weak explanation of the forms of imperial governance in the Americas. The English and Spanish empires, which both spanned the Atlantic, established different systems of legal communications that grew out of dissimilar political and social contexts. One goal of this chapter is to chart the presuppositions, nature, and implications (often inadvertent) of those divergent systems of legal communications – both of which, in different ways, responded to problems of distance.

reviewed misdemeanor convictions and civil cases, but only if they involved a substantial fine or amount in controversy – a variable figure, but typically more than £200 or £300.[11] The Council defined the subset of cases amenable to review not on the basis of their conceptual difficulty or the degree of injustice suffered by litigants. Instead, it used monetary restrictions to focus on the economically significant disputes of socially prominent people, a decision that excluded the vast majority of colonial lawsuits. Even within this narrow range of cases, the provision of justice to individual colonists ran second to other concerns. Joseph Smith, the closest student of the empire's appellate review, concluded that the Council concerned itself first and foremost with policing the boundaries of colonial tribunals and correcting their mistakes. The Council saw itself less as the last chance for colonists to get their due than as an administrative board devoted to keeping inferior jurisdictions in line.

Colonists could also bring to the Privy Council complaints about unjust laws and official misconduct (as opposed to judicial error). On behalf of the Council, the Board of Trade held hearings and considered charges, defenses, counter-charges, and written evidence. Agents or attorneys represented parties. Both sides supported their allegations by proof sent from America and authenticated by a colonial seal. The process of investigating and hearing complaints proved slow, complicated, ridden with delays, and expensive. A party could not compel witnesses to come to London. Should they be willing to give up months of their time to cross the Atlantic, the party needed to bear the cost of their voyage and lodging. Testimony given in America needed the governor's authentication, which did not inspire witnesses to speak freely about official malfeasance. Together, these features of the Council's procedure undermined its effectiveness.

The English government's limited mechanisms for providing justice to individual colonists and its relative lack of interest in doing so stand out when compared to the Spanish empire's practices. At first glance, one sees similarities. The Council of the Indies restricted appeals by imposing the same kinds of limitations as the Privy Council. The Council of the Indies would not reexamine criminal convictions, nor hear civil cases sent from intermediate courts below the level of the highest tribunals (the *audiencias*), nor review civil disputes involving less than a substantial amount in controversy (10,000 pesos). Yet, this surface similarity conceals different assumptions about the nature of colonial governance, which made the Spanish Crown more responsive to claims of injustice by individuals and groups. The Spanish empire valorized the King as a paternalistic and caring ruler of his American vassals, both Europeans and Indians. His supposedly personal

[11] The Privy Council could, at its discretion, waive these requirements.

oversight of the empire's legal system legitimated it, for the King had a duty to listen to aggrieved subjects in the interests of justice. Although the English monarch also had a duty to redress grievances, the empire did not turn on an intensely personal and paternalistic understanding of kingship in the Spanish style.

As a result of the Spanish empire's political presuppositions, its American subjects could find ways to approach the King and his Council of the Indies despite the limitations on civil appeals from *audiencias*. First, one might charge that officials in America acted contrary to religion and justice, the two key concepts legitimating the empire's legal system. Royal institutions conceived of their mission less as following promulgated law (*ley*) than as upholding justice (*derecho*) or giving subjects their due. Second, one might assert that tribunals or officials in America acted corruptly. The king and Council received frequent complaints about biased magistrates. These petitions offered a way to review, under another guise, the validity of an official's legal decisions when a claim of interpretive mistake could not be brought to the Council because of its restrictions on civil appeals. Petitions sent to the king directly were not bound by rules limiting who could apply, how, or why. If the king's staff took an interest in a petition, they would instruct the Council to consider it. These petitions abound in the Spanish archives. Contemporaries did not take them at face value. They knew that petitions demanding honesty, piety, and justice were often a vehicle for pursuing feuds and institutional rivalries. Still, the king and Council accepted, even encouraged, petitioning in order to uphold the values important to the empire's legitimation and to learn about the doings of American officials.

In the English empire, a private individual could not petition the Privy Council, Secretary of State, or the king himself by vaguely alleging the catch-all categories of injustice and impiety. We have seen that the Privy Council would hear appeals from the highest court of a colony and would investigate complaints of misconduct by those able to navigate its lengthy, formalized procedure and produce evidence authenticated by a colonial governor (possibly the patron of the accused official). Aside from these limited channels for hearing individual complaints, the English empire protected justice in the New World by overseeing the structures and procedures of colonial institutions. Consider a selection of the issues addressed in meetings of the Board of Trade, reviews of colonial legislation, and instructions to governors. Imperial authorities regulated colonial juror selection and qualifications, but left intact the verdicts of particular juries. They reshaped court organization, but did not consider the decisions of particular courts beyond the very limited subset of appealable cases. They prescribed the form of oaths, but did not ask whether officials, having taken the oaths, gave colonists their due. And they struck down colonial laws that gave judges too much discretion, but did not investigate how the judges used their discretion. The English empire's preference for regulating the structures and procedures of colonial institutions, rather than for assessing whether individuals obtained justice, helped insulate colonial legal decision making at the local level.

Strategies for Resisting Crown Authority

The dissimilar structure and purposes of legal communications in the English and Spanish empires encouraged their inhabitants to emphasize different strategies for resisting metropolitan oversight. Residents in Spanish America used various forms of consultation – appeals, correspondence, requests for guidance – as a device to delay or obstruct metropolitan policies. Aggrieved Spaniards, creoles, and Indians could cast their complaints as conflicts over jurisdiction needing review by the Council of the Indies. Two years might go by while the Council sorted out the situation. Officials invoking the "I obey, but do not execute" formula were supposed to inform the Council of their reasons for suspending operation of a royal order and present suggestions for fitting the Crown's instructions to local conditions. The Council would reply to these missives in a process that could take years. Those who wanted to hold off a Crown initiative could set rival bureaucracies against one another or ask the Council for instructions. Crown policies were deflected, therefore, by arguing over who should oversee them, or by asking advice on how better to implement them, or by offering counsel for improving them.

Although the English settlers did some of this, the structure of their empire's legal communications system encouraged them to use another strategy – delaying or withholding information.[12] Colonies, particularly chartered and proprietary colonies, proved reluctant to send their laws to England for review or submitted a paraphrase of a statute instead of the verbatim text. In periods of conflict between assemblies and governors (or proprietors), each side might try to block the appointment or funding of the colony's agent to hinder the other side's presentation of grievances. Agents resident in London who feared an unfavorable ruling from a royal official or board could delay proceedings by neglecting to provide needed evidence. Governors often ignored Board of Trade questionnaires on the state of their colony's economy, defense, and administration. Privy Council appellate jurisdiction also met with significant resistance, at least in the

[12] To be sure, Spanish American officials also hid information from metropolitan eyes. My point is about the relative balance of strategies in the two empires.

seventeenth century. Overt opposition faded in the early eighteenth century, but litigants continued to face obstacles. Governors and court clerks sometimes prevented the transmission of a written record to the Privy Council or else provided a deliberately scanty one.

In general, over the course of the colonial period, the deliberate withholding of information receded in importance as a legal and political tactic. From the late seventeenth century onward, the growth of imperial institutions and the increased density of trans-Atlantic ties through agents, merchant networks, and interest groups made lobbying both easier and more valuable. Increasingly, settlers and their London intermediaries tried to negotiate with Crown officials and Parliament to shape or deflect metropolitan decisions. Considered as one among a repertoire of strategies for dealing with the metropolis, deliberate withholding of information underwent a *relative* decline in importance.

Yet, the tactic never went entirely out of fashion. Deliberate withholding of legal information continued to work well because the English empire fastened its legal communications channels to the top of New World legal and political hierarchies. In comparison to Spanish colonial notables, local elites in British North America tried more frequently to starve metropolitan authorities of knowledge, rather than mislead and delay them by flooding them with questions, missives, and requests for guidance. Not simply the natural outcome of distance and irregular ocean crossings, English settlers were better able to preserve autonomy by keeping information *local* because of the structure of legal communications in the English empire.

Transatlantic Versus Intracontinental Orientations of Legal Communications

The English empire inadvertently promoted diversity and local control by orienting legal communication more across the Atlantic (between the metropolis and each colony) than continentally (among the various colonies). Trans-Atlantic interactions dominated seventeenth-century exchanges between England and the colonies – in commerce and the distribution of news no less than in legal communications. By the late seventeenth century, however, more intensive coastal trade, improvements in the postal system, and the multiplication of newspapers facilitated the dissemination of information and transfer of trade goods among the colonies. As intracontinental exchanges intensified during the eighteenth century, what was striking about law as compared to commerce or news circulation was the extent to which trans-Atlantic communications links continued to predominate over intracontinental contacts.

Why were legal communications distinctive in so heavily favoring trans-Atlantic over intracontinental channels? First, Crown officials commonly directed metropolitan review and discussion of law toward individual colonies, rather than toward regions or the continent as a whole. This emphasis on the colony as the basic unit of analysis and interaction was not a necessary feature of the English empire. By the later seventeenth century, trade increasingly passed through regional and continental networks; by the mid-eighteenth century, the empire often employed regional military commands. The customs official and merchant thought in terms of trade systems, the soldier in terms of theaters of operation (which cut across colonial boundaries). Law, by contrast, operated within jurisdictions. Colonies, not regions, served as the basic legal and political jurisdictions of the empire. As a result, the empire's major legal communications channels connected London to individual colonies. The Privy Council subjected the legislation of each colony to a separate review. It exercised its appellate jurisdiction, as Joseph Smith observed, "not as a court for an empire, but as a court of last resort for each particular jurisdiction." The Board of Trade dealt with each colony through its resident agents in London. It badgered those that failed to send an agent, and it resisted the stationing of multiple agents representing the governor, proprietor, or assembly alone, rather than the colony as a totality. England placed royal governors, attorneys general and chief justices, and vice-admiralty judges in given colonies, where they tended to stay until removed from power or reassigned. Spain circulated Crown servants by routinely and deliberately promoting officials from a lesser post in one part of the empire to a higher post somewhere else, a policy that England seldom followed before the nineteenth century.[13] Spain's posting of viceroys in particular *audiencias* elevated these centers relative to other *audiencias* that needed to stay in contact with the viceroy and take account of his policies. England did not encourage regional interactions by making one colonial capital the administrative center for its neighbors.[14] Its officials focused on the colonies in which they lived. Taken together, the English empire's choices downplayed intracontinental legal communications in favor of links between particular colonies and the metropolis.

Legal knowledge traveled through other routes as well – through law publishing and the training of practitioners. These too followed trans-Atlantic more than intracontinental courses. The printed legal materials available in the American settlements were a mix of imports from England, reprints of English titles, and limited domestic production (largely of statutes and

[13] Despite the circulation of royal appointees, legal communications in the Spanish empire flowed more heavily and rapidly across the Atlantic than between the viceroyalties of New Spain and Peru.

[14] There were exceptions – most prominently, the Dominion of New England – but these were unusual and short-lived.

primers for local officials). Apprenticeship within one's home colony provided the foundation of legal instruction, supplemented by the immigration of learned practitioners from England and the occasional American who attended the Inns of Court. The training of lawyers, like the dissemination of law books, largely took place within colonies, rather than regions. This would change. By 1820, universities and proprietary law schools (such as Litchfield) took in students from all around the country. Massachusetts and New York emerged as centers of law publishing, not only for their own state materials but also for texts of national interest. But in the colonial period, regional and continental law training and publishing, though not unknown, were of far less significance. The pre-Revolutionary settlements also lacked integrating mechanisms characteristic of the nineteenth century: national legislative and judicial institutions, judges riding circuit across a group of states, and courts engaging with decisions from other American jurisdictions (a difficult matter before the routine publication of American cases began in the Early Republic). In short, the patterns of colonial law training and publishing, like the practices of imperial governance, disposed Connecticut, Pennsylvania, and Carolina to exchange knowledge about law more with England than with each other.[15]

Given the prevalence of trans-Atlantic over intracontinental channels, what follows? From one perspective, this pattern facilitated the eighteenth-century "anglicization" of colonial law. The trans-Atlantic orientation of legal communications in the English empire encouraged a convergence of the diverse seventeenth-century colonial legal systems around metropolitan norms. From another perspective, though, the trans-Atlantic bias in communications inadvertently preserved local autonomy and diversity by retarding the capacity of any one colony to emerge as a standard for the others. Colonies might converge on the legal practices and values of the metropolis or of each other. The prevalence of trans-Atlantic legal communications facilitated the first of these possibilities (anglicization) while

[15] As always, there were exceptions – institutions and practices that encouraged the exchange of legal knowledge among colonies. The Board of Trade often standardized instructions about legal affairs, sending the same ones to governors in a variety of colonies for years at a time. The Customs Service appointed a surveyor-general who traveled among the colonies, in the process sharing expertise about trade regulation. A few of the agents residing in London served several colonies at once and learned to defend the legislation and judicial practices of multiple jurisdictions. Colonies borrowed statutory law from one another. Advocates preparing appellate cases for review by the Privy Council sometimes compared the law of their jurisdiction to that of other colonies in search of commonalities. My argument for the predominance of trans-Atlantic over intracontinental legal communications is ultimately a relative one; it is a point about balances.

discouraging the second (emergence of a colonial standard). Settlers knew less about the activities and assumptions of each other's legal systems than they did about England's. They constantly debated which provisions of England's law they should adopt, reject, or meld with their own, but they did not need to adopt a position on each other's legal practices – assuming that they could learn about more than published statutes, no easy matter. As a result, no colony served as the dominant clearinghouse of legal information for the others. None obtained a heightened power to block, redirect, or frame circulating legal knowledge. None provided the home for institutions that reviewed and interpreted law for the others or taught practitioners drawn from all over British North America. None emerged as the standard for the others to mimic or define themselves against. The patterns of communications in the empire, then, simultaneously encouraged anglicization *and* preserved a measure of diversity by muting the pressure on colonies to orient toward the legal cultures of their neighbors and rivals.

The Position of Native Peoples Within the Legal System

The English empire's relative lack of interest in the internal legal affairs of Native Americans reduced metropolitan incentives to oversee the settlers' laws vis-à-vis the Indians. This reluctance to intervene, which stands out strikingly in comparison to the Spanish experience, helped preserve local control and diversity in the colonists' legal systems. Native Americans maintained a variety of relationships to the colonists' law.[16] These can be placed on a spectrum. Indians who resided in colonial towns submitted to the settlers' legal system. Members of tribes that acknowledged English sovereignty but lived collectively in an Indian community near or within colonial borders maintained a more selective, ad hoc connection to the settlers' law. They commonly invoked or were forced into the colonists' legal system in intercommunal disputes between Native Americans and Europeans (typically involving crimes, sex and marriage, land sales and boundaries, and commercial exchanges). Colonial authorities were eager to expand the theoretical reach of their jurisdiction over Indian communities in order to pull important disputes into their courts at their discretion, but in practice they left largely untouched legal matters arising among Native American themselves. Finally, beyond the frontier of settlement, independent tribes exercised nearly unqualified sovereignty. They might accept the conclusions of the colonists' law in particular cases, such as

[16] For more on these matters, see Chapter 2 in this volume.

intercommunal crimes or land transactions, but only as a result of diplomatic negotiations.

Although the relationship of Native Americans to colonial law was highly variable, what stands out is the relatively limited scope of English ambitions, at least in comparison to the Spanish. English settlers aimed to define to their own advantage the terms of social and economic interaction – in particular, to regulate violence and oversee the dispossession or sale of Indian land. They sought their own protection, enrichment, and aggrandizement. However, settlers showed markedly less interest in reshaping the legal relations of Native Americans among themselves. The colonists made no systematic effort to anglicize the legal systems of Native American communities in the backcountry or beyond the frontier on the analogy of the (largely ineffective) campaign of Christianization.

The Spanish empire intervened more forcefully and self-consciously to reorder the law of Indian communities. Demography, reinforced by an ideological commitment to Christianizing unbelievers, proved decisive. Although historians disagree about the size and distribution of the indigenous and European populations, they agree that in the early decades of the conquest, tens of thousands of Spaniards confronted tens of millions of Indians. They also concur in finding that indigenous populations declined drastically in the sixteenth century before stabilizing and slowly recovering in the seventeenth or eighteenth century. In 1518, Central Mexico contained ten to twelve million native inhabitants (or perhaps as many as twenty-five million) before the population decreased to one or two million at the turn of the seventeenth century. Approximately nine million Indians (perhaps as many as eleven and a half million) lived in Peru in 1520. Only about 600,000 remained in 1630. Spaniards would remain a minority throughout the colonial period. When they established the political and legal institutions of their empire in the middle sixteenth century, they constituted a tiny minority.

The colonists of British North America encountered far smaller indigenous populations, which they supplanted in their core areas of settlement. Perhaps 700,000 Native Americans lived along the Atlantic coastal plain and in the Piedmont regions that provided a home to the European settlers. Their numbers declined by 80 to 90 percent over the course of the colonial period, falling from hundreds of thousands to tens of thousands. Meanwhile, European populations rapidly increased from approximately 70,000 in 1660 to about 1,270,000 in 1760. The displacement of Native Americans had not only a numerical but also a geographical component. Only a minority of the surviving Indians continued to reside in the core areas of European settlement. Most lived in the backcountry or behind a porous and rapidly shifting frontier.

Spread out in their vast American possessions and surrounded by large numbers of indigenous peoples, the Spanish did not want to drive their pool of laborers and potential converts beyond a frontier. Nor could they. There were Indian nations beyond the effective reach of Spanish power in the Americas, and in that sense, there was a frontier. But within the sprawling territory under Spanish control the colonists did not think that frontiers demarcated densely settled colonial areas from autonomous or semi-autonomous Indian areas, as in English North America. Spaniards and creoles instead expected native peoples to participate, if reluctantly, in the new colonial society.

As a result, powerful social and political forces encouraged Indians to learn to manipulate the settlers' legal system and helped introduce increasing knowledge of the colonists' law into indigenous communities. The Spanish empire replaced the upper reaches of the old native political and administrative hierarchies, reorganized Indian towns, and used legal institutions to mediate the colonists' demands for land, tribute, and labor. Although claiming to respect "good and just" indigenous customs, Spaniards reserved the right to decide which customs should be upheld and used this power to Hispanicize Indian customary law. In part to safeguard Indians out of a sense of paternalistic responsibility, and in part to prevent over-intensive exploitation by local settlers from interfering with more sustainable exploitation by provincial and metropolitan elites, the Crown set up institutions to protect the legal rights of native peoples. Viceroys in New Spain and in Peru created special tribunals, employing simplified procedures, to hear cases brought by Indians. They commissioned the *fiscal* [Crown attorney] of the *audiencia* or the *protector de indios* to provide representation in court to Indians and, in the process, teach principles of Spanish law. Within two generations after the Spanish conquests, native communities became adept and aggressive litigators over such matters as land ownership and boundaries, labor and tribute obligations, water and grazing rights, and succession to chieftanships. They challenged decisions of local officials by appealing to higher reaches of the bureaucracy. Although they resorted less frequently to the colonists' law for resolving disputes within a community, they did engage in repeated litigation against Spanish settlers, officials, and other Indians groups. In the process, the Castilian laws, procedures, and terminology used in the colonists' courts and bureaucracy seeped into native communities. The oversight of these communities by the *alcaldes mayores* and *corregidores* only increased the importance of Castilian law. By the beginning of the seventeenth century, native peoples were far along in fusing their traditional customs with elements of the colonists' law.

The situation in Spanish America highlights how seldom the English tried, for all their use of law to tilt political and economic interactions in their own favor, to reorder the legal folkways of indigenous peoples as an end in itself. The English typically did not encourage Native Americans to adopt the colonists' laws in their internal affairs or to submit intracommunal disputes to the settlers' tribunals. (The "praying towns" of Massachusetts, like other selected Indian groups embedded in the colonists' territory, were an exception to this generalization.) England's relative lack of interest in the legal transactions of Native Americans in the backcountry and on the frontier was possible because, unlike the Spanish, they did not expect most Indians to be enveloped within their empire under their paternalistic supervision. Whereas the Spanish empire styled indigenous peoples as vassals of the Crown whose "good and just" customs should be applied by the colonists' courts in intracommunal cases, the English considered Indians as foreigners, absent an affirmative act that changed their status. The English did not have a serious commitment to "civilizing" Native Americans by reordering their legal systems. Perhaps most important, although English settlers wanted Indian land, they did not live off the Native Americans' labor and tribute.

The implications of all these differences from Spanish America were significant. By Spanish standards, England had little incentive to project metropolitan law into Native American communities or oversee how its colonists' legal systems dealt with Indians. In English America, the legal system did not address in any detail the extraction of labor and tribute from indigenous peoples or coordinate large-scale economic enterprises (such as the mining and shipment of South American bullion) that drew on Indians from numerous local jurisdictions. The legal system did not oversee the "anglicization" of the Indians' legal folkways or protect them from heedless exploitation by local elites. As a result, one does not find institutions and offices along the lines of the General Indian Court of New Spain or the *protector de indios*. One does not see the empire purposefully disseminating English law to indigenous peoples. Unless colonists recklessly provoked Indian wars, the English empire saw little reason to intervene as colonists set the terms on which their legal systems regulated, or left alone, Native Americans. The scant presence of the metropolis in this critical area helped preserve diversity and local control in the colonies' legal systems.

Variation in Legal Communications Channels

From the mid-sixteenth century onward, the same group of royally authorized institutions were established throughout the Spanish empire's core regions of New Spain and Peru – viceroy or governor, *audiencia*, *corregidores* or *acaldes mayores, cabildos*, the fiscal administration, and the *residencia* and *visita* procedures.[17] The British North American settlements lived under a much more diverse set of governing institutions. The leading agencies of the English empire – the Board of Trade, Privy Council, Secretary of State for the Southern Department, Treasury, Admiralty, and customs service – exercised jurisdiction over all of British North America. Yet despite the continental scope of their jurisdiction, they were unable to maintain uniform legal communications channels with each settlement. These networks varied colony by colony. Although the Board of Trade continually recommended that all colonies be put on the same footing, this proved impossible, impeding imperial efforts to superintend the colonial legal systems.

The first, and most basic, form of diversity was the division of British North America into royal, proprietary, and corporate colonies. The eighteenth-century empire forged its strongest links with royal colonies and weaker connections with the proprietary colonies and the corporate colonies of Connecticut and Rhode Island. Consider Privy Council review of colonial legislation. The charters of most corporate and proprietary colonies did not require them to submit statutes to the Council for confirmation. By the early eighteenth century the Council had managed to develop a rationale for reviewing their ordinances, reasoning that because all charters forbad ordinances repugnant to the laws of England, the Council enjoyed implicit power to serve as the judge of "non-repugnancy." On this ground it struck down a handful of statutes from corporate and proprietary colonies (or else ordered proprietors to do so). But this makeshift process had its costs. Because royal charters explicitly required the submission of legislation to the Privy Council, and because royal governors were appointed by the Crown, compliance could be monitored routinely. In non-royal colonies, the Council had to contend with foot-dragging proprietors and elected corporate governors bickering over the constitutional legitimacy of legislative review without explicit warrant. The Board of Trade and the House of Lords several times proposed that all colonies be required to submit laws to the Council, contrary charter provisions or precedents notwithstanding, but without success. Predictably, the Council's oversight throughout was less sustained and effective in the proprietary and corporate colonies. Overall, it disallowed some 5 percent of the statutes of the continental colonies, but only three ordinances from the corporate colonies of Connecticut and Rhode Island were ever rejected in the eighteenth century.

The roles played by colonial agents in London also varied according to the type of colony that they represented. Agents were critical to the empire's legal communications. They supported (or deftly subverted) colonial

[17] To be sure, considerable political and institutional diversity marked the Spanish empire, particularly in the less settled peripheral and border areas.

statutes under review by the Privy Council, influenced Parliamentary legislation, passed along and interpreted documents, and forwarded (or delayed and undermined) colonial petitions and grievances. Assemblies in proprietary and royal colonies struggled with governors imposed from outside to make the agent their spokesman in London. Royal governors and their Councils wrestled with assemblies over the appointment and funding of agents and over control of communications to them. Royal governors and assemblies sometimes maintained separate agents or obstructed each other to the point where none could be appointed at all. Disputes over agents became even more pronounced in proprietary colonies because the people had no other reliable way to go "over the head" of the proprietor and bring grievances before the Crown. More vigorously than royal governors, proprietors opposed the selection of an agent they could not control. In corporate colonies, in contrast, the agent did not become an object of conflict. Governors were elected; hence constitutional tension between prerogative (or proprietary) executives and popular legislatures was lacking.

The type of colony that an agent represented and its changing internal balance of power determined his London agenda, for agents favored the views of those who selected, paid, and instructed them. An agent would attempt to reconcile the perspectives of differing power centers or find himself serving alongside competitors dispatched to discredit him. The colonial agent, then, did not reliably play a single role – he was not *necessarily* an ally of imperial administrators and royal governors, or a mouthpiece for the Assembly, or a guide to and mediator among the divergent factions of his colony, or the representative of a stable set of economic interests or ideological commitments. He could play one or several of these roles, his successor might play others, and the agents of neighboring colonies might play still others. Imperial administrators knew that agents' objectives shaped their management and coloring of information. But the differing, changeable allegiances of the agents made them an unpredictable vehicle for legal communications.

The ability of the English government to shape colonial law through governors' instructions also varied by type of colony. The Board of Trade used instructions to set forth its understanding of proper judicial organization, legislative procedure, and executive prerogatives. It dispatched these documents to newly appointed governors of royal colonies and updated them from time to time. Unlike royal colonies, however, proprietary and corporate colonies did not receive instructions as a matter of course. On occasion the English government included proprietary and royal colonies in circular instructions sent out to all American settlements. Sometimes the Privy Council dictated instructions to proprietors for transmission to their governors. Overall, though, proprietary and corporate colonies did not receive anything like the quantity and scope of instructions dispatched to royal colonies.

The distinction among royal, proprietary, and chartered colonies only begins to suggest the degree of variation in legal communications channels running between London and America, for the labels obscure differences among colonies in each group. Consider the two corporate colonies, Connecticut and Rhode Island. Connecticut's political culture disapproved of appeals to the Privy Council and few occurred. Neighboring Rhode Island, in contrast, favored appeals. As a corporate colony, Rhode Island was not bound by Privy Council instructions to royal governors to prevent appeals in cases involving less than, typically, £300. However, its legislation lowered the minimum amount required in controversy to £150, which encouraged its settlers to send more common law appeals to the Council than any other jurisdiction.

Peculiar features of charters introduced further variability into Privy Council review of legislation and appeals. Though the Pennsylvania charter required submission of legislation to the Privy Council, it gave the colony the unusually long period of five years in which to comply, which for a while enabled the legislature to pass limited-term ordinances and then repeal them before their disallowance. The charter also provided that a Pennsylvania statute would be valid unless the Council rejected it within six months of receipt (which made inertia and disorganization an ally of the colony). Massachusetts's 1691 charter also promised confirmation of statutes unless the Privy Council disallowed them, in this case within three years rather than six months. Both charters limited the Council's ability to let submitted ordinances "lie by probationary" without formal approval or rejection in order to invite comment from interested parties. The Massachusetts charter also allowed judicial appeals to the Council in personal actions (those not touching on real estate) worth more than £300. Through the middle of the eighteenth century, opponents of appeals read the charter strictly to permit appeals *only* in personal actions. In the late 1740s, Massachusetts Governor Shirley noted that colonial courts following this interpretation created a deliberately scanty written record in order to frustrate appeals in cases involving real estate.

The relatively standardized governing institutions of the core areas of the Spanish empire highlight the multiplicity of types of colonies and charter provisions found in British North America. The English empire was required to work with agents of changing and uncertain allegiance, to build circuitous legislative review procedures for corporate and proprietary colonies, and to confront the inapplicability of some of its favored devices for communicating about law – gubernatorial instructions and allowing statutes to "lie by probationary" while inviting commentary – to certain colonies. This unevenness helped preserve a measure of local control and diversity by undermining the empire's ability to exchange information, provide guidance and models of "proper" legal behavior, and nudge the colonial legal systems toward metropolitan norms.

Local Interpretive Leeway

It was no easy matter to determine what elements of English law – from Parliamentary statutes, equity and admiralty to ecclesiastical, merchant, and common law – actually applied in early America. Tribunals, interest groups, and officials routinely disagreed. High levels of uncertainty and local variability persisted in part because no metropolitan body authoritatively declared which elements of English law bound the colonists. In the Spanish empire, although all Castilian law automatically applied in the New World, the Council of the Indies from the early seventeenth century onward could specify the content of a supplementary "law of the Indies" particular to the colonies. (Of course, securing obedience to that law proved challenging.) The Council also decided which papal bulls and church documents could be promulgated in America. In the English empire, the Privy Council's review of legislation and judicial decisions provided a means for announcing that colonists had misunderstood the dictates of metropolitan law, but only in a particular instance and after the fact. No English imperial institution played a role analogous to the Council of the Indies by deciding, *in advance*, which elements of metropolitan law applied to the colonies. No imperial institution resolved conflicts between legal provisions in tension or determined that particular laws should be ignored because they were irrelevant or harmful given American conditions. Settlers were left to argue over these matters themselves. This interpretive leeway supported local control and variability in the colonial legal systems.

Reliance on amateur judges and administrators lacking legal education reinforced the colonies' interpretive freedom in ways that further compromised metropolitan oversight. Even if well disposed toward the empire, colonial lay officials often could not decode all the implications of imperial legal documents written in a professional idiom. Lawyers trained by apprenticeship and a handful of Inns of Courts matriculants occupied only a small minority of the main administrative and judicial offices in colonial America. Large landowners, merchants, planters, and scions of elite families provided the overwhelming majority of supreme, county, and probate court judges; governor's councilors; city mayors and selectmen; and justices of the peace.

By contrast, the Spanish empire used trained lawyers to staff major institutions of administration and judicature in America. *Letrados* (Spaniards or creoles educated in civil and/or canon law in a university) made up the corps of *audiencia* judges and Crown attorneys (*fiscales*) and supplied most of the deputies to *corregidores*. They also served as legal advisors (*asesores*) to governors, municipalities, local courts, and state-sanctioned monopolies. Along with laymen, *letrados* acted as *corregidores, alcaldes*, and councilman in town *cabildos*. They performed *residencias* and *visitas* and clustered around the *audiencia* as advocates. Although laymen ran most of the ground-level administrative and judicial systems, *letrados* heard appeals, guided lower tribunals and officials, and made major policy decisions in the bureaucracy. The power and prevalence of *letrados* at all levels of Spain's extensive imperial bureaucracy in the New World only emphasize how small a role trained lawyers played in governing the British North American colonies.[18]

What were the implications of the lack of trained lawyers for English efforts to project metropolitan legal understandings in the colonies? It is not clear that the multiplication of trained lawyers in American judicial and administrative institutions would have facilitated better imperial supervision of the colonial legal systems. Lawyers in the colonies sought less to help the empire than to help themselves. With few patronage appointments offered by London and the royal governors, lawyers turned to elective politics to get ahead. Most allied themselves with popular, anti-prerogative movements. Trained lawyers attended to the interests of the landowners, merchants, and planters who employed them, advancing or redirecting and undermining imperial policies as their clients' needs arose. We should note that Spain's American *letrados* could also prove less than dependable in the pursuit of imperial goals. Even those employed in the extensive imperial bureaucracy, reliant on the Crown for position and advancement, proved adept at deflecting or ignoring Castilian laws and royal orders in the service of personal or local interests.

From the perspective of a history of legal communications, the central consequence of the English colonies' overwhelming use of laymen in the government and judiciary may not have been a heightened propensity to disobey metropolitan directives so much as a reduced ability to see the background, context, and implications of the legal documents so critical to imperial regulation. We have seen that England transmitted expectations and goals to the colonies in a variety of forms, not least through legal documents. The concepts on which the constitutional relationship between England and the colonies was founded – for instance, the distinction between "conquered"

[18] The size and political influence of the colonial legal profession began to grow in the second quarter of the eighteenth century and accelerated in the third quarter. Even so, the vast majority of administrative and judicial posts remained in the hands of laymen on the eve of the American Revolution.

and "settled" colonies – emerged through court opinions and Privy Council rulings. Colonial charters set up the basic machinery of government; proclamations and governor's commissions added to it. Parliamentary statutes supplemented by judicial decisions set forth trade policy. Counsel to the Board of Trade and Privy Council advised them on legislative review and judicial appeals and drafted the reports that formed the heart of Council rulings. Even governors' instructions came full of legal terms of art.

Discrete provisions in legal documents presupposed a larger system of jurisdictions and remedies, officers and powers, and modes of proof and interpretive canons. The Navigation Acts, for example, proved difficult to administer because they assumed that the reader understood the difference between concurrent and exclusive jurisdiction, knew which tribunals in England could accept appeals from America in customs cases, and was familiar with the differing responsibilities of the courts of Admiralty, Exchequer, and King's Bench. Colonial officials, overwhelmingly laymen, had a shaky grasp of the vocabulary, interpretive methods, and institutional and doctrinal context presupposed by legal documents produced in England. Lawyers' training in "proper" modes of reading and contextualization created conceptual limits to the imagined meaning of a text. With less awareness of such limits, lay officials exercised heightened interpretive freedom. Thus, colonial lay officials might deflect imperial policies not only when they deliberately tried to do so – a skill they developed to a high pitch and that they shared with trained lawyers and Spanish American *letrados* – but also inadvertently, by proceeding in good faith without fully understanding what was asked of them. Disjunctions between the professional idiom of imperial legal documents and the lay idiom of most colonial officials thus blunted efforts to project metropolitan legal understandings into the colonies.

Scribal and Oral Transmission, Brokers, and Social Networks

Legal communications relied heavily on scribal and oral transmission filtered through social networks. Brokers of information enjoyed considerable power to bury, redirect, or alter metropolitan understandings of law flowing between London and the colonies. Thus, the English government could not be sure that discussions, reviews, and dissemination of law would reach colonial target audiences accurately or at all.

To illustrate, consider the behavior of the Privy Council, obviously a critical institution for imperial oversight. Though decisive in the individual case, the Council's decisions on judicial appeals and colonial legislation had an ad hoc quality that undermined their cumulative effect and limited their ability to reshape colonial law by providing an accessible account of metropolitan expectations. Nor, in any case, did the Council give any systematic attention to dissemination of its rulings. Orders were issued verbally or in sketchy written form supplemented and explained orally. Few were printed. Some circulated in manuscripts of uncertain distribution. Most spread by word of mouth in distorted and incomplete retellings. English government officials, let alone colonists, had trouble discovering what the Council had resolved and even greater trouble learning why.

The haphazard dissemination of Council rulings provides an example of two larger phenomena: (1) reliance on scribal and oral dissemination of law and (2) the importance of written or verbal interpretations (or "framings") that accompanied legal narratives and texts as they moved from place to place. Parliamentary and colonial statutes apart, only a tiny fraction of the laws and judicial and administrative decisions that governed public life were available in print. Most legal information circulated through handwritten manuscripts, whether traveling across the Atlantic (Privy Council rulings, governors' instructions, customs service interpretations) or within a colony (governor, Privy Council, and court decisions; responses to petitions; directions for local officials). Unlike printed materials, manuscripts were neither standardized nor generally available to the public. When the holder of the manuscript circulated it, he had to decide whether to send it verbatim, edit it, or combine it with other texts. He could add material that explained, undermined, or reinterpreted the main document. At each link in the circulatory chain, brokers of legal information could also add verbal commentary that "framed" a manuscript (or printed document) with views of its meaning.

A broker had to decide not only what to send but also to whom. He might routinely transmit documents to recipients selected because of their office (for instance, the secretary of a colonial assembly would routinely dispatch session laws to county clerks). Alternatively, he might distribute an edited and framed document only when politically or socially advantageous. He would consider the consequences of providing a given audience accounts of the Privy Council's rulings, or portions of the governor's instructions, or recent interpretations of the customs regulations. In turn, recipients would decide whether to circulate the document they received, to whom, and with what inclusions, exclusions, and changes.

Political calculations and personal sympathies influenced not only the dissemination but also the storage of legal information and governmental records. Officeholders sometimes denied their political and social rivals access to records. Given the incomplete separation of governmental and personal roles, officials tended to mix state and private papers. On retirement, they might take home public documents, compromising the institutional memory available to their successors. The English administrator most experienced in colonial affairs at the turn of the eighteenth century, William Blathwayt, removed much of his vast correspondence with colonial governors and deputy auditors after leaving office. Only slowly did officials come to think of official papers as a possession of the government to be housed in state repositories, rather than a form of private property. This transformation was underway during the eighteenth century, but incomplete. Throughout the colonial period, the preservation of legal knowledge, like its transmission, remained highly personal, unreliable, and politicized in British North America.

And not only there. Spanish and French America were only too familiar with the untrustworthy storage of legal information, self-interested brokers, and the haphazard dissemination of law through scribal or verbal chains of transmission. In light of these common limitations and inconsistencies in state administrative structures, social networks created by bonds of family, friendship, loyalty, common origin, and interest played a critical role in disseminating law.

Information moved readily between administrative and social pathways. An interpretation of export regulations sent from the English Treasury to a customs collector in New York passed through the empire's administrative system. But when the collector sent copies of the document to a lawyer who represented him in land speculations, to his merchant cousin in Albany, to a friend from church, and to an assembly representative sympathetic to the prerogative party, dissemination instead began to follow social networks.

It is tempting to observe that administrative structures and social networks fused at multiple points, but the observation would be misleading, in that it implies that they were otherwise separate. In fact, structures and networks were mutually constitutive. Early modern states expected and required social elites to assume governmental positions, not least to draw on those elites' formidable authority with neighbors, clients, and dependents. Officeholders competed for the favor of patrons whose approval won them desirable posts and promotions. Successful administrators discussed policy choices with the social and economic leaders of the community and cultivated their support. These interactions encouraged levels of compliance that could seldom be bought or forced, given the limited financial and military resources of early modern states.

The tight integration of administration and society encouraged officeholders to communicate law through social networks. They needed to describe local legal cultures to distant patrons and, conversely, explain metropolitan legal expectations to community notables. Officeholders also needed to inform allies about legal interpretations and disputes in order to prevail in the endemic factional disputes that spread from society into government (as a result of the weak separation of official role from social position). Additionally, local clergy, military officers, university scholars, and nearby gentlemen expected to be apprised of legal developments. Their social status made them the natural rulers of society no less than government officials. Political effectiveness and even continuation in office thus depended on dexterity in brokering information.

The centrality of scribal and verbal (as compared to print) media only reinforced the critical importance of social networks in shaping the patterns of legal transmission. The recipient of a manuscript either asked for it or held a place on the owner's distribution list. Dissemination of law through personal discussions, and verbal framings of manuscripts and printed documents, occurred in face-to-face interactions. Colonial governments promulgated statutes and proclamations through announcements at court day and fairs; and one could purchase manuscript copies of records, such as charters, statutes, and judicial rulings. But aside from state commands and a limited class of public records, colonists could not obtain legal information as of right or by the payment of a fee. Most knowledge about law moved through the possessor's networks according to the dictates of social obligation and political calculation.

Social networks transmitted far more than the formal materials of Anglo-American law, such as Privy Council Orders, court decisions, and parsings of customs regulations. They also transmitted the mores and dispositions that make up a legal culture: for example, commitments to particular types of dispute resolution, presuppositions about the nature and sources of justice and good government, opinions about imperial superintendence, and favored styles of interpreting legal materials. Schoolmasters and college tutors taught those under their charge how natural law constrained the state's positive law. Recently arrived Inns of Court barristers told their American business and political contacts what English statesmen thought the Glorious Revolution settlement meant for the colonies. Assembly representatives returning to their towns confided to their allies the compromises and limitations of newly passed legislation. Merchants recounted their London brokers' opinions about the Privy Council's agenda for colonial governance. Ministers advised their co-religionists about how to arrange their affairs to avoid ungodly secular courts.

The importance of social networks to legal communications, broadly construed, helped preserve local control and diversity in the colonial legal systems. Metropolitan legal understandings could spread through colonial social networks only after they were introduced in some fashion. The English empire, compared to the Spanish, maintained fewer points of contact from which diffusion could begin. Consider, first, the connections created by the institutions of imperial governance. As we have seen, the Spanish empire developed a multiplicity of alternative communications links that penetrated deep into the colonial governing structure and society. England maintained few points of contact outside the elites at the top of the legal and political hierarchies and beyond the colonial capitals and port cities. It lacked a robust inland bureaucracy.[19]

Metropolitan legal understandings could spread to colonial social networks not only through imperial governing structures but also through other institutions, such as universities and churches. Spanish colonists rapidly built universities in the Americas. Six were founded in the first fifty years of their empire and twenty-three by the middle of the eighteenth century. Many of the Spanish American universities established chairs of law and oversaw the study of Roman canon *ius commune* and of natural law (also offered in the arts curriculum). During the sixteenth and seventeenth centuries, the universities did not formally teach royal law. Their program of *ius commune* and natural law served metropolitan purposes obliquely by bringing a measure of unity to the legal culture of Spanish America and by providing a counterweight to local diversity in lawmaking. By the early to middle eighteenth century, universities began teaching royal law directly. They added chairs in that subject under the encouragement of the Council of the Indies. Knowledge of Roman, canon, natural, and royal law spread beyond the universities' students to the lettered segment of society, particularly those linked to the government bureaucracy and judiciary. By contrast, none of the handful of colleges in the English colonies offered a directed course of readings in law. Nor did they maintain chairs of law. Settlers who desired to learn law in an educational institution (rather than through apprenticeship) traveled to the Inns of Court in London. Compared to the number of Spanish America colonists exposed to Roman, canon, natural, and royal law in New World universities or through diffusion from those educational centers, they were few in number.

Churches and clergy could also introduce metropolitan legal understandings into colonial social networks. Unlike the pluralistic and frequently contrarian British North American denominations, the Spanish American church devoted itself to upholding the Crown's political and legal authority. Special papal dispensations gave the Spanish king more extensive supervisory powers over the church in America than any monarch enjoyed over the church in his European territories. Under the system of *Patronato Real*, the Crown nominated archbishops, bishops, and abbots directly and other clergy indirectly and controlled ecclesiastical revenues and governance. Catholic clergy dependent on the Crown for their positions and funding taught principles of law and constitutionalism through sermons, private instruction,

[19] I owe the phrase "inland bureaucracy" to a conversation with Prof. Charlotte Crane.

and example. They ran schools and the universities. Clerics served as advisors and advocates for Indians in secular legal and political affairs. Ecclesiastical courts also protected "wretched persons" – widows, orphans, and the poor – and exercised jurisdiction over marriage, inheritance, and sexual relations, as well as tithes and usury among other matters. Bishops and canon lawyers articulated legal principles as they fought for their jurisdictional rights against viceroys, *audiencias*, and state officials.

The diverse denominations and sects of British North America lacked many of the mechanisms that the Spanish American church used for tutoring residents in principles of law and constitutionalism. They did not formally instruct Indians in legal doctrines or run ecclesiastical courts. Yet, their role should not be underestimated. Through preaching, catechizing, and personal discussion, they formed "the minds of the people to the knowledge of both law and duty," as the minister William Smith put it. Sermons might convey constitutional principles and jurisprudence. They spoke, for instance, of the excellence of the "balanced" British constitution, the relationship of natural and positive law, the proper character of the magistrate, and the source and limits of colonial liberties within the empire. Church-supported mediation offered a site for clergy and laity to wrestle with legal doctrine, including the relationship of English and colonial law. New England Congregationalists, Quakers, Dutch Reformed congregants, and German Pietists particularly encouraged co-religionists to settle disputes under the auspices of the church rather than in the state's courts. Mediation addressed not only disputes about faith and sin but also quarrels about commercial dealings, property rights, marital obligations, and the proper sphere of officials' powers. Congregants worked through principles of secular law as these were used to define ethical duties. The Bible, for example, instructed believers not to covet thy neighbor's property; but the state's law defined the boundaries of thy neighbor's property and explained how it could be regulated and transferred.

When it came to imperial views of law and constitutionalism, however, the diverse denominations and sects in British North America proved at best uncertain allies, and sometimes opponents. All preached from Romans 13 in favor of hierarchical authority and justly constituted government. Aside from the Anglicans, however, their support of imperial policy was selective, self-interested, and changeable. As such, they diverged strikingly from the Spanish American church. The Catholic establishment suffered its own conflicts – between priests and parishioners, between bishops and parishes, between ecclesiastical courts and the Inquisition, and between "secular" priests in the dioceses and "regular" clergy in orders. But however much dioceses and churchmen clashed on particular points, their rivalries occurred within a theoretically integrated organization committed to the support of the Crown's government.[20] A parish in Peru and another in the valley of Mexico might disagree somewhat about the principles of justice and government. But how much more would opinions about justice and proper government differ between a Puritan gathered church and a Virginia Anglican parish, between a Sephardic Jewish congregation and a Philadelphia Quaker meetinghouse, between a German Pietist pastor and a Catholic priest in Maryland or a Dutch Reformed minister and a Baptist itinerant preacher? One need not claim that the Spanish American church aimed at or achieved a single, cohesive body of religious and legal principles to acknowledge that the variation among its constituent parishes, missions, and priests was less than among the strikingly diverse churches and clergy of British North America. The pluralistic theology, denominational structure, and ethnic foundations of the British colonial churches made them unreliable conduits for introducing metropolitan legal understandings into colonial social networks. In contrast to the Spanish American church, they stood outside the imperial apparatus, spreading inconsistent messages about jurisprudence, constitutionalism, and the proper relationship of colonies to the metropolis.

Considered together, the churches, universities, and royal bureaucracies offered the Spanish empire multiple and widely dispersed points of contact for introducing metropolitan legal understandings into colonial social networks. Each neglectful and self-interested social network decided how to reshape and explain what it chose to circulate. But the diversity of overlapping transmission routes reduced the power of each network to bury or alter beyond recovery the Crown's messages and outlook. How much less was this true in British North America. The churches and sects were unreliable allies of the empire. The handful of colleges played a far smaller role in disseminating law than their more numerous Spanish American counterparts. The English imperial administrative system maintained few points of contract outside the port cities and the elites who headed legal and political hierarchies.

The relative scarcity of points of contact gave local notables and social networks in British North America considerable power to influence the dissemination of metropolitan legal understandings. A small group of imperial appointees concentrated in colonial capitals and major ports (about twenty officials in a royal colony, fewer in a corporate or proprietary colony) spread and endorsed metropolitan legal understandings as a matter of duty. Most

[20] My emphasis here is on the political, social, and legal teachings of the Spanish American church. Parishioners, of course, interpreted those teachings in diverse ways, as the studies of indigenous peoples' "syncretic" religion have emphasized.

brokers of legal information did not. Assembly representatives, justices of the peace and sheriffs, vestries, merchants, clergy, lawyers of various degrees of training and professionalism, gentlemen who dominated their counties – these brokers, motivated by their interests and ideological commitments, screened or transformed metropolitan legal understandings while circulating them through social networks. If local brokers and networks were disinclined to cooperate, the English empire encountered real practical difficulty in projecting imperial versions of law. More often than not, metropolitan legal understandings reached colonists in fractured and competing forms. They did not enjoy the widespread presence and the perceived solidity and certainty that legitimates unfamiliar or unpalatable law. The empire's dependence on self-interested and unreliable colonial brokers and social networks helped preserve a measure of local control and diversity in the colonial legal systems.

CONCLUSION: AN "INDIVIDUALIZING" COMPARISON

My purpose in comparing English and Spanish America is not to assess their relative degree of obedience to royal directives or the relative degree of local control and diversity on the ground. To emphasize the many ways in which Spain created more varied and extensive means for legal communications with its American empire than England should not, in other words, be taken to mean that New Spain and Peru were more obedient to metropolitan directives than the British North American colonies. Indeed, historians of colonial Spanish America have long pondered why an empire with so elaborate a governing bureaucracy encountered such difficulty in getting New World officeholders and local elites to follow Crown policies.

Instead, I have used Spanish America as a contrast case. It sets up what Charles Tilly has called an "individualizing comparison," where one case brings out the distinctive and peculiar elements of the other. Contrasting the two New World empires highlights important features of legal communications in British North America whose existence or significance would not be apparent if examined in isolation.

This approach can shed light on early American politics and society as well as law. Historians have long wondered to what extent, and why, the colonies preserved a measure of local control and diversity despite oversight by the English empire and pressures to assimilate. One strand of scholarship has explored the foundations for resistance to overreaching prerogative and unwelcome imperial programs. Its themes are familiar. The growing authority of assemblies constrained the influence of royal governors and imperial administrators short on patronage and coercive power. Colonial notables (not metropolitan officials) staffed almost all administrative and judicial bodies, which could not function without active participation from local communities. Colonists valorized English freedoms and customary and consensual notions of authority while cultivating intense suspicions of prerogative (even when they were benefiting from it). The English empire's political divisions and modest fiscal, military, and administrative capacities inclined it to negotiate with colonial elites, rather than vigorously confront resistance.

Another strand of scholarship depicts pressures toward integration into the English empire. The first two generations of the imperial school charted the growth of the empire's administrative structures, and their successors explored the social and political developments that this apparatus inspired, from the elaboration of an Anglo-American patronage system to the mobilization of interest groups. Students of anglicization have noted the growing resemblance of the colonies' elite culture, legal and military structures, and consumption patterns to those of the metropolis, and their formation of a deeper, more self-conscious English identity. Recent studies of early American communications emphasize how improvements in the diffusion of information helped integrate the English Atlantic politically and culturally.

Both strands of scholarship capture essential features of colonial life. Historians have labored to bring the two together and explain their interaction. This study of the double nature of Anglo-American legal communications introduces another way to bridge them. At first glance, one sees the importance of legal communications in the administrative, political, and judicial structures of the empire. Imperial school historians a century ago began the exploration of this theme. Comparison with Spanish America provides a new perspective and reveals the particularities, omissions, and limitations that made Anglo-American communications practices anything but a reliable agent of imperial centralization. The Spanish American experience brings into sharper focus the English empire's preference for regulating governing structures, rather than assuring individual justice, and the colonists' ability to withhold legal information for strategic advantage. It underscores the trans-Atlantic (rather than intracontinental) orientation of the English empire's variegated (rather than uniform) legal communications channels and the relative scarcity of points for inserting metropolitan legal understandings in colonial social networks. And it suggests the implications of the colonists' reliance on lay (rather than legally trained) judges and administrators and the English empire's relative disinterest in the internal legal affairs of Native Americans. These are different types of observations. Some are about social and political strategies; others about institutional design, staffing, and priorities; and still others about the cumulative patterns of information exchange. Collectively, however, they reinforce one another.

Where the imperial school and its successors emphasized the centrality of legal communications in building an administrative apparatus and tying together the English empire politically and intellectually, the Spanish comparison brings out how and why these developments were incomplete and uneven. In particular, the study of communications reveals how decisively local notables and social networks controlled the dissemination of legal knowledge and commands. Scholars have long observed that the large degree of local control of legal institutions significantly influenced the shape of colonial politics and the Revolutionary movement. Yet, as we have seen, local notables exercised substantial control over the means of *communication* as well as the means of *administration*. They influenced which audiences would know what about imperial directives and about the legal heritage that supposedly united colonies and metropolis. They shaped the meaning of the shared heritage and of imperial directives in the process of disseminating them. Understanding the dynamics of Anglo-American legal communications (as well as legal administration) helps explain the persistence of a significant measure of local control and diversity in the colonial legal systems amid pressures toward integration into the English empire in the eighteenth century.

5

REGIONALISM IN EARLY AMERICAN LAW

DAVID THOMAS KONIG

Early Americans created regionally particular legal systems. Two centuries of nationhood have since brought a great measure of uniformity in certain areas of American law – the adoption of federal rules of procedure, the growth of a federal judiciary, a uniform commercial code, and a national system of legal education are just a few. Yet in certain respects American law remains regionally specific. The nation's ninety-four federal district courts, for example, are grouped into regional circuits whose decisions occasionally conflict and are not resolved. Perhaps in our own time regional distinctiveness is stronger in American culture and political discourse than in actual legal reality. Nevertheless, both its factual existence and its cultural potency are clear.

American regionalism has its roots in early America. In the case of law, the particular goals and variant experiences of unrelated colonization ventures led to the reanimation and recombination of English legal practices in different ways in the new environments. Colonists emphasized some English practices while rejecting others, resulting ultimately in the emergence of three new and distinct regional configurations – the Chesapeake and its Southern neighbors, New England, and the Middle Colonies.

The peoples of early America were – as those of modern America remain – as various as their land, and the regionally diverse legal systems they created gave meaning and order to their experiences. Their legal regionalism originated in a long tradition of diverse English practices and in the contingent exigencies of the unique historical "moments" of social change and legal crisis in which colonization efforts took place. These moments would produce the three distinct regions of legal culture on which we focus in this chapter. We examine and explain the creation and entrenchment of these plural legal orders not through an exhaustive catalog of their legal differences, but through an interpretive inquiry into particular areas of the law that demonstrate how the theory and reality of regionalism first created – and now continues to animate – law in America.

The first two great cultural hearths of American law – the Chesapeake and New England – emerged at a critical moment in English history when a "vexed and troubled" people turned to the institutions of law to reconstitute a body politic collapsing in disarray. Law at this moment stood as the bulwark both of identity and, indeed, survival. To those English who first settled North America, in particular, law would distinguish them from the peoples they encountered; it was a distinctive mark of the superiority of their free and Protestant civilization. They turned to it with enthusiasm as an instrument to settle North America – that is, to claim dominion and control over the land and the peoples they encountered there, whether "lawless" Indians, "heathen" Africans, or "Popish" Roman Catholic colonial rivals. The law provided different models for national recovery, and the two colonization ventures that began England's overseas empire – Virginia and Massachusetts Bay – took skillful advantage of the opportunities it offered; they self-consciously departed in many particulars from the law of the central courts at Westminster in their efforts to use law as an instrument to define their rights and secure their interests according to their particular goals.

This process had proceeded for two generations before war and political and economic revolution produced another, third, colonial moment – the creation and expansion of a seaborne commercial empire sustained in part by massive migration from diverse European origins into the new colonial ventures of the mid-Atlantic. There, English law had to accommodate the vestiges of prior colonial efforts, as well as a burgeoning population who accepted the authority of that law only with reluctance and who often greeted it with defiance.

Once underway in the seventeenth century, the process of regional differentiation continued apace in the next, shaped not only by the contingencies of the historical moments that had launched them but also by succeeding self-definitions – as settler societies developing in a hostile environment, as colonists joining together in collective separation from England, and finally as members of politically and culturally distinct entities in a federal republic attempting to balance the sovereignties of state and union.

I. THE DISCOVERY OF REGIONALISM IN EARLY AMERICAN LAW

Anyone traveling in Britain's North American colonies would have been struck by the diversity of its peoples, who distinguished themselves from each other in so many ways, whether by religion or race or by place of birth or of residence. Those same colonial populations, however, gave comparatively little thought to what distinguished their own governmental institutions from those of other mainland colonies. This was especially true of their law courts. The main business of courts was the protection of life and property, which rarely brought them into contact with courts in other colonies. Trade took people beyond the borders of their own colony, but most commonly brought them into contact not with fellow North Americans but with merchants doing business out of London or Glasgow, or perhaps the West Indies. The broad expanses of ocean seemed to stand as the real borders of legal cultures. When Parliament in the mid-eighteenth century began to impose more uniform legal rules in North America, therefore, Americans saw the contest as between two political and legal cultures – one in Britain and one spread along the coastline of North America. Virginia's conflict was with Britain, not with Massachusetts.

In mobilizing resistance to Parliament in the 1770s, the colonies were declaring their opposition to a new eighteenth-century "imperial constitution" that had altered long-established tradition by asserting a full legal sovereignty that required their complete compliance with English law. The colonists adhered instead to an earlier concept of constitution based on custom and express contractual agreement – that is, through court practice and colonial statute – and so had adapted the law to their needs, in the process gradually drifting away from the specifics and technicalities of the law as known and practiced in the central courts at Westminster Hall. Impelled by the needs of political contest, this colonial divergence from the legal orthodoxies of Westminster required legitimation by specific demonstration of consent and historical proof of custom.

To meet the need, Thomas Jefferson and others – including, not least, generations of legal historians – provided an account of American legal development that imposed a misleading unsophisticated uniformity on the regionally varied legal landscape of early America. To justify colonial departures from the orthodoxies of Westminster, Jefferson insisted that American legal development since the beginnings of the colonies had been a process of simplification by artlessly inexpert amateurs – a sort of legal regression to an ancient mean. According to this story – which has been embellished through time – the colonists devised a simpler, purer law better suited to the common needs of British North America. Theirs was a generic system of law lacking the complicated forms and actions of English secular and ecclesiastical law. Such a law was not only the product of nature; it was their right by nature. "Our ancestors . . . who migrated hither," wrote Jefferson in 1774, "were farmers, not lawyers." As both a farmer and a lawyer, he knew better, but such a national origins myth suited the strategy of denying the legitimacy of a metropolitan legal regime over Britain's North American provinces by elevating a more authentic expression of provincial culture in its stead. Jefferson, a close student of England's legal history, invoked the purity of a mythic Saxon past to extol a purer, simpler American system of law. Excusing the general American colonial practice of granting fee-simple tenures to land as "an error in the nature of our landholdings, which crept in at a very early period of our settlement," for example, he contrasted the allodial tenures of his Saxon ancestors to the feudal and "fictitious principle that all lands belong originally to the king." In so arguing, he laid a basis for perpetuating the idea that the legally inexpert "farmers, not lawyers," who colonized North America had been incapable of duplicating the technical niceties and fictions of English law and that a generalized rustic simplification guided early American law and reduced it to its common elements.[1] Out of that process emerged a shared foundation of truly American law, rid of its English corruptions and based on the universal "laws of nature & of nature's god."[2]

Jefferson's invocation of the first settlers as "farmers, not lawyers," artlessly natural simplifiers who improvised on a common fund of a liberty-loving tradition, served the immediate needs of political mobilization and emphasized a bright line between legal cultures separated by an ocean. But it intentionally neglected the English antecedents of a continuing American legal tradition of instrumentally crafted regional variation. Legal regionalism among the colonies had existed as a reality long before it became a consciously articulated ideal when Americans reexamined their colonial past in search of a workable foundation for a new legal order in the 1780s. The politics of unification forced James Madison as "Publius" to acknowledge the "different laws and circumstances" within his "extended republic of the United States" and led his co-author John Jay to address the danger that "three or four confederacies" might form among the different regions. Turning regionalism into an asset, however, "Publius" argued that regionalism within a federal union was a virtue that would prevent monolithic national consolidation.[3] Not only did this new concept prove more useful for the political needs of the new republic but it was also, in fact, far more accurate as history than Jefferson's artful Revolutionary polemic suggested.

Americans discovered their tradition of legal regionalism as soon as the question of imperial constitutional structure was replaced by the new

[1] Thomas Jefferson, "Draft of Instructions to the Virginia Delegates in the Continental Congress" [July 1774], published as "A Summary View of the Rights of British America," *The Papers of Thomas Jefferson*, ed. Julian P. Boyd, et al. (Princeton, 1950), I: 133. When printed as "A Summary View," "farmers" had been changed to "laborers."

[2] This is the form used in "Jefferson's 'original Rough draught' of the Declaration of Independence"; *Ibid.*, 423.

[3] Madison, *The Federalist*, No. 51 ("extended republic"), 53 ("different laws"), in *The Federalist*, ed. Jacob E. Cooke (Wesleyan, CT, 1961), 353, 363; Jay discussed regional confederacies at *Ibid.*, No. 5, 25.

problem of defining legal relationships between and among the newly independent states. Constitutional relations are, fundamentally, matters of competing sovereignties: as the sovereignty of King-in-Parliament was about to end in 1781 Jefferson revealed his own ambivalent identity, simultaneously "[a]s an American, as a Virginian."[4] Many times he had used the term "country" to describe both Virginia and the United States, but what seemed to augur a consolidation of law under the federal government drove him and others to emphasize the singularity of their own states' laws and legal systems. "Before the Revolution," he wrote to his future attorney-general, Edmund Randolph, "the nation of Virginia had, by the organs they then thought proper to constitute, established a system of laws. . . . " By contrast, he continued, "[b]efore the Revolution there existed no such nation as the United States," and thus no common legal system.[5]

Replacing the simplified natural uniformity of the first settlements with the more highly developed particularism of American state law, Jefferson joined a chorus of politicians and jurisprudents who acknowledged the distinctiveness – indeed, the conflicts – inherent in the many state systems of law framed after independence and who opposed any effort to assert a federal common law. Instead, it was axiomatic that "law" meant state law, especially in the area of private law. When Jesse Root of Connecticut wrote his introduction to the first law reports published in the United States, it went without saying that "a system of jurisprudence congenial to the spirit and principles of our own government" meant that of Connecticut. Revolutionary republicanism had left Americans suspicious of political motivations, especially those that threatened now to consolidate their communities and submerge their rights and identities within a national (and formerly, imperial) monolith. As Americans of different regions resisted the superimposing of a new national identity that threatened to efface local legal and political structures, they took refuge in a constitutional counter-narrative that sharply accentuated regional diversity.

Maintaining the union, paradoxically, would require the formal recognition of regional and local variation. "Nationalism in America," the historian Peter S. Onuf explains, "developed in tandem with opposition to centralized state power; sectionalism was its logical corollary." Only after independence had been secured did the difficulties of political union confront the aggregated states with the reality of the variations among their systems of law. Only then did the fact of their regional dissonance seize their attention and

[4] Jefferson to James Monroe, October 5, 1781, *Papers*, VI: 127.

[5] Jefferson to Edmund Randolph, August 18, 1799, in *The Life and Selected Writings of Thomas Jefferson*, ed. Adrienne Koch and William Peden ([1944] New York, 1993), 504–05.

gain pride of place as defining American identity. With the successful ouster of the imperial power against which all the colonies could unite in common cause and common identity, Ayers and Onuf point out, the "awareness of *other* regions in a competitive political context" finally led Americans to acknowledge – indeed, to celebrate – the enduring regional traditions of the colonial experience.

II. ENGLISH SOURCES OF REGIONAL LEGAL VARIATION

Early American legal regionalism reflected that of the English past, but the impact of that past was itself contingent and dynamic, and its product – a federal republic of constitutionally defined sovereignties – went well beyond English antecedents. The regional particularities of colonial legal practice did not reflect a direct, wholesale transplantation of English regional cultures, which were themselves too varied for easy replication even without the powerful forces of the colonization experience. Rather, it was the *concept and practice* of legal particularism, rooted in a history of English localism and given greater force by the peculiar exigencies of national crisis in the seventeenth century, which produced the different regional legal cultures of North America. English legal settlement of North America began at a particular moment in English history, a defining period of revolutionary change and deep crisis that evoked a range of desperate solutions. These responses, for all their impact at home, would have a much greater impact in the New World, where traditional institutions would have less of a restraining power. Isolated from each other and settled by dissimilar groups pursuing different goals, the various colonies of North America accelerated the process of legal change and diversification going on in England. The basic contours of English law and the self-conscious elevation of its importance, therefore, persisted and survived transplantation, leaving "an important paradigmatic legacy" that bore the exaggerated imprint of the particular changes overtaking England in the period before and during colonization, and of the forces introduced by the experience of colonization and settlement. Leaving an England in crisis in the first half of the seventeenth century, the settlers of North America brought with them a near-obsessive concern with using the law to achieve security of property and reestablish social order. Despite the changes that would occur in the eighteenth century, transforming the nature of colonial societies and bringing to them an overlay of a common transatlantic British culture, their founding moment left them with an indelible legacy.

The legal landscape that the first settlers left behind was itself variegated, the product of Britain's own diversity of geography, society, religion, and political organization. Though overwhelmingly rural and agrarian, the

British Isles encompassed different climatic zones and topographies that shaped the economic and political organization of its peoples, whose vastly different spoken dialects reflected their diverse social forms as well. Soil might be chalk, clay, or fen; communities might cultivate wheat and rye or barley and oats, or they might pasture livestock. At the onset of colonization, England alone (from which the vast majority of the earliest emigrants came) could count hundreds of boroughs and cities, 750 market towns, a capital town for each of its 40 counties, and 9,000 rural parishes containing numberless villages and manors. No one form could be called "typical" of English society, even within a county or region. Many manors followed an open-field form of agriculture, with holdings communally managed; in other communities people farmed their plots separately, according to a closed-field system. Even within those two basic forms, which were not confined to any particular area, great regional variation led to sharply differing local practices and customs. Moreover, the uneven effects of commercial change overtaking the realm were transforming its villages, towns, and cities. While some thrived, others withered; while some had to cope with the effects of prosperity and growth, others found themselves in deep crisis.

The protection of life and property, the two main goals of the law, thus took many different forms and made early modern England a patchwork of regional and even subregional legal diversity. Laws of descent varied by and within region, for example, deriving from custom as well as from common law. Although feudal tenures were the norm for the gentry, many exceptions existed. Land held by copyhold tenants, for example, might descend partibly according to manorial practice, rather than according to the rule of primogeniture, by which real property descended to the eldest male. Many legal backwaters were never affected by mainstreams of legal development; in some regions, as a result, the old Saxon principle of partible inheritance through gavelkind governed. In others, the peculiar circumstances of timing determined the shape and extent of legal practices. English boroughs obtained their charters at different times and under different circumstances from different monarchs, giving to each of them a different range of special privileges and varying degrees of autonomy that produced different local rules.

The effect of such variety was multiplied by the functional variations and political rivalries within the English legal system and the uneven force of the common law and its courts throughout the realm. England's common law – the law as applied in the central courts at Westminster – was only one of many systems operating in the lives of the peoples of early modern England, and it was not the only source of legal remedies. English suitors had before them a variety of options when they sought the remedies of the law, and they might frame the rights they claimed and the remedies they sought in different ways in order to choose among different, even competing, forums. The law courts derived their revenues from fees collected from litigants, and two of England's high courts of law at Westminster – King's Bench and Common Pleas – vied with one another for business. If it is too much to label England's legal system a free market in law, it remains true that courts competed with one another and provided options to forum-shopping litigants.

Although we speak of a "common law," the term misleads if it implies a uniform national law. In the first half of the seventeenth century Sir Edward Coke could list more than 100 different courts in the realm, including merchants' courts, ecclesiastical courts, and manorial courts, as well as courts that served specific locations, such as the Courts of the Cinque Ports and the Court of the County Palatine of Durham. Writing on the eve of American independence, Sir William Blackstone praised the "prodigious variety of courts" created in England. "The policy of our ancient constitution, as regulated and established by the great Alfred," he wrote, "was to bring justice home to every man's door, by constituting as many courts as there are manors and townships in the kingdom. . . ."[6]

The common law thus acknowledged local variation, and the reach of the central common law courts from Westminster varied according to local forces and practices. The common law, moreover, was not the only law available and had not fully supplanted the ancient Anglo-Saxon courts of the shire and the hundred. It coexisted, too, with non-common law courts such as civil (Roman) law courts that offered specialized justice for particular issues ranging from admiralty to marriage and the probate of personal property. Henry VIII, who viewed the common law courts and their lawyers with some suspicion, had sought to check their accumulating authority by encouraging the rival system of Roman civil law used in these numerous specialty courts. Henry also made great use of his Court of Star Chamber, where his Privy Councilors met and addressed matters affecting the security of the state or involving powerful magnates beyond the grasp of ordinary common law courts. Though its substantive law was that of the common law and common lawyers participated in its proceedings, its procedures were not bound by it. Such a court – known as a "conciliar" court because composed of a council – provided enormous advantages in furthering the interest of the state: the attorney-general brought prosecutions by information (not grand jury presentment), and no trial jury took part. Punishments also ignored the limits of the common law, and the court might order the severing of ears or the slitting of noses.

[6] Sir Edward Coke, *The Fourth Part of the Institutes of the Laws of England, Concerning the Jurisdiction of* Courts ([1641] London, 1797). Sir William Blackstone, *Commentaries on the Laws of England*, ([1765–69], reprint, Chicago, 1979), 3: 24, 30.

Star Chamber procedures reflected the impulse to escape the rigidity of the common law, and such departures – like those that would take place in North America – reveal less an inexpert simplification than a series of conscious choices to adapt legal institutions to particular and pressing needs by recombining forms and principles from preexisting courts. With good reason, then, Joseph H. Smith's observation that "English law has always made its new quilts from old rags" applies equally to the English colonists of North America. Early American legal innovation and regional variation must be seen as continuing an English legal tradition, one with which colonists were especially familiar given the specific timing of England's colonization project. It was no historical accident that expansion overseas coincided with an outburst of legal creativity and state-building in England: the three were indispensable to each other. In creating a more powerful state and effecting a veritable revolution in government, English monarchs created legal institutions adapted to their needs. Henry VII created the Star Chamber and established conciliar rule in Wales and the northern marches. His son Henry VIII continued the process by creating courts for wardships, augmentations, and for the better governance of the church, whereas his granddaughter Elizabeth established the Court of High Commission and the Court of Exchequer Chamber. Notably, the bench at Exchequer Chamber was drawn from other courts; sitting together, they unavoidably influenced each other.

It is of great importance in generating a useable and accurate model for the development of early American law, and especially its regionally particular aspects, that this dynamic and contested English background be understood. The rise of equity – the body of procedures and rules applied in the court of chancery – reveals a process of great interpretive value in comprehending the directions of early American legal growth and change. Guided by principles of fairness to temper the rigidity or limitations of the common law, chancery had steadily expanded its role as a rival to the common law courts. "By Tudor times," writes John Baker, "it was a trite saying that Chancery was not a court of law but of conscience." Indeed, chancellors were said to act "not to destroy the law but to fulfill it," embodying the monarch's obligation to right wrongs for which no common law remedy existed. They did so by providing simple alternatives to the common law's slow and complicated mesne process, its strict rules of pleading and evidence, or its lack of appropriate remedies. Chancery had a large staff, and in responding to grievances unmet by the common law it allowed petitioners to initiate an action by an informal "bill" rather than an original writ, and with a subpoena that commanded appearance, enforced if necessary by an attachment of property that might be forfeited. Chancery made itself available without regard to the formal designation of fixed terms, even conducting its activities in the home of the chancellor or bringing justice to the provinces by delegating to rural gentry the authority to try causes on commission outside of London. It allowed pleadings in English and offered relief in the form of direct *in personam* orders, such as compelling the production of a deed or enforcing an oral contract. Out of Chancery grew another court, the Court of Requests, originally established to provide justice for the poor and serving as a sort of small claims court. Its subsequent use by substantial parties who exploited its procedural simplicity should not obscure its origins nor the template of legal development that it and other courts would provide for English subjects beyond the seas.

Not all English suitors appreciated Chancery, and like many other courts and legal practices it was the target of legal reformers, especially Puritans and radicals, who saw it as an agent of prerogative power and an obstacle to further reformation. Chancery, for example, was so slow that one critic in the 1650s estimated that causes there averaged twenty-three years to complete. John Selden called equity "a roguish thing," an arbitrary system that followed the "uncertain measure" of the chancellor's personal sense of justice, "as if they should make the standard for the measure we call a 'foot' a Chancellor's foot." So, too, the ecclesiastical Court of High Commission, created in the sixteenth century to punish religious heterodoxy, was not bound by common law rules and provoked loud opposition when the Stuarts vastly expanded its jurisdiction to persecute Puritans.

But the common law, though it had many champions, also had its critics. It, too, was used to punish religious nonconformists. In civil matters the central courts of common law at Westminster could frustrate justice. Often painfully slow, the common law, with its mystification, technicality, and great expense, provoked widespread calls for its wholesale overhaul and simplification. The turn to the law accentuated the need "to bring justice home to every man's door" with less technical and less expensive pleading, and led to calls for compiling laws into "the bigness of a pocket book." Reformers assailed pleadings in Law French – the archaic Norman language brought with the Conquest – no less than the transcription of lengthy technical proceedings in an ornate "court hand," a service for which litigants paid by the number of pages copied. A diverse group of reformers, including some of the kingdom's most learned barristers and jurists, therefore called for an end to these relics of the oppressive "Norman yoke." They would achieve some success, both temporary and permanent, during the Puritan Protectorate. Indeed, it was Puritanism that provided the principal energy and commitment behind law reform, and it would be in Puritan colonies that the impulse to purify and rationalize law would see its greatest achievements.

Law, as a means by which people and communities negotiate and order their particular realities, therefore reflected the variety and dynamism of early modern England. It served too many masters to allow any particular attempt to impose conformity to succeed – if, indeed, any attempt had been made. In truth, the Tudor monarchy had only limited interest in achieving legal uniformity outside its needs for dynastic security, which in turn rested on fiscal strength and political stability. In consolidating power and building the foundations for the modern nation-state, the Tudors had acknowledged the limits of their own power in an age of fierce local attachments and unsatisfied baronial ambition, poor administrative mechanisms, and a limited treasury. They willingly delegated not only de facto power but de jure legal authority to local powers.

The conciliar model that served so well through Star Chamber had a particular legacy of utility in England's marchland regions in the north and in Wales, where marcher lords applied equitable relief in private matters as well as a mixture of common law and Star Chamber procedures to punish their own rivals and suppress enemies of the state. Delegating this power came with a cost: local wardens and marcher lords controlled their lands with more autonomy than a monarch would tolerate closer to home, but the discretion of regional elites was a bearable cost, and it served to insulate the particularities of regional law from any attempt to make it adhere to a common form, as long as order was achieved.

Though Parliament would reject this model in the eighteenth century, priorities in preceding centuries had dictated that royal (and professional) judges concentrate their energies on matters of national importance and that local governance be conducted by local men capable of trustworthy control, who in turn were forced to rely on the participation of local residents. Hundreds of justices of the peace, officials who have been aptly described as "men of all work" in the business of England's legal system, brought "justice home to every man's door." Despite recurring efforts by the Privy Council to supervise and control them, and despite the requirement that their appointments be renewed annually, their position in the community and the vast range of obligations heaped on them (by "stacks of statutes," groaned William Lambarde in his description of the office) allowed them to exercise enormous informal power. An amateur and a volunteer, the justice of the peace in Norma Landau's words "was both instrument of divine justice and defender of the state." His "commission of the peace" embraced administrative, civil, criminal, and religious matters: justices, wrote Lambarde, "exercise not the judgements of Men onlie, but of God himselfe."[7]

Despite the power of the sword and the authority of the Bible behind him, however, a justice derived only part of his true authority (as distinct from

[7] William Lambarde, *Eirenarcha: or of the Office of the Justice of Peace* (London, 1581), 57–8, cited by Norma Landau, *The Justices of the Peace, 1679–1760* (Berkeley, 1984), 335.

power) from his commission. The legitimacy of his office rested as much on his standing in the community and in his recognition of norms and standards accepted by those on whom the law operated and whose acquiescence in the system was vital. Blackstone conceded that the legitimacy of the common law "rests entirely upon general usage and custom." Though the local justice himself was "the depositary of the laws," his stature rested on more than his study of the law, for "the only method of proving, that this or that maxim is a rule of the common law, is by shewing that it hath been always the custom to observe it." His knowledge "of the existence of such a custom as shall form a part of the common law" legitimized his decisions, and it was precisely because of the force of custom that precedent formed the base of the common law. Justices of the peace embodied the "local knowledge" that only a resident *and* an amateur guided by such sensitivities would honor. Blackstone was using this legacy to defend the authority of the common law and its judges against challenges of arbitrary discretion, but the process by which he described the origin of customs for England was, ironically, easily applicable to American departures in a new environment: "what before was uncertain, and perhaps indifferent, is now become a permanent rule. . . . "[8] – a maxim that would, much to Blackstone's indignation, legitimize variant forms of custom-based provincial law in America. As Keith Wrightson reminds us, the "wide variation of practice and jurisdiction" in local courts contradicts any conclusions about uniformity that we might draw from the prescriptive literature of legal treatises and manuals. The legitimacy and utility of "local knowledge" in resolving disputes, defining the limits of acceptable behavior, and protecting property, therefore, caution us not to impose any grand theory of legal thought and behavior in early modern England or early America. Rather, the law they applied and the practices they followed thus bore a deep local imprint.

The imprint of local mores received still greater emphasis through the broad participation of ordinary individuals in the durable ancient institution of juries and jury-like bodies. The first settlers were not legal illiterates: as "farmers" they possessed considerable knowledge of the "practick part of the law" that defined *meum et tuum* – what was "mine and thine." As legally aware tenants and lay manorial officials they routinely employed law in the life of their communities. English agrarian society was organized around membership in a community, and that community was ruled by law. It depended on law to organize the property rights that defined not only an individual's material survival but also his (and secondarily, her) legal status. The seasonal rhythms of agrarian life demanded adherence to informal rules and formal bylaws created by the farmers who had to enforce land use practices, standards of neighborliness, and the descent of property

[8] Blackstone, *Commentaries*, 1: 68–9.

between generations. English local governance depended on a small army of lay officials and personnel to staff its courts and execute the commands and protections of the law. It needed viewers of fences and roads, wardens to report nuisance violations of many sorts, and reeves and constables to impose order. Churchwardens bore the responsibility to watch and censor moral offenses, an area into which community intervention became increasingly important with the rise of Puritanism.

Manorial bylaws conferred the legitimacy of collective agreement, but so, too, did the actual enforcement of rules and the resolution of conflict succeed best when decisions and orders were made by groups acting collectively. To mobilize this authority, the English legal system constituted a wide variety of institutionalized community norms. Most prominent of these was the jury, a body of laymen assembled to assist the court on factual questions. The use of lay groups of residents familiar with local matters reached far back into pre-Conquest England, and their durability attested to the importance of local norms and a community of awareness. Jurors were not judges; their role was to assist the court in determining matters of fact, and courts depended on their knowledge of the parties and witnesses to assess credibility and to consider reputation and the general beliefs of the community in making decisions. In criminal matters, especially where itinerant justices handled serious felonies, the personal knowledge of petit jurors was indispensable to legitimizing justice as meted out. They might be called on to inquire about a death to assist the coroner or to inquire into so mundane a matter as the adequacy of fences or the proper width of a sow's yoke. So valuable was the voice of the community that specialized jury-like bodies were entrusted with factual inquiries unrelated to judicial matters, such as taxation, where their knowledge of a neighbor's wealth provided a court with information necessary to assess a rate. Three thousand miles from England, distant from the crown and required to settle the questions that Blackstone referred to when he wrote of questions on which the laws of England were "uncertain, and perhaps indifferent," these men would not only wield their authority and articulate local norms as jurors but they would also do so as judges and legislators.

III. REGIONALISM AND LEGAL DIFFERENTIATION IN THE TRANSIT OF LAW TO NORTH AMERICA

The historical moment of English colonization in an age of legal response to crisis mixed these contingencies of context and timing with the determinisms of regionally different colonial impulses and circumstances to produce enduring regional patterns of consciousness and behavior. The historic legal template of localism, creative institution building, and reformist streamlining provided a basis for continued legal change and was reinforced by the process of colonization, in which, according to R. Cole Harris, settlers "experienced strong selective pressures that emphasized some tendencies and atrophied others." Following those tendencies in different, regionally specific directions as it adapted to the particular enterprises of different colonizing projects, colonial law showed itself to be, as a bewildered British official commented in 1708, "a strange sort of Proteus capable of putting on all shapes and figures as occasion requires."[9]

English visitors also derided what they perceived to be the rustic crudeness of colonial law, but they made such observations about all colonial institutions. In reality, the dire necessities of survival had compelled settlers to ignore many formalities of the law no less than those of other social arrangements. It would have been impossible, in any case, to duplicate the technicalities and distinctions that persisted in England by law and custom without a fully trained legal or administrative cadre even if anyone had attempted it. But it would be a mistake to oversimplify this process as artless or inexpert and explain it as the result of frontier degeneracy or unfamiliarity with proper procedures – the product of the "creolean degeneracy" that British officials invoked in their critique of provincial manners and culture. Rather, the selectivity apparent in the way that the founding generations drew on available English precedents reveals a far more skilled and self-conscious process, the product of experienced and practiced users of legal institutions in England. More accustomed to the convenience and affordability of local courts than to the technicalities and expense of those at Westminster, they replicated the less complicated instrumentalism of local justice, drawing on what they knew and applying it selectively to their specific regional imperatives in the New World. As in other colonial enterprises, no full-scale replication of specific English regional practice was possible. Rather, as Jack Greene explains, a process of "cultural reformulation" took place, by which all metropolitan "inheritances were modified by powerful elements inherent in the settlement situation." Rather than permitting a wholesale replication of the patterns of any particular English region, this process accelerated legal departure and hastened regionally adapted change suited to particular New World locales.

To be sure, common problems could draw on a common legacy to produce common solutions, but regional variation lurked just below the surface. As in England, the state relied on religious institutions for support in maintaining order: Virginia turned to its Anglican vestries, and Massachusetts to its congregations, for policing morals offenses and doling out poor relief.

[9] Joseph H. Smith, *Appeals to the Privy Council from the American Plantations* (New York, 1950), 475.

In neither colony were ecclesiastical courts established, though for different reasons: a lack of Anglican clergy in Virginia and a Puritan hostility to church courts in Massachusetts. The same reasons forced changes in the way marriages were solemnized: a lack of clergy in Virginia and a Puritan theological insistence on civil ceremony. Though the colonists might escape the bishop and his courts, they could not escape death, and both colonies vested probate authority– formerly an ecclesiastical jurisdiction – in their secular county courts. In assigning to secular courts the jurisdictions once exercised by church courts, the colonists were following proposals of English law reformers; they were also following them by decentralizing justice in local units of governance with an unprecedented range of authority and competence.

The near-obsessive concern for securing property reflects the resourceful selectivity of the colonists in establishing legal procedures that answered their imported fears and responded to newly confronted realities. Enclosure had left English tenants fearful of losing their lands, whereas the dissolution of English monastic landholdings had produced a new class of landowners also eager to protect their property. The recording of property interests – whether sale, mortgage, lease, will, or dower right – had existed as custom on many English manors, and English law reformers unsuccessfully sought to simplify the law when they demanded local title registries and the abolition of all estates in land but two, fee simple and for life. In both Virginia and Massachusetts these impulses led to the required recording of all land conveyances – and in the same year, 1640. Victimized by the costs of ancient tenures and buffeted by the economic pressures that had led landlords to displace tenants and enclose their fields, the New England colonists distributed land in freehold. Landholders would hold their property securely in fee simple and without the demands of quitrents or the threat of ouster. By the time the Puritans founded the Massachusetts Bay Colony and began to distribute land broadly to its settlers in freehold tenure, the leaders of the Virginia colony had had to bow to settler demands and distribute land there too, unencumbered by feudal dues and secured by freehold title. Though Virginians owed quit-rents – a demand that the New England Puritans refused even to consider – in practice they held their land with a degree of security and freedom known only to a minority in England. While the Tudor Statute of Enrollments (1536) had fallen into disuse and the Statute of Frauds (1677) was many years in the future, colonists in New England and Virginia thus were making formal recordation a legal fact of life. Taking ready advantage of the security that recording brought them, Massachusetts colonists recorded indentures and boundaries even when not required to do so, and Virginians had their local justices of the peace register not only their land transactions but also record the earmarks of their cattle or the terms of a bill of obligation.

The justices of the peace who controlled the colonial county courts were, like those who conducted quarter sessions in England, the men of affairs of the county. Lacking the social differentiation and long-established institutions that had made English local justice a patchwork of competing and parallel jurisdictions, the colonists had little choice but to concentrate control in institutions and in persons who could command respect. But as the products of the colonization process that had created them, the county elites of Virginia and New England embodied the differences behind the impulses and circumstances of the two colonies. In Virginia this elite emerged from the competitive race to control the tobacco boom. They were "winners in the servant sweepstakes" that ousted those chosen by the Company and successfully exploited those whose labor produced the wealth that supported the new planter aristocracy, and they guided legal affairs toward protecting their regime of acquisitive individualism. At Massachusetts Bay, the ruling elite was an imported phenomenon: the earliest colonization of the "Great Migration" resembled more a series of group migrations than a trek of individuals, and the distinctive coherence of the Puritan utopian vision preserved an acknowledgment of authority in the "godly." That vision also carried with it a distrust of human authority, following the Calvinist fear of "what desperate deceit and wickednesse there is in the hearts of men." For that reason, "well ordered liberty" meant "well-balanced authority in the magistrates" and further "that all power that is on earth be limited, Church-power or other." Before the founding generation died, they had devised a "Body of Libertyes" and then a frame of "Lawes and Libertyes" that specified limits on government as well as on personal behavior. They provided clear procedures to be followed in court, for example, and reduced England's list of more than 100 capital offenses to 15.

The pattern of rule by a hierarchy of status and wealth continued in both colonies, with power concentrated in a manner "which all men respect," remarked John Adams about Massachusetts, "and all men deride." Adams's comment reflected another colonial reality, one that reproduced an English reality in local courtrooms of both Massachusetts and Virginia: namely, that the practical needs of governance meant that local oligarchs had to share control with lesser men of the middling sort. If the county elites did not govern unchallenged, neither did they govern unassisted. In that respect activity at Virginia's county courthouses differed little from those in Massachusetts, where, as Adams noted of his own experience, "the practice of Law was grasped into the hands of Deputy Sheriffs, Pettyfoggers, and Even Constables, who filled all the Writts upon Bonds, promissory notes and accounts, received the Fees established for Lawyers and stirred up many unnecessary Suits."[10]

Wide participation in legal institutions was exceeded by an even wider participation in the market for land and other property in which emerging legal practices expressed local goals. The broad distribution of freehold meant that a much larger segment of the population enjoyed the advantages of property ownership. Colonists were thus able to buy, sell, mortgage, or rent their land much more freely than any generation of Englishmen could remember, but with that liberation of property came a greater need to secure it. Participation in a market economy brought with its advantages the risks not only of loss but also of fraud or otherwise unrecoverable obligations. John Locke was surely correct when he wrote that "in the beginning all the World was *America*" in its abundance of property unprotected by government, but once America became an English property-holding society it became necessary to provide for "*the preservation of their property*," and it was through the creative and synergistic reconstituting of English legal arrangements that they accomplished this objective. Laws that seem the sudden product of immediate action, wrote Sir Matthew Hale, actually reflect a process he observed in his study of English law; namely, that of "time, which as it discovers day after day Inconveniences, so it doth successively apply new Remedies; and indeed it is a kind of aggregation of the discoveries, Results, and applications of ages and events."[11]

Ordinary but extensive dealings in property over time thus led colonists in Virginia and Massachusetts to reach back to procedures from their experiences at church or manor courts for the legal mechanisms needed in a new land of property, presenting another example of Julius Goebel's observation that many colonial legal practices drew from "the backwaters of the mainstream of the common law." That these practices usually began as the responses of erstwhile tenants transformed into cautious smallholders must not obscure the legal knowledge behind them nor the way that intelligent assessment and calculation of possibility move legal change. The new bourgeoisie of landed settlers knew enough of the law to know that oral agreements or implied promises might not suffice in court to protect their interests. It was for this reason that a Virginia county court in 1682 prudently advised two men to convert their "verball agrement" into a written lease. Servants promised their freedom knew enough law, too, to insist that

[10] *The Diary and Autobiography of John Adams*, ed. Lyman H. Butterfield (Cambridge, MA, 1962), III: 274.

[11] Sir Matthew Hale, *Of the Alteration Amendment or Reformation of the Lawes of England* [1665], cited by Howard Nenner, *By Colour of Law. Legal Change and Constitutional Politics in England, 1660–1689* (Chicago, 1977), 15.

vows to free them were stronger if written down and specified the quid pro quo of consideration that made the contract valid. The nature of the agricultural economy and the aspirations of common people accelerated a turn to law and demanded effective legal instruments tailored to their needs. Simpler also meant better if it suited the basic needs of the face-to-face societies of the first settlements. If a lack of specie required Virginians to use tobacco as a medium of exchange, they also easily adapted to transatlantic bills of exchange. If keeping accounts in a ledger book sufficed for village life in early Connecticut, later generations of colonists had little trouble using more formal written obligations, which replaced the simpler procedures when commercial activity created debts of a more distant nature.

The disruptions of the Civil War and Interregnum gave Virginia and Massachusetts the benefit of additional time and relative isolation to continue framing new and regionally specific templates for the development of legal institutions. The problems they faced and the solutions they devised in this first wave of colonization set patterns that would serve well in the colonies that joined them to create two great regional aggregates in the Chesapeake and New England. The vastly differing patterns in employing this autonomy over time produced profound variations between these two earliest regional legal clusters – what the Virginia jurist St. George Tucker meant by the differing "motives and intentions of the colonists." "Two ships sailing from the equator to the opposite poles would scarcely pursue more different courses," he wrote, "or arrive at more opposite points."[12]

The Chesapeake and New England were the first two great cultural hearths of early America, and they forged regionally dominant legal regimes because the contingent timing of their founding transferred to North America the propulsively innovative force of the moment of seventeenth-century legal crisis and the varying responses applied to it. For Virginia and the Chesapeake, this would embody a regime of acquisitive individualism and the power of harsh and repressive magistratical authority to control labor. For New England, this would mean the force of a communal ideal fueled by the religious commitment to Puritanism. The influence of Massachusetts law was felt elsewhere in New England, especially in the colonies that "hived off" from it, confirming Tucker's observation that the "Massachusetts colony may be considered as the parent of the other colonies of New-England." Virginia's laws and structures were replicated elsewhere in the South, where its labor system became the basis of a distinctive regional

[12] St. George Tucker, "Of the Unwritten, or Common Law of England; And Its Introduction into, and Authority Within the United States," in St. George Tucker, *A View of the Constitution of the United States. With Selected Writings*, ed. Clyde N. Wilson (Indianapolis, 1999), 313–70, citation at 336–37.

economy based on its most significant "departure from the principles of the common law . . . in the establishment of slavery; a measure not to be reconciled either to the principles of the law of nature, nor even to the most arbitrary establishments in the government at that period."[13]

These two regionally specific patterns had formed even before England established colonies in the territory between them, where a later and different historical moment provided forces that would create a third legal culture in the Middle Colonies of New York, New Jersey, Pennsylvania, and Delaware. There, the remnants of Dutch and Swedish colonization and a rapidly increasing flow of non-English immigrants introduced an element of social diversity unknown to the north or south, where sharply reduced rates of white immigration left society more homogeneous. Although the English largely succeeded in imposing the formal legal institutions of the common law in these new colonies, they quickly discovered that they could not obliterate strong cultural legacies, especially skillful use of the law and defiant attitudes toward authority. The combination of forces that had shaped the older colonies not only continued but also gained momentum from the economic opportunities that had led English imperialists to covet the mid-Atlantic region and establish new colonial ventures there.

English attention had been drawn to the mid-Atlantic by the enviable success of Dutch interlopers using the port of New Amsterdam as a base from which to penetrate England's colonial markets to the north and south. The conquest of New Netherland (which had absorbed New Sweden) required three wars between 1664 and 1674, but it proved easier than establishing political control, as England's first governors found a diverse and uncooperative population of Dutch, Swedes, and Finns, as well as Jewish and Muslim religious refugees welcomed by the tolerant policies of the Dutch republic. Despite the efforts of military governors to impose autocratic rule there, the Dutch republic's tradition of political decentralization had left the colony with a legacy of independent-minded local settlements unwilling to yield to their demands. The Dutch, in fact, were a minority in their own colony, whose population was the most diverse of any in North America and also included a large number of Puritan emigrants from New England, who quickly dominated Long Island and defied Dutch control.

Dutch New Netherland, like its parent country, had thrived by encouraging trade and recognizing the contributions that a diverse population brought to a modern market economy. When Governor Peter Stuyvesant joined the Dutch Reformed Church's efforts against nonconformists, the Dutch West India Company overruled him. "Jesus Christ is good," so it was said, "but trade is better." The traditional usury limit of 6 percent was

[13] *Ibid.*, 323 (slavery), 331 (parent).

increased to 10 percent. Dutch law conferred full assignability on debts, including specialties, to facilitate exchange. Aspects of the Roman civil law that fostered economic growth allowed women to take part in trade on their own, without their husband's approval. Keeping their maiden names, jointly executing documents with their husbands, or signing obligations that bound their husbands (the civil law had no doctrine of coverture), they became partners who shared profit and loss in family business. Settlers there "love nothing so much as their freedom," noted a German visitor, and colony officials who tried to impose religious conformity met spirited resistance, as did attempts to control local courts, which retained their Dutch magistrates even after English conquest. The conquest of New York marked a new moment in English colonization – an envious acknowledgement of the Dutch model of commercial empire. The same men who urged the seizure of the Dutch trading colony, in fact, also backed the creation of the Royal Africa Company, which drew England officially into the slave trade. Urging English conquest of New Netherland, a powerful adviser to Charles II explained, "What matters this or that reason? What we want is more of the trade the Dutch now have."

Pennsylvania revealed other features of the Restoration moment. A proprietary colony given to William Penn in recognition of his father's aid to the Stuart cause, its success would be measured by its ability to attract large numbers of colonists to cultivate land, produce trade goods, and provide quitrent revenue to its proprietor. Restoration proprietors thus competed with one another in offering religious toleration and generous terms for land ownership. As also occurred in the case of the Carolina proprietary created to the south of Virginia, however, generous inducements of land and religious freedom unleashed a popular refusal to pay quitrents and overwhelmed proprietary goals. The slaveholding settlers who came to Carolina from the West Indies soon followed Virginia's pattern, whereas Penn's "Holy Experiment" drew Quaker colonists with a heritage of hostility to hierarchy and an adept use of the courts to assert and protect their rights and privileges. Long-suffering victims of Stuart persecution that used common law courts to imprison them by the thousands, the Quakers had responded to legal repression with tenacious and skillful legal defenses. They created a "Meeting for Sufferings," a legal defense unit that enlisted the aid of eminent barristers and judges to defend Quakers in the courts. Penn himself was party to a landmark in legal history after jurors acquitted him and another Quaker against the direction of the judge and were fined for their verdict. *Bushell's Case* (1671) established the principle that jurors could not be punished for their verdicts. Quakers schooled themselves in procedure, standards of proof, the role of witnesses, the limits of search and seizure, and exploiting technical error in indictments and prosecutions. Quakers were known for their legal adroitness, and "were thus hardly legal primitives when they contemplated settling the Delaware valley," writes William Offutt; "instead, they possessed a well-considered legal agenda grounded in both reform theory and personal experience."

Penn's colonial law reforms, which he introduced first in the Quaker West Jersey settlement in 1676, would reflect this past with their many protections of due process, leading Thomas Jefferson to call him one of the great lawgivers of all time. Penn's "Laws Agreed Upon In England" for Pennsylvania required "That in all courts persons of all persuasions may freely appear in their own way, and according to their own manner, and there personally plead their own cause themselves, or if unable, by their friends. . . . That all pleadings, processes, and records in courts, shall be short, and in English, and in an ordinary and plain character, that they may be understood, and justice speedily administered." In practice, moreover, juries decided law as well as fact, and judges in West Jersey had no authority to overturn verdicts.

By the end of the colonial period, this Quaker tradition of shrewd litigation had produced the image of the "Philadelphia lawyer." It also left a powerful anti-authoritarian streak that fueled quarrelsome rivalries and suspicions, especially among the many different ethnic groups Penn recruited for his colony. He proudly observed that Pennsylvania was "a Collection of divers nations in Europe: As, French, Dutch, Germans, Sweeds, Danes, Finns, Scotch, Irish and English. . . . And which is admirable," he added wishfully, "they live like People of One Country. . . . " Penn's ideals, unfortunately, could not erase ethnic rivalry and distrust, and diversity left the colony beset by "scurvy quarrels that break out to the disgrace of the province." Quaker replacement of oaths with affirmations did not satisfy suspicious Anglicans, who refused to honor them. Anglican court officials met with contempt from Quakers. Quakers regarded Pennsylvania's three Lower Counties as a "Frenchified, Scotchified, Dutchified place," and they had few regrets over the counties' decision to secede and become the separate colony of Delaware. "Be not so governmentish," Penn had urged his squabbling settlers, but to little avail. Ironically, they were taking his libertarian goals to a logical but unanticipated result. After his death, in fact, as the Quakers became a minority in their own province, they transformed their religious millennialism into a legalistic protectiveness of minority status that remains one of the Middle Colonies' most significant regional contributions to American law.

IV. THE ACHIEVEMENT OF REGIONALISM

In 1696 the Crown and Parliament cobbled together a system of imperial administration that they hoped would produce, among other positive results, a more efficient and uniform administration of law in the colonies. They failed, largely because of bureaucratic inefficiency, special interest lobbying by colonists and British traders, and resistance from colonial courts and legislatures. These locally entrenched legal departures defied any and all imperial attempts at uniformity, and in 1730 an exasperated imperial official could complain "that throughout the whole continent of North America, there are not two colonies, where the courts of justice or the methods of proceedings are alike. . . ."[14]

Parliament tried again, of course, in the 1760s. It was, appropriately, a conservative member of Parliament and agent for New York, that most fractious of North American colonies, who grasped more fully the course of colonial legal development when he urged abandonment of the plan in 1775. Representing New York's interests, Edmund Burke came to realize the necessity of recognizing the diversity of interests in the empire and the need to bring them together – loosely and in a de facto manner – under their common, broadly understood goals as demonstrated in their shared "history of liberty." Typical of Enlightenment historians, he understood how different conditions create different social and political forms, and he understood how the successful governing of British North America must not demand conformity to "abstract ideas of right" or "mere general theories of government." Rejecting the constitutional model of "a single state or kingdom" for the empire and colonies, he explained that Parliament must govern "according to that nature, and to those circumstances" prevalent in the separate colonies. Burke acknowledged the regional distinctiveness of the various colonies, noting the power of "religion in the northern provinces" as contrasted to the "high aristocratick spirit of Virginia," where experience with slavery made Virginians all the more jealous of their own rights. His plan of reconciliation rested on "a wise and salutary neglect" that conceded "the *legal competency*" of each colony to choose its own way. Only on that basis had the colonies survived and thrived, and only on that basis could the empire continue to retain their loyalty. His empire would follow a model with deep roots in England's legal past before 1700, one that the American colonists assumed to be an enduring constitutional norm and to which they would return when confronted with their own problems of shared sovereignty: an "aggregate of many states, under one common head" where "the subordinate parts have many local privileges and immunities."

Burke did not expect that such a system would function with no problems, and he anticipated the conflicts that have bedeviled American law with its regional variations: "Between these privileges, and the supreme common authority," admitted this historically informed observer, "the line

[14] Smith, *Appeals*, 484–85.

may be extremely nice."[15] With independence Americans suddenly had to confront such variety too, in their halting efforts to create an unprecedented federal system – one that Ayers and Onuf aptly describe as "a complex constitutional regime that would secure the equal rights of localities as well as of individuals." The legacy of early American local variation provided the necessary legitimacy and legal grounding for the federal system, with a template that simultaneously rejected English corruption and provided an alternative suited to the new states and nation.

St. George Tucker, in his effort to produce an edition of Blackstone's *Commentaries* purged of anti-republican doctrines incompatible with American political development, provided a general theory of colonial legal divergence from English law that also accommodated – indeed, emphasized – the resulting regional differences. His product, though motivated by the political impulses of the time, is nonetheless valuable as the thoughtful and careful analysis of two centuries of early American legal history. An ardent states' rights Jeffersonian, Tucker presented a theoretical model and factual narrative to justify regional prescription. The colonies had abandoned many of the rules of English law, he maintained, not out of legal naiveté but rather owing to the isolation that made consulting England on conformity impossible when "surrounded by hostile savage nations, and equally destitute of support from the Crown." Though he acknowledged the absence of a cadre of trained English lawyers in the settlement of the colonies, legal departures had occurred as self-conscious adaptations and the abandonment of rigidities that would have threatened the success of the ventures: "the colonies must either have been swallowed in the vortex of anarchy, or have expired under the *peine forte et dure* of submission to rigid, and impracticable rules."[16]

Tucker knew, too, that "the common, or unwritten law must have been in a state of continual change, from the first institution of parliaments, in the thirteenth century, to the present time," and that over the centuries of settlement colonial law had changed too. Freely interpreting the unwritten law during their colonial history, however, the colonists had done so in different ways. Changes in statute law also had had disparate impacts on the various colonies and had become a source of "endless variety, and disagreement, between the civil institutions of the several colonies." Because only those English statutes in force at the founding of a colony had legal effect there, he explained, older colonies had experienced less Parliamentary intrusion

[15] "Mr. Burke's Speech on Moving His Resolutions for Conciliation with the Colonies" [March 22, 1775], in [Edmund Burke] *On Empire, Liberty, and Reform. Speeches and Letters*, ed. David Bromwich (New Haven, 2000), 66–135, citations at 72, 79, 86, 94.

[16] Tucker, "Of the Unwritten, or Common Law of England," 321.

than newer ones. As a result, some enactments had "no effect or operation in Virginia" but did, say, in Georgia, the colony established most recently. "Those who are acquainted with the prodigious changes made in the laws of England, during the period above-mentioned, will at once discover that there could be no common rule of law between the two colonies, unless that rule could be deduced, without alteration, from a period antecedent to the charter of Virginia. The same observation will hold as to all the other colonies, neither of which were bound by any English law that was not in being at the time of its own establishment."[17]

Tucker added another – "and by far the most copious" – element fueling legal regionalism: "the power which the legislatures of several colonies were perpetually engaged in exercising, viz. that of making laws adapted to the views, principles, situation, and circumstances of their respective inhabitants and countries." Except for the requirement that colonial law be not repugnant to English law, assemblies had been free to pass any laws "deemed applicable to their respective situations and circumstances." Not surprisingly, "the application of this rule in the several colonies will be found to have been as various as their respective soils, climates, and productions." Any effort to understand American legal development, therefore, had to begin by acknowledging the historical force of regional variation and "must again abandon all hope of satisfaction from any *general theory*, and resort to their several charters, provincial establishments, legislative codes, and civil histories, for information."[18]

Tucker had a powerful and compelling reason to include his argument for regional variation with his edition of Blackstone – his abiding political animus against the Federalists. Like Jefferson, he feared what he perceived as a stealth campaign to undermine the true meaning of the federal union and replace it with a consolidated national government. The arch villain in this plot, he believed, was Massachusetts, and he devoted his greatest energies in emphasizing regional autonomy to demonstrating how incompatible were the legal systems of Massachusetts and Virginia, ignoring the colonies separating them. Following Jefferson's lead in emphasizing regional variation in the new nation, Tucker attributed this polarization to vastly differing "local circumstances," as well as to the "differing motives and intentions of the colonists, in their respective migrations." Unashamed at the acquisitive commercial impulse behind the Virginia Company, Tucker admitted that Virginia's settlers had been "allured by the hopes or prospects of immense riches, or a comfortable subsistence, at least." As a result, they had little reason to reject English law and acted to "conform as near as possible both in doctrine and in practice to all the institutions of the mother country."

[17] *Ibid.*, 321–22, 326. [18] *Ibid.*, 327–28.

Those who settled Massachusetts Bay, "[o]n the contrary," represented a dissenting tradition in all aspects of their life. They "fled from what they accounted tyranny, both in church and state" and established a veritable counterculture based on a "prejudice against the laws and government of the parent state, which would induce a general rejection of all such as were inimical to those principles, which prompted them to migrate." The result was a reformist legal culture far removed from the legal conservatism of Virginia. "And as two strait lines, which diverge from each other at the same point, can never after meet or become parallel, so the institutions of two countries, founded upon such discordant principles, could never after be assimilated to each other."[19] The rivalry between the Chesapeake and New England was a staple of the culture of the early republic, and Tucker's contrasts, though perhaps overdrawn, nevertheless reflected the cultural self-awareness of regional divergence that had driven the two apart and produced legal cultures differing in lesser degree in the colonies located between the two. Tucker's observations were not merely casual ruminations, but rather the product of careful research and inquiry, or what Ayers and Onuf would include in their general model of "reciprocal definition" or even mutual hostility – what John Adams described to Jefferson as a "damnable Rivalry between Virginia, and Massachusetts."[20]

Tucker observed a phenomenon no less familiar in his day than in today's post-modern awareness of historicized discourses. The charters of the two bay colonies, Virginia and Massachusetts, both specified that land was to be held "in free and common socage, as of the manor of east Greenwich in the county of Kent." When the two colonies interpreted this clause in diametrically opposite ways, however, Tucker attributed the divergence not only to the lack of "learned counsel" among the colonists but also to legal opportunism flowing from different agendas. The Puritans used the East Greenwich clause to import the local Kentish principle of partible inheritance through gavelkind, as well as an immunity to forfeiture on conviction of treason or felony – rejecting application of "the maxim, the father to the bough, the son to the plough." Only a legally astute legal draftsman – not an artless rustic unfamiliar with the niceties of English common law – would have pounced on such an opening that conformed so usefully to Puritan concerns. Cleverly, it protected the Puritans, whose religious heterodoxy and political fractiousness had exposed them to persecution and prosecution in England, if any among them were to be followed into the

[19] *Ibid.*, 326.

[20] Adams to Jefferson, June 30, 1813, in *The Adams-Jefferson Letters: The Complete Correspondence between Thomas Jefferson and Abigail and John Adams*, ed. Lester J. Cappon (Chapel Hill, 1959), 348.

New World by the Laudian policy that had driven them there in the first place. Moreover, partible inheritance promoted the Puritan goal of communalism by providing land and thus community membership within a broadly inclusive society. By contrast, Virginians, seeking to recreate a traditional hierarchical social order based on more concentrated land ownership, interpreted the clause to establish primogeniture. Protecting a regime of property holders who could jealously suppress and punish rivals, they also "adopted in its fullest latitude" the English law of forfeiture for treason or felony."[21] Memories of England's recent past thus provided the earliest colonists not only with the cautionary experiences of crisis but also with different agendas for the type of legal regime that would further their goals.

Those agendas shaped policy of land use and provided different instrumental designs for law. In Virginia from the beginning, land use had an economically instrumental purpose: the personal benefit of those individuals who owned it. Initially, this meant those investing as stockholders in the Virginia Company of London; with the collapse of the Company, land and its profits became the prize for those who gained control of the colony in Virginia. In Massachusetts land use adhered to more distributive impulses consistent with Puritan goals of a consociational godly community. A town was founded only after a congregation had been gathered, and all dwellings were to be built within a half-mile of the meetinghouse. The "fathers of the towns" were the legal proprietors of all undistributed land, and they granted it according to the godly goals of the gathered community. This took the form of favoring church members with larger lots and awarding land proportionally to the existing hierarchy of wealth – the "outward signs of inward grace" – as well as to family size. Stewardship was a corollary of Puritanism, and the town meeting, which included all heads of households, had to approve land sales to outsiders, who were expected to reside in the town and not enjoy its benefits as absentee landlords. Town bylaws meticulously governed day-to-day affairs, guarding the public trust by regulating the cutting of timber and the taking of fish. Some of these efforts came to naught – population growth quickly made the half-mile rule impractical – but they epitomized a legal culture that also set prices and wages in a committed effort to advance social purposes through property. Although the Bay Colony's first governor, John Winthrop, ultimately lamented that "it was a very sad thing to see how little of a public spirit appeared in the country, but self-love too much," the founding ideal would leave a potent legacy. Throughout the period the New England colonies continued to punish morals offenses that were largely ignored in the southern colonies:

[21] Tucker, "Unwritten, or Common Law," 336.

Maryland courts, in fact, prosecuted only one case of fornication in the seventeenth century.

The common pursuit of legally defined paradigms of social restoration, therefore, embraced competing agendas. For the Virginia Company of London, the model of the colonizing joint-stock enterprise provided a template for efforts to use employees to wrest profits, through commercial and extractive enterprise, from a hinterland inhabited by a hostile population perceived to be alien and intractably savage. Replicating the model of marchland conciliar rule, the Company provided a blueprint for exploitative control of a local laboring population. But even before the Company collapsed in 1624 its colonists had established their own conciliar rule through control of the council at Jamestown and had embarked on constituting themselves an English landed gentry governing through a legal system suited to their acquisitive ambitions. The Company's first councilors employed their powers to the fullest in protecting the financial interests of investors (including themselves), and their successors used them no less sternly to guard their own, now individual, self-interest. Sir Thomas Gates took literally his charge to govern "rather as a Chauncelor then as a judge" and to appoint lesser officials with unspecified and discretionary power as he wished. Gates made the fullest use, too, of the now infamous code known as "Dale's Laws," which conferred the powers of martial law when needed. A rival councilor was shot, allegedly for treason, and protests against Gates's rule were brutally punished. Though the martial code was terminated, it had set a pattern – reinforced by the inclinations and imperatives of a regime bent on re-creating a society ruled by a landed elite controlling the mechanisms of justice – that his successors could follow. Despite the formal authority of the common law, that of conciliar justice operated in tandem with it. And with no objection from England: throughout the 1620s Parliament distinguished the protections of the common law in England from their absence across the seas, advising the tyrannical head of a Cornish enterprise that "he was fitter to have a dominion in America than in this kingdom."

Departure from the common law allowed Virginia and Maryland, like their sister plantation colonies in the West Indies, to devise and refine that most deviant of anomalies in English law, human chattel slavery. Puritanism was not incompatible with slavery – Massachusetts enslaved Indians and Africans, and the Puritan colony of Providence Island in the Gulf of Mexico engaged heavily in the trade and use of African slaves. Lacking an economic demand for such labor, however, the New England colonies had little use for slavery and did not develop the comprehensive slave codes of the South. But the heavy demand for tractable labor on the Chesapeake made African laborers de facto slaves even before there existed any "law" of slavery there. The brutal regime of the first Virginia planters could draw on a tradition of martial discipline to compel work and to punish with discretion. Africans were bought and sold, treated more harshly than white indentured servants, and held to longer terms of servitude. Explicit legal distinctions between blacks and whites began to be made before the Civil War, and by the Restoration slavery existed in law in Virginia and Maryland. Within a generation, slavery would become a central feature of life in the new Carolina colony to their south, where émigré planters from the West Indies brought with them experiences and legal precedents of the islands, which they amalgamated with what they found on the mainland. "Colonial lawyers were analytically opportunistic," writes Jonathan Bush, in creating slave laws, adopting rules that had governed villeins, apprentices, and indentured servants, as well as property under the common law. While the common law for whites moved inexorably toward more freedom, the common law principle of legal thinking *in favorem libertatis* was reversed for blacks. Continental civil law also provided legitimacy for change where needed, making descent of status follow that of the mother, thus providing legal support to the social reality of white owners impregnating their female slaves. Civil law principles of slavery thus survived not only in those colonies settled by Continental kingdoms in New France and New Spain but also in that of New Netherland, where a "half-free" status obtained, in which slaves owned by the Dutch West India Company owed yearly dues and a specified amount of labor to the Company but worked for other masters and were entitled to keep part of their earnings, a relic of civil law *peculium*.

Though it is easy to ignore differences between Protestant Virginia and Roman Catholic Maryland, legal change in the Chesapeake thus moved along parallel lines guided by the needs of a plantation society and by the peculiar pressures placed on it. One especially notable pressure was the frightful mortality rate brought on by the climate and environment and by the demanding work regimen of tobacco cultivation, but aggravated by a persistent malarial pestilence imported from the Kentish lowlands. Early death combined with the sexual imbalance of an economy that attracted far more men than women as emigrants to drastically alter the shape of the family there. With sex ratios ranging from 3:1 to 6:1, it was difficult for families to form, and with mortality rates that usually killed one spouse or the other within seven years, Chesapeake society was one of orphans (defined as a child with one surviving parent) and widows or widowers, in which, Carr and Walsh have told us, "dying husbands were understandably anxious about the welfare of their families."

Colonists in the two Chesapeake colonies afflicted with such misery looked to their legal systems for support. The peculiar demography of the

Chesapeake left a population of widows who could remarry more easily and more often than widowers; on reaching the age of forty-five or beyond the age of reproduction, moreover, they were likely to outlive their husbands. At common law, however, widows were not the heirs of their husbands; to a far greater extent than their brothers in England, therefore, Chesapeake husbands often left their entire estate by will to their widows – up to 20 percent of them in Maryland by the 1660s. Other men in both colonies named their widows as estate executors, allowing them to keep control of family assets as long as possible. On remarriage, women sought legal protection of the property they brought with them to their new marriages. Although the doctrine of coverture, with its corollary of the unity of person, had invalidated contracts made by women before or during marriage, courts in the Chesapeake tended to honor them as expedients to assure property to a widow. In Anglicized New York, by contrast, where such demographic patterns did not exist, the strict application of coverture and other common law rules reversed Dutch practices on female property holding.

Chesapeake courts took a more active role, too, in protecting the assets of orphans. Though a widowed mother was legally the guardian of her children, she had no authority over property bequeathed to them; they were "orphans." In Maryland, where half of all children in the seventeenth century spent some part of their childhood under the care of a stepfather or other guardian, the English bishop's "ordinary court" served as a model for the creation of orphans' courts that examined and audited the arrangements made for orphans. Other powers designed to protect orphans, initially entrusted to the proprietor's Prerogative Court, devolved on county courts. In Virginia, too, the regular county courts assumed similar responsibilities.

The centrality of the family unit placed enormous pressure on the courts of both colonies to assure its survival amid relentless destabilizing forces. But the differing legal responses of the two regions throw into sharp relief the emergence of two regionally different legal cultures. The utopian religious impulse of the Puritans had made the family a cornerstone of their new godly commonwealth, and to make it so they revolutionized domestic relations. Though they never completely replaced the gender hierarchy of English society, they supplemented it with one of godliness. Though the male head of household would not be supplanted, his paternalistic control was to be directed to providing godly attention and concern. Marriage was to be a meeting of hearts before a meeting of hands, so went the axiom of companionate marriage, and husbands were assumed to be caring and protective of their wives. Where environment had produced in the Chesapeake a range of legal protections for a wife's individual property rights, Puritan social philosophy rejected the individualism inherent in such property arrangements. As a result, the Puritans saw less need to provide what they regarded as intrusive and protective legal rules that would diminish the paternal capacity of a husband and weaken the family bond. The ironic result of this philosophy was to entrust husbands with a much greater control over family property and to limit legal methods that wives might use to assure their own control over their own property. Connecticut, the most Puritan of the colonies, provided little or no protection to married women's property rights until well into the eighteenth century. On questions of female property rights, therefore, radical religious tradition refused to provide the protections seen in Virginia and her southern neighbors. Quaker ideals of marriage followed the Puritan tradition, for example, and Penn's laws retained strict rules of coverture.

Nowhere is this distinction illustrated more clearly than in the matter of dower, the common law right of a widow to a life estate in one-third of her late husband's real property, and a portion of his chattels. A husband in Virginia was barred from alienating any real property owned during marriage, as the income from that property (or the use of a part of a home) was assumed to serve as a type of pension for his widow. To sell land, therefore, a husband had to have his wife questioned privately by a magistrate to provide an uncoerced approval of the sale. Virginia and its southern neighbors adhered to the requirement of private examination to a far greater degree than Massachusetts or its New England neighbors, and more so than Pennsylvania or New York too. Maryland courts peremptorily rejected acknowledgments they deemed inadequate. The property subject to dower might be reinterpreted too: though generally dower applied to any land held at any time during marriage, Connecticut limited it to property held by the husband at his death and until 1723 wives lost all separate property rights in land they brought to the marriage. To the south, by contrast, Virginia went so far as to treat chattel slaves as real for the purposes of adding them to dower, assuring widows the labor needed to cultivate crops. Whereas the Chesapeake colonies were generally expanding and giving greater assurance to widows' dower rights, therefore, the New England experiment – especially in Connecticut – tended to limit them.

English wives enjoyed the benefits of the so-called separate estate, an arrangement in trust by which a woman's property was reserved to her use, though under the control of trustees. Separate estates became a useful protection for well-to-do wives in Virginia, but New England discouraged the creation of separate estates, as it also did private separation agreements. What those two arrangements had in common, in addition to the use of legal mechanisms to protect a married woman's property, was their reliance on the use of equity for enforcement. In coming to North America, the Puritans brought with them a distaste for equity and the broad authority of the chancellor, whereas the southern colonies, whose settlers had not supported radical English reform of the law, had no such tradition of resentment. Indeed, the need to protect wives from negligent or wasteful husbands drew on equity's long tradition of guarding the interests of the weak and vulnerable. The Chesapeake colonies, therefore, used equity to enforce separate estates and private separation agreements. To overcome the disabilities created by the common law doctrine of coverture and advance married women's property rights, therefore, English colonists had to resort to non-common law practices, whether through equity or statutory modification. Legal alternatives to the common law appear most clearly, of course, in the Dutch, French, and Spanish colonies. In following the Continental civil law tradition – where, Blackstone observed, unity of person did not exist and "the husband and wife are considered as two distinct persons" – women sued without their husbands and enjoyed community property rights.[22]

Ironically, this enhanced equitable protection of married women's property in the Chesapeake colonies paralleled – and perhaps resulted from – a strong aversion to allowing absolute divorce. Refusing to make absolute divorce an option, Virginia and Maryland equity courts instead enforced separate maintenance agreements unavailable at common law. By contrast, the Puritans' ideal of the companionate marriage led them to allow complete divorce long before it became available in England. Believing that dysfunctional marriage relationships threatened the godly community, they allowed irreparably damaged marriages to be dissolved and encouraged new marriages to form. Massachusetts and Connecticut, in fact, took the additional step of allowing divorce to men and women on the same grounds, whereas English law would perpetuate a formal bias in favor of husbands until 1923. Connecticut refused to grant separation agreements at all and instead led the colonies in granting full divorces, allowing nearly a thousand from 1670 through 1799. Rejecting the path taken by English law to keep divorce a legislative matter, these colonies also vested it in their courts. To the south, absolute divorce was impossible, and remained so in South Carolina until well into the nineteenth century.

Varying attitudes toward equity provide a touchstone for assessing regionalism in American law. Southern colonies established equity courts, whereas New England shunned them, giving only piecemeal equitable authority to common law courts to chancer bonds and to foreclose on mortgages and defeasances. In Pennsylvania, where Thomas Jefferson commented "that the two characters [of North and South] seem to meet and blend and to form a people free from the extremes both of vice and virtue," attitudes toward equity showed the same mixed quality. Indeed, equity amply demonstrates Jefferson's general proposition that the regional

[22] Blackstone, *Commentaries*, 1: 432.

peculiarities of the two regions "grow weaker and weaker by gradation from North to South and South to North." In Pennsylvania as well as in New York, hostility to equity courts rested not so much on ideology as on a practical aversion to their complexity and to the potential abuse by a proprietary government. "[A]s for the Court of Chancery," argued its opponents in the Pennsylvania assembly in 1736, "when well Manag'd is the finest in the world so on the other hand if managed by ignorance, prejudice, or Interest must be the worst." Penn's charter gave the governor and council authority to establish equity courts, but they did so only with the concurrence of the popular assembly, which chose to confer equitable authority only on locally controlled courts and gave the governor the authority of a chancellor only when it trusted him. Similarly, New Yorkers so distrusted their governors that they resisted their chancellor-governors and fought them relentlessly until the 1750s.

The reach of equity extended beyond matters of family and touched many aspects of life. Historically, direct attacks on equity usually identified post-judgment interference as the most irritating grievance. Josiah Quincy, Jr., a Bostonian visiting Williamsburg, Virginia's capital, in 1773, responded in amazement when told how judges of the superior court constituted themselves as a court of equity (sitting without a jury) and reversed the outcome of a case. "I am told that it is no uncommon thing for this court to sit one hour and hear a cause as a Court of Law; and the next hour, perhaps minute, to sit and audit the same cause as a Court of Chancery and equity: and if my information is good, they very frequently give directly contrary decisions. Voltaire, his Huron or Pupil of nature might here exercise their talent of wit and sarcasm."[23] Quincy's objections gave voice to a New England legal culture that favored creditors over debtors and regarded equity as an ill-conceived boon to the indebted. By the middle of the eighteenth century, Massachusetts courts relied heavily on the participation of juries to obtain a community sense of just obligation, and Massachusetts creditors were accustomed to bringing actions in assumpsit or case, where equity was barred. Their notion of a just obligation was incompatible with what Charles Gray has described as equity's help for "imprudent or unlucky debtors." Massachusetts showed little sympathy for debtors who tried to exercise their equity of redemption to stop foreclosure on mortgaged property and led the way in making it easier for a lender to recover such property. In a departure from the common law in property matters as significant as its turn to partible inheritance, Massachusetts allowed judgment creditors to take real property not secured by mortgage in satisfaction of private and public debts.

[23] Josiah Quincy, Jr., "A Journal, interspersed with observations and remarks" [1773], *Massachusetts Historical Society Proceedings*, 49 (1915–16), 465–66.

In Massachusetts, the writ of assumpsit suited a culture that saw a bargain as a bargain and stressed obligation to one's neighbors. Assumpsit, in its various forms, appeared in Massachusetts writs as "case," suggesting a generic simplification and obscuring from historians its more sophisticated content. It dominated the legal recovery of moneys lent and goods or services had and received in Massachusetts, and did so to protect lenders. By contrast, a very different legal culture drove Virginia suitors in another direction, that of putting limits on the claims of creditors. Instead of the written notes or contracts basic to assumpsit, it was more common for Virginia debtors to secure their obligations by giving a bond – a sealed instrument that admitted of no defense other than to deny its validity or plead performance. Virginia creditors were usually debtors too, and this system provided a legal mechanism consistent with a political and moral economy different from that of New England. As creditor-plaintiffs they rarely put their suits before a jury but preferred to allow the bench to assess damages, which in the writ of debt (used to recover on bonds) were calculated more strictly on the value of the undelivered amount and excluded any special damages related to the non-delivery. By contrast, damages in assumpsit might take into account the norms of New England, where juries more commonly heard civil litigation, and as John Adams learned from his practice, they might allow recovery "for more or less." New York, which fell under the economic influence of Boston, adopted this preference, but usually only for relatively small sums; it continued to follow the Dutch use of sealed obligations when larger sums were owed, thus demonstrating once more the meeting of North-South regional differences in the Middle Colonies.

CONCLUSION

It is worth emphasizing the legal precocity of the colonies and the particularities of their legal forms in order to underscore how deeply the process of legal change advanced ideological goals and to justify the claim that what appears to be inexpert rustic degeneracy in the law actually represents a more sophisticated eclecticism. The great changes in English commercial law at roughly this same time period are not seen as crude or rustic, though some at the time might have denounced such innovations as unwarranted: Sir John Holt's disapproval of legal innovation being "invented in Lombard Street" parallels the process of legal innovation in the courts of distant provinces, which anticipated changes later adopted in England. The "Duke's Laws" issued by the Duke of York (later James II) after the conquest of New Netherland, for example, accepted Dutch rules on the assignability of obligations well before English courts did.

Ultimately – when the newly independent states assembled to define a national legal system and establish a federal judiciary – slavery epitomized and solidified regionalism in American law. But the vast chasm between North and South over the law of human chattel was only one dimension of a larger historical process that drew on many English traditions and was accelerated by the contingencies of timing at an initial moment of protean legal innovation, when the pressures of social crisis led English peoples on both sides of the Atlantic to look to legal institutions for support and protection. When a moment of expanding market economy later in the seventeenth century threw together diverse and assertive peoples, a third such cultural hearth emerged in the mid-Atlantic colonies, combining many of the existing legal impulses and introducing innovations of its own. Within a century, regional distinctions had become so entrenched that even the powerful force of an anglicizing Parliament could not reverse them. Indeed, that effort ultimately precipitated an outburst of regional self-assertion and legal self-identification in the newly created American republic, one that exists to this day.

6

PENALITY AND THE COLONIAL PROJECT: CRIME, PUNISHMENT, AND THE REGULATION OF MORALS IN EARLY AMERICA

MICHAEL MERANZE

American criminal law was forged in the crucible of the colonial enterprise. Part British transplant and part American construction, the criminal law gave vivid and physical form to the effort to turn the Americas into an offshoot of Europe. Courtrooms and courthouses, gallows and whipping posts, jails and prisons all marked the American landscape with the material imprint of European institutions. In transporting British legal forms and traditions, colonial authorities aimed to maintain their own claims to civility on the borderlands of their cultural world while establishing their authority over natives and settlers. But no simple transfer of legal culture and practice was possible in the colonial world. Whatever the intentions of imperial officials or initial settlers, the process of colonization and the construction of unequal colonial societies produced legal systems that selectively appropriated and distorted tendencies unfolding in the metropolis itself.

During the seventeenth century, the crisis of the British state allowed disparate colonial legal systems and cultures to develop. The highly decentralized nature of British expansion, combined with the multiplicity of British legal traditions, led to a pronounced juridical diversity in early American law. Despite a shared acknowledgment of English sovereignty and the common law, British colonialism produced not a centralized system of criminal law but a variety of penal cultures. The religious conflicts that plagued the seventeenth-century English polity only exacerbated these developments as the founding of settler colonies during the post-Reformation struggles over religion and the pursuit of religious utopias charged the criminal law with particular sacred meanings. Combined with the British suspicion of political centralization, the lack of effective imperial oversight allowed local elites to turn the law to their own purposes, while the absence of meaningful police intensified the importance of publicly imposed corporal penalties. The fragmentation of the English polity was inscribed on the juridical culture of British colonial world.

During the eighteenth century, the growing power of the imperial state challenged the relatively autonomous and disparate character of colonial criminal law. The expansion of penal transportation after 1718 and the spread of vice-admiralty courts and imperial bureaucracies underlined the mounting presence of imperial authorities in colonial legal institutions. Imperial officials displayed an increasing assertiveness in their review of colonial legislation. The extension of British colonization itself meant that the reach of British law was extended throughout the North American seaboard, as colonial desires to mimic British gentility aided the spread of more complex legal forms, practices, and institutions. Colonial penality became more of a piece. To be sure, the reality of different colonies and legal cultures precluded a uniformity of law and practice. But compared to the seventeenth century, the eighteenth century witnessed an increasing imperialization of the criminal law throughout the mainland colonies.

Colonists' relationship to metropolitan power, however, was only part of the story of penal culture and practice; the colonial world and the contests of colonization played an equal role. Beginning in the seventeenth century, the criminal justice system became a forum for the adjudication of conflicts between settlers and Native Americans *and* a system for the assertion of colonists' authority. During the same period, the criminal justice system rapidly became embedded in the regulation and production of colonial labor systems and labor discipline. Whether enforcing the expansion of bound labor, or supplementing a father's power to demand family labor, or reinforcing the infliction of punishment aboard ship, the criminal law provided sanction for the labor coercion that made colonial expansion and maritime integration possible. Nowhere was the relationship between colonial law and labor organization more striking than in the ways that the criminal law echoed the spread of racialized chattel slavery in the late seventeenth and eighteenth centuries. The criminal law not only supported the master's right to physical punishment but through the development of dual systems of courts and dual practices of punishment, it also made material the reality that there was one law for free people and another for bonds-people.

All these systems – imperial and colonial, free and slave – were predicated on the degradation of the body. Whether in the hands of metropolitan or colonial authorities, violence traversed the criminal law. Early American criminal justice operated in a series of public forums (the courthouse, the jail, the whipping post, and the scaffold) to reinforce not only the power of the law but also the structures of locally dominant authorities. Punishment combined shame, pain, death, financial penalties, and forms of symbolic and physical exclusion to assert the authority of law and government. The repertoire of punishments changed little, though variation would be found in their deployment, valuation, and contexts. Throughout the colonial era the courts and the places of punishment were open to the community and spoke in its name.

The revolutionary crisis transformed but did not transcend these colonial patterns. The imperial reorganization that followed the Seven Years War included, among many other elements, a program to weaken the reach of local juries even as the violence that accompanied colonial resistance ultimately found its place in courtrooms. The result was a rapid politicization of the penal world on land and sea. During the 1760s and the 1770s British colonials and imperial officials debated the appropriate forms of criminal law and punishment, while independence spurred a search for new "republican" forms of penality. Paradoxically, the revolutionary upheaval fused penality and the American relationship to imperial culture even more tightly together.

The end result was a selective appropriation of colonial practices and legacies. During the Revolution and into the Early Republic, the diversity of local practices was not lost, but the larger milieu changed dramatically. Most obviously, the imperial context disappeared. As a result, criminal justice became even more the purview of individual states. But at the same time, critics building on a transatlantic genteel critique of public punishments overthrew the elite consensus behind publicly inflicted punishments of pain, shame, and death. The emergence of reformative incarceration, growing opposition to capital punishment, and efforts to simplify and moderate penal codes all combined to call into question criminal punishments throughout the new nation.

Contending penal theories and practices divided the new nation regionally. In the slave South, despite the emergence of penitentiaries, penality continued to parallel the colonial world of the British West Indies; in the North, penal practice identified itself with the bourgeois and religious reformers of metropolitan England. Equally significant, the different trajectories of reform, combined with the erosion of northern slavery, meant that criminal punishments not only divided according to region but also became a source of division among regions. In new and important ways, the ideologies and practices of punishment became linked to the dominant economic forms of the North and the South in the aftermath of revolution.

I. THE IMPERIAL BRITISH CONTEXT

Despite the variety of colonial settings and the vagaries of colonial encounters, English forms and imperial authorities determined the parameters of criminal justice in early British America. Although the peoples of the colonial periphery (Europeans, Africans, and Americans) were disparate, English standards defined legality and illegality in the colonies. In that sense at least, criminal justice in the British colonies was one imprint of the power of Britain's imperial power itself. Whatever alternate systems of punishment people brought to the colonies, once incorporated into the British colonial order, the peoples of America faced penal practices modeled on English ways. In particular, criminal justice in early America partook of England's distinctive emphasis on corporal symbolism. Famously lacking a "continental"-style police force, the English relied on the public display of state violence to assert the supremacy of the law. Their North Atlantic colonies would follow suit.

Throughout the seventeenth and eighteenth centuries, capital punishment stood at the heart of the British penal system. The English criminal code possessed an extremely long and continually increasing list of capital crimes – upward of 200 capital offenses by the eighteenth century. Not only murder, rape, petty treason, and serious crimes against property could lead to the ultimate penalty; British lawmakers extended the reach of capital sanctions in bewilderingly complicated directions. To be sure, many capital offenses were highly particular, such as offenses against particular forms of property or even against the property of specific companies. And their actual deployment was irregular. But the continued expansion of capital punishment points to an essential fact of British criminal law: the physical and symbolic center of punishment in Great Britain was the gallows.

Punishment stood at the intersection of political and moral authority in early modern Britain. Whether at the whipping post, the pillory, or the gallows, state-inflicted physical degradation of the body was a crucial site for the articulation of authority and for the fusing together of religious and political symbolism. England remained, however diffusely, a Christian country. The body under duress drew on powerful Christian symbols and narratives. As countless Divines reminded their listeners, magistrates were expected to "Beareth Not the Sword in Vain." Punishments maintained the social order; indeed they partook of the hand of God. In this world, the state stood in for the Divine and the Divine stood as justification for the state; the body itself stood as a crucial representation of the social order. The condemned body, in particular, figured in a wider political symbolism that imagined society itself as a great corporeal unity. Its sufferings were a microcosm of the sufferings the social body underwent through crime. The distresses of physical punishment thus achieved their great power not simply by virtue of the universal experience of pain; the body at the scaffold drew on some of the most powerful symbols of British culture.

Nonetheless, there were certain countervailing tendencies. The widespread availability of benefit of clergy and the frequent recourse to "pious perjury" (that is, the jury practice of devaluing stolen property so that theft did not reach the threshold of a felony) restrained the actual use of capital punishments. On the recommendations of the judges and prosecutors, the Crown frequently granted pardons. Throughout the eighteenth century – and with increasing frequency after mid-century – officials and commentators expressed deep concern over the efficacy of capital punishment. Indeed, by the 1770s and 1780s, the extent, if not the legitimacy, of the use of capital punishment was under serious question. Even William Blackstone (hardly the legal radical) expressed his own doubts over the reach of capital punishments:

> For, though the end of punishment is to deter men from offending, it never can follow from thence, that it is lawful to deter them at any rate and by any means; since there may be unlawful methods of enforcing obedience even to the justest laws. Every humane legislator will be therefore extremely cautious of establishing laws that inflict the penalty of death, especially for slight offences, or such as are merely positive. . . . Where the evil to be prevented is not adequate to the violence of the preventive, a sovereign that thinks seriously can never justify such a law to the dictates of conscience and humanity.[1]

Blackstone discreetly left it unsaid how far the sovereigns of England had met his test.

Most importantly for the colonial situation, from the early eighteenth century onward the penalty of transportation assumed greater and greater importance. The Transportation Act of 1718 expanded the use of penal transportation to the colonies while placing transportation firmly under the control of the government. Transportation allowed English authorities to lessen their reliance on secondary punishments, such as whipping, without being forced into dramatically expanding their infliction of capital sanctions. Despite the profusion of new capital statutes, in the years after the passage of the Transportation Act, capital punishment was most frequently inflicted for long-standing offenses (murder, burglary, robbery), rather than for the new more expanded list of crimes against particular forms of property. From the English vantage point transportation both rationalized and intensified penal powers while avoiding too great a reliance on sanguinary penalties. From the vantage point of the colonies, as we shall see, transportation looked very different.

Because the colonies were embedded within the empire, the colonial criminal justice system was never autonomous of imperial forces. Most obvious were the cases where royal officials overturned colonial efforts to reshape the criminal laws. Of equal significance was the imperial regulation of trade, which produced not only customs legislation and customs enforcement but

[1] William Blackstone, *Commentaries on the Laws of England*, ed. Thomas A. Green (Chicago, 1979), 4: 10–11.

also the whole system of vice-admiralty courts. Perhaps most important, the simple fact of empire systematically affected the social contexts of colonial justice. Colonial societies did not exist in isolation and could not ignore the geopolitical realities of intermittent warfare or the demographic realities of constant immigration. The cultural and social diversity of colonial societies existed because of empire, not despite it. Though local structures and interests guided the day-to-day operations of criminal justice in the colonies, the terrain on which the criminal law operated could never be fully separated from its imperial context.

II. CRIMINAL LAW, COLONIAL VIOLENCE

If the imperial context shaped the criminal law, the law itself played an ambiguous role in the process of colonization. Throughout North America the English sought to subject the native populations to English legal forms and institutions. Not surprisingly Indians, with their own very different senses of justice, did not always share the colonists' enthusiasm for English law. Whereas the English assumed that criminal justice was a state activity to determine and punish individual responsibility, Native Americans placed a far greater emphasis on community-based reconciliation and recompense. English notions of responsibility could conflict with native notions of responsibility; what determined justice in those instances was the balance of forces. As a result, the question of jurisdiction and of appropriate practice loomed large in the penal relationship between colonists and natives. In its very existence the law became a terrain of conflict between settlers and natives. To be sure, Native Americans did actively participate in colonial legal proceedings, often with great success. But of greater importance than individual cases or punishments was the larger colonial setting of legal practice and culture. And in that larger setting the colonists eventually determined the rules.

In the earliest years of settlement the reach of English law and the capacity of Englishmen to subject natives to their punishments and disciplines were limited. As they had demonstrated in Ireland, English elites were quite happy to subject dependent, or legally foreign, populations to practices unsuited for a "freeborn Englishmen." Within the limits posed by their relative military and political weakness, Virginia authorities, for example, were willing, when able, to subject Native Americans to coercive legal punishments. In both Massachusetts and Plymouth, colonial authorities aimed to ensure that natives would be brought before English courts and punished according to English law. Their success was mixed. Given the power of neighboring native groups, the English were not always able to ensure the delivery of natives they suspected of criminal offenses. Moreover, the

English authorities recognized the practical necessity of punishing colonists accused of crimes against Indians. But even in the earliest years colonists were able to make greater demands on the natives than the natives made on colonists. And the inequality of legal cultures would only grow.

Colonial authorities had to balance their desire to control the native populations with their equally strong desire not to provoke native violence. The result was to create a formally equal if contextually unequal criminal justice system. In New England, at least prior to King Philip's War, treatment of indigenous defendants was largely the same as treatment of colonial defendants. Punishments were not systematically different, the range of crimes that brought natives to the bar was for the most part similar, and both colonists and natives were subject to the same procedures. But the courts and juries rarely included native members, and the larger tendency of the legal system was to impose English institutions, laws, and regulations on the native populations. In this trajectory the criminal law replicated and reinforced the inequalities of the colonial relationship.

Coercive violence against Native Americans was recurrent in the seventeenth century. However, most violence took place in venues outside the criminal law. It does not appear, in other words, that the criminal law was a central tool for colonizing the native populations. To suggest that the criminal law played a marginal role is not to deny the everyday violence of the colonization process nor to ignore the incidents when Native Americans were subject to the punitive sanctions of the law. Nor is it to deny the manifold ways that the rhetoric of the law and its claims could be mobilized to cast the natives as savage. It is to suggest merely that relations between natives and settlers in the seventeenth century took place largely outside of the criminal courts and hence that the business of the criminal courts was not significantly concerned with Native Americans.

Still, colonists did deploy the rhetoric of the law and social discipline against the indigenous populations. Indeed, the spread of colonial power meant that over time the law did become a more important tool for colonizing the peoples of early America. In New England, to give but one example, colonial authorities in the latter part of the seventeenth century increasingly passed and enforced laws that regulated native access to alcohol and guns. And in the years following King Philip's War colonists took active steps to regulate and confine Indian populations. The increased control following King Philip's War was, in fact, the most dramatic example of the changing relationship between law and power. In the years following the war the Massachusetts government restructured Indian governance, created means for intensified oversight of the native population, and took steps toward limiting and defining Indian space. These actions were only the most concentrated moment of a much larger process: the ongoing reduction of autonomy for those native groups closest to the English. From that point on, everywhere that colonists and natives met the criminal law became a source of conflict as well as conflict resolution. By the eighteenth century, along the seaboard at least, those conflicts had been settled in favor of English law and English punishments. Natives and newcomers might be tried in the same way, but more and more that way was English.

III. THE PUBLICITY OF PUNISHMENT IN COLONIAL BRITISH AMERICA

For the most part, Britain's American colonists did not engage in any radical experimentation in the criminal punishments they imposed on the condemned. As members of the empire, they quite faithfully reproduced the repertoire of punishments in place in Britain. The number of capital offenses was not as great in the colonies as in the mother country, but the gallows anchored criminal justice in America as it did in Great Britain. From the earliest settlements in Virginia, Plymouth, and Massachusetts Bay, through the Restoration colonies from Pennsylvania to the Carolinas, and on to the utopian experiment in Georgia, capital punishment was a constant presence in social life. With the brief exception of early New England and Pennsylvania, hanging was imposed for crimes against property as well as persons. To be sure, in quantitative terms, the death penalty was not deployed on the same scale as in England. It was possible for counties, and even colonies, to go several years without witnessing an execution. Colonists imposed secondary corporal punishment and fines far more frequently than they imposed death. But as a threat the death penalty hung over the penal practices of the British in America as it hung over England itself. It was, after all, the point where power over life and death, the intersection of the state and the Divine, assumed its sharpest relief. Not simply as a legal category, then, but as social reality, the death penalty took up a settled position in the landscape of colonial British America.

Throughout the British colonies criminal punishments operated in a fundamentally public manner. Not only was justice imposed in the name of the public, it took place before the public and through the medium of denizens of the district. Courts were primarily situated in local communities, and their proceedings were open to the local population. Sentences were, for the most part, handed down by local notables and juries. For the free inhabitants of the colonies, criminal justice took place in public venues modeled on England. Although justices of the peace could hand down summary judgments for minor offenses, most criminal penalties against the body were inflicted under the authority of courts of Quarter Sessions or their equivalent. Capital cases took place in even more rarified surroundings.

The leading magistrates of the colony would oversee the trying of capital offenses in courtrooms marked by special ritual and pomp.

To be sure, these trials were often ramshackle affairs. Courts, especially in the early years of the colonies, frequently sat in commercial places (taverns, inns, etc.). Justice was both swift and decisive. Many sessions handled multiple cases in a day, trial testimony was brief, and the defendant stood at a grave disadvantage if he or she lacked support in the community. Procedure, though modeled on the English forms, was simplified. This situation meant that, like punishment itself, the process of criminal justice was eminently public. The community – through the jury and the audience – was implicated in the decisions of the courts. It may have been small comfort to the convicted, but the colonial court system prided itself on its openness to scrutiny. And there is little evidence that the legitimacy of the law was ever in doubt among the colonists.

As in England, hanging was an important communal practice. On execution day, crowds numbering in the thousands, some traveling hundreds of miles, could converge on the hanging scene. Authorities sought to manage these events with great care, careful to provide a detailed script in the hope of controlling the meaning and message of the hanging. In New England, especially, the execution itself was a highly ritualized event. A parade from the jail to the place of execution would wind its way through the town or city; sermons – some by the leading ministers of the area – would precede and follow the hangings; the condemned often provided last words and confessions; and prayers would be said for his or her soul. Reports of the deaths, even the briefest of comments, spread outward – by word of mouth, letter, newspaper, and, again especially in New England, by pamphlet.

The authorities aimed to ensure the greatest solemnity and dignity to the proceedings. On hanging day, after all, the state was taking up the sword and destroying the gift of life. In their justifications, ministers recognized the extremity of the law's actions. Nothing less than the good of all sanctioned the resort to force. Describing the purposes of an execution of a murderer in 1754, Charles Chauncy insisted: "And this is the Design of this Day's *Execution*. It is intended for the *common Good*, by exhibiting an Example of *public Vengeance*: Such an one as is fitted to curb the Lusts of Men, and prevent their breaking forth in *murderous* Attempts upon the Life of their Neighbour. We should view it in his Light and be deterred from *that Crime* which will expose us to be cut off by the Hand of *civil Justice*."[2] None, ministers and

[2] Charles Chauncy, *The Horrid Nature, and Enormous Guilt of Murder. A Sermon Preached at the Thursday Lecture in Boston, November 19th, 1754, The Day of the Execution of William Wieer, for the Murder of William Chism*. (Boston, 1754), 22.

colonial officials insisted, should mistake the absolutely necessary nature of the state's violence.

Throughout the colonial period, the legitimacy of these hanging days went largely unchallenged. Because people of different classes and races, men, and women attended, leading ministers (like Chauncy or, earlier, Increase and Cotton Mather) eagerly participated in the ceremony, seeing it – not without reason – as their best opportunity to speak to a mass of people. In 1693, for example, Cotton Mather noted in his diary that "by a very strange Providence" he was called to speak before an execution. "I did then with the special Assistance of Heaven, make and preach a Sermon.... Whereat one of the greatest Assemblies, ever known in these parts of the World, was come together."[3] Indeed, many attended executions quite matter-of-factly. Samuel Sewall, for one, repetitively noted executions (some of which he attended) with scarce an emotion. But that they were powerful rituals cannot be denied. Sewall may have kept his own emotions concealed, but others did not. Commenting on the execution of seven pirates in Boston Harbor on June 29, 1704, Sewall noted, "When the Scaffold was let sink, there was such a screech of the Women that my wife heard it sitting in our Entry next to the Orchard, and was much surprised at it.... Our house is a full mile from the place."[4]

Hanging was not the most painful death authorities employed. Some of the condemned were put to death by burning. Burning was apparently limited to crimes that the authorities considered outright attacks on the social order: witchcraft, wives committing petit treason, and slaves involved in (alleged) revolt. Nor did penalties end with death. Some criminals were hung in chains, others were dissected. Each additional penalty was designed to increase punishment's level of terror. Each powerfully reveals the extent to which the body was caught up in a public economy of punishment.

A wide range of public punishments symbolically surrounded the gallows. Throughout early America both capital defendants and state authorities mobilized a complex system of discretion to mitigate capital sentences. Pardons and reprieves were given frequently. Interestingly, they were frequently dramatized by the calculated display of last-minute mercy. Many criminals did not learn of their reprieve until they had already been taken to the gallows, some having already had the noose put around their necks (some who knew they had been pardoned were sentenced to stand on the gallows with the noose around their neck). In addition, the colonists

[3] *Diary of Cotton Mather*, ed. Worthington Chauncey Ford (New York, 1957 [1911]), 1: 165.

[4] Samuel Sewall, *The Diary of Samuel Sewall, 1674–1708*, ed. M. Halsey Thomas (New York, 1973), 1: 509.

also employed a varied repertoire of secondary corporal penalties. Colonial authorities aimed to inflict pain on the bodies and humiliation on the souls of criminal offenders. They inflicted whippings (sometimes at a whipping post and sometimes at a cart's tail), imposed time in the pillory (with or without additional duress from onlookers), branded, bored holes in tongues, defaced, and cropped ears. If the death penalty most dramatically imposed death, the more common public punishments wracked the bodies of offenders and did so with the intent of display. Whippings, after all, were not simply painful; they were public. In 1736, for example, the Philadelphia authorities made certain that one woman convicted of picking pockets during a market day was "exposed during the Market upon the Balcony of the Court-House with her Face towards the People, that every Body might know her; after which she received a Whipping."[5] Some sense of the disgrace a whipping entailed can be seen in a Dutch father's reaction to his son's sentence of a whipping for fornication in 1662. In his request to the New Haven magistrates to change the sentence to a fine he explained that the Dutch thought that "to be corporally punished was such an infamy . . . that they looked upon such noe better than a dog & not fit for Commerce with them & soe his sonne would be undone Thereby."[6] Humiliation and pain were the coin of this particular penal realm.

As in England then, public punishments operated on manifold levels. Clearly they imposed both pain and death. But they also turned the body into a symbol: of the power of the law, of God's love and anger, of the severity and mercy of the authorities. The body of the condemned was the meeting point for both sacred and secular authority, and reactions to it moved from the grimly satisfied to the indifferent through the mournfully sympathetic to the emotionally overwhelmed. Despite their relative infrequency, public punishments were central rituals to colonial authority and to the colonial imagination. In the New World setting, English forms of punishment may have been especially important. Through their violence to the body of the condemned, the authorities sought to reaffirm the community's commitments to the demands of God and of civilization.

Paradoxically, the intermittent and peripatetic nature of punishments inscribed criminal justice more widely on the social landscape. Lacking distinct and isolated penal institutions, early Americans witnessed punishments and judicial proceedings in a wide variety of venues. Spaces normally taken up by trade or recreation could be seized temporarily for the purpose of criminal justice. If the law lacked the majesty that it possessed in the

[5] *Pennsylvania Gazette*, October 21–28, 1736.

[6] Franklin B. Dexter, ed., *New Haven Town Records, 1649–1684* (New Haven, 1917–1919), 2: 12.

metropolitan countries, its very diffuseness signified that the law was remaking the new world in its own interest. The distinction between everyday and official spaces, between the secular and the sacred was blurred thereby. The criminal law and its violence could appear in unexpected places.

IV. THE SEVENTEENTH CENTURY: REGION, RELIGION, AND LABOR

The trajectories of criminal law in the seventeenth century established the diversity of penal practices that would remain present in mainland British North America through the eighteenth century. The fiscal limits of the English state meant that control over overseas organization rapidly devolved into the hands of colonial elites. And the lack of effective church oversight in post-Reformation England meant that unlike the Spanish case, the Church of England was unable to intervene powerfully into colonial affairs. As a result, the distinctive local influences of region, religion, and labor systems shaped colonial reorganizations of English practice. In the seventeenth century, both New England and the Chesapeake shared a common range of punishments and legal procedures. But the effects of local milieu inflected them in particular – and differently coercive – directions. Religion in New England and bound labor in the Chesapeake helped organize the criminal law as they did so many other aspects of the colonial project.

The Chesapeake Colonies

In the Chesapeake colonies, planter demands for labor powerfully shaped the development of the system of punishment and moral regulation. Drawing selectively on the English experience in Ireland as well as the evolution of systems of labor discipline, Virginians deployed the public punishments common to the Anglophone world in the interest of the planters' pursuit of wealth. The rapid development of a tobacco economy and the concomitant turn to servitude meant that Virginia's criminal law became significantly enmeshed in sustaining the power of masters. The instability of the ruling elite meant that the criminal law in both Maryland and Virginia was recurrently deployed to consolidate fragile authority. From its earliest years, criminal justice in Virginia was marked by a highly authoritarian streak. Maryland appears to have mimicked its neighbor. That the law was there to maintain the majesty of authority was never in doubt.

In large part, the Chesapeake colonies simply circulated the common penal coin of seventeenth-century England. Early on Virginians adopted the common forms of investigation and prosecution (indictment, arrest, coroner's courts, etc.), institutionalized both grand juries and magisterial investigations, and established a simplified system of courts (at the county and colony level) that assumed the myriad functions handled by the diverse judicial institutions of the mother country. The authorities certainly hanged offenders – especially in the colonies' early years – although it is impossible to tell with what frequency. The whip and the fine were frequent tools of authority. Most trials took place summarily or before county justices, and they took place swiftly.

Crime in the seventeenth century appears to have been limited. Records document more prosecutions for slander (suggesting the insecurity of authority and instability of society) than for theft. One case can indicate the dynamic involved in the protection of authority. One woman in Lower Norfolk County had been convicted of slandering a neighbor. Condemned to beg forgiveness in her church, she refused; she further refused to appear before the court itself to answer for her refusal. The Justices responded as follows:

> The sheriff shall take her to the house of a commissioner and there she shall receive twenty lashes; she is then to be taken to church the next Sabbath to make confession according to the former order of the court. If she refuses, she is to be taken to a commissioner and to be given thirty lashes, and again given opportunity to do penance in church. If she still refuses to obey the order of the court, she is then to receive fifty lashes. If she continues in her contempt, she is to receive fifty lashes, and thereafter fifty every Monday until she performs her penance.[7]

The support of authority was also marked in Maryland.

But within this general commonality, Chesapeake authorities fashioned their criminal laws in particular ways. Guided by English practice in the subjugation of Ireland, Virginia's early leaders had quickly turned to military models for governing the colony: the colony's formative years saw the routine deployment – or at least the threat – of hanging and beating. From the first charter onward, non-capital defendants were tried summarily and with little formality. Under *The Lawes and Orders, Divine, Morall, and Martiall*, commonly known as Dale's Laws, the colony's legal regime took on a visibly authoritarian tinge. Although the overt system of martial law expired in 1619, its basic emphasis on the coercive control of labor shaped Virginia's history throughout the seventeenth century. To be sure, throughout the seventeenth century, Virginia's lawmakers made greater and greater use of common law practices. But it must be remembered that common law rights did not necessarily translate into actual practice for all subjects. In the case of Virginia two factors came into play: the first was the

[7] "Lower Norfolk County Records, 1637–1643," quoted in Oliver Chitwood, *Justice in Colonial Virginia* (Baltimore, 1905), 89–90.

colonial setting, the second the demographic fact of a large servant population. These two issues defined the distinctiveness of the criminal law in the seventeenth-century Chesapeake.

The criminal law was crucially involved in cases involving labor discipline and the status of laborers. Having failed to find a sufficient labor supply among the native populations, Chesapeake planters found and held indentured servants. It is here, indeed, that one can detect the beginnings of a characteristic Chesapeake structure of punishment and moral regulation. From the early years of the seventeenth century, courts and officials deployed the criminal law either to debase freemen to the status of servants or to coerce servants into additional labor time. Although the number of criminal trials through the 1620s appears small, courts began to intervene in questions arising from fornication, Sabbath-breaking, and petty theft, among others. Authorities adopted the conventional elite English suspicion of young laborers and, in a situation where young unattached laborers were the predominant demographic group, magnified it. Given the thin state of institutional development in seventeenth-century Virginia, the law and its constraints assumed a large role in supporting planter discipline. To be sure, labor discipline remained primarily a task of masters. Still, the sanctions of the criminal law provided a powerful backdrop to the efforts of individual planters, and the law ensured that servants would not find an easy path to freedom. The criminal law in the Chesapeake, then, was powerfully implicated in master-servant relations and in upholding the structures of the labor system.

The dispersed population and an extremely hierarchical society combined to devolve great power into the hands of local justices of the peace. Although the General Court in Jamestown maintained control over felony prosecutions (and felony defendants were, for most of the seventeenth century, compelled to travel to Jamestown), local justices were sometimes empowered to act as special courts of Oyer and Terminer and were always expected to conduct preliminary inquiries into felonies and determine who should be sent to the General Court. Combined with their power over petty offenses and given the relative lack of detailed rules for adjudication (justices drew on practical manuals more than explicit rules), the local justices were crucial figures in the process of criminal justice. Given their ties to the planter class, they were equally crucial figures in the maintenance of local authority.

The New England Colonies

Those who governed the seventeenth-century New England colonies fused religion with the law by building on the Tudor and Stuart intensification of the powers of magistrates while infusing that structure with the Puritan critique of England's corruption. On the one hand, Massachusetts Bay and its offshoots constructed dual systems for the enforcement of law and morals: both church and state had important responsibilities to ferret out and punish sin and crime. On the other, they transformed their criminal justice systems in accord with their reading of biblical precedents: New Englanders significantly modified dominant English practice in the areas of evidence and statutory definitions of crimes.

The direct influence of religious doctrine on legal practice would not survive the seventeenth century. Nevertheless the importance of religion was unmistakable in the ways that the New England colonies dealt with crime, immorality, and transgression in their early decades. New England churches practiced a detailed surveillance over the lives of their members and regulated their morality through chastisement and excommunication. In New Haven the mechanisms of Puritan surveillance were especially strong. Under the leadership of Theophilus Eaton, New Haven authorities imposed a highly personalized and religious form of legal authority. Due partly to its small size and partly to its powerful patriarchal magistracy, New Haven produced a society remarkably free from violence. In Massachusetts, matters were more complicated. Early settlers may have hoped to create God's kingdom, but as the gradual expansion of the criminal code demonstrates, any expectation on the part of the colony's founders that they would govern an immaculately God-fearing and law-abiding populace diminished rapidly.

Throughout the century, both churches and courts remained deeply involved in the regulation of morals and crime. From violations of sexual propriety to crimes against persons and property, the importance of religion intersected with the law in a variety of crucial ways. Under normal circumstances, a parallel system of moral regulation existed: churches would probe into the moral behavior of their congregants, whereas magistrates would pursue and discipline violators of the colony's legal codes. But at times, as in the Antinomian crisis of the 1630s, the struggles with Quakers in the 1660s, or the witchcraft trials throughout the century, enforcing law on behalf of both the Divine and the human could prove explosive. Under these circumstances, the Puritan commitment to dual regulation meant that theological and religious differences intersected with political structures in ways that threatened the existence of the colony itself. In the aftermath of the revocation of the Massachusetts charter and the legal and cultural fallout of the witchcraft trials of the 1690s, criminal justice and religious orthodoxy would take separate paths. But that the criminal justice system of Massachusetts Bay should remain devoted to the policing of God's way was never in doubt.

Connecticut steered a course closer to Massachusetts than to New Haven. In fact, when the New Haven colony was absorbed into its larger neighbor the early emphasis on magisterial piety faded away. But in whatever variation, the Puritan emphasis on intrusive surveillance and magisterial inquisition was strong – as was the necessity for that surveillance and inquisition to be practiced.

Through their intense emphasis on the practice of conscience, the churches helped construct a culture of communal inquiry into guilt and accustomed early New Englanders to a culture of confession. As a result, New England authorities expected defendants to admit guilt without argument. In seventeenth-century New Haven, for example, the accused were subject to a series of intense interrogations by the colony's leading figures both before and during trial. The search for confession was quite successful. In the twenty years of the New Haven colony, over half of all defendants confessed to their crimes; indeed in the period from 1645–58 more than 80 percent of defendants confessed. New Haven was extreme in its success, but its emphasis on confession was not unique.

The New England colonies tailored their codes in accord with their understanding of Divine ordinance. In early Massachusetts, authorities transposed biblical penalties into the legal system. Adultery, worshiping false gods, and blasphemy among other offenses were capital crimes in the early years of the colony. But at the same time, the colony broke from the English tendency to impose capital punishment for crimes against property (initially no crimes against property were capital). In its *Body of Liberties* (1641), the colony limited itself to twelve capital offenses, each with appropriate biblical justification. As the seventeenth century progressed, however, the colony's code moved more in alignment with the English; by the latter part of the century the list had grown to at least twenty-five capital offenses. Not only did they include serious crimes against the person (rape, murder) but also an expanding list of crimes against property. Nor were capital sanctions the only tools at the hands of the state. The New England colonies could, and did, employ a wide range of other penalties, including whipping, pillorying, fining, branding, marking, boring the tongue, and banishment. The statutory history of those colonies that split off from Massachusetts Bay largely repeated the history of the Puritan Commonwealth.

If New Englanders insisted that crime and sin be dealt with publicly, that did not mean they insisted they be dealt with by juries. Throughout much of the seventeenth century, jury trials in non-capital cases were quite few in number. In New Haven, juries were effectively abolished; in Massachusetts and Connecticut their role was severely circumscribed. Only in Rhode Island did trial by jury in lesser criminal cases take a firm hold. Most criminal cases (short of capital crimes) took place either summarily or before magistrates in court. Guilt needed to be established in public, but that did not mean that it had to be established by the public. Although these trends (outside of New Haven at least) were never unchallenged, in the orthodox colonies of New England magistrates retained a firm control over the mechanisms of criminal punishment and social discipline. This control was largely in keeping with the growing English emphasis on summary judgment, but the Puritan emphasis on a patriarchal magistracy fused legal practice with the larger structure of authority in a particularly powerful way. Indeed, the magistrates had such authority in the early years of Massachusetts Bay that the question of magisterial discretion in criminal punishments was an ongoing – and also heated – issue. Although the gradual expansion of the written law may have curbed the autonomy of the magistrates somewhat, the continued importance of summary judgments demonstrated that their authority remained powerfully established.

The combination of an intensely confessional culture and a powerful and discretionary magistracy produced a highly personalistic system of punishment. On the one hand, the Puritan commitment to original sin led to the assumption that everyone needed to be disciplined. This sense of shared depravity precluded any simple sense of divisions between law-breaking and law-abiding individuals. But at the same time, the discretion of the magistrates meant that punishments were often geared toward the individual. How much guilt the accused had acknowledged, whether he or she was a first-offender, how the accused fit into the community – all affected sentencing and punishment. This system was perhaps most powerfully enacted in Theophilus Eaton's New Haven. But as the struggles over magisterial discretion in early Massachusetts suggest, it was not limited to that short-lived colony. And in early Massachusetts at least, social status affected punishment profoundly. Gentlemen were rarely subject to corporal punishment, and fines were often calibrated to an individual's status. These tendencies may have been an acknowledgment of the realities of the power of gentlemen or the demands of equity. But they also strengthened the hand of the magistracy.

The colonial relationship also shaped the exercise of discretion. Massachusetts magistrates were concerned to shore up not only their own but all forms of local authority. Indeed, one reason that Massachusetts magistrates resisted written laws was their fear that having such laws would intensify British scrutiny of colonial practices. Given the centrality to the local social order of patriarchal households seeking economic competency, it is not surprising to find that the magistrates were careful to support the prerogative authority of age and fatherhood. But they wanted to do so without risking a loss of labor. In the early years of Massachusetts Bay, imposed penalties frequently departed from declared sentences. It seems clear that the magistrates modified both corporal and financial penalties in acknowledgment of the colonial shortage of labor and money.

Sexuality marked a further legal intersection between religious scruple and colonial labor systems. Fornication, rape, and adultery were all punished severely throughout the New England colonies (rape often with capital punishment, the lesser offenses with some combination of whipping, fine, and admonition). Fornication especially marked a point of intense contestation. The seriousness with which authorities dealt with fornication bespoke not a shared cultural attitude but rather the extremely diverse practices and attitudes of the colonists (both Puritan and otherwise). Indeed, it was in the realm of sexuality (and in the case of fishing towns the issue of drink), that the reality of criminal justice as an argument appeared most regularly. The sanctions of the law represented one side in an ongoing, and perpetually unresolved, cultural conflict.

One striking component of criminal justice in seventeenth-century New England was its relative openness to women. In this regard, New Haven led the way. During this colony's years of independence, women frequently found their way to its courts to register criminal complaints. The New Haven authorities responded to these accusations and punished men for sexual assault rigorously and severely. By the same token New Haven's leaders were intolerant of fornication. But here the interesting point was that men were punished more severely than women. For both crimes, the whipping post was the favored penalty. But if New Haven was extreme it was not alone. The commitment of Puritan authorities to suppress transgressions of sexual codes combined with the Puritan commitment to overcoming the double standard in sexual matters meant that women's words were taken seriously and men's sins were punished openly. Still, even in this realm the power of the patriarch was foremost. Adultery after all was defined by illicit sexuality on the part of married women. Even rape appears to have concerned Puritan magistrates most when it involved wives. In both cases, although the crime was illicit or coercive sexual behavior, an important issue seems to have been the damage done to the husband's rights.

In the seventeenth century, then, the North American situation made possible a selective intensification and adaptation of the practices of English criminal law in light of specific colonial projects. Seventeenth-century colonial leaders drew on the Tudor intensification of the power of justices of the peace to further particular religious and labor systems. In New England, religious critiques of church courts and hierarchies meant that the criminal law was separate from religious discipline, while the importance of fathers in the family, economy, and society meant that the law reinforced the patriarchal power of Puritan gentry. In the Chesapeake, the widespread early modern concern with "masterless men" reinforced the capacity of Chesapeake planters to deploy the law in the interests of labor discipline. In both areas, colonial efforts to regulate sexuality in the interests of production and property placed the regulation of desire at the center of court practices. The primacy of the colonial situation was, in turn, a manifestation of both the diffuse nature of English jurisdictions and the relative weakness of the Crown to assure uniformity in colonial practice.

V. IMPERIALIZATION: GENTILITY, COMMERCE, AND SLAVERY

The changing structures of the empire and the changing system of criminal law mirrored each other during the eighteenth century. If religious utopianism and coercive labor relations helped shape the meanings of seventeenth-century criminal law, the eighteenth-century law manifested the values of gentility, property, and commerce. Whether in the increasingly secular culture of New England, the increasingly civil culture of the Chesapeake, or the manifestly bourgeois cultures of the middle colonies, more elaborate legal forms intersected with the repertoire of public punishments to create a more genteel penal realm. Equally important, the expansion and consolidation of systems of slavery heightened the everyday presence of force in colonial societies while transmuting the notion of dual legal systems in a new direction. At the same time, an increasingly powerful British state extended the reach of its criminal law through transportation and the expansion of the imperial bureaucracy. The diversity and localism that marked the seventeenth-century colonial project did not disappear, but it became submerged within an increasingly uniform imperial world of culture, force, and property.

From one perspective, little changed in practices of punishment during the eighteenth century. Courts continued to impose the same range of financial, shaming, corporal, and capital penalties. Fines and whippings remained the most frequently imposed penalties, although, not surprisingly, the numbers of hangings increased. As in the seventeenth century the vast majority of convicts were men.

As new colonies were established and consolidated, the English criminal law expanded with them. Whereas the reach of the law in the seventeenth century was as intermittent as English colonial holdings, by the eighteenth century English legal forms and practices held sway from Maine to Georgia. Throughout the colonies quarterly courts of record were held; sheriffs, coroners, and justices of the peace identified criminals and criminal activities; printers distributed English legal forms and writs; and appellate courts met regularly. As each colony matured so did the hierarchy of courts as legal officials mimicked the mother country. Closer connections with Britain also meant expansion of capital codes. Pennsylvania may have been the extreme case. Having begun with a single capital offense (murder) in the late seventeenth century, eighteenth-century legislators regularly added to a basic list of nearly twenty offenses. But if extreme the Pennsylvania story was not unique. Throughout the colonies the list of capital offenses grew across the late colonial period as the laws of England made their presence felt in the colonies.

Finally, across the century courts and magistrates remained focused on offenses against property and persons. Though nothing approaching a complete accounting of prosecutions in the eighteenth-century colonies exists, certain general propositions seem clear. For one, although the numbers of offenses varied widely in time and place, minor crimes against persons and property were ongoing issues throughout eighteenth-century British North America. In New York, to name only one example, the most prevalent problems facing the courts were crimes of violence and crimes against public order. Pennsylvania had a rate of personal violence that exceeded that of England. So did the southern colonies. Crimes against property were not, to be sure, on the scale of London, but colonial crime certainly was comparable to the rest of England. New England was the exception to this overall situation. New Englanders sustained a remarkably low level of crimes against persons and property. The same could not be said of the range of colonies south of the old Puritan enclaves.

Still, there were also departures from the seventeenth-century situation. For example, the colonial legal regimes and the English legal system were becoming more interconnected. From the earliest days of colonization, English judges and ministers had intervened in the legislative and judicial processes of the colonies. Beginning in 1718, however, the English government made the colonies an actual appendage of British justice. From that point on, the transportation of convicts from the British Isles to the American colonies was systematic and continuous. Over 50,000 convicts were transported between 1718 and the Revolution, most to Maryland and Virginia. Whether or not colonial fears that Britain (mostly England but Scotland and Ireland as well) was simply dumping its criminal problems on the colonies were borne out in practice, transportation did mean that British criminal justice directly impinged on colonial society. The spread of vice-admiralty courts through the eighteenth century, although of less importance to colonial society than transportation, was another example of increased imperial intrusion into colonial justice and colonial society. The seventeenth-century colonial legal systems had developed in relative autonomy. The same could not be said of those in the eighteenth century.

Even within colonial criminal justice there were changes in context and emphasis. For one thing, New Englanders' desire that the criminal law manifest a sacred drama of sin and its punishment declined. The famous epidemic of executions at Salem during the 1690s proved to be the last systematic deployment of the penal law to uproot witchcraft. In the longer term, the effort to control morals offenses through the criminal law moved from center stage of the penal theater. It was not that in the eighteenth century courts ceased to prosecute and punish individuals for adultery, fornication, prostitution, and like offenses. In quantitative terms violations of moral regulations consistently took up a significant amount of the time of county courts and justices of the peace in all of the eighteenth-century colonies. In Massachusetts, to name only one, fornication predominated among prosecutions until the Revolution itself. But across the colonies morals offenses no longer stood at the center of penal concerns. In Connecticut, men were rarely prosecuted for fornication by the middle of the eighteenth-century. Women, it is true, were still brought before the magistrates and their names publicized, but the idea that the courts enacted the public reaffirmation of a common ethical condemnation of fornication had passed.

A related transformation occurred concerning sexual assault in New England. Rape and other sexual assaults continued to be punished severely across the century, but it became increasingly difficult to gain convictions for those crimes. Whereas prosecutions for rape were almost always successful in seventeenth-century Connecticut, by the eighteenth century convictions were limited to Indians, slaves, foreigners, or strangers. To be sure, in what Cornelia Dayton terms the "eighteenth-century double standard," women continued to be held accountable for their sexual transgressions. But, as regards sexual assault and fornication, the law's desire to control the sexuality of men had diminished. The control of sexual behavior had been central to the symbolic economy of the seventeenth-century New England court system, and the court system had been central to the regulation of sexual morals in seventeenth-century New England. By the late colonial period this world had been lost. Whereas seventeenth-century New Englanders assumed that courts were an essential site of the public acknowledgment and punishment of sexual transgression, in the eighteenth century control of sexuality became a more diffuse, and hidden, social task.

What was true in New England was also true elsewhere. Indeed, the emphasis on the communal aspect of morals regulation had always been less extreme in other colonies. Again, it is not that the courts did not take cognizance of morals offenses. Courts in Pennsylvania, for example, punished numerous individuals for fornication, adultery, drunkenness, and prostitution. And Quakers, at least, created a second system to police marriage and sexuality within the various meetings. In Richmond County, Virginia, although offenses against morals remained the largest single category in the first half of the century, their overall importance declined dramatically following the 1720s. But the more secular societies of the middle and southern colonies never placed the same emphasis on making the prosecution and punishment of morals offenses a communal drama of sin and redemption. Instead, they treated them as mundane problems of law enforcement or left them to the cognizance of religious discipline. The authorities became increasingly concerned with the economic and social, as opposed to the more explicitly moral, aspects of "morals" offenses. Instead of the drama of sin, magistrates were more concerned with the commonplace burdens to the community. Bastardy, from this perspective, threatened less for its religious significance than for the costs it could impose on the town or county.

One indication of the changing emphases of criminal justice was the relationship between criminality and print. Across the northern colonies, if most dramatically in New England, printers printed and readers read an ever expanding number of criminal narratives, execution sermons, dying speeches, and court transcripts. To be sure, growth in the number of criminal texts followed growth in the number of printers. Nevertheless, the popularity of criminal narratives points to the deep fascination that matters of criminality and punishment held for eighteenth-century colonists. It points also to the changing contours of that fascination. The English, of course, had long distributed dying speeches. The Ordinary of London's Newgate prison supported himself, in part, by drafting and selling the biographies of the condemned. Seventeenth-century colonists introduced new twists. New Englanders led the way in developing the genre of the printed execution sermon. Reproducing the ministerial exhortation that took place before the hanging, execution sermons became a major technique through which ministers asserted their interpretation of the meaning of secular events. The involvement of leading ministers in crime literature gave it a cultural gravity and meaningfulness it lacked in England. During the course of the eighteenth century, however, sermons increasingly found themselves bundled with other forms of criminal narrative. At the same time, the growing popularity of criminal memoirs and dying speeches suggests the widespread allure of outlaws and others who challenged authorities. By the late colonial period ministers and their messages were pushed to the margins; crime and criminality on its own terms had taken center stage. The relationship between sin and crime had not disappeared from people's minds, but the cultural representation was increasingly secular, no longer infused with religion.

If the emphases of the criminal courts were changing, so were court practices. The eighteenth century witnessed increasing complexity in legal forms and practices. Although colonial courts remained pale versions of their English counterparts, over the course of the eighteenth century they became comparatively more sophisticated. Criminal defense attorneys began to appear intermittently in the colonies, law books and justice of the peace manuals spread, and the physical space of the courts themselves became more formal. If seventeenth-century court days were often ramshackle affairs held in ramshackle surroundings, in the eighteenth century court buildings and court rituals became more elaborate and formidable. Indeed, in Virginia the authority of the courts and the ritualization of court proceedings generated struggles between attorneys who wished to seize control of the law and lay critics who argued that the courts were becoming a world apart from the community. The growing pomp of court activities and the formalization of their spaces meant that criminal justice stood as a unique realm. The public nature of punishments, of course, continued to blur the distinctions between juridical and everyday space, but that there was a separate juridical space was less and less in doubt.

From all of these developments should we assume that the criminal law was becoming more "anglicized," to use John Murrin's famous phrase? Collectively, these developments do suggest that colonial criminal law and its practice were increasingly modeled on the central law courts of eighteenth-century England. The growing presence of attorneys, the increasing complexity of legal forms, the spread of legal education, and the heightened emphasis on property crimes all mirror developments in England. Still, there are reasons to doubt the notion of anglicization. For one thing, England's criminal law was itself changing. Transformations in the British economy and in Britain's place in the Atlantic world produced new emphases on financial crimes, and the elite's perception of growing social unrest from below stimulated the expanded capital code. For another, there had never been a single criminal law of England that could be transported as such to the colonies. Colonial legislators had always had a variety of legal traditions to choose from and had done so in light of their own peculiar projects. What was occurring in the eighteenth century was that imperial pressures toward uniformity and colonial desires for civility both promoted a growing adherence to a particular strain of English criminal law – the law on display in the sophisticated courts of the capital. In this way, it would be more appropriate to treat eighteenth-century transformations as an "imperialization" of the law.

And then there was the question of slavery.

The law of slavery and the criminal law were powerfully intertwined. Indeed, the expansion of slavery and slave codes constituted the single most significant influence on the transformation of the criminal law in the colonial eighteenth century. Not that the intersection of the criminal law and the law of slavery was new: it had begun at least as early as Virginia's efforts, during the 1640s, to regulate the sexuality of female slaves. And throughout the late seventeenth century, colonial governments had placed firmer and firmer criminal restraints on their enslaved populations. But during the eighteenth century efforts to control slave populations in the interests of the master class assumed new dimensions and complexity. From isolated efforts to confront specific problems related to the organization of slavery or the authority of slave owners to the establishment of special courts and policing powers, eighteenth-century legislators across British North America consolidated the power of the master through the authority of the law.

Slave codes shared certain characteristics. For one thing, slave punishments degraded the body. Slaves lacked property, after all, and the law could only seize their corporal being. But the range of legitimated punishments suggests that degradation of the body was not simply an extension of the more conventional criminal codes. Virginia allowed the maiming of runaways; South Carolina included nose slitting in its legal arsenal. Both Virginia and South Carolina codes contained provisions for castration and burning alive. Nor were these efforts limited to the South. Pennsylvania included castration among its penalties in 1705 (a law that was struck down in England). New York burned some condemned slaves alive. Moreover, the penalties for slaves who committed offenses that cut across criminal codes were greater. In South Carolina, a slave could be executed for causing a white person to be "maimed, or disabled."[8]

Just as the law allowed itself broad license to degrade the bodies of slaves, it did little to restrain masters in their similar pursuits. True, there were legal limits to a master's liberty in punishing slaves (and more stringent limits on the power of an overseer), but the presumption that masters would not willfully damage their own property meant that, in practice even more than in law, official restraints on the infliction of corporal punishment were negligible. Moreover, the ability of slaves to challenge their master's punishments was limited by their legal incompetence to testify against whites. Although slaves could testify against other slaves (in the interest of discovering conspiracies) their word could rarely, if ever, be mobilized against a Euro-American. When it came to whites, the rules concerning testimony against slaves were looser than in regular proceedings. Indeed, in New York, Virginia, and South Carolina, to name only the most important colonies, the authorities established separate judicial systems for slave crimes – courts with streamlined procedures and fewer restraints on acceptable testimony or legal safeguards for defendants than even the normal criminal court of the eighteenth century. For all practical purposes slaves received some sort of defense in these courts only when their masters decided that it was worth *their* while to provide it.

In all, the basic imbalance in power among prosecutors, justices, and defendants that was present in all court settings was dramatically intensified in the case of enslaved men and women. To be sure, there were constraints

[8] Thomas Cooper and David J. McCord, *The Statutes at Large of South Carolina* (Columbia, SC, 1836–1841), 7: 359.

on the exercise of the penal power. Some procedural safeguards were followed, and sentences were remitted in part or in whole. The slaves' status as property meant that some masters defended their slaves from the full rigors of the law. Nor was it impossible to prove the innocence of accused slaves or the guilt of masters who had exceeded the bounds of customary treatment. Justices might mitigate punishments to spare the public the expense of compensation, or because of doubts about guilt, or out of humanitarian considerations. Each colonial code, moreover, had its own specific trajectory. Virginia's, for example, moved in the direction of leniency and heightened security for the accused, whereas South Carolina heightened and tightened its slave code across the century. Nevertheless, in each case legislators designed the criminal laws of slavery with the same working principle in mind – ensure the maintenance of human property in the interest of the owner. From the extremity of punishments deployed, through the modified rules of evidence, to streamlined and ad hoc judicial proceedings, the criminal law moved with remarkable and incessant force against the bodies and freedoms of enslaved men and women. Even the terms on which masters might seek to protect their property reveal the basic structure of the criminal law of slavery. Colonies offered compensation to masters for the loss of their property in cases of execution or banishment. So for masters the question of their loss structured the calculation of intervention: was the alleged offense worth the loss of property, and was the compensation sufficient for the loss of that particular slave? Some masters may have intervened in the name of humanity. But structurally the issue was whether or not the criminal punishment sustained, or damaged, the property holding of the master.

The law's deployment of public force in support of masters' power produced a complex dual system of justice in the colonies. Most directly, colonies with substantial populations of enslaved men and women relied on special courts to deal with slave offenses. These courts paralleled the regular judicial apparatus and often had the same personnel as the regular courts, but they followed their own procedures, operated on their own rules of evidence, and could declare their own (often exemplary) punishments. More fundamentally, the power of the law served to reinforce and to replicate the powers already granted to the master. Most slave crime and most slave punishment occurred on the plantation. The legal system served as bulwark, but the prime locus of criminal punishments within slavery was the master's whip, not the colony's gallows. The role of the law was to legitimate the informal practices of plantation discipline and to intervene in those cases where plantation discipline was not sufficient to sustain the legal order and the master's authority. Only in extremely rare cases might the community intervene against excessive plantation discipline. The law's violence stood in a secondary, supportive relationship to the structures of plantation violence.

Indeed, the relationship between legal violence and plantation violence points to one of the primary structures of colonial penal law. Throughout the colonial period, the practice of public, corporal, and capital punishment took place in a world in which the infliction of corporal punishment by masters against servants was a commonplace on land and on sea. The institutionally established dual system of slavery's criminal law renders explicit what remained implicit elsewhere – that everywhere in the colonial world an effective dual system of justice and punishment existed. Whether linked to structures of family labor, relationships of master and servant, or the extremity of racialized chattel slavery, the practice of public punishments mirrored and intensified the quotidian employment of corporal correction by patriarchs. It is a commonplace of scholarship that we will never know the "dark figure" of unreported crime. Nor will we ever know the "dark figure" of extra-juridical punishments. Juridically imposed public punishments were the intense exemplification of authority's everyday use of violence. This is not to minimize the difference between legal punishments and the discipline typically meted out by masters. The latter could be a simple slap of the hand or blow to the body. In their actual physical force this discipline paled compared to a public whipping, let alone a hanging. But corporal correction was a ubiquitous element of the maintenance of authority in the colonial world, and its significance as such cannot be underestimated, for it could not help but support the sense that corporal punishments were reasonable.

To point to the widespread use of coercive violence against unfree labor in the colonies is not to deny the specificity of the master-slave situation or of the slave codes. As Josiah Quincy remarked of the slave codes of late colonial South Carolina, "Legislators enacted laws touching negroes, mulattoes and masters which savor more of the policy of Pandemonium than the English constitution."[9] The criminal law of slavery was not simply an extension of wider practices. It imposed punishments on slaves that were forbidden for others. In both its extremity and in its *explicit* ties to race it existed as a world apart. The dual justice system of racialized slavery highlights one of the striking paradoxes of the racial implications of early American criminal justice. In the case of Native Americans, formally equal access to the courts took place in the context of a systemic social effort to marginalize and exclude Indians from colonial society. For enslaved blacks, and for free blacks in the southern colonies at least, recognition of the practical centrality

[9] Mark Antony De Wolfe Howe, ed., "Journal of Josiah Quincy, Junior, 1773," *Proceedings of the Massachusetts Historical Society*, 49 (1915–1916), 457.

of African Americans to colonial society produced a system of separate and unequal legal standing. As a result, the dialectic of red, white, and black legal inclusions and exclusions took a variety of paths.

One might pursue this dialectic further. For example, it is worth speculating that the centrality of slavery to colonial society had crucial ramifications for the punishment of criminals in the eighteenth century. Although the criminal law and slavery had long and separate histories, in the eighteenth century acceptance of the whip and the gallows fused slavery and penal law in new ways. On the one hand, the growing importance and acceptance of slavery in the eighteenth-century colonies may have normalized the continued practice of publicly imposed corporal punishment. As slavery reshaped the societies of both northern and southern colonies, the general deployment of coercive violence took on ever greater public presence. Each setting reinforced the other. On the other hand, from the mid-eighteenth century onward, as the genteel on both sides of the Atlantic began to withdraw in disgust from the spectacles of suffering at the whipping post and the gallows, the centrality of the body in both the traditional system of punishment and in the discipline of the plantation meant that the connection between the two settings worked to undermine resort to violence in each. As in England, there is evidence of growing uncertainty about the legitimacy of public punishments in mid-eighteenth-century colonial America. The growing problematization of the public infliction of legal violence would prove to be an important legacy for the revolutionary period.

The imperialization of the criminal law transformed both the law and its relationship to the colonial project. The elaboration of transportation and the expansion of maritime courts directly intruded imperial authority into colonial society and trade. But more fundamentally, the colonists' consolidation of chattel slavery and their desire to partake of British gentility meant that the law assumed new tasks of civility and coercion that aligned the mainland colonies with the societies of the British West Indies and the culture of the metropole in new and unpredictable ways. The imperialization of the eighteenth century meant that the question of the colonial project would be inescapable in the history of American criminal law.

VI. COLONIAL TRANSFORMATIONS, REVOLUTIONARY LEGACIES

The American Revolution intensified and transformed the problematic status of legal – especially imperial-legal – authority. As the criminal law became a source of intense conflict between rebellious colonists and imperial officials, Americans not only redefined their relationship to imperial law but also began to fashion their own notions of republican law. Out of the cauldron of revolutionary conflict, the newly independent states solidified colonial practices in the South while departing in new directions in the North. But even then Americans did not escape the legacy of their British and imperial roots, for their search for republican penalties led them into alliances with English strategists and theorists of punishment. Like their early forbears, revolutionary-era Americans drew on disparate British penal traditions. The bonds of civility persisted beyond the rupture of revolution; the colonial relationship would not be left behind.

Nonetheless, the era of the American Revolution and Early Republic did witness important transformations in the structures and practices of criminal punishments and moral regulation. Most obviously, the British Empire no longer determined the parameters of criminal justice in the newly independent United States. Although the federal government did construct its own criminal code its influence was negligible outside the maritime arena. As full responsibility for crime and punishment fell to the states the regional diversities that were implicit in the colonial period became more explicit. What had previously been a case of different practices within a predominantly uniform system of punishment now became a matter of overt policy. The Northern states increasingly centered their penal systems on reformative incarceration while limiting the deployment of publicly inflicted capital and corporal sanctions. In the South, although penitentiaries emerged in all states outside the Carolinas they remained marginal to the central task of the criminal justice system, which remained to give support to the system of slavery. In the South, the dual system of justice inherited from the colonial period became even more entrenched and racially coded.

The criminal law had been at the center of the agitation that led toward independence. From the early efforts to expand vice-admiralty jurisdiction and limit the power of local juries in maritime cases, through the trials of the Boston Massacre, to the removal of accused British officials from the control of all local jurisdictions, the question of the power to punish and to define criminality haunted the revolutionary process. Popular justice, both real and symbolic, made manifest colonial consciousness while revealing the coercion that was intrinsic to the rebellion. During the war for independence, the power to punish and to define criminality lay at the heart of American claims to sovereignty – signified in the American army's execution of John André for espionage against a nation that he did not recognize.

Consequently, the Northern states began to restructure their systems of punishment with remarkable rapidity after independence. Removed from the structures of the empire, Northern writers and legislators demonstrated their attachment to the doctrines of penal reform that had been circulating through genteel Britain and Europe since the middle of the eighteenth century. They focused on two issues in particular. First, they drew on the transatlantic critique of penal uncertainty to argue that it was the consistency of punishment, not its physical severity, that would diminish crimes. Second, they incorporated the growing elite revulsion at the public display of physical suffering to argue that public punishments stimulated rather than prevented criminality and violence. At the same time, religious dissenters in England and their confreres in America insisted that the soul of the condemned should become a central focus in penal practice. Whether it was John Howard in England or Benjamin Rush in the United States, the language of redemption and sin gained a prominence in penal thinking that it had not had since the reform efforts of Puritans and Quakers in the seventeenth century. Whether the motivation was primarily religious or genteel, the body under duress ceased to be presumptively reasonable in the penal realm. Rooted socially in the professional, mercantile, and artisanal classes on both sides of the Atlantic, reform efforts and organizations spread throughout the late eighteenth-century British Atlantic. In their eyes, the body of the condemned would need to be punished in a new way. No longer emblematic of society as a whole, the punished body would be either avenue to the soul or target of discipline or both.

Northern legislators thus began to displace corporal and capital punishment from the heart of penal practice. Massachusetts (1785) and Pennsylvania (1786) began the process in the 1780s, and New York began in the following decade, altering its codes and establishing a new prison regime in 1796. Central to this process was a reduction in the scope of the capital codes. Although more limited than the English code, colonial capital codes – and indeed the colonial practice of capital punishment – had always extended to a wide range of offenses. But throughout the period of the Early Republic, states in the north increasingly limited their capital sanctions. Although it would be the middle of the nineteenth century before capital punishment was effectively limited to the crime of murder, the process was set in motion in the Early Republic. Pennsylvania, for example, limited capital punishment to first-degree murder in 1794. In 1796, New York limited it to murder and treason (arson was added a few years later). Similar steps were taken to limit publicly inflicted corporal punishments. Corporal punishment remained a legally sanctioned penalty at least through the 1820s and a punishment for infractions of prison discipline for considerably longer, but as with capital punishment the first steps to limit its ambit were taken in the very first years of the Early Republic.

In place of these publicly inflicted corporal and capital punishments, Northern states increasingly turned to reformative incarceration within prison walls. New York and Pennsylvania undertook experiments with public labor in the streets, but these were discontinued in the face of a remarkable consensus that criminal punishment should be based on labor within confined spaces. In theory, at least, the combination of labor and confinement would serve to deter crime and, in the best cases at least, reform character itself. Across the Northern landscape new prisons were built or older ones reconfigured and reformed. States established new governing boards, newspapers and journals debated the proper forms of prison organization, and visitors from around the Atlantic basin traveled to inspect the prisons of the Early Republic.

The new centrality of incarceration was a revolution in penal theory. In the colonial period, jails and prisons had largely been places of temporary confinement – subordinate staging areas for the true sites of criminal justice: the courts, the whipping post, and the gallows. Although occasionally criminals were condemned to imprisonment as part of their sentence, for the most part jails functioned simply to restrain the accused until they could actually receive their trials and sentences. And although jails did occasionally emerge into public consciousness and debate, this was largely a result of issues relating to jail conditions and security. The growing emphasis on reformation of character, a concern largely lacking in the colonial period, transformed all of that. It necessitated an increased attention to the actual regimes of imprisonment. One effect of this attention was a flourishing discourse – a true transatlantic discourse – on the problems and practices of incarceration. In this new world of punishment the prison became an ongoing problem.

Practice changed more slowly. The changes in criminal codes did translate into sentencing, but the process of prison reformation itself was more complex and intermittent. In Massachusetts, New York, and Pennsylvania – to name only the most significant – new systems of authority and new regimes of labor were instituted. The prison reformers who took charge of these efforts strove to improve prison discipline, establish labor regimens, and ameliorate the physical conditions of their charges. But the reliance on corporal punishments within prison continued, the labor regimes were erratic at best, and the health of prisoners was always at risk. Nor is there much evidence of serious efforts to prepare inmates for reentry into society. If anything, the more extended period of punishment separated convicts from everyday life more brutally and more deleteriously than had the common whipping. Despite the Enlightenment critique of pardons in the name of certainty, the pardon reemerged as a central tool for prison discipline. Officials used the pardon both as a carrot to encourage compliance and as a safety valve to control numbers. Finally, as prison reformers organized themselves into groups and boards, and sought to deploy the authority and power of the state to remake the prison, prisoners were not passive recipients of their efforts. Inmates constructed their own communities, struggled to control the everyday life of the institution, defended what they viewed as their customary privileges and rights, and resisted efforts to control their behavior. Arson and riots were only the most visible and dramatic examples of a regular practice of resistance to prison rules and authority. In certain fundamental respects, moreover, prison reform simply passed reality by. Despite the rhetoric of the emancipatory effects of prison life, prisons replicated the inequalities of the wider world. Most inmates were poor. In the most important of the early prison experiments, Philadelphia's Walnut Street Jail, blacks were present in numbers significantly greater than their presence in the city's population. And racial tensions followed inmates into the prisons.

Alongside these state efforts, the late eighteenth and early nineteenth century also witnessed a flourishing of private efforts to reform morality. Moral reform societies were not, of course new, but they grew in number and took on new importance in the Early Republic. By the 1820s and 1830s, moral reform groups composed of both men and women were remaking the discourse of personal character and the institutions of social discipline. Whether responding to poverty or prostitution, juvenile crime or drunkenness, the conditions of prison inmates or the sick in hospitals, the same social groups that had pushed for a rethinking of legal punishment also sought to impose a new moral hygiene on society. Concentrated largely in the urban areas of the Northeast, and in regular contact with their counterparts in Britain, these reformers set up yet another dual system for the regulation of morality. In their practices and institutions they aimed to deploy charity in the interest of personal transformation in accord with an emerging bourgeois ethos. Here was another reinvention of the seventeenth-century Puritan and Quaker projects on the soil of the new Republic.

If the North took important, if limited, strides toward reconfiguring the target of punishment away from the body and toward character, the South took another course. It is not that the South did not also construct penitentiaries. It did. Following the lead of Virginia in 1796, all of the Southern states except North and South Carolina built new penitentiaries before the Civil War. But the Southern states never put the same emphasis on prison reform nor did they make the penitentiary the center of their penal practice. Instead, the penitentiary emerged as a subsidiary institution supplementing the central form of criminal law – plantation discipline. In the Deep South, almost all inmates were poor white men, accompanied by a smattering of free blacks. In the Upper South, the majority of inmates were poor white men with a larger minority of free blacks. Nowhere in the South was the penitentiary the main mechanism to punish enslaved men and women. Workhouses and prisons held runaway slaves but only until they could be returned to their masters. Slaves remained subject to the dual system of punishment that had marked the colonial period. In addition, although Southern states did reform their criminal codes, their capital codes remained far more substantial than in the North.

The South, to be sure, partook in the culture of Anglo-American gentility. And powerful arguments raged throughout the Early Republican South over the place of public and corporal punishments. But far more than the North, the South built on the systems of colonial labor and colonial punishments. Whereas the Northern economies were breaking away from their dependence on English manufacturing, the Southern economies retained their dependent relations – now extended to Northern manufacturing as well. And whereas Northern reformers joined with British reformers in a transatlantic movement of penal transformation, Southern slave-owners continued to organize their societies on the model of the landed aristocracy. Their penal practices shared a common world with the British colonies of the West Indies. As regards their bondsmen and bondswomen – arguably the most important targets of Southern punishments – they saw little reason to transform their systems of penal discipline. In the relationship of the penitentiary and the whipping post stood revealed the racial divisions of the Early Republican South. Mixing the newer notions of incarceration for free citizens with the elaborately violent practices of public, corporal, and capital penalties for the bound, the South created a new hybrid penal apparatus, one that reflected its ambivalent relationship to the larger Atlantic world as a whole.

In an ironic way, then, the establishment of the United States reinstated the penal and juridical diversity that had marked the earliest colonies. If the trend of the eighteenth century had been toward imperial unification, independence meant a reassertion of regional diversity in penal practice. Whereas the Northern states reconfigured the discipline of the body and created an ongoing problem of penal discipline, the Southern states modified but retained the system of corporal and capital penalties that had flourished during the colonial period. The new nation, thereby, provided a stage to reinvigorate the religiously based penal projects of the seventeenth century in combination with the labor discipline of the mature slave societies of the eighteenth. The revolutionary period simultaneously transformed and maintained the intersection between penality and the colonial project.

CONCLUSION

Early American criminal law passed through three phases in its relationship to imperial power. During the seventeenth century, the weakness of the imperial state, the complexity of encounters with different Native American groups, and the diversity of colonial labor and family organization produced extremely localized and divergent systems of criminal justice. Throughout most of the eighteenth century, in contrast, the strengthened power of imperial oversight, the spread of racialized chattel slavery, and the colonists' desire to share in the forms and practices of British civility led to an increasing uniformity and sophistication of penality combined with the elaboration of dual systems of justice. Finally, following the politicization of the criminal law and the search for a republican form of punishment that accompanied the American Revolution, the governments of the new nation instituted a renewed diversity of penality. Despite a shared affirmation of eighteenth-century civility and humanity, increasingly their efforts diverged according to the presence or absence of slavery. States drew on different and often competing legacies of imperial and colonial practice.

But the relationship between the colonial project and penality ran deeper than the presence or absence of the empire or juridical diversity. As we have seen, early America's existence on the colonial periphery, in societies without long-standing lines of social authority, placed the law's power at the center of questions of labor, maritime discipline, family order, and the colonists' relationships with competing sovereignties – both European and Native American. But this necessarily placed those questions at the heart of the criminal law's own tasks and legitimacy. The form and trajectory of early American penality were thus inseparable from the struggles, divisions, and projects that accompanied colonialism – from religion to race, security to sovereignty, and from labor to life and death. And these struggles were inseparable from the colonists' place on the periphery of the Atlantic system designed to increase the wealth and power of European metropolises.

To trace the colonial origins of American criminal law and moral regulation, then, is to do more than sketch a chronological backdrop to an essentially national story. The continuing particularities of the American criminal law – its jurisdictional localism, its deep imbrication with moralism, its recurrent concern with vagrancy and labor discipline, and its explosive place in the racial struggles of the nation – all emerged during and out of the colonial setting. Without understanding these imperial roots it is possible neither to understand the later trajectory of the criminal law nor to comprehend the role it continued and continues to play in the wider Atlantic world. Penality in America was an intricate part of the colonial project from the beginning, and colonial projects were inscribed at the very heart of the law.

7

LAW, POPULATION, LABOR

CHRISTOPHER TOMLINS

English colonizers mobilized immense resources to take possession of North America during the two centuries following their first intrusions in the late sixteenth century. None was more important than people. Nearly 200,000 were shipped across the Atlantic during the seventeenth century, nearly 600,000 during the eighteenth. Richard Hakluyt the elder – Middle Temple lawyer, Member of Parliament, confidant of statesmen, propagandist for colonizing – said it first and best. To "keepe" the country, it had to be planted – occupied and rendered productive. But planting required people. Hence the country had to be "man[ned]." English purposes rendered the existing indigenous population, to Hakluyt, "of small consideration."[1] The objective in colonizing North America was conquest and possession, not simply gain through commerce. "Manning," that is, meant the introduction of alien populations not just as a reliable labor force to produce plantation commodities for European buyers, but also to establish the colonizer's general dominion through physical occupation. Because population had such an unsurpassed strategic importance, the organization of manning requires our attention.

The demographic history of Anglophone America is characterized by great continuities. The first is the ubiquity of *movements* of population – indigenous, European, African, and (in the second half of the nineteenth century) Asian. The nation of immigrants is better denominated a nation of incessant migrations, whether transoceanic or intraregional, small or vast, voluntary or coerced. Second comes the equally ubiquitous phenomenon – among the newcomers – of rapid *growth*. During the first two centuries, for example, the introduced populations of the mainland British colonies grew from zero to 2.7 million. Though rates varied across regions and

[1] Richard Hakluyt the elder, "Pamphlet for the Virginia Enterprise," in E.G.R. Taylor, ed., *The Original Writings and Correspondence of the Two Richard Hakluyts* (London, 1935), 333.

periods, natural increase quickly outpaced immigration in accounting for population growth. Incessant migration and rapid growth underlie the third continuity: relentless expansion. Migration and natural increase transformed the first little clusters of foreign strangers into teeming creole[2] populations, whose expansive mobility and constant craving for productive land pressed unremittingly on indigenous inhabitants decimated by disease and warfare. The British were "like Piggons" according to the Shawnee people of the mid-eighteenth century Ohio Valley. Suffer but a pair to reside, "thayd Draw to them whole Troopes" and take all the land.

The Shawnee encounter with the realities of manning, planting, and keeping helps expose one of the deep connections between law and political economy on which colonizing depended: legal ideas and instrumentalities facilitated the displacement of one population by another. The law of nature and nations furnished discourses of civility and barbarity upon which Europeans founded doctrines of just war and rightful occupation; together they created an aboriginal emptiness, the legal and spatial expression of "small consideration." Metropolitan documents such as charters and treaties, and metropolitan practices such as tenures and deeds, filled the emptiness on the colonizer's terms.

But law did not merely facilitate displacement of former occupants in otherwise spontaneous processes of settlement, or simply service those migrants who happened to show up. Rather, law furnished the institutional technology by which the process of migration was organized. Law established the conditions of departure and of transit. It established the conditions under which, on arrival, migrants became producers. Overall, law helped mold strangers' propensities for mobility into the actuality of empire.

When we investigate the relationship of law to the process of English settlement we tend not to focus on law's capacity to "frame" macrostructural development. We concentrate on the venerable trope that settlers carried with them the law they knew and applied so much as was appropriate to their new circumstances. We imagine bits of English law tucked away in the migrant's cultural baggage. The bits are unpacked on the far side of the ocean like the odds and ends of an incomplete tool set, one more element in the self-absorbed history of setting up shop in an empty landscape. The trope has proven resilient for the very good reason that it conveys an important truth about the legal-cultural awareness and resources of ordinary migrants. But English law did a great deal more than furnish settlers with customary "English ways" to organize and render familiar their new localities. Law was

[2] "Creole" is used here to signify persons of European or African heritage born in the country, as distinguished from migrants (European or African) and from the indigenous population.

the conceptual structure – the organizational discourse – by which their move was enabled. First, law established the context for their liberty to be mobile by prescribing the extent of their freedom to depart and move and settle elsewhere. Second, in chartering colonies law created new and complex jurisdictional and governmental structures into which migrants were fed. Third, within those structures law established the actual conditions and effects of mobility, largely determining who might go where, and on what terms. That is, law organized mobile masses into discrete socioeconomic strata with very distinct legal profiles – freemen, masters and servants, slaves, "Indians," the settled, the unsettled (vagrant) poor. This was perhaps the most important contribution law made to the British Atlantic empire, so far at least as creation of a macrostructural context for a colonizing process driven by the deployment of labor in the production of agricultural commodities was concerned, for this was nothing less than the organization of population into the labor force necessary, as Hakluyt had realized, to render land occupied and productive beyond subsistence. Finally, throughout the first two centuries of Atlantic expansion, law composed discourses of status that defined the legal and political standing of populations: discourses of subjecthood, citizenship, and sojourn in relation to authority, both local and imperial.

In all these ways – policing mobility, assigning place, defining social and economic roles, ascribing status, creating subjects and citizens, and regulating their behavior – law shaped and organized the demography of colonizing. Population was a vital resource for colonizers. It could hardly be left to its own devices. Nor was it, either in the terms and forms of its mobilization, nor in its activities once planted. Few social processes unfold autonomously. The "peopling" of British North America was no exception.

I. POPULATION AND MIGRATION: MAIN CURRENTS OF MAINLAND DEMOGRAPHY

In the late sixteenth century, at the very beginnings of English colonizing, the portion of the North American mainland that would eventually comprise the thirteen English colonies was home to approximately 500,000 indigenous inhabitants, organized in a plethora of extended family groups, clans, and regional ethnic federations and engaged in subsistence economies dependent (in differing degrees) on hunting, gathering, and cultivation. Indigenous societies were not sedentary but their mobility was purposeful, following a settlement pattern of periodic intraregional migration among different forest or forest-edge areas. Indigenous population was already in decline as a result of European contact. In the Southeast, population fell some 23 percent during the sixteenth century. In the Northeast, the decline over the same period amounted to less than 5 percent. The arrival of the English in strength during the seventeenth century would see a catastrophic acceleration of indigenous population decline overall and a relative shift in emphasis to the Northeast as the locale of greatest loss. By 1700 the indigenous population of English America had fallen by half. Eighty percent of the decline occurred in the Northeast, where population decreased from 346,000 in 1600 to 150,000 in 1700.

Massachusetts Bay

European disease wrought such devastation on coastal groups in the Massachusetts Bay region that travelers likened the bones and skulls of the unburied dead to those that littered the biblical Golgotha. The New England Charter (1620) invoked this indigenous disaster as a wonder worked by providence on "the Sauages and brutish People there" releasing "large and goodly Territoryes" into the hands of those who would "be directed and conducted thither." For as Oxford's Regius Professor of Civil Law, Alberico Gentili, wrote in 1588, "'God did not create the world to be empty'. And therefore the seizure of vacant places is regarded as a law of nature."[3]

English migration to Massachusetts Bay began seriously in the early 1630s, bringing some 21,000 people into the region during the decade. Early mortality and reverse migration winnowed this founding group to a resident population of approximately 13,500 by 1640, but although in-migration tapered off sharply thereafter, stable sex ratios and a relatively even distribution of wealth in the migrant population combined with the region's benign (to Europeans) disease environment to encourage high rates of natural increase and rapid population growth. By the 1670s New England's settler population approached 70,000; by the 1770s, 700,000.

Continuous population increase meant constant pressure on available land. Complaints of overcrowding in settled areas were heard by the mid-1630s, only a few years after migration began. Crowding generated outward mobility and, inevitably, conflict with the region's surviving indigenous societies. By the end of the 1670s, New England's settlers had fought two major wars – with the Pequots in 1637 and the Algonquians in the mid-1670s. Each culminated in the devastation of indigenous societies by massacre and the enslavement and deportation of survivors. Each removed a restraint on settler expansion. Each invoked a legal discourse of "just war." In *De Iure Belli* (1588–9), Gentili had written that those who violated canons of human society established by nature – kinship, love, kindliness, and a bond of fellowship – were brutes, on whom war might justly be made,

[3] Alberico Gentili, *De Iure Belli Libri Tres*, John C. Rolfe trans. (Oxford, 1933), 80.

their lands appropriated, their persons enslaved. In the better known *De Iure Belli Ac Pacis* (1625), Hugo Grotius declared that war might justly be undertaken against any who killed strangers that settled among them. This too was an offence against nature.

The Chesapeake

Continuous settlement in the Chesapeake region began in 1607 at Jamestown, under the auspices of the Virginia Company. Over the next twelve years migrants arrived in an irregular trickle, the region was far less healthy for Europeans than New England, and it was populated by well-established indigenous groups with whom the intruders became engaged in brutal, if intermittent, conflict. Mutual hatreds peaked in 1622, three years into a period of much more systematic influx that had brought nearly 3,600 migrants to the colony. The expansion of settlement and grazing provoked an attack on Jamestown that killed 347 colonists. In more deadly retaliation, the English then engaged in wholesale warfare to expel Indians from the region and secure their own permanence. As in New England, the cycle of a growing settler population that pressed on finite resources leading to warfare and coerced removal of indigenous groups was repeated in the mid-1670s, using the same justifications.

By then, the Chesapeake's white population was approaching 55,000. Immigration had picked up after the colony was secured, particularly after the successful establishment of tobacco cultivation. From the mid-1620s through the end of the century more than 100,000 English migrants entered the region. Actual population grew more slowly than immigration rates would suggest, to a total of some 80,000 at the end of the century. From the beginnings of settlement, the Chesapeake's demography was dictated by a disastrous (for Europeans) disease environment. Throughout the years of substantial European migration, from the late 1620s through the end of the century, up to 40 percent of the entering cohort would die during their first two or three years of residence.

Reliance on immigration to maintain population nevertheless declined as the century progressed, at least in relative terms. The Chesapeake's white inhabitants became divided into two distinct components – new immigrants who died at alarming rates and a slowly growing creole population whose demographic experience was more benign. As we will see, this division is of considerable importance in understanding the differentiated legalities of the Chesapeake's labor regime.

The late seventeenth century saw a third component forcibly added to the Chesapeake population – enslaved Africans. Africans both enslaved and free (Atlantic Creoles, in Ira Berlin's words) had been present in the

Chesapeake almost as long as the English, but their numbers did not begin to increase significantly until the 1660s. In 1670 the African creole population totaled about 2,500 (6 percent of the total non-Indian population); a decade later Africans numbered 4,300 (7 percent). That decade had seen the first significant importation of African slaves into the Chesapeake – some 3,100, a figure that suggests mortality rates in the entering cohort at least as high as among white migrants. Importation continued at a rate of some 3,500 per decade through the end of the century. Imports to Virginia increased to more than 7,000 per decade through 1720, then doubled to an average of 13,500 per decade over the next thirty years. Arrivals began tailing off in the 1750s and 1760s. The African population, meanwhile, increased for most of the century at rates substantially higher than could be accounted for by slave importation – rates of natural increase rose as the pool of survivors from earlier migrant cohorts grew larger. In 1700 the Chesapeake's African-origin population was 13,000 (13 percent of the total population). By 1750 it was 150,000 (40 percent), a proportion that remained relatively constant thereafter. As in the case of the European-origin population, Chesapeake slavery's demographic rhythms of importation and expansion broadly explain the particular legalities of labor in the region.

The Lower South

In the Lower South (the Carolinas and, later, Georgia) white settlement began in the 1660s, growing to 13,500 by the end of the century and nearly 300,000 by 1780. Initially building an economy based on trade with the region's indigenous inhabitants for hides and Indian slaves for West Indies plantations, in the 1700s white settlers began pressing hard for land, culminating in the Yamasee War of 1715–16 and the familiar process of expulsion of Indians for agriculture. Staple crop cultivation – notably rice – stimulated demand for labor, which meant the importation of African slaves. In South Carolina, slave importation began in the 1700s in numbers that approximated the flow of slaves to Virginia. In the 1730s, slave importation increased dramatically to more than 20,000, but then fell off almost completely in the 1740s, perhaps in reaction to the Stono revolt of 1739 and the role played in that revolt by newly arrived Africans. Arrivals surged again in the 1750s. Over the period from 1750 through 1790 slave arrivals averaged 17,000 per decade, compared with fewer than 6,000 per decade to Virginia.

The Lower South's reliance on slave importation for labor meant that for most of the century the region's white population formed a smaller proportion of total population than in the Chesapeake. Blacks comprised

17 percent of the introduced population in 1700 and peaked at 47 percent by 1740, before declining over the second half of the century to around 40 percent. Unlike the Chesapeake, natural increase did not contribute significantly to black population growth until after the 1740s. Throughout the first half of the century, slave importation accounted for virtually all growth in South Carolina's African population.

The Middle Colonies

The middle colonies – Pennsylvania, Delaware, the Jerseys, and New York – had the most diverse population of all the mainland regions. Indigenous confederations – Algonquian on the coast, Iroquois to the north and west – were strong and populous. European settlement was begun in the 1630s by the Dutch in the Hudson Valley and included Swedish-founded settlements in the Delaware Valley and English settlements on Long Island. By 1660 the European population stood at about 5,000, mostly concentrated in the Dutch settlements. About 500 Africans were also present. A more rapid influx began in the 1670s after the English took control of New Amsterdam and after the creation of English colonies on both sides of the Delaware River. In the fifty years after 1680 the regional population grew from 15,000 to approaching 150,000. By 1780 it had reached 720,000. Much of the late seventeenth-century growth came from Northern English, Welsh, and Scottish migrants moving to Pennsylvania and the Jerseys, while the eighteenth century saw the development of substantial migrant flows from Ulster, Southern Ireland, and in particular from the Rhine lands of Middle and Southern Germany, as well as continued migration from Scotland. All these flows developed most rapidly after the 1730s, creating the same expansionist pressure on indigenous populations as elsewhere. Feeding into the middle colonies principally through New York and Philadelphia, many migrants extended their mobility westward to the Susquehanna River and thence on toward the Ohio Valley, where they met others heading west from the Chesapeake. As in New England, however, middle colony population growth was far more a creature of natural increase than of migration. The region's black population, meanwhile, grew from 1,000 to 40,000 in the century following 1680, generally averaging 6–8 percent of the region's total introduced population. Slavery was not widespread in the middle colonies outside urban areas such as Philadelphia and New York. As elsewhere, the region's legal labor regime reflected its demography.

Over the two centuries after 1580, then, the English mainland colonies had been "manned" by between 470,000 and 520,000 English and other European migrants (about 10 percent of them convicts or prisoners) and approximately 311,000 forced migrant Africans. By 1780 the non-indigenous population stood at 2.7 million – 79 percent of European origin, 21 percent African. It had spread in tentacular fashion up and down western river valleys, well beyond the narrow coastal strip where Europeans had settled in the seventeenth century. Over the same period the indigenous population of the same regions had declined by more than half. Hit by repeated demographic disasters and military campaigns that disrupted established social and political organization, land use, and economic behavior, sucked into an economy of procuring for European trading and slaving networks, the tribes had lost much of their structure, cohesion, and group identity. The indigenous found themselves pushed and pulled together in newly created polyglot communities – temporary worlds "made of fragments" of what had been.[4]

Ironically, this new world of fragments created by indigenous decline had something of a parallel in the swarming polythetic encroachments of the colonizers. To become the resource ("manning") that Hakluyt had foreseen, however, movement had to be organized and disciplined.

II. "DIRECTED AND CONDUCTED THITHER": THE LAW AND POLITICS OF POPULATING

Law was foundational in the peopling of British America. We have already noted that the first stirrings of international law, the law of nations and of war, are to be found in juristic discourses that naturalized European expansion and pushed aside those on whom European arrivals intruded. In the actual movement of peoples the relationship between law and migration shifts from the conceptual – the creation of an ideal emptiness meet to be filled – to the instrumental: the means to direct and conduct thither those who would fill it.

Loco-motion

Basic to the instrumentalities of migration is the law's place in defining the very phenomenon – capacity for mobility – that is the essential condition of "peopling" itself. What Blackstone described as "the right which the king has, whenever he sees proper, of confining his subjects to stay within the realm" underscored the development, traceable to early modern England, of an attitude that population was a resource to be rendered mobile or

[4] Daniel K. Richter, "Native Peoples of North America and the Eighteenth Century British Empire," in P. J. Marshall, ed., *The Eighteenth Century*, vol. II of *The Oxford History of the British Empire*, ed. William R. Louis (Oxford, 1998), 359.

immobile according to the best interests of the state; this attitude was displayed in the English case through the general assertion of sovereignty and duties of ligeance embodied in the writ *ne exeat regnum*. Blackstone made much of the centrality of "the power of loco-motion, of changing situation, or removing one's person to whatsoever place one's own inclination may direct" to the Englishman's personal liberty, second only to personal security in the great catalogue of absolute rights of persons secured by English law. But it was, he noted, a right open to abridgment with sufficient cause and the law's approval, and his brief history of locomotion's legalities noted a history of restraints stretching over four hundred years to the fourteenth century. "Some persons there antiently were, that, by reason of their stations, were under a perpetual prohibition of going abroad without licence obtained" – peers, knights and ecclesiastics, and in addition archers and artificers "lest they should instruct foreigners to rival us in their several trades and manufactures." An Act of 1381 revised and extended the prohibition, denying departure without license to all save only "the lords and other great men of the realm, and true and notable merchants, and the King's soldiers."[5] That act was in its turn repealed in 1607, but its authority is evident in the first (1606) Charter of Virginia, which specifically licensed the departure to America of "Sir Thomas Gates, Sir George Somers . . . " and all who should willingly accompany them, "to travel thitherward, and to abide and inhabit there, in every the said Colonies and Plantations," provided "that none of the said Persons be such, as shall hereafter be specially restrained by Us, our Heirs or Successors." Nor did repeal appear to lessen the significance of the sovereign's claim to a general authority over departure. Thus the second (1609) Charter of Virginia granted explicitly "that it shall be lawful and free" for promoters of the colony and those they might take with them to depart and inhabit "the said Plantation," as in 1606. The grant was repeated in the third (1612) Charter. In the New England Charter, eight years later, the Crown in similar fashion expressly granted the New England Council lawful authority to take and transport to "the said Plantation in New England, all such and so many of our loveing Subjects . . . as shall willingly accompany them." Cecilius Calvert's Maryland Charter (1632) included a grant of "Power, License and Liberty, to all the Liege-Men and Subjects, present and future, of Us, our Heirs and Successors, except such to whom it shall be expressly forbidden, to transport themselves and their Families to the said Province." The same is to be found in the Carolina and Pennsylvania charters. The English Solicitor General again asserted the Crown's authority over its subjects' departures in 1718, when restrictions were imposed on

[5] William Blackstone, *Commentaries on the Laws of England: A facsimile of the First Edition of 1765–1769*, vol. I (Chicago, 1979), 130, 133–4, 255–6, 261.

the migration of skilled workers. Additional regulations on the migration of artisans were enacted in 1750 and 1765, and defended by Blackstone, for though "at present every body has, or at least assumes, the liberty of going abroad when he pleases. Yet undoubtedly if the king . . . thinks proper to prohibit him from so doing" it would be "a high contempt" to disobey.[6]

Blackstone's affirmation of crown authority came at a time of rising clamor over depopulation of the British Isles by unprecedented levels of transoceanic migration following the cessation of Anglo-French hostilities in 1760. The debates of the 1760s and early 1770s explicitly recognized population as a resource of the nation-state – its increase to be measured, its movements tracked, its capacities mobilized in the service of the nation's social and economic betterment. The calls for wholesale restrictions on migration to which the debates gave rise were spurred by competition between British and American interests to control this resource. Both sides recognized that increase of population, economic vitality, and territorial expansion were intimately related, that population was the ultimate foundation for national power. As Benjamin Franklin wrote in 1773, artfully speaking the parts both of an Englishman opposed to restriction and of an American lauding the country's development (and thus tempting the migrant), "New farms are daily every where forming in those immense Forests, new Towns and Villages rising; hence a growing Demand for our Merchandise, to the greater Employment of our Manufacturers and the enriching of our Merchants. By this natural Increase of People, the Strength of the Empire is increased; Men are multiplied out of whom new Armies may be formed . . . for the manning of our Fleets in time of War." The increase of colonial populations – whether by unrestricted migration or natural growth – would render both colonies and metropolis "more secure."[7]

Two hundred years earlier, debates over English population had been leading in quite the opposite direction – fear of its excess rather than its loss. Legal debates had focused not on the Crown's authority to restrain but to banish. The point agitated, that is, was not freedom to depart but protection against forcible expulsion. But even as the polarity of debate swung back and forth over the centuries, the point at the center of the contest – that movements of population were not autonomous of sovereign authority – remained consistent. Nor was this simply a question of movements beyond the crown's realm or to new domains claimed beyond the ocean. Large segments of early modern English law addressed quite precisely the police

[6] Blackstone, *Commentaries*, 256.

[7] Benjamin Franklin, "On a Proposed Act to Prevent Emigration" (December? 1773), in William B. Willcox, ed., *The Papers of Benjamin Franklin*, 20 (New Haven, 1976), 522–28, at 526.

of population within the realm. From poor relief and the control of vagrancy, through the disciplining of labor and mobilization of the idle, to the very enjoyment of civic capacity, the English state attempted to set the terms of social and economic organization under which people lived, moved, and worked.

In good part the impulse to police population was engendered by environmental trends and upheavals. English population history long followed a pattern of secular growth interrupted by outbreaks of catastrophic disease, the results of which – social and economic disorganization, dearth, mobility – threatened social order. The first population peak, at more than 3.5 million, came in the mid-fourteenth century. Growth during the previous seventy-five years had been particularly rapid, but interspersed with periods of increasing mortality from famine and disease. These culminated in the Black Death plague outbreak of 1348–51, which killed between one-third and one-half of the population. By the end of the fourteenth century the population stood at 2.1 million. Sustained increase did not resume until the early sixteenth century and accelerated after 1530, but was interrupted, as before, by periods of disease (notably the influenza outbreak of the late 1550s and serial plague outbreaks during the seventeenth century) and by famine and dearth. Between the 1530s and the 1650s, the English population had grown from 2.3 million to some 5.6 million, with a particularly rapid increase between 1560 and 1590.

Growing population meant rising food prices, periodic dearths, and basic alterations in the balance and location of arable and pastoral agriculture, resulting in increased internal movement and population redistribution. After the Black Death, conditions of acute labor shortage and suddenly plentiful land saw arable cultivation retreat from the marginal lands to which it had been extended in the previous half-century. These tendencies were accompanied by structural change in the organization of agriculture that reflected competition among landlords to attract scarce tenants, the consolidation of vacant smallholdings into enlarged farms, the commutation of labor services into rents, and the development of new forms of manorial land title (copyhold) to replace villeinage. All increased the mobility of the surviving rural population. After population growth resumed, and particularly as the rate of growth accelerated during the latter part of the sixteenth century, mobility continued to increase, but this time as a response to constricted rather than increased opportunity. Impoverished uplanders from the north and west headed south from crowded pastoral areas where relentless subdivision of smallholdings was exhausting local capacity to continue absorbing generational increases in population. Similarly, as the fielden parishes typical of lowland England found their capacity to absorb their own growing population increasingly constrained, their surplus inhabitants likewise searched for localities with substantial commons and wastes or moved to woods-pasture, fens, and forest regions, all offering chances to practice subsistence farming and to engage in by-employments. Cities and towns provided another destination, particularly London, whose population increased from some 50,000 at the beginning of the sixteenth century to some 400,000 by the middle of the seventeenth.

Increasing mobility meant increasing visibility. Inter-regional subsistence migration spurred anxiety for the stability of social order and attempts to tie individuals in place – geographically, through entitlement to poor relief; socially and economically, through the harassment of vagrants and enforced employment of the idle. Each policy hinted at an awareness of population as a resource to be managed for the benefit of the commonwealth – as did the taking of censuses. However, just as current was fear of the disease of "masterless" excess that could not be controlled through existing social and economic institutions, to which statutory criminalization was the first and only retort. The Elizabethan poor laws were central: beginning with the act of 1572, climaxing in those of 1597 and 1601, legislation established compulsory poor rates for the relief of the impotent, directed the unemployed to work, and severely penalized vagrancy. Vagrancy laws doubled as a police of the young. Half of all vagrants apprehended were under the age of 16, two-thirds younger than 21. Early in the seventeenth century "vagrant" was defined as any able-bodied wanderer over the age of 7.

Central authorities might pass all the legislation they pleased, but action depended on the localities, where variations in will to implement could make "uniform" policy look anything but in execution. Propagandists of colonization stepped into this debate, arguing that overseas settlement would remove the threat – indeed, put the excess to good use. In an important sense, their arguments invited a delegation of responsibility entirely in keeping with English state structure – colonies could be seen as new cooperative and productive localities for accommodating superfluous people. "[T]he Bees, when they grow to be too many in their own hive at home, are wont to be led out by their Captaines to swarme abroad," wrote the younger Richard Hakluyt in his preface to *Divers Voyages to America* (1582). His elder cousin emphasized how, through settlement overseas, those who were "burdensome or hurtefull to this Realme at home" might be made "profitable members" – particularly the young, with whom "the Realme shall abound too much."[8]

[8] Richard Hakluyt the younger, "Preface to Diverse Voyages" (1582); Richard Hakluyt the elder, "Pamphlet for the Virginia Enterprise" (1585, two drafts), all in Taylor, ed., *Original Writings*, 175–6, 234, 330, 340.

Organizing Mobility

By the time continuous English settlement in Virginia had begun, active Crown engagement in projects to penetrate the "rude parts" of the British archipelago – the Anglo-Scottish Borders, the Scottish Highlands and the Hebrides, Ireland – had already brought the establishment of plantations and, particularly in the case of the Munster and Ulster plantations, significant transfers of population. In embracing the North American colonizing project, the early modern English state added further to its capacities to manage domestic population by facilitating the mobilization of its "surplus" for productive use elsewhere. In the American case, the crown charters that created colonies established in detail how authority was to be exercised over population. Charters licensed departures, as we have seen. They also established jurisdictions to manage arrivals. Migration became a process of moving people from one jurisdiction to another. Colonial jurisdictions were embodied generally in the creation of structures of governance and relations of authority, and specifically in provisions establishing explicit powers over the movements of people – as in the first Virginia Charter, for example, which granted to its licensees authority to expel "all and every such Person or Persons, as without the[ir] especial License . . . shall attempt to inhabit" within the precincts of the territory assigned in the charter, and as in the third Virginia Charter of 1611, which added a clause granting the London-based Virginia Council broad authority to police migrants' departures to and returns from Virginia "for the well-ordering and good Government of the said Colony." The same clause appeared in the New England Charter.

As well as outlining powers to manage and govern population, charters also established the legal statuses into which migrants and their descendants would fit. Migrants and their children would be "subjects" of the English Crown, enjoying "all Liberties, Franchises, and Immunities . . . as if they had been abiding and born, within this our Realm of England, or any other of our said Dominions" (the first Virginia Charter); they were to be "free Denizens and naturall Subjects" with those same liberties and privileges (the second Virginia Charter, the New England Charter). Precisely what these terms meant was clarified in *Calvin's Case* (1608), which in the course of mediating the jurisdictional consequences of James VI of Scotland's accession (1603) to the English throne as James I also began – indirectly – to address the implications of overseas settlement for the compass of English law.

Calvin's Case was a contrived dispute, heard by a special court consisting of the Lord Chancellor and the judges of all the king's common law courts, intended to resolve the question of who should enjoy the liberties and immunities of an English "subject." Born Scots were natural subjects of the Scottish Crown of James VI, but what of their status in England under James I? The English Parliament declined the proposition that all natural subjects in each kingdom should be recognized as natural subjects of the other. The immediate concern was jurisdiction over the movements of population – parliamentarians imagined that mutual recognition would mean an unstoppable influx of indigent Scots, exacerbating English population excess. But they also opposed blanket recognition of the new king's Scottish subjects so as to avoid a "mutual naturalizing of all nations that hereafter fall into the subjection of the king, although they be very remote," an outcome that would "disorder the settled government of every of the particulars." *Calvin's Case* mapped the precise borders of English refusal by considering the status of a particular subset of Scottish subjects, the so-called *postnati*: those born after James's English coronation. With the Scottish king now ruling an additional English domain, the case tested the *postnati*'s status as subjects in that domain through an examination of the infant Robert Calvin's right to sue in English courts to protect his title to land in England of which he had been disseised.

Land holding in England was a privilege of English subjects, and also of denizens – that is, aliens granted the privilege of land holding, though not of heritability, by the Crown. It was agreed that Scots who were *antenati* – born prior to James's accession to the English Crown – were not English subjects and thus could not have recourse to English law. They were aliens. At best they could become denizens. As a *postnatus*, however, Robert Calvin's status was held to be very different. Sir Edward Coke, then Chief Justice of Common Pleas, published his opinion in the case, which as a result became authoritative. Calvin had been born within James's domain, of parents who owed James obedience (and enjoyed his protection). Hence Calvin was born into relations of ligeance. By the time of Calvin's birth in 1606, James's royal domain had grown to encompass England as well as Scotland. No political union had occurred. But ligeance was a personal bond prevailing between the natural person of the king and the natural subject wherever he or she might reside in the king's domain, and hence transcended whatever political and legal distinctions might exist among different constituent parts of the domain. Ligeance meant that the king's subject enjoyed the king's protection wherever the king ruled at the moment that the relation of ligeance was formed. Calvin was hence as entitled to seek remedies obtainable from the King's *English* courts within their sphere of jurisdiction as he was from the King's *Scottish* courts within their sphere of jurisdiction, or indeed from courts anywhere within the king's domain as it was constituted at the time of his birth.

Calvin's Case has long been read for its imperial implications. As Daniel Hulsebosch has pointed out, both colonists and, later, historians invoked the case as establishing that subjects of the English monarchy anywhere within the royal domain had access to the benefits of English law, interpreting Coke's opinion to mean that English law and liberties accompanied British settlers. Indeed *Calvin's Case* did have implications for overseas expansion, but not for the infinite extensibility of English law. Coke's discussion of expansion was couched in terms of kingly conquest of alien kingdoms, Christian and infidel, and of what a conquering king might do to the laws of a conquered territory.[9] To conquest Coke counterposed not settlement but inheritance. Monarchs who acceded to a throne by inheritance, as James had, could not alter a kingdom's laws except by consent of its Parliament. The "third case" contention that English subjects settling new lands carried with them the laws of England by dint of birthright would not be formulated for well over a century. Rather, *Calvin's Case* established that wherever they were within the king's domain, his subjects might have resort to the king's courts with jurisdiction in that place – a rather different outcome. Natural subjects in Virginia had access to and were ruled by the law as administered in Virginia according to the jurisdictional structure outlined in the Virginia charters. This was not "English law" but law "as near as conveniently may be . . . agreeable" to English law. So also in New England under the New England Charter: local law was simply to be "not contrarie" to English laws; so also in the Massachusetts Bay Company Charter: "not contrary or repugnant" to English law. *Calvin's Case* underlined that English law as such was available to all subjects, wherever within the king's dominions they might be born or domiciled, only in England.

The charters made the same pronouncement. Guaranteed the status of natural subjects, or denizens, migrants and their offspring would enjoy those rights on their return. When domiciled overseas and answerable to a local jurisdiction, however, settlers did not gain access to English law per se, but to such law that had been formulated according to the limits specified, and through the jurisdictional structures described, in the charters granting permission to proceed with settlements. Coke, Hulsebosch argues, did conceive of a certain core of English liberties and privileges accompanying the migrating subject – a right to hold land by the same tenures available in England, a right to some form of parliamentary governance – and both are prominent in the charters of overseas settlement. But *Calvin's Case* is concerned predominantly with the implications for English

[9] If it were Christian, the conquering king might alter the laws of the conquered kingdom, but until such changes were made its own established laws would remain in effect; and once English laws had been introduced to a conquered Christian kingdom the monarch's capacity to continue to alter its laws became subject to parliamentary consent. If it were Infidel, existing laws were abrogated ipso facto and the king might govern at his pleasure, restrained only by natural equity, until certain laws were established anew.

laws of the accession of an alien Christian monarch. Much of what has since been interpreted as a disquisition on the early implications of English transoceanic expansion was at the time a careful attempt to restrain James I's royal discretion and known tendencies to absolutism in his *inherited* land of England.

Eutopolis

Charters, then, granted migrants permission to depart, created jurisdictional apparatuses to receive and govern them on arrival, assigned them statuses, and established a relationship between the laws prevailing in overseas territories and those prevailing in England. At the same time by separating status from territory, the discourse of allegiance allowed natural subjecthood to become fully portable. The English state thus maintained its emigrants in a state of legal accountability. Each was a person (subject) who could be policed overseas no less than in the metropolis through structures of governance established for that purpose and peculiar to each locale.

In these respects, and others too, the charters dealt in detail with the architecture of license, power, and authority in colonial societies, from land tenures to the establishment of markets, manors, and churches, from the levying of customs to the distribution of arms. As such they gave expression not merely to the institutional practicalities of state formation but to a discourse of civic organization that Engin Isin has recently termed "eutopolis" – the dream of the rational city made a legal reality, where population was organized as subjects arrayed in a ranked spatial order that was simultaneously a political order singling out the ideal citizen, the free man, and separating him from the rest – the vagrants, the vagabonds, the beggars, the slaves. Articulated in the Old World but continually projected onto the New, eutopolis provided "a technology of citizenship by which dominant groups encased their position in the social order by fusing the political and economic orders that produced a legal order" and thence created the rational city "as a concrete spatial order," a housing, as it were, for their ideal.[10] Nowhere is the conjunction of eutopolis with colonizing better expressed than in the writings of Hakluyt the elder, for whom the city planted in the transatlantic wilderness provided a perfected representation of civil association and civilization, a seat for sovereignty, a center for commerce, and a citadel for evangelism.

From the Virginia colony to New England to Carolina to Pennsylvania to Georgia, the creation of cities and townships – ordered rather than

[10] Engin Isin, *Being Political: Genealogies of Citizenship* (Minneapolis, 2002), 153–4.

dispersed settlement – stood at the center of colonizers' strategies for securing territory and planning inhabitation. The first settlement in the Chesapeake was named James City (colloquially Jamestown), the second Charles City. The projectors of the so-called particular plantations, such as Berkeley Plantation, planned settlement based on the establishment of towns. In New England, famously, John Winthrop's *Arbella* sermon, "A Modell of Christian Charity," denominated the Massachusetts Bay colonizing project an exemplary eutopolis, a city on a hill. Townships, not dispersed settlement, were the key to the organization of New England's population. The proprietary colonies of the Restoration further elaborated the model. The creation of a city was central to the Carolina proprietors' plans for their colonizing project. Their *Fundamental Constitutions* created a dense complementary political order – interwoven layers of office, rank, privilege, obligation, boundary, and rule sorting and regulating all inhabitants. Penn's ambitions were not dissimilar – a city, contiguous concentrated settlement patterns, and an elaborated political order all planned well in advance of actual settlement. What was being created in all these cases was a spatially embodied political or civic order to receive and organize the migrating population.

Servants

While they are potent expressions of crown claims and colonizers' ideal designs, the charters are less helpful as guides to the jurisdictional mechanics of organizing migrating populations on the ground. Practically speaking, neither the crown's *subject* nor the eutopolis's *citizen* was the legal status of most immediate consequence for the majority of transoceanic migrants. All were subjects; some were free men. But both in England and in North America, the practicalities of migration and its distributional aftermath were managed by resort to a distinct body of law, the legal incidents of servitude, for here lay the most fecund cache of rules for policing populations on the move in English law.

That the law of servitude should furnish the primary institutional structures for trans-Atlantic migration is not odd – the immediate purpose of migration, after all, was to supply labor for the mainland colonies out of the surplus population of England. Further, the legal incidents of servitude were of a piece with the subordination to a sovereign that subjecthood meant and with the ranked order of eutopolis, simultaneously manufacturing servant-subjects for the bottom of social hierarchies and master-citizens for the top. Conceptually, that is, Hakluyt's recommended exports – the eutopolitan city and the surplus population of masterless vagabonds and vagrants – went together: the one a receptacle and an ordering device for the other.

Once migration got fully under way in the 1630s, therefore, it is no surprise to find that the body of law managing the transoceanic movement of population was law relating to servitude. Servitude became an efficient means for controlling the process of assembling migrants, financing their passage, and distributing them on arrival. Servitude proved, moreover, a highly flexible legal mechanism, applicable to the several varieties of relationship forged in the process of population transfer, from individually negotiated indentures, through terms dictated by statute, all the way to slavery.

III. POPULATION, MIGRATION, AND INDENTURED SERVITUDE

The legal basis of early American indentured servitude was a written agreement (indenture) committing one party to a series of payments benefiting the other – to settle their transportation costs, provide subsistence over the (negotiable) contractual term, and pay "freedom dues" in kind or cash at the conclusion of the term – in exchange for which the beneficiary agreed to be completely at the disposal of the payor, or the payor's assigns, for performance of work, for the term agreed.

Of the total European migration to the mainland colonies during the two centuries prior to American independence (some 500,000 people), more than half arrived committed to an initial period of servitude by indenture or similar form of agreement, or by sentence of transportation. Among Europeans, migration under condition of servitude was substantially more common in the seventeenth century, when it covered 60–65 percent of all migrants, the vast majority of whom ended up in the Chesapeake region, than in the eighteenth century, when it covered some 50 percent (including convicts), a plurality of whom entered the Middle Colonies. The eighteenth century, however, saw rapid increases in slave importation. Adding enslaved Africans to European servants, some 70 percent of all eighteenth-century migrants entered the mainland colonies committed to servitude for a negotiated or assigned period (European) or for life (African). The same overall proportion was true for seventeenth-century migration, although the predominance then of European migration meant servitude for a term prevailed over slavery's servitude for life.

Servitude as Regulatory Capacity

Historically, few areas of English governmental activity have proven more constitutive of state capacities than the regulation of work and labor. It is precisely in the ambition to control the performance and mobility of labor that one finds the historical point of origin of what Margaret Somers has called England's "national legal sphere."[11] The Ordinance (1349) and Statute (1351) of Labourers, adopted in response to the demographic catastrophe of the Black Death, stand as the primary statutory expressions of the attempt to establish cohesive government during the second half of Edward III's reign to hold the existing structure of society together. Before 1348, English common law did not police agricultural or artisan labor. Such regulation as took place was piecemeal and purely local, and dealt with labor in terms of incidents of service arising from personal status. The Ordinance and Statute of Labourers added parliamentary regulation to local, imposing compulsion to work at accustomed wages on a wide range of agricultural and artisanal occupations, setting wage standards and terms of hire, and creating office-holders to implement the measures. So, also, did the Statute of Artificers (5 Eliz. c.4, 1563) two centuries later, which in certain respects once more gave labor regulation national expression. Its stated intent – to reduce the several laws on the books into one comprehensive statute that "shouyld banishe Idlenes advance Husbandrye and yeeld unto the hired pson both in the time of scarsitee and in the tyme of plentye a convenient proporcon of Wages" – lends some support to conventional perceptions of the statute as the domestic key to a systematic mercantilist policy of labor regulation.

But there is more to the Statute of Artificers than a mercantilist explanation allows. In the case of wages, its intent was self-professedly benign. The Statute abandoned 200 years of fixing wage rates by statute because "the wages and allouances lymytted and rated . . . are in dyvers places to small and not answerable to this tyme." This acknowledged both general price inflation and regional variation in labor markets, and hence in wage and price outcomes. In other respects too, the Statute was less a systematically formulated national code than an unwieldy compilation of regionally distinct components, serving different purposes. In the case of craft apprenticeship, for example, it established a structure of rules that simply elaborated practices (control of entry to trades, limitation of numbers, the delegitimation of untrained rivals, discipline) long since developed by the urban craft companies to regulate apprenticeship and the craft itself for their own purposes.

Where no embedded interests held sway, however, the Statute was peremptory. In contrast to its careful navigation of craft apprenticeship, apprenticeship in husbandry – a quite different institution – was forcefully established. Apprenticeship in husbandry had no preexisting structure of

[11] Margaret Somers, "Citizenship and the Place of the Public Sphere: Law, Community, and Political Culture in the Transition to Democracy," *American Sociological Review* 58, 5 (1993), 596.

corporate control or organized interests. It was the state's to define. The state did so in the name of an objective – "the better advauncement of Husbandrye and Tillage" – that expressed a perception of population as a resource for the advancement of general interests. In pursuit of "better advauncement," the Statute required that "any pson above thage of tenne yeres and under thage of eightene yeres," and without other calling, enter the service of any householder "having and using half a Ploughe Lande at the least in Tillage" for apprenticeship in husbandry "until his Age of one and twenty yeres at the least . . . the seyd reteynour and taking of an Apprentice to be made and done by Indenture."

Apprenticeship in husbandry targeted the same stratum of the population – rural youth – as the better known institution of service in husbandry. But farm service and farm apprenticeship were very different. Servants in husbandry were effectively self-activating. Beginning in early adolescence they served by the year for board and wages, contracting on their own behalf with successive masters until reaching the age of majority or until they married. The institution was brought under the umbrella of the Statute of Artificers, which provided for the general enforcement of yearly hirings by justices of the peace or officers of municipal corporations, and required that those departing service in husbandry or other yearly hirings obtain and carry "testimonial of licence" – a certificate, pass, or other document – to prove to local authorities that their mobility was legitimate. But it was not substantively altered. By contrast, apprenticeship in husbandry was intended for surplus children unable to find positions as yearly servants; it required them to remain in the service of a single master for the length of whatever term of service was secured by their indenture – anything from three to eleven years – in a relationship supervised by local authorities.

Because English farm servants appear demographically similar to transoceanic migrant servants – male and youthful – indentured servitude has been taken to be an adaptation of contractual farm service to the economics of intercontinental labor transfer. In this view the intercontinental journey was no different from the annual journeys that youths made from village to village to enter or continue service, and the agreement a variation on a contract for credit to cover transportation costs that required the binding authority of an indenture because the only security on the loan was the servant himself. No doubt numbers of migrant servants were recruited in this fashion, particularly those in late adolescence who had gained experience negotiating contracts as English farm servants and who managed to exert a degree of influence on the terms of indentures agreed before embarkation. Nevertheless, indentured servitude was not simply a credit-driven adaptation of yearly farm service. Apprenticeship in husbandry had long since made indentured servitude well known in England as a means to manage idle or surplus youth. It provided the necessary statutory definitions, and the model of criminal compulsion enforcing a multi-year indenture as well.

Building the structure of trans-Atlantic migration on indentured servitude thus meant building migration on an English legal foundation designed specifically to ensure that the youngest and poorest layers of the rural population, beginning at age 10, or even younger in the case of orphans, were mobilized for work. Legal design was fulfilled in social outcome, for the migrant population recruited to service in the colonies overwhelmingly reproduced the demographic character of the population that apprenticeship in husbandry was intended to cover. Take migration to the Chesapeake – the main region of mainland reception during the seventeenth century – as an example. Single males were absolutely predominant (the male:female sex ratio among indentured migrants was 6:1 in the 1630s, dropping to 3:1–2:1 during the second half of the century). Self-supporting migrants tended to be single males, like the indentured, but older: 75 percent were below age 35 but they clustered in the 20–34 age range. Indentured migrants were considerably more youthful: 30 percent under 19 (increasing to 50 percent by the end of the century) and 80 percent under age 24. And in fact, servant migration was substantially more youthful than these figures indicate. "Typical" age ranges rely on details of terms of service recorded in indentures registered before departure. But many were transported to the Chesapeake as servants without formally entering indentures before departure, destined to serve according to standardized terms and conditions specified in local statute law, the so-called custom of the country. The earliest such statutes included provision for servants below the age of 12, indicating how young migrant servants might be. The records of local Chesapeake courts, responsible for determining the new arrivals' ages and terms of service, confirm that servants retained according to local statute were consistently younger, aged on average 13–14, than those negotiating indentures in England. One may conclude that throughout the seventeenth century a significant percentage of male servant migrants clustered well below the lower end of the 15–24 age range that has been considered the norm. On this evidence, the "typical" age range should be adjusted downward. Male servant migrants on the whole are more appropriately considered children than young adults. In the initial attempts of the Virginia Company to promote systematic migration, beginning in 1619, indigent children feature prominently. The association of children with migrant indentured servitude remains marked throught the entire seventeenth century.[12]

Although forced transfer of destitute children by English local authorities featured quite prominently in the Virginia Company's recruitment efforts,

[12] See also Chapter 9, this volume.

the mechanism by which the mobilization of population was managed in the transatlantic case was less one of direct state compulsion than of mercantile investment backed by legal enforcement. By specifying a salable quantity (period) of service over and above the capacity to perform labor, the indenture commodified the migrant laborer as an article of commerce. Migrant servants were exported to the colonies in the course of transoceanic trade. This status – article of commerce – was confirmed in statutes enacted by colonial legislatures to regulate trade. Migrant indentured servants, moreover, remained within the stream of commerce. Unlike servants in England, servants in the colonies could be bought and sold throughout their period of service. In all these respects, the legalities of the servant trade created a recognizable structure for the later trade in slaves.

The most elaborated role played by colonial statutes, however, was the policing of migrant labor as a segment of the population – that is, specifying terms and conditions of service, disciplining behavior, restraining mobility, enforcing subordination, and generally creating migrant labor as a factor of production. Such police statutes can be found in all colonies, their appearance prompted by the beginnings of substantial migration in the 1630s. The Chesapeake was the region of heaviest migration, however, so it is no surprise to find the greatest concentration of regulatory laws developed there.

The Chesapeake

In 1625, a census of the Virginia colony reported a total population of 1,227, of whom 487 were listed as servants (more than half of them owned by just ten people). Largely children and young adults, they prefigured what would emerge in the years of peak servant migration ahead. But at this point servant migration had hardly begun, and little attention was given to the details of their legal status. In its first decade the Virginia Assembly was less concerned with defining the condition of indentured labor than controlling the costs of hired labor, adopting from among the many provisions of the Statute of Artificers those that empowered magistrates to assess wages and that forbade laborers and artificers to leave work unfinished "unlesse it be for not payinge of his wages."[13]

By the early 1640s Virginia's hired labor statutes were no longer in force: they were not included in either the 1642 or 1652 Assembly restatements of Virginia law. Court records from the 1630s and early 1640s indicate that hired workers and some artisans were ordered to perform agreed terms of

[13] Act XXX (1631–2), in William Waller Hening, comp., *The Statutes at Large: Being a Collection of all the Laws of Virginia* (New York, 1823), I, 167. All subsequent text references to early Virginia statutes are taken from Hening's *Statutes*.

service or agreed tasks, but such orders peter out after the early 1640s, as the lapse of the statutes would lead one to expect. Isolated performance orders appear again in the 1660s, but far more often courts dealt with disputes over hired work in a civil realm of compensatory adjustments using damages and the apportionment of wages owed according to actual time worked as remedies for tasks or terms of service left unfinished.[14]

Over the same period, meanwhile, the Assembly's attention turned to migrant indentured servitude, establishing it as a distinct condition of explicit subordination to a sovereign master. Activities that implied an infringement of the immediate master's household jurisdiction – absconding, clandestine marriage, fornication – were rendered liable to severe punishment, usually including the addition of time to be served. Provisions directed at the free population reinforced servitude's jurisdictional hierarchy by penalizing those who traded with servants, harbored runaways, or enticed servants to abscond. Legislation prescribing terms for servants migrating without indentures had been adopted by 1642 (four years if over age 20; five years if over 12, seven if under age 12). Subsequently, the Assembly directed the county courts to determine the ages of servants imported without indenture. Servants completing their terms were required to obtain certification of their freedom from former masters before hiring or agreeing on shares with anyone else. Servants had few legislated rights, the Assembly merely allowing them to take grievances before justices.

Virginia's initial servant statutes were reaffirmed in the third general revision of colony statutes undertaken in March 1651/2, just as the colony was entering its heaviest period of immigration. The colony's fourth general revision (1662) shows that the subject was given additional detailed attention during the 1650s. Statutes passed during that decade confirmed the establishment of clear distinctions (of origin, age, and status) between migrant and other forms of labor, and regularized the local law of indentured labor. Old measures dealing with wage fixing and the performance of contracts by artisan labor remained dead and buried. Certification of freedom continued to be required of freemen entering contracts for wages, but penalties were directed at masters who harbored or entertained freemen in another's employ, not at the employee. Specific performance of labor contracts by free persons was not abandoned entirely, but it was confined in application to persons originating outside Virginia – former indentured servants or free migrants. In the case of indentured servants, clandestine marriage,

[14] This and other characterizations of early Chesapeake case law advanced in the text are based on research on the court records of York County, Virginia. See York County Transcripts, *Deeds, Orders, Wills* [*DOW*], I-XIX (1633–1746/7, with gaps); *Judgments & Orders* [*JO*], I (1746/7–1765, with gaps); *Order Books* [*OB*], I (1765–1768); *Judgments & Orders*, II (1768–1774); and *Order Books*, II (1774–1783); all located at Department of Historical Research, Colonial Williamsburg Foundation.

fornication, and runaway punishments were all reenacted, although physical disfigurement of persistent runaways (branding and hair cropping) was discontinued. The default terms of servants imported without indenture continued to vary: those above age 16 were now required to serve five years, those below until age 24. Age on entry was to be determined exclusively by the courts. Prohibitions on trading with servants were also reenacted. For the first time, however, servants gained specific protections in an enactment that ordered "compotent dyett, clothing and lodging," required "moderation" in correction of servants, and once more emphasized court oversight. In 1677, masters were foreclosed from renegotiating indentures with their servants outside the presence of a justice.

The terms confirmed during the 1660 revision remained in place for the rest of the century. The Assembly took up the subject again, however, in 1705. This renewed attention came toward the end of a momentous period of transition in the sources of Virginia's labor supply that had begun in the years after Bacon's Rebellion (1676), away from the youthful English servants who had provided the bulk of the colony's bound labor force since the 1630s toward overwhelming reliance on the importation of enslaved Africans. The capstone was "An Act concerning Servants and Slaves" a hybrid enactment that established a comprehensive legal framework for the slavery that would dominate the eighteenth century within a restatement of the statutory law of servants that had been developed during the seventeenth.

Slaves were most likely present in Virginia within a decade of the founding of Jamestown. But although slaves were distinguished from servants in daily life by the permanence of their servitude, nothing in the colony's early laws differentiated slavery from servitude per se. In fact, slaves and servants shared the distinction of originating outside the colony. Only when the slave population began to grow rapidly, and – equally important – when direct importation from Africa wrought substantial changes in its character, was slavery in the Chesapeake named, defined, and placed.[15]

The first reference to slaves as such in Assembly legislation cannot be found until 1655/6, when it was provided that Indian children taken as

[15] It is clear that almost as soon as they appeared in Virginia, Africans were considered legally distinct from whites. It is also clear that most were considered slaves – that is, permanently in bond to others – from the moment of their arrival, presumably because they were purchased and held as such. But it is less clear that Africans as a racial category were identified as slaves; some Africans were clearly considered servants, and some became freemen. Those who were enslaved were legally distinguishable by property law from those who were not. And eventually those who might be enslaved were identified by legal elaboration of racial categories. But neither property nor race concepts per se furnished the substantive content of slavery in Virginia law: that content came from the law of servitude, elaborated over time and adapted during the last three decades of the seventeenth century to the condition of persons serving for life as their numbers became sufficiently large to require distinct treatment.

hostages might *not* be enslaved. Other measures passed during the following decade strengthened the association of Africans with the condition of slavery while distinguishing others, notably Indians. Thus, in answer to the question whether children "got by any Englishman upon a negro woman should be slave or ffree," Act XII of December 1662 provided that "children borne in this country shalbe held bond or free only according to the condition of the mother." Five years later, Act III of September 1667 provided that no child born a slave could be made free by baptism. In October 1670, Act XII held that "all servants not being Christians imported into this colony by shipping shalbe slaves for their lives; but what shall come by land [that is, "Indians taken in warr by any other nation, and . . . sold to the English"] shall serve, if boyes or girles, until thirty yeares of age; if men or women twelve yeares and no longer."

Bacon's Rebellion ended the exemption of Indians. Nevertheless, the identification of slavery remained overwhelmingly with Africans from overseas. In 1682 the Assembly pulled together the piecemeal definitions of the past twenty years in its first comprehensive statement. Slaves were "all servants, except Turks and Moors while in amity with his majesty, which shall be imported into this country either by sea or by land, whether Negroes, Moors, mulattoes or Indians who and whose parentage and native countries are not Christian at the time of their first purchase by some Christian, although afterward and before their importation into this country they shall be converted to the Christian faith; and all Indians, which shall be sold by our neighboring Indians, or any others trafficing with us for slaves."

In 1660 the Chesapeake's indentured servant population stood between four and five thousand. The African population was less than one thousand. By 1680, the African population had risen to slightly over four thousand, and by 1705 it was approaching twenty thousand. The indentured servant population, meanwhile, was in decline from its 1670s peak of more than five thousand, and by the turn of the century sat in the mid-three thousands. The 1682 and 1705 statutes thus bracket a profound alteration in the composition of the bound labor force from youthful white migrants to imported African slaves. Indeed, the timing of the 1705 statute appears to be explained by the particularly rapid increase in resort to slave imports in the face of the renewed shut-down of the servant trade after 1701. Unlike the 1682 statute, the 1705 statute comprehensively reorganized the substance of the prevailing seventeenth century law of servitude around the new norm of slavery.

The 1705 statute elaborated the substantive implications of the series of distinctions already established in Virginia law between those servants who were slaves and those who were not. Beginning from the now familiar position that "servant" meant "imported servant," the statute repeated 1682's definition of slaves as imported servants who were not Christians at their time of entry into Virginia (subsequent conversion notwithstanding) and 1662's statement of matrilineal inheritance. Powers and duties common to all relations of servitude were specified, but discriminations in treatment and the availability of redress were prominent: for example, masters were forbidden to "whip a christian white servant naked," but could brutalize or kill a slave without fear of retribution. Servants, but not slaves, could complain to a Justice of a master's neglect of duty, or mistreatment, or non-payment of wages. Servants were also held entitled to maintenance if sick during their term of service, to freedom dues at the end of it, and to the protection of the courts in renegotiating indentures. All were required to obey their masters' just and lawful commands, neither servants nor slaves were allowed to trade without permission, and procedures for pursuit and punishment of runaways were specified without distinction. But miscegenation penalties and established racial categorizations of enslavement prescribed fundamental race separation.

The creation of distinct legal categories of origin (European/African, Christian/non-Christian) to manage the substantial shift under way in the composition of *imported* bound labor suggests that native-born whites comprised a third, wholly free, civic category. The substance of local legislation contains further indications to this effect. For example, the 1705 statute made no mention of artisans or tradesmen, and its requirements for certification of servants' freedom on completion of their terms distinguished "servants" from "poor people . . . [seeking] emploiment" in a fashion consistent with prior usages distinguishing bound (or formerly bound) migrant labor from creoles. Internally the statute was a hodge-podge of clauses inconsistent in their descriptions of the category "servant," including within its disciplinary reach those "become servants of their own accord here" and elsewhere referring to servants "whether by importation, indenture or hire here," or in another clause "by importation, or by contract, or indenture made here." Conceivably all such descriptions were meant to apply only to persons whose origins were outside Virginia – indeed, this was the sense of the legislation passed in the 1650s – or who had been designated community outsiders by legal process (criminals, bound-out paupers). As in earlier statutes there is support for this interpretation in those sections of the statute that deal with penalties.[16] But the ambit of "servant" is not completely clear.

[16] The 1705 statute's penalty provisions uniformly assume that those to whom they apply are all serving terms defined by "indenture, custom, or former order of court," rather than contract of hire. The only reference to servants by hire is in that section of the Act (10) confirming access to judicial determination of grievances and wages owed. No penalty provision applies to a servant by hire.

Twenty years later, however, the transformation of the bound labor force to one based on racial slavery was complete, and amendments adopted in 1726 altered the law dealing with runaways in a fashion that suggested "runaway" almost invariably meant "slave." They also added three clauses punishing refusals to work and misrepresentations of ability on the part of tradesmen and workmen "on wages," but the clauses were confined in scope entirely to migrants imported into the colony. (At this point craftsmen were about the only category of voluntary English labor still entering Virginia under indenture.) Thus the 1726 statute strengthened the association of whiteness and freedom from restraint in matters of work discipline already apparent in the 1705 statute while treating imported white labor as a partial and temporary exception. In 1748, the Assembly revised the 1705 provisions applying to white labor once more to make it unmistakably a regulation of labor imported under indenture. Servants were those who labored for others for terms set "by act of parliament, indenture, or custom." Hireling labor was nowhere to be found among the statute's categories.

The course of Virginia's statutory servant law shows that a specific form for indentured servitude emerged locally once the practice itself had been adopted as the best means to facilitate large-scale transoceanic transfers of youthful migratory labor. As Virginia's institutional complexity increased, the police of servitude took on a more closely observed and regulated character. But its early form – hierarchical, youthful, and extended – remained a constant. Originating in English law's coerced enlistment of orphan and pauper children in agricultural production, the general concept was clearly taken from the husbandry apprenticeship clauses of the Statute of Artificers and from the law of vagrancy. This set indentured servitude apart from other forms of Anglo-American labor relation: an indenture for services had no parallel in English law outside apprenticeship in husbandry.[17] Legally, the length of term required in the colonies to compensate for costs of transportation, subsistence, and freedom dues necessitated an explicit covenant setting the terms of the relationship, rather than a nod. That covenant in turn confirmed masters in the enjoyment of authority over the disposition of servant labor for extended periods and gave them an assignable property right in the person of the servant.

Over time, indentured servitude's development as a legal category distanced it from other forms of English work relation. That development also

[17] Craft apprenticeship contemplated multiyear terms, but accompanied these with training rationales beyond simple subsistence. Municipal and craft company regulation also ordained changes in the content of the apprenticeship over time, as the apprentice matured.

distanced it from creole work relations. In Virginia, explicit legal subordination to the authority of a master became a condition identified particularly with youth, as in England, but also with persons imported from elsewhere to labor for the resident population, rather than with anyone who undertook work at large. More obvious in the case of slavery's bestowal of conditions of comparative elevation on the unenslaved, one can see throughout the seventeenth century qualitative distinctions – youth/adult, migrant/creole, bound/free – being woven into Virginia's civic culture as a consequence of the presence of indentured servitude. It was slavery, nevertheless, that finally enabled Virginians to achieve a stable civic culture built on the distinction between servitude and other work relations. In the wake of Bacon's Rebellion, planter elites were torn between a need to secure and a need to appease their unruly white indentured labor force. Their eventual turn to a largely enslaved plantation labor force allowed pursuit of labor force security and white appeasement simultaneously. As Kathleen Brown has argued, white male servants could be promised a future as part of the social order as voters, citizens, and patriarchs. The enslaved were defined as incapable of enjoying any such status. In Virginia, the legal culture of work bestowed real civic capacity by simultaneously becoming a legal culture of race.

Virginia's half-century slide from servitude to an explicit and generalized law of slavery well illustrates how the institution could be given form through piecemeal local action adapting elements of the law of migrant servitude, which itself sat quite comfortably within a legal culture "as near" English law "as conveniently may be . . . agreeable." The Lower South offers a variation on the same trajectory. Influenced by slaveholders migrating from Barbados, slavery was written into Carolina's 1669 Fundamental Constitutions. No great influx of slave labor followed until the turn of the century, and the development of a generalized law of slavery awaited the moment that slave numbers began to increase. When they did, Carolina turned again to Barbados and drew on the island's "mature" slave code. Barbados had already proven to be an important influence on English Caribbean slave law, serving as a template for Jamaican law. But on close examination major aspects of Barbados' "mature" slave law turn out to have been constructed in much the same fashion as Virginia's would be, by using bits of sixteenth-century English law and practice policing the mobility of labor and the containment of threats to social order as points of reference, legitimation, and foundation.

English law, then, was no more segregated from the law of slavery – whether in the Caribbean or on the mainland – than it was from the law of migrant servitude. Its capacity to define and police population was what counted most. Indeed, as Sally Hadden has shown, many of the institutions that scholars associate with control of slaves' movements, such as slave patrols and the requirement that slaves carry passes or tickets when away from their master's plantation, had their origins in a more general police of movement extending to far wider categories of strangers and travelers, intended to forestall unauthorized departures from the colony, or simply mobility in general, among the suspicious – servants without tickets of leave, debtors, Indians. In time, of course, the unsupervised slave became the most suspicious and dangerous figure of all, identifiable by race and the object of virtually exclusive attention. But Virginia had already begun to turn toward a statutory policing of labor mobility when imported slaves were still no more than a small minority of the working population. In 1672, the Assembly embraced the Elizabethan vagrancy statute of 1597 (39 Eliz. C.4), which called for the erection of houses of correction in each county and imprisonment of rogues and vagabonds until they were employed or banished.

New England

The Chesapeake offers the clearest example of the use of the law of servitude to mobilize a population and manage the formation of a colony. Similar processes were on display elsewhere, but are delineated somewhat less clearly – the circumstances of different regions and colonizing projects producing different dynamics in the migration and police of population. Thus, in early New England indentured servitude was of much less significance in managing migration and labor force creation than in the seventeenth-century Chesapeake. Bound servants comprised a far smaller percentage of transatlantic migrants to New England than to any other mainland region, no more than 15–20 percent of the main wave of migration during the 1630s. Their numbers in population decreased rapidly thereafter as migration to New England tailed off to the merest dribble after 1640. Workers on wages, meanwhile, were never subject to much restraint. On two occasions early in the history of settlement in Massachusetts, the Massachusetts Court of Assistants proclaimed colony-wide wage regulation. But the proclamations were as quickly rescinded. Relations of hire generated complaints alleging breaches of contract, non-performance, or departure, but punitive strictures on hirelings are not in evidence in local statutes or case records. In 1655, for example, when Richard Jacob established that Mordecai Larkum (a married adult) had neglected his service, Larkum was neither imprisoned nor compelled to perform, but instead ordered to pay damages in lieu.[18] In

[18] This and other early Massachusetts cases discussed in the text can be found in *Records and Files of the Quarterly Courts of Essex County, Massachusetts* (*RFQE*), vols. 1–8, 1636–83 (Salem, 1911–21; repr. 1988).

September 1659, John Godfrey was found liable in damages to Francis Urselton for failing to perform work for which he had received an advance on his pay, but in November Urselton was non-suited when he attempted to have Godfrey penalized £5 for his departure and ordered to perform the outstanding service. The debt action can only have been an attempt to invoke the Statute of Artificers' penalties on laborers leaving work unfinished, and the non-suit indicates the Statute was considered inapplicable – indeed no other attempt to invoke it can be identified during the entire colonial period. From the other side of the hiring relation, when Thomas Rumerye sued John Norman for wages for sawing timbers, Norman defended himself by showing that he had paid in full, excepting only an amount withheld because Rumerye had departed before the work was completed. The defendant had not pursued the plaintiff for his premature departure nor withheld all his wages, but had simply refused to pay in full for incomplete performance. The court found no cause to answer.

The Massachusetts Charter described a basis for civil authority within the Commonwealth that rested substantially on the discretionary rule of local leaders confined only by the injunction that colony laws be "not repugnant to the laws and statutes" of England. Within this ambit the colony's police of labor sketched a set of provisions as much protective as coercive. The first attempt at a general statement of colony law, the *Body of Liberties* (1641), drafted liberties of servants that were exclusively concerned with the servant's welfare. The later *Lawes and Libertyes* (1648) approved these provisions verbatim while adding several rather more restrictive orders adopted piecemeal since the beginning of settlement by the Court of Assistants and the General Court. These prohibited servants from dealing in commodities without permission (1630), required "workemen" (paid by the day) to work a full day "alloweing convenient tyme for foode & rest" (1633), provided for the return of runaway servants (1635), allowed towns to assess wages (1636), allowed payment of wages in corn (1641), and enabled town constables to call on artificers and handicraftsmen not otherwise engaged to work in the harvest for wages (1646). The colony never adopted "custom of the country" provisions to deal with servants migrating without entering formal indentures because the phenomenon was virtually unknown. No requirement of compensatory service by runaways appeared until 1695, when courts were granted discretion to add up to one year's service in the specific case of "sons and servants" deserting the service of parents or masters to enter on board any ship or vessel.[19] As a code of conduct for those in service, the *Lawes and Libertyes* recalled aspects of English law but with

[19] A wider grant of discretion followed in 1759 that permitted courts "to order satisfaction to be made" by runaways "by service or otherwise, as to them shall seem meet."

little of its detail. Only covenanted servants – those explicitly bound by written indenture or other form of explicit contract to furnish services on demand for a prescribed term – were clearly subject to restraint. From the beginning most decisions were left to the discretion of local courts.

That statutory labor regulation should appear so circumscribed is not particularly surprising given the character of the New England population. Unlike the Chesapeake, the original migrant population for whom the *Body* and the *Lawes* were prescribed was one of families, in which the capacity to labor was represented by the head of household, accompanying children, and a thin stream of unattached servants laboring under indentures in return for passage and subsistence. As in the Chesapeake, nevertheless, the police of labor came to be identified with two specific categories of persons: youth and "outsiders." The migrant indentured servants of the 1630s were overwhelmingly youthful. But migration to New England was a short-lived phenomenon. When the supply of imported servants collapsed after 1640, creole youth became virtually the only source of deployable labor easily available to local inhabitants. The propensity for Massachusetts statutes in general to identify disciplinable service almost exclusively with youth is one of the most prevalent characteristics of the police of labor in the colony. Numerous seventeenth-century statutes singled out youth for watchful restraint while also identifying youth with service: "younge people," "children and servants," "young people, children, servants, apprentices," "men's sons and servants." Apprenticeship, both in husbandry and in craft, became the standard institutional means to mobilize youthful creole labor. By the eighteenth century "apprentice" and apprenticeship had become synonymous with "servant" and service in Massachusetts statutes.[20] Because youth was outside the community of household heads, and because youth is always everywhere considered simultaneously socially vulnerable and socially dangerous, justifications of its subjection to "authoritie" were easy to come by, as they never were for adult males.

As to outsiders, the *Body* and the *Lawes* identified three categories of people that could lawfully be subjected to the loss of liberty that servitude entailed. First came "lawfull captives, taken in just warrs" – that is, Indians such as the Pequots enslaved in the aftermath of the Pequot War (1637). Second were those "strangers" who "willingly sell themselves, or are solde to us" – imported indentured servants and/or slaves. Finally came persons "who shall be judged thereto by Authoritie" – that is, persons temporarily cast out through conviction for criminal offenses or debtors delivered by

[20] As elsewhere, apprenticeship was not confined to trade education in New England, but was the means that households used when they wished to convey a child's or youth's labor to others for an extended period.

court execution to serve creditors. None of these outsiders bulked large in local population. Indian servants are in evidence in Massachusetts, but enslaved Indian captives were mostly shipped to the West Indies. Imported indentured servants were rare after the first generation and African slaves present only in very small numbers. Debtor and convict service was not a realistic basis for a labor force.

Children, then, were the real basis of the early New England farm economy's labor force. This was no English-style service in husbandry, nor was it plantation-style indentured servitude – New England farms generated neither the demand for continuous labor imports common to the plantation regions nor the revenues to pay for them. Instead, close-knit patriarchal households retained their own male children in generational subordination over an extended period of household dependency from late infancy through adulthood and beyond. Where the labor of offspring was insufficient, the household might add an imported servant if one could be found, but migrant servants were distinctly supplemental and their "careers" followed the dominant household-familial pattern, coming into households young and remaining over extended periods of time.

Except for provisions aimed at policing youth, statutory disciplines structuring the population in hierarchical work relations were not much in evidence. As in the Chesapeake, statutory identification of specific segments of the working population as subordinate appears to have been accompanied by the development of exceptional degrees of legal freedom in work relations for others – for adult white males and, to a lesser extent, females. The difference was that in New England the subordinated population was defined by age and generational ties, rather than by a dense local law of work. The relative paucity of strangers or outsiders to be subjected to control is striking, compared with the Chesapeake. In the Chesapeake, the juvenile migrant indentured servitude of the seventeenth century and the more permanent and extreme subordination of race enslavement that succeeded it in the eighteenth were more clearly means to contain and control strangers.

Statutory controls on the behavior and general disposition of population remained focused predominantly on juveniles throughout the seventeenth and early eighteenth century. In 1651, for example, servants, children, apprentices, and scholars were all identified in a Massachusetts General Court order intended to preserve "the younge people of this country" from dissipation and idleness. Over the next thirty years, children, servants, and youth in general were made the subject of several public order measures policing behavior, work, and domicile. The colony's police of mobility was represented in its Act of March 1695 prohibiting masters of outbound ships from taking on board "men's sons or servants" without leave. A revision of the 1695 act passed in 1718 prohibited "Persons Under Age, Apprentices or Servants, Being Transported Out of the Province."

During the eighteenth century, regulation of mobility broadened beyond specific categories of people to address movement as a general phenomenon. For the first hundred years, the Massachusetts population had displayed relatively high cohesion and low mobility. Settlement had been administered through the towns, where the regulation of entry had limited dispersal. Even though restraints on western settlement were removed by wars to crush indigenous resistance, the wars themselves – notably King Philip's War (1676) – set back the creation and settlement of new western towns until well into the next century in favor of rising density in the eastern region. Inter-regional migration began increasing rapidly in the 1740s, but rising rates of purposeful population redistribution to the west were accompanied by rising rates of intraregional transiency as well – people without means of support, largely but not exclusively young and unmarried, moving short distances among existing towns within particular local areas. The population of strangers and outsiders was on the rise.

Transiency was not new to the eighteenth century. As well as policing their youth, Massachusetts towns had long regulated the movements of strangers considered suspicious – Indians, vagabonds, and "nightwalkers" – through sanctions and warning-out. But transiency driven by poverty (lack of employment or landlessness) was new. As the numbers of "strolling poor" increased, town expulsion of transients became routine and was supplemented by colony-wide control mechanisms. Customary town residency requirements to qualify for poor relief (three months continuous habitation without notice to leave) had been rendered uniform by colony legislation late in the seventeenth century and then extended to twelve months in 1701. Town officers had been responsible for finding and warning transients out themselves. New laws in the 1720s and 1730s placed the burden elsewhere, requiring townspeople to report transients lodging with them within twenty days of arrival. Residency qualifications became ever more restrictive, and by the colony statute of 1767, transients were required to report their own presence to town selectmen on first arrival. Each measure rendered more difficult the acquisition of a residency and hence qualification for poor relief; each made it easier to force transients back onto the roads. Finally, toward the end of the century, legislation established a colony-wide system for returning native-born transients to their towns of legal residence. Although a feature of previous colony laws, the return of transients to places where they might remain had long taken a back seat to their expulsion from where they might not remain. Those migrating from overseas without a place of legal residence within the colony became the responsibility of the colony government.

The police of population in New England was thus, as in the Chesapeake, a police of work and of mobility. Unlike the Chesapeake, however, race provided no new hard line by which to distinguish those with civic capacity from those without it. Instead the police of work continued to focus its attention largely on youth, while the police of mobility concentrated on those who could not show that their mobility was purposeful and that their purpose was backed by resources. Together these two aspects of population control defined subaltern others from whom the community was protected. Punishing deviation from familiar routines of family, residential settlement, and work cemented the latter as the definition of freedom.

The Delaware Valley

The police of population and work in the Delaware Valley provides a further variation on factors on display in the Chesapeake and New England. Pennsylvania was founded to be a society of Christian harmony. Along with William Penn's desire for a New World order of "love and brotherly kindness," however, came a certain nostalgia for an organic English past and belief in the inevitability of ranked hierarchy in relations among society's different orders. These sentiments found their way into plans for Pennsylvania's future population. Abhorring indiscriminate settlement, Penn planned agricultural villages of up to twenty families, each set in a 5,000-acre tract, recalling the nucleated, manor-centered settlement pattern of downland England. As to the organization of migration, Penn's earliest agreements with his co-investors identified indentured servitude as the means to facilitate labor transfers. The "Certain Conditions or Concessions" agreed in 1681 contemplated a headright system of land grants that would reward the first purchasers of Pennsylvania land for mass importations of servants along Chesapeake plantation lines; the *Laws Agreed Upon in England* (1682) sketched the beginnings of a regulatory system to control the process of servant importation. Approximately one-third of the first flurry of arrivals recorded between 1682 and 1686 were indentured servants.

At its first two meetings in 1682 and 1683, the provincial Assembly adopted a detailed set of disciplinary and police measures to frame servitude. These measures gave local courts direct oversight of servant discipline and conditions of work, established a servant registry, adopted a pass law, penalized harboring or trading with servants, and prescribed five days additional service for each day an absconding servant was absent, together with the costs of pursuit. The Assembly also established statutory terms of service and freedom dues for servants imported without indenture (five years for those 17 or older, and until age 22 for those younger than 17). Codified in 1700, these measures remained the core of Pennsylvania's statute law of servitude throughout the eighteenth century. None ever touched wage-workers or artisans. Wages were not regulated. Hirelings were not required to remain in their employment. Unauthorized departure might mean at most the forfeiture of unpaid wages.

The "eutopolitan" overtones of the proprietor's original plans are clear. Pennsylvania was an elaborately planned colony. Orderly settlement, the importation and control of population through the mechanism of servitude, detailed oversight of the performance of work, and provision for supervision of the movements of population in general (Pennsylvania's pass law required all persons traveling beyond their counties of residence to carry official certification of their place of residence on pain of incarceration as a presumptive runaway) were all part of a single vision of controlled harmony. But important contradictions existed between Penn's conception of the colony's organization and the conditions characteristic of the English pastoral uplands from which most of its early settlers actually came. Penn's nucleated agricultural villages were displaced by "sprawling townships" of dispersed farmsteads producing a wide variety of crops and home manufactures, typical of the pastoral uplands. The organization of labor, too, varied from the proprietor's model. First, the character of servant migration into Pennsylvania did not follow the pattern that had prevailed in the Chesapeake. In the earliest period, it was not dissimilar – a movement of children and adolescents, largely male. Most, however, were offspring of the first settlers' English neighbors, bound in England and brought along, as in early New England, as part of the migrating family group. Moreover, migration from England was slowing in the late seventeenth century, so the initial influx was not sustained. Again as in New England, after the first wave dried up, farmers looked to their own children and to children of Delaware Valley neighbors bound out as domestic servants and farm apprentices. Some farmers bought slaves during the early eighteenth century to fill the gap caused by the interruption of European migration, but never on a scale remotely comparable to the Chesapeake colonies. The region's economy simply did not stimulate the levels of demand for labor that had characterized the tobacco-planting, land-engrossing staple economy of the Chesapeake. When migration resumed in the 1720s, Pennsylvania's rural servant labor force quickly reverted to a mixture of creole children and migrants, the latter ranging from unattached youth to the offspring of incoming migrant families (predominantly German and Irish) to entire migrant family groups of children and adults. Other sources of bound labor – transported convicts – simply helped confirm that, for European settlers, servitude was a status demarcated (as in New England) by age and origin – a condition for children and outsiders. Public records of bindings show little incidence of servitude among creole adults apart from debtors and local convicts.

The incidence of servitude of any kind in rural Pennsylvania remained low. Servant labor was supplementary to the immediate nuclear family, and demand was dictated by the household's life cycle. In the century following settlement, fewer than 30 percent of households (usually fewer than 25 percent) ever contained servants, and rarely more than one at a time. In the Chester County town of Goshen, for example, twenty of twenty-eight purchasers recorded during the thirty-six years (1736–72) covered by the township's servant list bought no more than one or two servants. Only eight purchasers bought more than two; the largest number bought by any individual was five.[21] The contrast with contemporary Maryland, where 50–75 percent of estates reported bound labor (largely slaves) with a mean holding that ranged from eight to more than ten per estate, is marked. Despite high levels of wages, short-term hired labor was consistently preferred by farmers seeking assistance beyond that which could be supplied by their own children or an indentured boy. And it was consistently available. By the second half of the eighteenth century, free landless wage laborers called "freemen" (adult sons of resident landholders who were not heads of their own households) or "inmates" (cottagers) had become the fastest-growing segment of the rural labor force.

Similar patterns characterized the colony's primary urban area. Indentured servitude in eighteenth-century Pennsylvania was predominantly an urban phenomenon. By the 1760s servants were no more than 3 percent of the workforce in Lancaster, Chester, and rural Philadelphia counties. In Bedford and Northampton counties the proportion was far lower. In the Philadelphia workforce during the 1760s and early 1770s, the incidence of servants was two to three times greater. (The same urban concentration was true of slaveholding.) Greater density apart, however, city holding patterns appear to have replicated those in the country. No more than 20–25 percent of Philadelphia households included servants; of those city inhabitants owning servants, 75 percent owned no more than one.

The Delaware Valley: Policing Mobility and Discipline

Regular influxes of transatlantic migrants, and the contiguity of the Delaware and Chesapeake bays and the waterways that fed them, encouraged constant population dispersal and mobility throughout the Delaware Valley

[21] "Town Book" for Goshen, Chester County, 1718–1870 (Historical Society of Pennsylvania). Sixty servants are listed "Imported into this Province and purchased by the Inhabitants of this Township." The twenty-eight purchasers comprised but one-third of Goshen's farmers. Eleven purchasers only ever bought one servant; ten only ever bought two. Thirty percent of all purchases were made by one family and 50 percent by three families.

region. Many migrants entering through Philadelphia stayed in Pennsylvania, but others headed north toward New York and the Hudson Valley, or south to the Chesapeake, or west into Appalachia and beyond. Servants landing in Philadelphia moved into the city's craft shops and the surrounding farming regions, but also south to the Chesapeake or to the Jerseys and New York. Runaways were pursued into Pennsylvania from the Chesapeake; runaways from Pennsylvania headed in all directions. Geography, then, gave Delaware Valley labor more opportunity for movement than perhaps any other locale of settlement.

James T. Lemon has observed that Pennsylvania's "relatively open society" meant that people in motion encountered few obstructions.[22] In fact, Pennsylvania's relatively open society existed as such on the basis of quite sharply defined distinctions between freedom and restraint. As noted above, despite Penn's original ambitions the dispersed farm household became the locus of social order, not the nucleated village. But the impulse to control movement remained. Using the pass law, county authorities would regularly restrain and incarcerate travelers unable to prove that they were *not* runaway servants.

In practice, most controls of mobility focused on bound servants. In Chester County during the period 1715–75, for example, absconding accounted for 80 percent of all proceedings against servants initiated by masters in the county court. Virtually all were found in favor of the master. The severity of the statutory penalty – five additional days' service for each day absent – made runaway time a valuable resource. Masters recorded absences diligently, often presenting them for balancing at the end of a term of service, rather like book debt. At the same time absconding appears quite exceptional: the average number of proceedings was but three per annum: it has been estimated that 95 percent of all servants under indenture quietly completed their terms without incident.

Court supervision of the master-servant relationship stretched well beyond the police of mobility: Pennsylvania statutes made substantially greater provision for juridical oversight of the relationship than elsewhere. Nor were servants reticent in seeking intervention on their own behalf; they regularly appealed to the courts' statutory authority in an attempt to blunt the asymmetries of power inherent in their situation. That the courts chose to mediate settlements in the majority of disputes meant that petitioners could be vulnerable if justices were biased. But the evidence does not suggest bias: servant-petitioners never appeared reluctant to press complaints.

[22] James T. Lemon, *The Best Poor Man's Country: A Geographical Study of Early Southeastern Pennsylvania* (Baltimore, 1972), 71–97, esp. 96, 97.

Though the policing of disputes between masters and indentured servants was no more crudely one-sided in Pennsylvania than it was elsewhere, the courts acted within the compass of a general understanding that, both socially and legally, the relationship of master and indentured servant was legitimately one of authority and subordination. Emblematic of this understanding was the courts' almost mechanical processing of runaways, which exemplified the key characteristic of servitude, the legality of restrained mobility. But court intervention was conditioned on the existence of an indenture. In May 1732, for example, Jonathan Strange sought redress against one Humphrey Reynolds, who had neglected his promise to "faithfully and truly serve him" for three months in consideration of wages advanced by the plaintiff.[23] But Strange's action was a civil suit seeking damages for Reynolds' failure to perform, not an invocation of the criminal penalties applied so routinely to indentured runaways. And unlike the summary disposal of those runaways, Strange's suit (like most civil suits in Chester and elsewhere) simply languished on the docket (in this case for three years) before being composed, privately, by the parties themselves. In the same way, the court found that Martha Liggett was free to depart the service of James Caldwell without penalty because no indenture bound her; nor could Mary Broom be punished for "disobedience to the orders" of her master, for she too was not bound.

Whether workers on wages remained liable to loss of earnings in the event they broke agreements to serve – as observers alleged – cannot be determined easily. Civil suits seeking payment for work invariably alleged prior performance, but generally offered few details. The form of wage work transactions suggests the predominance of casual day work; work debts were either paid immediately at the conclusion of a task or accumulated over time to be presented in periodic mutual accountings in the normal fashion of book debt. Such a pattern is unlikely to generate disputes over the "entirety" of a contract. Moreover, the amounts in dispute were generally small enough to be settled by a hearing before an individual justice, of which almost no records survive before 1760, rather than in the county court.

All that said, there is good evidence that wage laborers in breach of individual employment contracts did *not* face loss of unpaid earnings in colonial Pennsylvania. In July 1767, for example, Eneas Foulk appeared before Richard Riley, JP, of Chichester township to seek payment for work undertaken on behalf of Isaac Pyle. Pyle replied that Foulk had not been

[23] This and other early Pennsylvania cases discussed in the text can be found in the records and files for cases heard at courts of Common Pleas and General and Quarter Sessions, Chester County, all available at the Chester County Archives, Westchester, Pennsylvania.

paid because he "had not compleated his work according to Bargain." Riley's decision was that payment was owed for what had been done – "that the value of the work done & due to the plantiff is but 15/- and no more."[24]

In the Delaware Valley as elsewhere, then, the indenture established a crucial line of legal status in the performance of work – a line of demarcation between enforceable and unenforceable obligation. The indenture signified when the assertion of capacity to control or restrain or penalize another was legally allowable. It signified what labor was not "free" and mobile, and what was. In the Delaware Valley, as elsewhere, the indenture existed in an environment crosscut by numerous intersecting lines of social demarcation – of age and gender, of race – to which the police of labor was intimately related. As elsewhere, too, the structure of labor was itself a hierarchy, one in which the legal freedoms of adult white creole males stood out against, and were buttressed by, enforceable obligations of service visited more weightily on others – the young, migrants, and slaves. We have observed the same hierarchy in the Chesapeake and in Massachusetts, so to encounter it in the Delaware Valley is no surprise. As in Massachusetts, however, the subordinations encountered in Pennsylvania were essentially temporary and life-cyclical. Not until African enslavement had established race as the cardinal measure of servility does one find a segment of the early American population designated as a permanent underclass of workers. It is racial slavery that finally renders "master and servant" not as a temporary and essentially contained legal hierarchy, but as an expansive polarity of freedom and its absence in early America.

CONCLUSION: CIVIC STATUS IN THE EARLY REPUBLIC

"I apprehend," Benjamin Franklin wrote in 1773, "that every Briton who is made unhappy at home, has a Right to remove from any Part of his King's Dominions into those of any other Prince where he can be happier. If this should be denied me, at least it will be allowed that he has a Right to remove into any other Part of the same Dominions."[25] Domestically, the claim of an ancient "right" to mobility had been hedged repeatedly by Crown pronouncement and Parliamentary action. Britons nevertheless had removed themselves across the Atlantic or had been removed, with comparative ease. Still, Britons' mobility was conditioned by structures that policed their migrations. And for other transoceanic migrants, transfer took place without choice of any kind.

[24] See, Richard Riley, *Record of Proceedings* (1765–1776), Historical Society of Pennsylvania, Philadelphia.

[25] Franklin, "On a Proposed Act to Prevent Emigration," 527.

Transfers of population were crucial to the success of English colonizing in North America because controllable labor was the key to permanent occupation. Hence it is unremarkable that early modern labor law – the law of servitude – should become the means to organize population transfers: the law of servitude was the early modern era's most efficient means to the control of mobility. In its turn, servitude became the line of demarcation on which civic status, its relativities (for men and women, adults and children, masters and servants), and absence (for enslaved Africans) were erected.

This basic set of relationships among servitude, the police of population, and civic capacity was reproduced in the new Republic – in its constituent states and localities, in its Federal Constitution, and in its social practices. Locally, the early modern ideal of the eutopolitan city was expressed anew as the "well regulated city" of "regular gradation" and "correct arrangement and subordination of the parts."[26] In Boston, Josiah Quincy's reflections on the relief of poverty would take as their point of departure the efficient employment of population in productive labor at the same time that the ownership of property was becoming institutionalized as the criterion for civic membership. Vagrancy laws remained on states' books. Meanwhile, the Federal Constitution famously embedded a commitment to the police of labor mobility in the Republic's fundamental law through the fugitive clause of Article IV. The so-called fugitive slave clause, it must be remembered, applied not only to slaves but to *any person* "held to Service or Labour." Article I, meanwhile, granted additional recognition to the hierarchy of civic capacity created by the laws of servitude while at the same time masking the expression of hierarchy by redefining persons held to service "for a Term of Years" as "free" for purposes of representation, which left slaves as the only [and now quintessential] fractional "other Persons." Those bound to service for a term of years might still be restrained, but were yet "free." Quotidian life reproduced constitutional law in its own earthily simple claim: "None but negers are Sarvants."[27]

As Samuel McKee put it, long ago but so well, in mainland America during the seventeenth and eighteenth centuries "free" labor came to mean "without public or private regulation."[28] That is, rather than create a regulatory regime from statute and common law for the performance of work as a whole, as in England, laws in each region of colonial settlement were targeted to particular segments of the available labor force – indentured migrants, apprentices, slaves – establishing by default interstitial zones of

[26] Peter Oxenbridge Thacher, *An Address to the Members of the Massachusetts Charitable Fire Society, at their Annual Meeting, in Boston, May 31, 1805* (Boston, 1805).

[27] Charles William Jansen, *The Stranger in America* (London, 1807), 88.

[28] Samuel McKee, *Labor in Colonial New York, 1664–1776* (New York, 1935), 179.

(unregulated) freedom. In this sense, "None but negers . . . " could indeed emerge from the colonial era's legal culture of work with the appearance of transcendent civic fact, particularly after the Constitution declared those bound for a term of years to be "free" for at least some of its purposes.

During the first half of the nineteenth century the quotidian claim became increasingly hollow. Rather than atrophy, the ambit of master and servant grew until it absorbed the employment contract as a whole, underwriting the employer's right and capacity, simply as one who had contracted with another for the performance of services, to assert magisterial powers of management, discipline, and control.

Ironically, given the American Revolution, English influence was felt strongly in this nineteenth-century alteration of the Republic's master/servant relationship. This was not a matter of statutory borrowing. Rather it resulted from the influence of authoritative English common law reports and treatises – the product of common law judging and reconceived common law doctrine – all of which encouraged American legal culture to reject earlier delimited, parochial, and regionalized approaches to master and servant in favor of a more expansive, universalized conception of law – a cosmopolitan aesthetic delightful to the Republic's appellate elites. During the seventeenth and eighteenth centuries, America's colonial legal cultures had severally felt the original influence of English laws, but had simultaneously refracted them through dissimilar regional cultures of settlement whose distinctive statutory regimes resulted in differentiated legal cultures of work. But the impulses of the nineteenth century lent themselves to nothing so much as an overpowering indifference to that earlier history. The new nation sought a new legal culture not of discrete differences but of transcendent universals.

The importation of common law master and servant doctrine into nineteenth-century employment law was an importation of a general conceptual structure and language of legitimate authority in work relations, not of English legislation's criminal disciplines. "Free labor" was not a meaningless designation. But the importation was nevertheless deeply significant, for what distinguished the nineteenth-century version from what had gone before was its all-encompassing quality, finding disciplinary authority in the contract of employment itself, rather than in the particular sociolegal status – youthful, indentured, and so forth – characteristic of the worker. Thus Timothy Walker wrote, "We understand by the relation of master and servant nothing more or less than that of the *employer* and the *employed*."[29] This had its consequences. Wage labor throughout the northeastern states, for example, was challenged by legal strictures that imposed economic

[29] Timothy Walker, *An Introduction to American Law* (Philadelphia, 1837), 243.

disciplines absent in the previous century. In the antebellum South, the status of "free labor" remained qualitatively distinct from slavery, but white workers found the claims to legal privilege and civic status they had built on their difference from slaves increasingly vulnerable. Indeed, what crept into their debates with local elites were intimations of a willingness to work *as hard as* slaves in order to keep racial privilege within their grasp.

After the Civil War, this antebellum common law regime was joined by new measures that greatly intensified the police of population in the market for labor and at work, underscoring the homologies of coercion and contract, North and South. In the South, criminal sanctions against idleness and vagrancy forced freedmen into wage work. In the North, new laws reconfirmed the criminality of purposeless mobility, prescribing imprisonment and forced labor for vagrants and beggars. Once secured in an employment relationship, the common law of master and servant confronted the employee with the reality of employer-designed discipline. If "free labor" in the colonial era had come to mean the absence of "public or private regulation," a century into the era of the Republic, free labor was apparently quite compatible with both.

8

THE FRAGMENTED LAWS OF SLAVERY IN THE COLONIAL AND REVOLUTIONARY ERAS

SALLY E. HADDEN

The striking fact about slavery in the sixteenth, seventeenth, and eighteenth centuries was its universality. Enslaving humans was legal throughout the western hemisphere in the early modern period, sanctioned by every major legal system in operation there. The right to hold another person in bondage depended precisely on legal definitions of who could be enslaved within a given civilization – the English, Spanish, French, Dutch, Portuguese, and Native Americans differed on this and other specific slave laws – but if one could enslave another, the economic advantages to be gained were great, and the status of the slaveholder generally rose or fell in proportion to the fluctuating number of bondsmen he owned. In each New World colony or nation, however, the elevation of the slaveholder depended on the diminution of the slave. Slave law granted slave owners virtually unlimited power over the enslaved, but those laws simultaneously diminished the personhood of the enslaved, as if the bondsman had in some degree endured, in the words of sociologist Orlando Patterson, "social death."

Two groups of people suffered this social death in disproportionate numbers: Native Americans and Africans. Native Americans enslaved Native Americans, Africans enslaved Africans, and Europeans took advantage of the extant trade on both continents, buying unfree persons in ever increasing numbers until the nineteenth century. Assessments of the magnitude of slavery among Native Americans remain approximate; however, historians suspect that in the southeastern part of North America during the seventeenth and eighteenth centuries, some 50,000 aboriginal captives ultimately ended up in the hands of European slave traders. The estimated total number of enslaved individuals exported from West Africa to the western hemisphere between the fifteenth and nineteenth centuries, 11.3 million, is quantitatively firmer. Approximately 9.3 million survived the arduous Middle Passage. Of these, 3.8 million men and women arrived in Caribbean colonies held by European powers, many destined for subsequent transport to other New World destinations. Another 500,000 went directly to the

North American mainland between 1600 and 1808, when the importation of African slaves finally became illegal under U.S. law. Slavery and the laws that sanctioned it thus bound together disparate nations belonging to the Atlantic world and provided the rationale for the coerced migrations of millions who left behind homes and families for uncertain futures wherever their owners might force them to go.

From these imported, involuntary migrants grew the massive unfree populations that fueled America's growing economy in the antebellum era. By 1810, nearly 1.2 million slaves were living in the United States; by 1860, that number had reached 3.9 million, with laws designed to restrict virtually every aspect of slave life. By comparison, slavery in the colonial and revolutionary era, whether in New England, the Chesapeake, or the Caribbean, was a much smaller affair, and the laws pertaining to slavery were more scattered and less organized. To understand slave law in seventeenth- and eighteenth-century North America, one must forget the full-blown plantation society that the antebellum South would become, and reach back to an era when societies with slaves (communities in which slave labor was present, but non-essential) were more common than slave societies (communities in which slave productivity was the economic base). In other words, slavery before 1800 differed significantly from antebellum slavery, and the same was true of laws governing the enslaved in each period. Antebellum slave law developed mostly through case law, and its main challenge was reconciling conflicts of comity between Northern and Southern law – a reflection of the growing sectional disagreements about slavery's morality in the nineteenth century. No such disagreements plagued early America. European settlers North and South assumed the universal acceptance of enslavement. Slave law evolved more or less at will, through invention, imitation, and appropriation from a variety of legal sources. Municipal ordinances, individual laws, and criminal codes, rather than case law, dominated its development. Widespread acceptance encouraged laws about slavery that were drawn originally from numerous fragmented sources – Spanish, English, and French – to commingle slowly in more unitary statements about the permissible behavior of bondsmen. Eventually this gave rise to the creation of codes – sweeping, near-comprehensive laws.

The scattered origins of slave law in early America mirrored the fragmented background of America's colonization. Yet these splintered European sources shared important cultural underpinnings that justified bondage. The legitimacy of slave law throughout the western hemisphere was built on common religious and philosophical principles that stretched back to antiquity. Only the slow, steady development of Enlightenment criticism and religious movements like Quakerism that rejected slavery as immoral would eventually shatter the near-universal acceptance that, until the late eighteenth century, slave law enjoyed.

The widespread support for slavery in the colonial period gradually disappeared in the revolutionary era, leading to a different form of fragmentation in slave law. As colonies gave way to states, America's founding generation divided on the morality of enslavement. Lacking a national consensus, sensible that state laws covered most foreseeable situations, federal lawmakers crafted no overarching national law of slavery, but instead left the matter of slave law to individual states. The movement toward gradual emancipation in Northern states and increasing penalties for those involved in the international slave trade created a rift between the North and South over the general acceptability of bondage. As Congress outlawed the African slave trade and new laws banned slavery north of the nation's capital, the trend toward nationwide acceptance of slave law began to reverse itself. Though new states from the Deep South entered the Union having adopted the slave codes similar to those of South Carolina and Virginia, each additional state admitted placed additional strain on the principle of comity, strain that would only grow in the antebellum era.

The historical analysis of slave law in America, whether in the colonial or the early national period, has tended to focus on the ascendancy of England and English common law, obscuring the multiplicity of legal systems that actually contributed to slave laws in America prior to 1800. Likewise, analysis has emphasized positive law – the edicts of monarchs, the enactments of legislative assemblies, the opinions of judges – reflecting the longstanding cultural bias of Western societies to privilege written texts over oral traditions. Emphasis on the written word parallels another long-familiar trend in legal history, the priority given to those who pronounce the law rather than those affected by its decrees. Variously, these scholarly preferences have retarded a thoroughgoing investigation of what Africans thought of slave law, either in Africa or in America – we know far more about white enslavers and how they sought to restrain their human property than what bondsmen thought of those laws.

I. BEFORE AMERICAN SLAVERY: AFRICAN AND EUROPEAN CONCEPTIONS OF SLAVERY

Unfree persons, whether serfs, villeins, or slaves, could be found in almost every society, European or African, before the fifteenth century. Laws governing their actions, or structuring their transfer from one master to another, were codified as written law became more widespread. In Africa, Muslims following Islamic law (*shari'a*) believed it legitimate to enslave only non-Muslims, and developed elaborate legal treatises like the *Mi'raj al-Su'ud ila Nayl Hukm Majlub al-Sud* that addressed multiple aspects of slave law. No distinct racial aspect of Muslim enslavement existed: the one requirement to be enslaved appeared to be "otherness" in belief – the difference in religious tradition between enslaver and enslaved. A fifteenth-century imam wrote that "slavery is a humiliation and a servitude caused by previous or current unbelief and [has] as its purpose to discourage unbelief." Like Spanish and other legal systems derived from Roman law, Islamic law encouraged manumission (*'itq*), and slaves could gain their freedom through several methods: self-purchase by contract (*mukataba*, comparable to Spanish *coartacíon*); declaration by an owner to take effect on his death (*tadbir*) or a simple declaration of freedom in the present tense (the slave is immediately freed); or release of the slave as penance for a master's wrongdoing. Under Muslim law, an enslaved woman who gave birth to her master's child would eventually be freed, and the child was automatically free.

Elsewhere in Africa, other thriving legal traditions regulated the slave trade. Unlike Muslim law, among most West African tribes the legal status of the enslaved depended not on religious difference, but on tragic, catastrophic events: wars and slave raids converted once-free men and women into chattel. The legal presumption that one could identify a slave by race, which came to dominate American law by 1800, had no direct parallel in African practices. The boundary between free and unfree also seemed mutable in West Africa, for multiple definitions of enslavement existed simultaneously among tribes of Senegambia, the Bight of Biafra, the Bight of Benin, and Loango and Angola (the principal source regions for Africans who became slaves in America). Among the Igbo people, there were religious slaves (Osu), slaves of men (Oru or Ohu), and pawn-slaves. Religious slaves almost never attained their freedom, for their service was pledged to a god. Bondsmen belonging to men might readily alter their status through self-purchase or intermarriage with the master's family. Pawn-slaves worked only until a specific debt was repaid and could not be sold, given, or traded away by the original debt holder. Laws affecting the treatment of slaves in Africa varied by tribal custom and region, but freedom and assimilation into the enslaver's family were often provided for through law or tradition. Since female slaves were preferred by many African tribes (for both their productive and reproductive capacities), these assimilation laws were routinely invoked. Preferences for emancipation and assimilation did not find their way into colonial laws of British North America, although enslaved African women may have wondered whether European colonists provided analogous legal means to change status from unfree to free.

The laws of slavery known to Africans had little impact on the laws created by their European enslavers, whose most frequent defenses of the enslavement of others were biblical texts or references to natural law and writers from antiquity. Few Europeans criticized the institution of slavery on theoretical grounds before the eighteenth century, and many defended it as the result of just wars. Although Christian tradition could readily be turned against slavery, in the early modern period Portuguese or Spanish slave raiders more frequently used it – with papal blessing – to legitimize their activities. A few Spanish theologians criticized slavery in the late fifteenth and early sixteenth centuries, including Cajetan, Francisco de Vitoria, Domingo de Soto, and the well-known Bartolomé de las Casas. Slowly they began to propagate the view that enslavement of infidels could not arise from necessity or be sanctioned solely by papal authority. Some of their theoretical opposition to slavery rested on firsthand observations. De las Casas had traveled to the New World and wrote in graphic detail about the horrors of bondage. But these critics were a minority in the Iberian tradition, and throughout the rest of Europe, the opinion prevailed – relying on references to men like Thucydides and Cicero – that enslaving one's enemies could be sanctioned following just wars.

European humanists in the natural law tradition, like Alberico Gentili and Hugo Grotius, argued convincingly that persons could lawfully be made slaves, even if they rejected slavery in general. In his best-known work, *De Jure Belli ac Pacis* (1625), Grotius rejected the idea that bondage could be rationalized as the natural state of any human being: "[A]part from human institutions and customs, no men can be slaves; and it is in this sense that legal writers maintain the opinion that slavery is repugnant to nature."[1] Despite this, Grotius still considered slavery valid as a "result of lawful causes," and his views gained rapid acceptance among individuals seeking to enslave Africans or Native Americans. Pirates, barbarians, cannibals, those who did not know Christianity, and those who killed settlers might all deserve to be slaves.[2] Grotius's writings and those of similar natural law theorists dominated mainstream European thinking about slavery in the context of warfare and developed the wide-ranging rationales needed to legitimate European aggression against their African or Native American victims. Colonizers as well as philosophers like Hobbes and Locke read and quoted Grotius with approval.

Such philosophical perspectives gained wide readership in places like seventeenth-century England where slavery per se had vanished except in ancient law texts. In England, common law before the fifteenth century had no provisions directly pertaining to slavery because English slavery, defined as such, had all but disappeared by the thirteenth century. Forms of servitude like serfdom or villeinage bound unfree persons to specific plots of land through the Middle Ages, but such tenures were increasingly rare by the fifteenth century and did not carry the full range of legal restrictions

[1] Book 3, ch. VII, § 1 and book 2, ch. XXII, § 12.
[2] Book 2, ch. XXII, § 11 and ch. XX, § 40.

commonly associated with slavery. The closest analogy in English law was apprenticeship law, by which a young person wishing to learn a craft was bound by indenture to a master's service for a term of years. During the period of service, the apprentice was under the full legal control of the master, who could punish him for neglecting service, absconding, or marrying without consent. However, a master who failed to provide food, clothing, or training to the apprentice could be fined and the apprentice freed from his indentures. Indentured servants brought from England labored alongside African slaves in the Caribbean and British North America through the mid-seventeenth century, and early colonial statutes frequently refer to both groups together when describing punishments for misbehavior or running away.

English law offered a few models for slave laws in the western hemisphere, but Spanish law would be the source for most early New World slave laws. In Europe, canon law and Roman civil law were engrafted into *Las Siete Partidas*, the thirteenth-century Spanish code compiled by Alfonso X of Castile that would serve as the legal foundation throughout Spain's empire in the Americas, including Spanish territories that became part of the United States like Louisiana, Texas, and California (and it remains Spain's central legal authority to the present day). An indication of slaves' lowly status in Spanish society is that laws about lawyers, women, and even abandoned children all precede laws about bondsmen, found in the Fourth *Partida*. Slaves were defined as captives of war "who are enemies of the faith," that is, non-Christian, or the children of female slaves of any faith. As in Africa, most slaves in Spain could not be distinguished racially from their masters, and Spanish law did not define servitude racially. The Spanish master was endowed with nearly complete authority over an enslaved person, but was restricted from killing, maiming, or seriously injuring a bondsman. Except for these few injunctions, Spanish codified law was silent on many points – the proper religious instruction for slaves, for example, or their right to marry, or their rights to food, clothing, and shelter at their owners' hands. These omissions resulted from the relatively small population of bondsmen found in early modern Spain, and possibly from the overarching presumption that slavery was not intended as a lifelong status, but a temporary one. Title XXII of the Fourth *Partida* specified numerous methods by which a slave could obtain her freedom, for strong presumptions pervade the code that "all creatures in the world naturally love and desire liberty," and that a Christian master would grant freedom to a worthy slave. These presumptions in favor of freedom over slavery would find their way into Spanish colonial laws, but would be lost in the sixteenth-century transmission of such laws from Spanish to English settlers in the western hemisphere.

II. SLAVE LAWS OF THE CARIBBEAN

The Europeans who settled the New World arrived with varying degrees of knowledge of slave law and various justifications for those laws. The French, Portuguese, and Dutch, like the English, set up colonies on Caribbean islands or the mainland, but at the outset had few laws and no comprehensive code to regulate enslaved persons. French *coutumes* proffered no law of slavery; the *Ordenaçoes Filipinas*, the Portuguese legal compilation of 1643, contained little more. The States-General assembly of the Netherlands issued virtually no laws about slavery; any slave arriving in the Netherlands was automatically free. The assembly preferred to leave such matters in the hands of the privately controlled Dutch West India Company, which in turn left slave control and punishment largely in the hands of individual masters. Only the Spanish came to the western hemisphere relatively well equipped. Their *Las Siete Partidas* mandated that children follow the condition of their mother, prohibited atrocities by masters, and preferred emancipation. Regardless of nationality, many European colonizers shared in the Christian assumption that the "curse of Ham" justified the enslavement of Africans. Though scholars such as David Brion Davis have questioned whether this specific rationale actually swayed Europeans in the sixteenth and seventeenth centuries, Winthrop Jordan and others have shown convincingly that racism and greed persuaded many European enslavers to prey on Africans as slaves to export to the New World.

As the size of the Spanish empire in the western hemisphere grew by leaps and bounds, so too did its slave population. With it came local regulations to control slave activities and mandate proper behavior by slave owners. King Philip IV ordered that all colonial Spanish law – including slave laws – be gathered, digested, and published. The result was the first *Recopilación de las leyes de los reinos de los Indias* (1681), commonly called the *Recopilación de Indias*. The French also collected their local slave laws together in 1685 and published them in the early eighteenth century as the *Code Noir*. But the *Code Noir*, like the *Recopilación*, was incomplete by itself. The slave codes had to be supplemented by each colonizer's national law, like Spain's *Las Siete Partidas*, and also by regulations crafted by district or city magistrates who had the power to enact local slave regulations. Colonial officials passed decrees that continued to encourage emancipation while placing numerous restrictions on slave masters, but the extent of their actions remains largely unknown. Because the sources of slave regulation were so numerous and the laws themselves so scattered, no complete collection of Spanish colonial slave law has ever been compiled.

For the Spanish colonial empire, the detail of local and regional enactments has not been much explored – the historical record is too fragmented.

It is known, however, that Spanish slave law expanded dramatically and encompassed many more subjects than did English law for bondsmen. Historian Elsa Goveia, expert on slave laws of the Caribbean, has asserted that "[t]he English government never, until the nineteenth century, showed so careful and sustained an interest in the subject of slave regulations as did the government of Spain from earliest times."

Despite the extraordinary diversity of slave law, each island, each colony developed laws to regulate the conduct of bondsmen. By the mid-seventeenth century, some islands colonized by the English, like Barbados, had enacted their own slave codes (1661). In part, code development was connected with the successful transition to raising a cash crop – sugar, in this case – that fueled the rapidly increasing number of African slaves imported by Caribbean colonizers. Careful examination of the Barbadian code's provisions reveals elements drawn partly from English legal conceptions about bound labor and from neighboring Spanish and French island slave laws. Barbadian colonizers who had not known slave laws in their home country invented, transplanted, and borrowed eclectically, as necessary. Codes, more common to the Roman legal tradition from which *Las Siete Partidas* evolved than in English law, thus became integral to slave control in English settlements.

In Barbados, the impulse to craft the code may have been inspired by the rising population of bondsmen, By the 1670s, Africans had become a majority on the island. However, the preamble to the "Act for the Better ordering and governing of Negroes" speaks neither of slave demography nor of fears of insurrection. White Barbadians instead stressed slaves' difference: their "heathenish brutish" behavior and tendency to run away had become insupportable. The scattershot slave laws previously enacted had not "mett the effect . . . desired" because masters and overseers had not "beene so carefull of their obedience and complyance" as they ought. By enacting a comprehensive code, Barbadian legislators hoped to draw the slave laws to the attention of all whites, so that slave conduct would be better regulated throughout the island.

Because the Barbadian slave code served as a model for codes enacted in other English colonies – Jamaica (1664), South Carolina (1690/1691), and Antigua (1697) – its contents merit close scrutiny. The twenty-three articles covered several broad topics, but focused on the regulation of slave movement, discipline, slave crimes, and protection of the enslaved. The code did not address legal issues like purchase, sale, mortgaging, or other financial transactions involving slaves: control, not commodification, was the legislators' paramount concern. The law dictated the type of pass or ticket slaves must carry when working away from their master's plantation and mandated that whites (owners and non-owners alike) were to inspect all slave passes. In effect, this made all white Barbadians responsible for restricting slave movement, a pattern that would be repeated elsewhere in English slaveholding colonies. Bondsmen were expressly forbidden to leave the plantation on Sunday – the one day when all slaves might expect a respite from work. The code offered slaves incentives to assist in recapturing fugitives: runaways would have to avoid not only whites, but their fellow bondsmen too. Lacking a police force, seventeenth-century white Barbadians enlisted all residents, white and black, against slave runaways. Fugitives, they knew, might lead a slave revolt; punishments for insurrectionary violence included the death penalty. If rebellious slaves were executed, however, the code specified that owners would be monetarily compensated for their property. Such was the pecuniary value of slaves that the colonial government effectively insured masters against loss from state-mandated destruction of mutinous bondsmen.

The Barbadian code provided that slave crime, up to and including murder, would be tried not by jury but by a panel of justices of the peace and several landholders, typically all slave owners. Penalties included whipping, nose slitting, and branding and escalated for each subsequent offense up to capital punishment. In reality the majority of slave crimes never reached these tribunals, for masters had both the right and obligation to control their bondsmen and could inflict whatever penalties they wished. The 1661 code offered no sanctions against masters who maimed or even killed slaves in the course of punishment except for a fine if it could be shown the master acted out of malice, a provision honored mostly in the breach. This lack of oversight into owners' behavior was consistent with the rest of the code, which included few requirements covering treatment of slaves. Food, shelter, and medical care were left "to the Discretion of the Owner." Relying on masters' own financial self-interest to guide their care of bondsmen, the code's creators sought only to control slaves, not slave owners. That masters' self-interest could not be relied on becomes apparent when one looks at the revised code of 1688: Barbadian lawmakers began to penalize owners financially for slaves convicted of crimes that resulted from systematic starvation. If bondsmen stole or murdered due to hunger, their masters were "in some measure guilty of their Crimes," and the colony would consequently lower the compensation paid after the slaves' executions.

The slave code of Barbados repeated several key features found in Spanish and French colonial slave laws: higher penalties for crimes committed by slaves than by free persons, extreme penalties for participating in insurrections, and even the creation of a code itself rather than continuing to rely on individual slave laws. But in governing masters' behavior, the English colonists did not follow Spanish or French example. Historians Frank Tannenbaum and Carl Degler have tracked the tendency in Spanish colonial laws to provide greater protections for bondsmen than English or, later, American law. Spanish slave owners were required to provide adequate food, clothing, and religious instruction to their bondsmen. If slaves wed, masters were required to honor the marriage vow and keep the couple together. French slave laws specified food rations for slaves and protected the Sabbath: no slave was to work on Sunday or any holiday observed by the church. The 59th article of the *Code Noir* even stipulated that emancipated slaves were to enjoy the same rights and privileges as the freeborn. Whether such stipulations mitigated the harsh practices of slavery within the French and Spanish empires is unclear, but no such demands or expectations were made on Barbadian slave owners. Laws protecting slaves may well have been ignored whenever masters chose, but their creation itself says much about societal priorities. Ultimately, Spanish and French colonial laws, influenced by the humanitarian efforts of the Catholic church, or by legal presumptions found in the *Recopilación de Indias* or the *Code Noir*, worked in favor of treating slaves humanely, with an eye toward the eventual manumission of bondsmen. No such religious or cultural influences, or common law tradition, informed the legal choices made by English colonial lawmakers.

The creation of a slave code did not preclude the creation of other laws to regulate bondsmen. Indeed, the enactment of a code may have made more obvious the areas where deficiencies existed in controlling slaves. Two specific matters surface repeatedly in later Barbadian laws and would reappear on the North American mainland once white Barbadians began migrating to South Carolina in the 1670s. Huckstering, the process by which slaves sold goods at market, grew as the agricultural productivity of the island increasingly focused on sugar. In an island society that exported a wealth-making cash crop by the ton, white farmers had little time or incentive to raise enough foodstuffs to support themselves or their slaves. Through the seventeenth and eighteenth centuries, plantation owners readily turned to the thriving slave-dominated market culture where one could purchase fish, fruit, and other agricultural products that bondsmen caught or grew in their few unsupervised hours. Yet masters resented the prices charged and voiced suspicion that goods vended had been stolen by their vendors. The huckstering market also offered support to the island's few free blacks, who represented a security threat from the masters' perspective. Consequently, repeated attempts were made to regulate, curtail, and even end the slave markets, although with little apparent effect, for huckstering had become too integral to the island's economy. Anti-huckstering laws appeared in various guises – laws regulating town sanitation, establishing days and times when markets could legitimately convene, supervising town officers, and creating market officials. Such regulations may appear to relate solely to towns and markets, yet embedded within them were many measures designed to dominate slave behavior. Characteristically overlapping and sometimes contradictory, the nature of these laws suggests that Barbadian lawmakers never managed to work out how to govern this aspect of slave life. Both their multiplicity and repetitiveness serve as a reminder that the laws passed for slave control were as much normative statements about what white legislators wanted to happen as guides to what actually transpired within slave culture.

A second deficiency in Barbadian law is suggested by lawmakers' recurrent complaints that whites were failing to enforce the slave code and control wayward bondsmen. Reliance on private, individual enforcement of slave laws left the job to all whites: clearly, some simply did not bother. While bondsmen certainly learned to distinguish between whites who would enforce slave laws and those who would not, it took the Barbadian assembly some time to recognize the deficiency. Eventually, lawmakers began to transfer some power over slaves to third parties, authorizing private slave catchers, and later militia-based slave patrols, to step in and control slave behavior when owners and other whites would not. These third-party enforcers of the law became essential as absentee ownership of both land and slaves in Barbados grew more common. New legal provisions were necessitated to empower slave hunters and quasi-police forces to question, capture, and punish slaves in the absence of their masters. As the dichotomous nature of master-slave relations was reoriented to include state-mandated officials who could and did act in the place of owners at the behest of other white community residents, protections for slaves from abuse at the hands of non-owners, as well as compensation statutes to repay owners for damaged slaves, would enter the law. Slave catchers and slave patrols would also appear in British mainland colonies: after emigrant Barbadians began arriving in South Carolina in the 1670s, they set out to craft laws that drew on their Caribbean experience.

III. SLAVE LAWS ON THE NORTH AMERICAN MAINLAND: INITIAL LEGISLATION

In the seventeenth and eighteenth centuries, slavery came to be acknowledged as legal and legitimate in all British mainland colonies. In 1700, approximately 30,000 slaves lived in British North America, almost 90 percent of them in the South; by the Revolution, some 450,000 enslaved persons lived in the colonies, with more than 400,000 (the same proportion) in the South. In contrast, the population of slaves in New England was quite small, approaching 4,000 in 1715, and clustered near the seacoast. But although the population of slaves was heavily skewed toward the South, at the time of the American Revolution bondsmen could be found in every colony. Bondsmen frequently lived in Northern port towns like New York, Newport, and Boston where their concentrated numbers led to specific laws regulating their behavior, though not always comprehensive slave codes.

Historians of slavery in colonial America have focused too much on slave codes. Much of the law binding enslaved persons developed in piecemeal fashion, in multiple places, and in diverse types of legislation. Though nine of the thirteen mainland colonies that would become the United States enacted slave codes in the seventeenth and eighteenth centuries (Massachusetts, Rhode Island, Connecticut, and New Hampshire were the exceptions) single, topic-specific slave laws began to appear shortly after the first Africans arrived at Jamestown in 1619. Colonies without slave codes still had laws to control bondsmen. Both the development of cash crops, like tobacco in Virginia or rice in South Carolina, and the colonial world's dire shortage of labor promoted the purchase of Africans in growing numbers. Whether out of racism, greed, or fear, white mainland colonists enacted slave laws to control African laborers.

The earliest mainland laws were created by Virginians, who drew on Caribbean ideas while also inventing their own laws to compensate for the absence of English models. Well before white Barbadians migrated to South Carolina, Virginia's assemblymen had begun passing laws regulating Africans in many areas of colonial life. Their laws prohibited Africans from keeping weapons (1640), defined the status of mulattos (1662), and declared that baptism did not automatically grant emancipation (1667). That such laws were deemed necessary at all suggests that some slaves did keep firearms, that whites and Africans (and Native Americans) engaged in interracial intercourse, and that Africans believed becoming Christian would alter their status from slave to free. In Virginia, the cultural boundary dividing slavery from freedom was crossed with greater ease before the mid-seventeenth century, perhaps due to the presence of so many European indentured servants and so few Africans in the earliest years of the Old Dominion's colonization. Indeed, it was not clear whether Africans in Virginia had to serve only for a term of years (like an indentured servant) or for life. Nor was it clear what the status of a child born to African parents would be. The 1662 statute, on mulattos, made the boundary line sharper and less easy to cross. "Whereas some doubts have arrisen whether children got by any Englishman upon a negro woman should be slave or Free" the assembly declared that "all children borne in this country shalbe held bond or free only according to the condition of the mother."[3]

[3] William W. Hening, *The Statutes at Large; Being a Collection of All Laws of Virginia from the First Session of the Legislature, in the year 1619*, 13 vols. (New York: R. & W. & G. Barton, 1809–1823), 2:170.

This statute, and the 1667 law on baptism, drew some of their inspiration from lawsuits commenced by bondsmen named Elizabeth Key in 1655/1656 and Fernando in 1667. In each case, Elizabeth and Fernando pursued appeals through the Lower Norfolk and Northumberland county courts and higher Virginia tribunals to gain their freedom. Fernando claimed that he had been a Christian for years and that he should serve no longer than an English indentured servant. The loss of General Court records leaves the final disposition of Fernando's case unknowable. More is known about Elizabeth, daughter of a slave woman and a free man, who petitioned for her freedom based on the common law tenet that children inherited their father's condition, that she was a Christian, and that she had served a period of years equivalent to an indentured servant. Although her initial trial ended unsuccessfully, her attorney appealed to the General Assembly, and the burgesses ordered a retrial, at which time her so-called owners did not appear and Elizabeth won her freedom. That Elizabeth and Fernando both petitioned courts, in different counties, to have their Christianity considered when judging their status as slaves suggests that Africans who became Christian in the earliest period of Virginia history could indeed win their freedom. This ran counter to the long-term agricultural and financial needs of Virginia planters and helps explain the passage of a 1667 law preventing conversion from freeing a slave. Likewise, Elizabeth's common law claim that her father's status insured her freedom (and other cases like it) most likely spurred Virginia's assembly to pass the 1662 law declaring that children would inherit their mother's status (*partus sequitur ventrem*). This civil law doctrine, which spread through the English colonies, trumped common law for the financial benefit of slave owners and simultaneously stifled lawsuits based on paternity – always less certain of proof than maternity in an era before DNA testing. After 1662, an African in Virginia claiming freedom would have to prove his mother was free at the time of his birth or, like Benjamin Lewis in 1691, produce a written set of indentures that ended his servitude after a term of years.

While white colonists in Virginia were sorting out who would or would not remain in bondage, colonists elsewhere were explicitly proclaiming their (short-lived) aversion to slavery through law. Massachusetts, Rhode Island, New York, New Jersey, and Georgia all initially had laws that marked slavery as an unwelcome institution in their colonies. Massachusetts in 1641 (in the *Body of Liberties*) and Rhode Island in 1652 passed the earliest and apparently most stringent laws barring slavery, but exceptions existed and in any case the laws never stopped slave trading in either colony. Massachusetts still permitted the sale of "captives taken in just warres," which included Native Americans, and Rhode Islanders developed the largest slave trading fleet in North America, moving captives to ready markets throughout the

Atlantic world. New York's law, likewise, had little impact: in 1644 the Dutch West India Company received a petition from eleven men it held in bondage in New Amsterdam, asking for their freedom. The company responded by granting half-freedom; the men were released but required thereafter to give a portion of their produce to the company annually and to work for wages whenever the company needed them. Georgia's law banning slavery actually emanated from the colony's English trustees after its founding in 1732. Free labor, it was thought, would benefit the colony more than the productivity of slaves. But colonists living in Georgia complained that they could not prosper like their South Carolina neighbors as long as slavery was prohibited and repeatedly urged the trustees to lift the ban on slavery. When the colony transferred from proprietary to royal hands in the 1750s, white colonists jettisoned the ban on slavery and adopted the South Carolina slave code (written in 1740) virtually wholesale.

Generally, laws prohibiting or limiting slavery fell into disuse. Slave owners in each of the five colonies where they existed simply ignored them. By the end of the seventeenth century, for example, New York City had become home to the largest enslaved population in the North. In 1706, New Yorkers passed a law specifying that Negro, Indian, and mulatto slaves who were baptized would not be emancipated, just as Virginia slaveholders had done some forty years earlier.

Anti-slavery sentiment – in any case uncommon until the 1680s – was routinely ignored in the seventeenth century. New World racism instead inspired laws to keep the races separate and unequal. Colonies erected legal barriers between the races by penalizing parents of mixed-race children and ministers who married interracial couples. In 1663, Maryland passed a law that imposed slavery on free white women or men if they had a mixed-race child and in addition declared the child a slave for life. The growth of Massachusetts's interracial population by the eighteenth century was rapid enough to move legislators to halt the mixing of races, lest a "spurious and mixt Issue" become commonplace. A 1704 law stipulated penalties for ministers who solemnized marriages between persons of different races and prohibited all future marriages between whites and blacks (whether slave or free). The early eighteenth century also saw several colonies pass anti-manumission laws to stop slave owners from emancipating slaves no longer capable of working. Connecticut, for example, required masters who manumitted their slaves after 1702 to support any freed slave in old age if he became unable to work and sustain himself. Clearly some owners thought little of using a slave during her productive lifetime and then emancipating her when she could no longer labor. Outside Connecticut, Massachusetts ("An Act relating to Mulatto and Negro Slaves," 1703) prohibited masters from manumitting their bondsmen unless they posted £50 as security, to prevent persons freed from becoming a welfare charge to the community. Maryland passed a similar law in 1752 to prevent owners from leaving elderly and disabled slaves dependent on the general community for their support.

It is important to note that "slave" law tended always to intertwine with laws meant to control all "marginal" groups. In town governance statutes, colony after colony created night watches and curfews to protect cities against suspicious fires, illegal slave gatherings, and the questionable activities of Native Americans and free blacks. Charles Town (later Charleston), South Carolina, had such a night watch by 1671, and Savannah, Georgia, had one after 1759. In 1703, Massachusetts enacted a curfew providing that no "Indian, Negro or Mulatto Servant or Slave may presume to absent from the Families whereto they respectively belong" after nine o'clock at night. Violators were to be imprisoned and whipped and then returned to their owners. In 1732, the Long Island town of Brookhaven forbade slaves to go out at night at all. In 1737, Maryland likewise prohibited Negroes or slaves from "Rambling, rideing or Going a Broad in the night." Most colonies mandated that bondsmen carry passes when they left their masters; Connecticut began requiring passes in 1690 and in 1723 forbade nighttime movement after nine o'clock with "An to prevent Disorder of Negro and Indian Servants and Slaves in the Night Season." That curfews, night watches, and passes became necessary indicates that Africans and African Americans were indeed out and about after dark and were frequently away from the direct control of white owners. Whether the laws prevented nighttime movement or slowed down slave mobility most likely depended on the locality and relative degree of white supervision found there. That so much law was directed at controlling these marginal groups suggests that white lawmakers prized order highly, and feared or mistrusted what a society without order might become.

Mainland colonies also encountered the same problem that confronted white Barbadians: servants and slaves selling goods that might or might not belong to them. In 1708, for example, New York barred bondsmen from selling oysters. Some colonial lawmakers recognized that laws might regulate slave huckstering more effectively if they targeted the purchasers of goods. In 1708, Connecticut began penalizing free persons who purchased any goods from "Indian, malattoes and negro servants" by setting the fine at double the value of the item purchased. A 1741 North Carolina law prohibited any person from trading goods with slaves. South Carolina lawmakers had adopted a similar law to prohibit servant and slave huckstering as early as 1687.

Laws treating slaves and indentured servants in similar fashion when it came to nighttime meetings or selling goods should not be seen as conflating the two groups. Though both were seen as marginal and hence "dangerous," other legal distinctions still set them apart. Servants retained the right to sue in their own behalf (rather than through an attorney, guardian, or owner), could give evidence in trials, hold property, and legally marry. All were actions denied to slaves in the Atlantic seaboard colonies.

Just as they granted servants and slaves different legal capacities, owners and legislators also distinguished between types of slaves. In the wake of the Yamassee war of 1715, Indians from the South were exported to New England for sale. Their violent behavior eventually caused Massachusetts lawmakers to prohibit their importation to the colony for sale as slaves. Connecticut took similar steps in 1715, blocking the sale of "Carolina Indians." Later, following the revolt on Saint Domingue (Haiti) in 1793, South Carolina, Virginia, and other Southern states barred the importation of slaves from the Caribbean island. Fearful that they would spread contagious ideas about freedom, white lawmakers sought to "quarantine" Saint Domingue slaves and prevent their contact with mainland bondsmen, who might otherwise become "contaminated" with ideas about freedom borne from violence.

Though Native Americans were caught up in the English colonies' regulation of marginal populations, and in colonists' slave trading through warfare both in New England and Carolina, the use of Native Americans as slaves in the English colonies did not compare numerically with the far higher incidence of African slavery. Native American slavery persisted longest in Spanish-controlled colonies west of the Mississippi, where slave law developed in relative isolation, cut off from English legal influences as well as information about formal regulations emanating from either Madrid or Spanish colonial outposts in the Caribbean. Slave raiding by tribe against tribe remained common through the seventeenth and eighteenth centuries, and even Spaniards ended up as slaves following native revolts against European colonization in 1680 and 1696. Pawn-slaves also appeared in native societies, as weaker Indian groups sometimes surrendered to stronger neighboring tribes in return for food, shelter, and protection. Racial boundaries between enslaved and enslaver seemed thin at best in the region, and among colonizers, a lack of formal legal knowledge prompted improvisation. In remote regions of Northern New Spain (near current-day northern Mexico, Texas, and New Mexico) in the seventeenth and eighteenth centuries, the absence of lawyers and trained judges turned local military officials into adjudicators of the law on all matters, including slavery. When possible, these military commandants referred to legal manuals if they had them, but the absence of books in many outposts doubtless increased the haphazard quality of legal knowledge regarding slavery throughout the region. Pressure from Catholic priests and native peoples who comprised the bulk of the slave population may have persuaded military leaders to continue the Spanish legal presumption in favor of freeing enslaved persons, but more research is needed to affirm this conclusively.

IV. SLAVE LAW ON THE NORTH AMERICAN MAINLAND: CODES AND CRIMES

In Louisiana, France governed its colonists and slaves from 1699 until 1766, when the Spanish took control of the colony. The few slaves present there in 1715 were Native Americans, although Africans were imported in significant numbers in the years that followed. By 1731, about 6,000 African slaves worked in French Louisiana. The majority of Louisiana's population remained both black and enslaved through 1780. Piecemeal laws issued from Paris and the 1685 code originally used in Saint Domingue together inspired the creation of the *Code Noir*, designed to regulate slaves and masters in the French Caribbean and Louisiana. Like the *Recopilación de Indias*, the *Code Noir* was more compassionate than the slave codes later created by colonists in British North America, and its numerous references to religion betray its origins in a Catholic society. For example, masters were ordered to baptize their slaves, keep enslaved husbands and wives together following marriage, and provide regular religious instruction for bondsmen. Recognizing slaves' basic humanity and personhood, the *Code Noir* nevertheless placed many restrictions on the enslaved. Bondsmen, for example, could not possess firearms and were prohibited from trading any goods without their masters' consent. Just as in Massachusetts, Maryland, and Virginia, sexual contact between blacks and whites in Louisiana was outlawed. Whites who attempted to marry slaves or free blacks were subject to fine and punishment, and priests were forbidden to perform marriage rites for interracial couples. Local ordinances passed in New Orleans eventually supplemented this imperial system of laws. Despite the penalties for interracial sex, cross-racial couples continued to flout the law through the eighteenth and nineteenth centuries.

Like codes created elsewhere in mainland colonies, provisions of the *Code Noir* also focused on slave crime, specifying the penalties to be imposed on slaves found guilty of assault, arson, theft, and murder. Indeed, the various codes created by mainland lawmakers all focused heavily on slave crime and punishment because the codes' white creators assumed slaves were inherently lawless. South Carolina's second slave code, enacted in 1696, declared that bondsmen had "barbarous, wild, savage natures" that must be restrained. In Louisiana, capital punishment could be used if a slave struck her owner or a member of her owner's family. Typically the first punishment for theft or possessing weapons was whipping, nose slitting, or ear cropping, whereas a second or third offense might merit branding or even death. Murder or insurrection could attract the death penalty immediately.

Codes frequently resulted from an effort to organize the sometimes incoherent mass of individual laws passed by legislatures in previous decades. As each colony adopted additional legislation to regulate slaves' conduct, the need to collate and systematize slave laws became stronger. Growing slave populations also spurred the development of codes: lawmakers in South Carolina (1690/1691 and 1696), Virginia (1705, 1723), and New York (1712) enacted slave codes before all other colonies in part because their enslaved populations were established early and grew rapidly. New Jersey (1713), Maryland and North Carolina (1715), Delaware (1721), Pennsylvania (1725), and Georgia (1755) all created slave codes in later years. Georgia's code was Barbadian at one remove: the colony's legislators borrowed the 1696 South Carolina code (largely based on the revised Barbados code of 1688) almost in its entirety. Codes were often published as separate pamphlets, sold individually by printers to interested whites and magistrates charged with enforcing their provisions. Some legislators may have pushed for codification to simplify conflicting provisions and to publicize slave laws to recent immigrants or those unfamiliar with the scattered, fragmented laws affecting bondsmen. In other instances, codes were updated or renewed in the wake of events perceived as disastrous by the white community. Following the Stono rebellion of 1739, in which twenty-five whites died, South Carolina lawmakers revised and republished its slave code in 1740. North Carolina followed suit in 1741, as did Virginia in 1748.

Typically, colonial slave codes stipulated that slavery was inherited through the mother (*partus sequitur ventrem*), lasted for life, and applied presumptively to Africans, mulattos, and Native Americans. Codes repeated and sometimes expanded on earlier laws that forbade interracial sex and marriage; Maryland, Virginia, North, and South Carolina all stipulated penalties for white women giving birth to mixed-race children in their codes. Likewise, laws that denied manumission to slaves following baptism or conversion usually were incorporated into slave codes. In the case of Virginia, for example, the 1667 law enacted after the Fernando and Elizabeth Key cases was included in Virginia's 1705 slave code. Some codes specified the precise manner by which manumission might be undertaken, usually making it quite difficult. Elderly or infirm slaves often could not be freed, and several colonies like New Jersey and Pennsylvania required the would-be emancipator to post high bonds to guard against a former bondsman's indigence. Manumission often meant exile. Both South Carolina and Virginia required the freed person to leave the colony or be reenslaved. By contrast, Spanish law encouraged manumission and freed slaves could readily remain part of the society where they were manumitted. In Spanish

Florida slaves could bargain with their masters to set a self-purchase price (*coartacíon*) that masters were obliged to honor contractually. But whether manumission was encouraged or frowned on, slave codes specified the course of action that masters had to follow, no less than they regulated slaves.

Codes also applied to free blacks and mulattos, not just slaves. The specific provisions in codes frequently used inclusive language to apply laws to "all negroes," such that free blacks were affected by slave code provisions. This continued the trend of earlier, piecemeal legislation that had indicated white lawmakers' determination to regulate and control all marginal groups within colonial society. Some slave codes also included penalties for whites who attempted to aid blacks in insurrection attempts or enticed slaves to run away from their masters. Disregard for property rights and a willingness to take slaves away from the control of owners put any such whites outside mainstream society; if they willingly colluded with rebellious slaves, such whites who chose to "forget" their obligations to other whites could expect harsh retribution. Punishments for whites who participated in insurrections were routinely the same as those applied to bondsmen. Harboring runaways and encouraging slave flight were also capital offenses in several colonies.

Inevitably, slave codes have come to be particularly associated with the severe punishments inflicted on slaves for various crimes and the specific tribunals by which bondsmen accused of felonies were tried. A white who killed a slave in the course of inflicting punishment could expect to be shielded from fines or trial in colonies like Virginia, North Carolina, and Georgia. Enslaved persons accused of killing received precisely the opposite treatment. In every colony, the punishments slaves endured were far more severe than those imposed on whites accused of similar crimes. In North Carolina, for example, a slave convicted of rape in 1770 was hanged, his head displayed on a pole at a nearby fork in the road, and the rest of his body burned. Castration was the alternative punishment to the death penalty for North Carolina slaves convicted of rape or murder between 1759 and 1764. Whites found guilty of rape or murder were neither maimed nor burned, nor publicly exhibited after execution. In a thirty-five year period prior to the Revolution, North Carolina courts sentenced more than one hundred bondsmen to execution or castration for a variety of offenses – murder, assault, theft, rape, arson, or flight. During times of rumored insurrections, as in New York in 1741 after the discovery of an insurrectionary plot, penalties imposed on slaves might be increased and their executions turned into spectacular public rites. Bondsmen found to have been involved in the conspiracy were sentenced to slow torturous deaths by such means as impalement, starvation, or breaking on the wheel.

Colonial lawmakers created special slaveholders' courts to handle all slave trials, not merely because they wanted the courts to convene without delay (particularly important during real or rumored revolts) but also because the special courts could adopt their own practices and procedures in gathering evidence and hearing testimony. In most cases, the slave codes reproduced practices already established in this area. Pennsylvania, for example, specified in early 1700 that two justices of the peace, together with "six of the most substantial freeholders of the neighborhood," should gather to try all offenses committed by slaves, well before its 1725 code repeated the provision. In South Carolina, slave courts included two or three justices of the peace and three to seven "substantial freeholders." Unlike trials of whites, from which black testimony was excluded, both whites and blacks might testify before slave tribunals. The use of torture to gather information and evidence was sanctioned by several colonial governments, and virtually no appeals were permitted. Punishments meted out were rapid and harsh, although how arbitrary such justice might have been is hard to estimate. The execution of a slave routinely required the colony to make good a slave owner's property loss, which would result in a higher tax bill for all members of the tribunal weighing a potential death penalty. One solution that required neither higher taxes nor freeing an accused slave was to mandate transportation out of a colony's territory. By requiring an owner to sell the convicted slave out of his home colony, a slave's potential for bad conduct in the future would be passed on to another locale. Throughout the colonial and antebellum eras, slave traders transported convicted slaves to the Deep South and the Caribbean, where labor shortages continued, the slave's prior offenses were unknown, and a higher price was obtainable at the auction block. Eventually, several Deep South states, like Alabama, Mississippi, and Louisiana in the post-Revolution period, passed laws barring sales of convicted slaves to prevent owners from dumping violent slaves in their region, though the efficacy of such laws remains debatable.

As is true in modern society, the number of lawless individuals in the colonial world was far outnumbered by those who were decent and law abiding. The same was true for bondsmen. Many more were affected by curfew restrictions, prohibitions on selling produce and other goods, or the rules established on plantations by individual masters than by the criminal law of slavery. Most slaves did not enter or testify before slave courts or endure the brutal punishments they handed out. Those who were punished by slave courts may have complied for reasons derived from their African backgrounds rather than any coercion applied by court officials. African tribal beliefs often fused together religious and legal proceedings, placing them in the hands of an expert truth-finder from whom falsehoods could not be hidden. What might Africans forcibly shipped to the New World have deduced from the rituals and forms associated with typical colonial American legal proceedings? If they saw judges entering a courtroom, perhaps dressed in robes, some Africans might have concluded that they were in the company of religious figures, shamans, or truth-finders, endowed with supernatural powers. The desire to tell the truth to such religious/judicial figures may thus help account for the direct testimony that some colonial slaves gave indicting themselves in legal proceedings. Confronted with testimony about their wrongdoing, some African bondsmen may have admitted their guilt to slave courts as a form of religious obedience – not because American laws compelled them, but because African belief systems required it. By ignoring the expectations or actions of slaves within the courts we overlook the significance of collisions of multiple legal cultures, African and European, within the realm of slave law. The criminal law of slavery, codified in all its cruelty, tells us much about the white lawmakers who felt compelled to organize and systematize their colonial slave laws. It says little or nothing about what slaves actually did or what they thought of law and of legal systems.

On their plantations, where their word had the force of law, colonial slave owners were no less domineering than their antebellum counterparts and drew up elaborate rules to guide the conduct of bondsmen. Indeed, some masters repeatedly ignored aspects of the slave codes in order to impose their own, sometimes contradictory, authority. Although North and South Carolina (and later other colonies) prohibited slaves from hiring their own time out for wages, masters – particularly those in cities like Charleston – frequently encouraged skilled slaves to seek paid employment so that their wages could be turned over to owners in cash. Even as colonial laws barred these hiring-out schemes, local ordinances diluted their impact, stipulating instead that such slaves could only live in certain areas of town or work in certain trades. Such refinements suggest that local lawmakers had a more realistic assessment of urban slavery and the rules that should govern it than colonial legislatures. Generally, slave masters exercised their powers to the fullest in rural as well as urban areas, disdaining slave courts at will or flouting slave laws, preferring the autonomy and sense of personal power that slave owning routinely gave them.

We have seen that the actual enforcement of slave laws, whether criminal or otherwise, fell to all white members of colonial society. This meant that masters enjoyed considerable discretion not only in the detailed regulation of slaves on their own plantations but also in determining how far they would actually comply with the provisions of enacted slave codes that policed the slave population at large. The earliest laws regulating the conduct of bondsmen named no particular person or office to regulate slave behavior: the assumption was that slave masters would simply impose enactments on their bondsmen. A later generation of slave laws, as in Barbados, specifically named all whites as law enforcers. All were to be responsible for checking slave passes and correcting misbehavior through physical punishment, not just slave masters. Gradually, colonial lawmakers realized that they could not rely on slave masters or whites throughout society in general (without compensation) to enforce police laws preventing slaves from gathering in nighttime meetings, huckstering goods, or moving about without passes. Masters simply could not be counted on to implement all the laws intended to bind slaves all the time. Beginning in late seventeenth-century South Carolina and continuing through the eighteenth and into the nineteenth centuries, colonial (and later state) governments and town councils created slave patrols to take specific responsibility for enforcing the varied regulations circumscribing slave conduct. Patrols, composed of owners and non-owners alike, were employed in three- or six-month rotations, time enough to gain detailed knowledge of the slave codes they were meant to impose. Slave patrols operating in the growing cities and towns of the colonial period routinely predated the creation of urban police forces in the South and in some cases operated in their place, all the while focusing their attentions specifically on the activities – legal and illegal – of bondsmen. Slave patrol tactics, which frequently included riding at night and punishing all slaves or free blacks they encountered, foreshadowed the post-Civil War behaviors of the Ku Klux Klan.

V. SLAVE LAW IN A REVOLUTIONARY AGE

Although slave revolts and insurrections usually resulted in tougher slave laws, as was the case after the Stono rebellion in 1739 and the New York insurrection of 1741, the most dramatic changes in the mainland colonies' regulation of bondsmen were precipitated by the stresses associated with the American Revolution. The arrival of British and Hessian troops during the war offered new hope to slaves seeking an alternative to a lifetime in bondage. In November 1775, the royal governor of Virginia, Lord Dunmore, proclaimed that slaves belonging to rebellious colonists who chose to serve the British army would be emancipated, triggering a flood of runaways bound for the British lines. In consequence, slave patrols stepped up their enforcement of the slave laws, and Virginia rebel authorities increased punishments for recaptured runaways. Where earlier fugitives might have been whipped by the patrols and returned to their owners, wartime runaways recaptured in Virginia were liable to permanent confiscation by the patriot authorities and placed at work in the state's iron mines, where many of them died. As the British army moved through different regions of America, however, attempts to enforce slave laws restricting mobility after 1776 met with limited success; wartime enlistments drained men from slave patrol rosters at the very time when slave runaway attempts skyrocketed.

Estimates suggest that as many as 50,000 slaves attempted to reach British encampments during the course of the Revolution. Slaves who actively aided the British and were subsequently recaptured were often executed for treason.

The British offers made to American slaves had no humanitarian impulse behind them, but simple expediency: a shortage of manpower and local knowledge made slave workers invaluable. Rebel forces recognized that the same potential source of labor could be put to work for their side, and several Northern states, Connecticut and New York among them, offered slaves their freedom if they enlisted with local militia units (with their masters' permission). Maryland and Virginia also permitted slaves to enlist, although emancipation was not offered. South Carolina and Georgia, meanwhile, resisted all efforts to arm blacks. But in Northern regions, with two groups, rebels and loyalists, effectively bidding for the military services of enslaved men and offering freedom as the ultimate bounty, male and female slaves may have realized that their moment to press for total emancipation had arrived. Perhaps sensing that political winds had shifted in their favor, slaves in Worcester County, Massachusetts, petitioned their local Committee of Correspondence for freedom in 1775. The committee in turn pledged its support to all efforts that might emancipate African Americans in the future. A group of bondsmen in Portsmouth, New Hampshire, urged the state legislature to end slavery throughout the state, but their petition was tabled. Emancipation in New Hampshire would only come after the Revolution.

In 1775, Samuel Johnson famously noted the irony of American patriots complaining of their political bondage (being taxed without Parliamentary representation) at a time when close to a half-million Africans or African Americans were held in literal bondage by those same patriots: "How is it that we hear the loudest yelps for liberty among the drivers of Negroes?" The irony was not lost on all white Americans, who in some cases began to take action against the laws enslaving their fellow man. Before the Revolution, the strongest advocates for emancipation had been the Quakers, who in the early eighteenth century had agitated against slavery, with little success. The spread of their egalitarian views on religion nevertheless coincided with growing anti-slavery sentiment elsewhere in Europe. The language of universal freedom and independence that flowered in the works of Enlightenment figures like Baron de Montesquieu found a ready audience in British North America. In his proposed Declaration of Independence, Thomas Jefferson urged that George III should be indicted for the slave trade, a "piratical warfare" conducted against "a distant people who never offended him" who were now urged to "rise in arms among us." He likewise proposed that slavery should be abolished. Jefferson's fellow delegates to the

Continental Congress, however, were divided on these ideas: delegates from Georgia and South Carolina blocked their inclusion in the final version of the Declaration, revealing an early rift on the future course of emancipation in the new nation.

Several states determined to strike out on their own course in abolishing the international slave trade, making it illegal for ships carrying Africans to enter their ports or sell their human cargoes. These actions were inspired, in part, by the 1774 Articles of Association, designed to boycott all British products and cargoes shipped in British ships. The second article asserted that Americans would no longer participate in the international slave trade. Virginia and Connecticut implemented the provisions in 1774, outlawing slave importation and setting steep fines for ship captains found violating the law. However, when emancipation bills were presented in the Connecticut assembly, they were rejected – in 1777, 1779, and again in 1780. Halting a state's connection with the international slave trade was not equivalent, in the minds of white lawmakers, with ending slavery altogether. Rhode Island, a long-term participant in the slave trade, never passed a law banning slave ships from its waters. However, after the Revolution several other states followed Virginia and Connecticut's lead: Maryland, for example, prohibited further slave imports after 1783, and New York halted importation in 1785.

Emancipation in Northern states would come through a mixture of constitutional declarations and court cases. The first North American government to end slavery by constitutional means was Vermont, which formed an independent republic and ratified its own constitution in July 1777. The first article of Vermont's constitution rejected slavery as inhumane and inconsistent with a free republic. Such rhetoric may have come easily in Vermont. Fewer than 300 African Americans were living in the state when it joined the United States in 1791. In Massachusetts, the first version of a state constitution proposed in 1778 foundered during ratification because it included language in its fifth article, on representation, that refused free "Negroes, Indians, and molattoes" [sic] the right of participation in elections. Other aspects of the draft constitution were also controversial, but the townspeople of Sutton, like residents of eight other towns, specified in their return that "the grand and Fundamental Maxims of Humane Rights" were diametrically opposed to slavery and that the new constitution must not add to the "Load of guilt" lying on Massachusetts for permitting slavery or the slave trade to exist. Citizens of Pittsfield instructed the next Massachusetts convention that a new constitution must end slavery, and in the 1780 state constitution, crafted largely by John Adams, the first right declared was that "all men are born free and equal." The interpretation placed on these words was unambiguous. William Cushing, the state's chief justice, urged in the

Quock Walker freedom case (1783) that "the idea of slavery is inconsistent with our own conduct and Constitution." Although some scholars point to *Quock Walker* as the end of slavery in Massachusetts, Cushing himself would date its demise some three years earlier, to the adoption of the 1780 state constitution.

Unlike Vermont and Massachusetts, most Northern states experienced the end of slavery as a gradual, not an immediate event, brokered through legislative compromise on the question how long slaves should serve their masters before being freed as adults. During the Revolution, Pennsylvania with its numerous Quaker residents took the lead in gradual emancipation, creating a law to end slavery slowly after 1780. The legislature responded not merely to the idealism of Enlightenment thinkers but also to pressure from the first anti-slavery society founded in America in 1775, established by prominent Philadelphians like Benjamin Franklin. Pennsylvania's law provided that all persons born to slave parents after 1780 would serve until 28 years of age, when they would be freed. Lower ages, of 18 and 21, were originally proposed, but the legislative history shows that a higher age was finally established to allow slave owners recompense for the expense of rearing slave children from infancy.

Pennsylvania's gradual emancipation model was reproduced in several other northern states after the Revolution. Rhode Island (1784), Connecticut (1784, modified in 1797), New York (1799, modified in 1817), and New Jersey (1804) all adopted gradualist laws designed to emancipate bondsmen while at the same time partially compensating slave owners for their lost property by guaranteeing them terms of service lasting anywhere from eighteen to twenty-eight years. The famous slave orator Sojourner Truth (Isabella Baumfree) witnessed this legal process and its effects firsthand. Sojourner Truth's *Narrative*, told through an amanuensis, recounts how her children only gained their freedom after serving their masters through adolescence and young adulthood. Many white observers considered gradual emancipation to represent a less convulsive (and therefore commendable) method of emancipation because it altered the legal status of slaves piecemeal, one person at a time. In 1794, the Connecticut state assembly considered abolishing its gradual emancipation program, begun in 1784 in favor of immediate emancipation, but despite strong support from advocates like Jonathan Edwards, Jr. and Theodore Dwight the measure never became law. The inspiration for the immediate emancipation project in Connecticut probably came from the Caribbean, where the ongoing slave revolt on Saint Domingue (which began in 1791 and ended with the abolition of slavery) had inspired a reconsideration of slavery throughout the French colonial system. France's revolutionary convention formally abolished slavery in its colonies in 1794.

Several other states considered ending slavery during the Revolution. The most notable was Virginia, where legislators debated abolishing the institution, but ultimately chose not to do so. In 1782, however, Virginia lifted its restrictions on slave manumission, and the number of free blacks in Virginia began to rise dramatically (from 3,000 in 1782 to 13,000 by 1792) as many masters took advantage of the law to free their slaves. But anti-slavery sentiments in Maryland and Virginia could never persuade the numerous slave owners who clung to their human property and defeated measures to abolish slavery entirely both during the Revolution and in the years that followed. The financial costs associated with compensating slave owners for lost property rights, as well as the racism that served as the foundation for many slave-related laws, swayed the Virginia assembly to abandon any discussions of gradual or immediate emancipation. Indeed, in 1806 Virginia's legislature reimposed certain restrictions on manumission by requiring manumitted slaves to leave the state in the year after their emancipation or face reenslavement. Given that in 1790 Virginia and Maryland were home to more than half of all mainland slaves (nearly 300,000 in the first U.S. census), the failure to abolish slavery in its greatest stronghold must be considered a lost opportunity of immense significance, one that, if seized, would have decisively altered the nation's history. Had Virginia decided to end slavery within its borders in the 1780s or 1790s, the impact of the decision on the rest of the South might have caused slavery to diminish rapidly in the early nineteenth century.

The American law of slavery became more plural and more complicated after the colonies achieved their independence from Great Britain, for now the lives of bondsmen could be regulated not only by state laws but also by national law. The Articles of Confederation (proposed in 1776, ratified in 1781) creating the first government for the United States acknowledged the existence of slavery, but only indirectly and in a fashion that restricted any potential national authority over the institution. The "privileges and immunities" clause (Article IV) applied only to the states' free residents; Article IX's "treaties and alliances" power forbade the Confederation Congress from making treaties that would affect the import or export of any "species of goods or commodities whatsoever," which meant that Congress could not enter into any international agreement to prohibit the Atlantic slave trade. In general the terms of confederation made state sovereignty supreme (Article II), so slavery and its abolition remained largely in the realm of state law.

After the Revolutionary War ended in the Treaty of Paris (1783), the new confederation faced important problems in governing lands gained from Britain as a result of the peace treaty. With England's cession of all land claims on the eastern side of the Mississippi, Congress found itself required to create laws for territories beyond the jurisdiction of the existing state governments. In 1784, Thomas Jefferson chaired a congressional committee created to draft a plan for governing the newly acquired lands. Jefferson's draft legislation proposed that slavery be barred from all western territories after 1800, but the provision was removed by Congress before the law's passage. Nevertheless, growing anti-slavery sentiments among Northern congressmen could not be restrained, resulting in a compromise that provided a temporary solution to the thorny problem. In 1787, Congress passed the Northwest and Southwest Ordinances, dividing the western territory along the Ohio River and mandating that slavery would be absolutely excluded from lands north of the river. South of the Ohio, where the Southwest Ordinance prevailed, the law was silent: in other words, Congress tacitly accepted that slavery would likely spread to the territories of Alabama, Mississippi, Tennessee, and Kentucky. The Northwest Ordinance also included a provision (Article VI) that runaway slaves captured north of the Ohio were to be returned to their slave masters. This language, later echoed in the fugitive slave clause of the U. S. Constitution, required that residents of Northern territories and states where slavery did not exist must still respect the laws of Southern states binding African Americans in slavery. As regional practices in the United States diverged on whether slavery was legitimate or not, the respect for Southern slave laws required of Northern "free" states would prove an increasingly divisive issue.

VI. FROM ARTICLES OF CONFEDERATION TO THE CONSTITUTION: SLAVERY IN THE NEW NATION

The impact of the Revolution on slavery in the United States should not be minimized, for it represented a clear rift in the universality of slavery that had prevailed hitherto. At the start of the Revolution, slavery remained legal in all mainland colonies. By 1804, plans for gradual or immediate emancipation were in place in each state north of the Mason-Dixon line. Gradual emancipation did not work flawlessly. First, it was extremely gradual: in 1810, there were nearly 30,000 slaves still living north of Maryland, awaiting the slow transition to freedom. Second, it could be highly arbitrary: take the case of Lucy, a slave given her freedom by a Connecticut court only to be reenslaved a month later. After her manumission her former owner returned to court to complain that he had not known he would remain financially responsible for Lucy, were she to become a pauper in her old age. The court agreed to reverse Lucy's emancipation. The court did not recognize Lucy, an African American, as a full citizen of the republic, so her agonizing journey from and then back to slavery caused it little concern. Nor, finally, did the slow elimination of slavery in the North make much impression on the racism endemic among whites toward African Americans living in their midst. Nevertheless, the critique of slavery as a violation of natural law by Enlightenment writers and the spread of gradual emancipation in Northern states, flawed as it was, would eventually reduce slavery from an unquestioned universal practice to a regional "peculiar institution."

The regional quality that slavery was acquiring after the Revolution became apparent in 1787 during discussions at the Philadelphia Constitutional Convention. Weaknesses that had become manifest in the Articles of Confederation since 1781 caused political leaders to propose a new form of national government. In their constitutional debates, Northern delegates found that they could not avoid discussing slavery, no matter how hard they tried. Southern delegates consented to the use of euphemisms in the Constitution in place of the words "slave" and "slavery." But though the words "unfree persons" or "such persons" were employed, slavery was clearly part of the Constitution, notably in its apportionment of representation and taxes (Article I) and its fugitive slave clause (Article IV). For purposes of apportioning delegates in the House of Representatives according to population, each state could quantify a slave as three-fifths of a white citizen; attributing federal taxes payable by each state (split among states based on total population) would likewise tally a slave as three-fifths of a white resident. Two other provisions in the Constitution directly affected American slavery. Article V restricted Congress's ability to pass any law restricting the international slave trade before the year 1808; Article IV required (as the Articles of Confederation had) that each state grant "full faith and credit" to the laws passed by every other state. Laws passed in Southern states like Georgia regulating slavery were to have full effect in Massachusetts and elsewhere in the North.

Ratification of the proposed Constitution did not come immediately. Delegates to some Northern ratification conventions pointed out that the new document implicitly approved and sanctioned slavery, even though the word "slave" might be missing from its pages. No clause generated more furor than Article V, the restriction on the international slave trade – some slavery opponents sought to ban transatlantic slave trading immediately on moral grounds, whereas others suspected that the continued importation of slaves would merely boost the South's population and hence add to its political power in the House of Representatives. Opposition to Article V's restrictions in the New Hampshire, Massachusetts, and Pennsylvania ratifying conventions was, strangely enough, duplicated in a few Southern states like Virginia and North Carolina, where continuation of the slave trade was thought likely to increase the possibility of slave insurrections. Ultimately, the twenty-year restriction on Congress's power to ban the slave trade remained part of the document.

Although Congress could not outlaw the international slave trade until 1808, some national politicians began immediately attacking slavery through other means. In 1794, the national government banned the building of ships for use in the slave trade or the use of existing ships in the trade. Ship owners found to have participated in the slave trade were to be fined double the value of their investment in the ship. American sailors who worked on American ships in the slave trade, if caught, were to serve two years in jail and pay a fine of $2,000. Later this law would be augmented to include American sailors working on ships of any country engaged in the transatlantic slave trade. Widespread support, North and South, for preventing the importation of African slaves in American ships made the passage of such laws relatively easy.

Non-American slave ships nevertheless continued to enter ports of the American South – with increasing frequency, as the ban on importation drew closer. Congress would pass "An Act to Prohibit the Importation of Slaves into any Port or Place within the Jurisdiction of the US," on March 2, 1807, effectively expelling the international slave trade from American ports as of January 1, 1808. In the twenty years before the ban, more than 200,000 new African slaves entered Southern ports, destined for lives of servitude on southern plantations. Their arrival in the South coincided with and may have been inspired by the invention of a more efficient cotton gin in 1793, making agricultural production simpler than ever before. The high level of world demand for cotton, coupled with the new gin, sparked a migratory boom across the South, as numerous slave owners relocated from the Atlantic seaboard to the fertile, cotton-growing Deep South. Flocking to build new plantations in the Southwest territories, slave owners' demand for slave labor grew rather than diminished in the early years of the new nation.

As planters moved from the eastern seaboard to the territories of Alabama, Mississippi, Arkansas, and Louisiana (and also pushed into Florida and Texas, territories still controlled by European powers), they brought with them the legal codes of their native states. Congress did not create slave law for the territories – territorial legislatures had to come up with their own. Just as the Barbadian code had been adopted by South Carolina in the seventeenth century, Deep South territorial governments looked for existing models of slave regulation to copy and make their own. In the early nineteenth century, South Carolina's slave code was rapidly adopted, either in whole or in part, as the slave law of virtually all the newly formed territories. Its racialized description of slavery, restrictions on multiple aspects of slave life, and imposition of capital punishment for slave insurrections and white murder spread rapidly throughout the Deep South.

Unlike the other trans-Appalachian territories, Kentucky chose to adopt portions of its slave code from Virginia and North Carolina. Subsequently it invented new restrictive laws for slaves living near the Ohio River. As the last great barrier between slave and free states, the Ohio River represented a final hurdle for bondsmen running away to freedom. Kentucky lawmakers responded by creating stronger slave patrols along the river's edge to enforce the slave laws there more effectively. New restrictions on bondsmen also appeared in long-settled states, like Virginia. In the wake of the unsuccessful insurrection known as Gabriel's Rebellion (1800), Virginia lawmakers in the early 1800s placed additional limits on slave literacy and mobility. Fear of slave rebellions continued to inspire Southern legislators to attempt these new controls on slave behavior, but the laws remained ideals. Slaves who already knew how to read could not be forcibly rendered illiterate; bondsmen determined to violate curfews would not always be restrained.

Towns on the Gulf of Mexico and the Atlantic instituted additional laws in the 1790s to prevent contact between local slaves and outsiders carrying seditious tales of freedom. Following the successful slave revolt on St. Domingue (Haiti) in the 1790s, several states restricted the movement of visitors from the island so that emancipated Haitian slaves could not circulate insurrectionary ideas among Southern bondsmen. Likewise, ship captains who employed free black sailors learned on arriving in Charleston and Savannah that their "negro seamen" were required to lodge in the city jail during shore leave. Until their ships left harbor, African American sailors who knew of a world beyond slavery could not be permitted to mingle freely with the enslaved population of the South. Other Southern port cities soon followed Charleston and Savannah's example. Predictably, abolitionist newspaper editors in the North reacted with rage and scorn on learning that free United States citizens were being jailed in the South for no reason other than the color of their skin.

Throughout the early period of America's nationhood, comity in the area of slave law became an increasingly difficult problem. Given that the bulk of slave law was state-based, should Northern states where slavery had ended (or would soon end) be required to respect the legal restrictions placed by Southern states on African American slaves? Travelers from the Caribbean or the South who arrived in states like Rhode Island or New York were routinely accompanied by "servants" who were in truth slaves. Should those slaves be immediately emancipated on arriving in free states, as slaves who visited England would have been following the 1772 *Somerset* decision? Each Northern state devised its own solution. Pennsylvania's gradual emancipation statute (1780) contained a six-month clause for just such a situation: slaves accompanying visitors sojourning in the state remained bondsmen for only six months. If a slave owner lingered in Pennsylvania longer than six months, his accompanying slave was rendered free. Pennsylvania abolitionist groups pursued an aggressive litigation strategy to free slaves who had been in the state beyond the deadline.

As legal distinctions between Northern and Southern states in the realm of slave law grew more pronounced, additional cases would test each region's commitment to maintain or abolish slavery. The fragmented nature of slave law in America, so haphazard in the colonial period when slavery was almost universally accepted, did not lend itself to the mediation of the growing antagonisms of the late eighteenth and early nineteenth centuries. With new states added in each decade of the nineteenth century, conflict between state laws – and the increasing strain on comity – was only liable to increase. The intensifying connections between Southern culture and slavery on one hand and the North and free labor on the other served additionally to highlight the gulf growing in state law. In the absence of a national law of slavery that might reconcile differences, ever-worsening conflicts over slave law between North and South seemed inevitable. That such legal conflicts could only be resolved (as John Quincy Adams put it) "at the cannon's mouth," by warfare, is suggestive of how strong each state's commitment to its own law of slavery or freedom became during the nineteenth century – and how vigorously Southern states would fight to maintain their slave laws during the Civil War.

VII. THE DIRECTION OF FUTURE SCHOLARSHIP ABOUT COLONIAL SLAVE LAW

Histories written about American slave law in the colonial and revolutionary eras have tended to cluster in two areas: the criminal law, as evidenced by cases that reached the highest courts on appeal, and slave codes considered in their entirety. A few historians, notably Thomas Morris, have also considered how slaves were the subject of a wide array of conventional legal disputes, as, for example, in the realms of contract, property, and inheritance. And a small but significant body of studies has highlighted connections between European legal regimes (e.g., Roman law, common law) and the laws of slavery enacted by Caribbean and American colonial assemblies. The triumph of English common law in the United States has submerged the multiple legal systems that served as sources for slave law in America's colonial past. Ultimately, all previous studies of law and colonial slavery have taken very seriously the formal, positive creation of law by colonizing elites, and the implementation of these restrictive slave laws by whites (acting either as individuals or in so-called slave courts) who punished bondsmen when they violated these ideal precepts. With the exception of Philip Schwarz's *Slave Law in Virginia*, the only perspective recreated or considered recoverable by the vast majority of historians of colonial slave law has been that of European enslavers and their white descendants. A signal deficiency in each of these studies, therefore, has been the failure to consider and describe the experience of American slave law from the perspective of recently enslaved Africans, who were of course familiar with law in their natal lands. It is reasonable to suppose that their legal knowledge affected their expectations, understanding, and acceptance of American slave law as applied by white slave owners. Histories of early America have increasingly emphasized transnational or world historical perspectives, as evidenced by the growing interest in Atlantic world connections. The parochial, top-down approach of studying colonial and revolutionary slave law in America (emphasizing either America's exceptionalism or the indebtedness of America's slave law to European legal sources) should also give way to a more inclusive legal-historical approach that acknowledges the legal expectations of enslaved Africans as well as the Americans who kept them in bondage.

Analyses that give equal consideration to the legal perceptions and experiences of the enslaved as well as the enslaver will need to accord greater importance to the particular demography of Africans placed in bondage. Of the roughly eleven million Africans taken captive and shipped to the New World, some tribal groups were predominant. Recent studies of slaves taken from Africa indicate that the ports of departure most frequently named on slave ship manifests were in the Bight of Biafra, the Bight of Benin, or the west-central region of Africa, near Loango and Angola. Some 60 percent or more of all ships carrying slaves out of Africa left one of these regions, bound for the Americas, whereas Senegambian captives (from the area between the Senegal and Gambia rivers, farther north) accounted for another 10 percent of all Africans sent to what would become the United States. From the Bight of Biafra, one large group well represented among the many Africans enslaved was the Igbo people. Therefore, it would make sense to concentrate our attention on the Igbo approach to law (among others) to try to determine what legal understandings of their own slaves taken from among the Igbo might have brought to the slave law of the British mainland colonies. In the case of Senegambian captives, similarly, we should learn more about Muslim traditions within slavery, since the trade in non-Muslim slaves was strong in that region.

In the future, scholars of slave law will be interested in more than just how these West African customary laws might impose the status of slave on a person or enable the status to be cast off. We must anticipate that Africans encountering American slave law would have known not only specific principles of law, but would have framed their conceptions of law within a legal philosophy, an overarching theory that made sense of the entire legal system within their society. We should look for indications of the underlying principles that guided legal relations, conceptions of guilt and innocence, and presumptions about human nature. For instance, the Igbo believe that there are both divine and man-made laws, but that the greatest penalties are reserved for breaches of divine law. Thus, a murderer would not be put on trial, because if the evidence were clear and convincing no earthly court could have jurisdiction. Indeed, the penalty prescribed by Igbo tradition is that the murderer is expected to hang himself. Igbos placed on trial by slave owners for certain crimes may have experienced some conflict in their own minds about the legitimacy or jurisdictional claim of the colonial court, for any Igbo guilty of breaking a divine law would be required to do penance personally to be restored to the good favor of the gods.

To learn more about how Africans perceived their own legal systems (and thus, what they may have thought on encountering American laws), analysis of firsthand African accounts will be necessary. As one example of what is possible, an excellent account of the early civil and criminal justice system of the Yoruba people, from the area of modern-day Nigeria, can be found in the words of Osifekunde, a man sold into slavery who eventually told his story to a French ethnographer, D'Avezac-Macaya, in the early nineteenth century.

Given the limited nature of firsthand evidence, investigation of African perceptions of the colonial legal system may not be capable of rising above the inferential. Nevertheless, if inference permits the construction of a more inclusive picture of the legal cultures in contact during the colonial and Revolutionary eras we should not hesitate. Rather than assume that the only perspective and legal culture that matters is that of the white colonizer, slave owner, and lawgiver, future studies in this area must pay more attention to the customary laws of slavery in Africa and the information to be gleaned from travelers, explorers, and traders who visited West Africa. Likewise, surviving local court records found in many state archives for criminal trials demand much more attention from scholars. Published legal reports of criminal cases decided on appeal cannot substitute for the entirely distinct legal world of the lower courts during initial trial hearings and the records they generate. These case files, though incomplete and sometimes frustrating, contain the information necessary to recapture the lost voices of Africans and African Americans encountering a European-designed legal system for the first time.

CONCLUSION

The creation of slave laws in the New World resulted from longstanding European intellectual and religious traditions that justified using coercion against strangers. The Bible, natural law, and just war theories provided the rationales used by enslavers to legitimate the capture or retention of bondsmen in the early modern period. These widely shared beliefs, buttressed by racism, fear, or greed, provided Caribbean planters, the first British colonizers to invest heavily in slave labor, with the mental framework necessary to craft slave codes in the mid-seventeenth century. Their codes did not include every possible area of slave law that could be addressed – they tended to focus on criminal activity by slaves, rather than the commercial aspects of slaves as property – and historians have fixated on them often to the exclusion of individual slave laws enacted locally or passed by colonial assemblies in piecemeal fashion. Slave laws typically affected many individuals besides bondsmen, such as free blacks and servants, because lawmakers, somewhat naively, hoped to regulate and control the behavior of all marginal groups. Their codes were idealized statements of what white lawmakers hoped for, rather than reflections of actual law in practice; this can be seen in the gradual shift in enforcement, from reliance on voluntary adoption by masters to compulsory requirement for all masters and overseers. Eventual resort to slave patrols as a supplemental enforcement group suggests that, whether acting under a voluntary or compulsory regime, masters and overseers failed in their duties. Ideal standards of lawful behavior were met by neither slaves nor their white masters.

The fragmented background to America's slave law, drawn from French, Spanish, and English sources, did not yield a unified or comprehensive slave law in the colonial period. Gaps and omissions always remained; colonies fumbled to create new regulations as they were needed. Laws to regulate huckstering, to prevent intermarriage, and to restrict freedom following conversion to Christianity came into being as novel situations arose and demanded legislative solutions. Even colonies that had no slave codes restricted slave movement through curfew laws; these regulations probably affected many more bondsmen than did criminal laws. As we have just seen, little is known about how Africans themselves viewed slave laws. The addition of new voices to the tale of early America's scattered slave law in the colonial period, the voices of African slaves describing the law or their legal expectations, may prove difficult, yet this basic shortcoming of extant scholarship on slave law must be redressed.

The universal acceptance of slavery in the colonial period gave way to discord in the Revolutionary era, as several Northern states moved to embrace gradual emancipation. A fundamental shift in the moral acceptability of slavery took place, as Quakers and other religious groups joined forces with Enlightenment philosophers like Montesquieu to undermine slavery's legitimacy in Europe and America. In the years after 1780, what had once been universally believed – that slavery was justified religiously and philosophically – no longer held true, at least in states north of Maryland. These states began to abolish slavery by repealing its legal underpinnings. Where the fragmented origins of American slave law had once given way to comprehensive laws and codes restricting the behavior of bondsmen, a regional breakdown in the acceptability of slavery began to erode commonality, giving rise to a new round of fragmentation. This splintering at the state level, with some states still supporting slavery while others abandoned it, was not superseded by a national law of slavery that would regulate bondsmen in all states. The Constitution, like the Articles of Confederation, left slave law to the individual states and required little more than that states give full faith and credit to the laws of other states. As the federal government moved to close off the international slave trade in 1808, new states in the Deep South lined up for admission to the union, each with a slave code that echoed restrictions found in the South Carolina or Virginia codes of the eighteenth century. Even as widespread acceptance of slavery and its legal underpinnings diminished in the North, in regions where enslavement was still permitted its supporters increasingly turned to the law for reassurance and reinforcement. Meanwhile, new states admitted under provisions of the Northwest Ordinance swelled the number of non-slaveholding states north of the Ohio River. The absence of a national law of slavery set the stage for greater conflict about comity in the antebellum era, when Southern and Northern states would battle to see which state laws would prevail in repeated contests over slavery.

9

THE TRANSFORMATION OF DOMESTIC LAW

HOLLY BREWER

Law has a peculiar tendency to normalize social relations that are in fact culturally distinct in different societies and eras. There is no better example of this tendency than domestic relations. Following common law norms, legal historians have largely portrayed a particular domestic order as peculiarly unchanging, indeed as private and ideally inviolate. In an abstract sense domestic order may thus seem to be outside the law. The law's very success in normalizing family relations has obscured its own agency in shaping them, rendering its own role in historical and cultural change mysterious.

In England and its colonies in the early modern period, the law – both common and statute – regulated domestic order in many and profound ways. That regulation was also the subject of intense dispute. Laws defining domestic order circumscribed many people's lives from birth through death, shaping their status and mandating appropriate behavior – for women and children; for workers, servants, and slaves; and indeed for husbands, fathers, and masters. Relationships, particularly the status of "dependent" groups, usually thought of as static throughout the colonial and early national periods of American history, and in early modern Britain too, were recreated over the course of the eighteenth century through common law justifications of a particular domestic order. These acts of creation occurred during a period of dramatic struggle over the basis of authority, not only over abstract political authority but over the rules that should govern the household and indeed over the very definitions of household and domestic. The results diminished the legal powers of lords and masters and increased those of fathers and husbands. These changes were accomplished with a legal sleight-of-hand that made the powers of husbands and fathers seem eternal within the common law and obscured the frequent conflicts between the authority of masters and those of fathers and husbands. The new legal regime was built on a fiction that the rights of kings, lords, and masters were essentially the same and that all were variations on the same patriarchal absolutism that was itself a celebration of fatherly authority. In reality the rights of kings, lords, and masters were often in conflict with those of common men, women, and children. Consequently, the struggle over domestic space and authority was central to a larger struggle over rights and political authority.

To understand how law could normalize a particular domestic order, one must first sketch the vision of that order that emerged in the late eighteenth century. This was a moment of peculiar influence for the common law, and especially for its main expositor, Sir William Blackstone. The first professor of law at Oxford University, Blackstone is best known for the grand synthesis of the common law he completed in the 1760s. Blackstone's synthesis was profoundly influential in America no less than in England. He was cited more in American newspapers of the 1790s – that critical period of the creation of state constitutions and legal norms – than any other thinker, including Locke and Montesquieu, the sages of previous decades. At the end of the eighteenth century, Tapping Reeve, founder of the first American law school in Connecticut and author of the first American treatise on domestic law, posed neat, parallel categories of domestic order under the common law drawn straight from Blackstone: child/wife/servant appear ranged beneath father/husband/master. The head of household speaks for, orders, and controls those under his roof: they are his property and speak (if at all) only through him.[1]

Reeve claims to be portraying the common law of household relations as they existed throughout the colonial period and in England. In fact, he is largely reproducing both Blackstone's categories and his portrayal of them as unchanging. Blackstone had ordered in parallel the powers of masters over servants (first), followed by the powers of husbands over wives, parents over children, and guardians over wards (a lesser category). In each category, Blackstone set up the same order of identity and obedience, consistently denying the ability of the lesser person(s) to have legally independent judgment. Take, for example, the rule of husbands over wives: "By marriage, the husband and wife are one person in law: that is, the very being or legal existence of the woman is suspended during the marriage, or at least is incorporated and consolidated into that of the husband: under whose wing, protection, and *cover*, she performs everything."[2] Blackstone even claimed that a married woman could not testify against her husband. In his eyes this act was equal to self-incrimination.

Blackstone's changes built on more than a century of common law arguments that had begun to prioritize the rights of persons and the idea of

[1] Tapping Reeve, *The Law of Baron and Femme; of Parent and Child; of Guardian and Ward; of Master and Servant; and of the Powers of Courts of Chancery* (New Haven, 1816).

[2] William Blackstone, *Commentaries on the Laws of England* [London, 1765], facsimile ed. (Chicago, 1979), 1: 430.

consent – at least for those he held to be able to consent. His efforts harmonized earlier treatises and decisions in a fashion that made the common law more coherent, but at the expense sometimes of those persons he considered "dependent" on others. With respect to children, his logic is more persuasive. In his attempt to rationalize norms across categories, however, he ended up excluding workers and women (whom he also categorized as dependent) from obtaining many of the rights – and the ability fully to consent – that he elsewhere privileged.

Historians have allowed that during the seventeenth and eighteenth centuries some change in the legal rules of domestic hierarchy occurred with respect to servants, employees, and slaves – more in America than in England itself. Masters' powers declined, it is generally thought, along with a tendency to glorify "free labor." With regard to the remainder of the head of household's powers, however, only very minor regional variations, or "deviations" arising perhaps from social factors, such as longevity, the frontier, or the shortage of women, have been admitted. Generally, the organization of households in places like Puritan New England has been treated as good evidence for unchanging patriarchal legal power.

In fact, common law rules of domestic hierarchy were far from static. Just as masters' authority over servants, slaves, and workers was debated, so were the other aspects of domestic order. Throughout the seventeenth- and eighteenth-century Anglo-American world, the norms of domestic authority changed in response to some of the same forces that shaped contemporaneous debates about political hierarchies. Reeve and Blackstone, in other words, represent not stasis but the winning side in a fierce argument over the proper boundaries of household government and of personal identity. So-called deviations often expressed hotly contested struggles over legal norms that had everything to do with political order, not simply with domestic order.

To understand these developments we must begin by focusing on the power of masters. Reeve's triptych is neat but misleading. When we separate the authority of masters from that of husbands and fathers we can begin to measure – and to imagine – the extent of the change in the law of household government.

The fundamental change that occurred during the seventeenth and eighteenth century was that the legal powers of masters (or as the legal guides of the seventeenth century called them, Lords) were extended to men as fathers and as husbands. While this was happening, the powers of masters were changing – ameliorating in some ways, consolidating (depending in part on whom the master had power over: slave, servant, or employee) in others. Despite the revolutionary challenge to hierarchies in the broader political order, standard invocation and interpretations of the common law tended to substantiate and increase many aspects of domestic hierarchy, including even that of employers over employees. Overall, the common law developed simple parallel categories that tended to increase the power of the patriarch. New hierarchies came into being alongside older ones.

Largely outside the common law, meanwhile, revolutionary reforms and principles undermined older assumptions about status by idealizing consent and equality. Ideally, relations between adult men would be based on contracts, freely entered. Contract challenged the principle that one was born into a status that the law would confirm. Instead, adult men would gain some influence over their status at work and more control over their wives and children. Men as fathers, that is, gained grounds to challenge men as masters, such that poor children, for example, might not be as easily removed from their fathers and forcibly apprenticed.

The heritage of the Revolution and the legislative reforms that followed in its wake proved to be more ambiguous for women and children. Their opportunities to choose their status were sharply limited: women could choose mostly at marriage, and children not at all. Also, for some adult men – and certainly for their wives and children – these norms did not apply at all. They were slaves, not "free laborers." They did not possess legally recognized marital rights or custodial powers over their children. Their master owned both. Slavery became the major continuation of older common law norms about the rights of Lords.

Once this history is unpacked, it is apparent that the domestic law of the early nineteenth century was more complex than Reeve's simple presentation suggests. Many of his categories highlighted the principle of consent. In the same breath they raised a fundamental question: whose choice? Blackstone's common law allowed choice for some, but not others.

A final preliminary. Both inside and outside the common law, we shall see, many of the principal reformers who rose to challenge the rights of Lords in the seventeenth century (who argued for the rights of men) were from Puritan or dissenting backgrounds. In both America and in England, the political and legal debates of the seventeenth century had religious dimensions. Puritans and dissenters voiced the most profound challenge to the rights of Lords and argued for the rights of husbands and parents. Migration and civil war created opportunities to put new practices in place, first in Puritan New England and then in England during the Interregnum. Many of the most important common law legal reformers, men like Sir Matthew Hale, came from dissenting backgrounds. Their arguments combined with the larger debate in democratic/republican political theory that challenged the rights of birth, of Lords, and especially of the divine right of kings. Religion, politics, and law were in many ways conjoined.

I. THE OLD COMMON LAW

In the sixteenth and seventeenth centuries, throughout Anglo-America, the family was the basic unit of society. Perhaps that has always been true. Yet, relations of power within families – and the question of who is to be considered a member of which family – have differed dramatically across time and culture. In England and in its North American colonies, the family unit was composed of a master, his servants and slaves, his wife and his children, and sometimes his children's or his servants' (and normally his slaves') families. In the earliest period, the household master's powers were defined most clearly in application to non-kin – servants. The household mistress (the master's wife) had similar powers. Thus, authority accorded primarily to rank. The powers of husbands and of fathers were much less well defined: the child of a servant usually did not belong to the servant, but, at least in a legal sense, to the master.

These basic statements reflect a profoundly hierarchical society. Within Anglo-America in the seventeenth century, however, a great debate raged over the powers of masters *qua* fathers and husbands and – more broadly – parents who questioned this hierarchy. The debate took place within a society torn apart by religious conflict. In areas where religious radicals gained control, notably early New England and later colonies like Quaker Pennsylvania, they adopted contrarian norms.

In taking seriously the mainstream rules that prevented servants and slaves from forming legal families of their own, we begin to grasp the broad picture of Anglo-American colonial life, particularly as it developed in the South, outside the dissenter colonies. To grasp it fully, we must also recognize how different the powers of fathers and husbands were from those of masters. The rights of wives, of children, and of servants were also distinct. Each step away from Reeve's normalized post-eighteenth century perspective can transform our view of authority, of liberty, and of the family, especially if we then pause to survey the panorama before us.

The Status of Servants in Anglo-America

Sixteenth- and seventeenth-century England had a well-developed principle and practice of legal servitude. Statutes made labor obligatory for many landless people. Inheritance laws that governed the transfer even of rented land privileged the oldest son and deprived others of the ability to own land themselves. Whereas small holders and tenants had held real claims on land, even if their property claim was part of a multilayered ownership, efforts to "enclose" land vacated their ancient common law use rights in favor of the "greater" claims of lords. These larger property rules and practices are critical because most people made their living from the land. Lack of access to land meant that many people had no choice but to work for others as farm laborers or domestics. If they refused to work, they could be forced under vagrancy statutes into contracts of a year, or of many years, depending on their age.

At the dawn of its seventeenth-century colonization of the New World, England suffered from significant poverty. By some estimates, half the population was poor. Primogeniture, enclosure, and the dissolution of the older Catholic system of caring for the poor with the Reformation added up to a near crisis. Contemporary tracts and court records dwell on the problem of vagrants. The laws were harsh. There was no minimum age for forced service: by Elizabethan statute, a child of any age could be imprisoned until he or she signed a contract agreeing to labor until the age of 24 for a boy or 21 for a girl. The only questions were the poverty of the family or individual and whether anyone actually wanted their labor. The laws did not always work to the advantage of landowners: stories were told of masters forced to accept unwanted laborers. Perhaps so. Yet it is clear that the laws that denied ownership of landed property to one group and simultaneously made them the partial property of others are central to understanding the legal principles undergirding authority and domestic order in England and its colonies.

By these principles, hierarchy regularly trumped kin-family relations. Masters and mistresses often had authority over others, including others' children and others' wives and husbands. The elements of domestic hierarchy that we tend to assume went hand in hand – the powers of masters and those of husbands and fathers – were thus often in direct conflict. This was not true of all families of course. England had many tenants and smallholders who were not directly "in" the household of others and had their own separate families. Servants who "lived in" with their masters and mistresses were of course much more dependent than tenants. However, landlords often had claims over smallholders that made these men and women dependent on them in various ways. To acknowledge this dependency, which was often legally explicit and had important cultural and political consequences (such that those who were dependent on others were not allowed to vote), is to begin to understand that domestic order had a broad, multilayered legality.

Principles of dependency were eminently transportable. Consider the fate of some of the first immigrants to Virginia. Faced with a shortage of voluntary immigrants and not much money, the Virginia Company persuaded a number of London churches to participate in a benevolent enterprise. The Company argued that children who had been apprehended for the crime of "vagrancy" (not having employment) should not be apprenticed locally.

Instead the churches should pay for them to go to the New World and work there. In exchange, the Virginia Company promised that at the end of their service of seven or more years, the children would be given land, a reward unheard of in England. The churches agreed to underwrite the costs of passage. Unfortunately, the laws of England in 1618 required that the children themselves sign the labor contracts, and many refused to do so. To circumvent this restriction, the Privy Council granted a special exemption, forcing the children to go to Virginia and serve masters. Neither the laws nor the Privy Council required the consent of their parents. Of course, on some level this was really charity by the London churches; the parishioners thought they were offering the children a chance at a better life, including not only land but also training in "husbandry" (farming). Children needed such training to make a way for themselves. The very premises of the policy, however, revealed a society in which the labor of some for others in a property relation was normal, rank was central, and the integrity of poorer families unimportant.

The story also incorporates the promise of free land – symbolic of New World opportunity. One of American history's most durable myths is that land was free and abundant throughout the colonial period, undermining like nothing else the status relationships of the mother country. Though land was free at times, access was often controlled. Virginia's initial promise of land to freed servants, for example, changed after 1618. Masters thereafter received a "headright" – free land for each servant imported – a very different bargain that offered much less opportunity to the servant. While other colonies, like Maryland, continued to allow freed servants to claim land, the claims still had to be surveyed and granted through the secretary's office, a costly process. Former indentured servants were more likely to end up long-term tenants than landowners. This was especially so in the Southern colonies, where migrants were largely servants.

Long-term tenancy was of course an improvement on servitude. For whites who survived their servitude, the colonies offered better opportunities than England. Yet, servitude remained widespread. Indeed, once we include slaves – blacks and captured Indians – in the calculation, the percentage of the population in servitude was much higher in the colonies, particularly in the South, than in England. Correspondingly, the laws circumscribing servitude of all sorts became increasingly complex and rigid over the course of the colonial period. Every English colony routinely sanctioned slavery and indentured servitude as well as local apprenticeships. The laws tended to be more elaborate in the Southern colonies, with more complex slave codes and more enforcement, but the legal structures of servitude – including the legal sale of people (both white and black) and the legal capture of runaways (both white and black) – were similar throughout

British North America. White servants could complain of mistreatment to authorities (unlike slaves), but masters could punish both servants and slaves corporally – indeed could even kill them without penalty if death occurred during the course of punishment.

While the authority of the head of household was strongest over his servants, a great deal depended on the type of servant or employee and the status of that person. In the colonies, many white laborers (if born there or once freed from their initial indenture) could negotiate contracts that gave fewer privileges to their employers and did not place them firmly under a master's control. In England, in contrast, by the early eighteenth century, new restrictions were emerging that brought more forms of employment within the rubric of master/servant relationships, including many proto-industrial occupations, such as piecework and weaving. Even employees who did not live with their employers began to be seen – both at statute and common law – as governed by master/servant relations, with masters being given much greater privileges over their workers.

How was the role of head of household acquired? Status (derived from land ownership, militia or other title, financial resources, or age) played an important part. A wealth of records and studies indicate that whether an individual became a servant – or a master – depended greatly on status. Service was partly a life-cycle phenomenon, in that many servants were adolescents or adults younger than 25, saving to marry. But not all youth underwent a period of service. Indeed, many masters were youthful themselves. Although service, then, has been properly recognized as a part of the life cycle of poorer and middling people in England, it was not a "natural" institution. Rather, service was an institution designed to benefit elites.

Though widespread, most people did not enter into service for others, even as children. Some entered high-status apprenticeships controlled by guild companies or became mercantile clerks – but access to those positions was restricted. Elite families, and landowners generally, did not place their children in service to others. In seventeenth-century England, domestic servants were perhaps 20 percent of the total population. Many of these were adolescent life-cycle servants, but by no means all: in some districts 25 was the average age of domestic servants. Even when adolescents entered adulthood and finished "official" domestic service, the wage labor they entered could be poorly paid, condemning the laborer to life on the margins, unable to support a family. Especially before 1660, harsh vagrancy laws forced people into labor, or even transportation, simply because of poverty. Circumstances changed somewhat after 1660, when the poor law system began to emphasize returning people to their place of settlement, but punishment for vagrancy remained an issue.

In the British mainland colonies, the proportion of those in servitude grew even higher. Some 44 percent of the white population of 1620s Virginia were servants. However by 1700 the proportion had fallen to perhaps 10 percent (about 4 percent indentured servants from England and perhaps 6–10 percent native-born apprentices, mostly to farm labor). If slaves are included, of course, by the middle of the eighteenth century in Southern colonies like Virginia and South Carolina, more than half the total population, white and black, were domestic servants or slaves. In mid-Atlantic colonies, such as Pennsylvania and New York, and in New England, the proportion of servants and slaves in the total population was always lower – lower migration rates of indentured servants, lower binding rates for apprentices, and lower numbers of imported slaves. To be white in England's colonies was to enjoy opportunities for advancement: cheap land in some periods and places and better wage labor possibilities.

Given the ubiquity of status considerations, it is hardly surprising that the Elizabethan Statute of Artificers, which governed relations between masters and servants, operated on the basis of status. Potential masters (who met a specified property qualification) could request that any child under 21, of poor and landless parentage, be bound to them as an "apprentice" until the child reached age 24 (for boys) or 21 (for girls) If the child inherited property, the apprenticeship would be void. If a justice of the peace agreed, the child could be imprisoned until he or she agreed to the contract. These strict rules moderated over the next half-century; justices were allowed to approve the indenture themselves (without imprisoning the child). Nevertheless, forced labor remained a part of the labor code in early modern England. Poor fathers and mothers had no right to their children's labor. Statutes instead emphasized the inability of parents to care "properly" for their children. Property-less unemployed adults could also be forced to enter labor contracts at set rates. Those with minimal resources could, of course, enter contracts at their own discretion. Those of higher status never had to work at all. In the seventeenth century youth per se was no bar to power. Teenage sons of peers were routinely elected to Parliament.

During the seventeenth century the status-driven laws allowing land-owning persons to obtain servants from impoverished families by imprisoning their children became slightly less severe. Proceedings had to be initiated by a justice of the peace and the unfitness of the parent shown and recorded. A matter of status had become one that gave slightly more attention to the rights of parents. Simultaneously, vagrancy statutes became less harsh and enforced less severely, especially for adult men.

If status thus shaped the composition of the labor force of the Old World, it should come as no surprise that status also helped shape that of the New. Both indentured servitude and slavery feature prominently. Perhaps half of the white immigrants to British North America (roughly 250,000 people) arrived as indentured servants. Still, only a minority of the white population (aside from the very early years) was actually indentured or apprenticed at any given time because white servitude was a temporary condition. For African Americans, in contrast, slavery was perpetual and hereditary. Although not many more slaves arrived than servants (300,000), the permanence and heritability of slavery meant a large proportion of the population was permanently in bondage.

Some white servants traveled willingly, signing contracts with "spirits" who lured them into seeing the New World as a land of opportunity. Others did not. Kidnapping was widespread, especially in the seventeenth century. In some ports officials clearly colluded with shippers. English laws against kidnapping gained some teeth by the early eighteenth century, though the practice continued on a reduced scale through at least mid-century. Thousands, perhaps tens of thousands, traveled without contracts, for which colony laws designated terms of service that varied depending on the servant's adjudged age. Most English authorities looked on the practice relatively benevolently, seeing it as a means of managing the lower sort and of keeping the vagrant population under control. Even for those who willingly signed labor contracts, their situation on arrival in the New World was arguably worse than in the Old. Their contracts generally specified longer periods of service, with strict punishments for absconding. Though the servant was free to complain about mistreatment before a justice of the peace, the terms of the indenture gave masters relatively more power. Perhaps the most important difference from the Old World was that their contracts were transferable. In England, servant contracts were individually between master and servant and not assignable. The very nature of the "indenture," however, often between a shipmaster and the new servant, meant that it had to be assignable to the future master. This innovation made servants ever more clearly property – movable property – than had the older, more personal rules. Apart from this critical difference, master/servant relations generally followed the laws on the books for England.

Husband and Wife in Anglo-America

The laws of master and servant were both well developed and tailored to the status of the worker. Neither is true for those relating to husband and wife. In practice, this meant that the husband's powers under the common law were not nearly as strong in 1600 as they would be two centuries later.

When legal historians touch on the history of women in early modern England they often find that the common law rules they anticipate are missing. Take, for example, Edward Britton's *The Community of the Vill*, a study of fourteenth-century Huntingdonshire:

> Whether one looks at landholding, business affairs, or the home, it is evident that the wives of Broughton were by no means wards of their husbands. The precepts of *Baron et Feme* are fascinating, and may be used by all who wish to depict all that is medieval and retrograde, but such legal theories held little sway in this village in darkest Huntingdonshire. There women were a strong social force, and the independence of married women was clearly recognized by the customary law.

Numbers of studies of women's legal status in early modern Britain have concluded in effect that the common law guidelines were purposefully ignored. Scholars refer to the "wide gap" between the theory of femme covert and practice. While confined (and indeed repressed) by some laws, in many other cases women apparently used the law for their own purposes and protections.[3]

Recent studies of seventeenth-century Virginia have drawn similar conclusions. Only some of the common law rules about femme covert applied there. Women went in and out of courts, even while married. The most consistent seventeenth-century application of femme covert dealt with the sale of property by married women without their husbands' permission. This was widely viewed as a voidable transaction (indeed women themselves sometimes invoked the rules of femme covert to avoid such deeds). Restraint on land sales provided husbands a means of control that could turn particularly harsh when a woman's husband had actually abandoned her. In two early eighteenth-century cases, the Virginia House of Burgesses attempted to ameliorate just such a situation (vetoed by the king on the advice of his Privy Council). Femme covert rules also restrained married women's capacity to make wills.

These situations apart, women in the colonies in the seventeenth and early eighteenth centuries enjoyed relative freedom from rules limiting their legal capacity, at least compared to the nineteenth century. Married women appeared in courts. They were sometimes active business partners who participated fully in building the kin networks that provided the basis for transatlantic commerce. Nor were married women completely at the mercy of their husbands. As in England, a woman who was physically mistreated by her husband could obtain an action of the peace against him (requiring that he post bond for his good behavior toward her) or seek a

[3] Edward Britton, *The Community of the Vill: A Study in the History of the Family and Village Life in Fourteenth-Century England* (Toronto: Macmillan, 1977), 33–5; Susan Staves, *Married Women's Separate Property in England, 1660–1833* (Cambridge, MA, 1990), 206; Tim Stretton, *Women Waging Law in Elizabethan England* (Cambridge, 1998), 33–8.

"bed and board" separation (not the equivalent of divorce) that required him to provide her with alimony payments. Still, we must also be conscious of limits. The fact that in separations the husband had to provide alimony – and that he often remained in charge of the land that both had brought to the marriage – is strong evidence of assumptions and power relations underlying marriage during this period. Neither the bond he posted to keep the peace (for which the wife's estate was also potentially forfeit) nor a separation that offered only maintenance could provide complete protection for a wife.

Women's own goods belonged to them in marriage, and afterward they had legal disposition of them. Men's wills did not include their wives' personal possessions. Consider the example of Magdalen Trabue Chastain, who lived in Virginia in the early eighteenth century. She owned several pieces of jewelry that were not listed in the wills or inventories of either of her two husbands, indicating she disposed of them herself.[4] Sometimes the presence of the wife's goods was evident in joint suits, where husband and wife were both listed in the attempt to recover a debt owed to only the wife before marriage. Wives were also often administrators of their husbands' estates, with legal responsibility for paying the debts and managing the whole process. Their legal activities, in short, were extensive.

One factor that historians have explored in explaining women's legal position in the colonies is the prevalence of unbalanced sex ratios. In Virginia, men greatly outnumbered women in the early years, putting a premium on marriage. An excess of men grants women a better negotiating situation in relation to prospective husbands, and hence opportunities for greater autonomy. High death rates meant that women were often widowed, sometimes even before bearing children, which increased their chances of accumulating their own property through inheritance of entire estates, adding to their attractiveness (and chances for autonomy) to potential husbands. Historians have also pointed to the legal exigencies of the frontier to explain women's relative autonomy – to colonial judges who found common law rules unreasonable given the circumstances of settlement.

Though such factors may have had an impact on women's relative legal opportunities in the colonial period, however, they were not decisive. A shortage of women could as readily worsen their collective situation as improve it. Those who seek a rare resource often try to control it once found. Fewer women could mean individual oppression and isolation, not collective strength. But the larger problem with interpretations that dwell

[4] Joan R. Gunderson and Gwen Victor Gampel, "Married Women's Legal Status in Eighteenth-Century New York and Virginia," *Willam and Mary Quarterly*, 3rd ser., 39 (1982), 127.

on unique colonial environments is that in England, where the common law originated, where the sex ratios were balanced, and where no special circumstances obtained, women should have been worse off. They were not: instead, the English also deviated from eighteenth-century common law norms. There too, women in the sixteenth and seventeenth centuries had more freedoms and legal responsibilities than the common law supposedly allowed. Such broad similarities in practice across such different regions suggest that we have yet to understand the nature of the common law before Blackstone.

We return to this below. For the moment, we can note that the decisive issue for contemporary law books lay less in the realm of behavior than of property: how much control were wives to exercise over land, even their own dower lands, without their husband's permission?

We have talked of broad similarities across different regions. However, Puritan New England was unlike either Virginia or England, in that it gave relatively more authority to husbands over wives. Separate estates for women were less likely to be found there in the eighteenth century than elsewhere, as work by Marylynn Salmon illustrates. There too, however, the seventeenth century at least was a period of greater legal equality, as shown by such scholars as Cornelia Dayton. Divorce, for example, was acceptable in New England, particularly in Connecticut. Expectations of wifely obedience prevailed, but husbands' authority was limited to a greater extent than it would be in the nineteenth century. Unlike servants, wives were protected from battery by their husbands (except in cases of self-defense), or at least women were allowed to complain about it. Above all, there as elsewhere married women can be found in court records engaging in many kinds of legal action. Take Elizabeth Creford as an example; she frequently signed promissory notes on her family's behalf.[5]

Yet, we cannot say that in the seventeenth century married women had equal power in marriage or that women had approximately the same rights as men in general. Too many gendered disparities are observable. For example, both women and men were found guilty of sexual offenses during the seventeenth century and punished relatively equally, but in Massachusetts adultery, which was punishable by death, applied exclusively in cases of sexual relations involving a married woman. A married man who had sex with an unmarried woman committed only "fornication," a much less serious crime punishable by fine or whipping. In one famous case, a married woman and her two lovers were all executed. Women were also more much more likely than men to be accused of witchcraft in New

[5] Laurel Thatcher Ulrich, *Good Wives: Image and Reality in the Lives of Women in Northern New England, 1650–1750* (Oxford, 1980), 41.

England (by a ratio of 4 to 1), especially if they owned land in their own right.

Inequalities in marriage are particularly clear in matters of estates. Women were more likely than men to bring money and goods to their marriages, but sons were more likely than daughters to inherit land and hence a livelihood – especially in New England. Only if women had no brothers – characteristic of roughly one-quarter of families –were they likely to inherit land. About 20 percent of marriages produced no children, in which case widows often inherited the whole estate. Otherwise, widows might receive only their dower thirds (the minimum portion decreed their due) during their lives and have to share the remainder of the estate with children or other heirs. The law generally allowed women only life estates (owned during the widow's life and reabsorbed into the original estate on her death); husbands were always reluctant to allow wives unencumbered inheritance for doing so risked the estate. If widows remarried without restrictions on control of their inheritance, new husbands were likely to press their new wives to allow land sales, so that they could gradually take control of the original family estate and defraud the first marriage's children. This is one reason why so many forms of encumbrance – life estates and entails – were popular during this period. Dower thirds themselves were often life estates to prevent successor husbands from obtaining control. Wives and heirs of the original husband could sue for "waste" of the land (felling too many trees, failing to maintain a mill, or damage).

Fathers could also create encumbered estates for their daughters and their daughters' children to prevent husbands from taking control of the property. Entails are often understood to exclude female succession. This was not so. Entails often originated with daughters, so that the father could prevent a husband from controlling the land (or selling it), preserving it intact for his daughter and her progeny (a common pattern in Virginia). Entails allowed testators to designate who would get land "forever" by the rules of primogeniture, a policy that normally favored the eldest son. If there were no son, however, daughters inherited – either jointly or in severalty. Entails thus favored the male line, but over time they limited the power of the husband-patriarch and often allowed elite and middling women control over large estates. Fathers (or first husbands) might also prevent future husbands from controlling wives' estates through the creation of a jointure, common in England in the early modern period. A jointure set aside a separate estate for the wife's exclusive use, guaranteeing her income (usually rents) and a dower right on her husband's death. A jointure was a form of trust; there were many others, some overseen by common law courts and others by Chancery (or Equity) courts. Both tribunals can be found in the English colonies.

From the evidence presented, we can conclude that women in early modern Anglo-America enjoyed relatively greater authority within marriage than they would in the nineteenth century, but were still at a significant legal disadvantage. Women could not usually vote, although sometimes they could inherit that right and designate a male to vote for them (depending on borough norms). They could not hold seats in Parliament. Women were not appointed judges, generally they did not sit on juries (except in the limited role of examining women's bodies in cases of witchcraft or rape), and they could not hold most political offices. Culturally, the husband was expected to be the "Lord" of the family.

But the husband's authority over his servants was much clearer in law and in practice than his authority over his wife. Indeed, though a truism it is important to point out that wives also had authority over servants, male as well as female. As this suggests, both within and outside the household, legal disadvantage was modulated sharply by status. The impact of hierarchy in society is obvious from any analysis of women's legal identity during this period. In some districts in England, for example, women controlled which candidates stood for election to the House of Commons. Women, particularly as widows, clearly played political roles in England's colonies. Women could not only have political influence as the wives of governors – as did the wife of Virginia Governor Berkeley in the 1670s – but could also play influential political roles at court. And of course, as Queen, a woman could reign over all.

Parents and Children in Anglo-America

Parents' custodial authority was weak in early-modern Anglo-America, far weaker than it would be by the late eighteenth century. Only after 1660, as we have already seen, does one encounter something approaching legal recognition of parental, which is to say paternal, custody rights. Parents possessed disciplinary authority: they were allowed to punish their children "without breach of the peace" throughout this period. In many ways, however, childhood itself was not a defined category. Once again, status proved all important.

As we have seen from the earlier discussion of servants, status – whether in the Old World or New – was largely determined by the family into which one was born. Young children in wealthy families had authority over adult servants. In "middling sort" families, children lived with their families and performed much of the household and farm labor. In poor families, children were likely to be removed and placed in service in a wealthier family – to learn a trade if one was lucky; otherwise simply as a servant, to learn "husbandry" or "housewifery." Service was comparatively more common for poor whites in the Southern colonies. More common, too, in the South were wealthy households whose children learned early the skills and habits of command. Thomas Jefferson acknowledged the phenomenon in order to criticize it, late in the eighteenth century.

Though custodial rights were weak, fathers might exert indirect control over their children through inheritance. In the colonies testamentary power was mediated by the availability of western lands, which meant that children were less dependent on inheritance for their livelihood than in England. Nevertheless inheritance was a source of real power, especially in New England where fathers lived to an advanced age. In Virginia, fathers had less testamentary power. In the seventeenth century, fathers often died young, and by the eighteenth century estates were often entailed, allowing fathers less choice in the disposition of their estates and hence less control. Inheritance practices in the middle colonies varied, but tended to be more similar to those in New England. There too, longer life spans meant fewer encumbrances on estates.

As a concept, custody in its modern sense of parental authority and responsibility simply did not exist, partly because the idea was not needed in a world where children could enter their own binding contracts and possessed a legal identity no different from that of adults. Children were rarely distinguished as such in legal records. They could be punished for many different crimes – especially once older than age 8 – and could form many kinds of contracts. Thus, pre-pubescent children could and did enter into marriage contracts, usually to cement family alliances or alleviate property concerns. (Children marrying younger than 12 or 14 could sue for divorce if the marriage had not been consummated.)

The category of a ward needing a guardian was an exception, for it specifically recognized minority; however, it was applied only to heirs of land and the guardian's responsibilities were limited in scope. At age fourteen a ward was empowered to choose his or her own guardian. Some guardianships ended at that point, some at age seventeen or eighteen. Some heirs and heiresses could evade guardianship if, for example, their father had made them executor of the estate. All that would happen is that the estate would remain in a holding pattern until the minor executor reached age seventeen. Advisors (usually also designated in the will) had little authority to dispose of or manage the estate without consulting the heir.

Childhood per se entailed few legal restrictions. Teenagers could be elected to Parliament in England or to the House of Burgesses in Virginia during the seventeenth century. Legally a male could hold most appointed offices at age eleven. Army and navy officers – a patronage appointment – were frequently in their early teens. In England and Virginia one qualified to sit on a jury at age fourteen (higher in New England). At least in the early seventeenth century, one could testify at any age. In this part of the legal landscape, as elsewhere, status trumped everything else. All criminal records, for example, stated the status of the accused: virtually none stated the age. Those who held positions of political and legal authority while still teenagers – John Randolph, for example, who was appointed king's attorney for several Virginia counties at age eighteen – came from the most powerful families. Those bound into apprenticeships by the churchwardens though both parents might be alive came from the least powerful, the families of the poor.[6]

As consent became more important to the law over the course of the early modern period (growing out of broad religious and political debates), childhood would emerge as a much clearer category of law and experience. Children lost their independent legal and political identity, and parents gained the power to make decisions for them. These changes challenged old elite practices that allocated authority by birth status irrespective of age. They also reflected changing norms about the meaning of consent that grew out of broad economic and political changes.

The best way to understand changes in practice is to examine the evolution of the common law itself as recorded in legal treatises. English common law changed dramatically in many ways over the seventeenth and eighteenth centuries, particularly as it concerned the rights of persons. In the late sixteenth century, it was concerned primarily with the rights of Lords. What the early nineteenth century would consider domestic hierarchies were important mostly as they concerned masters and servants. Treatises touched lightly on husbands and wives and hardly at all on the rights of parents over children.

The focus of early modern common law – laid out in excruciating detail – was on the privileges of landowners and the constraints on those who did not own land. In practice England had moved away from strict feudalism, but the law on the books bore its deep imprint. The first volume of Sir Edward Coke's *Institutes of the Laws of England*, undoubtedly the most important attempt at a comprehensive survey of English law in the early seventeenth century, was a commentary on Sir Thomas Littleton's classic fifteenth-century text on the law of landed property and the obligations and authority of Lords and villeins. Coke's commentary had short sections on femme covert and the relationship of guardian and ward, but property was the core of the feudal law. What kinds of restraints governed the selling and inheritance of property? Who inherited under primogeniture? When could land be willed and what land was encumbered? What powers did landlords have over tenants, or Lords over villeins? When could guardians act for

[6] Holly Brewer, *By Birth or Consent: Children, Law and the Anglo-American Revolution in Authority* (Chapel Hill, 2005), 28.

wards, and over what? When could husbands sell their wives' property and on what conditions? The volume is thick with answers to questions like these. Its sections explain what it meant to hold land in different ways and the varied implications of each landholding method for the use and ownership of land. They even reveal that ownership of land often implied a limited ownership of people – those who farmed it, leased it, and dwelt on it.

Coke wrote three additional treatises to complete his *Institutes*, inspiring Blackstone's similar four-volume synthesis 150 years later. The commentary on Littleton (volume I) anticipates elements of what would come, particularly volume II, which concerns the statutory law of England. The third volume concerns crimes, particularly high crimes such as treason. The fourth deals with the jurisdiction of England's many different courts, not only those of the common law but also of some fifteen other court systems that produced precedents (with often overlapping appeals) in the early seventeenth century, notably the canon law and equity (Chancery) courts. A survey of their substance is revealing. Coke was a reformer – he had Puritan sympathies and struggled with James I over the rights of Parliament – but his *Institutes* contain little about subjects we might now think of as central to the common law, such as the rights of persons. Reading the *Institutes* introduces the reader to a very different world.

Coke's predominant concern in the *Institutes* is the reciprocal duties and obligations of Lords with regard to their villeins, servants, and tenants. His brief exposition on coverture focuses on the way that property can be held and conveyed (or not) once men and women marry. Men can convey their own property (if not entailed or encumbered) without their wives' consent, he tells us, but wives need their husbands' consent and must be separately examined by judges about their wishes. If land is not freehold, it cannot be conveyed at all. Husband and wife are considered as one in the eyes of the law only in the narrow sense that if an estate is left to husband and wife and to another person, husband and wife should receive only a half between them. After the husband's death, the wife has the right to the use during her life of a third of the property belonging to the husband before marriage (her "dower"). After the wife's death, the husband has the right to the use of all his wife's property during his life, but only if she actually bore a living child during the marriage (called his "curtesy").[7]

[7] Sir Edward Coke, *Institutes of the Laws of England* (London, 1809), Sect 36 "Dower":

> Ten[an]t in Dower is where a Man is seised of certain Lands or Tenements in Fee-simple, Fee-tail general, or as Heir in special Tail, and taketh a Wife, and dieth, the Wife after the Decease of her Husband shall be endowed of the third Part of such Lands and Tenements as were her Husband's at any Time during the Coverture, To have and to hold to the same Wife in severalty, by metes and bounds of Term of her Life, whether she hath Issue by her Husband or no, and of what Age soever the Wife be, so as she be past the Age of nine Years a the Time of the Death of her Husband.

The *Institutes* contain almost no discussion of the powers of parents. In contrast, discussions of the powers of guardians fill many pages. But guardianship is mostly a matter of property management – most orphans did not have guardians. In other words, children per se were not thought to be dependent and incapable; it was the inheritance of land that created the requirement for a guardian. Even then, most guardianships were sharply limited and ended at age 14.

Other early seventeenth-century law books present a similar picture of the law while filling a few gaps. Like Coke's *Institutes*, Dalton's *Countrey Justice* – a guide for local justices of the peace, men usually without legal training – was extremely popular not only in England during the seventeenth century but also in the North American colonies. It contained large sections on the statute of artificers (sometimes called the poor law by historians), indicating, for example, how a landowner might force another to labor for him and what remedies protected him from the laborer's early departure from the covenant. It also underlined the centrality of status to criminal penalties: a servant who killed a master could be drawn and quartered for the crime of petty treason, whereas a master killing a servant in the course of punishment would usually be excused altogether. A master who beat a servant was within his rights; a servant who beat his master could be imprisoned for a year.

Dalton's attention to criminal issues is not surprising, given that the jurisdiction of a justice of the peace would routinely encompass petty crime. But a modern eye quickly notices his relative neglect of questions relating to wives or children. The silence suggests he had no broad vision of "domestic" law. Other important guides give the same impression. Systematic study of them is even more revealing. By pursuing three of the key issues that appear in parallel in later guides, we realize just how different the law was at this juncture. First, many guides compared the powers of a master to those of a husband in matters of petty treason, in which a servant or wife who killed a master or husband was considered comparable to a subject who killed a king and punished as though guilty of high treason (drawn and quartered before execution or burned alive). However, a son who killed his father was not deemed guilty of petty treason and would not be liable for such extreme punishment. Second, the guides contain no discussion of witnesses, and

[Dower only applies when the lands in question belonged to the husband beforehand. Note also, that there are some cases when the man owns entailed land, where the wife cannot claim dower.]

Sect. 35 "Curtisia Dengleterre"; "Tenant by the Curtesy of England is where a man taketh a wife seised in Fee-simple, or in Fee-tail general, or seised as Heir in Tail especial, and hath Issue by the same wife, Male or Female born alive, albeit the Issue after dieth or liveth, yet if the Wife dies, the Husband shall hold the Land during his Life by the Law of England."

one encounters no sense that age is relevant to testimony: children could testify at any age. Wives and husbands could testify against each other or in open court generally. Last, and probably most revealing, are the entries on allowable battery. According to William Lambarde's *Eirenarcha: Or of the Office of the Justices of Peace*, battery "is not in all cases a violation and breach of the peace: for some are allowed to have privately a natural and some a civile power (or authority) over others: So that they may (in reasonable manner onely) correct and chastise them for their offences." A parent might beat a child "within age," the master a servant, the schoolmaster a scholar, the a jailer a prisoner, the lord a villein. But the husband might not beat his wife – that allowance is conspicuously absent.[8] Although another early text does allow a man to punish his wife, servant, or child "reasonably" without a breach of the peace, it also excludes children from the crime of petty treason against their parents and has no section on witnesses.[9] Generally, guides of this period prohibited husbands from physically beating wives. When they did so, they used the word "chastise," which had the primary meaning of verbal reprimand. Even this concession is debatable (writers would hedge, noting "some authors hold that," and would always append the word "moderately"). Physical beating could provide wives with the basis for separation suits in the ecclesiastical courts, which could also force husbands to provide their wives with alimony or "separate maintenance."[10]

Despite these limited protections, assault generally (of any kind) was not a serious crime and usually had to be privately prosecuted, a course open to those with money, such as masters, but not to servants and the poor. What this means is that while the common law discouraged husbands from beating their wives it did so only in a half-hearted manner. Wives found it difficult to prosecute and especially to convict husbands: rarely in this period did assaults lead to convictions, unless of an inferior assaulting a superior. Likewise, within marriage, the crime of rape did not exist, and rape itself was rarely prosecuted even outside marriage. These attitudes toward assault are important to a broader understanding of the character of the law at this juncture.

We can now see that the common law did not have a fully developed conception of domestic power except with respect to servants and that the tripartite array of master/husband/father was not in place, at least when it came to criminal matters. In civil matters, Coke has shown us that femme

[8] Lambarde, (London, 1599), 130–1.

[9] [Fitzherbert], *L'Office et Auctoritie de Justices de Peace* (London, 1583), 89a, 13a.

[10] Henry Ansgar Kelly, "Rule of Thumb and the Folklaw of the Husband's Stick," *Journal of Legal Education* 44 (1994), 341–65. On the meanings of chastize, see the OED (the third meaning is corporal punishment).

covert had limited application, relating almost solely to the selling of freehold property that had no other restraints on it, to a married woman's ability to make a will over such property, and, to a much lesser degree, to her husband's liability for her debts. Of particular importance, in this period most land was not unencumbered freehold. Any land that was entailed or had other legal restrictions on heritability was not within the husband's control. This basic point is very strange to modern readers, where almost all land is freehold. Once we acknowledge the encumbered nature of most land (in England especially, and increasingly in the colonies as well) we can recognize the limitations of even this core principle of femme covert.

The concept that husband and wife were one in the eyes of the law, so important to Blackstone, is conceived very narrowly in Coke's writings 150 years earlier. It is not treated at all in most other legal writings of the seventeenth century. One exception, an obscure text misleadingly entitled *The Lawes Resolutions of Womens Rights* (1632), does appear to show that Blackstone's broad concept of *femme covert* indeed had some currency in the early seventeenth century. But the treatise is not very reliable as a report on current law. The legal texts of this period name their sources in almost every paragraph, usually in statutes or other treatises on the common law or other laws. In contrast, this treatise has few citations to contemporary laws and none in the sections most relevant to the matter at hand. It is not cited by later treatises, nor does it appear in colonial lawyers' libraries. Also significant, the author's name appears only as the initials T.E. at a time when authors of most legal texts gave their full names, and the treatise itself appears in only one edition. By comparison, *Coke upon Littleton*, the first volume of Coke's *Institutes*, had appeared in eleven editions by 1719; Dalton's *Countrey Justice* was reprinted in comparable numbers.[11]

It is important, nevertheless, that we take this volume seriously, not because it was an accurate rendition of current law but because it is an early argument against women's rights. As such it provides useful information about the sources of the changes that would occur in women's legal status and indeed suggests something about why New England in particular had more limits on women's roles and property ownership than the southern mainland colonies. For T.E.'s arguments are fundamentally religious. Under the title "The Punishment of Adam's Sinne" he invites his readers to "returne a little to Genesis." Eve seduced her husband. Hence "In sorrow shalt thou bring forth thy children, thy desires shall bee subject to thy husband, and he shall rule over thee. See here the reason . . . that Women have no voyse

[11] Herbert A. Johnson, *Imported Eighteenth-Century Law Treatises in American Libraries* (Knoxville, 1978). Despite Johnson's title, his review of legal inventories examines seventeenth-century (and earlier) treatises as well.

in Parliament, They make no Lawes, they consent to none. they abrogate none. All of them are understood either married or to bee married and their desires are subject to their husband . . . The common law here shaketh hand with Divinitie." Elsewhere T.E. proclaims that in marriage "Now Man and Woman are one," again citing only biblical authority, and he offers as example the sale of land to man and wife together, as one (like Coke). Most of the book, in fact, is best understood as a response to Coke. Revealingly, the author uses biblical citation, not legal references, to challenge the legal rules that he finds objectionable. For example, following Littleton, Coke acknowledges that heiresses can manage their own estates at age fourteen, if unmarried. T.E. recommends against this: he states that the common law is clearly wrong and urges that heiresses should be married young so as to avoid letting them control their own property.[12]

"T.E." was probably Thomas Edgar, a member of the Inns of Court. Edgar was not a prominent seventeenth-century lawyer. Educated as a Puritan in Ipswich, he is best known for his defense in 1649 of the legality of the Commonwealth in the wake of Charles I's execution, seventeen years after the publication of *The Lawes Resolutions of Womens Rights*. Edgar would later support the Restoration of Charles II, but in 1649 his views were radical, suggestive both of his religious impulses and political principles.

The Lawes Resolutions of Womens Rights was thus a religiously inspired commentary on current law with important political implications and overtones that sought to limit married women's status and strengthen their husbands' authority. Significantly, it includes sources external to the law, notably Puritan sermons about wifely obedience and the ideal marital relationship. In elaborating on the possible legal meanings of the unity of husband and wife and in emphasizing women's legal disabilities it is quite possible that T.E. influenced later thinkers. And indeed that was the goal, for the book imported into legal writing the genre of the Puritan prescriptive manual, along the lines of (and arguably influenced by) William Gouge's popular 1622 treatise on *Domesticall Duties*. Gouge's text was not a law treatise but a religious advice manual that described how the members of the household should behave, outlining the "duties" of wives, husbands, children, parents, servants, and masters, in that order, citing only the Bible. Interestingly, in Gouge's treatise we begin to see the first outlines of the late eighteenth century's familiar triptych: "for a family consisteth of these three orders,

Husbands,	Parents,	Masters,
Wives,	Children,	Servants,"

[12] T.E., *The Lawes Resolutions of Womens Rights* [London, 1632], (facs. ed. Amsterdam, 1979), 21.

Gouge attributes his analysis of the proper order of "private families" to "the Apostle."[13]

From all this we can conclude that, beginning in the early seventeenth century, common law ideas about domestic order were profoundly influenced by Puritan ideas. We can see this most clearly in how prescriptive works by such authors as T.E. and William Gouge challenged the prevailing common law norms outlined in the work of commentators such as Sir Edward Coke.

There can be little doubt that Puritan writers sought to increase husbands' powers. Debate was raging, particularly in religious circles, over the role of the household and all its members. Part of the challenge to older hierarchies posed by radical Puritanism lay in religious arguments about a different natural order to which the family was central. In this new order men as such not only had the right to exercise consent but also to remain with their own families and enjoy rights to their own wives and children, so that a husband might rule his own household and his children might no longer be taken away as servants to others. It is highly significant that in early New England the first paragraph on the first page of the first law book specifies that "no man shall be deprived of his wife or children" – along with other basic rights, such as not to be killed, arrested, or banished – "unles it be by the vertue or equity of some expresse law."[14] Here was a profound challenge to the older common law of England.

It was not only Puritan ideas that shaped the common law, however, nor was the influence always direct. Religious debates intersected with political controversies in England throughout the seventeenth century. The tracks are not easy to follow, but we can be sure that the Puritan emphasis on consent in religious matters influenced the emergence of ideas about government based on consent, which challenged the powers of Lords in that sphere, and that fathers' and husbands' claims of household rights challenged those of Lords and masters in *that* sphere.

The clearest example of this interaction is the landmark custody law of 1660, which built on Puritan precedents and which was an essential element in the settlement to which Charles II had to agree for the Restoration to proceed after the English Civil War and Interregnum. The law allowed fathers, for the first time, to designate who should get custody of their children up to the age of 21, should the father die. Before 1660, inasmuch as custody had existed, it had been concerned with the rights of guardians

[13] William Gouge, *Of Domesticall Duties* (London, 1622, facs. rpt Amsterdam, 1976), 17.

[14] *The Laws and Liberties of Massachusetts* [1648], ed. Richard S. Dunn (facs. rpt. Huntington Library, 1998), 1.

(in limited cases) and the rights of masters. A Lord, for example, would receive custody of a tenant's son up to the age of 14. Likewise one of the greatest sources of revenue for the Tudor and early Stuart kings had been the "Court of Wards," which had allowed them, essentially, to sell land use and guardianship rights on behalf of all those inheriting land held of the King in so-called knight's service – encompassing the land of all major peers – but who were too young actually to perform their service. The 1660 revision abolished the Court of Wards and allowed all men to choose a guardian for all their children.

Giving up wardship income was an important concession by Charles II and marked a major weakening of feudalism. Indeed the 1660 custody law is commonly thought of as marking the final abolition of feudal tenures in general. Advocates emerged not only from the remnants of Puritan reformers in the Rump Parliament but also from the recently reincarnated House of Lords, which had an obvious interest in such a change. The larger point is that the trade-off here – the King's surrender of important rights over his tenants and the similar surrender by Lords of rights over their tenants, which in each case increased the rights of fathers over children – was part of a larger challenge to the old feudal system. New ideas grounded on family order supplanted older ideas grounded on feudal hierarchy.

A new "domestic" or household law dealing with servants, wives, and children did not emerge all at once in the late seventeenth century. Indeed, at the end of the eighteenth century, its rules remained unfinished. The head of Cromwell's Interregnum commission on law reform, Sir Matthew Hale, who subsequently became Chief Justice under Charles II, would play a major role in reform, although initially his recommendations went unheeded and were only fully absorbed into the law by the mid-eighteenth century. Other treatise writers, notably Thomas Wood and Sir William Blackstone, would also play important roles. Their work synthesized precedents and rationalized the common law to create a coherently reformed system. The American Revolution, finally, would play a crucial role in rendering explicit the shift of norms that had been taking place, not only in the larger political order and in ideas about consent but also in the new domestic order, in the duties of servants, wives, and children.

II. REORGANIZING HOUSEHOLD AUTHORITY: THE EMERGING POWERS OF FATHERS AND HUSBANDS

By the end of the eighteenth century and the beginning of the nineteenth, Anglo-American domestic law had begun to take coherent form. As we have seen, Blackstone was key to this transition, although Blackstone built on other treatise writers, such as Hale and Wood, and others added to (and modified) his formulations, such as Tapping Reeve and, later, Chancellor James Kent. In the wake of the Revolution, state legislatures would also contribute, as did judges (often following the new treatises) case by case.

One major change that occurred in the wake of the Revolution was that most of the new American states legalized complete divorces (all had allowed legal separations, called divorce "a mensa et thoro"). Before, only Connecticut had allowed complete divorces ("a vinculo"), although some colonies had permitted "private acts" of the legislature to authorize the divorce of a particular couple, following English practice. After the Revolution, many states began to allow divorces when one side could show that the other had broken the marriage contract by infidelity. The resulting cases, as one can imagine, make for interesting reading, but the larger point is that the rhetoric of the Revolution itself could have radical implications for marriage rules and practices.

Yet, the overall impact of the Revolution itself on domestic order – at least in the short term – was actually minimal, largely because of the continued role the common law played in America in the years immediately after the break with Britain. Partly we may credit Blackstone's particular influence, partly the very character of common law decision making itself. Instead of passing to legislators, legal authority remained in the hands of judges. Judges rationalized their decisions by appealing to what they portrayed as an unchanging, unhistorical, universal law. Blackstone's *Commentaries* provided judges with the necessary material, minimizing change over time and shrouding historical origins in invariant legal certainties.

Blackstone's representation of an unchanging common law, of course, actually hid what had been years of fundamental transformation. The reorganization he summarized and synthesized is revealed most clearly in the contrast between his *Commentaries on the Laws of England* and Coke's *Institutes*. Blackstone began the *Commentaries* with the rights of persons (volume I), moved on to the rights of things (volume II), and devoted volumes III and IV to crimes, private and public. A common law that had been primarily about property and the rights of Lords 150 years before, now devoted itself – under Blackstone's careful hand – to the rights of persons.

We have noted Blackstone's profound influence on the new United States: he was the most widely cited author in American newspapers in the 1790s (following Locke in 1770s and Montesquieu in the 1780s); he was immensely respected among the intelligentsia for his *Commentaries*, which were published in their first American edition, with a list of some 600 subscribers, in 1772; and his work would become the template and point of departure for all the major American common law treatise writers of the early nineteenth century. Given all this influence, Blackstone's representation of domestic law to his American readers is crucial. He commences discussion of domestic law as follows:

> The Three Great Relations in Private Life are 1. That of *master and servant*; which is founded in convenience. . . . 2. That of *husband and wife*; which is founded in nature, but modified by civil society: . . . 3. That of parent and child, which is consequential to that of marriage, being its principle end and design: and it is by virtue of this relation that infants are protected, maintained, and educated. But since the parents, on whom this care is presently incumbent, may be snatched away by death or otherwise. . . . the law has therefore provided a fourth relation; 4. That of guardian and ward, which is a kind of artificial parentage, in order to supply the deficiency, whenever it happens, of the natural.[15]

In succeeding chapters, Blackstone laid out these parallel household relations. What is striking are the similarities: according to the ancient common law (so Blackstone contends) the master, husband, father can beat the dependent servant, wife, child. The master, husband, father is often responsible for the dependent actions of the servant, wife, child. The master, husband, father is also responsible for the maintenance of his dependents and, in the case of the wife and child, also responsible for their debts for necessities (but no more than that). Within the parallels there are a few variations: wives cannot testify against their husbands (or vice versa) in most cases because they are considered "one" in the eyes of the law; children under age 14 generally cannot testify at all, whether against parents or not; and servants can testify. Wives can "elope" from their husbands without the law forcing their return (unlike servants and children) or penalizing them except (if they flee to another man) the loss of their alimony and of any monetary claims against their husbands. One variation is of particular importance. Blackstone clearly sees servants as the property of their masters, so that if a servant leaves to work for another he can be forced to return and the master can sue his rival for damages. Blackstone never describes wives in that fashion. He does, however, grant fathers a property interest in their children's labor, which is a direct parallel to his discussion of servants on this question and is a new common law right. Blackstone's discussion of the rights of guardians, finally, is quite brief compared with the other relations. Guardians' rights are clearly less extensive than they had been (guardians have no right of battery, for example). Nevertheless, guardians' rights are rendered comparable to those of parents. Blackstone bases those rights in children's inability to form contracts, although he allows children their established common-law exemptions – contracts for necessities and labor contracts. (Once aged 14 they can be held liable for crimes too.) Generally,

[15] Blackstone, *Commentaries*, I, 410.

he concludes, children need guardians, which in some cases they can choose if their father has not done so.

What is extraordinary about the *Commentaries* is first, just how much is new in the sections on servants, wives, and children, and second, just how much Blackstone tries to universalize principles across all three categories of relationship. Admittedly, the parallels Blackstone develops are not all his own doing: it was Hale, for example, who, late in the seventeenth century, first developed the rules barring wives and children from testifying. But Blackstone's is the grand synthesis.

Though acknowledging in specific instances that changes had occurred over time (as in the case of guardianship) Blackstone hides change. He also ignores contrary precedents. There are limits, one could argue, to how extensively Blackstone could mold the common law to fit his synthesizing imagination. Yet the limits are not clear, for his reasoning is supple. Take the expanding legal-political ideology of contract. Blackstone emphasizes that the power to contract is essential for an individual's public legal identity. Most persons, therefore, must have it. What then of the "necessary" dependencies of the domestic relations? They are founded on contract. A servant contracts with a master, a wife with a husband. But once a servant has contracted with the master, a wife with her husband, they have exhausted their capacity to contract. Their contractual act turns them into equivalents of children; like children they are dependent on the will of the master/husband/father, at least insofar as what he requires is lawful. In other words, Blackstone envelops each relation in the new ideas about contract while actually allowing those ideas only a tenuous purchase: following the statute of laborers, he still permits force to be used in the forming of labor contracts – against the laborer. Likewise, he allows that labor contracts can be for shorter (or longer) duration than the customary one year, which gives greater flexibility to those contracting. In the wife's case, meanwhile, the concept of femme covert becomes fully realized in the law by her contract, her one self-willed act held to imply an abnegation of her legal identity.

In the new United States, such commentators as St. George Tucker in Virginia, Tapping Reeve in Connecticut, James Wilson in Pennsylvania, and James Kent in New York built on Blackstone's domestic relations blueprint. They made their own modifications: Kent, for example, strengthened a father's right to property in his child, further limited the ability of children to contract (even for necessities), and allowed mothers custodial rights due to their loving care for their children. Arguably, this last change helped precipitate later key custody battles where judges in divorce cases began to grant mothers custodial authority over their children. Tapping Reeve adopted an extreme approach to wives' dependency, contending that wives could never be held responsible for any contract and that husbands were always responsible for fulfilling their wives' obligations, even to the extent of caring for her children from a former marriage. Reeve saw husbands' powers as also incurring responsibilities.

In the case of master/servant relations in America, the authority of masters over white servants and apprentices had weakened somewhat in the colonial period, in part because the percentage of whites in such relationships in the colonies decreased. In the wake of the Revolution, however, the common law broadened the reach of masters in parallel to increasing the powers of fathers and husbands. Adult male laborers who remained in the category of dependents were now analogized to children, but a more general basis for the authority of masters was placed on the contracts of formerly independent working men. This reactionary response to the principles of the enlightenment and the American Revolution took place particularly within the common law.

The laws regulating master and servant during the seventeenth and eighteenth centuries were grounded in older norms about master and servant, which persisted into the modern period. In practice, the application of those norms expanded in range. While in the early modern period, many types of skilled or day labor had been seen as legally independent, by the early nineteenth century, hierarchical definitions of master/servant relations began to apply to them. Masters/employers were granted so many legal advantages that real freedom of contract did not exist. The trend followed Blackstone and to some extent earlier treatise writers, such as Burns' popular *Justice of the Peace* guide. Still, in the wake of the Revolution the scope of the application of these norms expanded rapidly in America through court rulings. Key court decisions in many states allowed masters, for example, to set the rules of departure and terms of labor and to limit their liability in the case of injury. These decisions were made by placing most worker issues within the older master/servant law, which had become a universal category under which most worker relations fell. Courts also restricted workers' combinations (unions) in decisions along lines formulated in 1834 by Massachusetts Judge Peter Oxenbridge Thacher, who condemned unions as conspiracies that would undermine public order comparable to the excesses of the French Revolution. Such rulings were openly anti-democratic.[16] They blunted the principles coming out of the American Revolution that had given strength to the working men's movement, fueling the impetus toward unions that challenged employers on grounds of equity and rights and contributed to the nineteenth century's ideology of "free labor." One change that did begin

[16] Christopher L. Tomlins, *Law, Labor and Ideology in the Early American Republic* (Cambridge, 1993), e.g., 193, 238, 263, 275.

to benefit working men, however, were court decisions that began to limit employers' ability to physically punish their employees.

Ideas about the equality of men – about their ability to consent to government – shaped the legal debate about the rest of the household and the pattern of authority within it. Forcing poorer children to labor for masters no longer looked so appealing to a broader electorate that included the fathers of those poorer children. As consent became more important to the law and to the ideal of society, it became more important to train future citizens, which led in the wake of the American Revolution to ambitious plans for public education in many states that were actually realized in the middle and Northern states. In the longer run these principles also led to general bans on child labor, following the principle that poor children should not be condemned to service and manual labor, but had rights to occupational opportunity and civic capacity.

These changes were part of a larger challenge to hereditary status. With the notable exception of slavery, laws determining status by birth largely disappeared in the new United States. The U.S. Constitution mandated that, on the federal level at least, political offices could not be hereditary. States passed similar laws, though in some cases – justices of the peace in Virginia, for example – formally appointive positions remained hereditary in practice as they passed from elite landowner father to eldest inheriting son, just as in the colonial period. Still, even in Virginia, laws challenged hereditary status, such as those abolishing entails and primogeniture. Apprenticeship laws that had removed poor children to work in wealthier families also became less common – for whites, at least.

White parents tended to gain custody of their children; black parents (especially those enslaved) generally did not. Free black families were often female headed, perhaps with an enslaved father, and poor. Poor free black children were often forcibly bound out, especially in the South. The children of slaves were of course owned along with their parents. Enslaved parents had no legal voice and no legal right to be married. The legal word "family" did not apply to them. This might seem obvious to scholars of antebellum slavery, but its roots lay in older norms of master/servant. Slavery was a continuation of those norms, challenged but unreformed by the Revolution, as defenders of the South's "domestic institutions" repeatedly revealed.

States offered many variations in the details of domestic authority, with the South assuming the most hierarchical stance in the powers it gave white fathers. In the wake of the Revolution, fathers in Massachusetts were allowed to bind their children into apprenticeships solely on their own authority if the child were under 14; for children between 14 and 21, both father and child had to sign. In Virginia, fathers could bind the child solely on their own authority until the child was 21. In Pennsylvania, a parent or guardian had no power to bind the child on their own authority at any age. Even a 2-year-old had to sign too before a labor contract could be valid. (In all three states, however, Overseers of the Poor could bind children until age 21 if they determined the children were poor or illegitimate or without proper care.) These different state laws, of course, all marked a shift away from the earlier practice that held the child's consent sufficient in itself – a norm still acknowledged by Blackstone, his extensive objections to children forming contracts notwithstanding.

Across the broad spectrum of the law, children lost legal capacity – they were no longer able to manage estates, to serve in political or appointed offices or on juries, to marry without parental consent, let alone under the age of puberty, to be criminally culpable (at least if under the age of 14), to make wills, to testify in a court of law, or even to make contracts for necessaries. These changes sometimes worked to a child's advantage, as in an 1806 case in which a 13-year-old girl accused of murdering her drunken father was deemed too young to have her confession admitted as reliable evidence and was acquitted.[17] Generally these new rules emerged out of legal policies that privileged informed consent – and legal independence – in the forming of all contracts and relations of responsibility and assumed that children lacked the competence to make such decisions.

The story of women's legal rights is somewhat grim. Blackstone's grand synthesis set up a situation in which women (particularly heiresses) could be exploited more easily by their husbands, a situation that fed the women's rights movement and paved the way for some of the women's separate property acts of the mid- and late nineteenth century. Blackstone's unqualified embrace of marital unity and the reformulation of property rights that gave the husband all authority over property – even personal possessions and property the women had brought to the marriage as dower – sharply altered the multiple ownership norms and encumbrances of the older system. Blackstone's injunctions were supported by revolutionary ideals that glorified simple property ownership and jettisoned many types of property encumbrances. Bans on one particular type of encumbrance, namely entails that conveyed only life estates to heirs, did advantage women in the sense that daughters were more likely to inherit. However this reform also came at the expense of wives who were heiresses because encumbrances like entail had formerly protected a married woman's separate property. In and of itself, the abolition of entails displays the mixed character of the revolutionary legacy for women as daughters and wives.

One important technicality for understanding this transition is the role played by equity courts (Chancery). Equity courts in England had long

[17] *State v. Mary Doherty*, 2 Tenn (2 Overt), 80.

provided a separate system of justice headed by the Chancellor of England, which technically served as an appeal to the King from common law decisions. In the late eighteenth and early nineteenth centuries, equity courts coming out of the English tradition had crafted a separate body of law that (among many other things) tended to recognize the different forms of separate or encumbered estates of wives that husbands could not/should not control. In fact, these equity decisions often simply recognized what the common law, prior to Blackstone, had itself largely honored. In the early nineteenth century, as the common law ceased to allow women separate property, equity appeals (through the separate equity courts that existed in many states) built on older precedents to challenge Blackstone.

Not all states had equity courts and even those that did often limited their jurisdiction. Still, equity jurisdiction helped shape the laws that began to emerge in the 1830s and 1840s in America collectively known as the "women's separate property acts," laws that allowed women to retain control over the property that they had brought into the marriage. They were fiercely debated in many states, often in state constitutional conventions. Arguments not only focused on whether wives should be able to own separate property but also on the fundamental principle of marital unity itself, and what it meant for republican government, the virtue of citizens, and the liberties of free men. Defenders portrayed Blackstonian common law as the fundamental and eternal order of family relations, claiming that "oneness" was the core principle of happy marriage and a virtuous public order. Just like seventeenth-century reformers, they appealed to biblical descriptions of husband and wife as "one flesh." Challengers pointed to the abuses that the (new) common law norm had allowed – men who married heiresses only to squander their estates and leave them ruined and homeless. One can imagine that many men – as fathers of daughters – supported the women's separate property acts precisely as protection from such abuses.

The story of marital violence is more complicated. Most state courts held that men could not beat their wives, but their decisions varied and always found a way to repeat Blackstone's dictum that the ancient common law had allowed it. Some lawyers defending husbands in such cases actually argued that men should be allowed to beat their wives as much as they wanted, and even to kill them, on the grounds that "oneness" meant the man was beating or killing himself, which was simply suicide and not prosecutable. That argument was generally dismissed, but it remained part of mid-nineteenth-century popular and legal consciousness, and material for many jokes. In the masculine democracy of the new republic, where gender trumped rank, male "ownership" of the family arguably made abuse of both wives and children culturally and legally acceptable.[18] Nevertheless, the rights of persons were generally becoming more important to the law, and assault a more serious crime.

Ironically, perhaps, the injustices to women sanctioned by Blackstonian common law fueled women's rights advocates. Had Blackstone not cast the common law so starkly, they would have had less to protest. And indeed, the women's movement tended to ignore equity court decisions so as to focus more sharply on the injustices of the common law. The famous Seneca Falls Declaration of Sentiments of 1848, seen by many historians as the official start of the women's rights movement, plays on the 1776 Declaration of Independence, substituting "all men and women are created equal" for the Declaration's "men" only, and replacing George III's crimes against the colonies with men's crimes against women. The list is a fair summary of Blackstone's description of a husband's powers over his wife in marriage – a tyranny, according to the authors, like that of a king granted too much power. The very definition and history of the common law, as Blackstone had portrayed it, now shaped the legal debate not only in practice, in other words but also in theory. Tradition had become a weapon for people on both sides of the struggle.

But tradition was neither as unchanging nor as exploitative as either side believed. Why? Arguments about the basis of governmental authority convulsed England during the seventeenth century. Should government be based on consent or heredity? Constitutionally, from the thirteenth-century founding of the House of Commons onward, English government had been a mixture of the two, but it had leaned more toward heredity. Both the monarchy and the House of Lords determined the next heir according to primogeniture, or birthright. Too, most of those elected to the House of Commons were prominent landowners, many the eldest sons of peers. Powerful families often controlled which candidate stood for election, and the suffrage was sharply restricted. No more than 10 percent of adult males could vote, and qualification was often hereditary, whether directly, through descent, or indirectly, based on land ownership. Only sometimes could suffrage be earned, by, for example finishing an apprenticeship and becoming a "freeman" of particular cities.

Even that was not enough for hereditarian ideologues of the mid-seventeenth century such as Sir Robert Filmer. Filmer claimed that the sole purpose of Parliament was to advise the king and that its instructions were not binding. His arguments were challenged by many mid-seventeenth-century religious and political reformers, such as John Milton – and of

[18] Hendrik Hartog, *Man and Wife in America: A History* (Cambridge, MA, 2000), 103–5.

course by Civil War defenders of Parliament in general. Authors of political tracts in the 1680s renewed the assault, most prominently John Locke, whose arguments against Filmer greatly strengthened the contentions of those whose theory of government emphasized consent. His entire *Two Treatises of Government* (1689) was a sustained attack on birthright and birth privilege.

The problem, of course, lay in defining who should be able to consent. Hereditarians argued that all human beings were born into a state of natural dependence, and that dependence should (and did) order society. Building on earlier arguments about religious choice, Locke developed an answer that contested universal dependence by conceding the difference between children and adults. All men were by nature born equal, but while children men were dependent for a period of time and incapable of independent judgment. Dependence ended at the age children attained reason; that is, became adults. Reason then supplied the principle underlying the formation of society. In a society founded on reasoned consent, all men would be equal under the laws. Children would be dependent on their parents to make decisions for them until they could make decisions for themselves in a free and uncoerced manner. Parents should not be able to bind their children irrevocably: all contracts should be temporary. Children could not be born into servitude, even if their parent was a servant or slave to another. Likewise children could not be born owing political obedience.

Locke had a good deal to say about children, but much less about the rights of masters or husbands. What he did say indicated that even in those cases consent had to be given freely. Locke hinted that a woman, while reasonable, might, in choosing a husband, also be choosing a political representative (in that he would vote on her behalf). He also suggested, however, that women should have the right to divorce. As to servitude, Locke held that in only one case – the crime of engaging in an unjust war – could a person be forced to serve another without consent, for the captive had in effect forfeited his life to his captor. Still, the captive was to be treated with respect by his master, was required to labor only for a set term of years, and retained a primary obligation to his family.

The point that emerges here is that what we would now regard as fundamental democratic political theory – who could consent, under what circumstances, who could not, who had authority over those who could not – was being worked out in arguments over family order. In this merged arena, the idea that unjust contracts were voidable challenged tyrannical government by kings and also by husbands, fathers, and masters. To be just, consent to anything had to be meaningful – fully informed and free from coercion. Obviously such arguments would have invalidated many Elizabethan and seventeenth-century labor contracts. At the same time, such arguments demarcated a very clear space for childhood and underlay arguments for expanded custody. Other norms of authority could also potentially be justified by comparing wives, slaves, and servants to children in their inability to make independent judgments. Thomas Wood's *Institute of the Laws of England* (1720), popular in colonial libraries, appears to follow precisely this strategy by exploring in parallel the rights of masters, husbands, and fathers.

As Wood's "prequel" to Blackstone suggests, the new synthesis of the common law under way in the eighteenth century was deeply influenced by Locke. Blackstone's crowning edifice – the *Commentaries* – cites Locke (and also Continental natural law theorists like Pufendorf) repeatedly. For years, scholars have debated the political meaning of this development: whether, crudely, the new common law synthesis should be considered conservative or radical in its implications. The debate admits no clear answer, for the *Commentaries* are an artful mixture: Blackstone upholds hereditary status and the obligations of inferiors to obey their superiors, but he also argues that slavery is immoral and should be illegal (at least in his first edition). Some sections seem to express pure Lockean contract theory, notably Blackstone's argument against the wide use of the death penalty. Others adapt contractarianism to hierarchical precepts. With respect to domestic law, for example, it can fairly be said that Blackstone made it more hierarchical and gave hierarchy broader, more universal application.

Blackstone was thus influenced by emerging contractarian ideas at the same time as he adhered to hierarchical principles and older precedents. His objective was to create clarity and consistency within the common law in a way that strengthened the legal authority of many adult men, especially with respect to their wives. His domestic law was not the work of a misogynist: by all accounts Blackstone had a close and loving relationship with his own wife. It is not clear that Blackstone gave much thought to the practical effects of the powers he attributed men as husbands and fathers. What is clear is that Blackstone sought to bring order to a disorderly, haphazard, and neglected mass of statutes and common law precedents that appeared to obey no principles. Locke supplied principles that could be useful in imagining the balanced organizational framework Blackstone desired to create, whose particular twist appealed to Blackstone's own sympathies for hierarchy. The twist increased the powers of fathers and husbands and masters, for it established that those who cannot reason, like children, cannot consent. Wives can consent, but they consent to their husbands in marriage, who thereby becomes their representative and acts for them. Servants consent initially to labor and then are bound, unless the master releases them. Blackstone cemented hierarchy into the setting of consent by interpolating an element left over from the medieval common law: the idea of people as property. Locke had carefully avoided that idea in the case of wives and children and had hedged it even for servants – more so, at least, than did the law of his own time. Blackstone was not so shy. Here was a broad exception to the principles of "All men created equal" for it meant that the contracts were not entered into in equal terms. It would prove a powerful legal tool, at least for those who sought to maximize its potential.

CONCLUSION

Anglo-American domestic law was not a timeless category: the powers of fathers and parents were not fixed in an unchanging common law between 1600 and the early nineteenth century, but significantly strengthened. Those powers increased at the same time as the powers of Lords and masters weakened (though applied more broadly), and the underlying cause was the same in each case: the political ideas that powered the three Anglo-American Revolutions (the Civil War and Interregnum, the Glorious Revolution of 1688, and the American Revolution of 1776). The new revolutionary principle of authority based on consent grew out of religious arguments that emphasized the authority of the father/husband and the principle of meaningful consent as corollary propositions. Political debates affected the common law and legal practice to reshape the boundaries of domestic authority. In the common law one finds both accommodation of the new principles of authority and elements of reaction.

The American Revolution added force to the legal changes whose path we have observed. Particularly in the late eighteenth century, changes in legal norms were occurring virtually hand in hand with the development of democratic-republican ideas about consent. They also occurred hand in hand with the emergence of new forms of capitalist industrial organization. The ubiquity of contractualism made it easier to identify and prosecute debtors, confiscate estates for debt, streamline finance, facilitate mortgages, and generally increase both circulation of and access to capital. Freedom of contract could aid transactions by unraveling tangled lines of property ownership, simultaneously simplifying the lines of responsibility of owners for debts owed. Freedom of contract could also advance the circulation of labor, while restrictions on the ability to contract could enable employers to retain effective control of their workers. We should note that America offered more possibilities for free labor before the Revolution and that Americans in the wake of the Revolution never adopted some of the harsh restraints developed in English law. The Revolution and attachment to the principles underlying it help explain the latter, whereas opportunities for westward movement helped forestall the coercive restraint of white labor.

Anglo-American common law innovation reified and reorganized old and ubiquitous norms about the power of lords and masters and then preserved them within the law as a new category, "domestic law." This category (especially with regard to minor children) was intrinsic to the newer political ideas of a government based on meaningful consent. Given its construction, we should not, indeed cannot, understand domestic law as if it were a phenomenon lying outside politics. Principles of domestic authority connect intimately with principles of public authority; public debates and legal decisions shaped private relationships.

10

LAW AND RELIGION IN COLONIAL AMERICA

MARK McGARVIE AND ELIZABETH MENSCH

English religious conflict influenced law in the early British colonies; so too, however, did commercial ambition and English legal traditionalism. That inherently unstable combination produced significant reconfigurations in the eighteenth century, when religion became less obviously formative and public in relation to law, but no less intermeshed with legal culture and political conflict. Protestants in America reenacted many Old World religious conflicts as they struggled to integrate commercial gain, the coercions of law, and the promise of Christian freedom – or, put differently, as they sought the right relation between the City on Earth and the City of God. Their various solutions to that Augustinian dilemma took widely different forms.

In England Tudor political skill had, for a time, muted religious tension. Church and commonwealth became a single all-enveloping unity. That unity, however, masked both Catholic resentment and mounting Calvinist pressure to distinguish the church from the realm – to "gather out" and purify the true church of the redeemed. Early Stuarts exacerbated these tensions exactly when England was extending commercial ventures into America. Protestants feared the Catholic leanings of the Stuart kings, and Archbishop Laud's persecution of dissenters coupled the Church of England with Stuart assertion of unlimited prerogative. Puritans, viewing Christ (and the free consent of believers) as the only true source of church authority, denounced a hierarchical Anglican episcopacy rooted in Crown prerogative. Meanwhile, lower ecclesiastical courts, charged with enforcing morality, veered from laxness to corrupt and discretionary intrusiveness. Their disrepute was almost matched by that of English law, with its capriciously enforced multitude of capital crimes.

Religion drove many dissenting Protestants and some Catholics to America. In England, civil war (beginning in 1642) led to Puritan Parliamentary rule, which was followed by the Restoration of Charles II in 1660. Restoration brought renewed imposition of Anglican uniformity and fear of Catholicism until 1688, when the Glorious Revolution established both Parliamentary supremacy and a Protestant Church of England, with (limited) toleration of non-conformists. The consequent easing of religious tension provided a backdrop for the rationalism of the English Enlightenment – embraced by many Anglican clergy – but also for renewed religious fervor. Both of those developments in England were reinforced by similar developments in the colonies.

English settlers came, however, not just as Protestants but also as colonizers. They arrived under the authority of two written texts: the Bible and the Law. The first charter of the Virginia Company stated, as its primary purpose, to bring the "Christian religion to such people [Indians] as yet live in darkness and miserable ignorance. . . ." Metaphors of darkness and ignorance filled colonial descriptions of the wilderness, juxtaposed to metaphors, common in Europe, of noble savages in a state of Edenic innocence. Linked to metaphors of darkness and ignorance were images of death, idleness, the void, chaos, wild beasts, and Satan. Thus a Virginia tract described Indians as in "the arms of the Devil" and "wrapped up unto death, in almost invincible ignorance." Into the darkness the settlers brought the Word, and with it, they believed, light, knowledge, order, and industry.

Metaphors of visibility and darkness perhaps come naturally, especially to literate cultures, but they carried special power for Protestants schooled in the primacy of texts (*sola scriptura*), and deeply familiar with such particular texts as the Bible, Augustine, and Calvin, in which images of light and darkness abound. Attitudes shaped and reflected by such metaphors affected legal treatment of Africans as well as Indians, and also of those who practiced in the shadows, so to speak, those (pre-literate) arts of the occult called witchcraft.

Written legal and religious texts embodied authority and reinforced white male dominance over less literate groups – Africans, Indians, and women. Massachusetts Bay had a government printer by 1638 chiefly to print laws and religious works, and New England villages often required a Bible in every household; similarly, the Church of England inundated colonies with books of common prayer. Laws were to be read, Massachusetts magistrates stated, not just in print but in the lives of the people themselves – inscribed in the heart, like scripture. Throughout the colonies laws and public announcements were read in churches. After the 1750s a republicanized, secular print culture emerged, with vigorous debate of public issues; but in the early colonies written texts embodied a unified political and religious authority.

Outsiders to the dominant culture suffered catastrophic ostracism. Indians who survived white diseases often had two options: conversion or death. Massachusetts Puritans, for example, published enough native language

Bibles for one of every $2^1/_2$ Indians, and set up more than thirty "praying towns" with regular schedules of work and worship; but they also invoked "light" from the Word of God to justify igniting the flames that burned (alive) an entire Indian village. Anglicanism offered an elaborate spiritual defense of brutal race-based Southern slave codes, and execution (by burning, hanging, and the wheel) of rebel New York City slaves underscored the legal violence even of Northern slavery. All colonies founded before 1660 had laws against witchcraft, which were enforced most rigorously in New England: occult practices were implicitly associated with the wilderness and with African and Indian pagan "darkness." English enforcement of equivalent laws died out well before colonial enforcement.

The colonists' legal and religious relation to outsiders, of course, was not one of pure conquest. Indians resisted conversion, were shrewd partners in war and trade, and litigated in colonial courts; slaves negotiated rights, became adept at passive resistance, and learned to invoke the implicit egalitarianism of Christian baptism; and legal excesses at Salem were sufficiently embarrassing to end New England witchcraft trials, despite lingering enforcement in the South. Nevertheless, colonial elites undeniably used religion in relation to law to legitimate social control – not just as colonizers but also within their own white communities. "Social control" as an explanatory category, however, is excessively reductionist: it denigrates sincerity of belief and ignores difference. Most early colonists used law to construct Protestant community – to give concrete embodiment to faith. The chief purpose of law was not to protect individual rights (the preoccupation of a later period) but to build a Christian polity. Indeed, for many, liberty itself meant the liberty to form a godly community, which necessarily required, however paradoxically, a high degree of social control.

The first section of the chapter describes some general features of the interaction of law and religion in the colonies and some common historical changes. Subsequent sections, describing six distinct colonies, explore significant differences that those commonalities mask.

I. COMMON THEMES

Most British colonizers came to America for profit and expected law to serve that purpose. Like other Europeans, however, they assumed the value of a Christianized culture in which self-interest was subordinate to God's will, as served by hierarchy, order, and Christian communalism. To reinforce Christian values eleven of the original thirteen colonies legally established Protestant churches, requiring tax support and regular attendance. All colony-wide religious establishments were either (Puritan) Congregationalist or Anglican, but some colonies created a "multiple" establishment, which allowed each locality to establish its own churches. Often, only the established church could promulgate creeds taught in schools or perform weddings or baptisms, and only members could vote or hold office. Notably, the two colonies that rejected establishment (Rhode Island and Pennsylvania) did so on specifically theological grounds. Therefore "establishment" in the colonies is best appreciated not as a particular legal arrangement but as the cultural reflection and promotion of Christian values – values that competed with economic and military influences, as well as English legal traditionalism, to form colonial law. Throughout the colonies, including those with no official establishment, churches played a central role in educating the young, establishing community norms, and shaping law.

The egalitarianism latent in Reformation theology sometimes came to the fore and, especially in New England, cut against hierarchical extremes. Nevertheless, to the early colonists community implied some social hierarchy, with each station performing its sanctioned role. Ministers from Massachusetts to South Carolina preached both deference to social betters and the obligations entailed by privilege: when social position was ordained by God, attendant duties did not seem a violation of "earned" private right. A pervasive model for hierarchy was the household, where the father's loving governance of family, servants, and economic production ideally eased the Christian tension between enforcement of ethical norms and the requirement of boundless forgiveness – between the demand of law and the promise of grace. Law reinforced household authority by imposing public corporal punishment to control servants and slaves, and to strengthen family-based moral discipline, while also imposing duties on the wealthy to give support to workers, orphans, or the indigent. Early Virginia records document the prosecution of a "runaway master" who "fled from his servants" to evade supporting them and show parish assignment of poor boys to work for wealthy individuals, whether needed or not. Ironically, such laws foreshadowed later Anglican defense of race-based slavery as a paternalistic embodiment of Christian love and charity, yet even in the North charity reflected a pre-modern understanding of hierarchy and deference; it was intended to relieve individual suffering, not transform the social order.

Colonial laws relating to economic activity further reinforced communitarianism. Clergy not only admonished greed and encouraged charity but also specifically endorsed commercial restrictions that were even more rigorous than those endorsed by their Catholic counterparts in Europe. Some historians have recently argued that colonial Massachusetts flourished by linking communitarian ethics with an emerging capitalism. Nevertheless, the Bay government structured its markets to serve community in a manner unfamiliar to modern capitalism: it limited land distribution to "worthy" recipients, controlled prices and wages, prosecuted merchants for seeking unjust profits, and limited all business activity to prescribed times and places.

Most colonies adopted the Reformed view that government, as an "ordinance of God," should protect the individual's moral as well as civil welfare. Criminal law in Virginia and in New England referred to "sin," implicitly accepting the obligation to construct Christian conscience, not just preserve civil peace. Penal law provided the moral definition of community, and the earliest colonies instituted significant reforms. They eliminated lower ecclesiastical courts (despised by Puritans), virtually abolished execution for property offenses as inconsistent with scripture and level of moral blame, and heightened criminal liability for personal misconduct. Corporal punishment provided public moral instruction, often including sermons at executions.

Even a rough contrast between early New England and Chesapeake penal law, however, shows the difference between Puritan and Anglican influence. New Englanders, shaping their polities on the model of ancient Israel, adopted English legal categories only if consistent with the Bible and used scripture as the direct source for roughly half their criminal law. New England also dropped capricious mitigating pleas, like benefit of clergy, since literacy and wealth implied heightened moral accountability, not privileged excuse. The earliest Puritans trusted magistrates ("Gods upon earthe," said Winthrop) to apply law with equitable Christian discretion; admonishment was often sufficient punishment. Codification followed later, with its own didactic value.

By contrast, Southern Anglicans often reintroduced a modified ecclesiastical court system by entrusting church officers to report personal misconduct to county courts. Reflecting the public, political nature of Anglican ecclesiology, discretionary legal enforcement aimed more toward preserving outward public peace than building inner righteousness. Particular laws were usually taken from England, not scripture, and defined judicially, in the name of paternal authority, not by codes. Judges, eschewing mere admonishment, allowed traditional English mitigating pleas and relaxed punishment for gentry while operating *in terrorem* in relation to the large servant classes who, before the huge slave purchases began in the late seventeenth century, constituted roughly three-fourths of Chesapeake immigrants. The only two early colonial executions for theft, for example, were of Virginia laborers. Thus, put generally, early Puritans used penal law to serve scripture, whereas Anglicanism used religion to spiritualize English traditionalism; Anglicans sacralized law and a paternalistic social order, Puritans prepared the godly for salvation. Nevertheless, in each case the goal was a version of Christian community.

By the late seventeenth century, communitarianism showed the strains of entrepreneurial efforts to recruit new inhabitants, even as disaffected second and third generations felt the pull of commercial opportunity and unsettled land. Religious diversity also became common, leading to accommodation. Nevertheless, pluralism did not automatically produce a high level of toleration. Throughout the seventeenth century nearly all colonies had laws to deter heterodox religious practice, and prosecutions for blasphemy, heresy, sedition, contempt, passion, breach of the Sabbath, or religious deviance continued into the eighteenth century. In 1703 South Carolina made blasphemy a crime, defining it as "defaming any person of the Trinity, denying the truths of Christianity, or denying the divine authority of the Bible." New York prosecuted a blasphemy case pursuant to an already existent statute during the same year. Delaware brought a blasphemy suit in 1705, Maryland in 1710, and North Carolina in 1717. Protestants who dissented from established churches could be prosecuted, along with agnostics, Jews, and Catholics; Connecticut passed a new law in 1742 against itinerant preaching to stifle evangelicalism.

While establishment waned between 1660 and 1690, that waning was followed by fresh efforts to establish Anglicanism, vigorously supported by England and by colonial officials. Especially when coupled with the imposition of English law, Anglicanization of other Europeans often meant a significant reduction in women's legal rights and cultural influence. Meanwhile, Congregationalism remained strong in New England, where most people still lived within six miles of a church. Congregationalism also had the advantage of well-educated, locally ordained ministers. In 1690, 90 percent of all colonial congregations were either Congregational or Anglican.

In the next eighty years that reality changed dramatically as immigrants from Germany, France, Ireland, and Scotland came to the middle colonies. By 1770 only about 20 percent of congregations were Congregational and 15 percent Anglican. Meanwhile, commercialism led to the increased use of law to structure competitive property and exchange relationships, not the godly life. The eighteenth century brought a vast proliferation of printed law forms, which preceded the dramatic expansion of a professional lawyer class in mid-century.

Several historians have seen in these changes a breakdown of the communitarianism once premised on religious homogeneity and the seeds of an individualistic ideology that prompted political revolution. The Great Awakening, starting in the 1730s, can be seen either as consistent with those trends or as a reaction against them. During the Awakening, New Light preachers combined human-centered emotional appeals with invocation of a God-centered communal existence. Preachers became a "means of grace," exciting listeners to frenzies of repentance that bent their wills toward conversion. Despite its flirtation with Arminianism – the human capacity to achieve righteousness – New Light doctrine restated human depravity and dependence on divine grace. Yet, Jonathan Edwards argued, people could hasten the coming of the millennium by forming a new, perfected social order, a "union of believers" joined together in regenerate love. Awakening preaching was radically egalitarian while simultaneously evocative of an earlier, legally structured Christian communitarianism. To a degree especially surprising in the South, Awakening congregations broke down barriers based on race, gender, class, and even literacy.

Established churchmen reacted with alarm, even describing New Light emotionalism as Satanic. Governments helped head off the assault. Several New England legislatures, for example, enacted laws in the 1740s to discipline government officials and ministers who endorsed separatism, itinerant evangelicalism, or emotional piety. Similarly, in the South planters feared the Baptist and Methodist challenge to legally structured inequality. Gentry seized control of churches to strengthen the Anglican establishment, but persecution only fortified New Light dissenters: convinced by faith, they calmly accepted martyrdom.

Established churches could not absorb the force of the Awakening's piety. Dissenters migrated to other churches, such as Baptist, Presbyterian, or Methodist, sapping power from integrated corporate systems of church and state. A crucial development of this post-Awakening period was the vigorous growth of non-established American denominationalism, with its combination of hierarchy and autonomy, cross-colonial ties, and local independence. Denominational associations were at the forefront in adapting legal categories still on the border of an emerging distinction between public and private (such as incorporation, trust, and property) to fashion their identities as private, voluntary institutions protected by law to serve a quasi-public moral role. As their institutional structures became increasingly intermeshed with existing legal and social structures, denominations typically gained respectability but lost New Light perfectionist zeal; old divisions of class, race, and gender reemerged.

Although it united some evangelicals within denominations, the Great Awakening isolated many from the traditional established churches and also from commercialism and rationalism. By mid-century the market economy had outgrown the parameters of providentialism and communalism. New Lights who sought to perpetuate an archaic model of religious community viewed the new economy with disdain, condemning its greed, inequality, and self-indulgence. Equally great was the shift New Lights precipitated within the established churches, in which Congregational and Anglican exponents of rational religion united with traditionalists in opposition to evangelicalism. As in England, Arminianism combined with natural law to direct established religion toward secular, Enlightenment rationalism. In effect, the social radicals, the evangelicals, became the religiously orthodox, whereas the social conservatives in established churches became the religious liberals. By the middle of the eighteenth century religion had divided American society and positioned itself as a vehicle for social change.

II. REGIONAL VARIATIONS

Generally drawn comparisons and contrasts do not do justice to the richness and nuance of colonial religious difference. For example, in New England, Puritan theology was a decisive force, in effect subordinating civil government to religious truth; during the colonial period New England struggled against the amoral effects of commerce on its legally structured religious community. Yet internal struggles arising from paradoxes within Reformed theology itself produced Rhode Island's extraordinary Baptist experiment in religious liberty, the unusual but consequential history of which cannot be captured under a general heading, "New England."

Similarly, the Middle Colonies, subject of recent historical attention due to their diversity and rapid commercial development, cannot be described by reference to pluralism and commerce alone. Pennsylvania's legal history, shaped by Quaker, pietist, and other sectarian influence, is different from New York's, with its often-violent struggles between a forced Anglican establishment and Dutch and dissenter resistance.

Finally, in the South, Anglicanism demonstrated its expansive capacity to envelop and spiritualize the legal and social order by sanctifying even the privileged moral license and slave laws of gentry culture. Anglicans refused to convert slaves, despite pressure to do so by clergy in England, and thereby reinforced the white construction of Africans as a heathen "other." Only Awakening evangelicals rekindled Christians' latent, egalitarian longing for a true community of believers, challenging Southern traditionalism. Yet Anglicanism in Maryland was different from Anglicanism in Virginia, being more Calvinist and also shaped by an extraordinary preoccupation with the perceived threat of Catholicism. Maryland's legal conflicts, often carried back to England, were utterly unique but at the same time representative of the extent to which America's Protestant culture still defined itself by opposition to Catholicism – a fact of lasting historical significance.

Despite those differences, regional commonalities are helpful in characterizing general forms of colonial establishment. New England townships attempted to preserve Christian homogeneity and communitarianism until well into the nineteenth century. Congregationalists, Presbyterians, Quakers, and Baptists shared a common Reformation heritage, imbuing New England with cultural similarity despite sectarian differences. Religious establishment persisted in New England longer than elsewhere, usually into the second or third decade of the nineteenth century; Massachusetts continued public support of churches until 1833.

The mid-Atlantic colonies were the most diverse: Germans, English, Irish, Dutch, and Scots migrated to New York, Pennsylvania, Delaware, and New Jersey. Yet, diversity did not necessarily inhibit religious establishment. Dissenters were often taxed to support an established church and accepted its role in public functions, and the wide variety of sects led to more congregations, relative to population, than in any other region. Nevertheless, residents chafed at laws that restricted individual freedom and economic initiative. By the mid-eighteenth century, New York City and Philadelphia had become major cosmopolitan centers of business, ideas, and entertainment. Economic expansion and religious diversity eroded the authority of religiously inspired law, and most mid-Atlantic states disestablished their churches in revolutionary-era constitutions. In the process, churches were also removed from performing vital public tasks like education, poor relief, and record keeping. The states were slow to assume those responsibilities, leaving them to the (unreliable) beneficence of the wealthy.

By 1703 Anglicanism was established in each of the Southern colonies. Southern Anglicanism reflected both the influence of the English Enlightenment and the deference to gentry domination that characterized the South's paternalistic honor-based society. Anglican devotion to social order served as the glue within a society divided by wealth, race, and culture. Along with frontier Indian wars and race-based slavery, Anglicanism helped define white culture as a unified, inclusive, morally based community, notwithstanding inequalities in wealth and education far more extreme than in other regions. Under the parish structure churches assumed a significant role in governing, but the autonomous moral authority of the church was never strong and declined in the eighteenth century when religious growth occurred almost exclusively among rural Baptists and Methodists. Southern colonies disestablished their churches during the constitutional era, 1785–1800.

New England: Massachusetts

English Puritans were convinced that a true church of the elect (those redeemed by God's grace) could not survive within a church ruled by the Crown rather than Christ, and they believed that the (predestined) elect, servants of Christ on earth, must be free to shape their churches to conform to the gospel. In America, therefore, self-governing congregations formed the colony's primary social structure. Civil authority, exercising coercive force, gained legitimacy only to the extent that it governed consistently with church teachings. Puritan ventures to Massachusetts thus sought not only to secure churches conducive to Puritan worship but also to form civil societies that would adhere to scripture; like Calvin in Geneva, Puritans designed their governments to serve the church. While Puritans scrupulously separated realms of church and state authority, their polity suppressed heresy, enforced laws of Christian morality, and acceded to advice of church leaders; conversely, ministers used sermons to reinforce civil authority, preaching strict obedience to civil law.

Puritans believed God provided natural reason so people could comprehend the world, if not its Creator. Yet, as inherently sinful, people must subordinate their ambition to God's will. Piety, the proper human attitude, required devotion of natural talent to furthering God's will as expressed in scripture. While nobody could merit salvation by works, God's covenant required that people serve God in return for the possibility of salvation for some, and held each person responsible for the welfare of the whole. Taking love of neighbor to be a sign of salvation, Puritans put group above individual and used scripture to shape legal definitions of the public good.

Massachusetts began as two separate colonies, which were not united until the late 1600s. Pilgrims, who were radical Puritans seeking complete separation from the Church of England, reached Plymouth in 1620. Since the colony had no specialized police, law enforcement in early Plymouth meant imposition of community norms by group action. Civil law was integrated with church doctrine, and disputes were resolved in three institutions with overlapping jurisdiction: town meetings, church congregations, and law courts. Any dispute could be brought to any forum, but town meetings generally resolved the few cases that set policy for the entire community. In each forum the goal was the same: restoration of community through extirpation of sin, which was, by definition, whatever caused division and antagonism, civil or criminal.

In 1630, less radically separatist Puritans settled a second Bay colony. The newly elected Governor, John Winthrop, arrived with a charter signed by Charles I that created a joint-stock company dedicated to earning profits; it allowed the company to establish any laws not in conflict with English law. Immediately, however, the colonists ignored even this minimal limitation, looking chiefly to the Bible, not England, for direction. The charter authorized the creation of "one greate, generall, and solempe Assemblie" known as "The Great and Generall Courtes," with executive, legislative, and judicial authority. Court members, or magistrates, bound by law to serve God and Gospel, exercised essentially equitable authority. Ministers were regularly summoned to advise magistrates, even on matters of trade and foreign relations. Moreover, the body politic itself was constituted only of (male) church members. While membership rates for early years are uncertain, by

1652 perhaps half of adult males were church members, a percentage that declined during the century.

Colonists brought private disputes to the General Court, which had original, and later appellate, jurisdiction over criminal and civil matters. The use of a consent-based political body to adjudicate personal disputes reflected the communitarian attitude that all matters were public and also the Puritan belief that the soundest "law" was the discerning judgment of the godly people. Church elders served as a final court of appeals, resolving disputes over charter interpretation and General Court authority; possibly, this process was a reflection of the religious origins of appeal rights (to Rome). Growth of the colony required division of the General Court into two houses in 1634. Further growth led to formation of county courts in the 1640s, whose chief function was to maintain "an able and faithful ministry" and remove any "perniciously Heterodox" preacher.

Early laws secured conformity by requiring support of congregational churches and attendance at services; full church membership came only with proof of conversion. Massachusetts, unlike Virginia, did not immediately regulate church attendance: until 1635 no compulsion was necessary. Each Bay settlement asserted authority to banish heretical groups or ministers and to regulate behavior to conform to Christian virtue. Laws of the 1630s and 1640s, before codification, already punished idleness, stubbornness, card playing, fishing out of season, bowling, drunkenness, lying, swearing, and taking the Lord's name in vain. Other laws punished single women for entertaining men at home or corrupting youth. Notably, however, enforcement of sexual morality was largely free of gender bias: eradication of sin meant male as well as female sin.

Laws also fostered communal interdependence. In 1635 the General Court ordered that no home be built more than one-half mile from a church. This proved impractical, but later modifications served similar goals. In business dealings, subordination of private interest to common good meant merchants and artisans faced criminal fines and civil liability for the "oppression" of charging more than a "fair" price for goods or services. Leaders also discouraged controversy and litigation. Before the 1670s most disputes were arbitrated by clergy and resolved on principles of equity and community norms, with the goal of preserving the integrity of the community.

Puritans did not think that this communitarianism compromised individual liberty. Rather, they defined liberty as the freedom necessary to conform one's life to God's teachings. Liberty, which they cherished, was a pre-condition to the construction of godly community – the opportunity to fuse Christian piety with service to the public good. Communal peace and reciprocal charity were the ends of liberty, not alternatives to the protection of individual freedom. Accordingly, disputes resolved in law tribunals were not subject to different goals than those which proceeded to arbitration. As late as the 1740s, judges charged juries "to use law to create 'a civil and Christian state'" so as to eliminate "vice, profaneness, and immorality" and reform mankind "with a Due Regard to God."

Later generations, beginning perhaps with Hawthorne, have looked with morbid fascination on Puritan laws that attacked free expression and sexual license. Such laws, however, simply recognized widely shared Christian norms; similar laws existed in England and other colonies, but were enforced mainly when public peace was threatened. New England is distinctive chiefly for its prosecutorial rigor and consistency (with enforcement rates between 200 and 400 percent higher than in the South), and extended retention (sometimes into the nineteenth century). Massachusetts law texts explicitly noted their dependence on religion: in 1665 the General Court stated that "subjection to ecclesiastical discipline is necessary for the well-being of any Christian society," and until 1672 the title page of the code book often carried a quote from Romans 13:12 – "Whosoever therefore resisteth the power, resisteth the ordinance of God: and they that resist shall receive to themselves damnation." Even in exacting punishment the colony conformed to scripture. Deuteronomy provided punishment with up to forty stripes; Massachusetts's judges usually assessed up to thirty-nine strokes, always to a bare back, but sometimes "well" or "severely laid on."

Sex offenses and offenses against marriage constituted over half the prosecuted crimes and covered a wide range of behaviors, reflecting the crucial role of family as a microcosm of the public moral order. Puritans were robustly enthusiastic about sex in marriage, but they feared its errant, defiant tendencies (mirroring human disobedience of God) and its consequent capacity to disrupt community. John Hobell in 1641 and Robert Crocker in 1642 were each whipped for breaching promises to marry. In 1640, Margery Rugs was given "39 lashes, well-laid on" for behaving in "enticing and alluring" ways. Two years earlier Alice Burwoode was whipped for "yielding" and "not crying out" during apparently consensual sex with John Bickerstaffe, who received thirty-nine lashes for fornication.

The General Court in 1677 required towns to appoint tithing men to inspect the lives and homes of neighbors, looking for Sabbath-breaking, intemperance, sexual misconduct, and profanity. These oversight duties, moreover, were assumed by all townspeople: in 1682, 19-year-old Mary Brown testified to seeing James Creeke kiss and tickle the wife of another man. Speech laws not only protected the names of God and Jesus but also Calvinist doctrine. In 1684, during heated debate between two Calvinists,

Joseph Gatchell argued that if Christ had spoken as his companion asserted, He was "an Imperfect Saviour." Gatchell was taken to the pillory, where his tongue was drawn and pierced with a hot iron.

The history of the Bay colony can be summarized as a tenacious struggle to perpetuate Calvinist doctrine within a community radically altered by immigration, aggressive territorial expansion, Enlightenment thinking, and a market economy based on profitable international trade. Whether one sees persistence, declension, or reformulation of Calvinist doctrine depends as much on perspective as on record. In 1646, confronting declining church membership and increased heresy, ministers met in synod and drafted the Cambridge Platform to reassert that all public institutions were derived from the "Word of God" and were dependent on the true church of visible saints. Church elders were still to make and enforce the laws, control church discipline, and shape political debate. The problems did not end, however. In 1657, again at synod, the ministers adopted the "half-way covenant," which gave partial participation in the church and hope of salvation to baptized persons unable to give testimony of regeneration. More willing than men to give experiential accounts of conversion, women had become the majority in full church membership. The half-way covenant provided the inclusiveness expected of an established church and perpetuated clerical power.

As compared to other colonies, Puritan New England preserved much of its ethnic and religious homogeneity and even its relative economic equality, but it was not exempt from change. By century's end, growth and land scarcity led to family dispersal, extended governance, and impersonal trade relations. Accommodating business transactions between strangers and even people with different languages, transactional law imposed new objective standards, reflecting and contributing to rising individualism. Preachers saw in these changes the erosion of communal ideals: sermons excoriated listeners for the selfish pursuit of luxury and described plagues and Indian violence as proof of God's wrath.

The quest for cultural homogeneity sometimes took a desperate tone. The witchcraft scares of the late 1600s, for example, may evince the depth of desire to perpetuate communitarianism amidst fears arising from increased diversity, social change, and religious uncertainty. Authorities applied old concepts of law, which integrated Calvinist doctrine and communal values, both to define and eliminate problems of non-conformity, but the law, the doctrine, and the values were found wanting. Salem ended its persecutions with grave doubts about the efficacy of spectral evidence (visions and spiritual forms), bringing into question the extent to which law could fully incorporate religious belief. That question hung as a Damocles' sword over the viability of a jurisprudence rooted in Calvinist doctrine, but even in the mid-eighteenth century, Massachusetts' courts still admitted hauntings and spiritual presences as evidence in valuing real property.

Challenges to the Puritan establishment also mounted from outside Massachusetts. After the English Restoration, Charles II demanded suffrage rights for Anglicans. The Bay colony, in response, repealed its restrictions, but then passed new ones requiring all voters to prove, by card or letter from an orthodox minister, that they were Calvinist in religion, virtuous in lifestyle, and current in paying taxes and taking communion. In 1684 the Crown vacated the charter for the colony's failure to conform to charter prescription and the laws of England: in support, London cited the Bay's refusal to extend the franchise to non-orthodox Christians, its punishment of dissenters, its use of scripture as the primary source of law, and its incomplete fidelity to the King. James II installed royal governors to rule Massachusetts.

The Revolution of 1688 was thus as "glorious" in Massachusetts as in England, but it did not help the colony regain its old charter. Increase Mather agreed to a second charter in 1691 that provided for a Crown-appointed governor with veto power over all legislation. The General Court survived as a single house of representatives, popularly elected, but all Protestants could vote and practice their own religion and all legal decisions were ultimately appealable to London.

The laws of 1692 accommodated England's demand for limited religious toleration, consistent with its own new Act of Toleration. Each town was ordered to appoint and support an "able learned, orthodox minister or ministers." Costs of the minister's salary, church, and teaching were paid by general taxes, but dissenters were free to attend and support their own churches. In 1727, in response to petitions to England, Massachusetts also created tax exemptions for dissenters, although to be eligible a taxpayer needed a document from his minister stating he attended a dissenting church located within five miles of his home and objected to the established religion as a matter of conscience. Dissenting churches also needed legislative recognition to receive tax support from an exempt taxpayer. The paucity of dissenting churches, even in the 1720s, limited the effectiveness of the exemption provision; Baptist churches had become common in Massachusetts, but members of less popular sects often had no nearby church, and irreligious people were required to support their town's Congregational churches.

Massachusetts adopted a new court system after consolidation of the colonies and imposition of the new charter. Even then, struggling against change, it perpetuated the jurisdictional overlap between law courts and churches, and churches continued to urge members to resolve disputes over property and tort among themselves. Also, until the mid-eighteenth century, election to the jury, by town meeting, required attending a

Congregational church: the jury, like the congregation of the elect itself, approximated God's voice on earth and decided law as well as facts.

Massachusetts consistently sought religious conformity despite growing resistance. As late as the mid-eighteenth century, laws were passed to give Jesuits only weeks to remove themselves, and throughout the century crimes against morality dominated criminal courts. On average, 50 percent of criminal prosecutions addressed sex offenses (other than rape), violations of Sabbath, and use of profanity. Until the Revolution Massachusetts punished adultery with up to forty stripes and the black letter "A." By mid-century all colonial America confronted the tension between an emerging modern economy and the communitarianism of an earlier era, but nowhere was this tension so great as in Massachusetts, where communitarianism retained such powerful Calvinist vibrancy.

New England: Rhode Island

The colony of Rhode Island emerged after the legal prosecution of dissenters had revealed theological dilemmas deep at the core of Massachusetts's experiment in applied Calvinism. After banishment, Roger Williams founded Providence, and Anne Hutchinson settled in Portsmouth. As other dissidents followed, religious quarrels soon intersected with land disputes, leading to disruptive township controversies and border conflicts with Massachusetts and Connecticut. Outside observers saw only anarchy in the absence of religious establishment. Routinely invoking images of cesspools and contagion (metaphors of defilement from within), they cited Rhode Island as proof that toleration of schismatics would always lead to civil chaos. Nevertheless, by moving from radical church/state separation to legally protected denominationalism, Rhode Island in fact achieved a high level of stability by the mid-1700s.

With no charter from England, Rhode Islanders confronted the question of legal legitimacy as a theological matter of first principle. Williams had denounced the Massachusetts effort to use law, even law based on the Old Testament, to serve religion. Such use, he argued (with a characteristic reversal of metaphor) contaminated Christian freedom and defiled the purity of Christ's church with the coercions of the earthly city. Some Rhode Islanders were eager to take the next logical step: if Christian freedom superseded the law when the New Testament superseded the Old, then the true Christian should not be bound by any law. Thus arose the famous Rhode Island tendency to see even the most minimal civil restriction as yet another instance of illegitimate tyranny – an antinomian zeal for liberty no less rooted in Protestantism than the Massachusetts zeal for coerced moral conformity. In contrast to some of his followers, however, Williams himself did not dispute the need for secular law; he disputed law's contamination of the sacred, and its claim to divine sanction. Unlike the true church founded by Christ, he insisted legal authority, tainted by coercion, was a merely human construction, a concession to human imperfectability. Thus its legitimacy was no more than provisional: while individuals could be baptized and redeemed, the state could not.

Given their commitment to Christian liberty the earliest Providence settlers relied on equality, not religion, to foster community and showed their Baptist aversion to coercion by trying to minimize the role of formal law. Government originated as a fortnightly meeting of household heads. When the first newcomers arrived, villagers laid out equal house lots, fields, and commons – the New England village without inequality or common church. The guiding principle was complete religious toleration and church/state separation. Householders agreed to land distribution and dispute settlement by five arbitrators, a method considered more rooted in true natural law than fixed rules. Early records show little crime, with freemen collectively subduing the rare delinquent. Rhode Island (not uniquely) was slow to build jails.

Subsequent newcomers were compelled to sign an agreement to obey the original freemen, who claimed, as a right automatically flowing to risk-taking founders, the privilege to structure their community by limiting others' suffrage and land ownership. Newcomers challenged this freeman definition of "equal" rights and "free" consent, which was never approved by Williams. The contested inequality at the core of Providence society produced fateful conflicts that soon reached out to neighboring colonies – as any Protestant schooled in Augustine should have predicted. The meaning of religious liberty was itself contested when a woman attended more of Williams' religious meetings than were sanctioned by her husband. The town tried to protect the wife from her husband's beatings, which he considered his religious privilege to administer. When Rhode Island law refused to recognize this husband's freedom to perform his "religious duty," he led his wife back to Massachusetts with a rope.

Radical theologians pushed Rhode Island into ever more radical realms of social liberty. Portsmouth settlers avoided the problem of legal legitimacy by establishing no secular government at all. Eschewing political authority, for a time they simply conveyed governance to William Coddington, who like Hutchinson sought his own direct communion with Christ. Samuel Gorton, espousing a similar antinomianism, was serially banished from Plymouth, Portsmouth, and Providence for denying the legitimacy of all civil authority. Welcome nowhere, he and followers founded Warwick to live with God as their only judge. In Rhode Island community was achieved more often by withdrawal and reformation than by law.

Contested definitions of liberty led to conflicts that threatened the whole colony with invasion. Rhode Islanders finally asked Williams to seek a patent from England, by then the only available source of legal legitimacy. Granted in 1643/4 and reconfirmed after the Restoration by corporate charter, the patent conveyed full lawmaking and judicial authority. Rhode Island government could claim English legitimacy, even if not, as Williams insisted, divine sanction. After the grant of the patent, Warwick and Providence loosely joined the governments of Newport and Portsmouth, which had, without complete success, attempted reconsolidation under the hopeful motto, "Amor Vincet Omnia."

In 1647 Rhode Island enacted its first Code of Law. The Code established a superior court, the Court of Tryals, which for a time simply consisted of a general assembly and later became a traveling sessions court that heard both criminal and civil disputes. The prickly question, as always, was legitimacy. The (unknown) drafters of the Code implicitly rejected the Old Testament model, as superseded by gospel freedom. Instead, they looked to scriptural authority for their recourse to English law by basing organization of the Code on 1 Timothy 9–10, wherein Paul explains that law is not for the godly, but for the sinful – for those who kill their father or mother, for murderers, whoremongers, sodomites, and the like. The Code therefore organized crimes by following those headings, as in "Touching Murdering of Fathers and Mothers" and "Touching Whoremongers." This reference to Paul presumably justified Christian recourse to secular forms of legal coercion. Then, more than in any other colony, the drafters used English law as their source, specifically Dalton's manual for justices of the peace. Approximately 85 percent of Rhode Island criminal law had its direct source in England; by way of contrast, Massachusetts took only about 40 percent of its penal law from England and roughly the same from the Bible.

Consistent with separatist principles, the Code recognized no crimes of heresy, Sabbath violation, or blasphemy. Reflecting its recent history and still irrepressible Christian desire for community, however, it did give unusual attention to crimes of general disorder. For example, it not only retained the law against riot (dropped by other colonies) but also described with specificity how riots and breaches of the peace should be handled. Assault, slander, and defamation were criminalized under the general category of disturbing the peace, and contempt was described as a "kind of Rebellion." Notably absent were offenses against trade, such as fair price violations, perhaps suggesting the conceptual link between religious disestablishment and free markets.

The 1663 Charter affirmed Rhode Island's "livelie experiment" to prove that a "civill state may stand and best bee maintained . . . " with religious liberty and that "true pietye rightly grounded upon gospel" will give sufficient "security to sovereignetye . . . " A further clause released the colony from conformity to the Church of England. Rhode Island was, indeed, utterly unique in its degree of church/state separation. It had no parish taxes or boundaries, no land grants to churches, no tax exemption for church property, no laws requiring church attendance or urging family devotion, no clergy authority to license marriages, no public support for education, and no oaths in court or for swearing in officers.

The disruptive early years might have suggested that Rhode Island's "livelie experiment" was doomed to failure; the Christian charity required to sustain community seemed to require some degree of legal compulsion. While some groups, notably the Quakers, provided communal cohesion and mutual support, elsewhere basic services like education and poor relief, publicly supported within a parish structure, were often neglected. Williams was forced to urge aid for specific cases of need, suggesting the lack of routine care. Eventually, however, a new set of legal understandings began to emerge that would remain workable even for the post-Revolution state government. By the mid-seventeenth century, radical separatism had left churches with minimal institutional structure – often not even a building – and no ties to the legal order. This stark separation began to change in the late seventeenth and early eighteenth centuries in ways that shaped legal culture, even as a proliferation of printed legal forms and an expanding legal professionalism began to shape religion.

One example, recently traced, serves as an illustration. In 1676 John Clarke, a leader of the First Baptist Church in Newport and Charter negotiator, died leaving a large bequest in trust for relief of the poor and education of poor children, with instructions to trustees to have special regard for those who feared God. A charitable trust specifically to benefit poor Baptists was arguably precluded by English law, which prohibited donations to religious uses outside the Church of England, and by Parliament's Charitable Uses Act of 1601, which limited permissible charitable uses largely to the secular, underscoring their public nature. Charter language about repugnancy to English law therefore might void colonial bequests to a non-Anglican church. While Clarke had not confined charitable benefits to Baptists, he had clearly wanted First Baptist oversight of the trust and its uses.

Trouble arose when an irresponsible Baptist trustee used trust land for his own benefit. A fellow congregant sought the Newport Council's help, and the Council tried to seize the property for town use. Extensive legal proceedings, including threatened appeal to England and two Acts of the Rhode Island General Assembly, produced Rhode Island's first charitable trust law, which uniformly protected charitable bequests in trust to any religious denomination or secular charity. In practice the law allowed extremely broad trustee discretion while also authorizing legal supervision to prevent corruption. Subsequent trustees of the Clarke bequest submitted accounts to prove honest management, but otherwise owed nothing to the public and in fact used the trust for a building and for clergy salary, not just charity.

Starting with complete disestablishment, early Rhode Island law thus began to pre-figure reconceptualizations of church/state relations in post-revolutionary America whereby religion would support charity and moral community from within a realm of private ordering, with resources protected by the (public) law of property, corporation, and trust – and ultimately by the Constitution. The public construction of moral community, and of conscience itself – a task central to Puritanism – would drop from view, as would the public nature of private law categories themselves.

Another aspect of the Clarke case also illustrated emerging trends. When litigation produced church conflict, a sister Baptist church was called to arbitrate. Arbitration exerted moral pressure on the wayward trustee to surrender authority, averting Council intervention. This move strengthened denominational ties, once almost non-existent among Baptists, and illustrated the subtle coordination of (public) legal action and (private) religious persuasion – pointing toward religion's future role in the new republic.

Institutionalism grew quickly. Baptists owned property, erected buildings, paid educated ministers with endowments, and founded a college (now Brown University) – all activities that embroiled them in the legal system to a degree that would have shocked John Clarke no less than Roger Williams. This involvement with law strengthened the legitimacy of legal professionalism while protecting the strength of professionalized institutional religion. Denominationalism advanced on a foundation of institutional strength secured by legally protected wealth and autonomy, producing structures of hierarchical authority that roughly paralleled, and subtly reinforced, the formalized hierarchical legal order under the charter. Other denominations, especially Congregationalists, brought links to other colonies, and even Baptists formed intercolonial ties. Quakers flourished, as did a Jewish synagogue at Newport. Anglicanism was popular among the upper classes, although Rhode Island resisted all moves toward its establishment.

Incorporation paralleled trust law. The Anglicans' Trinity Church in Newport was the first to seek incorporation. Other Anglican, then Congregational, and one Baptist church followed. Incorporation guaranteed property protection and some degree of state coercion to enforce church rules, as with pew rents, but never became the instrument of political establishment it was in some colonies. Quakers, rejecting the government support that incorporation still implied, achieved similar goals by the adept use of trust and property law.

With no established church, Rhode Island experienced Great Awakening intra-denominational controversy, but not upheaval. Even the Revolution did not destabilize forms of governance that had become traditional. Church and state achieved a mutual accommodation and reinforcement that strengthened both law and religion without undermining a shared cultural commitment to religious freedom, as it was understood. Ironically, given the quarrels that led to Rhode Island's founding, "as it was understood" meant as defined, in large part, by the state's legal culture.

The Middle Colonies: New York

The story of law and religion in New York is in part the story of America's future. From the start the colony dedicated itself to trade and profit, not religious purity, and its population was characterized by a religious and ethnic diversity unimaginable in New England. On the eve of the Revolution, however, the shared culture of mutually defining and reinforcing legal and religious forms, which had finally emerged in Rhode Island, still eluded New York. Instead, religious quarrels intersected with quarrels over the meaning of crucial legal categories like property and corporation. New York had accommodated rampant diversity; nevertheless, it still struggled over a basic question of governance – freedom's relation to hierarchical authority and the coercions of law.

The Dutch preceded the British to New York and profoundly influenced the province. The charter founding New Amsterdam in 1628 stipulated an established Calvinist Dutch Reformed Church: no other religion could be publicly admitted, and the West India Company (WIC) pledged to provide suitable preachers under supervision of the church governing body, the Classis, in Amsterdam. The first minister, or dominie, arrived promptly, expecting to build a structured religious life coordinate to the structured polity planned by Governor Stuyvesant – tight burgher regulation of both civic life and economic activity. Stuyvesant assumed that civic control depended on religious uniformity and cooperated with the dominies by stamping out dissidents: he jailed Lutherans just for conducting home worship services.

Nevertheless, by the 1640s this tidy model of cooperative church/civic control confronted a social reality of inhabitants from at least a half-dozen countries speaking eighteen languages and practicing religions that included Catholicism, Judaism, and a dizzying variety of Protestant sects. The WIC, eager for the profits that accompanied population growth, directed Stuyvesant to lift regulation over both religion and trade. The dominies despaired but after mid-century abandoned the goal of unity and successfully built up their own thirteen Dutch churches – until the English takeover.

The English seized New York in 1664 and ruled under a proprietary patent from Charles II to his brother, James, which conveyed virtually unlimited political, economic, and religious authority. James delegated authority to a series of English governors who established a small provincial aristocracy: huge manorial land grants, with the option of manor courts, were combined with commercial monopoly privileges and government contracts to consolidate aristocratic power.

Anglican and some Dutch clergy located themselves within this aristocracy, but during the first years of English rule there was no move toward establishment. Instead, under the plural structure of the early Duke's Laws, limited toleration masked subtle forms of civil control. The Laws mandated a parish system wherein each parish elected overseers who called (chose) an ordained Protestant minister – not necessarily an Anglican. Overseers, backed by courts, collected money for church construction, salary payment, poor relief, and general management of parochial affairs. These civilly elected church officials also reported, in open sessions, all "swearing, prophaneness, Sabbath breaking, drunkenness, fornication, adultery, and all such abominable sinnes."

Governors and courts rigorously enforced support for churches, but taxes were resented and local ministers became identified with the colonial political order. Moreover, officials easily exerted pressure over potentially disruptive ministers: dissenting preachers who moved in anti-Anglican directions of greater church purity (for example, by refusing infant baptism) could be threatened with no salary. In consequence, often Tory ministers preached to rebellious congregations. Antagonism ran high, linking political grievances to religious dissent.

Dutch resentment was especially intense. Close ties linked Dutch and English upper classes to conservative Dutch and English clergy, but the majority of the Dutch still resented English rule. Resentment mounted when the English instituted aggressive Anglicanizing measures, closing Dutch schools and imposing English Law and a Naturalization Act. Under English coverture law women lost their legal identity at marriage and could no longer manage property. By contrast, Dutch women were accustomed to owning property, engaging in trade in their own names, and enjoying the benefit of inheritance laws that reflected their relatively strong position in Dutch culture. The economic and cultural subservience expected by the English was alien to them.

New Yorkers stubbornly resisted English attempts to impose uniformity. An "anti-Catholic" rebellion, waged with Dutch leadership in the name of Calvinism and England's Glorious (Protestant) Revolution, succeeded briefly between 1689 and 1691. When it was quelled, the new governor, Benjamin Fletcher, convinced the Assembly to pass a Ministry Act, which he interpreted as establishing the Church of England in New York City and four provincial counties. Nevertheless, elected vestry and wardens, backed by the Assembly, refused to call an Anglican minister. Fletcher then granted a corporate charter to Trinity, New York City's new Anglican church. Under that charter the elected civil vestrymen were required to collect funds for Trinity's rector from city inhabitants; the rector could sue them for refusal. The corporate body of Trinity elected separate vestrymen, so that the governing body of the church was insulated from control by the (usually dissenting) elected civil vestry – an ironic move in the direction of privatizing the corporation even while publicly enforcing Anglican establishment. In a parallel move Fletcher incorporated the Dutch Reformed Church, so that Dutch and Anglican churches, both under the control of conservative ministers, formed a mutually congenial elite. Both Trinity and elite Dutch churches received extensive land grants; one Dutch dominie with close ties to the Anglicans also received a personal grant of 700,000 acres.

The Fletcher grants of land and corporate privileges, given exclusively to Dutch and Anglican churches and to a few powerful individuals, contaminated religion and politics for decades. Identified with a monopolized and Crown-controlled economy and at odds with growing commercialization, the grants left many inhabitants disillusioned with religion in general. Poor relief and education, entrusted to churches, suffered from conflict and indifference. The result was quiet alienation among the Dutch (who resented their own privileged clergy's alliance with the English) and also among most of the English (who were never majority Anglican).

During the early eighteenth century the Society for the Propagation of the Gospel in London dedicated new resources to Anglican missionary work. With London financing and provincial government support, Anglicans could proselytize on a scale no other religion could match. Books of Common Prayer, many in Dutch, inundated the province. Anglicans made inroads among French Protestants and also among Long Island Congregationalists, as Cotton Mather noted with dismay in 1706. So too, they finally converted many disheartened Dutch. Missionaries taught children English while catechizing them: the goal was cultural as well as religious conversion. To aid Anglican education, the governor under Queen Anne pressured the Assembly to pass an Act for Encouragement of a Common Free School, with the salary of an orthodox Anglican schoolmaster paid by a general tax.

In reaction, there was a brief resurgence of Dutch culture. Indeed, the first stirrings of the Great Awakening in America occurred among the New York Dutch, brought by Theodorus Frelinghuesen of the Raritan Valley. Frelingheusen attacked the hierarchical structures and formalized worship that characterized both the Church of England and conservative Dutch churches, and his emphasis on the intense awareness of sin that must precede the experience of grace led him to challenge upper-class complacency. Preaching for a time in a barn when conservatives took over his church, he drew on the ordinary experience of Dutch farmers, not the conventions of formalized worship, to convey his radicalized message of sin and redemption. Soon, however, he was just one of many New Light preachers forming evangelical alliances across denominational and cultural boundaries; Dutch distinctiveness dropped out.

By 1750 the colony's embrace of commerce had influenced its law, and many New Yorkers did not attend church: the unchurched, the New Lights, and religious traditionalists emerged as three separate political forces. Religious splits had also been exacerbated by the pressure of extensive grants on land availability. Whereas some governors favored the Fletcher policy of achieving legal/religious control through land conveyance, others, following Crown policy, disfavored huge grants because they stifled development, despite lenient tenancy terms. The Crown also defended Indian land claims for the sake of retaining Iroquois allegiance; attacked by the French and their Indian allies, the Iroquois were not protected by white settlers, whose main concern was land, not the honor of alliance. Repeated government grant revocations and rerevocations rendered titles uncertain; so too did vague boundaries, Indian claims, and frequent failure of proprietors to honor semi-feudal obligations like quitrent payments – even while tenants were pressured to honor theirs. Conflicts arose as settlers, often with governor approval, established dissenting New England-type townships on lands claimed by proprietors.

Such conflicts, often violent, became commonplace after mid-century. They dramatically juxtaposed two models of religious life, Anglican and dissenting (with unchurched liberals often joining dissenters). And they illustrated, in externalized form, the same Protestant tension between hierarchical public order and radical Christian egalitarian freedom that the Puritans tried so hard to contain. Legally, such conflicts dramatically pitted ownership by title against ownership through labor and use. In handling resulting disputes, lawyers began to construct a conception of rights that could protect property from either religiously sanctioned political hierarchy or disruptive, dissenting, leveling usurpation. But that process was far from complete on the eve of the Revolution.

Similar conflicts occurred in relation to incorporation, which in Rhode Island already meant impartial legal protection for a variety of independent associations but in New York still represented religious and political privilege. During the King's College debates, right before the Revolution, a famous "Triumvirate" of Enlightenment Whig journalists of the type represented by Franklin in Pennsylvania joined with Presbyterians to argue that an educational corporation should mean a self-governing corporate body chartered by the Assembly, not, as proposed, a delegation of Crown authority subject to and incorporating Anglican ecclesiastical authority; the Triumvirate made explicit comparison to an economy weighed down by monopoly privilege and Crown control, in contrast to the vigor of free commerce. They lost the battle, and King's College (now Columbia) was incorporated under the Crown. They lost because conservative Dutch clergy, promised an endowed professorship, helped urge Assembly passage of the Anglican corporate form. Debates during the 1769 elections compelled the Assembly to extend incorporation rights to all Protestant churches and to allow exemptions from church taxes in the four counties where they were still collected. The governor vetoed even those changes, however, although fewer than one in ten New Yorkers attended an Anglican church.

Thus, the much-cited (and very real) pluralism and materialism of New York masked lingering vestiges of starkly hierarchical conceptualism, incorporating ecclesiology, legal form, and social/economic ordering. That hierarchy had suffered repeated challenge. Resulting conflicts remained unresolved but an evolving legal conceptualization had started the process of aligning religious and market freedom, each as associated with an emerging privatization of property and corporation rights.

The Middle Colonies: Pennsylvania

Pennsylvania emerged from paradox. Founded by a pacifist sect that shunned worldly power, it quickly produced a sophisticated legal framework for government, an effective system of social control, and a learned and prosperous group of leaders. In short, it mirrored the paradoxes of its founder, a dedicated Quaker who was also a skilled profit-seeking gentleman lawyer. Pennsylvania contained such sectarian diversity that visiting ministers commonly likened it, with New York, to Babel – a reference once reserved for quarreling Europe. In contrast to the hierarchy/voluntarism conflicts of New York, Pennsylvania's competing religious directions moved horizontally, so to speak, from all-inclusive spiritualism to strict Biblicist separatism. Quakers were its dominant influence, but that influence created a legally secured spiritual ecumenicalism that precluded religious establishment and opened the way for the rationalized ecumenicalism of the Enlightenment.

By the 1680s, when they came to Pennsylvania in large numbers, Quakers were already dispersed throughout the colonies but usually as a despised sect. Quakers publicly ridiculed hierarchy in church and polity, taking it as sign of sinful pride. Three New England colonies passed laws banning

Quakers; when they reappeared in Massachusetts magistrates resorted to tarring, ear cropping, and, in four cases, hanging. The named crime was sedition.

Quaker theology was Protestant, but tended toward universalism by describing grace, not as an unearned gift to the elect, but as living spirit present in all. Quakers believed this spirit, or light of grace dwelling in each person, could overcome original sin, but in the fallen world carnal pride had led to hierarchy and violence. Eschewing that violence, Quakers stressed the role of family and community in nurturing the inner light: tender conversation, free from self-serving pretenses, could perfect children's spirits and maintain the community in near-Edenic innocence. Given this Quaker emphasis on domesticity – as well as the role of Margaret Fell as almost co-equal founder of the movement, with George Fox – women equaled men in influence.

William Penn's own background was a complex mix of spirit and worldliness. Son of an admiral favored by the Stuarts, Penn learned law and became a Quaker against his father's wishes. In England he challenged Quaker persecution by appealing to traditional English legal rights; one of his victories helped establish juror independence. Granted Pennsylvania in payment for a debt owed his father, Penn set out to found a "Holy Experiment" in religious toleration, which he conceived in terms of legally protected liberty. As profit-seeking proprietor he also retained traditional feudal legal rights like quitrents, escheat, and tax exemption, which soon led to conflict with the Quaker-dominated Assembly. Nevertheless, Penn's effort to use law in service of liberty served as one precedent for American constitutionalism.

Penn's first "Frame of Government" was a Quaker document informed by both liberal and republican political theory. After addressing, in typical republican fashion, the nature of monarchy, aristocracy, and democracy, Penn incorporated all three in an institutional framework with a governor (Penn), an elected Council of 72 to propose law, and a rotating Assembly to accept it – a separation of "debate" from "result" possibly taken from Harringtonian republicanism but also consistent with decision making in Quaker meetings, where debate was followed by a separate "sense of the meeting." (Later the Assembly demanded a more powerful unicameral legislature, granted in a 1701 Charter of Liberties that included amendment rights.) In a "Prologue" Penn laid out his theology of government, starting with the Augustinian assumption that the unfortunate reality of evil in the world justified legal coercion, which was required for order but was never itself free of sin. Penn also proposed, however, the ideal of a tender government, used not just to terrify evildoers but also to "cherish those that do well," and he argued for "kindness, goodness, and charity," in cares "more soft, and daily necessary." Since social nurturing would have occurred without the Fall, presumably it escaped the taint of sin otherwise implicit in law.

A "Great Law" followed the Frame, laying down Penn's goal of toleration among Christians and making notable changes in penal law. The Law's rights-based purpose was to preserve "Christian and Civill Liberty" against both private injustice and government tyranny. The first law guaranteed freedom of conscience (since God alone is "Lord of Conscience") for all who acknowledged a Supreme Being; all but atheists were citizens, no taxes supported churches, and abuse of another's religion constituted breach of the peace. Nevertheless, only Christians could hold office and the Law prohibited blasphemy, profanity, and breach of the Sabbath along with the usual sex offenses, drunkenness, and "harmful" games like cards and cockfighting. Thus the Law reflected Quaker belief that the spirit cannot be coerced, but should be protected from worldly sin – an uneasy combination.

Penal law reform was equally Quaker. Elsewhere physical punishment was the norm, including flogging, cropping, and the rack. Public corporal punishment instructed the community's conscience as well as the offender's; except in capital cases, a quick return to community followed and prisons played a minor role. The Great Law, by contrast, eliminated the death penalty for all crimes except premeditated murder; and, except for whipping in cases of adultery, rape, or sodomy, limited punishment to fines and imprisonment (with labor) in a house of corrections. The Christian purpose was rehabilitation – a rekindling of the spirit through removal from the carnal world and direct communion with God. (Repealed by England in 1718, these reforms were reintroduced with the Revolution, becoming the penitentiary system.) Also consistent with honest Quaker conversation were reforms like plain language in pleadings, open publication of laws and official salaries, and protection of Indians from liquor-induced land sales; such reforms became well known in the colonies, while Penn's Christian goal of a "cherishing" government was reflected in Pennsylvania's unusual civil provisions for poor relief.

Religion was a powerful coordinate means of social control. At monthly meetings Quakers considered no concern too "private" for intervention: excessive ornamentation, prideful speech, untender childrearing, harsh treatment of servants, indebtedness, or the need for charitable relief. Marriage, which provided nurture for children's tender spirits, was of particular importance; committees carefully monitored a couple before granting approval, and parents encouraged "in meeting" marriage by rewarding couples with ample land.

Given that reward system, Pennsylvania became a rural landscape of large separate family farms, linked by invisible but effective family and religious control. Accordingly, government operated at the county, not township, level, and both taxation and participation in public life were minimal. Despite Penn's defense of law, most Quakers disliked legality. They discouraged suits against each other, refused to take oaths (assuming honesty in all speech), and as pacifists might refuse to apprehend criminals. Early Assemblymen were notorious for a reluctance to pass laws and a refusal to speak except when moved by the spirit. County courts were used chiefly to register deeds, wills, or transactions and to recover debts; letters to Europe praised the near absence of government. For disputes that did go to court, over debt or fences or occasional crime, records indicate a high level of compliance (as with uncontested debt recovery); Quaker legal reforms apparently helped induce cooperation.

Despite its egalitarianism, a hierarchy emerged not explicitly based on wealth and power, but incorporating both. Wealthy Quakers were the ones most successful in keeping children in meeting, thus earning moral prestige. Chosen for high-level meeting tasks, they were also, in practical effect, chosen at meeting for Assembly and judicial office. Notwithstanding formal disestablishment, meeting authority and political power became intertwined. As the prestige of a selective Yearly Meeting in Philadelphia grew, paralleling Philadelphia's growth as a commercial center, a powerful, religiously based political force emerged: the "Quaker Party" was arguably the first major American political party.

The Quaker family model of land distribution, more than either the (dissenting) township or (Anglican) estate model, provided extraordinary surplus productivity and hence the foundation for Quaker trading wealth and political dominance until the 1750s. It was also the foundation for an increasingly privatized conception of property, at odds with Penn's own feudal model. By mid-century, however, Quakers were only a fourth of the population, and Germans close to half. The intersection of German with Quaker culture produced complex, sometimes conflicting, currents of influence. For example, German Moravians shared the Quaker tendency toward spiritualized universalism, but not the emphasis on protected domesticity and distinct community. Moravians effectively embraced Indians, given the shared spiritualist interest in trances, and they sought to unite all Pennsylvanians in one ecumenical Community of God in the Spirit. At the other extreme, sectarian perfectionists sought separation from the world for the sake of strict conformity to scripture. Between those ecumenical/separatist extremes were large numbers of Lutherans. Some brought (from the influential Prussian Halle academy) a tradition stressing public life as service and property as responsibility. More common, however, was a pietism that defined property and liberty, for both church and individual, in negative terms – as protection of the pious household, not opportunity for public virtue, and as protection from plunder, not public obligation. Abused by local German rulers, these settlers sought in Pennsylvania's promised liberty a household and religious freedom from official demand for services, funds, and conformity.

This negative conception of liberty was reinforced by the colony's corrupt land system. Escaping otherwise effective law reform, Penn's sons vigorously enforced escheat and quitrent privileges and refused to curtail dishonest speculator ejectments based on false surveys and uncertain boundaries. Specialized land-dispute tribunals earned only disdain. In reaction, German immigrants, who were highly literate, engaged with Philadelphia's emerging legal culture to give liberty a legal, property-based definition, and their emphasis on property protection helped shift Pennsylvania's focus from community to individual. A pietist printer, Christopher Sauer, sold a widely read paper containing technical advice on avoiding English intestate law (which disfavored widows), and on using English law both to protect inheritances in Germany and to secure title to colonial land. He encouraged naturalization, which protected families against proprietor escheat and, with property ownership, also secured voting rights. Sauer's periodicals combined piety, practical household advice, and technical English law – all representing some part of the pietist meaning of liberty.

Sauer's experiment in legal education through journalism was carried forward by Henry Miller, a cosmopolitan ex-Moravian who learned printing in Europe and from Ben Franklin. He published a widely distributed legal handbook that precisely translated English legal categories to German. Knowledge of law, the book explained, paralleled knowledge of scripture; both protected the pious household from injurious error. In his paper, moreover, Miller also moved beyond negative liberty by pressing the connection between Christian virtue and its secularized, republican parallel, with increasing emphasis on the latter. When the Stamp Act imposed a double tax on foreign-language papers, it reached an audience well schooled in protecting (negative) legal rights through (positive) political action, with the tension between those two directions unresolved. By then German culture had effectively combined legal self-protection with political clout. After mid-century the Quaker Party, with Franklin's support, had sought a royal charter to undercut proprietor power. To split the usually pro-Quaker German vote, Thomas Penn instituted property law reforms that provided first-purchase rights for squatters, surveyor supervision, and an impartial board to settle disputes. Germans, accepting increased quitrents in return for secure titles, provided the decisive votes for Penn – who now represented legal security for property, not its opposite. When the Crown threatened that same security, Germans rallied to the Revolution.

Church incorporation provided another legal vocabulary for emerging, if not always consistent, conceptions of liberty. Henry Muhlenberg, an influential Halle minister, knew his church lacked sufficient legal status to secure property or delineate internal authority. Familiar with the use of English law to cheat unincorporated New York Lutherans, Muhlenberg assiduously studied law and sought incorporation for his church – despite his astute suspicion of incorporation's lingering dependence on political influence. He fashioned a constitution that defined spheres of pastoral and vestry authority and stipulated free annual elections and an expanded lay right of veto – claimed by his congregation as part of the religious liberty Penn had guaranteed. This incorporation of the church as a predominately private organization with considerable legally protected lay self-determination aligned the legal protection of religious freedom with both property protection and consent-based governance. While still incomplete, this process of protected privatization and internal quasi-constitutionalism advanced further in Pennsylvania than in other colonies outside Rhode Island and paralleled an emerging political conceptualism that would surface during the Revolution.

In Pennsylvania the Great Awakening was more complex than a simple challenge to structured authority. Penn had provided a legal framework for tolerance but no religious or political direction. By 1700 the result had been a confusion of competing sectarian influences that opened the way for mounting materialism and indifference; people mocked the rampant diversity of religious messages, and even Quaker discipline grew lax. During the Awakening strict separated sects died out or, like Mennonites, survived intact, still separated. Quakers simply excluded Awakening participants and achieved reform from within. Awakening fervor did, however, empower Protestant denominations that had once played a muted role in Pennsylvania's sectarian Babel, and Pennsylvania's material success contributed to denominational strength as congregants gained influence and respectability. Pennsylvania became the institutional center for the organization of intercolonial denominationalism, but another Awakening effect was equally important. Those who crossed sectarian lines had experienced religion as a matter of private choice, not communitarian authority. As distinct Protestant denominations grew in the Awakening, the goal of universalism was transferred to secular society. Ecumenicalism became a rationalist, philosophical ideal, typified by Franklin's promotion of a print-dominated public citizenship – a project much advanced, not coincidentally, by Franklin's publication of Whitefield's Awakening sermons.

By mid-century, in fact, a tradition of non-sectarian voluntary civic organization had already grown, due to weak local government, religious diversity, and the absence of parishes. Schools, for example, while usually started by churches, were by 1750 often maintained across sectarian lines. So too with cemeteries, fire companies, and even some libraries. County courts assigned public overseers of poor relief, but charity was often handled semi-privately by inhabitants in groups with indeterminant legal status. Thus, in this most sectarian of colonies, non-sectarian cooperation had become a norm. Franklin built on that civic tradition by promoting interdenominational groups like the Philosophical Society and Library Company, creating, in effect, a public secular version of the ecumenical community of believers, a secularism with its own millennial zeal to promote progress through reason and science. A telling symbol: to promote education Franklin skillfully arranged transfer, to a set of secular trustees, of a valued building once built for Whitefield's tour and then quarreled over by Presbyterians and Moravians; it became the academy that was later the University of Pennsylvania.

One vocabulary for emerging patriotic secularism was, of course, law. After mid-century, men from the best Pennsylvania families studied law in London. In 1764 alone ten lawyers were admitted to practice, and they used the Enlightenment vocabulary of natural rights, not just common law writs. This vocabulary drew people together more than did theology. Sauer had already explained natural law to German readers, and Muhlenberg, while distrusting the atheistic Franklin, had read law texts and he supported Franklin in the Revolution despite Lutheran reservations. In other words, after the Great Awakening people joined denominations with new enthusiasm, but they united across denominational lines under legal, not biblical texts.

The Southern Colonies: Virginia

The written laws and formal administrative procedures of early Virginia evince a superficial similarity to New England's religious establishment. The Anglican Church was established by charter prior to the landing of the first settlers at Jamestown in 1607. Virginia's early governments compelled church attendance and the maintenance of orthodoxy. By the 1650s elected vestries enforced moral discipline in their parishes, collected taxes to support the church and its minister, and maintained the only birth, death, marriage, and tax records of the time. As in New England, laws integrated religion and civil government in providing Christian education, care for the poor, and the preservation of social tranquility. The General Court had jurisdiction over both ecclesiastical and civil causes of action and relied on biblically derived concepts of morality and popular conceptions of equity and good conscience in reaching its decisions, as well as on rules of secular law. In this way, Virginia common law came to embody religious teachings. Statutory laws reflected a similar orientation, as moral standards of equity and fairness were imposed on commercial activities. Even after its second decade, when widespread cultivation of tobacco as a cash crop fragmented Virginia society, laws perpetuated the myth of communal integrity and social interdependence. Virginian's law code restricted the hours people could work, the prices that could be charged, and the number of economic ventures that could be pursued simultaneously.

Leaders of the Virginia Company believed that settlers in the New World required religious instruction and discipline. They were also committed, at least in part, to spreading the gospel, a commitment derived from the practical need to fight Popery (France and Spain) in the New World. Anglican minister Robert Hunt was among the first 105 men who disembarked at Jamestown in May of 1607. A temporary church was the first structure erected, and Communion was held there on the third Sunday after landing. In 1610 and 1611 ministers accompanied new settlers to the colony. Governor Dale arrived with the latter group and immediately employed martial law to enforce productive labor and religious practice. All men and women were required to attend church services morning and evening and were subject to the watchful eyes of churchwardens, magistrates, and soldiers for moral conformity.

Virginia's first House of Burgesses in 1619 met in the Jamestown Church and took an oath of office swearing fealty to God. In its first session the Burgesses passed laws requiring church attendance and punishing idleness, gaming, and immoderate dress. This legislative body also divided the colony into four parishes, set aside glebe lands for the support of the Anglican Church, and prepared to support missionary efforts to the Indians. Within the parishes elected vestrymen were responsible for enforcing moral laws, which included not only those passed at the first session of the Burgesses but also sexual offenses, blasphemy, and various forms of antisocial behavior, such as lying and shrewishness. The vestrymen selected churchwardens, prominent members of church and community, to investigate the morals of the parish and present written findings in the county court. County judges usually ordered public whippings for breach of moral laws.

Yet, despite the apparent priority given to religion in its early laws, Virginia never fully embraced its mission as a religious one. The growth of the colony after 1620 far exceeded the increase in Anglican clergy. Parishes could be fifty miles long, making church attendance and enforcement of religious discipline nearly impossible. Virginians frequently buried their dead in family plots and married without clergy. Responding to instructions from England, the General Assembly in 1664 ordered that all ceremonies and rites "be according to the orders and canons of England, and the Sacraments . . . performed according to the Book of Common Prayer." The law was seemingly forgotten before the ink was dry. The extent of religious laxity is evident in the few attempts made by religious leaders to impose greater conformity to Christian teachings. In the 1680s, James Blair, an official of the Church of England, arrived in Virginia under orders to manage ecclesiastical affairs so as to establish uniform discipline in the colony. The ministers with whom he met complained that the courts had ceased enforcing moral laws and sought his aid in creating a more consistent system of ecclesiastical courts to punish "all cursers, swearers, blasphemers, all whoremongers, fornicators and adulterers, all drunkards, ranters and profaners of the Lord's day." This proposal never reached the stage of government debate at any level.

Subordination of religion to economic pursuits is evident in the Virginians' relative toleration of religious dissent. While compelled to contribute to the established church, dissenters were seldom troubled in their own religious practices. After Massachusetts warned the Virginia burgesses of a likely southern influx of Quakers after banishment from New England, the Virginians welcomed the newcomers as laborers. In the 1630s Virginians protested the creation of a haven for Catholics to the north, but their reaction resulted more from the loss of land than from fear of Catholics. Moreover, limits to economic activity and social amusement were rarely enforced. In 1650 a grand jury in Lower Norfolk County, when presented with a case of alleged Sabbath-breaking, chose to indict the entire town rather than single out an individual for punishment.

By 1700 colonial Virginia showed few signs of following the strict religious prescriptions of its founders. Virginia had built sixty-two Anglican churches by 1662, and clergy reported attendance rates of about 60 percent, indicating more attention to religion than some historians have recognized. Nevertheless, churchgoing for many became a social function more than an exercise in piety; true piety was a sentiment reserved for the old and dying. Household religious practices like family prayer declined as gambling, cockfighting, and horse racing came to characterize Southern culture. Sponsorship of these activities by local gentry reinforced their stature at the head of a society premised on norms of honor and prestige, not Christian selflessness. A hierarchy thus arose very different from that which evolved in New England. Property ownership bestowed social rank and semi-feudal political power, with prominent gentry acting, in effect, like manor lords – untitled, but very much responsible for the livelihood and behavior of those who worked on their estates. In the absence of influential clergy and local town governments, the gentry assumed economic, intellectual, and political leadership.

The gentry also provided the Church's financial support, not so subtly influencing the nature of religion in the colony. The gentry preferred secular law to scripture and their own individual authority to social responsibility. Virginia judges obliged by emphasizing property rights and owner freedom; they worked to secure gentry rights over land and servants or slaves, not to foster a community of reciprocal benevolence. In 1749 the clergy approached the Virginia Assembly seeking to escape economic dependence on the gentry. In an action indicative of religious sentiment in the colony, the legislators passed a law providing taxpayer support of Anglican clergy, but at an extraordinarily low salary: the bill was derisively known to as the "Two Penny Act."

During the Great Awakening the established Anglican Church came under attack from Virginians who bemoaned clerical laxity in doctrine and morals. Dissenters, mostly poor farmers, the less educated, and a small number of merchants, flocked to hear traveling evangelical preachers. Itinerant Presbyterian ministers such as William Robinson found a ready audience for their passionate revivals in western Virginia. Baptists, with energetic and emotional preachers Shubel Stearns and Daniel Marshall in the vanguard, garnered even more converts while Anglican converts to Methodism in the 1760s developed a stronghold in Brunswick County.

Even as dissenters were attacking the established clergy for its liberality, the gentry was scolding it for failure to control the masses: the disruption of the Great Awakening, with its emotional egalitarian message of self-empowerment, challenged gentry control of Virginia society and the hierarchical code of honor and prestige on which it was premised. In response, acting through the Assembly, the gentry secured, after 1740, complete political domination of the church, eschewing the need for bishops and other ecclesiastical offices. Under gentry control the church preached a message equating legitimate paternalistic authority with ethical responsibility. This message at once questioned the legitimacy of British rule while it augmented the local authority of the gentry who provided for the welfare of the populations: liberty, virtue, and paternalism were interwoven.

The Anglican Church in Virginia consistently supported both slavery and laws directed toward brutal slave control. Like frontier wars against the Indians that provided land for white settlers, slave laws were instituted in part to gain the solidarity of lower class whites who, in the 1670s, had demonstrated a dangerous capacity to rebel. In 1680 the Assembly reinforced the construction of lower class "whiteness" by forbidding slaves to defend themselves against whites, even when bullied; in 1705 it passed a law allowing vestries to seize any livestock claimed by slaves, to be sold for the benefit of poor whites. Interracial marriage and sex were forbidden, except of course for the freedom that male slave owners could in secret exercise over slaves. Free Africans, in turn, lost many of their earlier privileges, ensuring unremitting inequality. Many fled to escape Virginia laws.

In 1670 the legislature justified slavery in part by reference to Africans' paganism, but the church, despite urging from London, made insignificant efforts to minister to the slaves. This inaction protected the legislature's expressed justification for slavery, while the church's message of sacralized hierarchy provided slave laws with religious sanction. Many slaveholders rationalized their authority as the exercise of an obligation to care for "heathens" of an "inferior" race who could not care for themselves. When dissenters succeeded in converting slaves during the later eighteenth and early nineteenth centuries, however, the church and the slaveholders reversed position, arguing that slavery offered to African heathens the means of salvation through Christ.

Dissenters, especially Baptists, challenged both the Anglican refusal to convert slaves and the church's privileged legal status in Virginia. Baptists openly attacked the colony's establishment as early as the 1760s, arguing that faith cannot be legally compelled. Practical grievances also fueled the Baptist crusade: dissenters were forced to support a church they did not accept, and they could not secure for their own churches the legal right to incorporate, to receive and hold bequests, or to proselytize. To gain these rights, dissenters aligned themselves with Enlightenment reformers, often deists, atheists, or humanistic Unitarians who were using a secular vocabulary of rights to advocate greater protection of individual liberty – encompassing rights of property ownership as well as freedom of conscience. By the 1770s law provided a common vocabulary that united these two very distinct cultures. Their anomalous alliance brought disestablishment after the Revolution, but did not usher in the Christian nation the Baptists envisioned.

The Southern Colonies: Maryland

Maryland is often cited as early precedent for religious toleration in America. Yet, for many years Maryland maintained the strongest Anglican establishment in North America; its earlier, limited religious toleration masked de facto Catholic control. Maryland represents, in fact, not toleration, but the bitterness of Catholic/Protestant antagonism. Indeed, to the extent that Maryland embraced toleration, it did so only at the command of England and not on colonial initiative.

Initially, for political and economic reasons, Maryland did not rely on religion as a foundation for community. James I had intended to give the colony to George Calvert, a devout Catholic, the first Lord Baltimore and trusted servant of the King. When Calvert died, his son, Cecilius, inherited the title, and in 1629 Charles I gave him Maryland. Immediately, representatives of the failed Virginia Company, fearing further land devaluation, protested this grant to a Catholic as a violation of English law and an invitation to Spanish or French intervention. Protests delayed settlement until

1633 and shaped the religious character of the colony. The new Lord Baltimore, knowing his estate was precarious, tried to minimize the influence of religion altogether. He insisted Catholics "preserve unity and peace" by refraining from public discussion or practice of religion, a policy that precluded not only Catholic establishment, but even construction of Catholic churches.

Baltimore exercised extraordinary proprietary authority. Owning all land, he was also sole source of legal authority. He appointed the governor, a council of advisors, magistrates, and judiciary; his authority to promulgate laws was limited only by the requirement that no law be "repugnant to English law" or violate English rights. In recognition of those rights Baltimore created an Assembly that at first only reviewed legislation proposed by the Lord Proprietor, but soon began initiating bills and later established two courts.

Baltimore managed Maryland as a profit-generating enterprise, with income from taxes, fines, and fees. It appealed to younger sons of the English Catholic gentry who wanted land and influence without compromise of belief, a combination impossible in England. Calvert gave the largest tracts and most powerful political positions to Catholics, but to attract laborers he encouraged religious diversity, leaving Catholics a distinct minority.

Tension between Catholic rulers and Protestant settlers arose almost immediately. Many Jesuits migrated to Maryland in the 1630s, settling without legal title. Committed to reclaiming Catholic universalism, they traveled the colony, converting Indians and threatening Protestant laborers with eternal damnation. Catholic landowner toleration of Jesuits prompted claims of persecution by Protestants, who appealed to Virginia to rescue them, militarily if necessary, from Jesuit harassment. Maryland's governor, Lord Baltimore's brother, acted quickly to suppress unrest, convicting one of the proselytizers of "offensive and indiscreet speech" for warning Protestants of damnation.

Legal action to temper Jesuit enthusiasm pacified workers but also attracted dissenters to the colony. Religious diversity, however, did not mean toleration: each religious enclave exercised its own rules regarding conformity with a sectarian defensiveness that stemmed from the precarious state of any religion in Maryland. Only one Anglican minister preached in the colony before the late 1650s, and most Protestants could not afford to support a minister, build a church, or maintain a school. For three generations most people did not attend a single formal church service, and responsibility for public services vested instead in the gentry. As a result, prior to 1700 Maryland maintained practically no poor relief, schooling, or records and lacked the usual signs of community – churches, town squares, or schoolhouses – that foster public life. Nevertheless, every town had stocks, pillory, and a whipping post, while vacant country homes served as jails.

Laws in Maryland were similar to those in Massachusetts, but enforcement was not. Drunkenness was a crime in both colonies, but Maryland only punished one who "abuse(s) himself by frequent drunkenness," and required multiple witnesses to repeated incidents. Many penal statutes addressed sex offenses, but most actual prosecution resulted from unusual circumstances – forced miscarriages or infanticides, a husband accusing wife and lover, or a female servant charging a master for child support.

Conflict in England profoundly affected Maryland. During the English Civil War nervous Maryland Catholics acted to solidify their position with a 1649 "Act concerning Religion." Known for providing religious toleration, the Act in fact was explicitly designed to protect Catholics from the "dangerous consequence[s]" they feared. Specifically incorporating protection of Catholicism into criminal law, the Act prescribed execution for any who openly denied the Trinity; it also ordered that the Virgin and Apostles be spoken of with reverence and prohibited slanderous religious designations, with particular mention of the term "papist."

By 1651, however, the Protestant majority controlled the Assembly, which abrogated the Toleration Act of 1649 and also passed laws reflecting Puritan influence, with strict penalties for drunkenness, profanity, swearing and cursing, adultery, fornication, blasphemy, and violating the Sabbath. Only the governor's veto prevented a tax-supported Protestant establishment. In 1654, angered by persistent interference from Calvert, the Assembly launched its own civil war by repudiating the Lord Proprietor's authority to govern. The governor raised an army to defend his proprietary rights, but was defeated in 1655. Now unencumbered, the Assembly made Catholicism a crime. Radical Puritans plundered homes of Catholics and forced them and their priests into exile, executing at least four who resisted. Thus self-government in Maryland resulted in violent religious persecution, not toleration. Refusing defeat, Baltimore worked through a hostile Puritan Parliament to reestablish dialogue with the Maryland Assembly: he regained control but on radically modified charter terms, which included installation of a Protestant governor. Baltimore retained his income, but his role in governance was never the same.

Charles Calvert succeeded his father as Lord Baltimore in 1676 and took advantage of the Restoration in England by trying to exclude Protestants from Maryland government. In response, the Assembly complained to London that Baltimore overused his veto, filled powerful offices with Catholics, and denied Protestants their rights of self-government. With continuing Puritanical zeal, the Assembly also prohibited Sabbath labor and required church attendance or private worship. While not explicitly anti-Catholic, the legislation was so perceived.

In the political skirmishes that followed, the Lords of Trade generally favored the Protestants, especially after a report from an Anglican minister, John Yeo, was forwarded by way of the Archbishop of Canterbury. Yeo described Maryland's lack of churches, its general irreligion, and its "notorious vices . . . soe that it is become a Sodom of uncleanness and a pest house of iniquity." Baltimore, however, stubbornly resisted pressure from the Lords to stop favoring "those of the Papish Religion to the discouragement of his Majesties' Protestant subjects."

As in New York, England's Glorious Revolution of 1688 brought revolution to Maryland. An anti-Baltimore assemblyman, John Goode (variously spelled "Coode"), a one-time Anglican minister, planter, and businessman, recruited a small army with support from Protestant lawyers and merchants who had recently fled the English Restoration. Goode's band marched toward the capital, and the Council and Governor surrendered without resisting. The rebels, called the "Associators," were not anarchists. They claimed only to object to a government that rested on a charter rendered invalid by Parliamentary supremacy, and that now refused to recognize the new Protestant monarchs as the lawful Crown. Immediately congratulating the Crown, the Associators implored them to stabilize a Protestant Maryland government. Only near the end of 1689 did the Protestants, claiming fear of violence, also close Catholic churches and imprison priests; in addition, Associators undertook investigation of the Baltimore administration, turning up evidence of misused funds and abuse of power, which they reported to England. In 1690 Whitehall charged Baltimore with fifty-two Articles of mismanagement; the Privy Council recommended suspension of his charter, with retention of only a small portion of the colony's income. A new governor, Copley, arrived in 1692, and the Lords of Trade selected a Council containing many Associators.

English diplomacy, however, imposed limits on Protestant triumph in Maryland. Seeking good relations with Spain, his military ally against France, King William promised Spain that Catholics would be free to worship both in England and the colonies. After the Associators' attacks on Catholics in 1689, Spain pressed William to act. William extended to the colonies the limited religious freedom guaranteed in the English Act of Toleration (1689) and ordered Governor Copley to restore liberty of conscience to Catholics. In response the Assembly passed a bill establishing Anglicanism; Copley refused to implement it.

Toleration during the period of royal control did not amount to religious freedom. Non-Christians had few rights; they could not bestow property by will, vote, or hold office. The Governor and Assembly renewed laws against Sabbath-breaking, sexual misconduct, alcohol consumption, and various forms of gaming and entertainment, all with the expressed purpose of ensuring Christian morality. Catholics were an isolated minority, shorn of political power. They could practice their faith in public, but were not granted full rights of property ownership or political participation until the Revolution. Many, feeling betrayed, supported a return of Baltimore and Stuart restoration. Jesuits aggressively asserted proselytizing rights in 1697, resulting in then-Governor Nicholson's private condemnation of Catholicism as an "idolatrous religion," but Nicholson's hands were tied by royal policy and he incurred Protestant wrath by tolerating Catholics.

By the turn of the century Catholic plantation owners, mostly Calvert friends or relatives, had witnessed the decay of Maryland's manorial system. Local government replaced manor courts in administering justice and providing social needs. The colony remained religiously and ethnically diverse, with Quaker and Catholic "undesirables" from other colonies, along with immigrants from Scotland and slaves from Africa. The 1692 "Act of [Anglican] Establishment" had never been implemented, despite growing Anglican influence; three times the Lords of Trade under William rejected it. Then, when Queen Anne succeeded King William in 1702, she confirmed the 1692 Act and revoked orders securing freedom of religion for Catholics. As in other colonies, Queen Anne's reign represented a period of intensified Anglicanism, embraced by Maryland's Assembly because of its implicit anti-Catholicism. When Anne's royal governor, John Seymour, arrived, his first action was to arrest and threaten Catholic proselytizers; he then urged adoption of criminal laws to address the "audacious misbehavior of Romish Clergy," resulting in prohibition of Catholic worship in public and severe penalties for Catholic proselytizing.

Legally the Anglican establishment was relatively weak. It permitted practice of any Protestant religion and did not require attendance at Anglican services. The Assembly did, however, support establishment by organizing vestries as quasi-governmental organizations in twenty-two of the thirty parishes and provided new church buildings for most of those parishes. Elected vestrymen collected taxes to pay for churches, poor rates, support of a minister, and, often, a church school. A 1715 law allowed vestrymen to remove children from a Catholic mother if their Protestant father died, so they "be Securely Educated in the protestant religion." For funds to pay for the French and Indian War, the Assembly taxed Catholics double for their land and allowed lower tax rates on trade among Protestants.

Only after the fourth Lord Baltimore converted to Protestantism and successfully petitioned for return of his family's land did Anglicanism flourish as the chosen religion of the proprietary family. For the first time, social status attached to participation in the Anglican Church; legal establishment, formally weak, was coupled with real political clout. Anglican establishment, however, did not prefigure the colony's future. Western Maryland grew dramatically from 1720 to 1776, but Anglican attempts to benefit from establishment there failed. Westerners were largely recent immigrants – Germans, French Huguenots, and Scots-Irish – who were disinclined to adopt Anglicanism. Some brought solid commitments to home churches, such as Dutch Reformed, Moravian, Mennonite, or Lutheran. Others followed Great Awakening preaching, which, as in Virginia, appealed openly to lower classes and slaves. Participants usually became Baptists or Methodists, and local churches, with their growing strength, served as de facto established churches throughout the frontier: they collected money for the poor, funded education and medical care, delivered mail, and kept records. One church task was to construct schools and hire teachers; Bibles served as texts until the decline in Christian education in the 1770s. In 1750, the Lutheran Ministerium also founded an orphanage for children of deceased German immigrants. Government performed none of these functions on the frontier, and even along the seaboard dissenting churches assumed many such tasks. Disturbed by dissenters' success, the Anglican ministry sent missionaries to the west, but they chiefly encountered hostility to Anglicanism's official establishment.

Limited toleration existed throughout most of the colonial era, but it was frequently imposed by a distant government primarily concerned with political and economic goals. Even in its more liberal incarnation, religious toleration never became the freedom to believe and to practice any or no religion without the loss of political, economic, or civil privileges. On the eve of Revolution, Maryland stood as an Anglican establishment that relied on churches to perform many public functions, relied on Christian teachings for many of its laws, and persecuted non-Christians and non-Anglican Christians to varying degrees. Maryland, in this way at least, was a typical British-American colony.

CONCLUSION

Four main themes emerge from these accounts. The first is the theme of Christian community and its erosion. Yearning to regain lost community is, of course, a recurrent American motif. The historian is challenged to separate fact from myth; complete separation may be impossible. Yet, clearly in colonial America religion was integrated with law as a means of building communities rooted in common Christian values, and many colonists lamented when their contemporary reality fell short of an idealized past or failed to prefigure the millennial future.

A second theme is the shift in influence from public religious establishment to a "private" denominationalism with complex links to the public order. Denominational linkages to the public realm were achieved partly through legal forms that would soon be located, like religion itself, within a sphere of private ordering – property, corporation, and charitable bequest. As denominationalism became the dominant model for American religious life it employed and reinforced those legal categories, thereby shaping reconfigurations that would later transform American conceptions of private right and public authority. For example, tasks considered both public and religious under colonial establishment – charity, education, promotion of morality – would be redistributed across a public/private divide, posing dilemmas with which we still wrestle.

The third theme is the one of difference. American colonies were overwhelmingly Protestant, but Protestants fiercely disputed the role of political authority in relation to Christian freedom – in other words, the relation between law and grace or between the City on Earth and the City of God. Those dilemmas deep at the core of Christian theology were illustrated in the colonies, as theological differences shaped the legal structuring of communities and became inseparable from social and economic differences. It might fairly be said that American Protestants did not solve the problem of law, but at least many took it seriously, as a question of theological legitimacy.

Finally, of course, is the theme of colonization. The meaning of "Christian community" in the colonies was inextricably linked to the constant presence of those who had been conquered. In confronting the colonized, white Christians reenacted yet another Augustinian paradox as they found themselves defining communitarian inclusion by its flip side – by exclusion and by the coercion of enforced boundaries. Without boundaries, the pious community seemed to dissolve into the corruptions of the world, and thence into pagan darkness. That radical dissolution was embraced by Roger Williams when he took up residence among the Indians and declared Massachusetts to be the real pagan wilderness, since coerced exclusions had replaced true Christian love. For most colonists, however, community came to be defined in part by an "other" that could be both racially identified and variously described as heathen or Satanic. That "otherness" united whites and reminded them of the vigilance needed to build Christian community. As a result, "community" increasingly rested on foundations of bloody conquest and enslavement. For example, during the attacks of the 1670s Puritans believed God had unleashed Indians as a punishing force from Satan, in part because, in the wilderness, Massachusetts had itself become too heathen and was no longer a godly community. Puritans slaughtered

Indians to prove God's power and their own worth and sold Indian children ("young Serpents") as slaves.

These inclusion/exclusion decisions, defining the meaning of Christian community, set in motion ironic forces and cross-currents that played themselves out for decades in post-Revolutionary Era America. For example, the all-enveloping, anti-Puritan Anglican church in the South embraced both unregenerate masses and privileged elites, the former frustrating New Englanders' conceptions of a true church, the latter asserting a status New Englanders found unchristian. Yet, Southern Anglicans rejected African slaves the New Englanders might well have welcomed. By contrast, dissidents during the Great Awakening excluded from their definition of Christian community New England latitudinarianism, commercial wealth, and the values of elite Southern culture, which they labeled immoral, while including slaves and the lower classes. Ensuing struggles to define the "true" meaning of community in America would last until the Civil War, and beyond.

11

THE TRANSFORMATION OF LAW AND ECONOMY IN EARLY AMERICA

BRUCE H. MANN

Scholarship on law and the economy often has a chicken-and-egg quality. Is law a tool wielded instrumentally to effect specific economic ends, or does it emerge functionally from particular economic needs? Most such writing addresses the nineteenth century, but it serves as a caution for earlier centuries, despite, or perhaps because of, the comparative paucity of work on law and the economy in the colonial period. What makes the caution necessary is that, notwithstanding a certain heuristic value, the dichotomy misleads and oversimplifies. It could hardly be otherwise, given the pervasiveness in society of both law and economy. Things legal and things economic are everywhere any moderately perceptive historian looks, by their very profusion interacting in complex ways. Moreover, one cannot talk of law and economy in the seventeenth and eighteenth centuries as though each was a single, unitary construct. There were many laws – or, perhaps more helpfully, many legalities – and many economies, as diverse and diversified as we now know British North America itself to have been. The task at hand is to sort out the myriad strands and see if they can be woven into a coherent story or set of stories about law and the economy in the seventeenth and eighteenth centuries.

The only clear generalization one can offer is that law and economy at the close of the eighteenth century looked very different than they did at the beginning of the seventeenth. This is not the same as saying that the relationship between them changed over that span, although it did; but how it changed is less clear than the fact that law and economy themselves changed. To indulge in the sort of crude oversimplification just criticized, in the seventeenth century the relationship between law and the economy played out on a level one might loosely call public, while in the eighteenth century it was more clearly private.

The legal activities of greatest consequence for the economy in the seventeenth century were the establishment of legal institutions and attempts at economic regulation. The two were related. Many of the regulatory measures emanated from legal institutions that were called courts, but that blended judicial and administrative functions. Defined broadly, economic regulation included wage and price controls, fencing regulations, land distribution rules, land-title recordation, regulation of labor relationships, and the like. By way of contrast, private law activity – matters of debt, contract, and property – were generally subsidiary to public rules. Property law was the most "developed" of the private law areas, in the sense of being more articulated and formalized. Debt and contract were, by comparison, almost rudimentary. This difference reflected the centrality of land and the highly localized, relatively undeveloped nature of the economy. The relationship between law and economy did not have a transactional basis in the sense that law shaped or influenced how economic actors dealt with one another. Rather, it rested on regulation and on the growing protection of private rights in land.

Changes toward the end of the seventeenth century began to affect the relationship between law and economy. Local court functions became more differentiated, with the result that courts focused more clearly on disputes between individuals. Local economies began to turn outward, as the production and accumulation of things to sell and the spread of markets in which to sell them promoted the expansion of the coasting trade and the development of a trans-Atlantic trade. These economic changes shifted the focus of law to transactions between individual economic actors. Issues of debt and contract came to predominate.

Part of the eighteenth-century story is how the transformation of formerly local economies made credit and failure the dominant legal issues. Economic development required credit, which in varying ways was supplied by paper money, written credit instruments, and tobacco warehouse receipts. The expansion of credit necessarily raised the question of how to assure its repayment, which law tried to address through mortgages, sureties, tighter procedural rules, and other such devices. Under the time-honored principle of what-goes-up-must-come-down, the expansion of credit and of the economic activity that ran on it meant that law also had to learn how to handle economic failure. The private-law focus of the relationship between law and economy made this more difficult. The notion of credit as something created in bilateral contracts enforceable through similarly bilateral litigation complicated insolvency and bankruptcy, both of which required rising above the transactional origin of each debt to achieve some degree of cooperation among creditors. Long-standing beliefs that insolvency represented moral failure rather than economic risk and that debtors thus bore a moral obligation to repay their debts in full further complicated the ability of law to deal with failure. Moreover, the large-scale speculation schemes that were the primary investment vehicles of the 1780s and 1790s quickly outstripped the ability of the legal system to deal with them, both in terms of how they mustered capital and of how to sort through the consequences of their collapse – a dilemma that foreshadowed the legal struggle to define and contain the great economic and political phenomenon of the nineteenth century, the business corporation.

In the broadest and most summary of outlines, that was the shape of the changing relationship between law and economy in the seventeenth and eighteenth centuries. Giving it content and coherence, not to mention credibility, requires rather more explanation. Any explanation can, of course, only be partial. The literatures of law and of economy for the era rarely overlap. There is more for New England, less for the South, and little for the colonies in between. But there is enough to hazard a beginning.

I. LAND AND LAW IN THE EARLY ECONOMIES

While most of the British North American colonies shared roughly similar dates of settlement, they did not necessarily share similar laws or economies. Eventually the former would converge, but not the latter. The Southern and Caribbean colonies began as explicitly commercial ventures with different postures toward law than was the case in the northeastern colonies, where economic activity was more a means than an end. For example, whatever profit-making ambitions the original investors in the Plymouth or the Massachusetts Bay companies might have had quickly evaporated in the face of land and resources that were suited only to household production, a limitation that dovetailed nicely with the communal aspirations of the settlers themselves. Not all who migrated to the New England colonies in the first decades of settlement were Puritans or Pilgrims or families or congregations, but enough were that the laws and economies they established were theirs. Others had to conform or live on the margins. Similarly, the Quakers, Presbyterians, and German pietists who settled Pennsylvania and New Jersey later in the seventeenth century found land that was much better suited to commercial agriculture than any in New England, but like the Puritans they arrived with a religiously shaped vision of society that placed the family, and consequently the household economy, at the center. This is not to say that trade or the marketplace were anathema – far from it. But they were contested spheres that some people pursued and others attempted to contain – a tension that often found legal expression.

Apart from rapidly depleted stocks of beaver pelts, the natural resources of New England could be counted most generously as trees and fish, neither of which promised great riches. The soil tended to be rocky and uneven, cultivable only in relatively small patches with little commercial potential, though reasonably well suited to small-scale farming. Rather than distribute land under the headright system common in the southern colonies, the New England colonies promoted concentrated settlement by granting town-sized tracts to quasi-corporate bodies of proprietors, which in turn allocated land to male heads of households in combinations that included house lots clustered in town centers, more dispersed farm lots, and pasturage rights in the town common lands. The allotments varied in size and choiceness according to social status, family size, and wealth. In Massachusetts, the General Court underscored the purpose of the grants in 1634 by declaring that it would seize the land of any grantee who did not build on or otherwise improve it within three years and re-grant it to someone who would.

Initially, the proprietorship was coterminous with the town, an identity reinforced in some towns by town covenants that ranged from hortatory professions of godly fraternity to blueprints for public participation, all phrased in contractual language and signed by the landowning inhabitants. In time, the arrival of new settlers who could purchase land but not shares in the proprietorship and the coming of age of sons of proprietors who similarly were excluded from the benefits of proprietorship – the most valuable of which was the right to share in future land distributions – caused significant problems for town governance and citizenship, which need not concern us. What matters is that the prevailing pattern of land distribution created a landscape of small farms in close proximity to one another, in sharp contrast to the dispersed plantations that came to characterize the Chesapeake. There were, of course, always outliers – fisherman, trappers, and others who preferred to live beyond the reach of godly neighbors – but their preference for the margins also made them marginal to the main development of law and economy.

If the land itself and the manner in which it was distributed determined that the economy would be shaped primarily by household production, the legal form in which land was distributed influenced how law touched on the economy. Throughout New England, land grants to individuals were almost exclusively in free and common socage, which meant that grantees owned the land without owing any continuing personal or financial obligations to anyone else, whether as rents or personal services – the beginning, in effect, of the American dream. Tenancy existed, most notably in William and John Pynchon's Springfield in western Massachusetts. But it was not the norm. Instead, people typically held land in a legal form that not only allowed them to farm it but also to treat it as an asset and a commodity, a part of their wealth that could be bought, sold, mortgaged, and inherited. This helps explain the early appearance of land recordation statutes, first in Plymouth in 1636, then in Massachusetts four years later.

Recording statutes protect landowners and facilitate land transactions by creating public evidence of title on which prospective purchasers and creditors can rely. In their modern form, they do this by designating an office to which purchasers and creditors can present their deeds from the owner/seller or owner/debtor to be copied into the public records, where they constitute legal notice of their interests and establish their legal priority over anyone who later asserts a competing interest in the land. Recording statutes are notice statutes. They do not require people to record their deeds or other instruments of title for the documents to be valid as between the parties to them – as between, say, the seller and buyer or the mortgagor and mortgagee. Rather, they require buyers and creditors to record their instruments if they want to establish their priority over third-party claimants. Once an instrument is recorded, anyone contemplating a transaction involving the same land is deemed to have notice of the prior claims and so will not prevail over them. Thus, buyers who record their deeds from their sellers need not worry if someone later claims to have an earlier but unrecorded deed to the same land. And creditors thinking of lending money to a landowner on the security of a mortgage can determine if other creditors have already recorded mortgages in the same land to secure their own loans to the owner and who therefore would have first claim to the mortgaged property in the event of default.

The first recording statutes were much less detailed than their modern equivalents. They did not, for example, require that the full text of the deed be recorded and so were of little help in boundary disputes. And they could be of little practical comfort in frontier areas where distance to the courthouse often discouraged recording altogether. But they nonetheless established the important legal principle that priority of record guaranteed priority of title, thereby helping redefine the economic value of land. Whereas the value of land had traditionally been measured in straightforward terms by what could be extracted from it, either in rent or what it could produce, a proper land title system broadened the understanding of economic value to include land as a commodity that could be bought and sold, and land as an asset that could be tapped to secure credit. It was these new understandings of economic value that in the eighteenth century helped drive land speculation and the efforts of squatters to secure paper recognition of their claims. This redefinition, however, lay in the future.

II. REGULATING THE MARKETPLACE

At the very beginning of settlement in New England, when land mattered most for the families it could sustain, the primary impact of law on the economy lay in its attempts to regulate the economy by restraining what would later be apostrophized as market forces. In early modern England, a regulated economy was an important element of a moral economy that preserved order and stability within the traditional social hierarchy. What later writers referred to as "the restlessness of the market place" was thought inimical to a well-ordered society. In Massachusetts in the 1630s, regulation meant, most saliently, the enactment of wage and price controls. The former were a response to the scarcity of non-family labor, the latter to a combination of remembered English regulations and theological concerns about just price. Both attempted to deal with the strains placed on the economy by the Great Migration, which propelled the European population of New England from a few hundred in 1630 to twenty thousand a mere decade later.

Later generations made much of the contrast between free labor in the North and bound labor in the South, as though the difference stemmed from innate moral differences. It is true that bound labor, whether as indentured servants or as slaves, never reached the scale in New England that it did in the plantation colonies, but that was not because of moral scruple. Bound labor was too common in the Northern colonies to believe it would not have spread had economic conditions supported it. Although not on a par with the voracious demand for labor of the plantation economies, New England had its own labor needs, but little wherewithal to meet them. Even small farms were labor intensive, but they did not generate sufficient surplus to purchase bound labor, which required a capital investment that was beyond the means of most landowners. Farmers relied instead on family labor, which could include less fortunate relatives, dependent sons and daughters, or, for certain tasks, apprentices. When these sources fell short, landowners turned to wage labor, whether for unskilled field work or for skilled labor such as carpentry. There the market prevailed. Whether skilled or unskilled, labor was scarce and demand was high, thereby raising the wages workers could command. It was in part to counter this market response, which observers thought of as greed, that the legislature enacted caps on daily wage rates. Other corners of New England addressed the problem differently: the Pynchons in the Connecticut valley used immigrant servants and dependent tenants in what often resembled debt peonage; large-scale sheep and dairy farmers on Narragansett Bay used Indian and later African slaves. But they were just that, corners.

Price controls were known in England, primarily in the form of periodic efforts to regulate the price of bread, but in Massachusetts their brief imposition owed more to the theological idea of just price – a price determined not solely by the market but also by considerations of intrinsic value and godly restraint. Just price notwithstanding, price controls often gestured toward the market. For example, prices of foodstuffs were more likely to be regulated in Boston than in the more self-sufficient rural areas that supplied Boston. Prices of perishable items tended not to be regulated, their perishability giving buyers leverage they did not have in more durable items.

In truth, wage and price controls were more hortatory than binding. Stephen Innes has calculated that peacetime wage and price controls were in effect in Massachusetts for only forty-three months between 1630 and 1684, primarily in the first decade of settlement. Even when nominally in force, controls could be toothless. The General Court declared in September 1634 that employers who violated the mandated wage limit would not have to pay the fine prescribed by statute. By 1636, the General Court had largely withdrawn from centralized wage regulation and directed the towns to set and enforce wages. Prosecutions at both levels were few and far between. This ambivalence toward regulation arose from different sources. One was the inability of the legislature to abrogate the laws of supply and demand, which although not understood or even named nonetheless inhibited compliance. Another was that wage limits sometimes had non-economic goals. For example, when the General Court in 1633 reimposed wage and price limits it had previously rescinded, it did so in response to complaints that laborers were using their unregulated, and consequently higher, wages to get drunk and buy "superfluities." Wage limits for such class purposes went hand in hand with sumptuary laws, which just as ineffectually attempted to limit the consumer impulse for lace and other fineries to people whose social status merited them.

The futility of the controls illustrated the limits of law. It did not, however, imply an unrestrained marketplace. If the market could not be tamed by law, perhaps it would bend to the influence of the traditional moral economy in which profit had to be tempered by the good of the community. The legislature periodically tried to establish normative restraints by exhorting the population to observe suggested limits. Individual towns encouraged voluntary compliance. The 1639 prosecution and conviction of the wealthiest and arguably greediest merchant in Boston, the reviled Robert Keayne, for price gouging rested more on general principle than on statute and was seconded by the formal censure of his church. Law still had a place, even if for exemplary purposes.

Although New England legislatures had to concede that they could not restrain market values by fiat, there were other legal mechanisms for regulating the economy. These other mechanisms could facilitate market exchanges or limit their consequences. Among the former were regulatory measures to assure the quality of goods traded and the fairness of the people trading them. Chief among the latter were usury laws, which restricted the cost of credit by criminalizing the charging of interest above the statutory maximum.

In England, policing quality in the marketplace had generally been the responsibility of craft guilds. But guilds never took root in the American colonies. For all of four months in 1635, Massachusetts created a merchants guild of sorts by giving nine men the exclusive right to board arriving ships, examine whatever goods they had for sale, agree on the prices, and purchase the goods for resale to the inhabitants at a 5 percent mark-up. The magistrates quickly conceded the unenforceability of such a monopoly, which few but the nine appointees favored, and replaced it with a similarly short-lived system that applied only to imported foodstuffs, in which the colony government had the right of first purchase and licensed wholesale merchants that could buy whatever remained. Massachusetts experimented again in 1648 by granting the coopers of Boston and Charlestown guild privileges to enforce standards of packing fish, pork, and beer for export, complete with the customary English guild privileges of regulating entry into the trade and judicial authority over their members. The General Court declined to renew the coopers' charter four years later and assumed responsibility for regulating the quality of export goods, a responsibility it had never relinquished over other goods or at most had delegated to the towns. The colony and individual towns variously appointed fish cullers to grade the quality of the catch, leather searchers to inspect the hides and skins supplied to tanners and shoemakers, flour inspectors to test the quality of bread, and, most pervasively, inspectors of weights and measures so that purchasers would not have to rely solely on the integrity of vendors for the accuracy of their measurements. In short, public officials oversaw most aspects of commercial activity.

Usury laws, in which the colonies followed centuries of Western tradition, were just one consequence of two related facts that shaped much of the relationship between law and economy in early America – namely, that merchants conducted business on promises and that they controlled the available supply of money. The former is fundamental. Unless commerce consists of simultaneous exchanges of goods or services and the payment for them – that is, unless buyers immediately pay their sellers in cash or in kind – people must conduct business on promises, whether promises to pay, promises to deliver, or promises to perform. The promises create debts and transform the people who make and receive them into debtors and creditors. The full ramifications of this belong to the eighteenth century, but the immediate impact in the seventeenth century derived from the facts that all debts carried interest in one form or another and that they required formal enforcement mechanisms in the event of non-payment.

A perennial complaint throughout the colonial period of everyone who ever bought or sold anything – rich and poor alike, debtors and creditors all – was the scarcity of money. The colonial economies never had enough specie and rarely any paper currency to serve as a circulating medium of exchange. In their absence, people paid for goods and services in agricultural produce, or "commodity money." Unless one assumes a landscape of people routinely pushing wheelbarrow-loads of produce the way modern Americans carry wallets, commodity money necessarily turned all transactions into credit transactions in which people delivered goods or performed services and were paid later. Until the beginning of the eighteenth century, the predominant mode of memorializing these transactions in the northeastern colonies, with the possible exception of Dutch New Amsterdam, was by book accounts, which enabled people to purchase goods or services on credit with payment postponed until they could harvest their crops or otherwise acquire commodity money items.

Books were running accounts of the dealings between creditors and their debtors. Each entry chronicled a transaction – the purchase of goods, the performance of labor services, occasional payments on account. In legal terms, the defining features of book accounts were that they did not contain an explicit promise by the debtor to pay for the goods or services received and did not stipulate a time for repayment. Instead, books recorded debts for which the law implied a promise to pay, albeit at a time uncertain. That the promise to pay was implied rather than express did not compromise the popularity of book accounts, but it did shape their salient features. Books were only presumptive, not conclusive, evidence of the debts they recorded. That is, when sued, debtors were free to counter their creditors' claims with a wide range of controverting evidence, allowing juries to sort out who owed what to whom. Book accounts thus had too much intrinsic uncertainty to permit the calculation of interest, even though creditors who sued typically prevailed. On the other hand, vendors compensated for their inability to levy interest by charging higher prices to credit customers than they did to cash customers.

The first government intervention in the debtor-creditor relationship was prompted by the same scarcity of money that underlay routine dealings on book. In October 1631, a scant sixteen months after arriving in New England, the Massachusetts magistrates made corn legal tender at the market rate for all debts except those in which the parties had expressly contracted for payment in money or beaver pelts, the latter an acknowledgment of the growing importance of the fur trade. Six years later the General Court fixed the price at which corn would be accepted in payment of any future debts, although it subsequently compensated at least some creditors who suffered losses when the market price of corn fell below the statutory tender price.

In 1640, the sudden prospect of a Puritan future in England stemmed the Great Migration. The economy it had supported spiraled into depression. The price of corn, which had been driven upward by demand as long as immigration flowed, plummeted. As a result, corn lost most of its value as money, throwing credit into disarray. During the years of booming migration, settlers had supplied themselves on credit, often secured by mortgages on their lands, crops, or cattle. When crop prices fell, they lost the ability to repay their creditors, who then seized the mortgaged land or crops, thereby truly impoverishing their debtors. Unsecured creditors could wreak the same damage by winning court judgments against their debtors and levying execution on the debtor's property. As John Winthrop wrote in his journal, "men could not pay their debts, for no money nor beaver were to be had."[1] In its second intervention in the debtor-creditor relationship, the General Court moved quickly in October 1640 to extend at least some protection to debtors by requiring that creditors accept a debtor's property at values determined by three "understanding and indifferent men" and that they exhaust the debtor's movable property before seizing his land, thereby giving at least temporary protection to the ultimate source of the debtor's livelihood. For debts contracted thenceforward, the Court stipulated that creditors could not compel payment in money, but rather had to accept commodities at such rates as the Court determined or, if the Court failed to act, by the appraisal of "indifferent men." Connecticut enacted a similar law four months later.

By May 1646 Massachusetts legislators decided that the worst of the crisis had passed and repealed the law that had permitted contracts for money to be paid in kind. They had already eased credit by relaxing the restrictions on usury, and to facilitate international trade they had lifted the ceiling on interest rates for bills of exchange. In 1650 they repealed another law from the same era that had allowed debtors to stymie the attachment process simply by failing to appear in court. Nevertheless, while in force, the laws shielding debtors were a very Puritan gesture of the Christian charity that leaders such as Winthrop felt creditors should have shown on their own.

On a broader scale, depression forced a shift in government efforts to regulate the economy. Wage and price controls were largely abandoned. Massachusetts overcame its early antipathy to monopoly rights and began offering franchise monopolies for limited terms of years to budding entrepreneurs to encourage economic development. These included straightforward market monopolies, such as guarantees of exclusive markets to fur traders who agreed to pioneer routes to new sources of furs; market monopolies combined with quasi-patent protection, such as grants of exclusive rights to sell iron conditioned on building ironworks that used advanced technologies; and outright protection of intellectual property rights in the form of patents to inventors of manufacturing machines, who could then charge for their use. The colony also granted tax abatements and direct subsidies to spur growth in commercial endeavors as varied as

[1] Richard S. Dunn, James Savage, and Laetitia Yaendle, eds., *The Journal of John Winthrop, 1630–1649* (Cambridge, MA, 1996), 342.

planting hemp and flax, clothmaking, mining, raising sheep, and building bridges and wharves. Towns chipped in grants of land for gristmills, sawmills, and ironworks, often sweetened by tax exemptions and freedom from militia duty. The effect was to socialize the start-up costs of economic development by creating legally enforceable rights – some of which resembled property rights – in selected grantees. Regulation did not disappear. Town or colony governments continued to set ferry tolls and tavern hours, regulate the weight of loaves of bread, and oversee exports. But promoting development became paramount.

There the relationship between law and economy in New England remained for the rest of the seventeenth century: a mixture of government stimulus and regulation that tried, with mixed results, to overcome the limitations of land, labor, resources, and money within the framework of covenanted communities that emphasized not the individual, but the individual's obligations to God and to others, while at the same time seeing a person's financial success as a sign of God's favor.

III. THE LAW OF TOBACCO

New England's efforts to promote and regulate a diversified economy stood in sharp contrast to Virginia, where regulation of the economy in the early years operated within the framework of martial law. Until 1618, all land was owned by the Virginia Company and worked by strictly supervised, military-style gangs of laborers bound to the Company by indentures for specified terms. Only when tobacco took root as the engine of the Chesapeake economy did the Company introduce the headright system by which each settler received fifty acres of land for himself, each member of his family, and each bound laborer he imported. Tobacco soon dominated the economy so completely that every point at which law touched on the economy had something to do with tobacco, whether it was labor, finance, exchange, or regulation.

Tobacco was a labor-intensive crop – an attribute that, when coupled with its huge profitability, sharply raised the demand for, and consequently the value of, labor. Contract law sailed to the rescue. Beginning in 1619, the Virginia Company recruited labor in England by providing passage to Virginia as a loan that workers agreed to repay with their labor services for a specified term of years, usually four but sometimes as high as seven. The contracts of indenture they signed memorialized the terms of their agreement. The Company then transported the now-indentured servants to Virginia, where it auctioned or sold the contracts and the labor they promised to planters who agreed to furnish the servants with food, clothing, and lodging and, at the end of the term of indenture, "freedom dues" – a suit of clothing and a small allotment of land. Private agents and ship captains soon took over recruitment and transportation from the Company. Indentures were freely assignable; that is, they could be transferred from one master to another, whether by sale, gift, inheritance, or as stakes lost at cards, with each subsequent owner acquiring the servant's labor for whatever term remained under the contract.

From a lay perspective, and perhaps also from the perspective of masters and servants themselves, indentured servants resembled a species of property, sold from one master to another without the servant's consent. But they were not. Even as indentured servitude developed into a distinctive legal institution, it remained a creature of contract law, not property law. Workers had some latitude within which they could negotiate the terms of their indentures, depending on what skills they offered, and the master's rights were in the servant's labor, not the servant's person. This did not mean that masters and servants were equal contracting parties, as modern contract law would presume, but the indentures were no less contracts for the imbalance. In one key respect, the law did acknowledge that labor indentures were not ordinary contracts. Whereas the standard legal remedy for breach of contract was monetary damages, courts routinely ordered specific performance of indentures, requiring the breaching party, whether servant or master, to perform the labor or deliver the maintenance that he or she had promised in the indenture. In the seventeenth century, at least, there was no monetary substitute for bound labor.

White indentured servants initially supplied the labor needs of the Southern and Caribbean colonies. However, within a short time in the sugar colonies of the Caribbean and by the end of the seventeenth century in the tobacco colonies of the Chesapeake, indentured servitude had yielded to African slavery as the dominant labor system. Part of the persistence of indentured servitude in the Chesapeake was a function of differences in the conditions of cultivation; tobacco was not suited to the routinized labor of work gangs and could be grown profitably on small farms as well as on large plantations. Part was a function of timing. Only toward the end of the century did Virginia and Maryland, with their dwindling supplies of land, have to compete for immigrant labor with Pennsylvania, where an abundance of cheap land promised greater post-indenture opportunity for small farmers. There were other economic factors, too, and some political ones as well, but critical to the emergence of slavery as the dominant labor system in the Chesapeake was the evolution of a clear and unambiguous legal definition of slaves as property. Slavery had certainly existed before, but it was the legal articulation of slavery as a status of lifetime, heritable servitude that applied to all Africans and only to Africans that firmly bound property law to the tobacco economy.

Tobacco also shaped the law of finance and exchange in the Chesapeake. As the only crop of consequence, the entire export trade – and therefore the entire wealth – of the region rested on it. Tobacco gave British merchants a direct involvement in the Chesapeake economy that they did not have in the colonies to the north. It also gave planters a familiarity with sophisticated commercial credit instruments that most economic actors in New England did not have. Bills of exchange, the workhorse of trans-Atlantic commercial credit, penetrated local credit transactions to an extent unmatched elsewhere. This suggests a somewhat higher level of legal and financial sophistication in the plantation economies, but it also reflected an important structural difference between the Southern and Northern economies that had far-reaching consequences. Almost from the beginning, settlers in the plantation colonies, where the economies revolved around single staple crops – tobacco, rice, or sugar – did more business with consumers and suppliers in Europe and less with one another than did settlers in the Northern colonies, which of necessity developed more diversified, if less profitable, economies.

IV. CREDIT AND ITS CONSEQUENCES

This description of the plantation economies points toward what became the overriding legal and economic issue of the eighteenth century: credit. Virtually every significant development at the intersection of law and economy bore a direct or indirect relationship to credit. Indeed, one could, without exaggeration, write the entire history of law and economy in the long eighteenth century through the lens of credit. Credit was the wheel of commerce, both foreign and domestic. It was the engine of internal development. It was the foundation of finance, both public and private. It drove the settlement of the frontier and fueled vast land speculation schemes. It enabled farmers to buy land and livestock and planters to purchase land and slaves. It made possible the specialization of business activities that distinguished urban towns and cities from rural areas. It gave wing to the consumer revolution. And its withdrawal shattered lives and economies.

What gave credit legal, rather than just economic, significance was its conjoined twin, debt. The two were inescapable, integral facts of daily life in early America, whether one was an Atlantic merchant or a rural shopkeeper, a tidewater planter or a backwoods farmer. Debt cut across regional, class, and occupational lines so completely that everyone stood somewhere on the continuum of indebtedness that ran from prosperity to insolvency, either in their own right or by their dependence on a husband, a father, a master, or an owner. One can see this in the pervasiveness of debts owed and owing in probate inventories, in the predominance of debt actions in civil litigation, in the vast number of account books that have survived but never found their way into litigation, and in the fact that promises to pay were themselves a medium of exchange, circulating as money through factoring of open accounts and assignment of notes and bonds. Relations between debtors and creditors, and consequently the economy itself, were shaped by such matters as the legal form of the debt, whether a debt was secured or unsecured, the procedural rules of debt collection that came into play when debtors failed to pay debts when they were due, and the laws of insolvency, bankruptcy, and imprisonment for debt that governed the disposition of the debtor's person and property. If credit was the lifeblood of the economy, law was the framework within which credit and the economy operated.

Each of the different legal forms used to extend credit played a different role in the economy, a role that in large part turned on the differing degrees to which each one facilitated repayment. Throughout the colonial period, the form of debt that virtually everyone – rich and poor, urban and rural, even servants, many women, and some slaves – was familiar with was the account book. But book accounts did not dominate economic exchange in the eighteenth century as they had in the seventeenth. As running accounts of face-to-face dealings between creditors and their debtors, they were creatures of relatively insular local economies in which conditions of land, labor, and transportation kept trade largely within well-worn channels. By their very nature, book accounts recorded the transactions of people who dealt with one another repeatedly and who thus knew, whether through trust or merely familiarity, what to expect of one another. Within this context, the comparative informality and the procedural and evidentiary flexibility of book accounts gave them enough legal indeterminacy that payment was often more a matter of negotiation than of legal compulsion. However appropriate book accounts may have been for local economies, they were ill suited for more complex commercial transactions or for the direct extensions of credit at interest that constituted investment. There, formal written credit instruments supplied the economic need.

Written credit instruments came in several precisely defined forms, in all of which debtors, over their own signatures, expressly promised to pay specific sums to creditors, either on demand or by a certain date. Bonds, for example, could be conditioned or simple. Both were contracts under seal by which the obligor bound himself to pay a stipulated sum to the obligee on a stated date. Conditioned bonds, which were the more common and useful of the two, differed from simple bonds in that they predicated payment on the obligor's failure to perform a specified condition before the date set for payment. That condition, known as a condition of defeasance, could be either the performance of some act or the payment of a sum of money. Conditioned bonds guaranteed the conveyance of land, the delivery of commercial goods, and the repayment of loans. Their guarantee lay in their *in terrorem* effect. Failure to perform the condition made the obligor liable for the full amount of the bond, which was typically twice the sum lent or twice the value of the items to be delivered.

Bills obligatory and promissory notes or notes of hand were promises signed by the debtor to pay the creditor a specified sum within a stipulated time or on demand. Bills generally acknowledged the debt and recited what we would now regard as consideration for the debtor's promise – that, for example, the obligation was for goods received – whereas notes were simply unadorned promises to pay the named amount, much like I.O.U.'s. Bills obligatory were signed by witnesses; promissory notes were not.

Bills of exchange were a further variant and, for commercial purposes, a very important one. The precursors to modern checks, bills of exchange facilitated long-distance commercial transactions by serving as vehicles for borrowing money, making third-party payment of debts, and moving money from one place to another without having to do so physically. In its plainest form, a bill of exchange was a written order by one person instructing a second to pay a third. Or, in legalese, a drawer drew on a drawee in favor of a payee. The drawee, whose position in the transaction approximated that of the bank where one has a checking account, became liable for payment to the payee only by agreeing to do so when physically presented with the bill; that is, again in legalese, by accepting the draft. The person who presented the bill for payment was, technically, the holder of the bill. He might be the original named payee, or someone to whom the payee had endorsed the bill, or a subsequent endorsee from intervening endorsers. On acceptance, the drawer became liable to the drawee for the amount of the draft. A drawee's refusal to accept a draft had serious consequences for the drawer, the magnitude of which is best captured by the fact that rejected bills were referred to as "dishonored." Drawees sometimes refused drafts because they lacked funds to pay them. More often, however, they did so because they lacked confidence in the drawer's ability to reimburse them; in other words, they doubted the drawer's creditworthiness. A dishonored bill of exchange thus reflected directly on the honor and reputation of its maker and, by extension, on all his other bills.

Unlike book debts and oral promises, written credit instruments carried interest, either by contract or by statute. If by contract – which is to say, by agreement between debtor and creditor, whether the agreement was truly negotiated or imposed by the creditor – the rate of interest and when it would begin to accrue were stated in the instrument. If by statute, it usually took the form of a maximum legal rate, above which lay the forbidden realm of usury. Also unlike book debts and oral promises, written credit instruments were assignable; the creditor could transfer the instrument by endorsing it to a third party, who would then have the right to collect the amount due on it from the debtor, interest and all.

Assignability plays a crucial role in commercial economies. A proper credit system requires that debts be transferable, most importantly because the ability to transfer a debt permits the transferors to pay their own debts. With assignability, the debtor's promise to pay becomes a kind of currency that circulates from one assignee to another, coming to rest only when whoever holds the written evidence of the promise asks the debtor to make good on it. Local traders can thus satisfy their debts to their suppliers by endorsing over to their suppliers the promissory notes they have received from their local customers in payment for goods purchased – thereby transferring to their creditors the promises to pay that their customers have made to them. The one who ultimately demands payment of the note from the debtor whose note it is will then be the more distant supplier, not the local trader with whom the debtor had originally dealt. For this process to work, promises to pay must be severed from the transactions that give rise to them and be treated as essentially fungible. Only then can written credit instruments circulate in the economy. Assignability thus promoted economic efficiency by depersonalizing the relationship between debtor and creditor, part of the social cost of commercialization.

Notes, bills, and bonds were instruments of a commercial economy. But different colonial economies commercialized at different times and in different ways. For example, in the seventeenth century the Dutch in New Amsterdam, which was established essentially as a trading post, applied the same formal writings obligatory executed by the debtor before a notary and two witnesses, then recorded in the notary's register, used in Amsterdam itself, which was rapidly becoming the leading financial center in Europe. Less formal debt obligations became common only after the transfer to English rule in 1664. Similarly, virtually from their inception, the plantation colonies of the Southern mainland and the Caribbean produced valuable export crops for the European market – sugar in the Caribbean, tobacco in the Chesapeake, rice and indigo in South Carolina – which meant that they were full participants in the trans-Atlantic economy.

The economics of sugar and rice cultivation more or less compelled large-scale operations, creating capital-intensive plantation economies to which entry was very expensive, primarily because of the high cost of slave labor. To meet these costs, planters relied on credit, which, because of the large sums required, was usually trans-Atlantic rather than local in origin. Large planters were thus doubly bound to the trans-Atlantic economy for their markets and their credit, both of which relied on promises formally embodied in commercial credit instruments. Planters typically paid for purchases in bills of exchange drawn against the planter's credit balance with a metropolitan merchant or, more often, against the anticipated value of commodities shipped to market but not yet sold or even landed when the bill was drawn. The purchase of slaves was usually a credit transaction in which planters paid in bills of exchange payable two, four, or six months after acceptance, or in bonds due at specified future dates. The length of time required for payment, like the prices of the slaves themselves, was a market phenomenon governed by conditions of supply and demand both in the slave trade and in the trade in the staple crops produced by slaves.

The bills of exchange and bonds used in these transactions were sophisticated commercial instruments designed to facilitate long-distance credit. They also penetrated local transactions because of the many planters who dealt directly with English merchants rather than with local intermediaries and so were accustomed to using them and, in the case of bills of exchange, for the very practical reason that the funds and credit on which a planter's bill of exchange drew lay on the books of the British merchant to whom the planter shipped his tobacco. Yet it would be misleading to describe the plantation economies as commercial economics in any true sense, despite their use of commercial instruments. To be sure, trade in sugar, rice, and tobacco could be enormously profitable. Because of them, the plantation colonies were the only North American colonies to trade with England on anything approaching an equal footing. They were the only colonies from which the ships that had brought consumer goods could return to England laden with valuable cargo. Planters made large capital investment in land and slaves and often amassed considerable wealth, much greater than farmers or even merchants in the colonies to the north. But "commercialization" describes a set of economic practices and values, not merely a profitable trade. Their wealth and use of commercial paper notwithstanding, planters self-consciously adhered to a traditional set of agrarian values that regarded participation in the market as primarily a means to the end of presenting oneself as a gentleman, which by definition meant holding oneself apart from, and above, the marketplace. So deeply ingrained and enduring was this posture that even after the Revolution Southern Jeffersonians disdained commerce while embracing trade. "Trade" was an accumulation of exchange transactions. "Commerce," to its detractors, was a world view dominated by the pursuit of profit for its own sake.

The seeming anomaly of planters entirely dependent on trans-Atlantic trade using commercial credit instruments while disdaining commerce makes more sense when viewed against the vagaries of the tobacco and sugar markets and the legal responses to them in the eighteenth century. Debtors and creditors in the Chesapeake – or, more precisely, Chesapeake debtors and their local and foreign creditors – lived in a state of mutual dependence possible only in a highly leveraged economy, where the fortunes of borrowers and lenders were so thoroughly intertwined that they often seemed more like partners. Debt was a constant companion of the successful and unsuccessful alike; few planters after 1660 managed to avoid it. Planters purchased slaves with promises to pay for them at a future date. They shipped tobacco to British merchants on the understanding that the payment they ultimately received would be based on the market value of the tobacco when it arrived. They bought supplies and consumer items from British merchants and local traders by promising to pay for them with anticipated future profits. They bought tobacco from and resold goods to lesser planters who did not have their access to British markets, with all parties exchanging promises as well as goods. The flow of commodities, goods, and slaves within the Chesapeake and across the Atlantic thus rode on debt; that is, on promises that were, at least in theory, legally enforceable. Similar credit patterns prevailed in the sugar and rice colonies to the south.

The large role of English credit in the plantation economies occasioned a wide range of legal responses, most of which were shaped by the more or less continual decline in commodity prices from the closing decades of the seventeenth century onward. The link lay in the fact that lower prices for sugar or tobacco tended to drive planters deeper into debt, which creditors periodically attempted to collect. To deter creditors, colonies resorted to various legal and legislative measures, the most important of which recognized the economic centrality of land and labor. For example, land in the plantation colonies, Jamaica included, typically enjoyed a statutory exemption from attachment. Creditors could not seize a debtor's land and sell it out from under him unless the execution was pursuant to a mortgage foreclosure, in which case it was the debtor who had put the land at risk by pledging it to secure a debt. All other property, apart from a few small exemptions, was vulnerable to a creditor's levy. But land was worthless without the labor to work it, as the Virginia House of Burgesses recognized in 1705 when it formally reclassified slaves as real property – that is, land – which meant they could not be reached by creditors unless their owner had mortgaged them. Also in 1705, the Virginia burgesses enacted two additional impediments to creditors: a statute of limitations barring them from recovering sums due on judgments or bonds after a certain period of time, and a requirement that attorneys suing local debtors on behalf of English creditors post bond to cover court costs and damages. The spirit of these was not new. At various times in the seventeenth century Virginia had allowed debtors to spread payments to their creditors across three harvests, and the assembly had twice suspended collection on debts contracted in England. For its part, Maryland shielded its planter-debtors when the tobacco crop failed in 1724 by imposing a general stay of executions, thereby preventing creditors from collecting on judgments they had won in court. Jamaica tried a similar protection in 1728 by requiring creditors to accept commodities in payment of debts at fixed prices, but the law died without approval by the Board of Trade.

In addition to addressing the problem of tobacco-related debt by limiting private law remedies, Virginia and Maryland adopted regulatory measures as well. Both colonies tried to boost the sagging price of tobacco by reducing the quantity and improving the quality of the tobacco exported each year. Their efforts to do so – banning the inferior second-growth tobacco leaves and barring export of trash tobacco (stems, pulverized leaf, and other scraps) – proved unenforceable. The Virginia burgesses briefly added teeth to the restrictions in 1713 by requiring inspection of all tobacco at central warehouses and destruction of all trash tobacco. But planters who produced the targeted grades of tobacco protested, and the Board of Trade disallowed the law four years later. When depression returned in the 1720s, both colonies reimposed the prohibitions on seconds and on exporting trash and limited the number of tobacco plants each worker could tend. These, too, proved unenforceable, partly because of the resistance of poor planters and planters in areas where inferior grades of tobacco predominated, who rightly feared that the consequences would fall disproportionately on them, and partly because lower exports would have reduced the duties and fees collected by the Board of Trade and the Maryland proprietors.

There matters might have rested but for William Gooch, the royal governor of Virginia. Gooch was dispatched to Virginia in 1727 with instructions to ask the assembly for a bill that would permit British creditors to recover sums owed in Virginia to their bankrupt British debtors, which both Virginia and Maryland barred. Gooch's failure to win such a bill helped persuade British merchants to join him and wealthy planters in lobbying for and winning passage of an inspection act in 1730. The act had far-reaching consequences for both public and private law in Virginia. It required all planters to take their tobacco to government-owned warehouses. There, public officials would inspect the tobacco; pass only what they judged good, merchantable, and free from trash; and burn the rest. The inspectors then weighed the good tobacco and gave planters tobacco notes or warehouse receipts denominated by weight that added up to the amount of tobacco they had deposited for export to Europe. The notes circulated within the colony as legal tender for taxes and private debts. Maryland, whose planters generally grew lower quality tobacco, did not enact a similar law until 1747, after years of growing price differentials between inspected, quality-certified Virginia tobacco and its uninspected Maryland counterpart.

The implications of the Virginia inspection act for private law lay in the tobacco notes it authorized. The economies of the British North American colonies suffered from the lack of an adequate circulating medium of exchange. Led by Massachusetts in 1690, several colonies issued paper currency in the form of bills of public credit. Paper money redressed chronic shortages of specie and credit, stimulated internal trade, and facilitated consumption, but it was also prone to crippling depreciation, especially in New England, as few colonies had the fortitude to tax old issues out of circulation before emitting new ones. Virginia was the last colony to issue paper currency, in 1755. Until then, it relied on bills of exchange, bonds, and the new tobacco notes. Tobacco notes, which were backed not by promises but by hogsheads of quality-certified tobacco, and bills of exchange, which drew on planters' accounts in England, enjoyed a modicum of stability because their value was ultimately determined by the value of the tobacco crop in pounds sterling. This comparative monetary stability gave lenders a measure of security that a depreciating currency could not. It also permitted borrowers to give bonds for their obligations, whether for cash advances or to refinance existing debts by rolling book accounts with local traders over into the more certain promises of bonds.

Bonds, tobacco notes, and bills of exchange all circulated in Virginia as the equivalent of money. Bonds offered protections to debtors that promissory notes did not. The procedural rules of the action of debt by which bonds were litigated limited the creditor's recovery to the contract amount and barred additional claims for damages, and equity rules permitted judges to chancer the contract sum stipulated in the bond to a lower amount. Ironically, in 1732 debtors lost other protections they had enjoyed when Parliament passed an act "for the more easy Recovery of Debts" in the colonies that made land, houses, chattels, and slaves liable for satisfying sterling debts due by bond (the debts most commonly owed to British merchants), any colonial law to the contrary notwithstanding.

Although the 1732 debt recovery act applied throughout the colonies, its greatest impact was on the plantation economies. By exposing slaves to the claims of their masters' creditors, it enhanced the legal efficacy of the bonds planters gave to buy them, thereby encouraging expansion of the credit-based slave trade. It also facilitated the expansion of the store system that was the foundation of Scottish merchants' success in the tobacco trade. Scottish factors aggressively established stores far upstream in the Piedmont region, selling supplies on credit to smaller landowners while engrossing much of their tobacco crops for the Glasgow firms. Although the initial credit was usually on book accounts, a substantial portion of this short-term credit was converted into long-term obligations, primarily bonds or mortgages. When the Scottish factors sued for these debts, which they did not hesitate to do, they not only had the colonial debts act behind them, but as local creditors of locally contracted obligations they also sidestepped the procedural impediments that Virginia regularly threw up against foreign creditors.

Mortgages performed different credit functions in different colonies. For example, Jacob Price has described mortgages in the Caribbean as "the last stage in the ontogeny of debt: book debt, bond, judgment, mortgage."[2] When a planter ran up accounts on book too large to be cleared by the next crop or two, he might give his creditor – a local or British merchant or trader – a bond to guarantee repayment and, incidentally, to gain time. If the planter failed to pay the bond, the creditor could then sue and win judgment. To forestall execution on the judgment, the planter would give his creditor a mortgage on some or all of his land and slaves. Mortgages used in this fashion, to secure payment of a judgment, performed a very different economic function than did mortgages given to secure credit. As an example of the latter, consider the transformation of South Carolina from an unimpressive outpost in 1690 to a wealthy colony whose great planters produced rice for the European market by 1740, which was driven in part by mortgage-backed credit, as small farmers expanded their operations and became planters by mortgaging their land and slaves to secure loans to purchase more land and slaves. These were mortgages to finance development, not to secure prior past-due obligations. As the mortgagees were often Charleston merchants and the mortgagors rural farmers and planters, mortgage lending in South Carolina represented investment by urban merchants in country plantation development. Investors also included artisans, widows, and, in time, institutional investors, such as local parish vestries and even the Society for the Propagation of the Gospel in Foreign Parts – a sure sign of the growing maturity and sophistication of the credit market. The mortgage market did not finance the agricultural development of the South Carolina lowcountry by itself, but it was a major source of the capital that did.

Mortgages played yet another role in New England and the middle colonies, where they were the essential security mechanism in every attempt to establish a land bank. The object of a land bank was to create a stable circulating medium of exchange by issuing paper money backed by the security of mortgages on land. The idea itself circulated as early as the 1650s. In 1684, Massachusetts became the first colony to consider, and to reject, a proposal to establish a private land bank. Other attempts to create private land banks generally met stiff opposition, but in the quarter-century from 1712 to 1737 ten colonies created public land banks, usually labeling them loan offices. Only Delaware, Virginia, and Georgia did not.

[2] Jacob M. Price, "Credit in the Slave Trade and Plantation Economies," in Barbara L. Solow, ed., *Slavery and the Rise of the Atlantic System* (Cambridge, 1991), 35.

The colonial loan offices lent provincial paper money to citizens on the security of their land, farms, town houses, or other real estate, with the hope of promoting trade and industry. Despite the popularity of the loans, the effect on business was uncertain, although the interest paid by the borrowers did meet a variety of government expenses, such as poor relief, schools, public buildings, and the like. By and large, land banks succeeded in the middle colonies and failed in New England. Land – the irreducible core of mortgage-backed lending – was simply more valuable in the middle colonies than in New England because of the region's profitable commercial agriculture, and loan directors there were much more rigorous in requiring that the lands mortgaged were ample security for the money borrowed. In addition, the middle colonies showed significantly more restraint in the volume of currency issued, sparing themselves the ruinous depreciation that characterized New England currency, which at times seemed to be printed with near-abandon.

V. COMMERCIALIZATION AND CREDIT

Commercialization of the New England economies proceeded along different lines and employed different legal forms than in the Southern plantation economies. The middle colonies partook of both, though with a greater affinity for the New England model. Internal trade in New England expanded dramatically in the first half of the eighteenth century, spurred first by a boom in international trade through Boston in the 1690s and later by rapid population growth and periodic military expeditions to Canada and against the Indians. The rate of population growth outstripped the availability of new land for settlement. The resulting pressure on land encouraged more specialized cultivation to adapt to the different types of land. Specialization in turn led to commercial farming, both because of the inherent need to market crops and the development of large markets for foodstuffs in the West Indies. Market farming and agricultural specialization did not develop as fully in New England as they did in Pennsylvania or the Chesapeake. Nonetheless, the agrarian economy of the region developed enough to change the contours of commercial activity. With more products available for export, secondary ports and market towns grew to accommodate the demands for markets and transportation. The concentrated population and market orientation of these towns encouraged the appearance of artisans and shopkeepers. The lure of greater local trade opportunities encouraged people to enter the lists as small traders and challenge established merchants. This was the process of commercialization: people trading across greater distances, credit networks snaking through the countryside, the specialization of business enterprise, farmers and craftsmen trading on the side, artisans supporting themselves primarily by their crafts.

Commercialization was also an embrace of different values. To take just one prescient example from the beginning of the economic transformation, in 1699 the ministers of the Cambridge Association in Massachusetts formally abandoned their categorical objection to usury – opposition to which had been a cornerstone of Puritan commercial theology since the founding of the colony – conceding that "Humane Society, as now circumstanced, would sink, if all Usury were Impractable." They now justified moneylending, at least at reasonable rates, in terms appropriate to a commercial economy; namely, that it is only equitable for a lender to reap some benefit from a borrower's use of his property and that money is a commodity, an asset, and as such "is really as Improvable a thing as any other."[3]

As the New England economies changed, credit transactions rested increasingly on promissory notes, not on the more elaborate bonds common in Virginia. The advantage of written credit instruments in the new economy was that the debtor's liability on them rested not on the substance of the transaction, as it did in book debt, but rather on whether the note or bond itself met the legal requirements of form. Except for pleas that were limited in scope and often technical in nature, notes and bonds bound debtors to what they had signed. As a consequence, the outcome of litigation on them was more predictable. Rates of contest declined as debtors increasingly admitted liability by confessing judgment against themselves or by not appearing in court at all and allowing judgment to go against them by default. Most actions on notes and other written instruments were not disputes at all but rather fairly routine reductions of debts to judgments.

All of this reflected a world of relations between debtors and creditors that was rather different from the world of book debt. The exchange recorded by book accounts was often, though not always, commercial in nature. It might represent trading on account with a local shopkeeper, but it could just as easily arise from labor services by a neighbor. The exchange covered by notes and bonds, on the other hand, was always commercial. It arose from trade transactions, from direct extensions of credit, or from contractual undertakings. With their comparative precision and certainty, notes and bonds were instruments of increasingly commercialized economies in which trade and credit networks spanned greater distances. This was as much the case in Pennsylvania, where merchants were much more likely than farmers to formalize economic transactions, and New York, where

[3] Quoted in Perry Miller, *The New England Mind: From Colony to Province* (Cambridge, MA, 1953), 309.

economic relationships were increasingly contracted in writing and enforced according to their terms, as in New England.

One factor in the preference for notes over bonds was the advent and spread of paper money, which itself was both a cause and a symptom of commercialization. Bills of public credit were, in effect, public variants of private promissory notes. Their very appearance signaled growing involvement in a commercial economy. From the time Massachusetts first issued bills of public credit in 1690 as an emergency revenue measure after a series of costly imperial wars, people recognized their value as a circulating medium of exchange independent of any government revenue potential. For farmers and new traders who ran marginal operations with little capital support, paper money eased the chronic shortages of currency and credit that limited their growth. It answered the demands for capital of farmers who wanted to buy land or livestock and of traders who needed goods to trade. It provided an alternate source of credit for retailers, shopkeepers, and others in the domestic market that enabled them to bypass large wholesalers. With paper currency, new merchants entered towns and competed with established traders by offering farmers cash for their goods. Farmers, in turn, used the cash to repay debts they owed to the merchants with whom they usually ran up long book accounts – a relationship that could resemble economic bondage when they fell far enough behind.

As paper money circulated through the New England economies, touching people whose previous participation in the economy had been conducted by commodity exchanges, it democratized credit, allowing local traders and entrepreneurial farmers to share the aspirations of Atlantic merchants. Early proponents had recognized that ordinary people, not just large merchants, wanted to engage in commerce. But what some saw as opportunity, others viewed with concern. Cautionary writers argued that the credit made freely available by paper money encouraged people to spend beyond their means, to consume rather than invest. Rather than be satisfied with a competency appropriate to their station, they complained, people sought to emulate their betters, in the process incurring indebtedness that threatened both their moral and economic independence. To their minds, credit and everything it entailed – the right to engage in commerce, to borrow, to consume – should be limited to the privileged few.

The most vocal opponents of paper money objected on other grounds. These were the great Atlantic merchants, whose direct connections to England gave them ready access to credit. Paper currency was of no use to them in their international trade, since their foreign creditors would not accept it. In their domestic transactions, they were the ones who stood to lose the most if legal tender laws compelled them to receive paper money from their debtors in payment of their obligations, given the tendency of New

England bills to depreciate. Moreover, competition from new merchants with the growing contacts in the countryside that paper money facilitated threatened the dominance of established import merchants at the same time that it drove up commodity prices, which made it more expensive for Atlantic merchants to assemble cargoes for export. Complaints to England by the large Atlantic merchants eventually attracted the scrutiny of Parliamentary regulators, who moved to bar or restrict additional emissions of paper currency.

Agents of commercialization appeared on both sides of the issue. They all assumed the existence of competing economic interests in society – an assumption alien to earlier ideas of the covenant and an organic body politic. The controversies over paper money and banks were an emphatic rejection of the Puritan jeremiad, with its religious theme of declension, as a means of explaining commercial change and an embrace of the secular language of political economy. Even ministers who contributed to the debate wrote in terms of the role of money, the balance of trade, and political virtue, not of sin and punishment. This in itself was a fundamental change. But the debates also raised issues and questions that continued to occupy law and economy well into the Early Republic: Who had the right to participate in commerce, to borrow, to consume? Would easy credit undermine industry and frugality? Did consumption threaten the social order? Did debt compromise independence and political virtue? What was the proper role of government in financial and economic affairs? Was credit necessary to a commercial economy? What was the proper role of commerce? Was depreciation a moral issue, an economic issue, or a legal issue?

VI. THE LAW AND ECONOMY OF FAILURE

Written credit instruments and paper money were elements of a commercial economy based on contractual exchange. As they spread through the economy, the focus of law inevitably shifted to transactions between individual economic actors. Issues of debt and contract came to predominate, one measure of which was the overwhelming proportion of debt-related actions in civil litigation, not just in New England, but throughout the northeastern colonies. However, the law of debt and contract had a converse that was just as important to a commercial economy – the law of failure. The increasingly commercial economies of the eighteenth century created new opportunities for success. They also multiplied the risk of failure. Commercial development rode the crest of a rising tide of indebtedness, otherwise known as investment. It was a tide that reflected the confidence of prosperity as farmers and planters, artisans and shopkeepers, traders and merchants borrowed against anticipated profits to finance the undertakings that they knew – not hoped, but knew – would create them. Not surprisingly, some faltered while others soared. In highly leveraged, largely uninsured economies, even single misfortunes can bring ruin. However great the wreckage, debt always remains, and with it questions that only law can answer: What should become of debtors and their property when what they owned was not enough to pay what they owed? Did creditors' claims to repayment of what they had lent extend to the bodies of the debtors to whom they had lent it? Could creditors imprison their debtors or bind them to service? Could insolvent debtors ever hope for release from their debts, short of repayment in full?

Whether a society forgives its debtors and how it bestows or withholds forgiveness are more than matters of economic or legal consequence. They go to the heart of what a society values. At the beginning of the eighteenth century, people believed in a moral economy of debt that assumed the dependence of debtors and the omnipotence and inherent justness of creditors. Within that framework, inability to pay was a moral failure, not a business risk. Ministers preached that debtors must, if necessary, dispose of everything they own to repay their debts. God was the "Great Creditor" who casts insolvent souls into the debtors' prison of hell. As one minister wrote, a debtor who failed to pay "not only lost his Religion, but his Morality too."[4]

For these men and for the people to whom they preached, debtors were morally bound to pay their debts. Insolvency, although pitiable, warranted no relief other than what creditors might be inclined to grant out of the goodness of their hearts. Not surprisingly, the law agreed with them. Every colony, and later every state, permitted imprisonment for debt, most on *mesne* process and all on execution of a judgment. Several colonies – all in the North – bound insolvent debtors to their creditors as indentured servants to work off their debts. A handful of colonies flirted briefly with true bankruptcy discharges, others with insolvency laws that distributed the debtor's property while leaving his debts intact. Unlike criminals and paupers, imprisoned debtors had to provide their own food, fuel, and clothing – supplied from their own resources, the generosity of family or friends, begging, or the beneficence of a local relief society – or they did without. The state owed debtors nothing; not food, not clothing, not heat, not sanitation, and certainly not a discharge.

Quite apart from any moral reservations, attempts to enact insolvency or bankruptcy laws were complicated by the nature of credit itself. Credit was created in bilateral contracts that were enforceable through similarly

[4] Samuel Willard, *Promise-Keeping, A Great Duty* (Boston, 1691), 18.

bilateral litigation. One creditor, one debtor; one plaintiff, one defendant. Insolvency and bankruptcy proceedings, however, required transcending the transactional origin of each debt to achieve cooperation among creditors. Cooperation meant apportioning their losses among themselves, not securing repayment.

In fits and starts, colonies began to regard an insolvent debtor's financial and material remains as rightfully belonging to all of the debtor's creditors rather than to the creditor who was quickest to seize them. In part, this recognition was shaped by the growing geographic complexity of credit. Trading networks and the assignment of debt obligations swept debtors into larger economies. Whether or not debtors themselves traveled, their debts did, so that debtors often owed money to distant creditors as well as near ones. By the 1750s, the old moral economy of debt had begun to slip. For the first time one finds people arguing against imprisonment for debt and for bankruptcy laws. What prompted the change was failure. Economic growth enabled more people to fail owing greater sums of money to larger numbers of creditors than had been possible in the smaller, more insular local economies of the seventeenth century.

The legal landscape changed dramatically with the Seven Years' War. Wartime economic expansion, coupled with wartime economic risk, followed by postwar economic contraction, created the sort of fluid economy in which both success and failure could flourish. Shortly after the war began, several colonies experimented with new statutory schemes for discharging debts as well as debtors, the first concerted effort to do so. Within a two-year period, 1755 to 1757, New York, Rhode Island, and Massachusetts enacted bankruptcy systems that distributed insolvent debtors' assets among their creditors and discharged them from further liability on their debts. Connecticut followed suit in 1763. The experiments were short-lived or restrictive in their application or both. Each one expired or was repealed, leaving behind at best mechanisms for distributing debtors' assets without relieving debtors themselves, and at worst nothing at all.

The economic uncertainties of war were prelude to those of peace. Economies that had expanded to meet wartime needs and opportunities contracted. In addition, the demands of British creditors for payment in specie accelerated its depletion. To make matters worse, tightened enforcement of British imperial policy, together with high taxes by the colonies themselves to repay war debts and new Parliamentary measures to bind the colonies more closely to Britain, notably the Currency Act of 1764, combined disastrously to block sources of hard currency, drain paper money from the economy, and prevent new emissions of paper currency. As the supply of money shrank, commercial transactions required hopelessly long credits or reverted to commodity money, taxes could not be collected, and debts could not be paid. The colonial economies could not function smoothly or profitably without an adequate circulating medium of exchange. The postwar recession deepened into a depression that, in Carl Bridenbaugh's colorful phrase, "deranged the entire credit structure."

The war and its aftermath demonstrated to all how far tremors in foreign markets rippled through the colonial economies. One consequence was to demystify economic success and failure by clarifying economic cause and effect, which in turn pushed insolvency farther from moral failure and closer to simple economic risk. The accompanying flurry of statutes suggests a new willingness to create a law of failure that was something other than mere debt-collection process. With the economic impact of war and its aftermath clear for all to see, it became harder to stigmatize insolvency as moral failure. But there was a twist. Writers continued to warn against the dangers of debt in moral terms, but their target now was consumer debt, not commercial debt. When Benjamin Franklin railed against debt in *Poor Richard's Almanack* – "He that goes a borrowing goes a sorrowing," "The Borrower is a Slave to the Lender, and the Debtor to the Creditor" – he was exhorting his readers not to buy consumer goods on credit.[5] Commercial debt was different. Commercial creditors and debtors were, after all, partners in "the Race of Commerce." The redefinition of insolvency from moral failure to economic risk thus applied principally to debtors who were themselves entrepreneurs in the changing economy. So, when Americans began to question the efficacy of imprisonment for debt and consider the utility of bankruptcy discharges, their animating concern was the people who trafficked in credit, not those who merely purchased on it.

The American Revolution drove these lessons home with a vengeance. Like all wars, the Revolution was fought on credit. The Continental Congress and state governments issued massive volumes of paper money and loan certificates to sustain the war effort, which of course led to equally massive depreciation, which in turn was aggravated by inflation, as large-scale government purchases drove prices upward, prompting Congress to print even more currency. Private debts were only slightly less daunting. The war had disrupted foreign trade, which was the linchpin of the entire economy. After the war, prices declined and the economy contracted. At the same time, British merchants flooded the market with higher quality, lower priced goods and pressed commercial credit on coastal import merchants to enable them to feed the pent-up demand for consumer items. The tentacles of credit followed the goods from importers to wholesalers to retailers to

[5] [Benjamin Franklin], *Father Abraham's Speech To a great Number of People, at a Vendue of Merchant-Goods; Introduced to the Publick by Poor Richard* (Boston, [1758]), 14.

consumers, from the ports to the backcountry. Exports fell, imports grew, income and wealth declined, and debt increased.

The instability of paper currency in the 1780s generated several responses. The most immediate was proposals to charter banks that could issue bank notes as a form of private currency that would be backed by something more substantial than the traditional hope-and-a-prayer of government issues. From the beginning, calls for a bank emphasized the importance of public credit and a stable paper currency to commerce and industry. Thus, when Robert Morris procured a charter for the Bank of North America in 1781, the venture had widespread support among merchants, as did similar banks organized or incorporated in New York and Boston in 1784 and Baltimore in 1790. Agrarian interests, however, attacked banks as undemocratic concentrations of wealth and succeeded in revoking the state charter of the Bank of North America.

A second response, corollary to the first, was the enactment of state tender laws, which required creditors to accept paper currency at face value in payment of debts, no matter what the actual depreciated value of the currency. Paper money as legal tender for public obligations such as taxes was familiar enough before the Revolution, but as legal tender for private debts it remained controversial. Although often cast as debtor-relief measures, tender laws generated more complex reactions, largely because debtors were themselves often creditors, which made any tender law a double-edged sword. In addition, hostility to a state tender act varied with the rate of depreciation. Tender laws in states with reasonably well-supported paper currency did not encounter nearly the opposition they did in states with notoriously devalued currency. Initially, tender laws seemed an unavoidable, if drastic, solution to the problems debtors faced in how they were to repay prewar and wartime domestic debts when the only currency available, when any was available at all, was depreciating paper. Legislatures did not set out to "defraud" creditors. Rather, they sought to bolster the value of the only currency they had. The difficulty, of course, lay in attempting to legislate the value of something that had no intrinsic worth.

A third response was the rapid spread of speculation, which grew at a fevered pace at the close of the war when soldiers were sent home with settlement certificates as their pay. Speculators quickly bought up most of the certificates for as little as ten or fifteen cents on the dollar. In short order, and aided by a decline in prices that limited the appeal of trading opportunities, speculative activity spread to every kind of government issue that contemplated future redemption, whether land warrants or debt certificates. Within just a few years, a very large proportion of the state and national public debt was held by speculator-investors who had bought warrants, certificates, and indents from the originals holders at steeply discounted prices, with the result that people began debating issues of debt equity long before controversy swirled around Alexander Hamilton's plan for funding the public debt in the 1790s.

Alongside the "spirit of speculation" in the 1780s was a renewed acquaintance with failure. The decline of prices, the scarcity of cash, depreciation, competition from British manufactures, the obstacles to establishing export markets when no longer part of the British empire, and efforts by British commercial creditors to collect prewar debts all contributed to a wave of business failures after the Revolution. Following as they did so closely on the heels of a steep rise in mercantile activity, the business collapses deepened the understanding of failure as the downside of entrepreneurial risk. This made failure the potential common fate of all merchants. In these circumstances, merchants recognized the value of asserting mercantile control over failure, much as the law merchant rested on the principle that matters of commerce were best adjudicated by men of commerce under procedures that accommodated the demands of commerce. For merchants, the attempt to control the consequences of failure led to the first postwar bankruptcy law, enacted by Pennsylvania in 1785. The Pennsylvania statute offered the holy grail of debt relief – discharge of unpaid debts – only to commercial debtors who owed a large minimum amount.

The rise of speculation as the investment of choice in the 1790s fundamentally transformed indebtedness. Speculators stood at the center of a financial vortex. Their competition for capital drove up the interest rates they had to offer to investors, which in turn attracted investment from ever-widening circles, both demographically and geographically. When they failed, the effects of their failure rippled outward, engulfing those who had loaned them money. The two financial crises of the decade were triggered by the collapse of speculation schemes – the bursting of William Duer's speculations in bank stock and government securities in 1792 and the failure of large land ventures in 1797, many of which involved Robert Morris. The resulting economic distress far surpassed any that had occurred before. For the first time numerous prominent men found themselves imprisoned for their debts or fugitives from their creditors. Their presence in the pool of insolvent debtors confounded the normal expectations of social and economic status and altered the political dimensions of debtors' relief. As a result, the debate over debtor relief was recast as a debate on the merits of bankruptcy. In part, this was because the sudden increase in the number of people imprisoned for their debts generated new calls for ending the practice, which necessarily raised the question of how else to deal with unpaid debts. In addition, the widespread popularity of speculative investment had helped speed the redefinition of debt from a moral failing to an economic one for which imprisonment seemed an inappropriately criminal punishment. Perhaps most important, the prominence of the speculator-debtors dovetailed with the traditional ambit of bankruptcy in England, where relief was available only to merchants, traders, and brokers whose debts exceeded a minimum that itself exceeded the typical indebtedness of farmers, laborers, and shopkeepers – in short, of most ordinary debtors.

The first national bankruptcy act in 1800 thus applied only to commercial debtors whose success had allowed them to amass debts that were far beyond the means of less prosperous debtors. The statute was, in effect, a national statement of the "principle" that release from debts was a boon reserved for capitalist entrepreneurs, while simpler debtors should, by implication, remember the sanctity of their obligations. However much men of commerce might dun their own debtors, the law decreed that for them, and them alone, the hazards of the market trumped moral obligation. Only they could fail. All other debtors merely grew poorer, their insolvency the result not of risk but of their reach exceeding their grasp. The Bankruptcy Act of 1800 was a declaration that the new nation was, emphatically, a commercial republic. It was also short lived. The traditional restriction of bankruptcy to elite merchants hinted at aristocratic privilege and so made bankruptcy untenable in the new democratic politics that erupted from the election of 1800. Congress repealed the statute in 1803, eighteen months before it would have expired on its own.

The Bankruptcy Act of 1800 highlighted an important fault line in the American economy. Merchants and other commercial figures tended to favor bankruptcy legislation because it offered them an entrepreneurial safety net if they failed – release from debtors' prison, an orderly apportionment of their assets among their creditors, who were thereby compelled to share in the losses, and discharge from liability for their debts, with the consequent promise of being able to start afresh in business unburdened of past debts. Planters and farmers, on the other hand, opposed bankruptcy because it threatened their livelihoods by exposing their land to their creditors' claims if the trading all of them did on the side swept them within the ambit of the law by turning them into commercial debtors. Indeed, the Southern hostility to bankruptcy – the Southern colonies and states never experimented with insolvency or bankruptcy relief with the urgency that their Northern counterparts did – may have been a symptom of the region's inability to maintain its colonial economic supremacy after independence.

VII. CAPITAL AND INVESTMENT IN THE EARLY REPUBLIC

There was more to law and economy in the 1790s than dealing with failure. The decade also saw the emergence of a capital market that financed economic development in the Early Republic and paved the way for the corporation to become the engine of the economy in the nineteenth century. And there was, of course, the corporation itself. The capital market had three parts: government bonds first issued as part of Alexander Hamilton's plan to fund the national debt, stock of chartered private banks, and insurance company equities. All three were investment vehicles; indeed, the first two were objects of the speculative frenzy that culminated in the Panic of 1792. But that was only part of their utility. Banks, for example, quickly became the primary source of commercial credit, at least in the North. Planters in the Southern states drew on the same European sources of credit they had before the war, which is one reason why the South never developed significant financial services firms and had little control over development capital. Banks were created by government charter, both federal and state. Their initial capitalization came from the sale of shares, the number of which was limited by charter. The twenty thousand shares in the Bank of the United States offered to the general public in 1791 at the high price of $400 per share sold out the very morning they were issued. Together with the five thousand shares retained by the federal government, they created a financial institution with $10,000,000 in capital. Banks also accepted deposits from governments and individuals. Governments usually deposited specie, while individuals typically deposited promissory notes, bills of exchange, and other securities, which the bank would accept at a discount and which the depositor could then draw on by writing checks.

What mattered, of course, was what banks did with the money. Quite simply, they lent it to borrowers. Banks made business loans to artisans, tradesmen, manufacturers, shopkeepers, carpenters, shipwrights, blacksmiths, painters, masons, brickmakers, sailmakers, farmers, and others. They helped finance the creation of a transportation infrastructure by investing in (in effect, making long-term loans to) the private internal improvement companies that built turnpikes, canals, bridges, waterworks, and, eventually, railroads. Banks were not the only source of investment capital – insurance companies were another – but they were an indispensable source of commercial credit. Moreover, the bank notes they issued functioned as paper money – a circulating medium of exchange backed by fractional specie reserves. Some banks issued their notes in sufficiently high minimum denominations that only wholesalers could use them. Others, mechanics' or farmers' banks, operated under charters that required them to issue notes in denominations low enough to be useful to artisans, shopkeepers, and farmers in retail transactions. These bank notes filled the gap abruptly created in 1789 when the Constitution prohibited state governments from emitting bills of public credit. In the absence of a federal currency, they remained the only circulating paper currency until the Civil War. They were also the mechanism by which the Bank of the United States acted as an unofficial bank regulator, the equivalent of a central bank. There were 32 chartered banks in the United States by 1800, and 210 by 1815, all of which issued bank notes, accepted deposits, and made loans. Until it closed in 1812, the Bank of the United States, because of its size and branch network, routinely accumulated large sums in notes issued by the state-chartered banks. By periodically presenting these notes to their issuing banks for conversion into specie, the Bank of the United States kept enough pressure on the banks' specie reserves to hold their loan and currency volumes within sustainable limits.

The corporation, like banks, was not a creation of the 1790s. Both had much deeper roots. But also like banks, the 1790s is when corporations began to reshape the economy. Variants on the corporation had existed in America from the beginning of settlement, which had been undertaken by chartered joint-stock associations, such as the Virginia Company, the Massachusetts Bay Company, and the Plymouth Company. Massachusetts, in particular, had long experience with corporate forms, from creating entities such as town proprietors that resembled corporations in the seventeenth century to formal grants of corporate privileges to bodies as disparate as schools, parishes, church officers, marine societies, and overseers of the poor in the eighteenth century. So routine were corporations that in 1753 Massachusetts enacted what was, in effect, a general law of incorporation, nearly a century before such laws became the norm. The statute allowed owners of land that lay outside existing towns or precincts to form associations to promote its settlement and improvement simply by petitioning a justice of the peace to issue warrants for the first meeting – a much simpler process than the standard mode of incorporation, which was by petition to and charter from the legislature.

Incorporation is a private-law version of the political maxim, "*e pluribus unum*": out of the many, one. It authorizes a group of individuals to join together in a new entity that is itself a legal person, a self-governing body capable of holding property and of suing and being sued. The Massachusetts legislature granted more than one hundred acts of incorporation in the 1780s, the first full decade of statehood. Nearly two-thirds constituted individual towns, districts, parishes, and precincts as legal "bodies politic." Most of the remainder created various religious societies. Others incorporated educational institutions and charitable societies. Only a few formed business corporations – the Massachusetts Bank in 1784, the Charles River Bridge Company in 1785, the Beverly Cotton Manufactory in 1789. In the 1790s, the legislature doubled the number of acts of incorporation it passed. "Bodies politic" still dominated, but their proportion fell to half. The number of incorporated religious societies, educational institutions, charitable societies, and professional associations increased. Most significantly, nearly one-fourth of the acts of incorporation granted that decade created business corporations organized to construct internal improvements, such as bridges, canals, turnpikes, and waterworks. The legislature also incorporated seven banks, six insurance companies, three manufacturing companies, and two mills.

The sharp rise of the for-profit business corporation in the 1790s continued in the ensuing decades. The stated purpose of the business corporation was not to make money, however much that may have been the unstated purpose. Instead, the legislature conferred corporate status to serve a public purpose. Thus, banks, turnpike companies, manufacturing companies, insurance companies, and bridge companies all existed, according to their charters, for the benefit and good of the public, as did incorporated colleges and universities, religious societies, charities, and institutions such as the Massachusetts Historical Society. However, the proliferation of business corporations soon left this commonality behind. Their numbers grew as opportunities for capital-intensive enterprise increased. The spectacular failure of Robert Morris's land companies in 1797 demonstrated the limits of what one man could accomplish, even one as wealthy and creditworthy as Morris. By way of contrast, the ability of the corporation to muster large quantities of capital through the sale of stock and corporate borrowing – larger quantities than individuals alone could supply – and to apply it in a concerted fashion were what permitted business corporations to capitalize on the opportunities presented by the emergence of national markets. As Pauline Maier has observed, the corporation empowered individuals "whose resources were unequal to their imaginations" and thus represented "the most significant form of collectivism to emerge from the Revolution." How to restrain its power would be a question for the nineteenth century.

CONCLUSION

The relationship between law and economy is dynamic, not static. So to say that the focus of law shifted in the eighteenth century to transactions between individual economic actors is not to say that it remained there. The rise of the administrative or regulatory state toward the end of the nineteenth century and the resulting struggle between public and private would mark yet another stage in the ever-changing relationship between law and economy. Nonetheless, the transactional focus of law in the eighteenth century and its intimate connection to credit had far-reaching implications for American society.

Scholars differ on the nature and even the existence of economic growth in the eighteenth century. Undeniable, though, is that the American economies were becoming more commercial, particularly in the North, as trade reached across greater distances, credit networks spread through the countryside, business enterprise grew more specialized, farmers and craftsmen traded on the side, and people embraced the market as a value in itself rather than as a distastefully necessary means to a traditional social end. In legal terms, these commercial economies consisted of thousands of contractual exchanges, large and small. Each exchange, whether the purchase and sale of goods or services or the extension of credit, was a bilateral transaction between two parties, enforceable through similarly bilateral litigation. Contractual exchange drew more people into a marketplace in which law was the ultimate arbiter of economic relations.

Commercial law drew no distinction among persons, even though the economy itself did. The benefits of commercialization were not distributed evenly, either within or across regions. Economic actors were thus equals in legal form despite often being unequals in material substance. This duality formed the basis of two great social, political, and economic developments in the eighteenth century. One was the growing claim to equality that helped spur the Revolution and shape the constitutional order that followed. The other was the gradual coalescing of economic differences into class distinctions, a process that accelerated with industrialization in the next century. The two came together in the claims of ordinary men to political equality that made the Early Republic such a tumultuous era. Their claims reflected a democratization of American society that might fairly be said to have had roots in the democratization of credit that accompanied the intertwined economic and legal changes of the century.

12

LAW AND COMMERCE, 1580–1815

CLAIRE PRIEST

Was empire-building an animating objective of the U.S. government in its early years? Was the Constitution enacted to achieve mercantilist purposes? Were early federal government policies mercantilist? In the early twenty-first century, scholars have been answering these questions with a resounding "yes." Their answers suggest that American colonialism of the late nineteenth century and the record of U.S. military interventions abroad since then are a continuation of values held since the founding.

The scholarship contending that the federal government in the Founding Era was by nature mercantilist (or "neo-mercantilist") and imperial, however, is imprecise and anecdotal. Moreover, it raises complex historical questions that scholars have not addressed. Why would a nation of colonies that fought a revolution against an imperial power immediately adopt the core values of the mercantilist government it had rejected? How "radical" could the Revolution have been if the framers of the U.S. Constitution viewed empire-building as a primary objective? More broadly, if that were indeed the objective, why did the United States avoid the European race for colonies in Africa, Asia, and the Middle East for most of the nineteenth century?

Here, I provide a detailed history of British mercantilism and explain why its core principles were *rejected* by American political leaders in the Founding Era. Part I follows Adam Smith's *Wealth of Nations* in defining "mercantilism" as the policies in force during British imperial history in the seventeenth and eighteenth centuries. According to this definition, mercantilism comprises several interrelated positions: first, a commitment to the belief that political power and national strength are achieved by government regulations that improve the home country's balance of trade; second, the acquisition of colonies that are monopolized and regulated to further improve the mother country's trade balance; third, the maintenance of active military policies to defend these colonial holdings; and fourth, the adoption of a financial system that supports military campaigns to secure and protect markets abroad. Most prominent political leaders in Founding Era America (and likely the general public) subscribed to the first element of mercantilism: that national prosperity and liquid credit markets depended on a favorable trade balance. There was, however, little support for the acquisition, monopolization, or the defense of colonies and colonial markets, three core features of British mercantilism.

The rejection of mercantilism in Founding Era America was rooted in the economic and institutional development of the British colonies in North America. Part II describes how, from the outset, colonial legislatures exercised authority independently as sovereign powers, although subject to the regulation and supervision of the royal government. Colonies competed with one another for trade and enacted independent commercial and economic legislation. Until the colonies joined together to throw off English colonial rule during the American Revolution, discussed in Part III, there was little unity among them, either economically, politically, or through a sense of a shared colonial identity.

Not surprisingly, after the American Revolution, the states emerged as the locus of the citizenry's allegiance and as the primary institutions dedicated to economic promotion. Part IV shows how hostility to past Parliamentary regulation transformed into immediate suspicion of federal government power. Under the Articles of Confederation, individual states retained the authority to enact trade regulations and had sole authority to impose taxes. State sovereignty with regard to commercial and foreign policy, however, left the former colonies financially and militarily insecure. The weakness of the state sovereignty model of the Articles led to the movement for a stronger federal government, which resulted in the ratification of the U.S. Constitution.

The U.S. Constitution left *internal* commercial regulation principally to the states, but constrained the states by preventing them from negotiating independently with foreign governments and from (at least explicitly) discriminating against each other's goods. The U.S. Constitution prevented the states – which remained the most important units of government – from adopting mercantilist policies.

The federal government's power to adopt a mercantilist agenda was curtailed for much of the nineteenth century not, like the states, by constitutional provision, but by regional diversity, national political ideology, and electoral choices. The vast differences in the economies of the North, Middle Atlantic, and South meant that their economic interests were often opposed to one another. Tariff policy, one of the principal devices available to structure national economic policy in the nineteenth century, reflected a constant compromise between regions with diametrically opposed preferences (Northerners favored tariffs; Southerners were generally hostile to them). Moreover, the growing dominance of Jeffersonian republican values translated into limited resources for the United States to play a central role in global imperialism: through the first quarter of the nineteenth century import tariff levels were relatively low, the citizenry was hostile to federal direct taxes, and the Bank of the United States was severely limited in its ability to establish a permanent federal debt that would have allowed the finance of military action similar to that of England and France.

Expansionist principles were embodied in the conquest of Native American tribes in the West. But the conquest of the West, perhaps counter-intuitively, represented the rejection of classical mercantilist ideals. Subsidization of the conquest and settlement of the West by the federal government reflected the dominant Jeffersonian view that American economic growth should be advanced by means of the expansion of agriculture, not by the capture of markets abroad. Moreover, Western expansion was a popular policy in part because the proceeds from the sale of public lands were earmarked to reduce the size of the federal debt. Thus in the early nineteenth century, the conquest of the West was a means of expanding the country's size while respecting the citizenry's hostility to taxes and to the federal government. The American government could easily have competed with European powers for colonies in Africa, the Middle East, and Asia in the nineteenth century, but it did not. For much of the nineteenth century, federalism and republicanism prevented American mercantilism and imperialism.

I. BRITISH MERCANTILISM

"Mercantilism" is a term derived from the critique of British political economy that Adam Smith advanced in *The Wealth of Nations*. Smith showed that centuries of British commercial regulations and military policy had been justified by inherently flawed ideas about the sources of national wealth and global power. A principal object of his critique was the widespread acceptance of "bullionism," the view that the wealth of a nation is embodied in the quantity of bullion (specie) circulating within the nation's borders. Bullionists believed that the primary means of increasing national wealth was to draw specie into the national economy from the outside. The sovereign could help attract specie by enacting policies that improved the country's balance of trade – the value of exports in relation to the value of imports.

Under mercantilist assumptions, merchants served as "agents" of the state in improving the balance of trade. As described by Thomas Mun, a London merchant and author of a classic 1664 mercantilist essay entitled *England's Treasure by Forraign Trade, or the Balance of our Forraign Trade is the Rule of our Treasure* (singled out by Adam Smith as exemplifying the faulty assumptions he critiqued), merchants were "the Steward[s] of the Kingdom's stock [of specie]." The object of government policy was to help merchants "sell more to strangers yearly than wee consume of theirs in value." Those in the government who espoused mercantilist beliefs were amenable to enacting legislation on the merchants' behalf.

Mercantilist assumptions justified military interventions to conquer colonies and to exclude adversaries from colonial markets. The acquisition of colonies was believed to improve the balance of trade because colonies provided exclusive access to natural resources or locally produced goods, like tobacco or spices, that the home country's merchants could export at a profit to other parts of the world. Moreover, colonial markets were regulated to promote the sale of the home country's manufactured exports.

Mercantilists typically believed that a fixed amount of trade existed in the world and that a nation could expand its relative wealth and power only by "taking" trade away from other nations through the capture of colonies. The expenses of war were justified on the ground that the loss of trade or of colonial holdings meant a decline in national wealth and power both in absolute terms and relative to the nation that "acquired" the trade of the colony. Winning wars, however, required both a competitive military and a competitive financial system. Classic mercantilism therefore involves a possible vicious circle: government subsidizes private investment in trade with colonial producers; greater private investment in the colonies increases the exposure to loss when colonies are threatened by foreign powers; greater investment in the colonies requires the government to increase military expenditures to protect its colonial holdings; increased military expenditures must be justified by increased investment in the colonies; and so on.

The History of British Mercantilism

How did mercantilism develop? Mercantilist regulatory systems did not appear immediately, but emerged alongside the centralized European state. In Britain, Parliament enacted individual pieces of special interest legislation benefiting merchants as early as the fourteenth century. By the second half of the sixteenth century, the Crown began regularly granting monopolistic corporate charters to groups of private investors and individual mariners interested in trading ventures abroad. The principal purpose of these early companies was to run trading posts, delivering goods from the British Isles to sell abroad and bringing back high-demand items in return. These trading ventures were typically financed through the vehicle of a joint-stock company. Money from the sale of shares to the public provided the initial capital. In the late sixteenth century, the joint-stock company device was used to finance trading ventures in Russia, Turkey, the Levant, and the East Indies.

In this "first" stage of mercantilism, the Crown provided little military support to the trading companies it chartered. The chartered companies were required to invest in ships capable of self-defense. The Crown viewed these private ships as a reserve force that it could use, when necessary, for its own military ends. Military benefits rarely flowed from the government to the private sector.

The first English colonies in the Americas were organized as for-profit, joint-stock companies. For example, the Virginia Company of London (chartered in 1606), which created the first settlement at Jamestown, and its companion Plymouth Company, which attempted to settle at Sagadahoc, were both joint-stock companies. Theirs was a far more complicated type of business than the traditional trading posts. Unlike the companies trading in the East, which had traded for goods for which they knew a market existed, the companies operating in America had to discover and develop lucrative items for export. Finding such goods in North America proved difficult. The original economic ambition of the British colonies, as reflected in many colonial charters, was to find gold and silver mines on the scale of those that had been discovered in the Spanish colonies. But the minerals were not there to be found. The types of goods that appeared to be marketable, such as tobacco and rice, required labor. The companies' ventures thus became complicated by the need to transport laborers to the New World and establish permanent settlements with governance structures and legal institutions. Laborers were initially recruited by means of indentured servant contracts, later by slavery. Estimates suggest that indentured servants constituted possibly 50 percent to 66 percent of white males immigrating to the American colonies between 1630 and 1776, or approximately 300,000 to 400,000 people. Slave importation to British North America – primarily an eighteenth- century phenomenon – is estimated at just over 255,000 between 1701 and 1775.

In the initial years, the Virginia Company, the Massachusetts Bay Company (chartered 1628), and the companies that created the first colonies in Bermuda (1609–10), Newfoundland (1610), and Nova Scotia (1610) were not highly profitable. By mid-century, however, goods like tobacco grown in Virginia, sugar produced in Barbados, and fish in the Northern colonies proved to be important export items justifying further settlement, investment, and military support. Joint-stock investments became so profitable in the seventeenth century that Britons from all classes – from the monarchy and landed aristocracy, to the urban elite, to the middle classes – increasingly invested in foreign trade ventures. Those investments, in turn, translated into increased political support for government military protection of colonial trade.

The growth of the navy was a consequence of, and a necessary condition for, a new, "second" stage of mercantilism. Under Charles I, the state's first-stage role had been limited to granting and enforcing monopolistic charters and providing partial financing for trading ventures. During the Commonwealth period, in large part due to merchant lobbying, the government for the first time assumed responsibility for military protection of merchant vessels trading abroad. The British navy consisted of 39 vessels in 1648, 80 in 1651, and 287 in 1660. The state monopolized trade with entire colonies, but British merchants developed open, competitive markets among Britons within the ports of those colonies. Colonies became the military responsibility of the state; the British citizenry in theory received a corresponding benefit through customs revenues and free opportunities for trade and immigration abroad. With a few exceptions, such as the East India Company and the Hudson's Bay Company, monopolistic joint-stock companies that governed as well as traded declined in importance by the end of the seventeenth century.

Mercantilism and Political Reform

The commitment of the British government to protecting overseas trade eventually led to an overhaul of government finances and democratic political reform. English kings, like other European monarchies, responded to financial difficulties by compelling wealthy individuals to loan money to the government, by changing the terms of existing loan agreements, or by unilaterally repudiating their debts. Bad credit terms also led them to obtain funds by means of fines and land confiscations. Monarchs historically faced severe public skepticism about any increase in general taxes needed as security for government debt obligations. However, the adoption of the Navigation Acts (described below) threw Britain into its first major trade wars – that is, wars not involving the conquest of land: the Anglo-Dutch wars of 1652–4, 1664–7, and 1672–4. Government debts incurred during these wars were unsustainable under the traditional model of English finance. Britain ultimately expanded its financial capability through the transfer of power from the monarch to a legislature whose members maintained the integrity of the government's financial promises. Parliamentary control over finances was secured with the ascension to the throne of William and Mary in the Glorious Revolution of 1688–9. Their acceptance of the Declaration of Rights and Bill of Rights abolished the royal power to suspend and overrule enacted law. Parliament took control over the government's finances and increased government transparency and accountability. The Bank of England emerged by the 1730s as the primary institutional source of government borrowing. Its notes and bonds were sold to the public and traded like a currency, which increased the liquidity of the economy and made the government financially accountable to the public. Britain entered further wars, this time with France, in 1689–97 (King William's War), 1702–13 (Queen Anne's War), 1744–8 (King George's War), and 1754–63 (French and Indian, or Seven Years War). These wars led to unprecedented levels of government debt in both countries. Britain, however, was able to borrow at terms twice as good as those available to France.[1]

The Navigation Acts

The British Empire was defined by the reach of comprehensive trade regulations enacted to advance the mercantilist goal of improving England's balance of trade. As one act stated, the regulations were intended to keep the colonies "in a firmer dependance" upon England, and to render them "more beneficial and advantagious" to the mother country by furthering the "imployment and increase of English shipping and seamen," the export of "English woolen and other manufactures and commodities" to the colonies, and by making England a clearinghouse for colonial imports (the "commodities of th[e] plantations") and for "commodities of other countries and places" that English merchants could "supply" to the colonies.[2] The commercial regulations were enacted in piecemeal fashion and were often the product of highly contested political debate in England. They are, however, collectively referred to as the "Navigation Acts."

The 1660 "Act for the Encouraging and Increasing of Shipping and Navigation" was the central statute defining British mercantilism. A 1651 ordinance had required that the produce of the British colonies be transported in English-owned ships. The 1660 act extended the 1651 ordinance and prohibited all non-British ships from entering colonial ports. It also prohibited non-British subjects from acting as factors or merchants in the British colonies and, therefore, from promoting foreign-produced goods. The act cemented control over colonial markets by requiring that certain lucrative items – originally, sugar, tobacco, cotton-wool, ginger, and various dyes produced in the New World – be exported only to ports in England

[1] Britain was also able to outspend France. It spent £73 million on the Seven Years War to France's £53 million, and £112 million during the War of American Independence as compared to France's £40 million.

[2] An Act for the Encouragement of Trade, 15 Charles II, c. 7 (1663).

or to another British colony prior to reexportation. Later acts extended this requirement to molasses, rice, coffee, coconuts, cacao-nuts, pimento, whale-fins, hemp, raw silk, beaver and other pelts, hides, and skins, potash, pearl ash, and all naval stores, such as masts, yards, tar, pitch, pig and bar iron, copper ore, and turpentine. Colonial merchants thus were prohibited from directly exporting these commodities to a foreign port.

The Staple Act of 1663 led to further control over colonial markets by requiring all European goods, with minor exceptions, to be imported into the British colonies by way of an English port. European goods thereafter had to be unloaded in England, duties paid, and reloaded and shipped to the colonies.

MONOPOLIZING THE CARRYING TRADE

What was the underlying logic of this complex system of acts? The first grouping of acts related to the regulation of the nationality, crews, and ownership of the vessels in which goods were shipped. They gave British ship-builders and merchants almost exclusive dominance in the carrying trade within the British Empire. In the seventeenth and eighteenth centuries, goods were sold in colonial ports at prices that were on average 20 percent higher than in English ports, reflecting the costs of transportation. Monopolizing the carrying trade improved England's balance of trade by reserving the revenue generated by the carrying trade to British merchants, at the expense of the colonists who would have benefited from greater competition.

At the time of the 1651 ordinance, the Dutch dominated the carrying trade between Europe and the Atlantic colonies. English ships were a minor presence. The Navigation Acts sought to capture this business from the Dutch fleet. The Anglo-Dutch trade wars of the second half of the seventeenth century reflected, in part, Dutch resistance to the acts and its attempt to regain the carrying trade. Britain's ultimate defeat of the Dutch secured a monopoly of colonial ports for British shipping and led to the acquisition of new colonies, such as New Amsterdam, renamed New York.

The near-monopoly on shipping within the British Empire imposed by Parliament was initially met with colonial resistance because the Dutch offered shipping of imported goods at lower rates and on better credit terms. Southern colonies suffered from the loss of competition in the tobacco export business. At the same time, the stimulus to ship-building generated by the monopoly helped boost the New England economy. The lower relative cost of materials in New England led it to become the center of ship-building within the British Empire. Over time, rapid expansion of the British mercantile fleet and increased competition meant British shipping rates and credit terms fell to levels equal to the rates formerly charged by the Dutch. The British shipping monopoly also made it easier to combat piracy. Limiting all colonial ports to English-owned ships reduced the bases from which pirates and privateers in foreign-owned ships could operate. Insurance costs for shipments lowered.

REGULATING COLONIAL EXPORTS

From the perspective of the colonies, the most onerous regulations were those that impaired trade with Europe. As mentioned, the Navigation Acts required that certain enumerated items, including tobacco, rice, indigo, and other goods, be exported directly to England to enable English merchants to dominate the international marketing of the goods and thereby to improve England's balance of trade. London and Glasgow, for example, became global centers for the marketing of tobacco and rice. The goods subjected to this requirement were typically the most profitable items produced in the colonies, the importation of which would not adversely affect the English economy through competition with goods produced in England.

This requirement increased prices for colonial goods in European markets because of the additional costs of unloading and reloading in English ports. It also gave English merchants a monopoly on factoring to Europe, further reducing colonial returns by comparison to what might have been earned had the colonists had been able to trade in European markets directly: more than 80 percent of colonial enumerated goods brought to England and Scotland were subsequently reexported to northern Europe.

SUPPRESSING COLONIAL MANUFACTURING

Colonial manufacturing ran contrary to the goal of increasing England's balance of trade because it both reduced colonial demand for English goods and, in some cases, created competition with English manufactures. The Crown and Parliament never enacted a blanket ban on colonial manufacturing; it would have been unrealistic to do so, if only because colonists needed the wherewithal to buy British goods. Nevertheless, they selectively sought to suppress colonial competition in manufactures. For example, statutes prohibited shipping among the continental colonies of raw wool, woolen manufactures, and hats in order to increase the demand for English woolens and English hats.[3] The Crown also invalidated colonial statutes that sought to promote local manufacturing. As an example, Pennsylvania in 1700

[3] An Act to Prevent the Exportation of Wooll out of the kingdom of Ireland and England . . . for the encouragement of the woollen manufactures in the Kingdom of England, 10 and 11 William III, c. 10 (1699); An Act to Prevent the Exportation of Hats out of any of his Majesty's colonies or plantations in America . . . for the better encouraging the making hats in Great Britain, 5 George II, c. 22 (1732).

prohibited the export of ill-tanned leather (a basic material for making shoes) in order to encourage local shoe-making. The Board of Trade required that the legislature repeal the act, explaining that "[i]t cannot be expected that encouragement should be given by law to the making any manufactures in the plantations, it being against the advantage of England."[4]

Parliament and the Crown also imposed high import duties on colonial *manufactured* goods and reduced duties or subsidies on colonial *raw materials*. For example, Parliament established a tiered structure of import duties for sugar, which were lowest for raw, unrefined sugar and prohibitively high for refined sugar. The tariff structure was effective. Little sugar refining developed in the English West Indies. By comparison, the French had no such structure of duties, and sugar refining became an integral part of the French Caribbean economy. Parliament did prohibit colonial steel manufacturing, but encouraged the production and export of raw materials, such as pig and bar iron, by exempting them from normal import duties.[5]

Initially, the colonies' comparative economic advantage was in extractive industries, such as fishing, lumbering, and fur trapping, and in the agricultural production of tobacco, rice, and food products. The suppression of manufacturing, therefore, likely had little impact during the early stages of colonial development. As the colonial economy expanded, however, it became clear that these English policies would eventually impair colonial economic interests. More broadly, imperial policies designed to improve *England's* balance of trade and to benefit *England's* economy were strong symbols of colonial dependence.

REGULATIONS HELPFUL TO COLONIAL ECONOMIC GROWTH

Not every commercial regulation discriminated against the colonies. The Navigation Acts allowed an entirely free trade between colonial merchants and merchants of foreign countries in all commodities that had not been enumerated for exclusive export to England, so long as the goods were carried in British ships. Free trade was permitted in many important colonial goods, including grain of all varieties, lumber, salt, fish, sugar, and rum. These commodities could be transported directly to cities in Holland, France, Portugal, Spain, and Africa and to any of the European colonies in the Caribbean.[6]

[4] Objections made by the Commissioners for Trade and Plantations upon Several Acts of Pennsylvania (Endorsed August 3, 1705), *The Statutes at Large of Pennsylvania from 1682 to 1801* (PA, 1896), 466.

[5] An Act to Encourage the Importation of Pig and Bar Iron from his Majesty's Colonies in America [and to prevent the erection of iron mills, forges and steel-making furnaces in the colonies], 23 George II, c. 29 (1750).

[6] A 1766 Act prohibited the direct export of any colonial good north of Cape Finisterre, on the west coast of Spain.

Why did the Crown permit any colonial free trade? First, protecting industries in England often did not require a complete ban on colonial trade. Wheat, for example, was an important colonial product that was barred from importation to England in order to protect English wheat producers. English wheat growers, however, exported chiefly to Europe. Thus they were not harmed by allowing Philadelphia merchants to sell wheat in French Caribbean colonies. Second, as mentioned, it was not in the interest of England to suppress entirely the colonial economy. Colonial merchants depended on exports to secure the specie necessary to pay for the vast quantities of manufactured items imported from England. Allowing colonists to make profits on goods not desired in England led to stronger demand for English imports.[7]

Under the Navigation Acts, just as all colonial goods had to be unloaded and reloaded in England, all European goods were required to be unloaded and reloaded at an English port prior to reexport to the colonies. The price of European goods in the colonies reflected the additional transportation costs as well as the import duties paid in English ports.[8] The British, however, reduced the magnitude of import duties by allowing "drawbacks" (typically refunds of 50 percent to 100 percent of the import duties) on foreign goods reexported to the colonies. At times, the drawback provisions were criticized for providing inadequate protection to English manufacturing concerns by, for example, allowing German linens to fully supply the colonial market at the expense of the nascent English linen industry. Indeed, in a few cases, Parliament approved export subsidies that made English-produced goods less expensive in the colonies than in England.[9] These laws are inconsistent with mercantilist theory and likely reflected advantages merchants held over manufacturing interests in influencing government policy with respect to particular products.

MONOPOLIZING THE SUPPLY OF COLONIAL CREDIT

The Navigation Acts led to an English and Scottish monopoly over the supply of credit to the colonies. Colonists were not prohibited by law from

[7] This might explain Parliamentary legislation giving colonial tobacco a de facto monopoly in England: Parliament adopted prohibitively high tariffs on Spanish and other foreign tobacco and banned growing tobacco in England, Scotland, and Ireland. By stimulating colonial production of tobacco and by banning its growth in England, Parliament directed native Englishmen toward specialization in economic activities that would lead to greater profits abroad, such as manufacturing, while simultaneously expanding colonial specialization in agricultural production.

[8] The colonies purchased 75 percent of their imports from England, of which 20 percent were goods originally manufactured in Europe or Asia.

[9] Adam Smith, *An Inquiry into the Nature and Causes of the Wealth of Nations*, 2 vols. Edwin Cannan, ed., II: 96–97.

obtaining credit outside Britain. But by monopolizing shipping, by prohibiting non-British subjects from acting as factors or merchants in the colonies, and by requiring that European goods be imported into an English port before reexport to the colonies, the Navigation Acts made it extremely difficult for colonists to obtain credit from European sources, either directly or through a middleman. Colonists from all regions were steady consumers of imported manufactured goods and were therefore perpetually in debt to English or Scottish creditors.

The central problem of the trans-Atlantic trade was the distance between England and the colonies and the informational problems that attended credit relationships. It was very difficult for merchants residing in London to be familiar with market conditions in America or the creditworthiness of colonial debtors. One solution to the problems of distance and lack of information was that transactions were structured whenever possible so that risks relating to legal enforcement were contained within England. Bills of exchange payable in London served as the basic currency in all large commercial transactions within the Atlantic trade. The ultimate liability for the bills therefore resided with an individual who had an account in London. To obtain major loans, colonists were often required to find guarantors in London. London-based insurance companies were preferred to such an extent that the colonial insurance industry never developed beyond small operations in the major cities. Moreover, financing within the empire took the form of short-term commercial credit, rather than long-term repayment arrangements backed by colonial property, such as by means of mortgages.

Trading with colonial producers, of course, also involved operations within the colonies. English credit typically originated with an English export firm that financed the costs of transporting goods to the colonies.[10] To handle sales in the colonies, English merchants typically hired factors who resided semi-permanently in the colonies. Once English goods arrived in the colonies, factors typically sold to planters (in slave colonies) or, in the Northern colonies, to retailers or storekeepers who, in turn, sold the goods directly to consumers.[11] To reduce the agency problem inherent in the merchant-factor relationship, merchants often hired family members or acquaintances or worked through factorage firms, which typically charged higher rates, but had better established connections and more to lose through a diminished reputation.

[10] The credit terms from England were generally twelve months. In order to pay their English debts on time, goods were offered locally on shorter credit terms; customarily the terms of credit ranged from six to twelve months, and possibly less.

[11] Factors typically earned a small percentage (such as 2.5 to 5 percent) of the gross sales of the goods. Factors remitted the proceeds of the sale (gross sales minus the commission, duties, and other expenses) either by purchasing bills of exchange or by providing a return cargo.

The primary responsibility of factors was to develop information and contacts and to seek out the highest prices for the goods they sold on the merchants' behalf. The "price" they received, of course, also included consideration of the terms of credit and the creditworthiness of the purchasers. To be competitive, factors often remitted payments to the British merchants immediately, in advance of actually collecting debts from those to whom they sold goods. The factors assumed the role of creditors on the ground, who could navigate the informal and formal means available to collect debts.

THE ROLE OF THE COMMON LAW COURTS IN TRANS-ATLANTIC RELATIONS

Every colony in the British Atlantic Empire established common law courts. The enforcement of debt agreements dominated the business of the courts. The existence of formal institutions that enforced contracts strictly was of tremendous importance to the economic development of the colonies. The structure of credit transactions between the English and their colonial counterparts, however, reveals a strong aversion to the formal legal system. Family relationships, personal acquaintances, and the spread of information about an individual's reputation and honor were its centerpieces.

For British creditors, finding recourse in the colonial courts was close to a last resort.[12] Not only were colonial courts highly inconvenient for English creditors and costly, but colonial juries were biased in favor of local residents. The common law courts met only four times each year and were often criticized for their excessive delays. Fees were imposed to compensate officials for every aspect of the paperwork involved, reducing creditors' incentives to litigate. Filing a lawsuit, however, was the only way a creditor might establish priority in claims on a debtor's assets. In times of general economic recession or uncertainty, litigation volume skyrocketed as creditors scrambled to get a place in line. As an example, 800 cases were reported to be pending in the Barbados Court of Common Pleas in 1699.

In response to the problems posed by the common law courts, merchants in some colonies developed legal institutions that gave quick decisions in convenient locations. The Mayor's Court in New York and the Hustings Court in Virginia, for example, were common law courts that specialized in

[12] The vast majority of credit arrangements involved unsecured book credit. Obtaining secured credit was typically a second step, after a debtor had failed to pay his debts, and usually after many extensions in time. The process of debt collection began with written requests for payment of the unsecured credit. After a failure to pay, a creditor would request a debt on a penalty bond or specialty (a signed and sealed credit instrument). The next step was a debt established by a judgment in court. As a final step, the creditor would require a mortgage.

merchant-related disputes and that relied on merchant-friendly juries. One merchant wrote that, in the Hustings Court, "[s]uits have seldom remained undetermined longer than 3 or 4 months . . . when they have remained undetermined almost as many Years in most of the other Courts."[13] In New York until 1801, special merchant juries were the norm in commercial matters.

Arbitration was also a common way to avoid the costs and delays of jury trials in the colonial period. Business contracts, such as insurance contracts, often included arbitration clauses. In the absence of an arbitration clause, the parties might also agree to arbitration by reference, in which the judge referred the matter to a panel of arbitrators. The New York Chamber of Commerce was created in 1768 and almost immediately appointed a Monthly Committee to arbitrate disputes brought before it.

British creditors complained about debt collection in colonial courts, but courts in the British colonies had a reputation for greater formality and even-handedness than courts in other colonies. Although those entering commercial dealings naturally tried to avoid litigation in order to settle disputes, the presence of a legal system that would strictly enforce debts if necessary was an essential feature of the economy of colonial British America. Adam Smith compared British colonial courts favorably with those of the Spanish and Portuguese colonies where "irregular and partial administration of justice, [. . .] often protects the rich and powerful debtor from the pursuit of his injured creditor." Indeed, Smith continued, these justice systems "make the industrious part of the nation afraid to prepare goods for the consumption of those haughty and great men, to whom they dare not to refuse to sell upon credit, and from whom they are altogether uncertain of repayment."[14]

The greater formality of English law may explain some of the differentiated growth of the American slave systems. Slaves were a highly costly investment, and creditors would only lend money for slaves when they believed the legal system would enforce debt agreements. Barbados could become the largest sugar export market in the Americas in part because

[13] John Tazewell to John Norton, July 12, 1770, John Norton & Sons Papers (Colonial Williamsburg). In 1736, the Virginia legislature enacted a law that allowed any debt case within the colony to be brought in the Hustings Court in Williamsburg. An Act . . . for Enlarging the Jurisdiction of the Court of Hustings in the City of Williamsburg, *Statutes at Large*, William Waller Hening, ed. (Richmond, VA, 1814), IV: 541–42, 542.

[14] Smith, *Wealth of Nations*, II: 125. In listing the reasons why English colonies flourished economically, Adam Smith emphasized "above all that equal and impartial administration of justice which renders the rights of the meanest British subject respectable to the greatest, and which, by securing to every man the fruits of his own industry, gives the greatest and most effectual encouragement to every sort of industry."

strict enforcement of debt agreements encouraged British merchants to lend money to Barbados planters to buy slaves. In contrast, the Portuguese permitted more extensive debt relief legislation that dissuaded investment in large quantities of slaves. Sugar planting in Brazil remained dispersed and relatively inefficient throughout the colonial period. Slavery, of course, is only one example of economic investment in the colonies promoted by the enforcement of the common law.

ENFORCING THE NAVIGATION ACTS: THE VICE-ADMIRALTY COURTS

Without effective enforcement, the Navigation Acts would have had significance in letter only. Overseeing colonial trade from the vantage point of England presented innumerable problems. The amount of shoreline to monitor was immense. The financial incentives to evade the Navigation Acts were high.

The Navigation Act of 1673 authorized the formal organization of a colonial customs service. It appointed collectors and surveyors to those colonies that produced enumerated commodities and required local collection of all duties payable in London. Ship owners were required to execute bonds guaranteeing that enumerated commodities would be transported to England. The bonds became the basis for enforcement suits in the local courts if violations were later discovered. The salaries of customs officials were set as a percentage of total revenue collected (from one-eighth in the lucrative colony of Virginia, to one-half in the Carolinas).[15]

The colonists were hostile to the 1673 Navigation Act. Within a few decades, three collectors were killed, two imprisoned, and one tried for treason. Prosecuting Navigation Act cases in the provincial courts was, in a typical depiction, "trying one Illicit Trader by his Fellows, or at least by his well-wishers," and routinely resulted in an acquittal. The direct trade between the British colonies and Europe (in British ships) flourished.

As a remedy, Parliament enacted the Navigation Act of 1696, which created a separate court system, the vice-admiralty courts, to enforce the Navigation Acts. The Act of 1696 authorized customs officers to exercise general search warrants, known as writs of assistance, and permitted the right of forceful entry in cases of suspected concealment of illegally imported goods. It authorized seizure of the vessels used in violating the act, with one-third of the proceeds distributed to the King, one-third to the governor, and one-third to the informer.[16]

[15] An Act . . . for the Better Securing the Plantation-trade, 25 Charles II, c. 7 (1673).

[16] An Act for Preventing Frauds, and Regulating Abuses in the Plantation Trade, 7 & 8 William III, c. 22 (1696).

Prosecuting Navigation Acts cases in the vice-admiralty courts was immediately controversial. In England, Navigation Acts cases were prosecuted in the Court of Exchequer, which provided a jury trial. The lack of juries in the vice-admiralty courts was viewed as a violation of England's customary constitution or fundamental law, and the convictions and fines they imposed were widely viewed as illegitimate. Until the 1760s, however, colonial merchants had a variety of means at their disposal to stymie prosecutions in the vice-admiralty courts. The merchant community pressured colonial governors to appoint as judges people friendly to them who would overlook Navigation Act violations. (Colonial governors' salaries were paid out of colonial treasuries, which gave colonial legislatures some power over them.) Merchants often illicitly recaptured property that had been seized as evidence. Merchants also harassed customs officials by suing them in their individual capacities. Another popular device was to have a sympathetic common law judge issue a "writ of prohibition," which removed the case to the common law court for a decision as to whether the vice-admiralty court properly had jurisdiction over the matter. If the common law judged decided that the vice-admiralty court lacked jurisdiction, the judge could hold the customs official in contempt of court. Until the 1760s, colonists and customs officials existed in a hostile but viable relationship.

The vice-admiralty courts, however, were also the forum of choice for the resolution of disputes relating to maritime issues in general. The courts offered summary procedures and resolved cases far more quickly than the county courts, in part because they had no juries and in part because they were open all year, as opposed to the common pleas courts, which met on a quarterly basis. About 50 percent of the business of the vice-admiralty courts was enforcement of the Navigation Acts. The remainder was admiralty cases relating to seamen's wages, salvage, prize, bottomry (a form of mortgage for ships), partnership disputes, and disputes relating to building and insuring vessels.

ADAM SMITH'S CRITIQUE

One of the principal contributions of Smith's *Wealth of Nations* was to describe the seemingly ad hoc regulations governing trade within the British Empire as the embodiment of a system of political economy that, while coherent in itself, rested on flawed assumptions and empirical beliefs. Smith explained that European governments' bullionist emphasis on specie flows misunderstood the deeper basis of economic growth. The wealth of a nation derived from the value of the goods and services that the nation produced, not from the amount of specie circulating within its borders.

The effort by a government to micro-manage trade in order to improve its balance of trade did not enhance basic productivity and often diminished it. Government trade regulations distorted incentives by inflating profits in particular areas and thereby diverting investment into them, which would generate decreased investment in activities or products that provided greater economic return.

Smith's criticism of what he referred to as Britain's "mercantile system" focused on its negative effects on the English, not the colonial, economy. In Smith's account, the primary beneficiaries of the Navigation Acts were English merchants, whom he believed controlled British policy, and colonial subjects. The enumeration of goods – which constrained their export directly to England or Scotland – increased profits for English and Scottish merchants dealing in those goods and led to excessive investment in their production.

As a consequence of these policies, the English citizenry not involved in the colonial trade suffered net losses. Smith argued that the British domestic economy would have been more prosperous had less of the national wealth been invested in the colonies.[17] Moreover, the Navigation Act system required continued military expenses for colonial defense. According to Smith, the colonists were free riders benefiting from English military protection and not contributing their share.

Smith advocated a world free of mercantile regulations. In such a world, the colonies were likely to play a large role. He believed that exchanges between British creditors and colonial producers greatly stimulated English industry. Writing in 1776, however, Smith opposed fighting to retain the American colonies. Smith believed that a better course would be to negotiate a trade treaty with America so that trade relations would be maintained without the costs of Empire.

Unlike Smith, the colonists began to emphasize the direct, tangible costs that the Navigation Acts imposed on their economic activity. Until the 1760s, however, colonial citizens were generally content with their status within the empire. Colonial residents appreciated the advantages of membership in the British Empire. The two principal counterfactual alternatives – colonial sovereignty during the eighteenth century (holding European foreign policy steady) or colonial dependency on another European government – might each have been inferior in terms of economic growth when compared to remaining a colony of Britain. Seventeenth- and eighteenth-century English commercial regulation had dual effects: the laws were designed to ensure that the English would receive the principal financial benefits of trade within the empire, but the imperial system

[17] Smith, *Wealth of Nations*, II: 109–44.

worked to the advantage of the colonies as well. The vice-admiralty courts, which were established for the purpose of enforcing the Navigation Laws to the detriment of individual colonists, greatly benefited colonial economies by applying a consistent body of law to resolve disputes emerging on the seas. The existence of a uniform law of bills and notes allowed payments by bills of exchange anywhere in the empire. Finally, in very crude terms, British bankers and merchants financed operations in the colonies because the colonies shared a legal tradition of formalistic enforcement of contractual obligations.

Residents of the colonies, however, viewed themselves as supporting the English economy in four ways: by stimulating English industry through the purchase of imports; by paying the interest costs of the goods they bought on credit; by paying import duties when applicable; and, particularly in the South, by suffering the English monopoly on goods like tobacco and rice. The next section describes the colonial legislatures' economic regulations and the events leading to the American Revolution.

II. LAW AND COMMERCE IN COLONIAL AMERICA

A new political economy emerged in Founding Era America. It arose from the federalist system designed by the framers of the U.S. Constitution and was developed over years of contested political debate after the Constitution's ratification. The American federalist system, in turn, was the product of institutional developments that took place during the colonial period. For more than a century, the colonial governments behaved as quasi-independent sovereign powers. They enacted their own laws regulating commerce and relating to slave property, reformed English property and inheritance laws, issued paper money and regulated their currencies, and dealt with Native Americans.

Vast economic, social, and cultural differences divided the colonies. There was little intercolonial trade, and the colonies' closest economic ties were with England and other foreign markets. An English clergyman visiting America in 1759 was skeptical that the colonies could ever unite in a "permanent union," because "fire and water are not more heterogeneous than the different colonies in North America."[18] The competitive character of the colonies' policies led many to fear, after independence, that the colonies would replicate the cycle of trade competition and warfare that had plagued Europe.

[18] Andrew Burnaby, *Travels Through the Middle Settlements in North-America in the Years 1759 and 1760 with Observations upon the State of the Colonies* (Dublin, 1775), 202–4.

The British Empire was governed in a highly decentralized manner in comparison to, say, the Spanish Empire.[19] Nonetheless, Parliament and the Crown, through its advisory boards, the Privy Council and the Board of Trade and Plantations,[20] were strongly interested in monitoring the colonial legislatures to protect the revenues afforded the Crown under the Navigation Acts and the interests of English creditors. In each of the primary areas of colonial policymaking, acts of Parliament or decisions by the Crown-appointed Board of Trade created resentment toward English rule decades before the movement for independence. Beginning in the 1760s, however, for the first time mutual hostility toward Parliamentary and Crown oversight gave the colonists common grounds for seeking independence. This history, of more than a century of relative colonial independence and sovereignty, and the shared resentment toward Parliamentary regulation exacerbated in the 1760s, is essential to understanding the rejection of mercantilism and the creation of a new political economy in the Founding Era.

The Economic Policies of Colonial Legislatures

Each colony enacted an independent economic policy. Colonial legislatures derived their lawmaking authority by charters issued by the Crown, by proprietary grants to individuals under patent, or by direct rule of the Crown. In all cases, they were constrained only by a proviso or an understanding that the laws they adopted "would not be repugnant to" the laws of England and by a broader imperial understanding that their laws must not conflict with the interests of England, which usually meant the interests of English creditors and merchants.

COLONIAL COMMERCIAL POLICIES

As described above, commercial regulations were a primary instrument of mercantilist governments. In this tradition, every colonial legislature collected revenue through duties as part of a broader trade policy. The colonial legislatures, however, were subject to two substantial constraints. First, tariff policies (duties on specified imported goods) and tonnage duties (duties on vessels unloading at a port based on cargo capacity) were constantly monitored by English merchants selling wares locally. The merchants complained to the Board of Trade about colonial legislation that taxed them or diminished their trade. The Board of Trade often invalidated colonial duties that treated local merchants more favorably than English merchants.

[19] See Chapter 4, this volume.

[20] The Board of Trade and Plantations was established in 1696 to supervise the colonies and to advise Parliament on matters relating to colonial economic regulation.

A second, and equally powerful, constraint was intercolonial competition. The major ports were in constant competition with one another for trade. Colonists wanted to encourage trade in order to expand the market for their exports and to increase the products available for internal purchase and consumption. Non-competitive duty taxation drove imports to other ports.

Typically, colonial legislatures confined import duties to three luxury items: wine, hard liquor, and slaves. Colonial tonnage duties typically did not increase general revenues: they were earmarked for port-related projects, such as the construction of lighthouses, digging channels, and the maintenance of wharves. The import and tonnage duties were often reduced for merchants who resided locally.

On some occasions, colonial legislatures imposed special, retaliatory tariffs on goods produced in other colonies. As an example, in the early eighteenth century, New York and Maryland enacted a special tax on goods from Pennsylvania. Pennsylvania then retaliated with a 10 percent tax on products imported from New York and Maryland. Retaliatory tariffs were often imposed in relation to some other dispute between the colonies, such as a boundary dispute. Again, intercolonial competition for trade constrained the extent to which colonial legislatures generated revenues through tariffs.

The two constraints on colonial trade regulations – English oversight and intercolonial competition – led to an emphasis on legislative efforts to *promote* locally produced goods in foreign markets. Most prominent among these efforts was the establishment of mandatory inspection systems, based on the belief that minimum quality standards for exported goods were essential to a colony's competitiveness. The export of inferior goods was believed to taint the reputation of the colony as a whole. The laws authorizing inspection also required that all export goods bear the mark of a registered brand and established standardized quantity and weight regulations.

Pennsylvania, for example, required inspection of bread and flour; beef and pork; lumber items such as "staves, headings, boards, planks and shingles"; and shad and herring. The inspectors were given the power to condemn items not meeting the standards they adopted. Pennsylvania's regulation led New York merchants to lobby in the 1750s for higher local standards, explaining that the French and Spanish islands "absolutely" refused to purchase flour from the colony of New York "if any Pennsylvania Flour could be had. . . ."[21]

Other colonies adopted inspection systems to establish commodity money. Because English merchants typically demanded payment in specie,

[21] Petition of Merchants to New York Assembly, Oct. 26, 1750, *Journal of the General Assembly of New York* (New York, 1764–1768), II, 294–295.

gold and silver coins were often scarce in the colonies as a currency and as a taxation base. As a consequence, many colonies denominated commodities to serve as a currency, especially for purposes of taxation. New England, at various times, designated farm products, typically called "country pay," as commodity money. In 1720, for example, Massachusetts responded to a currency shortage by allowing taxes to be paid (at rates set by the General Assembly) in "good Barrel-Beef or Pork, Or in Wheat, Pease, Barley, Rye, Indian Corn, Oats, Flax, Hemp, Beeswax, Butter in Ferkins, Cheese, Hides, Tann'd Leather, Dry Fish, Mackrel in Barrels, Oyl, Whale-bone, Bayberry Wax, or Tallow."[22] The system had an inherent problem: the incentive of the taxpayer was to pass off the worst quality goods to the collectors.

In the 1730s, Virginia adopted a sophisticated inspection system to establish a form of tobacco currency. Individuals brought their tobacco to a local warehouse. If the tobacco met the quality standard, the farmer would be given "tobacco notes," which could be used to pay taxes or used as a currency. Virginia did not adopt a paper money with legal tender status outside of the tobacco note system until 1755.

The relative prominence of government inspectors and the support for inspection and standardization are striking in a period in which government bureaucracy was almost non-existent. The importance of inspection systems in colonial economic life is reflected in the U.S. Constitution that, though denying the states the power to "lay any imposts or duties on imports or exports," permits states to impose duties when necessary for executing inspection laws, again, important for certifying quality in markets with very uneven information.[23] Inspection systems are a revealing predecessor to later state programs for economic promotion.

PROPERTY REGULATION

Each colony enacted its own property and inheritance law. Colonial legislatures established land registries to demarcate rights more clearly to land than the existing system in England. Land was the principal form in which wealth could be held, and mortgage markets were central to colonial liquidity.

Legislative approaches to inheritance and real property were important sources of social, economic and cultural difference. In general, land was distributed far more widely among the colonial population than in England,

[22] Resolve for Emitting £5,000 in Bills of Credit and Order for Rec'g the Tax in Several Species of Goods (July 22, 1720, ch. 28), reprinted in *The Acts and Resolves Public and Private of the Province of Massachusetts Bay* (Boston, MA, 1902), X: 16.

[23] U.S. Constitution, Art. 1, sec. 10, cl. 2.

and the majority of colonial citizens held their land in fee simple absolute. The widespread availability of land for purchase meant that children were often less dependent on a family homestead and were more likely to obtain their own land. The Northern colonies (with the exception of New York and Rhode Island), however, eliminated primogeniture and moved to a system whereby children divided their father's property evenly at the time of his death, though some provided a double share to the eldest son.

The New England colonies also eliminated traditional English immunities on title to real property from the claims of unsecured creditors. English law incorporated a default rule that protected property owners' title to land from the claims of all unsecured creditors. In England, unsecured creditors enforcing their debts in the common law courts could claim only debtors' chattel property and temporary possessory interests in part of debtors' real property. The law also extended this rule so that, at the death of a debtor, the debtor's real property holdings descended to the heirs and devisees free of all claims of the deceased debtor's unsecured creditors. The New England legislatures (with the exception of Rhode Island) rejected this body of English law and retained only negligible property exemptions from creditors' claims. The Southern colonies, in contrast, maintained traditional English laws related to real property and inheritance: They affirmed primogeniture and the body of creditors' remedies that made title to real property immune from the claims of unsecured creditors.

In the early 1730s, however, English creditors began to aggressively lobby Parliament for legislation that would provide more protection to English creditors than was available under English law. They lobbied for a repeal of all exemptions from the claims of unsecured creditors on real property. Parliament, in 1732, enacted "An Act for the More Easy Recovery of Debts in America," which required that land and slaves be treated exactly like chattel property for the purpose of satisfying both secured and unsecured debts. The statute radically changed the law in Rhode Island, New York, Maryland, and in all of the Southern colonies. It diverged from English law by providing that, in all of the British colonies, unsecured creditors could claim against the real property holdings of their debtors. Perhaps most important, it modified the English inheritance laws by giving creditors priority to land over heirs and devisees when debtors died. By clarifying that all forms of property were subject to the claims of creditors, this statute likely expanded the amount of credit extended in the colonies. It coincided with the expansion of slavery by expanding the availability of loans to colonial planters for slave purchases. It was also an important example of Parliamentary interference with colonial domestic matters. Alexander Hamilton later wrote that this act, "Admitted more then our Legislature ought to have assented to; it was one of the Highest Acts of Legislature that one Country could exercise over another."[24]

CURRENCY POLICIES

Each colony adopted independent monetary policies, and these policies often reflected intercolonial competition. The colonial economy largely functioned without the use of cash. Imports from England exceeded colonial exports, and coins were generally required as balance-of-trade payments to English creditors. Initially, various colonies competed for specie by enacting legislation that overvalued Spanish pieces of eight and other foreign coins (in relation to sterling), predicting that a favorable legal exchange rate would attract traders to the colonies seeking to buy goods with cash. As an example, in 1652, Massachusetts opened a mint that created "pinetree shillings" out of the metal of coins from other nations. The colonial mint offered a profit to individuals, including pirates, who brought in foreign coins to be reminted.

Competitive colonial legislation that debased the local currency, however, was viewed by the Crown as conflicting with the mercantilist ambition of keeping coins in England and of maintaining currency stability in the colonies. The Crown shut down the Massachusetts mint in 1684. In 1695, Parliament prohibited the export of English sterling to the colonies, reflecting, again, the bullionist belief in the importance of keeping specie within English boundaries. In 1708, Parliament attempted to suppress colonial legislatures' competitive use of monetary policy by requiring a uniform exchange rate in the various currencies in relation to English sterling throughout the North American colonies.[25] This statute, however, was difficult to enforce and had little impact.

Throughout the late seventeenth century, many colonists began lobbying their legislatures for paper money. Colonists thought that paper money would increase the ease of transacting and expand the supply of credit. From the perspective of local government officials, collecting taxes payable in paper money had obvious advantages over collecting taxes in commodity monies like corn. The costs of war against the French created financial pressures that led colonial legislatures to adopt paper money policies with the tacit consent of Parliament. In 1690, Massachusetts issued the first paper money in the colonies to pay soldiers returning from battle in Quebec. The

[24] Alexander Hamilton, *Practical Proceedings in the Supreme Court of the State of New York*, in Julius Goebel, Jr. ed., *The Law Practice of Alexander Hamilton* (New York, 1964), I: 55–166, 97 (emphasis added).

[25] An Act for Ascertaining the Rates of Foreign Coins in Her Majesty's Plantations in America, 6 Anne, c. 30 (1708).

"bills of credit" in which they were paid would give the bearer a 5 percent premium if used to pay taxes in 1691. The experiment was successful and the government issued more bills of credit the next year. In subsequent years, without protest from England, other colonies quickly adopted independent paper money policies: South Carolina in 1703; Connecticut, New Hampshire, New Jersey, and New York in 1709; Rhode Island in 1710; and North Carolina in 1712.

Paper money often crossed colonial boundaries, and colonists were highly aware of the monetary policies of neighboring colonies. Perhaps the most egregious example of a colony trying to profit through its currency policies was Rhode Island, which infamously flooded the New England market with its notes from the mid-1730s through the mid-1760s. Currency policy, however, was also a great source of tension with England. When England faced periods of economic decline, English creditors shortened the terms of colonial credit or called in their debts, creating corresponding credit problems throughout the colonies. It was at these times that the pressure for debt relief legislation, in the form of greater currency issues and legal tender laws, was strongest. The volume of paper money in circulation and the extent to which the paper money was "backed" by regular taxation were highly political issues. During periods of economic recession, colonists clamored for more paper money to resolve liquidity pressures, and the policy decisions made by legislatures could exacerbate economic problems.

An important currency dispute preceding the Revolutionary movement occurred in Massachusetts. Upset by Massachusetts' currency instability, the Board of Trade in 1730 issued an Instruction to the Massachusetts governor to substantially reduce the supply of paper money in the colony. The Instruction was viewed by many Massachusetts residents as entirely unresponsive to their economic predicament. To remedy the scarcity of money during a recession starting in 1738, Massachusetts residents developed plans for a Land Bank, which would issue notes backed by the real property holdings of close to 400 private individuals. The bank was put into operation in 1740. On March 27, 1741, Parliament suppressed the Land Bank by applying to the colonies the Bubble Act – enacted in the wake of the South Sea bubble – which banned joint-stock companies. John Adams later claimed that the "act to destroy the Land Bank scheme *raised a greater ferment in this province than the Stamp Act did.*"[26]

[26] John Adams, "Novanglus: Or, A History of the Dispute with America, from Its Origin, in 1754, to the Present Time," in Charles Francis Adams ed., *The Works of John Adams, Second President of the United States*, 10 vols. (Boston, 1851), IV: 3–177, 49 (emphasis added).

The colonial monetary crisis throughout the 1740s culminated in the Currency Act of 1751, which prohibited New England governments from issuing bills of credit with legal tender status.[27] Merchants in England quickly began advocating extension of the paper money prohibition to the Middle Atlantic and Southern colonies. They ultimately succeeded with the enactment of the Currency Act of 1764.[28] Received with great protest, particularly by merchants in New York City and Philadelphia, the Currency Act was one of the most unpopular and disruptive Parliamentary measures of the immediate pre-Revolutionary period. It was eventually repealed in 1774.

REGIONAL VARIATIONS IN ECONOMIC STRUCTURE

The colonies lacked a sense of national unity, in part, because their economic systems differed so greatly by region. These regional economic differences played a central role in trade policy and were central to national politics from the 1780s through the Civil War.

The Southern continental colonies and the West Indies conformed most closely to the model of dependent staple crop producing colonies, dominated by slave labor. The economies of Virginia and the Carolinas were highly specialized in the production of tobacco and rice, and the West Indies in the production of sugar. The relationships between planters in these colonies and their British and Scottish creditors were extremely close: English merchants typically provided planters with financing both for the production of staple crops and for imports of English goods sold to the planters in advance of return shipments. The English merchants sold the crops in England under a consignment system, satisfying the colonial planters' debts with the proceeds of the sales.

Southern merchants controlled only a small local fleet of ships. Moreover, Southern planters did not fully control the internal marketing of imported goods. In the early years "Scots peddlers" wandered the countryside selling goods and purchasing tobacco directly from small farmers. The "Glasgow system" was developed by the mid-eighteenth century, when Scottish factors had set up chains of stores throughout the Chesapeake that sold imported goods in return for payments of tobacco. This system involved, first, sending traders throughout the Chesapeake region to deal directly with small planters and farmers, and second, a willingness to accept

[27] An Act to Regulate and Restrain Paper Bills of Credit in his Majesty's Colonies, 24 Geo. II, c. 53 (1751).

[28] An Act to Prevent Paper Bills of Credit, hereafter to be Issued in Any of his Majesty's Colonies or Plantations in America, from Being Declared to be a Legal Tender, 4 Geo. III, c. 34 (1764).

low-quality tobacco. English merchants never replicated the Glasgow system. They dealt with larger planters and dominated the market for higher quality tobacco.

In contrast, the Northern colonies in many respects resembled European mercantilist nations, although on a smaller scale. Their economies were highly diverse. Northerners commanded a large fleet of ships and invested in shipping and marketing their exports abroad. Northern merchants were exporters, importers, wholesalers, retailers, purchasing agents, bankers, insurance underwriters, and attorneys. In contrast to Southern colonists who allowed their internal markets to be dominated by Scottish importers, Northern colonists controlled the internal markets of their colonies. Transactions with English merchants and factors relating to the importation of goods typically took place in major port towns.

Prior to the 1760s, merchants in the Northern colonies were free to market most of their goods anywhere in the world. They never managed to produce a profitable staple crop desired by the English. As a consequence, England imported only a portion of their exports. In the period 1768 to 1772, for example, only 17.8 percent of commodity exports from New England and 22.8 percent of commodity exports from the mid-Atlantic colonies were exported to England or Ireland. In contrast, during the same period, 81.8 percent of the commodity exports of Virginia and Maryland and 71.6 percent of the commodity exports from the Carolinas and Georgia were exported directly to England or Ireland.

Their import markets, however, were dominated by goods from England. To pay for the English imports, the merchants of New England and the mid-Atlantic colonies exported foodstuffs, such as wheat, corn, and meat products, to colonies and nations that had a favorable balance of trade with England. The most important markets were in the West Indies and Spain and Portugal. Sugar was so profitable that the six sugar islands – Jamaica, St. Kitts, Barbados, Montserrat, Nevis, and Antigua – contributed almost as much (more than 9 percent) to Britain's external commerce as the thirteen continental colonies combined (approximately 10 percent). The Northern merchants sold their goods there in return for cash (bills of exchange payable in London) or products, such as molasses, sugar, and wine, which could be used to pay English creditors directly. The profitability of the slave system of labor and sugar production in the West Indies and wine production in the Iberian Peninsula meant that these areas had more liquid markets (greater available currency) than New England and the Mid-Atlantic. Thus the British Empire of the eighteenth century consisted of dispersed constituencies, integrated loosely by a shared cultural and legal tradition, by market relationships, and by the relatively weak superstructure of Parliamentary and Crown rule.

III. PARLIAMENTARY REGULATION AND THE AMERICAN REVOLUTION

By the time of the American Revolution, the colonies were separated by a history of intercolonial rivalry, independent trade regulations, property laws, currency policies, and vastly different economic structures. Why did the colonies join together to rebel against British rule?

At the conclusion of the Seven Years War, a consensus emerged in England that the colonies should increase their financial contributions to the expenses of the British Empire. In 1763, the British debt was massive. The costs of the Seven Years War had doubled its size. Annual interest owed by the government was £5 million alone; the ordinary British peacetime budget was £8 million. Most of the war had been fought in the New World, and the colonists were its central beneficiaries. Vast new territories (Canada and Florida) had been acquired from France and Spain. As English settlers moved west, the British feared large-scale conflicts between settlers and Native Americans that would require costly military involvement. The decision was made to maintain a standing army in America for deterrence, even though it would be highly expensive to feed, clothe, and pay. George Grenville, the new Chancellor of the Exchequer, reported that the customs service in America was costing more than it was collecting in revenue. In the years that followed, Parliament passed several statutes that fundamentally changed the nature of imperial regulation of the colonies.

In 1763, Parliament passed a statute that gave captains and officers of the Royal Navy stationed in North America the power to be sworn in as customs officers who could prosecute Navigation Acts violations including seizing offending vessels (earning, as a commission, one-half of the net proceeds after condemnation and sale of the goods and the ship).[29] The act also adopted a "hovering" provision, allowing the seizure of vessels that carried illegal goods offshore, even if they showed no inclination to enter the ports. Enforcement of the British monopoly by a fleet of naval officers prowling the seas was a shocking development to colonial merchants up and down the Atlantic seaboard.

In 1764, Parliament enacted the Revenue Act, which came to be called the "Sugar Act."[30] The act reduced the duty on foreign molasses from six to three pence per gallon in an attempt to generate greater revenue through

[29] An Act for the Further Improvement of his Majesty's Revenue of Customs, 3 George III, c. 22 (1763).

[30] An Act for Granting Certain Duties in the British Colonies . . . in America . . . and More Effectually Preventing the Clandestine Conveyance of Goods to and from the said Colonies and Plantations, and Improving and Securing the Trade Between the Same and Great Britain, 4 George III, c. 15 (1764).

fuller compliance. More controversially, however, the act shifted the burden of proof in Navigation Act trials to the accused (the claimant of the seized property). It gave informers and prosecutors immunity from liability so long as they could convince the admiralty judge that probable cause had existed for a seizure. This took away the primary weapon in the merchants' legal arsenal against the enforcement of Navigation Acts: harassment of officials through litigation.

The 1764 Sugar Act also imposed onerous regulations on ships involved in the coastwise trade that had previously applied only to ships crossing the Atlantic. All vessels traveling more than seven miles from shore were required to present bonds and acquire loading certificates before taking cargo on board their ship. They were also required to carry official inventories listing each item in their cargo (called cockets), certified by a customs official. Each addition to the inventory of a ship required an additional visit to a customs official and more fees. The likelihood of having one's ship searched had increased dramatically after 1763, and owners of smaller vessels in the coastwise trade, in particular, resented the new paperwork and costs. The assemblies of eight colonies sent petitions to English authorities claiming that the Sugar Act was harmful to colonial trade.

The next year, in 1765, Parliament went further, enacting the Stamp Act, which required that most formal legal documents be drafted on special stamped paper printed in a central stamp office in London and sold by the colonial governments locally. As Franklin later testified before Parliament, this law was particularly threatening because it was a direct tax on internal colonial legal affairs and therefore was far more invasive than customs duties, which allowed the colonies autonomy over internal governance. Moreover, Stamp Act violations were to be prosecuted in the vice-admiralty courts, where colonists would not have the shield of a jury trial.

The colonists responded to the Stamp Act with a widespread, voluntary movement to cease importing English goods in the winter of 1765 and 1766. The non-importation movement of 1765 and 1766 was the first coordinated intercolonial effort. The boycott of British goods in 1765 and more extensive boycotts in 1767 and 1774 represent the beginnings of a "national" American political identity. This identity was closely connected to the status of colonists as consumers of English exports. Under the Navigation Acts system, the colonists viewed themselves as contributing to the empire in multiple ways. They contributed to the profits of English manufacturers and producers by consuming English goods. They paid the interest costs of purchasing on credit both directly and in the price of goods. The economies of many colonies were dominated by the production of goods that were legally required to be shipped to England. Moreover, the colonists contributed to the English shipping business by complying with the monopoly given to English ship owners and sailors. Given these many contributions, to protest the Stamp Act by refusing to buy English goods perfectly reflected the colonists' central concerns. That protest prevented the English from profiting from colonial purchases, colonial credit, and tariffs all at once.

Again, the world of the late eighteenth century was one in which a "mercantilist" mentality toward economic activity prevailed. It viewed merchants who "owned" the trade as skimming the profits off of those with whom they traded. Money spent on English consumer goods represented payments of specie to English merchants and producers that increased the wealth circulating in England at the expense of the specie-poor colonies. Taxes imposed by Parliament for revenue purposes threatened to draw even more wealth away from the colonies. As described by the New York Assembly in 1764, "all Impositions, whether they be internal Taxes, or Duties paid, for what we consume, equally diminish the Estates upon which they are charged. . . . *The whole Wealth of a Country may be as effectually drawn off*, by the Exaction of Duties, as by any other Tax upon their Estates." The scarcity of specie in the colonies reinforced the bullionist view of trade. The sense of England skimming the wealth from the colonies was exacerbated by the Currency Act of 1764, which, as mentioned, prohibited all colonial governments from issuing legal tender paper currencies.

In his efforts to obtain the repeal of the Stamp Act, Benjamin Franklin proposed that Parliament instead generate revenue in the Americas by establishing a profit-seeking central bank that issued currency. After the Revolution, Franklin was challenged about his proposal, and he conceded that this central bank would have led to Parliamentary interference with the colonial economy to a degree that was undesirable. But his proposal when initially presented was on the mark. The Americans would likely have endured government action that was viewed as promoting economic exchange and lowering the cost of credit. Instead, the Sugar Act of 1764 and the Stamp Act of 1765 constituted taxes that depleted the colonies' monetary wealth. Revulsion to a revenue-generating statute from a formerly loyal population is understandable if one recognizes that colonial citizens viewed themselves as having their wealth drained from them as consumers and debtors in a monopolized market.

The Stamp Act was repealed in February of 1767, but the colonists' victory was overturned by Parliament's enactment of the Declaratory Act, which stated in general terms that Parliament had the right to legislate for the colonies "in all cases whatsoever." With the thought that perhaps the Stamp Act was offensive because it was a direct tax – which Franklin had argued – Parliament in 1767 enacted the Townshend Act, which sought to obtain tax revenues through duties on imported goods, such as tea, lead, glass, paint, and paper. To ensure adequate revenue, Parliament again increased local supervision of customs collection. In 1767–8, Parliament created the American Board of Customs, which reported directly to the Treasury. Superior vice-admiralty courts, to which appeals from the lower vice-admiralty courts could be made, were established in Boston, Philadelphia, and Charleston. Salaries of new customs officials as well as of other Crown appointees, such as the colonial governors, would come from the revenues they collected, relieving them of their longstanding dependence on colonial legislatures.

The Townshend Acts represent, not a response to colonial demands, but an attempt to reinforce Crown authority and clamp down on colonial resistance. They were eventually repealed, but the tensions between customs officials and colonial residents escalated. The colonists increasingly resented the enforcement of the Navigation Acts in the vice-admiralty courts, which they viewed as a violation of their constitutional right to a trial by jury. John Adams's representation of John Hancock, in a trial involving the question of whether he smuggled Madeira wine off his boat late at night to avoid customs duties, became a multi-month publicity event focused on the injustices of the vice-admiralty courts. Adams stated that the system "takes from Mr. Hancock this precious Tryal [by jury], and gives it to a single Judge. However respectable the Judge may be, it is however an Hardship and severity, which distinguishes my Clyent from the rest of Englishmen."[31]

Collective resentment toward English transgressions brought the colonies together to fight for independence. But what type of national government would they support after the goal of independence had been achieved? The colonial legislatures were accustomed to having authority over their economic, monetary, and commercial policies and were often rivals and competitors. The U.S. Constitution, however, limited state power in relation to foreign commerce.

Uneasy compromises would characterize American federalism in its early years. The political system that emerged prevented both the states and the federal government from pursuing an aggressive foreign policy on the British model. The new American political economy, fully implemented under Jefferson and Madison, linked westward expansion and the spread of agriculture to diminishing federal government debt and lowering taxes, and consisted of a tariff policy constrained by fierce inter-regional tensions. The legacy of the colonial (and then state) sovereignty model and the political hostility to a strong federal government shaped American foreign

[31] "John Adams's Copy of the Information and Draft of His Argument, *Jonathan Sewal v. John Hancock* (Oct. 1768 – March 1769)," in L. Kinvin Wroth and Hiller B. Zobel, eds. *Legal Papers of John Adams*, 3 vols. (1965): 2: 194–210, 202.

policy – and prevented mercantilism and the acquisition of foreign colonies – for much of the nineteenth century.

IV. THE POLITICAL ECONOMY OF THE FOUNDING ERA

The Navigation Act system came to an end in 1775, when Parliament prohibited entirely British trade with the American colonies.[32] The American patriots viewed this as a liberation. The 1770s were a time of extreme optimism about America's economic future. On April 4, 1776, the Continental Congress opened American ports to the traders of all foreign nationalities, except the subjects of Great Britain. This was the first time that American ports had been fully open to non-British ships in more than a century. John Adams optimistically wrote, "Foreign nations, all the world I hope, will be invited to come here, and our people permitted to go to all the world. . . . "[33]

Independence and Free Trade

Leaders like John Adams and Benjamin Franklin were committed to an open trade policy because they believed that the colonies would benefit most from low tariffs and a position of neutrality with respect to European powers. The primary models for the Americans were the Dutch, neutral, free-trade ports in the West Indies that had enjoyed instant success as international markets during the European wars. Many believed that low tariffs and neutrality would, similarly, stimulate American markets and allow a global trade to develop in the void left by the English.

The colonial legacy of specialization toward agricultural exports and dependence on imported manufactured items was viewed as an advantage in the effort to expand trade relations abroad. It was believed that Europeans would place high value on having close commercial relations with a country that actively sought the importation of manufactured goods. Indeed, America was offering more developed countries some of the benefits of colonialism without the costs of governance and military protection. As Thomas Paine stated in *Common Sense*, "It is in the interest of all Europe to have America as a free port." In 1776, a committee of Congress led by John Adams drafted a Model Treaty that was intended to be used as a platform to negotiate trade treaties with various foreign governments. Under the Model Treaty, Americans would impose no duties on foreign merchants trading in

[32] An Act to Prohibit all Trade and Intercourse with the Colonies [in America], 16 Geo. III, c. 5 (1775).

[33] John Adams to James Warren (March 21, 1776), in *Letters of Delegates to Congress*, Vol. 3: 422.

American ports beyond those imposed on American merchants trading in American ports, and Americans would enjoy the same advantages in foreign ports.

The legacy of colonial sovereignty, however, became a barrier to the adoption of a "national" foreign policy. In 1781, the colonies – now states – ratified the Articles of Confederation, which was the first formal union of the states as the United States of America. Under the Articles of Confederation, state governments were responsible for collecting all revenue. The federal government had no power to tax and was compelled to rely for funds on requisitions from the states. State governments were responsible for regulating trade and collecting revenue through independent state tariffs. State governments, as well as the Congress, had the power to issue currency. The Articles gave Congress the exclusive power to negotiate with foreign nations and Native American tribes. Congress, however, had no effective means of coercing the states to adhere to its treaties and policies.

During the 1780s, Americans experienced a foreign affairs crisis that revealed the weaknesses of the state sovereignty model of finance and trade regulation. Lord Sheffield in England pinpointed these weaknesses in a pamphlet entitled *Observations on the Commerce of the United States*. Sheffield advocated severe punitive measures against the former colonies, to which, he predicted, they would be unable to respond. The pamphlet influenced public opinion, and in 1783, the British enacted a decree prohibiting Americans from accessing the West Indies. The ban on trade to the West Indies – the Americans' primary export market – to which the Americans, lacking a uniform trade policy and a navy, could not respond, had a devastating impact on American agriculture. In addition, the Spanish held the southern parts of the Mississippi River and, in 1784, forbade access to Americans in order to limit settlements in Kentucky and Tennessee. The Mississippi was a crucial means by which western farmers exported their agricultural products.

With British exclusion of American ships from the West Indies and the closure of the Mississippi, many merchants hoped to expand trade in the Mediterranean. They were prevented from doing so by the Barbary pirates. Prior to the Revolutionary War, American ships had been protected from the pirates by annual British tribute payments to the North African governments. In October of 1783, however, the American ship *Betsey* was seized by Moroccan pirates. In 1785, three more ships were captured, and many of the crewmen were enslaved. Americans at the time were horrified by the idea of white, Christian crews being sold into slavery to Muslims. Various political leaders, including John Adams, Benjamin Franklin, and Thomas Jefferson, negotiated with three of the four leaders of the pirates (from Algiers, Tunis, and Tripoli), but could not raise the money needed to reach an agreement. Algiers declared war on the United States in 1785. In

1790, Jefferson concluded that, because of the "unprovoked war of Algiers," American trade "into the Mediterranean, has not been resumed at all since the peace [of 1783]."[34]

During this crisis, the states often behaved in ways that weakened Congress's authority in foreign affairs. Efforts by the newly created Congress to portray itself as sovereign over the states were undermined by expressions of sovereignty by state legislatures. Virginia, for example, weakened the federal government's standing abroad by ratifying the Treaty of Peace with Britain after Congress had formally ratified it (implying that Virginia was a sovereign government). Virginia further embarrassed American political leaders when it disobeyed Congress and violated international law by harboring a French pirate wanted by Louis XVI.

As predicted by Sheffield, interstate competition weakened the ability of the states to retaliate collectively against punitive policies adopted by foreign governments. As an example, in response to Britain's exclusion of America from the West Indies, nine states adopted tariff and tonnage policies that discriminated against British ships and goods. Five other states, however, either chose not to discriminate against or imposed negligible tariffs on British goods. Merchants imported British goods into the states with favorable policies, and the goods were then distributed across state lines, undermining the impact of the discriminatory policies of the nine states that wanted to retaliate against the British. One Congressman later accused Vermont of harming the joint effort of the states to strike back against Britain by being "leagued with Canada in pouring in upon the interior country the manufactures of Britain."[35]

Many also feared that the states' commercial policies would lead to counter-productive interstate discriminatory taxation, hostility, and possibly even war. New York, for example, imposed taxes on trade with New Jersey and Connecticut. Connecticut imposed heavier duties on goods from Massachusetts than those from Great Britain.

Finally, Congress needed an independent revenue source to pay its Revolutionary War debts. Many states failed to impose the taxes necessary for their requisition payments to the federal government. Congress was forced to stop paying interest on its debts, and the credit standing of the United States abroad declined rapidly. Americans had to borrow from the Dutch and French at very high interest rates. Outstanding debts to a variety of European countries made the Confederation generally insecure because,

[34] Thomas Jefferson, Report of the Secretary of State relative to the Mediterranean *Trade* (Dec. 28, 1790), 1st Cong., 3d Sess., *American State Papers, Foreign Relations*: 1, 104–105, 104.

[35] Boudinot, U.S. *House Journal*. 1st Cong., 1st sess., April 11, 1789, p. 123.

according to international law at the time, non-payment of debts by a country was an acceptable ground for invasion. John Adams wrote that, unless the federal government paid its debts, "it will be but a few years . . . before we are involved in another war."[36] Congress was powerless to deal with the crisis caused by Spain's closure of the Mississippi. The government also needed money to address the humiliating Barbary pirate crisis, and in preparation for future emergencies.

The U.S. Constitution

The U.S. Constitution represented in large part a response to the problems of the state sovereignty model of finance and trade. The states ceded their control over many central economic and commercial policies to the federal government. At the same time, the federal Congress was prohibited from using trade policy to discriminate against any of the states. The outcome was the creation of an internal free trade zone throughout the states. Under Article I, Section 10, the states might not independently "lay any imposts or duties on imports or exports, except what may be absolutely necessary for executing . . . inspection laws," or "lay any duty of tonnage," or negotiate independently with foreign governments.

The Constitution gave Congress the power "to lay and collect taxes, duties, imposts and excises," "to regulate commerce with foreign Nations and among the several states, and with the Indian tribes," and, by making treaties the supreme law of the land, to negotiate with foreign powers. The individual states were protected, however, by the requirement that the duties and imposts "be uniform throughout the United States," by a prohibition on taxes and duties imposed on "articles exported from any state" and a prohibition on "preference[s] . . . given by any Regulation of Commerce or Revenue to the Ports of one State over those of another." The Constitution further stated that "Vessels bound to, or from, one State [shall not] be obliged to enter, clear, or pay Duties in another."

The Constitution did not end interstate competition. It prevented explicit state imposition of discriminatory tariffs and tonnage duties (except to finance inspection). It thereby channeled state government involvement in the economy into internal improvements and the promotion and subsidy of local economic activity. The Constitution forced the state legislatures to cede control over many of the central areas of policymaking that had been under their control since they originated as colonies. The states could no longer collect revenue by means of tariff and tonnage policies (again, except to fund inspection). They could no longer issue paper money or enact

[36] Quoted in Marks, *Independence on Trial*, 46.

commodity money policies by means of legal tender laws. They were required to respect federal law, federal trade treaties, and federal law relating to Native Americans. The states – the institutions of government to which the citizenry felt the most allegiance – were prevented from acting in the areas of foreign trade and foreign policy.

What type of commercial policy did the Constitution's framers intend for the federal government? Although the U.S. Constitution unequivocally established a free-trade regime within the United States, the document was open ended on the issue of foreign policy and of America's role in world affairs. The Constitution did not set express limitations on the use of protective legislation to regulate external trade. It gave Congress an unlimited power to borrow on the credit of the United States, but was silent on the issue of the appropriate government financial infrastructure that would dictate the extent of federal borrowing. The Constitution placed few limitations on the executive branch's power to make military decisions. Under the Constitution, isolationism and aggressive expansion were equally acceptable.

The Northwest Ordinance of 1787, enacted months before the Constitution was ratified, however, sheds some light on the founding intent with respect to American trade policy. The Ordinance explicitly adopted an anti-mercantilist stance with respect to frontier land. Prior to its enactment, questions existed as to the proper role of the American frontier in relation to the original states: should the frontier areas be treated as colonies of the United States? The Northwest Ordinance announced a new, republican style of expansion that dispelled doubt. It provided a mechanism for the territories to join the U.S. "empire," not as dependent colonies, but as equal participants in the nation as states. As James Monroe wrote in a letter to Thomas Jefferson, the Ordinance creates "a colonial government similar to that which prevail'd in these States previous to the revolution, *with this remarkable and important difference*" that the districts "shall be admitted into the confederacy" when they reached a certain population.[37] The text of the Ordinance stated that when a state reached sixty thousand free inhabitants, the state would be admitted to the Congress of the United States "on an equal footing with the original States in all respects whatever." Because of the concern that the frontier areas might be treated as colonies, the Ordinance, in contrast to the U.S. Constitution, provided a bill of rights. It stated that the inhabitants of the territory were entitled to the right of *habeas corpus*,

[37] James Monroe to Thomas Jefferson (May 11, 1786), in Julian P. Boyd and Mina R. Bryan, eds., *The Papers of Thomas Jefferson* (Princeton, NJ, 1954), vol. 9: 510–12, 511 (emphasis added).

trial by jury, and a host of other liberties on which, the colonists had felt, Britain had reneged.

The Ordinance of 1787, however, was internal; it did not prevent American political leaders from pursuing aggressive foreign policies – financial and otherwise – elsewhere. John Adams, Benjamin Franklin, and others in the 1770s believed that America might bring about a revolution in international commercial relations based on free-trade principles. Their ambition, it turned out, was quickly suppressed by historical events; Britain would not recognize American neutrality in subsequent European wars. Given the circumstances, American political leaders might have mobilized support for an aggressive foreign policy, leading, perhaps, to America entering the European race for colonies in the early nineteenth century. But, federal government policy in the Founding Era was constrained by lingering hostility to centralized governmental authority and taxation.

Federal Government Trade Policy in the Founding Era – The Tariff of 1789

Tariff policy was the central means available to a government to define its foreign trade policy in the late eighteenth century. As exemplified by the English Navigation Acts, tariff policies enacted to promote the balance of trade are a quintessential feature of a "mercantilist" government. When the First Congress of the United States met in 1789, it was immediately obvious that collecting tariffs would be essential to resolving the country's desperate financial problems. The federal tariff was the first non-administrative item on Congress's agenda when it first met in April 1789. George Washington signed the Tariff Act of 1789 on July 4, signaling, on the new republic's most revered day, that it was derived from true American sovereignty and independence from Britain.

Americans were generally supportive of the tariff because relying on tariff duties for revenue was more palatable than any other form of taxation. The citizenry was far more hostile to federal direct taxation of property because that would have involved droves of government officials roaming the countryside, assessing the value of the citizenry's property, and foreclosing on the property of those who failed to pay. Tariffs were paid by merchants at the time of import and were therefore "invisible" to the ultimate consumer. Allowing the federal government to rely on tariffs for revenue also catered to the Southern states' preference to avoid Congressional discussion of slaves – how their numbers would affect the revenue or at what rates slaves should be taxed – which inevitably would have arisen in debates over direct taxes. In each year between 1791 and the War of 1812 more than 85 percent of the federal government's tax revenue was collected in the form of tariffs.

For ten of those years it accounted for 100 percent of federal government tax revenues.

Early American tariff policy, however, reflected not an aggressive stance on trade policy designed to improve the balance of trade, but rather an attempt to collect the minimum required revenue to support the government while delicately balancing competing regional interests. During the debates over the first national tariff, a consensus emerged that the burdens of taxation should be divided as evenly as possible among the states. As one Congressman put it, "Whenever a tax on a particular article seems to bear harder on one State than another, we must endeavor to equalize it by laying some other to restore an *equilibrium* to the system."[38]

Regional interests among the states differed substantially. The South wanted tariffs kept low. Like most regions dominated by the export of staple agricultural goods, Southern states feared retaliatory taxes by foreign governments. If European nations were to levy high tariffs on tobacco (or later, cotton) in retaliation to American duties, the Southern economy would bear most of the costs. Southerners also depended more heavily on imported manufactured goods, and tariffs on such goods would harm them as consumers. Madison represented the Southern interests in stating that the regulation of commerce "ought to be as free as the policy of nations will admit."[39]

The Middle Atlantic states, in contrast, promoted a moderately protectionist agenda. Initially, the "manufactures" these colonies wanted to protect were goods like cheese, cider, and leather goods produced on local farms.[40]

The central concern of the New England states was protection of their ship-building enterprises by means of tonnage duties that discriminated against foreign-built and foreign-owned ships. New Englanders advocated a mercantilist American monopoly of shipping, similar to the monopoly enjoyed by British merchants under the Navigation Acts.

Southern politicians viewed any protection of manufacturing as a transfer of wealth from South to North. According to one Southern representative, "By the encouragement given to manufactures you raise them in price, while a competition is destroyed which tended to the advantage of agriculture."[41] Similarly, a shipping monopoly ran directly against the interests of Southerners dependent on less costly English and European shipping for the export of staple goods in the trans-Atlantic trade.

[38] Fitzsimons, U.S. *House Journal*. 1st Cong., 1st sess., April 14, 1789, 136 (emphasis added).

[39] James Madison, U.S. *House Journal*. 1st Cong., 1st sess., April 9, 1789, 107.

[40] U.S. *House Journal*. 1st Cong., 1st sess., April 9, 1789, 111.

[41] Moore, U.S. *House Journal*. 1st Cong., 1st sess., April 16, 1789, 160.

The initial tariff legislation adopted by Congress granted New England the discriminatory tonnage duties it wanted.[42] Ultimately, Madison built a consensus around the notion that it was in the national interest to impose discriminatory tonnage duties, not for explicitly mercantilist purposes, but as defense legislation. America lacked a navy and through the practice of privateering – when government permitted private ships to capture ships of the enemy – private ships could be used for military purposes. (Indeed, the military ends of navigation were viewed as so important that Congress decided to subsidize fish exports to encourage an expansion of the fishing industry, because fishing was a "nursery for seamen."[43]) The Tariff Act gave the Middle Atlantic states moderate protection on many items they produced (ranging from a high of 15 percent on carriages, to 10 percent or 7.5 percent on other goods). It placated the South with low rates of tariffs overall. The protective tariffs were not generally prohibitively high, and a low duty of 5 percent ad valorem was imposed on all items not specifically enumerated.

Overall, tariff legislation of the Founding Era reflected the rejection of the British model of mercantilism. Like the Navigation Acts, the tariff included protectionist elements. The central focus of the tariff debates and of the tariff legislation, however, was to generate the revenue the federal government needed to pay its debts. In contrast, mercantilist tariff systems were designed to improve the balance of trade, typically by promoting the export of manufactured items. The dominant lobby within the United States, however, was agriculture, and tariff rates in the late eighteenth century were low.

HAMILTON'S FINANCIAL SYSTEM: THE MERCANTILIST MOMENT

Alexander Hamilton became Treasury Secretary in 1790 and, at the request of Congress, developed a financial plan that would both resolve the country's immediate financial problems and enable it to protect itself in the event of a future war with European powers. His plan was outlined in three reports presented to Congress: the *Report on Public Credit* (1790), the *Report on a National Bank* (1790), and the *Report on Manufactures* (1791). Hamilton's plan had a lasting impact on the country, both because Congress approved of and adopted most of his proposals and also because a new American

[42] The Tonnage Act of 1789 imposed a duty of fifty cents a ton on vessels that were both foreign built and foreign owned; a duty of thirty cents a ton on vessels built in the United States, but foreign owned; and a duty of six cents per ton on vessels built and owned by Americans. If the vessels were employed in the fisheries or coasting trade, they were required to pay the duty only once a year.

[43] U.S. *House Journal*. 1st Cong., 1st sess., April 28, 1789, 222–23 (Wadsworth) and May 4, 249 (Madison).

political economy emerged out of the fierce public reaction to Hamilton's proposals and to the Federalists who supported it.

The *Report on Pubic Credit* proposed a redefinition of the balance of power between the state and federal governments by having the federal government assume all state war debts. To Hamilton, federal government assumption of state debts was a vehicle for rallying local economic interests to support the federal government. Satisfying the war debts would require the sale of bond issues. If the federal government assumed the state war debts and issued its own federal bonds, as Hamilton proposed, these bondholders would have a direct interest in the financial security of the federal government. State issues of bonds, in contrast, would have led to greater economic interest in and, ultimately, allegiance to the state governments.

Hamilton's *Report on Public Credit* also insisted on making markets for government debt stable and highly liquid, so that the debt instruments would function as an infusion of capital in the economy. The price of the government bonds issued during the War had dropped to a fraction of their initial worth. By 1790, speculators betting on full redemption, including several prominent government officials, rapidly bought up the bonds at very low prices. Hamilton's *Report* energetically defended non-discrimination between those who had purchased government bonds directly from the government at face value in specie (the primary debt holders), and those who had purchased the bonds in the bond market later (the secondary debt holders). Hamilton's plan of full redemption for secondary debt holders anticipated profits for these speculators in the tens of millions of dollars in contemporary values.

Madison and others, in contrast, believed that *foreign* creditors should be paid at par, but *domestic* debt holders should receive no more than the price they had paid for the bonds plus interest. Madison found it offensive that the "profits" handed out to the bond speculators – many of whom were government insiders – would be paid for by taxes on the general population. Hamilton prevailed, however, asserting that maintaining the highest standards with respect to government credit obligations, whether to foreign or domestic creditors, ultimately saved taxpayers money through lower future interest rates and more available credit.[44]

[44] Hamilton's *Report on Public Credit* explains that discrimination against secondary bond holders "would operate a diminution of the value of stock in the hands of the first, as well as of every other holder. . . . For this diminution of the value of stock, every person who should be about to lend to the Government, would demand compensation. . . . Every compensation of this sort . . . would be an absolute loss to the Government." Alexander Hamilton, Report on Public Credit (Jan. 9, 1790), Finance, 1st Cong., 2d. Sess., *American State Papers*, 15–29, 17.

Assumption of the state debts and securing the public credit had an additional polarizing implication: the federal government would need greater revenues to meet expanded obligations. It was widely acknowledged that the revenues from the import tariffs of 1789 were insufficient to pay the government debts on the terms Hamilton outlined.[45] Federal assumption of the state war debts brought the taxation issue to the forefront of discussion. To raise further revenues to cover the costs of the assumption of state debts, in March 1791, Congress imposed an excise tax on whiskey. The whiskey tax was Congress's first experiment in federal direct taxation.

Hamilton's *Report on a National Bank* presented his plan to create a privately run national bank to hold the government reserves and to use government debt to stimulate the economy. The bank would have the ability to make loans and to issue notes that would circulate as a currency. The bank could be relied on to service the government with loans in cases of national emergency, and it would make taxation far more administrable, since bank notes would be accepted as tax payments. Congress granted the First Bank of the United States a twenty-year charter in 1791. The First Bank, however, was controversial. Many, including Madison and Jefferson, initially believed it to be unconstitutional. It gave the federal government and its private managers financial powers resembling those of the privately run Bank of England, which held most of the British government reserves.

Hamilton's final major report, the *Report on Manufactures*, though more equivocal than his other reports, presented the case for a system of tariffs and bounties that would stimulate manufacturing in America. It asserted that free-trade policies would be ideal if other nations could be counted on to also adopt such policies. Hamilton viewed tariff policy as a response to the "numerous and very injurious impediments to the emission and vent of [our] own commodities." He also believed that government incentives to develop manufacturing (such as import substitution policies) were particularly necessary in America because manufacturing had been suppressed under British colonial rule. To Hamilton, the "simplest and most obvious improvements, in the most ordinary occupations, are adopted with hesitation,

[45] As William Grayson, an anti-Federalist senator from Virginia described,

> The creditors of the domestic debt (the great supporters of the new government) are now looking steadfastly on their friends for a permanent provision for their interest – But how is this to be accomplished – The Impost . . . will not yield after supporting the expenses of government, more than will pay the French and Dutch interest, if so much – what is then to be done? Ah! There is the question.

William Grayson to Patrick Henry, 12 June 1789, quoted in William D. Barber, "'Among the Most *Techy Articles of Civil Police*': Federal Taxation and the Adoption of the Whiskey Excise," *William and Mary Quarterly* 25 (1968), 58–84, 67.

reluctance, and by slow gradations. . . . The spontaneous transition to new pursuits [is] . . . attended with proportionably greater difficulty."[46] In the *Report*, Hamilton argued that manufacturing would benefit the society because it would lead to greater independence from European manufactures, greater division of labor, and more jobs (especially for women and children), which would increase demand for agricultural goods. Perhaps most important, the federal government was in desperate need of revenue. Why not earn revenue with a measure that would jump-start American manufacturing?

The Federalist foreign policy vision, more generally, was characterized by a pragmatic commitment to building on the strengths of the American economy as it existed in the 1790s. Hamilton and the other Federalists supported furthering close economic relationships with Britain. The ability to repay the public debts and honor the obligations of the bond issues rested on continued revenues from import tariffs. Maintaining trade relations with the English would ensure Hamilton of the tariff revenue he needed to fund his financial plan because English merchants would willingly extend credit to the Americans for imports. From the vantage of public credit, relying on new trade relations with the French and Dutch was much more risky.

To defend American commerce, however, the Federalists were committed to a much stronger military and advocated federal expenditures on a navy. Hamilton suggested to John Adams that he might lead an army to conquer Louisiana and Florida to give Americans access to their rivers and outlets. However, Hamilton and the Federalists opposed any immediate western expansion. They believed that the capital resources of the country should be invested locally to develop manufacturing and American industry. Expansion would dissipate these resources. Referring to the settlement of "the vast tracts of waste land" in the West, Hamilton stated, "while it promises ample retribution, in the generation of future resources, diminishes or obstructs, in the mean time, the *active* wealth of the country. It not only draws off a part of the circulating money, and places it in a more passive state, but it diverts, into its own channels, a portion of that species of labor and industry which would otherwise be employed in furnishing materials for foreign trade, and which, by contributing to a favorable balance, would assist the introduction of specie."[47] Still partly a mercantilist – note his emphasis on specie – Hamilton opposed federal subsidization of western expansion.

[46] Alexander Hamilton, Report on Manufactures (Dec. 5, 1791), 2d. Cong., 1st Sess., *American State Papers*, Finance, 123–44, 128.

[47] Alexander Hamilton, Report on a National Bank (Dec. 14, 1790), 1st. Cong., 2d Sess., *American State Papers*, Finance, 67–76, 71.

Had the Federalist vision of American economic growth been implemented, the United States might have become a major force internationally by mid-century. The national debt in 1790 was only 40 percent of gross national product, smaller than that of most countries in the early twenty-first century, and the economy was booming. During the 1790s, under Hamilton's plan, 40 percent of federal revenues were used to pay down the government's debt obligations. By 1800, the national debt was reduced to 18 percent of gross national product. Hamilton can be credited with creating an institutional structure that would have allowed the U.S. government to finance expenditures on the scale of the leading European powers.

The institutional features of American public finance were a great success in economic terms. Politically, however, the implementation of Hamilton's scheme proved disastrous, provoking the emergence of Republicanism in reaction. A speculative frenzy developed during the subscription to the stock of the Bank of the United States and to the new government bonds. The speculation was viewed by many skeptics of the Bank as scandalous evidence of its inherently corrupt effect. More deeply, many thought that the existence of the Bank would create an aristocratic court party and financial class that would usurp popular government authority. The mad scramble for the Bank stock in the opening hours of offer suggested that the institution would gain high monopoly profits. Speculators in government debt drove up the price to par value, which meant millions in profits for speculators who had bought at substantial discounts from par. In the spring of 1792, however, nervous European investors began to sell the government bonds, and major speculators lost money. This first financial collapse, though inconsistent with the opposition to profit-making, only increased the opposition to Hamilton and his ideas.

In this context, Hamilton's *Report on Manufactures* of 1791, coinciding with his creation of a corporation called the Society for Useful Manufactures that would promote manufacturing in Pennsylvania, created deep suspicion that the U.S. government would be used by Federalists, as the central government had been used in Britain, to advance mercantile interests. Moreover, Hamilton's 1794 direct tax on whiskey distilleries was wildly unpopular. Although in New England the tax was levied on large molasses distilleries, in the corn-growing regions of the West and South, farmers often kept small distilleries on their farms. The intrusion of federal tax collectors into these regions brought open rebellion against the government. George Washington, general of the American Revolution, and Hamilton, who had been his principal aide, personally suppressed the Whiskey Rebellion with 13,000 troops in 1794. Jefferson's campaign in 1800 emphasized a promise to repeal all federal government internal taxes.

Jefferson's *Notes on the State of Virginia* laid the groundwork for the Republican theory of political economy. To Jefferson, British prohibitions on American manufacturing were fortuitous in that they led to the dominance of agriculture and extractive industries throughout the colonies. This agricultural base supported the creation of a society free of the miseries and corruptions of European life. The *Notes* famously stated that "those who labor the earth" are "the chosen people of God." To Jefferson and many of his contemporaries, manufacturing involved work that only people without property would willingly perform. Manufacturing was "resorted to of necessity not of choice." American greatness lay in the rejection of domestic manufacturing. America would import its luxury goods from European countries that lacked the land to offer their citizenry the life of the independent farmer. By its "immensity of land," the expansion of agriculture, and the virtuous nature of its citizenry, America would achieve the "happiness and permanence of government."

Jefferson preserved Hamilton's basic financial system, but reduced its impact on the lives of the citizenry. On entering office, Jefferson brought about the repeal of Hamilton's internal taxes and appointed Albert Gallatin as Secretary of Treasury with a specific mandate to pay down the federal debt. Under Gallatin's direction, the federal debt was reduced without taxes by funds from the sale of public lands earmarked for the purpose. By the outbreak of the War of 1812, the government debt was $45 million, only 8 percent of the country's gross national product. To the Jeffersonian-Republicans, a balanced budget reflected a popular desire to limit the size and power of the federal government and to protect the authority of the states. By repealing the internal taxes and paying down the debt, Jefferson at least temporarily blocked federal government expansion.

In terms of foreign policy, Republicanism turned mercantilism on its head. European mercantilism had traditionally focused – to a fault – on the capture of markets where manufactured exports could be sold. The Jeffersonian-Republicans sought to use government influence to negotiate treaties that would indirectly suppress manufacturing by expanding agriculture. They were not isolationists, far from it. Foreign trade and engagement with the world were essential to Republican ideology. The successful creation of the Republican economy depended on close commercial relations with foreign merchants who would purchase American agricultural goods and, in return, supply Americans with the manufactured items they needed.

The conquest of the West might seem to replicate British colonialism of the eighteenth and nineteenth centuries. It is essential to remember, however, that in the Founding Era it was the Jeffersonian-Republicans, not the Washington-Hamiltonian Federalists, who were the party of expansionism.

Jefferson agonized over the Louisiana Purchase because he viewed it to be beyond the powers of the federal government under the Constitution. There is no question, however, that the Louisiana Purchase, and the conquest of the West more generally, fulfilled his vision of America and could be justified as necessary acts by government to ensure enough land to spread the agrarian ideal and to forestall industrialization. Indeed, Jefferson and other Republicans proposed conquering Canada immediately prior to the War of 1812. Jefferson believed that Canada was so ready for "liberation" that conquering it would be "a mere matter of marching."[48]

The distinction between the Federalist and Jeffersonian-Republican parties is also highlighted by the manner in which the crisis with the Barbary pirates was ultimately resolved. The Federalists tried to resolve the crisis through monetary payments only. The hostage-taking persisted, however, and in 1805 Jefferson built a navy for the express purpose of crushing the Barbary pirates. Jefferson wanted to break ties with Europe and viewed access to the Mediterranean as central to the Republican goal of an economy based on exporting agricultural goods. He was willing to use military means to achieve his objective and he succeeded.

More generally, however, the West was not conquered because of the traditional mercantilist belief in the need to capture markets. The West was conquered to expand agriculture. According to Madison, "By a free expansion of our people the establishment of internal manufactures will not only be long delayed but the consumption of foreign manufactures long continue increasing; and at the same time, all the productions of the American soil required by Europe in return for her manufactures, will proportionably increase."[49] The federal government's investments in western expansion might be criticized for draining resources from the domestic economy and for inflating the incentives for settlers to move to the frontier (as well as for atrocities committed against Native Americans). In contrast to classic mercantilist policies, however, westward expansion was not pursued for the purpose of achieving national power at the expense of other world powers.

In sum, commercial regulations in the Founding Era were not used to enhance government power and reflected a compromise between conflicting regional interests, the use of military to expand westward did not conform to the traditional mercantilist objective of securing markets, and the financial apparatus that could have been used to vastly increase federal government power was severely constrained.

[48] Thomas Jefferson to William Duane, Aug. 4, 1812, in Paul L. Ford, ed., *The Writings of Thomas Jefferson*, 10 vols. (New York, 1892–9), IX: 366.

[49] James Madison to Thomas Jefferson, Aug. 20, 1784, in Gaillard Hunt, ed., *The Writings of James Madison*, 9 vols. (New York, 1901), II: 64–76, 72.

The Rise of Tariff Levels and Manufacturing Prior to the Civil War

We can consider tariff levels a proxy for the pursuit of mercantilist-like goals of protecting manufacturing and improving the balance of trade. In the Founding Era, tariff levels gradually, but steadily, increased as the manufacturing sector developed and its lobbying capabilities became more powerful. The Revolutionary War provided the first stimulus to manufacturing. American manufacturing grew exponentially during Jefferson's 1808–9 Embargo of Britain and the War of 1812. Tariff legislation became increasingly protective after these crises. Between 1789 and 1812 twelve tariff laws were enacted. Each increased the number of dutiable articles and the overall level of duties.

Northern manufacturing interests lobbying for tariffs, however, faced increasing opposition from Southerners, who persistently viewed protection as a transfer of wealth from North to South. Every tariff bill adopted in America prior to the Civil War reflected a compromise based on conflicting regional interests. Southern hostility to the duties escalated as tariff legislation increasingly became identified as a federal legislative precedent that might eventually threaten slave interests.

With the growth of manufacturing during the 1820s, New England leaders adopted highly protectionist positions, abandoning their prior, more moderate views. When Southern interests were disregarded in 1832, South Carolina charged that the tariff was "intended for the protection of domestic manufactures, and the giving of bounties to classes and individuals engaged in particular employments at the expense and to the injury and oppression of other classes and individuals." South Carolina analogized its situation to that of a colony of the North. Guided by Calhoun's *Exposition* on state nullification of federal legislation, South Carolina held a state convention that made it unlawful after February 1, 1833, to collect tariff duties within the state. The nullification crisis was suppressed by Andrew Jackson's threat to invade the state. The crisis was the breaking point of a decades-long interregional conflict over tariffs.

The movement for western expansion did not face similar opposition. As already mentioned, revenues from federal land sales were earmarked to pay down federal government debt. Land sales led to a steady reduction of the federal debt between 1812 and 1833, when the federal debt was fully paid off. Western expansion was "imperialism" of a peculiar kind. In the minds of the people, western expansion in the early nineteenth century directly reduced the size and scope of the federal government, as reflected in government debt, and the institutions, such as the Bank of the United States, that managed the government debt. There was no strong economic interest to oppose western expansion. True American colonialism did not take place until after the Civil War when the Southern states, the primary economic lobby that would have opposed American colonialism overseas, were far less economically and politically powerful than before.

V. CONCLUSION

The global economic and political dominance of the United States today make it tempting to look for traces of imperialism and colonialism in America's early history. There is superficial evidence to support the claim. A desire for stronger tariff policies was a pressing issue underlying the ratification of the U.S. Constitution. Hamilton's financial system was based on the English model that financed the creation of a global empire. Westward expansion was an integral part of the American experience from the start. The account on which it relies, however, is historically misconceived; it overlooks the long history of institutional and legal development during the colonial period and the fragility of the federal government that emerged when the colonies united.

In 1818, reflecting on the formation of the U.S. government, John Adams remarked,

> The colonies had grown up under constitutions of government so different, there was so great a variety of religions, they were composed of so many different nations, their customs, manners, and habits had so little resemblance, and their intercourse had been so rare, and their knowledge of each other so imperfect, that to unite them in the same principles in theory and the same system of action, was certainly a very difficult enterprise. The complete accomplishment of it, in so short a time and by such simple means, was perhaps a singular example in the history of mankind. Thirteen clocks were made to strike together – a perfection of mechanism, which no artist had ever before effected.[50]

Adams' metaphor emphasizes the tenuous nature of the federal union in its early years. Arguably, the federal government reflected the lowest common denominator of what was palatable, given the public's hostility to federal power. Its policies were a product of constant compromises among states representing vastly different interests. Scholars' attempts to give the federal government of the Founding Era a mercantilist or neo-mercantilist gloss is inconsistent with the reluctance of the United States to become a global power until the end of the nineteenth century. Western expansion was a popular policy in part because the earmarking of public land sales to the reduction of the federal debt was a means of expanding the country's

[50] John Adams to Hezekiah Niles, Feb. 13, 1818, in Charles Francis Adams, ed., *The Works of John Adams, Second President of the United States*, 10 vols. (Boston, 1856), 10:282–89, 283.

size while respecting the citizenry's hostility to federal government power. One consequence was a much more rapid conquest of the West and Native Americans than might have taken place otherwise. But a second consequence was almost a century of relative isolation from global events. The history of colonial institutional and legal development, and of Founding Era politics, had a long, but of course far from permanent, legacy.

13

LAW AND THE ORIGINS OF THE AMERICAN REVOLUTION

JACK P. GREENE

The revolution that occurred in North America during the last quarter of the eighteenth century was the unintended consequence of a dispute about law. During the dozen years between 1764 and 1776, Britons on both sides of the Atlantic engaged in an elaborate debate over the source and character of law within the larger British Empire. Whether the King-in-Parliament, the ultimate source of statute law in Great Britain, could legislate for British colonies overseas was the ostensible question in dispute, but many other related and even deeper legal issues involving the nature of the constitution of the empire and the location of sovereignty within the empire emerged from and were canvassed thoroughly during the debate. On neither side of the Atlantic was opinion monolithic, but two sides, one representing the dominant opinion in metropolitan Britain and the other the principal view in the colonies, rapidly took shape. The failure to reconcile these positions led in 1775 to open warfare and in 1776 to the decision of thirteen of Britain's more than thirty American colonies to declare their independence and form an American union. This chapter examines the nature and shifting character of this dispute and its place in the larger process of imperial legal and constitutional thought and practice.

I. THE COLONIAL BACKGROUND

At the conclusion of the Seven Years War, constitutional arrangements within the British Empire were deeply ambiguous. Recurrent disputes over the extent of the Crown's colonial authority had punctuated the public life of the empire throughout its first century and a half. The colonizing process had produced in each province a system of governance and authority loosely modeled on that of the English. In each of these systems, elected legislative assemblies asserted the claims of their constituents to all the rights and legal safeguards enjoyed by English people at home. When, beginning in the 1650s, London officials sought to impose metropolitan authority on these provincial centers of authority, they evoked a profound mistrust of central authority and a widespread demand for legal and constitutional limitations on metropolitan power among American settlers, who insisted that, as English people or the descendants of English people, they were entitled to enjoy all the rights and legal protections of English people in the home island.

The recurring arguments over this issue gave rise to an extensive constitutional debate in which colonial spokesmen early developed an elaborate argument to support their claims to what they thought of as their inherited rights as English people. According to this argument, recently dubbed the doctrine of settlement, the original settlers of the colonies had, with authorization from the English monarchy, migrated voluntarily to America, where they quickly turned a wilderness into thriving and well-inhabited settlements and thereby, at little or no cost to the English government, greatly enlarged the territories, wealth, and power of the English nation. In the process of migration, this argument claimed, settlers took their English rights and liberties with them, rights that had been guaranteed to them by their charters and were secured by their respective civil governments. Colonial charters, in this view, did not grant new rights but only confirmed that settlers would continue to enjoy in their new polities across the sea their inherited rights as English people. Among the liberties thus inherited by and confirmed to them, settlers considered none more essential than the rights, in the words of New York justice William Smith, "to choose the Laws by which we will be Governed" and "to be Governed only by such Laws."[1] They saw their elected assemblies as the primary instruments for the exercise of those rights, the provincial equivalents of the metropolitan House of Commons with the same broad lawmaking and rights-defending authority within their respective jurisdictions.

This line of thought implied a conception of colonies as extensions of Britain overseas and of colonists as Britons living outside the realm but enjoying the very same liberties and rights to the very same extent as those who remained at home. From this perspective, the British Empire was a free empire based on consent, and colonists were fellow subjects who, though "living in different parts of the world," together with those residing in Britain, formed, as the political economist Arthur Young remarked in 1772, "one nation, united under one sovereign, speaking the same language and enjoying the same liberty."[2]

But metropolitan officials always remained ambivalent about, not whether, but to what extent English colonists were entitled to English

[1] William Smith, *Mr. Smith's Opinion Humbly Offered* (New York 1734), 34.

[2] Arthur Young, *Political Essays Concerning the Present State of the British Empire* (London, 1772), 1.

law and liberty. They were never willing to admit in their fullest extent the colonists' claims to enjoy all the rights of the English constitution. For that reason, the exact nature of the colonial constitutions rapidly became the main point of contention between Crown and colonies in much the same way that, in the previous century, the nature of the English constitution had been at the heart of the struggle between Crown and Parliament. The many contests that everywhere developed over this issue revolved around two principal questions: whether colonists were entitled to all the benefits of the laws of England and whether the representative assemblies that settlers established early in the history of every colony to make laws for the local populations enjoyed the same status in the colonial constitutions as the House of Commons did in the English constitution.

Crown officials never accepted the settler demands for explicit statutory guarantees of their rights to the benefits of English laws. Nevertheless, through the extensive use of English legal precedents and statutes by colonial judges, colonists seem eventually to have managed to secure those benefits through custom, usage, and practice. Most of the empirical research necessary to nail down this point and to show fully the precise extent and character of the transfer of English law to the colonies remains to be done. Nevertheless, the diminution of demands for explicit guarantees of English laws in the colonies after 1730 strongly suggests that provincial and local courts had by that time effectively established the customary rights of the colonists in this broad area.

In much the same way, the colonial assemblies succeeded in establishing their strident and often reiterated claims to constitutional authority within their respective jurisdictions equivalent to that of the House of Commons in Britain. Although Crown officials consistently recognized the assemblies' authority to pass laws, they always insisted that those bodies were subordinate institutions, much like the governing bodies of English corporations and without the full rights and privileges of the English Parliament. According to metropolitan theory, the very existence of the assemblies depended, not on their constituents' inherent rights as English people, but on the favor of the Crown as extended to them by royal charter or some other official document, such as the King's commission or instructions to his governors; from the late 1670s London authorities often condemned colonial assemblies for regarding as rights what had only been granted as favors. Repeatedly affirmed by the Crown's law officers in London throughout the eight decades between 1680 and 1760, this doctrine served as the favorite defense for colonial executives trying to combat the assemblies' pretensions to full legislative powers in the colonies, the clear implication of their argument being that the Crown might change the constitutions of the colonies whenever and however it saw fit.

This view of the colonies saw them less as societies of Britons overseas populated by free settlers of English and European descent than as outposts of British economic and strategic power. In this restrictive conception, explicit in the Navigation Acts of the late seventeenth century, the colonies were principally workshops or, in the words of the former Massachusetts governor, Thomas Pownall, "mere plantations, tracts of foreign country, employed in raising certain specified and enumerated commodities, solely for the use of the trade and manufactures of the mother-country." Increasingly after 1740, and especially during the Seven Years War, this view gave way to a complementary emphasis on the colonies as instruments of British national power. Between 1745 and 1763, intensifying rivalries with France and Spain and the growing populations and wealth of the colonies produced, for the first time among metropolitan analysts, an intensive discussion about the nature and workings of the empire, but that discussion only reaffirmed the view that, as Charles Townshend declared subsequently, the very word "colony" implied not the equality claimed by colonists but subordination. This conception suggested that colonists were something less than full Britons, not "fellow subjects," as Benjamin Franklin put it in 1768, "but subjects of subjects."[3]

Because they controlled the power of the purse, however, and because the Crown's colonial governors found it impossible to govern effectively without their consent, the colonial assemblies slowly managed to obtain in practice the authority that Crown officials denied them in theory. Like the English House of Commons had itself managed during the seventeenth century, the colonial assemblies by the middle of the eighteenth century had through precedent and custom been able to establish their authority and status as local parliaments, the most important institutions in the colonial constitutions, and the primary guardians of the colonists' inherited rights as Englishmen – including especially the right not be subjected to any taxes or laws relating to their internal affairs without the consent of their representatives in assembly.

The growth of legislative power in the colonies during the colonial era was paralleled by the localization of authority within each of the colonies. As each of these overseas entities developed its own peculiarly provincial constitutional tradition, each one's localities played a significant role in the creation and perpetuation of those traditions. Perhaps to an even greater extent than in contemporary Britain, where the Glorious Revolution had

[3] Thomas Pownall, *The Administration of the Colonies* (London, 1768), 282; Benjamin Franklin to the *Gentlemen's Magazine*, January 1768, in Verner W. Crane, ed., *Benjamin Franklin's Letters to the Press* (Chapel Hill, NC, 1950), 111.

paved the way for a profound reassertion of the authority of local governing institutions, local magistracies in the colonies exercised a pervasive jurisdiction over many of the constitutive elements of the colonial polities, including law enforcement, in which local magistrates and juries had broad powers to determine what, in their respective communities, was – and was not – law. The constitutional order in the colonies was at once local, consensual, participatory, lay-directed, and customary. This diffusion and localization of authority ensured that, in contrast to those of contemporary continental monarchies, Britain's expanding empire, like the emerging British national state itself, would not be founded on methods of centralization and absolutism.

These developments provided American settlers with another powerful foundation for their arguments in defense of colonial rights against intrusions of metropolitan power: the ancient English legal doctrine of usage or custom. Custom had enormous authority in the British legal and constitutional tradition. Both the common law and Parliament derived their authority from the force of custom, and the British constitution was itself based as much on custom as on statute law. Whether the colonies had been settled long enough to be able to claim their rights and liberties on the basis of immemorial custom was a matter of some doubt, even among colonial partisans. Yet, in asserting that their right to representative institutions was inherent in them as Englishmen, the colonists were claiming, as Justice Joseph Murray of New York declared in 1734, that the assemblies derived "their Power or Authority . . . from the common Custom and Laws of England, claimed as an English-man[']s Birth Right, and as having been such by Immemorial Custom in England; and tho' the People" in the colonies could not "claim this by Immemorial Custom here, yet as being part of the Dominions of England, they are intitled to the like Powers and Authorities here, that their fellow Subjects have, or are intitled to, in their Mother Country, by Immemorial Custom."[4]

From very early on, however, colonists had defended their rights to assemblies on the basis not just of English custom but of their own. By the early 1720s, colonists commonly based their claims for legislative rights and practices on the basis of ancient custom or uninterrupted usage, which in some colonies went back almost a century. "One would think," wrote Connecticut governor Jonathan Law in 1728, that rights "of so antient standing" – constituting a "universal custom" stretching back "beyond the memory of man" to the very beginnings of the colonies – "would . . . have the like

[4] Joseph Murray, *Mr. Murray's Opinion Relating to the Courts of Justice in the Colony of New-York* (New York, 1734), 7, 15.

foundation with the general and particular customs of England."[5] When they were "general, and . . . long continued," explained Jonathan Blenham, attorney general of Barbados, in 1742, "particular Customs and Usages" became "in a manner Lex Loci" and were "not at once to be overthrown, merely because" some Crown official happened to find them at variance with his instructions.[6] Quoting Sir Edward Coke, colonial protagonists often argued that the Crown could lose a right by never having enforced it, and they challenged the Crown's authority to infringe rights and liberties that they had long enjoyed.

Although the Crown's law officers sometimes agreed with the colonists that custom gave legal sanction to colonial practices that seemed to undermine the prerogatives of the Crown, the usual metropolitan attitude was that, no matter how long they had prevailed, such customary deviations from British practice and royal prescription were unconstitutional and without legal standing. Repeatedly they argued that such deviations might be altered by the unilateral action of the metropolitan government, especially when they represented obvious encroachments on the prerogatives of the Crown.

Nevertheless, the trajectory of colonial constitutional development over the course of the colonial period was powerfully in the direction of consensual governance with strong legislative checks on the royal prerogative. While the prerogative in Britain was reduced considerably as a result of various statutory restrictions following the Glorious Revolution, it remained, at least theoretically, extensive in the colonies. But over the seven decades from the Revolution to the early 1760s, the assemblies in most colonies had managed, through a combination of statutes and custom, largely to neutralize the prerogative, and some of these achievements had been sanctioned not only by custom but also even by rulings of Crown law officers, who often upheld the doctrine of usage in colonial cases. The result was the continuing fragility of royal power in the colonies.

The corollary of this weakness of royal power through a combination of custom and the recognition of custom's legally binding character by metropolitan law officers was the failure of Parliament to take an expansive role in colonial affairs. Except in the areas of general trade regulation, imperial defense, and a few other minor matters, Parliament had taken little interest in the colonies and very little interest indeed in internal colonial governance. Combined with the example of the reduction of royal

[5] Jonathan Law to Jonathan Belcher, June 18, 1728, in "Talcott Papers," *Collections of the Connecticut Historical Society*, 4:122–23.

[6] [Jonathan Blenham], *Remarks on Several Acts of Parliament Relating More especially to the Colonies Abroad* (London, 1742), 17.

authority in England itself, the limited nature of Parliament's interest in the colonies strongly suggested the reduction of all external power in the colonies, that of Parliament as well as of the Crown. But the fact was that before the mid-1760s the nature of Parliament's relation to the colonies had never been examined explicitly.

II. THE STAMP ACT CRISIS

Parliament's efforts to impose revenue taxes on the colonies in the mid-1760s thus precipitated the first intensive and systematic exploration of this problem on either side of the Atlantic. On the surface, the issue raised by these efforts, especially by the Stamp Act of 1765, was no more than whether, in the succinct words of Massachusetts Governor Francis Bernard, "America shall or shall not be Subject to the Legislature of Great Britain."[7] But the controversy moved on rapidly to a broad-ranging consideration of fundamental issues involving the nature of the constitutional relationship between Britain and the colonies and the distribution of power within the empire. Far from producing either a theoretical or a practical solution of these issues, however, the Stamp Act crisis revealed a deep rift in understanding between metropolis and colonies, a rift that would never be bridged within the structure of the empire.

Some metropolitan supporters later admitted that the Stamp Act was an innovation. For at least three decades, however, metropolitan officials had casually assumed that Parliament's colonial authority was unlimited. For more than a century, moreover, Parliament had routinely laid duties on colonial exports and imports for the purposes of regulating trade and protecting metropolitan interests. But Parliamentary legislation for the colonies had been confined almost entirely to commercial and other economic regulations of general scope. The only precedent for any other sort of revenue tax was the Post Office Act of 1710, and revenue was not its primary objective. If, before the Stamp Act, there were no precedents for Parliament's taxing the colonies for revenue, neither had anyone explicitly articulated a theoretical justification for the exertion of Parliamentary authority in that area.

The traditional link between taxation and representation in British constitutional thought and practice made this problem potentially troublesome – for metropolitans as well as colonials. Indeed, metropolitan disquiet over this problem was clearly revealed during the Stamp Act crisis

[7] Francis Bernard to Richard Jackson, August 18, 1764, in Edmund S. Morgan, ed., *Prologue to Revolution: Sources and Documents on the Stamp Act Crisis, 1764–1776* (Chapel Hill, NC, 1959), 29.

by proposals from several writers for colonial representation in Parliament. More important, the administration of Prime Minister George Grenville itself implicitly acknowledged the importance of the matter by the pains it took to deal with it. During the winter of 1764–65, in the months just before the passage of the Stamp Act, Grenville's lieutenant, Thomas Whately, ingeniously invented the doctrine of virtual representation, according to which the colonists, like the many residents of Britain who had no voice in elections, were nonetheless virtually represented in Parliament.

When Grenville first brought the proposal for colonial stamp duties before Parliament the previous March, however, neither he nor Whately had apparently thought of applying the doctrine of virtual representation to the colonies; his initial attempt to finesse the problem created by the lack of colonial representation in Parliament was a categorical assertion of Parliament's right. Indeed, by insisting on that occasion that Britain had "an inherent right to lay inland duties there," Grenville himself first raised the question of Parliamentary right. In addition, by going out of his way to assert that the "very sovereignty of this kingdom depends [up]on it," he also managed to establish the framework within which most metropolitans would subsequently consider the issue by ensuring that they would thenceforth interpret colonial opposition to the exertion of that right as a challenge not simply to the authority of Parliament per se but to the sovereignty of the metropolis in general.[8]

As soon as it was raised, the specter of Parliamentary taxation produced enormous unease in the colonies. Arguing that it was unprecedented, colonial spokesmen insisted that no community of Englishmen and their descendants could be taxed without their consent, an exemption they claimed as a right and not as a privilege. They dismissed the idea of virtual representation out of hand and argued that no legislature had any right to legislate for any people with whom it did not have a common interest and a direct connection. For people on the peripheries of an extended polity like that of the early modern British Empire, this emphasis on the local foundations of legislative authority made sense. Whatever Parliament might declare, few colonists had any doubt that their rights as Englishmen demanded both that they be exempt from taxes levied in a distant metropolis without their consent and that their own local assemblies have an exclusive power to tax them.

In analyzing the colonial response to the Stamp Act crisis, scholars have long tended to treat the colonists' claims as demands for their individual

[8] Commons Proceedings, March 8, 1764, in R. C. Simmons and P. D. G. Thomas, eds., *Proceedings and Debates of the British Parliament Respecting North America* (New York, 1980–87), 1:492.

rights as Englishmen, as indeed they were. As several recent writers have stressed, however, this emphasis has tended to obscure the very important extent to which, especially during the Stamp Act crisis, the colonists seem to have believed that the security of individual rights depended on the security of corporate rights, which they thought of as virtually synonymous with the rights of provincial assemblies. Throughout the colonial period, the status and authority of the assemblies had been a prime subject of dispute between metropolitans and colonials, and colonial legislators and political writers had produced a rich and extensive body of literature, thereby building a solid and thoroughly internalized political tradition on which resistance leaders in the 1760s and 1770s could draw. Whereas earlier the conflict had been between the assemblies and the Crown, after 1765 it was between the assemblies and Parliament.

Throughout the Stamp Act crisis, colonial spokesmen put enormous stress on the traditional conception of their assemblies as the primary guardians of both the individual liberties of their constituents and the corporate rights of the colonies. Noting that it was precisely because of their great distance from the metropolis, which prevented them from being either incorporated fully into the British nation or represented in the metropolitan Parliament, that their assemblies had been established initially, they insisted that each of their own local legislatures enjoyed full legislative authority and exclusive power to tax within its respective jurisdiction.

The identification of individual rights with the corporate rights of the assemblies ran right through the entire colonial argument. Thus the Connecticut Assembly argued against Parliamentary taxation on the grounds that it would both deprive their constituents of "that fundamental privilege of Englishmen whereby, in special, they are denominated a free people" and, no less important, leave them with "no more than a shew of legislation." "May it not be truly said in this case," it asked, "that the Assemblies in the colonies will have left no other power or authority, and the people no other freedom, estates, or privileges than what may truly be called a tenancy at will; that they [will] have exchanged, or rather lost those privileges and rights which, according to the national constitution, were their birthright and inheritance for such a disagreeable tenancy?"[9]

The colonists based their claims for exclusive taxing authority and exemption from Parliamentary taxation almost entirely on the traditional legal supports that they had relied on in their struggles with the Crown throughout the colonial era: their rights as Englishmen, their royal charters, and,

[9] [Tobias Fitch, et al.], *Reasons Why the British Colonies, in America, Should not be Charged with Internal Taxes* (New Haven, 1764), in Bernard Bailyn, ed., *Pamphlets of the American Revolution, 1750–1776* (Cambridge, MA, 1965), 392–94.

especially, longstanding custom. Even those writers who, like the Massachusetts lawyer James Otis, made extensive use of natural rights theory, tended to equate natural rights with English rights. For more than a century, they explained, they had uniformly exercised and enjoyed the privileges of imposing and raising their own taxes in their provincial assemblies, and such constant and uninterrupted usage, it seemed to them, was, in the best traditions of English constitutional governance, sufficient in itself to make a constitution. With these arguments, colonial spokesmen merely turned against Parliament defenses they and their ancestors had developed over the previous century to protect colonial rights against abuses of prerogative.

Whatever the sources of the legislative authority of the assemblies, the most significant questions posed by the new intrusion of Parliament into the domestic affairs of the colonies and the most vital issues raised by the Stamp Act crisis vis-à-vis the constitutional organization of the early modern British Empire were how extensive that authority was and how it related to the authority of the British Parliament. Linking authority to consent, few colonists could accept the metropolitan position that there were no limits to Parliament's colonial authority. Although some argued that Parliament's authority was purely local and did not extend beyond the bounds of Britain, most colonists in 1764–66 took a far more cautious approach, admitting, as the Virginia lawyer and political writer Richard Bland put it, that the colonies were "subordinate to the Authority of Parliament" but denying that they were "absolutely so."[10] But what was the nature of that subordination? Where should the line be drawn between the authority of Parliament at the center and that of the colonial legislatures on the peripheries of empire?

The traditional view has been that during the Stamp Act crisis the colonists drew that line between taxation and legislation, that they denied Parliament's authority to tax the colonies for revenue but not its authority to legislate for the colonies. Neither the Stamp Act Congress, a gathering of delegates in New York in the fall of 1765, nor many of the assemblies commented explicitly on Parliament's authority outside the realm of taxation. But the failure of most of these bodies to challenge Parliament's legislative authority outside the area of taxation by no means constituted an admission of that authority, especially in view of the fact that several official bodies denied that authority explicitly.

Indeed, considerable evidence suggests that the colonists' strong initial impulse was to exclude Parliament from all jurisdiction over the domestic

[10] Richard Bland, *An Inquiry into the Rights of the British Colonies* (Williamsburg, 1766), in William J. Van Schreeven and Robert L. Scribner, eds., *Revolutionary Virginia: The Road to Independence* (Charlottesville, NC, 1973), 1:41, 43.

affairs of the colonies. Denying Parliament's right to pass laws respecting either taxation or their internal polities, early protests from the Connecticut and Virginia legislatures and later declarations from the Virginia, Rhode Island, Maryland, Connecticut, and Massachusetts assemblies claimed for their constituents a right not merely to no taxation without representation but even to no legislation without representation. Several writers, including Bland, Governor Stephen Hopkins of Rhode Island, and Samuel Adams of Massachusetts, wrote elaborate statements in defense of this position. An analysis of their work suggests that the supposed colonial distinction between taxation and legislation was less important to the colonial attempt to delineate the jurisdictional boundaries between Parliament and the colonial assemblies than a distinction between internal and external spheres of government.

Bland provided the most extensive and systematic examination of this distinction. Claiming for the colonists the authority "of directing their internal Government by Laws made with their Consent," he argued that each colony was "a distinct State, independent, as to their internal Government, of the original Kingdom, but united with her, as to their external Polity, in the closest and most intimate LEAGUE AND AMITY, under the same Allegiance, and enjoying the Benefits of a reciprocal Intercourse."[11] Though Bland did not specify precisely what matters were subsumed under the respective categories internal and external, he implied that Parliament's authority – to legislate as well as to tax – stopped short of the Atlantic coast of the colonies and did not extend over any affairs relating exclusively to the domestic life of the colonies. Such matters, according to Bland's formulation, were the exclusive province of the several colonial assemblies.

Nor was Bland peculiar in explicitly arguing that the limitations on Parliament's authority extended to all of the internal affairs of the colonies, and not just to taxation. "The general superintending Power of the Parliament over the whole British Empire," four members of the Massachusetts Assembly, including Samuel Adams and James Otis, wrote to a London correspondent in December 1765, "is clearly admitted here, so far as in our Circumstances is consistent with the Enjoyment of our essential Rights, as Freemen, and British Subjects."[12] As Adams explained in another letter, however, this general superintending power did not extend to the internal affairs of the colonies. Claiming an "exclusive Right to make Laws for our own internal Government & Taxation," Adams argued that if the colonists

[11] Ibid., 38–39.

[12] James Otis et al., to Dennys De Berdt, December 20, 1765, in Harry Alonzo Cushing, ed., *The Writings of Samuel Adams* (New York, 1904–08), 1:67.

were "indeed . . . British Subjects, (& they never can brook to be thought any thing less) it seems necessary that they should exercise this Power within themselves; for they are not represented in the British Parliam[en]t & their great Distance renders it impracticable."[13] Only if each legislature within the empire had an exclusive legislative authority within its own jurisdiction, the Massachusetts Assembly declared in elaborating on this point, would it be possible to ensure "that equality [of rights and legal status] which ought ever to subsist among all his Majesty's subjects in his wide extended empire."[14]

Stephen Hopkins carried this point still farther. "In an imperial state, which consists of many separate governments each of which hath peculiar privileges and of which kind it is evident that the empire of Great Britain is," Hopkins observed, "no single part, though greater than another part, is by that superiority entitled to make laws for or to tax such lesser part." That was the reason, Hopkins believed, why each of the colonies had to have "a legislature within itself to take care of its interests and to provide for its peace and internal government." Yet, like Bland and the Massachusetts representatives, he recognized that there were "many things of a more general nature, quite out of the reach of these particular legislatures, which it is necessary should be regulated, ordered, and governed." Among those general matters, Hopkins included regulations concerning trade and good order of "the whole British empire, taken collectively," including "those grand instruments of commerce," money and paper credit. With regard to all such general matters, he thought it "absolutely necessary" to have "a general power to direct them, some supreme and overruling authority with power to make laws and form regulations for the good of all, and to compel their execution and observation." Within the British Empire, this general power, according to Hopkins, could be lodged only in the British Parliament.[15]

The underlying conception of the empire suggested by these writers was, perhaps, spelled out most clearly by one of the colonists' supporters in Britain. "Our Constitution is so tender of the Rights and Liberties of the Subject," wrote the anonymous author of *A Vindication of the Rights of the Americans* in 1765, "that the People of England have their Repr[esentative]s, the Scotch theirs, the Welsh theirs, the Irish theirs, [and] the Americans theirs, for they have Assemblies and Parliaments, each of which represent the

[13] Samuel Adams to Reverend G[eorge] W[hitfield], November 11, 1765, in ibid., 1:28–29.

[14] Massachusetts House to Francis Bernard, October 23, 1765, in ibid., 1:20.

[15] Stephen Hopkins, *The Rights of the Colonies Examined* (Providence, 1765), in Bailyn, ed., *Pamphlets*, 512, 519.

Bulk of the People, of that Generality, or Division, for which such Assembly or Parliament is appointed to be held." The reason why it was "necessary to have so many Houses of Representatives in the several Departments of Government" was "obvious." "In extensive Territories not confined to one Island, or one Continent, but dispersed through a great Part of the Globe," he explained, "the Laws cannot be put into execution, nor the Rights of the People preserved, without their being arranged into several Classes" of coordinate legislatures, each, presumably, having exclusive jurisdiction over the internal affairs of the territory for which it was responsible.[16]

This distinction between internal and external spheres effectively described the pragmatic and customary distribution of authority within the empire as it had developed over the past century and a half. Notwithstanding metropolitan efforts to limit the extent of local self-government in the colonies, the colonists had continued to enjoy considerable local authority. In the exercise of metropolitan authority, Crown and Parliament had, in fact, usually intervened only in matters of general import and with the final review of actions undertaken by colonial legislatures and courts. All powers relating to the internal affairs of the colonies, by contrast, were under the control of local governing institutions. In view of this situation, it was only natural for settlers to conclude that, insofar as their respective internal affairs were concerned, no part of the empire could be subordinated legally and constitutionally to any other part.

If, at the beginning of the Stamp Act crisis, the questions, in Benjamin Franklin's words, of "how far, and in what particulars" the colonies were "subordinate and subject to the British parliament" were "points newly agitated [and] never yet thoroughly considered,"[17] that was no longer the case by the time of the repeal of the Stamp Act in 1766. Over the preceding two years, the colonists had slowly begun to construct what John Adams later called "a formal, logical, and technical definition" of the imperial constitution under which they lived.[18] As a result of this "great inquiry," they had learned, as Bland put it, that it was "in vain to search into the civil Constitution of England for directions in fixing the proper Connexion between the Colonies and the Mother Kingdom."[19] The main underlying principles of that constitution were certainly relevant to their inquiry, but

[16] *A Vindication of the Rights of the Americans* (London, 1765), 10–11.

[17] Benjamin Franklin, "On the Tenure of the Manor of East Greenwich," January 11, 1766, in Verner W. Crane, ed., *Benjamin Franklin's Letters to the Press* (Chapel Hill, NC, 1950), 48.

[18] Earl of Clarendon [John Adams] to William Pym, January 27, 1766, in Charles Francis Adams, ed., *The Works of John Adams* (Boston, 1856), 3:477.

[19] Bland, *Inquiry*, in Van Schreeven and Scribner, eds., *Revolutionary Virginia*, 1:34.

the British constitution was not, in and of itself, a suitable constitution for an "extended and diversified" empire.[20]

Instead, in their efforts to understand the nature of the relationship between Britain and the colonies, the colonists turned for guidance to the traditional rights of Englishmen and to their own experience with the actual pattern of customary relations within the empire as it had developed over the previous century and a half. They agreed with the Cambridge natural law theorist Thomas Rutherforth that, as he wrote in the late 1750s, the best "way of determining what form [of constitution] has been established in any particular nation" was to examine "the history and customs of that nation. A knowledge of its present customs will inform us what constitution of government obtains now," Rutherforth wrote, "and a knowledge of its history will inform us by what means this constitution was introduced or established."[21] Indeed, one of the central conclusions of their inquiry – and one of their most vigorously pressed arguments against the intrusion of Parliamentary power – was that, like Britain itself, both the individual colonies and the empire as a whole had longstanding constitutional traditions that, at least from the point of view of the colonies, seemed to supply legitimacy to their determined efforts to resist what Bland referred to as the "new System of Placing Great Britain as the centre of Attraction to the Colonies."[22]

In 1764–66, only the most advanced thinkers among the colonists were willing to argue that Parliament had no role in either the imperial or the several colonial constitutions, to suggest that there was "no dependence or relation" between Britain and the colonies except "only that we are all the common subjects of the same King."[23] What all colonial protests did have in common, however, was a clear concern to fix the constitutional and legal boundaries between the authority of the metropolis and that of the colonies, between the power of Parliament and that of the colonial assemblies. If Parliament had a constitutional role in the empire, they were persuaded, that role had to be a limited one. They were virtually unanimous in agreeing that that role did not include authority to tax the colonies for revenue, and a substantial body of sentiment also held that it did not include authority to legislate for the internal affairs of the colonies.

The colonial case against the Stamp Act got a generally hostile reception in Britain. Few seemed to understand that the colonists' challenge

[20] J. M., *The Legislative Authority of the British Parliament with respect to North America and the Privileges of the Assemblies there, briefly considered* (London, 1766), 11.

[21] Thomas Rutherforth, *Institutes of Natural Law*, 2nd American ed. (Baltimore, 1832), 296.

[22] Bland, *Inquiry*, in Van Schreeven and Scribner, eds., *Revolutionary Virginia*, 1:43.

[23] "Letter from a Plain Yeoman," *Providence Gazette*, May 11, 1765, in Morgan, ed., *Prologue to Revolution*, 73.

to parliamentary authority went beyond the realm of taxation, and even with regard to the more restricted conception of the colonial position, only a few men in Parliament agreed with the colonists that there were limits on Parliament's colonial authority. Most both rejected the colonists' contention that they were unrepresented in Parliament and dismissed the argument that inheritance, charters, and custom exempted the colonies from parliamentary taxation. Lord Mansfield sounded the predominant argument when he flatly declared that, "as to the power of making laws," Parliament represented "the whole British empire" and had "authority to bind every part and every subject without the least distinction."[24]

From this point of view, colonial claims for exemption from Parliamentary taxation seemed, as Grenville had defined them when he first proposed to levy stamp duties on the colonies, to be nothing less than a challenge to British sovereignty. As it had gradually developed over the previous century and a half, the conventional conception of sovereignty was that in all polities, including "an Empire, extended and diversified, like that of Great-Britain,"[25] there had to be, as Blackstone wrote, "a supreme, irresistible, absolute uncontrolled authority, in which the *jura summi imperii*, or rights of sovereignty reside[d]."[26] Because, most contemporaries seem to have believed, the King-in-Parliament was sovereign in the British polity, it could accept no restrictions on its authority without relinquishing the sovereignty of the nation over the colonies. By definition, there could be no limitation on a supreme authority: it was either complete or non-existent. For that reason, it seemed obvious that the King-in-Parliament had full authority over all matters relating to Britons everywhere. For the same reason, it also seemed evident that no clear line could be drawn between Parliament's power to legislate for the colonies and its power to tax them.

In the metropolitan view, there was thus no distribution of authority within the empire. "As the sovereign of the whole," the King-in-Parliament had "control over the whole British empire."[27] To most metropolitans, in fact, the colonial position appeared incomprehensible because it seemed to imply the existence of more than one sovereign authority within a single state, and sovereignty, according to conventional theory, could not be divided. An *imperium in imperio* – a sovereign authority within a sovereign authority – was a contradiction in terms. As Lord Lyttleton put it, the colonies were either "part of the dominions of the Crown of Great Britain"

[24] Mansfield's Speech, February 3, 1766, in Simmons and Thomas, eds., *Proceedings and Debates*, 2:128–30.

[25] J. M., *Legislative Authority of the British Parliament*, 11.

[26] Sir William Blackstone, *Commentaries on the Laws of England* (London, 1822), 1:50–51, 178–80.

[27] *Letter to G. G.* (London, 1767), 74.

and therefore "proper objects of our legislature," or they were "small independent communities," each operating under its own sovereign authority.[28] According to metropolitan theory, there was no middle ground between these two extremes.

The intensity of colonial opposition to the Stamp Act forced Parliament to repeal that measure, but it accompanied repeal with passage of the Declaratory Act, modeled on the Irish Declaratory Act of 1720, asserting Parliament's authority "to bind the colonies and people of America . . . in all cases whatsoever." But this fiat from the center by no means resolved the question of the distribution of authority within the empire. As Colonel Isaac Barre announced in the House of Commons early in 1766, the Stamp Act crisis had provoked "the people of America to reason . . . closely upon the relative rights of this country and that,"[29] and the undefined and "loose texture"[30] of Britain's extended and diversified empire had fostered the development of two widely divergent interpretations of how authority was distributed between metropolis and colonies. Whereas most people in the former thought the empire a unitary state, most people in the latter thought it a federal polity in which the authority of the center was limited by the authority exercised by the peripheries.

III. THE TOWNSHEND MEASURES CONTROVERSY, 1768–72

If the Stamp Act crisis "first led the colonists into [systematic] Enquiries concerning the nature of their political situation" in relation to Parliament,[31] its resolution in early 1766 by no means put an end to those inquiries. Indeed, Parliament's renewed efforts early in 1767 to tax the colonies through the Townshend Acts quickly reopened the question. For the next six years, people of all persuasions on both sides of the Atlantic dug deeper into the difficult problem of the constitutional organization of the empire. Their chief reaction to their findings was a fundamental ambivalence.

During the crisis over the Townshend Acts, this ambivalence helped generate a considerable amount of pragmatic flexibility, manifest, on both sides, in a pronounced concern to contain the dispute within a narrow compass.

[28] Lyttelton's speech, February 3, 1766, in Simmons and Thomas, eds., *Proceedings and Debates*, 2:126–27.

[29] Barre's speech, February 24, 1766, in ibid., 2:296.

[30] *The Political Balance, in which the Principles and Conduct of the Two Parties are weighed* (London, 1765), 45

[31] William Hicks, *The Nature and Extent of Parliamentary Power Considered* (New York, 1768), in Merrill Jensen, ed., *Tracts of the American Revolution, 1763–1776* (Indianapolis, 1967), 177.

At the same time, however, the length and intensity of the dispute pushed some analysts on the colonial side to think through the nature of the connection between Britain and the colonies more thoroughly than anyone had ever done before. Although these thinkers regarded their conclusions as no more than an articulation and rationalization of longstanding practice, they represented a radical challenge to the metropolitan belief in Parliamentary supremacy over the entire empire, a belief that, for most members of the metropolitan political nation, continued to be nonnegotiable.

Notwithstanding a palpable crystallization of informed colonial opinion around what was, from the perspective of the center, a radical view of the constitutional organization of the empire, the spirit of conciliation ran so deep that constituted authorities in no colony officially endorsed it during the Townshend Acts crisis. Indeed, Parliament's repeal of most of the Townshend duties in 1770 and the rapid subsidence of overt colonial opposition to Parliament over the next three years provided dramatic testimony to the depth of that spirit. Yet those same years were also marked by a revival of the much older controversy over the scope of the Crown's prerogative powers in the colonies. This revival underlined the fundamental problem of the distribution of authority between Britain and the colonies as a continuing major source of tension between metropolis and colonies.

The vast majority of people in the metropolitan establishment, in both Britain and the colonies, adhered strictly to the position articulated by Grenville and his supporters during the Stamp Act crisis. Interpreting all suggestions for any limitations on Parliament's colonial authority as a challenge to the British constitution of Parliamentary supremacy and to metropolitan sovereignty over the colonies, they continued to insist, as they had throughout the Stamp Act crisis, that sovereignty was indivisible and the maintenance of the supremacy and legislative authority of Parliament in its fullest extent over the colonies was essential to the existence of the empire. Undersecretary of State William Knox, one of the few metropolitan officials who had actually served in the colonies, spelled out the full implications of this line of reasoning in his influential *The Controversy Between Great Britain and her Colonies Reviewed*, published in 1769. "If the authority of the legislature be not in one instance equally supreme over the Colonies as it is over the people of England," he wrote, "then are not the Colonies of the same community with the people of England. All distinctions," he continued, "destroy this union; and if it can be shown in any particular to be dissolved, it must be so in all instances whatever."[32]

[32] [William Knox], *The Controversy Between Great Britain and her Colonies Reviewed* (London, 1769), 50–51.

Notwithstanding the tenacity with which they held to this point of view, metropolitan authorities resisted the impulse to take sweeping coercive measures against the colonies during the late 1760s. Sensing the expediency of Thomas Pownall's declaration that "You may exert power over, but you can never govern an unwilling people,"[33] they instead wound up in 1770 taking what they regarded as a conciliatory approach. At the same time that they indicated that they would seek no new Parliamentary taxes and guided through Parliament a repeal of most of the Townshend duties, they retained taxes on tea and sugar products to stand as symbols of Parliament's colonial authority.

If anything, the urge toward conciliation during the crisis over the Townshend Acts was even more powerful in the colonies. This urge was evident in the grudging willingness of colonial merchants throughout the crisis to pay an unrepealed Parliamentary tax on molasses. On both sides of the Atlantic, John Dickinson's *Letters from a Farmer in Pennsylvania*, published in 1767, was certainly the most widely circulated expression of colonial opinion. Obviously intending to confine the controversy within the narrowest possible bounds, Dickinson, a Pennsylvania and Delaware lawyer, addressed his pamphlet exclusively to the issue of the moment – Parliament's right to tax the colonies for revenue – and did not consider the wider problems of the relationship between metropolis and colonies or the distribution of authority within the empire.

By focusing debate so narrowly on the question of taxation, Dickinson helped to deescalate the controversy. The widespread acceptance of his definition of the situation seems both to have inhibited the sort of wide-ranging discussion of the nature of the metropolitan-colonial relationship that had occurred during the Stamp Act crisis and to have been in no small part responsible for the fact that all but a few official colonial challenges to Parliamentary authority during the late 1760s and very early 1770s were confined to the single issue of taxation for revenue.

If, during the crisis over the Townshend Acts, most colonial assemblies, as the Massachusetts legislator Thomas Cushing later observed, "acquiesced in the distinction between Taxation and Legislation and were disposed to Confine the dispute to that of Taxation only and entirely to wave the other as a subject of too delicate a Nature,"[34] a number of thinkers in both the colonies and Britain took a much deeper look at the controversy. As Benjamin Franklin wrote his son in March 1768, they concluded that "Something

[33] Pownall's speech, April 19, 1769, in Simmons and Thomas, eds., *Proceedings and Debates*, 3:156.

[34] William Cushing to Benjamin Franklin, May 6, 1773, in Leonard W. Labaree et al., eds., *The Papers of Benjamin Franklin* (New Haven, 1959–), 20: 204.

might be made of either of the extremes; that Parliament has a power to make all laws for us, or that it has a power to make no laws for us," but that "no middle doctrine" of the kind proposed by Dickinson could be maintained successfully.[35] Although these thinkers regarded their conclusions as no more than an articulation and rationalization of longstanding constitutional practice within the empire, they in fact represented a radical challenge to the metropolitan belief in Parliament's supremacy over the whole empire.

This radical interpretation proceeded from three underlying assumptions. The first was that Parliament's claims to colonial jurisdiction had to be proved and could not simply be taken for granted or permitted to rest on an obviously contrived concept like virtual representation. The second was that the civil constitution of Britain by no means determined the constitutional connection between Britain and the colonies. The third was that the history of the colonies and of their relationship to the metropolis was the most authoritative guide to the exact nature of that connection.

Adherents of this interpretation put particular emphasis on the history of the colonies, which seemed to them to make clear that the colonies had never been incorporated with Great Britain in a legislative capacity. This being the case, it seemed equally obvious that Great Britain and the British Empire were distinct political entities. As the Georgia minister Johan Joachim Zubly explained, the British Empire was a far "more extensive word, and should not be confounded with the kingdom of Great Britain." Rather, it was a "confederal" polity that consisted of both the home islands and a number of "extrinsic Dominions," including "several islands and other distant countries, asunder in different parts of the globe." As the "head of this great body," England was "called the mother country" and "all the settled inhabitants of this vast empire" were "called Englishmen."[36] But those phrases by no means implied that the empire was a single state. On the contrary, each of its many separate entities had a legislative power within itself, and the several legislative bodies of Great Britain, Ireland, and the British colonies were entirely independent of one another.

In the view of its proponents, the real virtue of this emerging conception lay not in its foundations in past practice, but in its appropriateness for the governance of an extended polity. The "Excellency of the Invention of Colony Government, by separate independent Legislatures," Franklin

[35] Benjamin Franklin to William Franklin, March 13, 1768, in ibid., 15:75–76.

[36] John Joachim Zubly, *An Humble Enquiry Into the Nature of the Dependency of the American Colonies upon the Parliament of Great-Britain* (Charleston, 1769), in Randall A. Miller, ed., *"A Warm & Zealous Spirit": John J. Zubly and the American Revolution, A Selection of His Writings* (Macon, GA, 1982), 57.

wrote in 1769, was that it permitted "the remotest Parts of a great Empire" to be "as well governed as the Center." By guaranteeing maximum autonomy to peripheral polities and thereby helping prevent wholesale "Misrule, Oppressions of Proconsuls, and Discontents and Rebellions" in those areas, the authority of the British monarch seemed to be infinitely expandable, capable, in Franklin's words, of being "extended without Inconvenience over Territories how great soever."[37]

This conception of the British Empire as consisting, in Benjamin Prescott's words, "of a great and glorious King, with a Number of distinct Governments, alike subjected to his royal Scepter, and each governed by its own Laws,"[38] also seemed to its proponents to offer a solution to the problem of the indivisibility of sovereignty. Posed by metropolitan protagonists during the earliest days of the Stamp Act controversy, the logical dilemma of an *imperium in imperio* had remained at the heart of metropolitan resistance to colonial claims for exemption from Parliamentary authority. According to the emerging conception of empire among the most advanced defenders of the colonies, however, sovereignty within the extended polity of the British Empire resided not in Britain and not in the King-in-Parliament but in the institution of the monarchy alone. In the imperial realm, according to these writers, the theory of coordination, of the legal sovereignty of the King-in-Parliament, did not apply.

To its proponents, this view of the empire as many polities under one sovereign seemed thoroughly defensible on the basis both of the terms of the colonial charters and the customary constitutional arrangements that had grown up since the establishment of the colonies. For more than a century and a half the colonists, without interruption, had been trusted in good measure with the management of their internal affairs. Of course, as they recognized, the doctrine of usage on which their developing conception of the empire rested so heavily cut two ways. If Parliament had no role whatever in their early history and if, subsequently, Parliament had not customarily interfered in their internal affairs, they could not deny that, from the mid-seventeenth century on, Parliament had exerted an authority to regulate colonial trade and later to direct their exterior policy. Furthermore, they had to admit that, even though Parliament's authority had sometimes been applied with great prejudice to the colonies, they had always submitted to it and thereby consented to it in this external realm.

[37] Benjamin Franklin to William Strahan, November 29, 1769, and Franklin, Marginalia to *An Inquiry into the Nature and Causes of the Present Disputes* (London, 1769), in Labaree et al., eds., *Franklin Papers*, 16:246, 17:322.

[38] Benjamin Prescott, *A Free and Calm Consideration of the Unhappy Misunderstandings and Debates* (Salem, 1774), 30, which was written in 1768.

Deriving from a century and a half of experience, custom thus seemed to prescribe a clear allocation of authority within the broad extended polity of the early modern British Empire, an allocation precisely along the lines identified by Bland and other colonial writers during the Stamp Act crisis. The many provincial governments – Ireland in the near periphery and the several colonies in the distant American periphery – had full jurisdiction over their own particular local and internal affairs, while the metropolitan government at the center had authority over all general matters, including the external relations of the several provincial governments.

In the absence of any impartial tribunal to settle constitutional disputes between the center and the peripheries, there was, as Pownall lamented in 1768, "no means of deciding the controversy" by law.[39] Unwilling to give in, metropolitan leaders were, as yet, also unwilling to resort to force. They still understood that, in the words of Edmund Burke, there was "no such thing as governing the whole body of the people contrary to their inclinations,"[40] and such considerations were behind Parliament's decision in the spring of 1770 to repeal all of the Townshend duties except the tax on tea. This essentially political resolution of the crisis in effect went back to the settlement adopted in 1766. That is, it left the issue of the extent of Parliament's colonial authority to rest on the Declaratory Act and token taxes on sugar products and tea, with an implicit understanding that, as in the case of Ireland, Parliament would not thenceforth levy any further taxes on the colonies.

Like the Stamp Act crisis, the controversy over the Townshend Acts had helped illuminate still further the ancient question of how, within the extended polity of the British Empire, authority was distributed between metropolis and colonies. To be sure, it produced little change in the metropolitan position as it had been articulated in 1764–66, while the conciliatory thrust of both Dickinson's *Letters from a Pennsylvania Farmer* and most of the official colonial protests helped obscure the radical drift of sentiment among spokesmen in both America and Britain who supported the colonial side. For, pursuing the logic of the customary constitutional arrangements that had obtained in the empire over the previous century, a great many writers between 1767 and 1770 had worked out detailed arguments to prove what a few colonial thinkers had already implied in 1764–66: that the British Empire was a loose association under a common king of distinct political entities, each having its own legislature with exclusive jurisdiction over its own internal affairs. As in 1764–66, a major constitutional

[39] Thomas Pownall's speech, April 19, 1769, in Simmons and Thomas, eds., *Proceedings and Debates*, 3:154.

[40] Edmund Burke's speech, November 8, 1768, in ibid., 3:7.

crisis had thus functioned to intensify, rather than to resolve, differences in interpretations of the constitutional organization of the empire.

Nevertheless, repeal of the Townshend Acts brought a temporary respite from the turmoil that had beset metropolitan-colonial relations over the previous six years. For the next three and a half years, debate over the respective jurisdictions of Parliament and the several peripheral legislatures in Ireland and the American colonies fell into temporary abeyance. Yet, throughout the early 1770s, constitutional relations within the empire remained troubled. Coincident with the repeal of most of the Townshend duties, a series of quarrels over the scope of the Crown's colonial authority erupted in several colonies, punctuating the so-called period of quiet during the early 1770s and revealing that the debate over the extent of the Crown's prerogative in the colonies was still thoroughly alive. Quarrels in Massachusetts over the governor's right to transfer the meetings of the legislature from the traditional site at Boston to Cambridge and in South Carolina over the assembly's authority to issue money from the treasury without executive approval were particularly serious and resulted in long interruptions in the legislative process. Like more limited controversies at the same time in Georgia and North Carolina, these disputes revolved around metropolitan efforts to use royal instructions to curb the power of local assemblies.

From the perspective of the crises over the Stamp and Townshend Acts and the debate about Parliament's new pretensions to authority over the internal affairs of the colonies, however, these old questions about the Crown's relationship acquired a new and heightened urgency in the colonies. If, as an impressive number of colonial spokesmen had begun to argue during the late 1760s, sovereignty within the empire rested not in the King-in-Parliament but in the Crown alone, then it became especially important for the colonists to establish the boundaries not just of Parliamentary but also of royal authority in the colonies. For that reason, colonial defenders in all of the battles of the early 1770s revealed a pronounced tendency to build on their own particular local constitutional heritages to argue, as their predecessors in earlier generations had often done, that, no less than in Britain itself, the Crown's authority – the freedom of its "will" – in the colonies had been effectively limited over the previous century by specific idiosyncratic constitutional developments in each of the colonies. Again just as in Britain, these developments had led irreversibly, colonial leaders believed, in the direction of increasing authority in the hands of the local legislatures and placing greater restrictions on the prerogatives of the Crown. By this process, they argued, the rights of the inhabitants in the peripheries had gradually been secured against the power of the center.

As refined and elaborated during the contests of the early 1770s, this view of colonial constitutional history powerfully helped reinforce traditional views of the colonial legislatures both as the primary guardians of the local rights of the corporate entities over which they presided and, like Parliament itself in Britain, as the dynamic forces in shaping the colonial constitutions. Insofar as the constitution of the empire was concerned, this emphasis on the peculiarity and integrity of the several colonial constitutions certainly constituted a vigorous defense of constitutional multiplicity that had profound implications for the ongoing debate over the nature of sovereignty within the empire. For, together with the emerging conviction that Parliament had no authority over the colonies, the renewed contention that the Crown's authority in the peripheries was likewise limited by local constitutions – constitutions that had emerged not just out of the colonists' inherited rights as Englishmen and their corporate or proprietary charters but also out of local usage and custom – pushed the colonists still further in the direction of a wholly new conception of sovereignty in an extended polity like the early modern British Empire. That conception implied that ultimate constitutional authority – sovereignty – lay not in any institution or collection of institutions at the center of the empire but in the separate constitutions of each of the many separate political entities of which the empire was composed.

IV. CONDITIONS OF LAW IN THE COLONIES

Explicit in these formulations was an underlying preference for a system of authority in which local law, institutions, officials, and populations had ultimate authority over local and provincial matters. Nor was this preference confined to the lawyers, opinion leaders, and other members of provincial and local political establishments who produced the essays and pamphlets that laid out the emerging colonial case. Repeatedly, beginning with the Stamp Act crisis, many crowds, denominated "mobs" by metropolitan representatives and their supporters, used force and intimidation to prevent the enforcement of metropolitan laws contrary to local customs and interests. These popular gatherings, commonly a broad cross-section of the free population, sometimes wreaked considerable damage on the property and persons of people associated with those laws. The sackings and burnings of the houses of Stamp Collector Andrew Oliver and Lieutenant Governor Thomas Hutchinson in Boston on August 14, 1765, were only the most dramatic and destructive of the popular protests that occurred in opposition to the Stamp Act. For a decade thereafter, similar crowds acted as an adjunct to local officials in resisting the efforts of metropolitan officers to enforce metropolitan law when it seemed antagonistic to local interests or at variance with local law.

Such actions occurred in every major colonial city on the mainland and even in rural Virginia, but they were particularly prevalent in Boston and in eastern New England, where crowds acting in defense of local interests often interfered with the enforcement of customs regulations and sometimes brawled with British soldiers. The "rescue" of the cargo of the merchant Job Smith's sloop *Polly* from custom officials in Dighton, Massachusetts, on April 7, 1765; the prevention of a customs search of Captain Daniel Malcolm's house in Boston on September 24, 1766; the riot over the new customs commissioners' seizure of John Hancock's sloop, *Liberty*, on June 10, 1768; the confrontation with British troops at the so-called Boston Massacre on March 5, 1770; the burning in Narragansett Bay of the grounded royal naval schooner, the *Gaspee*, by Rhode Islanders on June 10, 1772; and the Boston Tea Party of December 16, 1773, were the most prominent of these incidents.

Traditionally, these and similar incidents have been depicted as evidence of mounting disorder and lawlessness in which the rule of law was steadily supplanted by rule of the mob. But such characterizations are based on an anachronistic conception of the law as sovereign command, a modern conception that derives from a positive jurisprudence that was only just coming into vogue during the last half of the eighteenth century and would not gain full ascendancy until the nineteenth and twentieth centuries. For Britons on either side of the Atlantic during the pre-Revolutionary crisis, law did not always mean command or will, and legal theorists, judges, and lawyers did not necessarily associate law with sovereignty. Rather, in the context of British and British-American legal traditions, law in the 1760s and 1770s was still as much thought of as custom and community consensus as sovereign command. Eighteenth-century law throughout the British world was considerably less coercive and considerably more dependent for its enforcement on community support than most historians once thought.

Consider the extensive legal limitations on government in late colonial Massachusetts. Restraint of governmental power and affirmation of the security of individuals in their lives, liberties, and property were among the most intense concerns of free colonial British Americans of all social classes. In Massachusetts they managed, to an extraordinary degree, to construct a polity that thoroughly reflected these concerns. Because Massachusetts, like the other colonies, had no permanent police force and only a tiny bureaucracy, the provincial courts were the only governmental institution with much coercive power. However, because they wanted to be ruled by law, not by judges possessing vast discretionary powers that could be turned to the service of arbitrary rulers, legislators were careful to limit judicial discretion too. In part, legislators were aided in this task by longstanding custom, according to which courts never went against precedent. As in England itself, precedent, usage, or custom had the force of law and was invariably used to fill the interstices in statute and common law. But legislators also gave juries wide jurisdiction in both civil and criminal cases and, even more important, vast authority to find both the law and the facts in cases in those areas. The virtually unlimited power of juries to find law in effect meant both that judges had little lawmaking power and that representatives of local communities assembled as jurors generally possessed effective power to control the content of substantive law in the localities.

Other officials, both provincial and metropolitan, had even less power than judges. Almost entirely without coercive power of their own, they were, in fact, subject to common law actions for damages whenever they committed a "wrong" in the exercise of their duties. In effect, then, officials were unable to exercise their powers without the consent of local communities. Even the sheriffs and constables responsible for enforcing court judgments could do so only when local communities were willing to allow the judgments to be carried out. Colonial Massachusetts was thus a standing example of one of early modern British political theorists' favorite maxims: all government depends on opinion. No less than in Britain itself, Massachusetts, and presumably all the other British-American colonies, thus functioned within the venerable Anglo-American tradition of a government whose limited law enforcement personnel relied on the public to assist them in implementing the law.

The implications for understanding the origins of the American Revolution, in Massachusetts and elsewhere, are profound. Law was bicentric, not unicentric. Generated by Parliament and royal officials and judges in London, metropolitan law was anemic. With no effective legal institutions at their command, Massachusetts officials charged with its enforcement were helpless without the support of the local community. Already weak before the Revolutionary crisis, metropolitan law became even more so over time, as local opinion increasingly came to perceive it as in large part a series of arbitrary measures intended to undermine their traditional constitutional rights and their economic and political autonomy.

But the decline in respect for metropolitan law did not lead to a breakdown in respect for law in general. On the contrary, at the same time that metropolitan law was becoming steadily weaker, local law – those provincial statutes, judicial precedents, and customs that were upheld by the courts, grand jury, traverse juries, magistrates, and other institutions that comprised the colony's effective legal system – retained its full vigor. The two essential features of that law were that it was a reflection of community consensus and that it was under local, not metropolitan, control.

No less than metropolitan law, local law lacked strong formal instruments of coercion and depended on public support for its enforcement. Throughout Britain's American colonies during the eighteenth century, popular uprisings had repeatedly acted to defend the urgent interests of communities, both to enforce the will of local magistrates and to compensate for the inability of constituted authorities to act on their own. In this regard, the colonies were not all that different from contemporary Britain, where it was a well-established tradition for people to take matters into their own hands in two different types of situation: first, when they had no other means to nullify arbitrary, unconstitutional measures, and, second, when ordinary legal processes failed to function or did not exist.

So long as popular uprisings served a public function and confined their actions to harassing those charged with enforcing unconstitutional statutes of Parliament, they were thus perfectly in accord with British legal traditions as expressed in the contemporary doctrine that it was legal to resist unlawful government power. So far from being outside the bounds of law, popular uprisings actually functioned as the police unit, the posse comitatus, of local law. No wonder that throughout the colonies between 1765 and 1776 the institutions of provincial and local government almost always supported such uprisings. No wonder that provincial political establishments everywhere depended on informal bodies, such as the Sons of Liberty, that sprang up during the Stamp Act crisis or, beginning in 1774, public associations and popularly elected committees of safety to enforce non-importation agreements and other sanctions designed to nullify metropolitan laws and regulations.

Of course, customs and other metropolitan officials and supporters who were the victims of public uprisings or patriot committees saw them as open violations of law – lawless violence. But their perspective was not that of the majority. Far from being illegal, resistance to metropolitan law was actually undertaken in defense of local law. American crowds thus served largely as an auxiliary enforcement agency for locally dominated legal institutions. Acting in concert and with overwhelming popular support, the formal instruments of law – juries, magistrates, and the like – and the informal instrument – the crowd – managed in one incident after another after 1765 to nullify those many Parliamentary statutes and metropolitan regulations that were deemed both arbitrary and contrary to the vital interests of the colonies. In the process they effectively underlined the impotence of metropolitan agents to enforce any measure opposed by locals.

The rescue of the contents of the sloop *Polly* provides a case in point. When Collector of Customs John Robinson in Newport decided in April

1765 that the master of the sloop *Polly* had probably underreported the number of hogsheads of sugar imported from Surinam, he chased it up Narragansett Bay, overtook it at Dighton, searched it, and, after finding twice the reported amount of sugar, seized it along with the undeclared part of its cargo for the King. But no local mariners would agree to take the ship back to Newport where it was to be condemned in court, and Robinson had to leave the vessel in the hands of two of his subordinates. No sooner had those subordinates left the *Polly* to refresh themselves at a shore-side tavern than locals stole their boat and proceeded to unload the entire cargo; divest the sloop of its sails, rigging, cables, anchors, and other marine equipment; and, by boring holes in the hull, render it wholly unseaworthy. When Robinson heard what had happened, he returned to Dighton with a party of royal marines and sought to obtain a writ of assistance to enable him to search for the missing cargo. But local magistrates refused his request on the grounds that only the Massachusetts Supreme Court could issue such a writ. Nor could the few marines with him prevent his arrest on a legal action brought by the *Polly's* owner, Job Smith, who sued Robinson for £3,000 in damages for the loss of his ship and cargo, and Robinson spent three days in the Taunton jail before his Boston superior could send money to bail him out. Robinson subsequently found and seized 8 of Smith's more than 120 hogsheads of sugar, refloated the *Polly*, and succeeded in having it condemned in Newport. But this incident revealed the limited extent of metropolitan authority in the colonies and the ways in which local populations mobilized and functioned as auxiliaries to local officials in resisting metropolitan efforts to enforce regulations from London.

Nor was the force of metropolitan law in New England in any way strengthened by the stationing of British troops in Boston after 1768: that event did not lead to arrests and executions of resistance leaders. Never empowered to act as a police force, the army remained subject to civilian control. The result was that it could not be used as an instrument of coercion and was easily neutralized by the same agencies of local law that had already – by legal means – rendered metropolitan law a dead letter in the colony. The neutralization of metropolitan power after 1765 occurred not because metropolitan representatives were restrained or timid in their use of power, but because they were immobilized by local law so rapidly and fully.

Although they usually acted in cooperation with or even under the direction of provincial political leaders and rarely veered out of control, the participants in crowd actions clearly had opinions, interests, and objectives of their own that sometimes diverged from those of provincial or local figures of authority. In several actions, for example, antagonism to impressment into the British naval service was the crowd's principal motivation, dramatically swelling its numbers. But however great the divergence in interest, opinion, and goals between the leadership and the other participants, these crowds demonstrated a remarkable solidarity with provincial leaders on the desirability of preventing the enforcement of metropolitan law whenever it conflicted with local law and opinion and of retaining local control over all matters affecting local interests.

V. THE CRISIS OF IMPERIAL AUTHORITY AND INDEPENDENCE, 1773–76

When Parliament's passage of the Tea Act in May 1773 revived the dispute over its colonial authority, colonial resistance to that measure provoked the crisis that would, in a mere two and a half years, lead to the dismemberment of the early modern British Empire. At no time during this crisis did either side show much disposition to compromise. As each quickly took a determined stand on the position marked out by its most extreme proponents during the previous crises, the spirit of conciliation that had characterized the crisis over the Townshend Acts rapidly gave way to complete intransigence. While the metropolitan political nation refused to back down from its insistence that the King-in-Parliament was the supreme sovereign of the empire, the colonial assemblies and the First and Second Continental Congresses, composed of delegates from the thirteen colonies from Georgia north to New Hampshire, gave official sanction to views that had been developed by Franklin and others during the late 1760s and early 1770s and called for complete colonial autonomy over colonial internal affairs. By 1776, what had begun as yet another crisis over Parliament's right to tax the colonies had become a crisis over whether the colonies would become independent, and the empire foundered over the inability of Britain and the colonies to agree on a formula for governance that would give colonists the same legal and constitutional rights as those Britons who remained at home.

In both Britain and the colonies, supporters of Parliament's right to legislate for the colonies insisted, as they had ever since the beginning of the controversy during the Stamp Act crisis, that the British Empire, consisting of Great Britain and all its territories, was a single state composed of one people, living under one constitution, and governed by one monarch. Reiterating the same central contentions that had underlain their argument from the beginning, they continued to interpret the controversy as a dispute over sovereignty. They dismissed the doctrine of no legislation without representation as "an obsolete maxim" that had no applicability to the distant parts of an extended polity like the British Empire, and persisted in asserting that "no maxim of policy" was "more universally admitted, than that a supreme and uncontroulable power must exist somewhere in every state." In the British Empire, they insisted, that power was vested "in King, Lords, and Commons, under the collective appellation of the Legislature," which, as the polemicist James Macpherson phrased it, was merely "another name for the Constitution of State," was, "in fact, the State itself."[41]

Thus, if the colonists refused obedience to Parliament, they were "no longer Subjects, but rebels" who, by arrogating "to themselves all the functions of Sovereignty," were obviously endeavoring to put themselves "on the footing of a Sovereign State." "The question between them and Great Britain," then, as Macpherson noted gravely in summarizing the dominant position within the metropolitan political nation, was nothing less than "dependence or independence, connection or no connection."[42] With "no common Principle to rest upon, no common Medium to appeal to," wrote Josiah Tucker, the dispute seemed to have no middle ground.[43] To admit any qualification in "the controuling right of the British legislature over the colonies,"[44] its proponents devoutly believed, would mean nothing less than the abandonment of "the whole of our authority over the Americans."[45]

The colonial position, as it was enunciated in mid-1774 and elaborated over the next two years, was founded on a complete rejection of the prevailing metropolitan theory of an omnipotent Parliament. By ignoring the vital and traditional British constitutional principle of consent, or no legislation without representation, this theory, supporters of the colonial position declared, was at total variance with both the ancient rights of Britons and the long-settled practice of imperial governance within the empire over the previous century and a half.

No less important, when applied to distant and unrepresented colonies, this new doctrine, it seemed to the colonists, obviously also represented a total contradiction to every principle laid down at the time of the Glorious Revolution. Indeed, by its insistence on exerting a supreme jurisdiction over the colonies, Parliament seemed not merely to be violating the most essential principles of the Revolution but actually to have assumed and be acting on precisely the same high prerogative doctrines against which that Revolution had been undertaken. Thus, the colonists believed that, if by

[41] [James Macpherson], *The Rights of Great Britain Asserted Against the Claims of America* (London, 1776), 3–5, 11.

[42] Ibid., 3, 11.

[43] Josiah Tucker, Tract V, *The Respective Pleas and Arguments of the Mother Country, and of the Colonies, Distinctly Set Forth* (Gloucester, 1775), 38.

[44] Nathaniel George Rice's speech, May 17, 1774, in William Cobbett and T. C. Hansard, eds., *The Parliamentary History of England from the Earliest Period to 1803* (London, 1806–20), 17:1159.

[45] Charles Cornwall's speech, April 17, 1774, in ibid., 17:1213.

resisting Parliament they had become rebels, they were rebels in the same way and for the same reasons that the people of Britain had been rebels during the Revolution.

By 1774, few colonial leaders any longer had any doubt that, over the previous decade, it had been proven clearly and fully that the colonial assemblies had an exclusive right not only of taxation but of legislation and that the British Parliament, so far from having a right to make laws binding the colonies in all cases whatsoever, had no legal right to make any laws in any way binding on the colonies. Far from being subject to the supreme authority of Parliament, most American leaders now believed the colonies had always enjoyed their own supreme legislatures and had always claimed an exemption from the jurisdiction of the British Parliament. Not the King-in-Parliament, wrote the Virginian Thomson Mason, but the "King, at the head of his respective American Assemblies," constituted "the Supreme Legislature of the Colonies."[46]

Whether Parliament had any authority even over the external affairs of the colonies now became a point of contention. Already during the Townshend Act crisis, some colonial supporters were beginning to suggest that Parliament had no authority whatsoever over the colonies. By 1774, many of the most influential tracts, including those written by lawyers James Wilson of Pennsylvania and Thomas Jefferson of Virginia, unequivocally took this position. The legislative authority of each of the many independent legislatures within the empire, including Parliament, wrote Wilson, was necessarily "confined within . . . local bounds" and could not be imposed on any of the other areas of the empire without their consent.[47] During the early stages of the crisis of independence, however, most American leaders seemed still to believe that Parliament did have authority over external affairs. Alexander Hamilton and John Adams were two prominent writers who acknowledged that authority derived from the long usage and uninterrupted acquiescence by which the colonists, since the middle of the seventeenth century, had given their implied consent to the Navigation Acts and other trade regulations.

But, if few of their protagonists yet claimed for the colonists external as well as internal sovereign jurisdiction as independent polities, virtually everyone now agreed with those people who had begun to argue during the late 1760s that all the different polities within the British Empire

[46] [Thomson Mason], "The British American," nos. VI–VII, July 7, 14, 1774, in Peter Force, comp., *American Archives* (Washington, 1837–53), 4th ser., 1: 522, 544.

[47] James Wilson, *Considerations on the Nature and Extent of the Legislative Authority of the British Parliament* (Philadelphia, 1774), in Robert Green McCloskey, ed., *The Works of James Wilson* (Cambridge, Mass., 1767), 2:741, 743–46.

were distinct, independent of each other, but connected through allegiance to the same sovereign. On close examination, they had discovered that, as an entity composed of extensive and dispersed dominions, the empire was a new phenomenon in British political history that required a form of governance appropriate to its own circumstances, outside conventional notions of government. Separated by vast distances, inhabited by different people, living under distinct constitutions of government, with different customs, laws, and interests, the empire's several constitutional elements could not possibly comprise a single civil state. Rather, each part had to be considered not as a set of individuals, but as a distinct people. Presided over by its own legislature, each of these corporate entities was a separate realm. According to this line of thought, no part of the empire was subordinate to any other part. As Franklin had remarked in 1770, there was no dependence among the several parts of the empire, "only a Connection, of which the King is the common Link."[48]

In view of the economic success of the empire, both Americans and their supporters in Britain regarded it as absurd for the metropolis to risk so many palpable advantages in pursuit of what increasingly appeared to them to be nothing more than an academic and irrelevant political abstraction. Sovereignty might appear to be the grand question in dispute to the vast majority of the metropolitan political nation. Throughout the pre-Revolutionary debates, however, most colonial leaders had resisted such reductionism and had endeavored, unsuccessfully, to focus debate on the seemingly more tractable and certainly less abstract problem of how power was or should be allocated in a polity composed of several related but nonetheless distinct corporate entities. For the colonists, resolution of their dispute with the metropolis had never seemed to require much more than the rationalization of existing political arrangements within the empire.

For them, the "great solecism of an imperium in imperio" seemed, as the North Carolina lawyer James Iredell declared, to be little more than "a narrow and pedantic . . . point of speculation," a "scholastic and trifling refinement" that had no relevance to the situation at hand. "Custom and continual usage" seemed to be "of a much more unequivocal nature than speculation and refined principles." Notwithstanding the fact that it had been "so vainly and confidently relied on" by their antagonists, that "beautiful theory in political discourses – the necessity of an absolute power residing somewhere in every state" – seemed, as Iredell wrote, to be wholly inapplicable to a situation involving "several distinct and independent

[48] Benjamin Franklin, Marginalia to Matthew Wheelock, *Reflections Moral and Political on Great Britain and Her Colonies* (London, 1770), in Labaree et al., *Franklin Papers*, 17:393.

legislatures, each engaged in a separate scale, and employed about different objects."[49]

Colonial protagonists thus called on the metropolitan government to abandon its pursuit of the "vain phantom of unlimited sovereignty" and content itself with "the solid advantages of a moderate, useful and intelligible authority."[50] As long as all members of the empire adhered to the customary arrangements that had developed over the previous century and a half, as long as the king was the supreme head of every legislature in the British dominions, they suggested, he would always have it in his power to direct the various governments to the reciprocal advantage of the empire as a whole and, by his authority to veto laws, could always prevent any positive law in any part of the empire from injuring the whole.

In their efforts to explain – and to rationalize – existing constitutional relationships within the empire, colonial protagonists, between 1764 and 1776, had discovered that the locus of authority necessarily had to reside in each of the separate corporate entities that composed the empire. Contrary to metropolitan theory as it had developed following the Glorious Revolution and, more especially, after 1740, authority, they now clearly understood, had never been concentrated in a sovereign institution at the center. Rather, it had always been dispersed among the several Parliaments that routinely had been established to preside over, and express the collective will of, each new polity within the empire. Indeed, this proliferation of legislatures was the only way that those traditional English rights that had been confirmed to the inhabitants of the metropolis by the Revolutionary settlement – especially that most fundamental right of no legislation without representation – could be extended to people in the peripheries of a large extended polity like the early modern British Empire. For the inhabitants of those, by then, quite ancient corporate entities, English liberty and their specific local corporate rights were identical. Just as it had been throughout the colonial era, the integrity of those rights and of the constitutions and assemblies that embodied and protected them was thus, not surprisingly, the central theme of colonial constitutional protest during the 1760s and 1770s.

Although this insistence on the autonomy and integrity of the several colonial constitutions was certainly a defense of constitutional multiplicity within the empire, the ancient and continuing association of its several

[49] James Iredell, "To the Inhabitants of Great Britain," September 1774, and "The Principles of an American Whig" [1775–76], in Don Higginbotham, ed., *The Papers of James Iredell* (Raleigh, N.C., 1976), 1: 254, 264–67, 332.

[50] Jonathan Shipley, *A Sermon Preached before the Incorporated Society for the Propagation of the Gospel in Foreign Parts* (London, 1774), in Paul H. Smith, comp., *English Defenders of American Freedom, 1774–1778* (Washington, 1972), 38.

separate polities clearly implied the existence of a larger imperial constitution, a constitution of the empire. Though this constitution was obviously based on and expressed the same fundamental constitutional principles, it was emphatically not identical to the British constitution. By the 1760s the British constitution had become a constitution of Parliamentary supremacy. But the emerging imperial constitution, like the separate constitutions of Britain's many overseas dominions, remained a customary constitution in which, according to the colonial point of view, sovereignty resided not in an all-powerful Parliament but in the Crown, the power of which had been reduced considerably over the previous century by the specific gains made in the direction of self-determination by each representative body within the empire.

Regarding any diminution of Parliamentary sovereignty as a prelude to the eventual loss of control of the colonies that seemed to be associated so intimately with Britain's rise to world power, the vast majority of the metropolitan political nation found it impossible to accept such arguments. In addition, from the perspective of Britain's own internal constitutional development during the previous century, colonial theories about the organization of the empire seemed dangerously retrograde. By placing the resources of Ireland and the colonies directly in the hands of the Crown and beyond the reach of Parliament, those theories appeared to strike directly at the root of the legislative supremacy that, for them, was the primary legacy of the Glorious Revolution.

In 1774, the Coercive Acts produced an astonishing union among the colonies. So alarmed were the colonists that those measures would deprive them of "every essential privilege" that, as the Massachusetts Committee of Correspondence wrote Franklin in the spring of 1774, "the whole Continent" was united "in Sentiment and . . . Measures."[51] Already, in the initial response to those acts, a few writers, notably Thomas Jefferson of Virginia and William Henry Drayton of South Carolina, pointed out that many of the most egregious colonial grievances were attributable directly to the Crown. By thus raising the old question of the extent of the king's authority in the colonies, a question that had been given new force by the many local controversies of the early 1770s, they thereby both issued a new challenge to the Crown's long-standing claim for more extensive prerogative in America than it could legally exercise in Britain and, implicitly at least, questioned the wisdom and viability of the emerging argument that a continuing connection with Britain through the Crown could provide an adequate basis for the security of colonial rights.

[51] Massachusetts Committee of Correspondence to Franklin, March 31, 1774, in Labaree et al., eds., *Franklin Papers*, 21: 165–66.

As it became increasingly clear in 1775–76 that Parliament would not abandon its claims to imperial supremacy and that George III was every bit as committed to those claims as was the rest of the British political nation, more colonials began to think of a new course of political action that included both independence from Britain and the creation of a grand American commonwealth. Notwithstanding the old conviction that every colony was so fond of its own distinctiveness that they could never unite into one state, they more and more came to the conclusion that there was no other way for them to preserve their legal and constitutional rights and liberties. Whether or not independence would be the first step toward the establishment of a viable union that would enable them to resolve the problem that had brought the British Empire to grief, the problem of how in an extended polity authority should be distributed between center and peripheries was still an open question when the colonies declared independence in July 1776.

CONCLUSION

Driven by the specter of Parliamentary taxation to investigate the constitutional organization of the empire, American colonials quickly turned in the 1760s to the defense, fully elaborated during the colonial era in efforts to limit the Crown's prerogative powers in the colonies, that they were governed by a customary imperial constitution based on the ideas of principled limitation and government by consent. Metropolitan officials refused to take the colonial case seriously, but this refusal does not mean that they were right about the law. Constitutional arrangements within the British Empire were far from precise, and in the debates of the 1760s and 1770s, each side could marshal effective legal arguments in behalf of its position. In this unsettled situation, constitutional questions were by no means as clear as they were said to be in London.

The early modern British Empire was by no means yet a modern unitary state. Imperial institutions in the colonies had little coercive power and depended for their effectiveness on the consent of local populations. Authority within the empire had long been dispersed into the hands of authoritative, powerful, and largely autonomous local institutions. Not dependent for their effectiveness on the support or the acquiescence of a central authority and highly resistant to central control, these institutions were regarded, both by those who composed them and those whom they served, as largely independent agencies of constitutional power and authority. In this diffuse and decentralized political entity, institutions on the periphery were as free to determine the nature of the constitution as authorities at the center.

When Thomas Jefferson and his colleagues in the Second Continental Congress produced the Declaration of Independence in the summer of 1776, they made extensive use of natural rights theory. In that way the Declaration represented something of a departure from the impressive political tracts and state papers they had been producing over the previous twelve years. Natural rights theory had not been absent from that literature, but it had never been much more than a complementary strain to their principal argument, which rested on law. Specifically, that argument, following logically from the colonists' own heritage of legal and constitutional thought over the previous century and a half, was largely founded on the English jurisprudential conception of government as limited government and of the British constitution as a constitution in which law confined the discretion or will of monarchs, judges, and legislators; a conception that, even after the rise of the doctrine of Parliamentary supremacy, still had much vitality in Britain itself. Indeed, much of this literature was the work of colonial lawyers. Richard Bland, James Otis, Daniel Dulany, John Dickinson, James Wilson, Thomas Jefferson, John Adams, Alexander Hamilton, Charles Carroll of Carrollton, James Iredell – these were only the most prominent lawyers who contributed to the colonial case. Even more impressive, lay leaders, merchants, printers, and planters, including Stephen Hopkins, Benjamin Franklin, Samuel Adams, William Hicks, and William Henry Drayton, displayed a deep familiarity with the common culture of legal thought and constitutional culture that made the entire English-speaking world into a single discursive community. If, as the controversies of the 1760s and 1770s dramatically underline, that world did not always agree on the definition of crucial concepts, it did possess a common vocabulary. Throughout those controversies, colonial spokesmen demonstrated extraordinary learning in legal and constitutional matters, conducting their case like a common law litigation in the court of Anglophone public opinion. Displaying a tough law-mindedness, they had no doubt that the law, as they knew it from their metropolitan heritage and their own experience, could be marshaled in their favor and, for that reason, never hesitated to make law the foundation for their view of the constitutional organization of the empire.

14

CONFEDERATION AND CONSTITUTION

JACK N. RAKOVE

In both its origins and principal consequences, the American Revolution was a profoundly constitutional phenomenon. It began in the mid-1760s as a characteristically Anglo-American dispute over the extent of the rights of self-government that the colonies could claim in the face of new assertions of Parliament's legislative jurisdiction over America. When the ensuing dispute proved irresolvable, Americans declared their political independence from Britain and simultaneously embarked on a radical experiment in constitution-making that thereafter distinguished their ideas and practices of governance from those they had once shared with the mother country. A decade later, dissatisfaction with the state and federal constitutions adopted in the mid-1770s led to the calling of the Federal Convention that met at Philadelphia in May 1787. The new Constitution it proposed after four months of strenuous deliberation reflected a careful reconsideration of what one of its leading authors, James Madison, called "the vices of the political system of the United States," vices that had become evident only through the experience of self-government since 1776. The ensuing struggle over its ratification in turn gave rise to an extended public debate that revealed how far some Americans had moved in their thinking over the previous decade and how closely others adhered to beliefs that had led the colonists to revolt in 1776.

The revolutionaries themselves were deeply conscious of the significance and novelty of these accomplishments. No one expressed this awareness better than John Adams. In the spring of 1776, Adams snatched time from his numerous duties in the Continental Congress to write a short pamphlet sketching the constitutions of government that the colonies should begin drafting. Adams closed his *Thoughts on Government* by rejoicing at being "sent into life, at a time when the greatest law givers of antiquity would have wished to have lived." When else had a people enjoyed "full power and a fair opportunity to form and establish the wisest and happiest government that human wisdom can contrive?"[1] Thomas Jefferson agreed. A few weeks before Congress saddled him with the task of writing the Declaration of Independence, he wondered whether Virginia's congressional delegates could do better service by being recalled home to work on the province's new constitution. "In truth it is the whole object of the present controversy," Jefferson observed; "for should a bad government be instituted for us in future it had been as well to have accepted the bad one offered us from beyond the water without the risk and expense of contest."[2] Eleven years later Alexander Hamilton struck a similar note in opening *The Federalist*: "It has been frequently remarked that it seems to have been reserved to the people of this country, by their conduct and example, to decide the important question, whether societies of men are really capable or not of establishing good government from reflection and choice, or whether they are forever destined to depend for their political constitutions on accident and force."[3]

In both 1776 and 1787, this sense of opportunity and exultation masked the problematic circumstances under which the enterprise of constitution-making proceeded. The conventions that wrote the first state constitutions were simultaneously preoccupied with an urgent array of legislative duties required to mobilize their societies for war. Their innate inclination to create strongly republican or "popular" governments that vested a near monopoly of authority in the legislature hardly accorded with the immediate and urgent circumstance that Americans were waging war against the great power of the Atlantic world. A decade later, the advocates of national constitutional reform faced the daunting challenge of proposing a wholesale transformation of the structure of the Union after three successive efforts to amend the Articles of Confederation had failed to attain the requisite approval of all thirteen states. Their solution to this problem was to ignore the formal rules of amendment and hope that Americans would accept the novel procedures for ratification that the Federal Convention proposed in their place.

Of course, in the end, the Convention did meet, and under the stern eye of its presiding officer, George Washington, managed to hammer out a Constitution. That Constitution was in turn subjected to ten months of

[1] [John Adams], *Thoughts on Government* (Philadelphia, 1776), in Philip Kurland and Ralph Lerner, eds., *The Founders' Constitution* (Chicago, 1987), I, 110.

[2] Thomas Jefferson to Thomas Nelson, May 16, 1776, in Julian P. Boyd *et al.*, eds., *The Papers of Thomas Jefferson* (Princeton, NJ, 1950–), I, 292.

[3] Alexander Hamilton, *Federalist* 1, in Benjamin Wright, ed., *The Federalist* (Cambridge, MA, 1961), 89.

public debate, at the end of which it had been ratified by eleven states – two more than the Convention had required for the Constitution to take effect. Whether or not this decision was in some sense "illegal" – as some intrepid scholars have alleged – it was widely recognized as legitimate, and by the winter of 1789 elections were well under way for the new government that would go into operation in March.

The adoption of the Federal Constitution in 1787–88 is often seen, with good reason, as the fulfillment of the Revolution. It prevented the revolutionary alliance that secured national independence in 1783 from devolving into a set of petty, bickering republics or regional confederacies. It laid the basis for the orderly settlement and development of the trans-Appalachian interior, the great territorial prize that was secured with the peace treaty of 1783. And it marked the point of departure for the ongoing constitutional conflicts that have been a hallmark of American law and politics ever since. For as the disputes that erupted in the 1790s quickly made clear, the boundary between the realms of the political and constitutional proved difficult to discern and easy to cross. Disputes over policy repeatedly escalated into quarrels over the meaning of relevant constitutional clauses, and the existence of a written Constitution adopted in living memory made it easy for partisans and polemicists to accuse their opponents of trampling constitutional values in the name of party advantage.

Any event that embodies so many consequences and implications naturally acquires an aura of historical inevitability. Over two centuries later, American political culture still pays homage to this conviction by portentously calling this epoch "the Founding" and its leading lights "the Founding Fathers." This in turn makes it difficult to restore a due measure of contingency to key developments of the Revolutionary era. Back in the 1760s, the colonists had not set out to foment crises that would enable them to seize their independence. They reacted instead to a set of British miscues and miscalculations that produced the opposite result of what the successive ministries of George III intended. Nor did Americans think they were inventing a new model of constitutionalism, relying on the supreme authority of a single text, when they began writing new constitutions of government in 1776. They were driven to write constitutions because they were anxious to restore legal government; only afterward did they begin to ponder the implications of what they had done. So, too, the advocates of federal constitutional reform in the mid-1780s did not set out to establish a national Leviathan with powers akin to those once claimed by Parliament. Had any of the modest amendments to the Articles of Congress proposed before 1787 ever been ratified, the case for calling a general convention like the one that gathered at Philadelphia would have been far more difficult to make. Even then, many sensible observers believed that the

Philadelphia convention would be a forum more for discussion than concrete action.

There was, nevertheless, a deep logic to the constitutional transformation that unfolded in America after 1765. The absence of a determinate imperial constitution specifying the respective powers of the empire and the rights of its colonies was one reason why the controversy that began with the Stamp Act proved so resistant to resolution. Both sides appealed to principles that were embedded within a common constitutional heritage and represented equally legitimate strands of that tradition. Once the colonists seized the opportunity to begin writing constitutions, they began to discover that documents used to establish government could also be used to limit its authority. But the question of how power could be both effectively constituted and safely limited could not be resolved by appeal to principle alone. It required reflecting on experience, and that was exactly what a decade of self-government after 1776 provided.

I. FRAMING THE CONFEDERATION

The controversy that ultimately led Americans to declare independence in July 1776 began as a dispute over taxation. In the Stamp Act crisis of 1765–66, the colonists denied that they could ever be taxed by a Parliament in which they were not, nor ever could be, represented. This dispute quickly escalated into a debate over the location of sovereignty, after the Declaratory Act of 1766, adopted to ease the repeal of the Stamp Act, asserted that Parliament retained jurisdiction over the colonies "in all cases whatsoever."[4] Most colonists conceded that Parliament could continue to regulate imperial commerce. But by 1774, the prevailing American position was that the separate colonial assemblies were the virtual equivalents of Parliament.

This claim would not have converted the individual American provinces into fully sovereign governments, however. Prior to 1774, no one would have regarded the colonies as sovereign in the conventional sense of the term. Although they had long enjoyed substantial legislative autonomy, their powers of government were derived from the British Crown, which retained the legal right not only to annul colonial legislation but even to revoke the charters under which it had organized the separate colonial governments. Had it been the Crown, rather than Parliament, that altered the royal charter of government of 1691 with the Massachusetts Government Act in 1774,

[4] Danby Pickering, ed., *The Statutes at Large* (Cambridge, Eng., 1762–1807), XXVII, 19–20.

Americans would have found it more difficult to protest that the King and his ministers were acting either unlawfully or unconstitutionally.

Along with the Boston Port Act and the Administration of Justice Act, the Massachusetts Government Act that Parliament passed in response to the Boston Tea Party provoked the crisis that led to the calling of the First Continental Congress in 1774. From its inception, Congress managed the external relations of the united colonies it represented. After civil war erupted outside Boston in April 1775, Congress converted the Massachusetts provisional forces into a Continental Army commanded by George Washington. In effect, foreign affairs and war, the two principal markers of sovereignty in the international sense of the term, were effectively concentrated at the inter-colonial or national level of governance. As the crisis deepened, local resistance leaders grew anxious to replace the extra-legal committees and conventions that had effectively ruled since 1774 with legal governments. But they did so only after securing permission from Congress, not by invoking the sovereign authority of their own people.

The state constitutions were hastily drafted by provincial conventions that had other pressing duties to perform. Some thought was given to submitting these documents to the people for discussion, perhaps even for approval, but the notion that a constitution had to be ratified by a sovereign people was at this point no more than a theoretical glimmer. From the start, some Americans believed that the received conception of a constitution was inadequate. "The truth is, the English have no fixed Constitution," observed the anonymous author (possibly Thomas Paine) of *Four Letters on Interesting Subjects*.[5] Because the first constitutions were drafted by bodies that were also acting legislatively, it became possible to argue that these charters had no greater authority than other statutes. The distinction between a constitution and a statute was not firmly established until the Massachusetts constitution of 1780 was drafted by a convention called for that sole purpose and then submitted to the towns for their approval.

At the national level, constitution-making was a more protracted process. Individual members of Congress began thinking about the problem as early as 1775, when Benjamin Franklin and the Connecticut delegates prepared drafts of a confederation. But Congress balked at action until June 1776, when it appointed three committees to prepare a declaration of independence, a plan for foreign treaties, and a confederation. The last committee, with one member from each state, was chaired by John Dickinson, the prominent Pennsylvania moderate who resisted declaring independence and feared the potential for disputes among the states. It delivered its report in early July, and Congress debated it actively into August. Then the subject

[5] *Four Letters on Interesting Subjects* (Philadelphia, 1776), in Kurland and Lerner, eds., *Founders' Constitution*, I, 637.

was postponed, not to be resumed until the spring of 1777, and then tabled again.

Three issues appeared intractable: the rule of voting in Congress, the formula for apportioning common expenses among the states, and the control of interior western lands. In each case, palpable interests divided the states into well-defined blocs. In 1774, Congress had adopted a rule that gave each state an equal vote. That decision made sense in the absence of reliable data about population and property; initially, it also seemed more important to reach decisions by consensus than by simple majorities. Once it became evident that a lengthy war loomed, however, delegates from the larger states complained of the inequity of giving each state an equal vote when their own constituents would have to contribute more manpower, money, and matériel to "the common cause." Delegates from less populous states insisted that they were committing "their all" just as much as the larger states, but the "all" of some states was obviously larger than the "all" of others. In the case of apportionment of expenses, Northern and Southern delegations disagreed over whether the best measure of wealth was simple acreage (which would impose heavier burdens on Southern states) or the value of improved land (which would penalize the more intensively farmed lands of the North). As to interior lands, those states whose western limits were bounded by the terms of their charters argued that unappropriated "waste" lands in the interior should become a common national stock that would help defray the expenses of the war. States with claims to the interior, however, were reluctant to yield them to the Union.

These three issues delayed completion of the drafting of the Articles until late 1777. Then, hoping that the recent victory at Saratoga would bring France into the war as an American ally, the delegates mustered the will to complete the work. Even then, decisions were grudgingly accepted, rather than fashioned through compromise. The small states gained their point on voting. The landed states prevented Congress from acquiring authority over western lands. On the difficult question of expenses, the delegates approved an impracticable New Jersey scheme to allocate the financial burdens of the Union among the states on the basis of the assessed value of improved lands, a formula that could never be implemented in wartime. In the event, opposition from the "landless" states of Maryland, Delaware, and New Jersey delayed ratification of the Articles of Confederation until March 1, 1781.

Throughout these discussions, little was said about the abstract question of the location of sovereignty in the federal system. At first glance, the lack of attention to this issue seems surprising. Given the central place that claims about sovereignty had occupied in the imperial debate, Americans might have been inclined to ask just where ultimate authority would reside in the hybrid federal system they were creating.

The one exception to this silence occurred in May 1777, when Thomas Burke, a newly arrived member from North Carolina, forced the subject to the attention of Congress. Burke's inexperience did not prevent him from suspecting that his colleagues, either by design or inadvertently, might foster designs to encroach on the authority of the states. He accordingly proposed the addition of an article affirming that each state would retain "its sovereignty, freedom, and independence, and every power, jurisdiction, and right, which is not by this confederation expressly delegated" to Congress. After a somewhat confused debate, Congress adopted this formula as the second Article of Confederation.

Its approval, however, could not unilaterally define the location of sovereignty in the American system in any way that would have made sense to eighteenth-century thinkers. For the orthodox understanding of sovereignty remained closer to the potent, awesome definitions worked out by thinkers like Jean Bodin and Thomas Hobbes in the late sixteenth and seventeenth centuries and codified by Sir William Blackstone in his *Commentaries on the Laws of England*. The problem of sovereignty, in their account, was essentially a matter of locating the ultimate and indeed absolute source of authority within a polity. The powers attributed to the sovereign could be classified and analyzed, but the idea that these powers could be distributed broadly among different governments within a single polity remained difficult to grasp. The traditional language of sovereignty was a language of absolute, ultimate, and final power.

Americans had been groping to fashion a different dialect since they first tried to explain why they were not subject to Parliament. They did not really wish to deny the supremacy of Parliament as recognized by the Glorious Revolution of 1688. They simply wanted to explain why it could not bind them, even should they remain part of the same polity within which Parliament was the highest lawmaking authority. But during the crisis of 1774–76, they had effectively assumed every sovereign power that mattered, declining to renounce their allegiance to the Crown – their original and proper bond to the empire – until King George III had made clear his own commitment to repression rather than negotiation.

Those powers, however, had been divided tacitly and pragmatically between the novel institution of Congress and the emerging states. To Congress had fallen the responsibility for diplomacy and war, while the states retained full legislative authority over their "internal police," as matters of domestic governance were commonly described. Neither before the Articles were ratified nor after could Congress cast its decisions in the language of statutes. The most it could do was to adopt "ordinances," a legal term of art that ranked somewhere below statute in the hierarchy of authority, and even then to regulate only matters over which the law of the states did not extend. In its dealings with the states, Congress relied on recommendations and requisitions that it expected the separate legislatures to implement. As a system of federalism, then, the theory of the Confederation was that Congress would propose and the states dispose. But this disposal did not mean determining whether Congress had acted rightly or wrongly. It did not presuppose that the states were entitled to reject Congressional decisions as a matter of preference or policy. It assumed, rather, that only the states could finally determine how best to implement particular Congressional decisions within their boundaries. In this sense, the state legislatures were to act as administrative auxiliaries of Congress, while Congress itself was less a legislative body than a collective form of executive power (drawing on that strain in separation-of-powers thinking that treated war and diplomacy as essentially executive functions).

The war sorely tried this assumption and found it wanting. But in the mid-1770s it seemed eminently reasonable. For one thing, Americans could not fashion a national administrative apparatus out of whole cloth, especially under the urgent conditions of the early years of the war. For another, it was naïve, but not implausible, to think that the states would patriotically do what was expected of them. This assumption reflected the republican enthusiasm with which Americans acted in 1775 and 1776, years that became a rosy memory the longer the war went on.

In many ways, then, Americans initially approached the problem of locating sovereignty within a federal system as a pragmatic matter of dealing with the exigencies of war and the legacy of colonial governance. A Congress that typically muddled along with two to three dozen members in attendance, and high rates of turnover, lacked the capacity to operate as a genuine national government. There was no political infrastructure in place to coordinate its activities with those of the states. Congress conducted much of its administrative business through numerous committees and a handful of executive boards with specific functions. Not until 1781 did it begin to establish executive departments.

II. EFFORTS AT AMENDMENT

So long as the Articles remained unratified – as they did until March 1, 1781 – Congress could still be classified as a revolutionary body. Its authority was political, not constitutional; its ability to direct the struggle against Britain depended on the survival of the Continental Army and the capacity of the state governments to command the allegiance and support of their constituents. With each passing year, patriot leaders spoke more frequently about the mounting "disaffection" of the people, but by that they meant war weariness rather than disloyalty. There were significant pockets of loyalist strength in individual states, but at no point after 1776 were patriot leaders in the position of losing political control of the state governments.

After 1780, two critical developments encouraged a rethinking of the structure of federalism envisioned by the Articles of Confederation. The first stemmed from the difficulties that Congress and the states jointly experienced in raising adequate revenues and supplies to sustain the army in the field. The second derived from the issue that posed the chief obstacle to the ratification of the Articles of Confederation: the control of interior western lands that different states claimed under their original colonial charters.

Under the Confederation, Congress had no independent authority to levy taxes. This critical omission was justified for two reasons. First, it comported with the fundamental constitutional principle that taxes could be levied only by the people's directly elected representatives – and members of Congress, appointed as they were by the state legislatures, were only delegates of delegates. Second, determining which modes of taxation would prove most productive within particular localities during the dislocations of the war was obviously a task beyond the competence of Congress. The Articles accordingly authorized Congress to impose requisitions for revenues on the states, which in turn would levy the appropriate taxes. In practice, the spiraling demands of the war outran both the administrative capacities and, to some extent, the political will of the states. Congress accordingly relied on its power to issue bills of credit, which became its preferred method of financing the war. The inevitable consequence was a depreciation of the specie value of this paper currency, exacerbated by wartime shortages that drove prices relentlessly higher. In 1779, with the value of paper currency to specie approaching 200:1, Congress resolved to cease emitting bills of credit and instead to require the states to provide "specific supplies" of food, clothing, and other matériel needed by the army.

One long-term solution to the financial woes of the federal Union, some thought, could spring from the establishment of a national domain on the "waste" lands north of the Ohio River – "waste" in the sense that they were occupied only by native American peoples who, by the standards of Euro-American agriculture, were not using these lands productively. In his first draft of articles of confederation (June 1776), John Dickinson proposed giving Congress authority to limit the states' western claims, resolve interstate disputes over boundaries and other matters, and control relations with Indian tribes. But during the ensuing months of intermittent discussion, a bloc of "landed" states had gained and held the narrow advantage on these matters. Congress was given no authority to limit the states' western boundaries. The procedures for mediating interstate disputes made Congress only an agency for convening courts to be appointed by the contending parties.

And the clause governing relations with Indians came saddled with qualifications that seemingly gave Congress jurisdiction, for the time being, only over Indians living beyond any state's boundaries – "not members of any of the States" – that is, with no Indians at all.

Early in 1780, however, New York launched an initiative to induce states with western claims to surrender their title to Congress. New York's own claims to interior lands were problematic. Unlike other colonies, New York, acquired by conquest from the Dutch in 1664, had no charter specifying its boundaries. The successor state's western claims instead rested on the former royal colony's historical relationship with the Five (later Six) Nations of the Iroquois confederacy, and the fiction that the Iroquois in turn were overlords of other native peoples in the Ohio Valley. To secure the territory it wished to retain – essentially everything now lying between Albany and Buffalo – the New York legislature ceded its problematic Ohio Valley claims to Congress. It did so, in part, for narrow purposes of state policy. But New York's political leaders, including Governor George Clinton, also had nationalist inclinations, and they hoped this cession would break the impasse over ratification of the Articles of Confederation.

The principal target of this maneuver was Virginia, whose own claims rested on the original 1606 charter of the antecedent Virginia Company. If New York grounded its claims on the colony's fictive relationship with the Iroquois, Virginia relied on legal fictions of the right of discovery and ignorance of North American geography. But as with New York, key Virginia leaders were willing to cede their state's extravagant claims above the Ohio to Congress, if the state could bar various groups of speculators from retaining objectionable land purchases they had made from assorted Indians prior to the Revolution. By late 1780, the Virginia legislature was preparing its own cession of lands lying north of the Ohio and west of Pennsylvania. This in turn cleared the way for Maryland to ratify the Articles. Although another three years passed before the Virginia cession was accepted, it was now evident that Congress eventually would have its own territory to govern.

Taken together, these two developments – the perceived need for independent sources of revenue and the prospective creation of a national domain – suggested that the powers and purposes of the Union might evolve beyond the expectations of 1776. A month before the Articles took formal effect, Congress submitted its first proposed amendment to the states, seeking permission to collect a 5 percent impost duty on foreign goods. This measure was seen not as a source of operating revenue, but as security for foreign loans. Governance of a national domain would make Congress more than a body to coordinate the struggle for independence. It would make key aspects of the economic and social development of the country objects of national concern, and necessarily raise the question of the future constitutional status of interior territories.

There were other constitutional dimensions to both issues. Like the original Articles of Confederation, the impost amendment required approval of all thirteen legislatures, and this proved impossible to attain. In 1782 Rhode Island rejected the impost, and Virginia subsequently rescinded its ratification. This first effort at amendment thus demonstrated that the unanimity rule for ratification imposed a formidable obstacle to any constitutional reform. The cession of western territories, on the other hand, revealed that a Confederation premised on the explicit delegation of power to the national government could not wholly cabin the expansion of national authority. Although many framers of the Articles had expected such cessions to occur, they made no explicit provision for the acquisition of territory or its governance. The cessions that created the national domain, therefore, had notably expanded the authority of Congress, but arguably by extra-constitutional means.

The decisive Franco-American victory at Yorktown in October 1781 did not free Congress of its financial problems. It still had major obligations to public creditors at home and abroad, to unpaid soldiers, and to the officer corps of the army. In 1781, Congress appointed the wealthy Philadelphia merchant and former delegate, Robert Morris, as its first superintendent of finance. Morris had played a critical role in keeping the army in the field during the year of victory, at times relying on his own private credit. In July 1782 he drafted an ambitious plan to establish public credit by asking the states to grant Congress permanent land, poll, and excise taxes. But Morris had dogged detractors in Congress, some of whom believed he had used his public office to garner private profits exceeding what even the tolerant standards of the era allowed. Morris tried to advance his program first by mobilizing political support from public creditors and then, more riskily, by abetting discontent among officers at the main army encampment at Newburgh, New York. In this scheme, the so-called Newburgh Conspiracy, Morris may have had the assistance of Alexander Hamilton, formerly aide-de-camp to General Washington, now a New York delegate to Congress. But Washington himself broke the officers' defiant mood with a single dramatic appearance at a meeting called to discuss their grievances. In the end, the Morris program failed to muster a majority within Congress. Instead on April 18, 1783, the delegates approved a compromise set of measures that included a second request for an impost, the substitution of a population rule for apportioning expenses among the states for the unwieldy assessment set down in the Articles, and the laying by the states of taxes dedicated to the use of Congress. The key architect of this proposal was James Madison of Virginia. This package would also require approval in its entirety by all the state legislatures, which would deliberate in peacetime as constituent members of the new federal republic whose independence was internationally recognized by the Treaty of Paris ending the Revolutionary War.

III. THE "CRITICAL PERIOD" AND MADISON'S CRITIQUE

The years that immediately followed have long been called "the Critical Period," a label bestowed by the historian John Fiske in 1888, during the centennial of the Constitution.[6] Scholars have ever since debated just how "critical" this period truly was ever since. Some of Fiske's successors, for example, disparaged his label as an echo of the abuse the supporters of the Constitution had heaped on the Confederation. In their view, the adoption of the Constitution was a virtual coup staged by an elite anxious to regain power from insurgent democratic forces and upstart leaders in the states. Given that the country was recovering from an eight-year war, their skepticism has merit. Yet the fact remains that in late 1786 a movement did coalesce to call a plenary convention to revise the Articles; that its leaders persuaded state legislatures and citizens alike that the proposed Constitution deserved serious consideration; and that within ten months of public deliberation, eleven of the thirteen states had ratified the proposed Constitution. Political activity and constitutional change of this kind could not have occurred had Americans believed that the nation was enjoying sound governance, political stability, and prosperity.

Three sets of factors explain how this transformation became possible. The first, and perhaps most prosaic, begins with the various difficulties that beset Congress after 1783, which fed a growing perception that the Confederation was verging toward "imbecility." These were the essential problems of *federalism*, that is, of the division of authority between the Union and the states, and the adequacy of the powers that Congress possessed. A second set of difficulties involved the internal governance of the states. These were problems of *republicanism*, that is, of the nature of the constitutions established at the outset of the Revolution and of the capacity of American citizens to act with the virtuous restraint that republican theory demanded. These concerns loomed particularly large in the thinking of James Madison, the one political actor who most shaped the agenda of constitutional reform. A third set of concerns could be subsumed under the broad heading of federalism, but merits separate mention. These required defining the essential interests that the national government should pursue,

[6] John Fiske, *The Critical Period of American History, 1783–1789* (New York and Boston, 1888).

identifying the principal threats to those interests, and asking what kind of nation-state the emerging American *imperium* should form. These concerns involved the demands of *state-building*, and those who took them most seriously included George Washington and his former aide-de-camp, Alexander Hamilton.

With the coming of peace in April 1783, Americans were eager to restore old channels of trade and develop new ones wherever possible. Two adverse developments soon threatened the interests of American merchants and artisans. Britain closed its West Indian ports to American ships, thereby reserving to its own merchants the profits of carrying American foodstuffs to the slave economies of the Caribbean. And long-desired British goods, carried in British ships, flooded American harbors, often underselling local artisans. In response, Congress in April 1784 framed two further amendments to the Confederation to follow the revenue measures it had proposed a year earlier. Carefully drawn, they would have enabled Congress to impose moderate restrictions on foreign merchants from nations pursuing discriminatory commercial policies against the United States. The essential purpose of these measures was to buttress the bargaining position of John Adams, the American minister to the Court of St. James, as he vainly sought to restore favorable commercial relations with Britain.

After submitting these amendments to the states, Congress adjourned for the first time since September 1775. To manage whatever national business occurred, it left behind a Committee of the States, comprising one member from each state, as provided by the Articles. But with little business to transact, that committee also dissolved, leaving only the secretary of Congress, Charles Thomson, and a handful of executive officers to constitute a skeletal national government. Since July 1783, the national government had become peripatetic. It had first decamped from Philadelphia to Princeton after a crowd of unpaid Pennsylvania soldiers staged a threatening protest outside the Pennsylvania Statehouse. Then it abandoned tiny Princeton for a more accommodating but torpid Annapolis. Late in 1784, the new Congress reconvened in Trenton, but Trenton was also found wanting. So Congress decamped for New York City, only recently liberated from British occupation, where it finally settled. A number of congressional bachelors turned to spending the better part of their time scouting for brides among the city's mercantile families.

Once settled in New York, Congress confronted two disturbing facts. Neither of its proposed sets of amendments had attained the requisite approval of all thirteen states; and the flow of revenue from the states had slowed to a trickle. In the meantime, commercial depression was settling on the port cities of the North. In the southwest, Spanish authorities at New Orleans closed the Mississippi to the shipment of American produce into the Gulf of Mexico, threatening both the welfare and loyalty of thousands of settlers occupying territory south of the Ohio River. Further north, British authorities in Canada retained control of the frontier posts on the Great Lakes. Under the peace treaty, these forts were to be surrendered to the Americans, which was essential to the settlement of the new national domain because of the influence the British exercised over Indian peoples above the Ohio River. But the British argued that they were entitled to retain the forts because various American states were also violating the treaty by preventing suits for the recovery of prewar debts owed to British creditors and of property confiscated from American loyalists. Moreover, without adequate revenue, Congress could not station a military force on the Ohio frontier large enough to overawe the Indians or prevent squatters from swarming the territory, and thereby thwarting its plans for orderly and profitable settlement.

Urgent as they were, these concerns – revenue, foreign commerce, treaty enforcement, and western development – were consistent with the understanding of the purposes of the Union that had emerged by the early 1780s. To supporters of an effective national government, the basic challenge remained to secure adequate revenues and a modest increment in the formal authority of Congress. While the various amendments made their slow circuit of the states, Congress could only hope that the manifest difficulties it faced would convince its member states to do the right thing.

Supporting pro-federal policies was one of James Madison's principal goals after he entered the Virginia legislature in 1784. His experience there in the mid-1780s explains the fusion in his thinking of the distinct problems of federalism and republicanism that ultimately led him to expand the agenda of constitutional reform. By early 1787, Madison had concluded that this agenda had to extend beyond merely providing supplemental powers to Congress. Rather, it required a wholesale restructuring of the national government and its relation to the states and the citizenry at large.

Madison had entered Congress in March 1780, amid its transition from currency finance to the system of requisitioning "specific supplies" from the states. As a delegate from Virginia, he participated in the land cessions that led to the ratification of the Confederation. But as a member of Congress, he was also troubled by the states' failure to meet their national responsibilities. By 1781, Madison was actively contemplating the idea that delinquent states should be coerced, by armed force, into performing their duty. Over the next two years, however, his views moderated with experience, as his role in fashioning the revenue compromises of April 1783 suggests.

In the fall of 1783, Madison became one of the first victims of term limits in American history, mustered home by the clause of the Articles of Confederation restricting service in Congress to three years out of six.

Once elected to the Virginia assembly, he played the leading role in its deliberations. Letters from his replacement in Congress, James Monroe, kept Madison well informed about national politics, and he consistently worked to persuade his fellow legislators to support Congress. At the same time, he was deeply involved in projects of internal legislative reform. Madison took on the added duty of enacting the comprehensive revisal of the Virginia statutory code that Thomas Jefferson, now American minister to France, had compiled in the late 1770s.

In both efforts, Madison enjoyed significant successes. Yet his experience had the effect, first, of souring his opinion of his fellow legislators, and then, more significantly, of encouraging him to analyze the underlying defects of republican politics and legislative deliberation within the states. Between the summer of 1785 and the early spring of 1787, Madison began to think systematically about the "vices of the political system of the United States." One part of this analysis led him to ask how the history of ancient and modern confederacies illuminated the difficulties Congress was facing. But Madison drew primarily on his own experience in Congress and Virginia and a probing mind that was equally capable of reasoning empirically and abstractly about events.

Having served as a member of the Virginia provincial convention of 1776, Madison recalled the haste with which the constitution had been drafted. More important, he understood how poorly the framers of 1776 had anticipated the realities of governance in the years to come. The early constitutions seemed deficient in two basic respects. They did not encourage sufficient care and deliberation in the legislative process, and they left the weaker executive and judicial branches vulnerable to legislative encroachments. Writing to a college friend seeking his advice on the constitution that Kentucky might write when it was finally separated from Virginia, Madison made his first recommendation the creation of a true senate that could provide the "*wisdom* and steadiness" so conspicuously absent from ordinary legislation.[7] He liked the idea of instituting an executive-judicial council of revision like the one provided in the New York constitution of 1777, which could exercise a negative on legislative acts, or even requiring the establishment of special committees to see that legislation was drafted properly. Madison also questioned the fundamental republican norm that made annual elections of legislators the people's best security against the abuse of power by their rulers. In his view, "triennial" elections might be preferable.

This concern with the character of legislation and legislators critically shaped Madison's political thinking after 1785, and it led him to fashion

[7] James Madison to Caleb Wallace, August 23, 1785, in Jack N. Rakove, ed., *James Madison: Writings* (New York, 1999), 40.

a quite modern understanding of the nature of representative government itself. In traditional Anglo-American constitutionalism, the first task of a representative assembly was not to make law in the positive sense. Rather, it was to prevent the executive from acting arbitrarily, from imposing law by fiat without the consent of the people's representatives. This had been the great issue in the constitutional struggles of seventeenth-century England, and it still resonated in eighteenth-century America in the recurring battles between royal governors and colonial assemblies. The memory of those controversies, Madison believed, explained why the constitution-makers of 1776 had naturally sought to confine executive power and therefore paid too little attention to the construction of the legislature. The past decade had demonstrated how misplaced that concern had been. The urgent business of conducting the Revolution repeatedly forced legislatures to act, and to enact laws more extensive and intrusive in their impact than Americans had ever known previously.[8] But, in Madison's view, the circumstances of revolution alone did not explain the active lawmaking of the republican assemblies. In a republican government, a supreme legislature would always be responsive to the pressures and preferences of the electorate. The people themselves were the real force in a republic, and in peacetime as well as war, they would expect the legislature to act instrumentally in pursuit of their interests.

For Madison the people were neither a mere abstraction nor an undifferentiated mass. Citizens had their individual interests, opinions, and passions, and the political coalitions they formed would reflect the interplay of all three. Republican politics, at the state level, was a politics of fashioning popular majorities. Once those majorities coalesced, they would persuade legislators to pursue their particular interests. The adverse effects those interests might have on the legitimate rights of minorities would be no deterrent to majority action. And if they conflicted with the larger public good of the Union, these majorities would prefer their own parochial concerns to the national interest.

This assessment of state politics had critical implications for the agenda of constitutional reform. First, it brought the discrete issues of federalism and republicanism together in one analysis. At bottom, what Madison derided as the defects of state legislation derived from the same causes as the reluctance of the state legislatures to ratify amendments to the Confederation, abide by the peace treaty, or provide adequate revenues to Congress. This judgment in turn led to a second, equally fundamental conclusion: Any system of federalism resting on the voluntary compliance of the states with national measures was doomed to failure. The radical omission of the Articles, Madison reasoned, was in depriving Congress of authority to

[8] Except, of course, for the most noteworthy and innovative category of American legislation, the novel statutes instituting and maintaining a system of chattel slavery.

compel the states to do their duty or to sanction them when they failed. So long as Congress had to rely on the states, a non-compliance of some legislatures would be the norm, not the exception. Not all states would have an equal interest in seeing particular national decisions implemented. Some state-based politicians ("courtiers of Popularity") would always find it convenient to oppose national measures. And even when the states generally agreed on a particular policy, "a distrust of the voluntary compliance of each other may discourage the compliance of any, even though it be the latent disposition of all."[9]

A proper national government, Madison concluded, would be organized under a different principle. It would have to become a government of law, operating not through recommendations addressed to the legislatures, but through ordinary statutes enacted, administered, and adjudicated by its own officials. This would mean replacing the unicameral Congress and its dependent executive departments with the bicameral legislature and independent executive and judiciary that Americans expected to find in any proper government. That reconstitution could benefit from all the critical appraisals of the state governments that had been forming over the past decade. The project of federal constitutional reform would thus provide an opportunity to assess the shortcomings not only of the Articles of Confederation but also of the republican constitutions adopted with independence.

Madison was not alone in thinking that the state governments merited critical review. That process arguably had begun much earlier, with the drafting of the New York constitution of 1777 and the Massachusetts constitution of 1780 (largely written by John Adams while home after his first diplomatic posting to Paris). Both of these documents, for example, had provided for the popular election of the governor, thereby making that officer politically independent of the legislature. Each armed the executive with a limited legislative veto, thereby restoring a controversial monarchical prerogative. (In New York, this negative was to be exercised through a council of revision including other executive and judicial officers.) Each therefore marked a somewhat "conservative" reaction against the republican enthusiasms of 1776.

The Massachusetts constitution was notable in two other respects. Following the precedent of the Pennsylvania constitution of 1776, it made its Declaration of the Rights of the Inhabitants an integral part of the constitutional text, rather than stand alone as an independent statement of uncertain authority. It was also the first to be proposed by a convention appointed for that purpose alone and then submitted to the people, gathered

[9] Madison, Vices of the Political System, in Kurland and Lerner, eds., *Founders' Constitution*, I, 167–68.

in their town meetings, for approval. That had not been the intention of the Massachusetts General Court – the legislature whose authority had been reestablished in 1775 by an act of the Continental Congress. Rather, this novel procedure was forced on the lawmakers by protests from individual towns arguing that it was improper for a legislative body to frame the very constitution that would define its own powers.

In taking this position, the protesting towns were invoking the common law maxim of statutory construction that resolved conflicts between two legislative acts by making the later one legally superior to the earlier one (*quod leges posteriores priores contrarias abrogant*). A constitution promulgated by a legislature possessed only the authority of a statute. A later law violating the constitution would thus be legally superior. By invoking this maxim, the protesting towns identified the dominant vector along which American constitutionalism developed in the decade after 1776. The impetus to think of a constitution as higher law, superior to ordinary legislation, was primarily a reaction against the dominant principle of legislative supremacy that had shaped the first constitutions.

The emerging doctrines of American constitutionalism were thus driven by a critical engagement with the experience of republican government within the states. But an agenda of state-building also deeply affected the movement for constitutional reform. Determining the shape and extent of this agenda required drawing a different set of lessons from the experience of the past decade.

The original American nation-state of 1776 – if that term can even be used – was a confederation of autonomous jurisdictions, united for the great purpose of securing independence from Britain. Although that paramount goal did not stifle the expression of particular state and regional interests, it generally discouraged such interests from being asserted too forcefully. There was never a moment when any of the new commonwealths considered defecting from the interstate alliance for independence.

Once independence was secured, it became easier to ask whether a genuine national interest still existed. Issues of commercial policy exposed significant differences between the regional economies of Northern and Southern states. The former rested on family farms producing modest surpluses that local merchants would carry (if permitted) to the slave societies of the Caribbean. The latter featured slave-driven plantation agriculture raising tobacco, rice, and indigo for European markets. New England had a special interest in gaining access to North Atlantic fishing banks, especially those off Newfoundland. Southern planters looked toward the southwestern interior, imagining a commodity-exporting society extending into the fertile bottom lands between the Ohio River and the Gulf of Mexico.

For the time being, these lands remained within the claimed jurisdictions of Virginia, North Carolina, and Georgia. Eventually, however, these lands were expected to fall under national jurisdiction, just as the territory above the Ohio River had come to form a national domain when Congress finally accepted the Virginia cession in 1784. It was the prospect of sustained expansion into the trans-Appalachian interior, on both sides of the Ohio, that arguably formed the principal impetus for a new conception of a post-Revolutionary nation-state.

In consenting to the establishment of the national domain, the ceding states had in effect admitted their own inability to maintain effective republican government over too extensive a territory. But this willingness to contract their boundaries, though in part a confession of state weakness, left the states in a mutually secure relation with each other. In effect, the states had converted problematic territorial claims that might have generated conflicts both among themselves and with restive frontier settlers into a system whereby they would collectively recognize each other's legitimate boundaries. Rather than becoming a source of interstate rivalry, the interior had become a stimulus to an expansion of national jurisdiction that left the states more, not less, secure in exercising the substantial legal authority they retained.

The creation of a national domain destined for future settlement shaped American state-building in other ways. Were these territories to be organized as internal colonies, subordinated to the confederation of existing provinces along the seaboard? Or would they be allowed to join the Union as equal members? In a series of committee reports and ordinances, beginning with a provisional measure drafted by Thomas Jefferson in 1784 and culminating with the Northwest Ordinance of 1787, Congress began to plan to divide the interior territory into potential new states, to be admitted on terms of equality with the original thirteen states. The national government would be responsible for administering the territory in their preliminary phases of settlement. But at some point, the power to govern would revert to the people, who would draft new constitutions as they made the transition to statehood.

For this visionary policy to succeed, however, the United States would have to project its own power across the Appalachians. From the north, Congress still faced significant competition from British authorities in Canada. Unless their influence over the Native American peoples of the Great Lakes region was checked, Congress could not expect to proceed with orderly settlement north of the Ohio. To the south, Spanish control of New Orleans placed a choke-hold on the flow of American produce into the Gulf of Mexico for sale. Without Congressional action to counter Spanish restrictions, western settlers would have little incentive to remain loyal to the confederation of seaboard states. Instead, they would have to seek an accommodation with Spain.

The potential continental empire of the United States thus found itself in competition with the older Atlantic empires of Britain and Spain. In the mid-1780s, there was every reason to worry that this competition might continue indefinitely. The challenge Americans faced, if they were to remain Americans and not merely residents of individual states, was to develop a government with the resources to overawe the native peoples of the interior while preventing the relatively weak colonial establishments that Britain and Spain maintained in Canada and Louisiana from checking expansion into the interior. At the minimum, that seemed to require the capacity to sustain an adequate military force under the authority of Congress. But provisioning troops on a distant and extensive frontier was not cheap (as the British had learned before the Revolution). It required revenue, which was exactly what Congress lacked in the mid-1780s. Three years after Congress proposed its financial amendments of April 1783, the hurdle of unanimous state ratification had still not been surmounted.

IV. PHILADELPHIA

In the end, the apparent impossibility of overcoming the obstacle of unanimity persuaded the advocates of constitutional reform to pursue a more radical strategy. Ideally, they might have preferred to wait to allow the adoption of individual amendments to clear the path for the consideration of others. But when neither the revenue amendments of 1783 nor the commercial amendments of 1784 secured approval, other options had to be considered.

The initiative came from the Virginia legislature. In January 1786, it invited the other states to appoint commissioners to meet at a conference to consider how to vest Congress with authority over commerce. By the summer, eight states had agreed to send delegates to Annapolis, the site the Virginia commissioners chose for the meeting. However, only a dozen deputies from five states appeared at the appointed time in mid-September, too few to pursue the proposed project. Rather than simply adjourn, the commissioners present (who included Madison and Edmund Randolph from Virginia, Alexander Hamilton, and John Dickinson) endorsed a risky gambit. Seizing on a clause in the credentials of the New Jersey commissioners, they proposed that another convention should meet at Philadelphia in May and that its agenda extend beyond commerce to consider the defects of the Confederation more generally.

Although the commissioners had no reason to think this stratagem would succeed, three conditions worked in its favor. One was the recognition that an impotent Congress could not survive indefinitely and that the amendment route was an exercise in futility. The second was a serious fissure within Congress, sparked by a request from Secretary of Foreign Affairs John Jay for a revision of the instructions under which he was negotiating a commercial treaty with a Spanish emissary. Jay had asked Congress to allow him to relinquish American claims for a free navigation of the Mississippi River. This request was supported by Northern delegates anxious to see a treaty concluded, but sharply opposed by Southern delegates who saw the continued occlusion of the Mississippi at New Orleans as an impediment to expansion into the southwest. In repeated votes on this issue, Congress divided along starkly sectional lines, and that division made it easier to imagine that the existing Union could devolve into two or three regional confederations.

The third condition favoring the idea of a general convention was the unrest in Massachusetts. However one explains Shays' Rebellion (a protest against court-ordered seizures of the property of indebted farmers) its occurrence in Massachusetts, generally regarded as one of the best governed states in the Union, was a cause for alarm. Massachusetts had been pursuing a policy of levying taxes to retire its own public debt incurred during the Revolution. Its constitution, adopted only in 1780, had avoided some of the republican enthusiasms of 1776, notably by granting the popularly elected governor a limited veto over legislation, thereby making its government better "balanced" than those of other states.

Against this background, twelve of the thirteen state legislatures eventually appointed delegates to attend the convention at Philadelphia. Rhode Island was the lone holdout. In 1782, it had blocked the first attempt to amend the Articles of Confederation. Since then, its politics had been dominated by a party committed to a program of making paper currency legal tender for the payment of private debts, a policy that proto-Federalists like James Madison regarded as the hallmark of "vicious" legislation because it seemed to attack the fundamental rights of property. But Rhode Island's opposition to the convention in fact proved strategically useful. A state that refused even to attend the convention was unlikely to approve anything it recommended, and this consideration in turn gave the delegates at Philadelphia a powerful incentive to abandon the unanimity rule for amending the Confederation.

In the months leading up to the convention, there must have been many private discussions of its potential agenda. "It is not uncommon to hear the principles of Government stated in common Conversation," Samuel Osgood, a former member of Congress, informed John Adams. "Emperors, Kings, Stadtholders, Governors General, with a Senate, or House of Lords, & House of Commons, are frequently the Topics of Conversation," he added.

"Many are for abolishing all the State Governments, & for establishing some Kind of general Government."[10] But the extant *documentary* record of what was being said is surprisingly thin. The most important evidence of what was being prepared is found in the papers of James Madison, who had returned to Congress in the winter of 1787. As a politician who understood the importance of shaping a legislative agenda, Madison set himself the task of fashioning a broad framework for the convention's deliberations.

Madison developed his ideas in letters to three fellow Virginians – Thomas Jefferson, the American minister to France; Edmund Randolph, the state's newly elected governor; and the nation's most distinguished citizen, George Washington, whose attendance at the convention Madison deemed crucial to its success – and in his memorandum on the "Vices of the Political System of the U. States." Madison took as his point of departure the need to find "some middle ground" between a system predicated on the "individual independence of the states" and one designed to produce "a consolidation of the whole into one simple republic." The states should be preserved "wherever they can be subordinately useful," but a "due supremacy of the national authority" also had to be established. That supremacy would no longer be exercised by a government acting through the states, but by one empowered to act directly on the population, effectively bypassing the state governments. This in turn justified turning Congress into a true representative body, where members would be apportioned among the states on the basis of population and speak not for the state legislatures but the people themselves.[11] Moreover, the national "supremacy" should be vested not only in the legislature but also in its coordinate departments of the executive and judiciary, each of which would also act directly on the population. This was a system of federalism, in short, that would define the relation between the national and state governments in terms of boundaries more than connections.

The most radical (or reactionary) element in Madison's thinking, however, did involve a new connection between the two levels of government. This was his proposal to give the new legislature "a negative *in all cases whatsoever* on the legislative acts of the States."[12] That negative could be used to prevent individual states from interfering with national measures that they opposed. But more intriguingly, Madison hoped this negative would enable the national government to protect minorities *within* individual states against unjust laws passed by their own legislatures. In advancing this

[10] Samuel Osgood to John Adams, November 14, 1786, Adams Family Papers, Massachusetts Historical Society, microfilm reel 368.

[11] Madison to Washington, April 16, 1787, in Rakove, ed., *Madison: Writings*, 80–83.

[12] Ibid., 81.

proposal, Madison moved beyond the conventional understanding which held that the principal problem in securing rights was to protect the people as a whole against the arbitrary power of government. Historically that meant shielding the people against the concentrated power of the monarchy. But in a republican government, where the legislature dominated, the real problem of rights would be to protect minorities among the people from whatever popular majorities managed to dominate the government. Because such majorities were more likely to form within the smaller compass of the states, Madison believed that the most effective remedy for the abuse of rights would be to empower a "sufficiently disinterested" national government to protect individuals and minorities against unjust laws enacted by the people's own representatives.

Madison's analysis formed the basis for the plan that the Virginia delegates drafted while they waited for the other delegations to straggle into Philadelphia. The convention was due to open on May 14, but a quorum of seven states was not formed until May 25. Once assembled in the same ground floor chamber of the Pennsylvania Statehouse where Congress had declared independence eleven years earlier, the delegates' first actions were to adopt rules of deliberation and to elect George Washington as their presiding officer. Having previously announced his retirement from public life, Washington had attended the convention only reluctantly. Madison, too, had worried that Washington's prestige might be wasted if the Philadelphia convention proved a replay of Annapolis. But once it was clear that the convention would be well attended, his presence, even if he never said a word, became an invaluable political asset.

While drafting the plan that Randolph formally introduced on May 29, the Virginia delegates, in consultation with the Pennsylvanians, had considered proposing that the convention not follow the one state, one vote rule used by Congress since 1774. To insist on that point from the outset, however, would have been a formula for confrontation, not deliberation. Instead, the Virginia and Pennsylvania delegates believed they could persuade the small states that principles of proportional representation should be applied to *both* houses of the bicameral legislature that the Virginia Plan would create. This assumption, which followed the strategy Madison had sketched before the convention, effectively shaped the first seven weeks of debate. Along with such allies as James Wilson of Pennsylvania and Rufus King of Massachusetts, Madison insisted that the principle of bicameral proportional representation had to be approved first, before the convention considered exactly which powers to vest in the national government. On this point, the Virginia Plan proposed that the new legislature should inherit the existing powers of Congress, and be further authorized "to legislate in all cases to which the separate States are incompetent, or in which the harmony of the United States may be interrupted by the exercise of individual Legislation." If not quite equivalent to the legislative sovereignty of Parliament, this formula nonetheless suggested an open-ended grant of power that would make the national legislature the discretionary judge of its own authority. Moreover, that discretion would extend to the exercise of a negative over state laws "contravening . . . the articles of Union."[13]

The principal limit on the abuse of that discretion would come from a joint executive-judicial council of revision, modeled on a similar institution established by the New York constitution of 1777 and which would be armed with a limited negative over national legislation, including the negative on state laws. Madison's rationale for uniting the two "weaker" departments in this council was that they might collectively discover the will to counterpose their judgment to the superior political influence of the legislature. But in debating this proposal in the first week of June, most of the delegates indicated they preferred fortifying the two other departments separately, not jointly. With little dissent, the executive alone was given a limited veto over national legislation – thereby revealing how far the framers had moved from the evisceration of executive power in 1776. Equally revealing, criticism of the council of revision demonstrated that many delegates assumed the judiciary would enjoy the authority to test the constitutional validity of legislation after its enactment. Involving the judiciary in the passage of legislation, some delegates objected, would weaken the judges' ability and will to assess its constitutionality once a proper legal case presented itself. Here, too, the delegates drew on the experience within the states, where, in a tantalizing handful of cases, judges had begun to assert their authority to subject legislative acts to constitutional review.

Until mid-July, however, the question of representation preoccupied the convention. There was broad agreement that seats in the lower house of the new national legislature should be apportioned among the states on the basis of population. Back in 1776, John Adams had declared that a representative assembly should be "in miniature, an exact portrait of the people at large,"[14] and that principle had since become something of a cliché in American thinking. It did remain a question, however, whether the enslaved African American population concentrated in the Southern states should be counted for purposes of representation.

The greater difficulty involved the upper house. Delegates from the less populous states insisted on retaining the equal state vote of the Confederation in at least one house of the legislature. Without that security, they

[13] Max Farrand, ed. *Records of the Federal Convention of 1787* (New Haven, CT, 1966), I, 21.
[14] [Adams], *Thoughts on Government*, in Kurland and Lerner, eds., *Founders' Constitution*, I, 108.

argued, a government dominated by the larger states would run roughshod over the interests of their constituents. The presence in the Virginia Plan of a negative on state laws made that concern plausible. Delegates from the more populous states replied that individuals were the only proper units of political representation, not corporate entities like states. The interests of a state were simply the aggregates of the interests of its citizens and residents, and a formula for treating states with disparate populations as equal units would be an injustice to the inhabitants of larger states. Perhaps the small states' concerns would deserve consideration if the interests of their citizens really were different from those of citizens of the larger states. But they were not. It was not the size of a state that would determine how its citizens or their representatives would vote, but rather the array of specific interests each state possessed. If some security were required to protect the state governments in the exercise of their proper powers it could be provided by allowing the legislature of each state to elect its delegates to the upper house – a procedure the convention roundly endorsed on June 7.

In mid-June, delegates from the small states responded to the looming impasse over this issue when William Paterson of New Jersey introduced an alternative plan of reform. Rather than establish a wholly new government, the New Jersey Plan would modestly augment the powers of the existing Congress, where the equal state vote would remain in force. Paterson's proposals were less a serious alternative to the Virginia Plan than a warning that if the small states were not satisfied on their key point, the convention might have to accept a more modest agenda of reform if it wanted to maintain an appearance of consensus. After minimal debate, the New Jersey Plan was rejected on June 19.

Over the next four weeks, the convention continued to debate the issue of representation. After a July 2 vote produced a deadlock of five states each on a motion for an equal state vote in the upper house, the convention appointed a committee to seek a compromise. Its report of July 5 did just that, calling for proportional representation in the lower house, an equal state vote in the upper, and a restriction on the authority of the latter to alter appropriation measures. The large state delegates rejected this ostensible compromise, noting that so long as the upper house had to consent to appropriations, the proposed restriction on amendments was superfluous.

At this point, the convention looked more carefully at the issue of apportionment in the lower house. Another committee had proposed an initial apportionment, first of fifty-six and then of sixty-five representatives, but its inability to explain the basis of this apportionment made Southern delegates in particular nervous about protecting their region's interests. Two concerns were foremost. First, they assumed (wrongly, as it turned out), that migration trends into the interior would favor their region, reducing or even eliminating the disparity with the more populous Northern states. Second, Southern delegates forthrightly insisted on having their slave populations counted for purposes of representation. Slaves might not be citizens, they conceded, worthy of representation in their own name. But because they were productive workers sustaining a prosperous segment of the national economy, the states where they resided deserved political compensation for the contributions they would make to the national welfare. Southern delegates took particular alarm when Gouverneur Morris of Pennsylvania suggested that the seaboard states should unite to guarantee that they would always retain a majority in the new legislature, which they might do by leaving the question of whether, when, and how to reapportion to its discretion. But that would also allow the current Northern majority to maintain the Southern states as a permanent minority. In response, Southern delegates sought and secured two major concessions. First, the convention agreed that the basis for reapportionment should be a decennial census, constitutionally mandated. Second, a constitutional rule for reapportionment would also be set, counting "other persons" (a euphemism for slaves) at the ratio of three-fifths of the free population. The same ratio would be used, in theory, to apportion "direct taxes" (such as a poll tax) among the states. But the delegates believed that direct taxes would rarely, if ever, be laid. The inclusion of a provision for taxation was designed to make the counting of slaves for political representation less offensive.

In late June, Madison had used the difference between the northern and southern regions to demonstrate why the small states' claims for special protection were specious. The existence of economies rooted in free or slave labor represented lasting differences that would shape political behavior and that would therefore need to be accommodated for the Union to survive. The size of a state would have no such durable influence. But the efforts of the Southern delegations to secure their interests as a regional minority nonetheless helped legitimate the claims of the small states, by suggesting that the protection of all identifiable minorities was a legitimate object of representation. In the critical vote of July 16, the small states carried their point, but not by convincing their opponents of the merits of their claims, or by securing a genuine compromise. In fact, the key decision found five states in favor of the equal state vote, four opposed, and Massachusetts, presumably a member of the large state bloc, divided.

With this decision finally taken, the convention turned its attention to other issues previously neglected. Its first decision, coincidentally, was to eliminate the negative on state laws that remained Madison's pet proposal. In its place, it adopted a weak statement of the principle of the supremacy of federal law, first expressed in the New Jersey Plan. During the second half of July, the delegates devoted most of their attention to the election of the executive. In early June, they had agreed to vest the executive power in a single individual (rather than a plural council), with a limited veto over legislation. But the political capacity of the executive remained largely unexplored.

The framers faced two great difficulties in designing the office to which they eventually gave the title of president. One involved rethinking the nature of executive power under a republican constitution. The other required fashioning a suitable mode of appointment or election, which in turn implicated other questions about length of term, eligibility for reelection, and mechanisms for removal. On the first point, the delegates expressed an array of opinions. Roger Sherman of Connecticut, for example, regarded the executive simply as an agency for implementing the legislative will. A few delegates, such as George Mason of Virginia, feared concentrating executive power in the hands of a single person. At the other pole, Alexander Hamilton favored an executive who could act as a great minister of state, fashioning public policies for legislative consideration and exercising significant discretion in matters of war and diplomacy. As the early decision to grant a limited veto suggests, the convention was prepared to restore some measure of prerogative – as the inherent powers of the British Crown were often characterized – to the executive. Yet well into August, the delegates also assumed that the power to appoint judges and other high officials, and to make treaties, would reside in the Senate.

The framers were hard pressed to agree on a satisfactory mode of election. When they took up this issue in late July, they considered three alternatives without reaching consensus on any one of them. The idea of a popular election was dismised on two grounds. First, the delegates doubted that a highly provincial electorate would be able to identify truly national "characters" or make an effective choice between them. Second, a popular election in a single national constituency would disadvantage Southern candidates because so much of the population of their region consisted of African American slaves who could have no vote. An appointment by the national legislature would avoid the information problem that militated against popular election, but it proved vulnerable to other objections. As the restoration of the veto suggests, the framers wanted to create an office capable of resisting legislative intrusion in the administration of government. But an executive elected by the legislature would lack the requisite independence, unless limited to a single term. Because it would take time to master the business of government, that term should be relatively long, but a long term smacked a bit of monarchy. Instead, some delegates, including Hamilton, thought that a shorter term with an opportunity for reelection would give the executive the strongest incentives to perform admirably in office. That, however, required placing the power of appointment outside the legislature. Accordingly, the convention briefly endorsed a scheme to establish a separate corps of presidential electors. But almost immediately doubts arose about their competence, leading the convention to return, on July 26, to the initial proposal for a legislative appointment for a single seven-year term.

This uncertainty reflected the difficulty Americans faced in reconciling a strong conception of executive power with republican principles. Contemporary models of executive power were either monarchical or ministerial, and American political culture disparaged both. Nevertheless, during the convention's final weeks, the presidency acquired new authority, less because the framers had adopted a Hamiltonian view of executive power, but rather in reaction to growing concern about the Senate (as the upper house was now called). The turning point came on August 24, when the convention deadlocked over a motion to restore appointment by presidential electors. Further discussion took place in a Committee on Postponed Parts. Its report of September 4 proposed two significant changes. First, it placed the powers of appointment and treaty making in the presidency, to be exercised with the "advice and consent" of the Senate. Second, it provided for a system of presidential electors, to be apportioned among the states on the basis of their total membership in Congress. The electors would not gather to deliberate and vote until they reached a decision. Rather, they would meet in their separate states, cast their ballots, and disperse. Should the electoral vote fail to produce a majority, the final decision would fall to the Senate.

This report had the advantage of replicating the compromises (as the weary framers now thought of them) that had been reached over the composition of Congress. The large states would hold an advantage in the electoral round (though the small states would be over-compensated by the two votes each gained for its senators). But should the electors not produce a majority – which many delegates suspected would often occur – a decision by the Senate would favor the less populous states. But this arrangement proved vulnerable to a telling objection. It would make the executive politically dependent on the Senate, the institution with which it would jointly exercise the appointment and treaty powers. Three days of heated debate on this point ended only when Roger Sherman hit on the ingenious solution of placing the contingent election in the House of Representatives, voting by states. A constitutional basis had thus been laid for creating an independent presidency that, if less than monarchical, would still have seemed ominous by the republican standards of 1776. Yet so many questions remained about the political potentiality of this novel office that few of the framers left Philadelphia confident that they understood how it would function.

The convention took other momentous decisions during its final weeks, but few generated the sustained debate that accompanied the disputes over representation and the presidency. Some of the most important were relatively uncontroversial. The Supremacy Clause, for example, originated as a weak alternative to Madison's negative on state laws. But with little discussion, it evolved into a robust statement of the supremacy of the Constitution, federal statutes, and national treaties that state judges were bound to enforce, "any Thing in the Constitution or Laws of any State to the Contrary notwithstanding." Whether state judges would have the fortitude to exercise this responsibility was uncertain. But the framers believed that *federal* judges would discharge that duty conscientiously, because the Constitution granted them the same tenure of good behavior that had shielded English judges from royal manipulation since 1701.

Two other sets of decisions deserve special notice. One dealt with the legislative authority of Congress, the other with the procedures for adopting the Constitution itself. As previously noted, the Virginia Plan left Congress to judge the extent of its own power. Although Madison may have intended this formula to serve simply as a placeholder until the key issues of representation were resolved, it nonetheless could be read as an American variant of the British conception of Parliamentary supremacy. In the wake of the July 16 decision on the Senate, however, this broad grant was replaced by a list of specific powers, first enumerated in the Committee of Detail that met from July 26 to August 5 and then expanded, again with little debate, during August. Foremost among these were the power to regulate interstate and foreign commerce; to levy a wide array of taxes, exempting only duties on exports; and to declare war and take a number of other actions relating to the domestic and foreign security of the nation. In the last area of jurisdiction, a brief but much-studied debate of August 23 led the convention to replace a clause authorizing Congress "to make war" with one empowering it "to declare war." The most plausible interpretation of this amendment is that it was designed to prevent Congress from meddling with the president's authority, as commander-in-chief of the armed forces, to conduct war once initiated or authorized by the legislature. But that understanding has not prevented numerous presidents since from asserting that their authority as commander-in-chief subsumes significant discretion to commit forces to combat without prior Congressional approval.

This enumeration of legislative powers in Article I, Section 8 of the Constitution ended with a clause permitting Congress "To make all Laws which shall be necessary and proper for carrying into Execution the foregoing Powers," and it was followed by two additional sections restricting the legislative powers of Congress and the states. Together, these three sections reflected and advanced the evolution in constitutional thinking that had occurred since 1776. Then it would have been understood that a government, once constituted, possessed plenary legislative power, and it would have been difficult to identify areas where that power could not intrude. The bills of rights that accompanied many of the first state constitutions did not formally limit this power, but were rather regarded as expressing principles guiding its exercise. But the delegation of specific powers to Congress, accompanied by restrictions on the legislative authority of both the national government and the states, established a new understanding of legislative power itself. It was no longer a plenary grant, but an assignment of specific duties to particular institutions and levels of government. The republican idea that all government rested on a primal grant of authority from the people now took a different, more precise form. The people granted and distributed only specific powers while retaining the capacity to retain others or redistribute those already granted.

This was popular sovereignty in a more radical form than the theorists of the social contract had envisioned. Nor was the concept of popular sovereignty confined to the delegation of legislative power alone. For the framers also deployed another, more immediate, but equally powerful application of this concept to assure not only the legitimacy but the deep legality of the Constitution itself.

In the strictest sense, the convention was an extra-constitutional device, unknown to either the Articles of Confederation or the state constitutions. That, in fact, was how the Anglo-American tradition ordinarily understood conventions of any kind. The Convention Parliament of 1688, for example, was a defective meeting of Parliament, made necessary by the flight of James II, but for that very reason extra-constitutional because it was the king who had to summon Parliament and approve its acts. The American convention of 1787 did have important sources of legitimacy. Twelve of the thirteen state legislatures had appointed delegates, and Congress had also endorsed the meeting. Moreover, the convention could not promulgate a constitution of its own authority; it could only propose, not conclusively act. But imposing hurdles remained. Amendments to the Articles of Confederation required approval by nine states in Congress and ratification by all thirteen legislatures, and Rhode Island had balked at attending the convention itself. For the Constitution to be approved in the orthodox manner, Congress would have to consent to its own demise, the state legislatures would have to accept new limitations on their own authority, and Rhode Island, a province that had always pluckily pursued its own ways, would have to relent.

Rhode Island's expected opposition was a sufficient reason to abandon the amending rules of the Articles and devise a fresh solution to the other potential obstacles as well. The solution the framers adopted involved a direct appeal to popular sovereignty. The convention would submit the Constitution to Congress, which would then transmit it intact and unrevised to the state legislatures. But the latter were asked only to arrange for the election of ratification conventions. Adoption of the Constitution would require approval by nine state conventions. The framers and their supporters, who seized the label of Federalists, insisted on one other crucial point. The state conventions would have to approve or reject the Constitution in its entirety.

This resort to popularly elected ratification conventions combined political ingenuity with a theoretically potent method of distinguishing a constitution from ordinary law. In one sense, the idea that a convention would provide a purer expression of the popular will than the legislature was a legal fiction. But a convention that would meet only once and then forever disband could not be accused of having the same incentives to protect its own privileges as a legislature. More important, the resort to a convention would free the Constitution of its legal vulnerability under the *leges posteriores* doctrine. If the Constitution secured only legislative approval, later sessions of the state legislatures could, in theory, lawfully violate its provisions, the Supremacy Clause notwithstanding. The potent fiction that the people had directly assented to the Constitution obviated that possibility.

V. RATIFICATION

The Convention adjourned on September 17. Of the forty-two delegates still present, all but three – George Mason and Edmund Randolph of Virginia and Elbridge Gerry of Massachusetts – signed the completed Constitution. A number of delegates then repaired to the Continental Congress in New York, the Constitution's first stop en route to ratification. There the framers' strategy was briefly challenged by Richard Henry Lee, who thought that the Constitution should be amenable to amendment by Congress, and accordingly introduced a number of changes he would like to see made. Madison and other supporters of the Constitution adamantly resisted this suggestion. By altering the text, they argued, Congress would also become a partial author of the Constitution, which might imply that the amending procedures of the Articles of Confederation should be invoked. Madison and other Federalists beat back Lee's challenge, but his idea that the Constitution should not be approved unless it were amended became a leading strategy of its Anti-Federalist opponents.

On September 28, 1787, Congress sent the Constitution on to the state legislatures. Over the coming months, twelve of the thirteen legislatures endorsed the proposed ratification procedures. Rhode Island, predictably, was the exception, but in the name of popular sovereignty it went the other states one better by submitting the Constitution to a referendum that roundly voted for its rejection. But the discussions and decisions of these conventions were also only the culmination of a broader public debate that began as soon as the Constitution was published. Nearly a year passed before the final states of New York and North Carolina, both dominated by Anti-Federalists, held their conventions. In the meantime, the Constitution was subjected to prolonged public examination.

Many Federalists were content to defend the Constitution on the most general lines possible, contrasting its promise of revitalized national government with the manifest feebleness (or "imbecility") of Congress. For their part, many Anti-Federalists seemed to assume that utter depravity was the normal condition of mankind and that self-aggrandizing officials would manipulate every loosely worded clause of the Constitution to acquire despotic power at the expense of the rights of the states and the liberties of their citizens. Such fears echoed the language with which colonial leaders of the 1760s and 1770s had interpreted the motives underlying British policy, a language that still resonated deeply within American political culture. But the most compelling Anti-Federalist criticisms grappled honestly with the significant ways in which the Constitution departed from the orthodox understandings of 1776.

Foremost among these criticisms was the idea that the Constitution would lead to a *consolidation* of all real power in the national government. Consolidation, as Anti-Federalists used the term, had two meanings. One was that the national government would be consolidated simply because it could act directly on the people, independently of the states. The other invoked the image of a relentless competition between the governments in which power would ineluctably move from the states to the nation. If the states survived at all, they would be hollow jurisdictions, lacking the resources to compete effectively with the national government for the loyalty of the people. To support this conclusion, Anti-Federalists tried to identify all the clauses of the Constitution that would aid and abet this shift in power. The most ominous were the clauses of Article I, Section 8 giving Congress broad authority to raise its own revenues, to command an army independent of state control, and to "make all laws necessary and proper" for implementing its enumerated powers. Coupled with the Supremacy Clause of Article IV, this "sweeping clause," as it was often called, seemed to assure that the power of Congress would infallibly trump the reserved authority of the states.

That power would be wielded, Anti-Federalists also argued, by two legislative houses that would owe little to their respective constituents. The Senate appeared to be the most dangerous institution of all. Notwithstanding its election by the state legislatures, its members' extended six-year terms, free from instruction or recall, would render them politically independent. Moreover, the Senate posed a particular affront to the orthodox idea of separation of powers. In addition to the legislative powers it jointly exercised with the House, it would enjoy the executive powers it shared with the president and the judicial authority to try impeachments – which it could abuse to shield malefactors content to do its evil bidding. This concentration of the three forms of power in one institution met the very definition of tyranny laid down by the celebrated French political philosopher, Montesquieu, in his canonical *The Spirit of the Laws*. Nor did Anti-Federalists think it likely that the popularly elected House would counter the "aristocratic" Senate. Compared to the state legislatures, the scale of representation in the House seemed so large as to fray every bond of "sympathy" that should unite lawmakers with their constituents. For his part, the president would find it in his interest to collude with the Senate. Similarly, federal judges serving on good behavior would develop their own incentives to favor the claims of national governance over the states.

These criticisms were trenchant enough to merit serious answers. The greater difficulty faced by Anti-Federalists lay in the realm of political strategy. For one thing, their goals were not easily defined. Outright rejection of the Constitution meant continuation of a Confederation believed to be drifting into impotence. But there was no obvious way to alter the Constitution prior to its ratification. Failing to hold a convention or caucus of their own, Anti-Federalists could never agree on the changes they desired or the means to attain them. Some, like Edmund Randolph (who eventually returned to the Federalist fold), favored holding a second convention. Others came to prefer the idea of recommending that amendments to the Constitution be considered as soon as it was adopted. Whichever strategy they pursued, Anti-Federalists suffered from a lack of effective leadership. Their ranks did include such major revolutionary figures as Samuel Adams, Elbridge Gerry, George Clinton, Patrick Henry, Richard Henry Lee, and George Mason. But their efforts at coordination were few and feeble.

The Federalist campaign for ratification, by contrast, was highly coordinated. Their strategy was predicated on using early victories in states where they enjoyed decisive majorities to limit Anti-Federalist options in others where public opinion seemed more divided. By the new year of 1788, five states had ratified the Constitution over token opposition: Delaware, Georgia, New Jersey, Connecticut, and Pennsylvania. Serious Anti-Federalist opposition first appeared in Massachusetts, whose convention assembled in the early January dead of winter. Though Anti-Federalists enjoyed a potential majority, the Constitution's supporters gained the upper hand by courting the state's dominant political figure, John Hancock, and assenting to a variety of amendments to be proposed to the first Congress to meet after ratification. In the spring of 1788, South Carolina and Maryland also accompanied their ratifications of the Constitution with recommendations of amendments. That left the ninth and decisive vote for adoption to come from one of three states where Anti-Federalists had actual or potential majorities: New Hampshire (whose convention had met once but adjourned), Virginia, and New York.

While the Constitution made its circuit of the states, the public debate over its merits continued unabated. Perhaps the most influential Federalist positions were those developed by James Wilson, first at a public rally held in early October outside the Pennsylvania Statehouse where the convention had met, then in the ratification convention at Harrisburg in late November. As a known framer of the Constitution, Wilson's *public* (and published) statements in its support appeared authoritative in ways that other pseudonymous writings could not. Though hardly a populist in his politics, Wilson now emerged as the leading advocate of a new theory of popular sovereignty, which he deployed to rebut the argument that the Constitution was severely flawed both because it contained no declaration of rights and because it radically diminished the sovereignty of the states. Wilson's arguments on these points gave a new and more precise meaning to the idea that all government depended on a delegation of authority from the people. It would be dangerous to include a bill of rights in a constitution, he argued, if the provision made for the protection of freedom of speech or conscience, for example, could be read to imply that the national government had been given some authority to regulate those areas of behavior. In fact, Wilson observed, the national government had been given no such power; it was a government of limited, delegated authority only, with no claims to the plenary legislative powers formerly claimed by the state assemblies. But neither did it make sense to argue that the states had lost their former sovereignty, Wilson further asserted. In a popular government, sovereignty should not be regarded as an attribute of government. It was properly vested in the people, who retained at all times a right to allocate specific powers and duties to whichever level of government they wished to exercise them. The proclaimed supremacy of the Constitution may have altered this distribution of power between the national and state governments. But sovereignty, properly understood, was always vested in the people.

The most comprehensive defense of the Constitution was organized by Alexander Hamilton, who recruited first John Jay and then James Madison to join him under the pen-name Publius as co-authors of *The Federalist*. In eighty-five essays written between the early fall of 1787 and the spring of 1788, the authors first laid out a broad case for the necessity and advantages of a federal union fully capable of carrying out its assigned responsibilities and then turned to a sustained discussion of the composition and powers of each of the three departments of the national government. A veritable cottage industry of scholarly commentary has been dedicated to the best-known essays: Madison's argument about the superior merits of an extended national republic in *Federalist* 10, his recasting of the doctrine of separation of powers in *Federalist* 47–51, and Hamilton's argument for the judicial review of constitutionally dubious legislation in *Federalist* 78. But the authority of *The Federalist* also rests on the breadth of its examination of the Constitution, which has no parallel in the larger literature of the ratification debate, the special prestige of its authors, and the extent to which their essays reflected their deepest analyses of constitutionalism, federalism, and republicanism.

The two states where these arguments were most needed were Madison's Virginia and Hamilton's New York. The Virginia convention met first, in early June 1788. The New York convention, solidly dominated by Anti-Federalists who suspected Hamilton's authorship of *The Federalist* but found his reasoning unpersuasive, came to order at the end of the same month. Before either could vote, the second session of the New Hampshire convention provided the ninth vote necessary for the Constitution to take effect. But rejection by either populous Virginia or New York, obviously poised for major population growth, would seriously impair the new government from the start. In closely divided Virginia, Federalists led by Madison had to parry the rhetorical fireworks of Patrick Henry and the learned arguments of George Mason, as well as the anxieties of delegates from the Kentucky district upset by the Spanish closure of the Mississippi. Rather than risk rejection, Madison acceded to the Anti-Federalist insistence that the convention recommend a number of amendments to the Constitution. That concession produced an eight-vote majority for the Constitution, making Virginia the tenth state to ratify. In New York, by contrast, the Federalist minority, led by Hamilton, had no room for maneuver. It was the Anti-Federalists who had to decide, among themselves, whether the combined news from New Hampshire and Virginia warranted abandoning their strong opposition to the Constitution. On this issue, the Anti-Federalist ranks sundered, with more moderate delegates joining the beleaguered Federalists to produce a three-vote majority for ratification.

CONCLUSION

Could public opinion polls have been taken, a majority of the free American population might well have opposed the Constitution. Federalist success can be attributed to several factors. Their opponents' lack of coordination and effective leadership clearly was one; it stood in clear contrast to a Federalist movement that could summon the prestige of Washington and Benjamin Franklin as well as the political skills of Madison, Hamilton, Wilson, and other framers of the Constitution. Federalist domination of the press was another advantage. Just as impressive, however, was the skill with which the Federalists managed to limit the authoritative acts of the ratification conventions to a simple up or down vote on the Constitution in its entirety. Adoption of the Constitution would have been far more difficult had individual conventions made their acts of ratification contingent on the prior approval of amendments or insisted on summoning a second convention to improve on the first. Agreeing merely to recommend amendments to a future Congress gathered under the authority of the Constitution was a small price to pay to secure unequivocal acts of ratification. Many Federalists, in fact, denied they had made any explicit promise to pursue amendments.

Much of the credit for assuring that the First Federal Congress would even consider amendments belongs to Madison. Although intent on preventing any structural changes to the Constitution, he was willing to support the inclusion of additional articles affirming the recognition of fundamental rights. He did so, however, not because he believed that the omission of such articles was a genuine defect in the Constitution, but rather because the speedy adoption of amendments would reconcile well-meaning if misguided Anti-Federalists to the Constitution.

Taken together, the unequivocal nature of the ratification decision and the early attention to amendments gave the Constitution an immediate legitimacy that trumped whatever residual doubts remained about the strict legality of the proceedings of 1787–88. This was no small achievement. It meant, among other things, that the numerous controversies over constitutional *interpretation* that accompanied so many of the political disputes of the Early Republic crested below the level of challenging the constitutional regime itself. For decades to come, the American propensity to convert political disputes into constitutional controversies would be safely contained within the four corners of the original text. It would take the intractable and ultimately irresolvable issue of slavery to produce a fundamental challenge to the decisions of the late 1780s.

15

THE CONSOLIDATION OF THE EARLY FEDERAL SYSTEM, 1791–1812

SAUL CORNELL AND GERALD LEONARD

To celebrate the ratification of the new Federal Constitution, Federalist Francis Hopkinson composed "The Raising: A New Song for Federal Mechanics." In one verse he exhorted America's artisans to rally to the Constitution's standard. In Hopkinson's musical ode, citizens mustered with their tools, not muskets.

> COME muster, my lads, your mechanical tools,
> Your saws and your axes, your hammers and rules;
> Bring your mallets and planes, your level and line,
> And plenty of pins of American pine:
> *For our roof we will raise, and our song still shall be*
> *Our Government firm, and our citizens free.*[1]

Hopkinson also helped stage Philadelphia's elaborate procession in honor of the Constitution. As many as 5,000 marchers representing the city's many trades, professions, and different religious denominations assembled to demonstrate their support. Similar but less elaborate parades and celebrations occurred in other cities and towns. These carefully staged rituals were designed to symbolize harmony and promote consensus in the wake of the sometimes bitter ratification debates. Although these public displays of consensus never managed to obliterate fully the lingering traces of Anti-Federalist antagonism and suspicion, the rapid acceptance of the Constitution was nothing short of remarkable given the rancor of the ratification process. Even in Rhode Island, a strongly Anti-Federalist state that would not ratify the Constitution for almost two years, the new language of American constitutionalism permeated public discourse. Thus,

[1] Francis Hopkinson, "The Raising: A New Song for Federal Mechanics," in *The Miscellaneous Essays and Occasional Writings*. 3 vols. (Philadelphia, 1792), 2: 320; see also "A Grand Procession in Honor of Ratification," *Maryland Journal* (Baltimore) May 6, 1788 in Bernard Bailyn, ed., *The Debate On the Constitution*. 2 vols. (New York, 1993), 2:430–38.

one commentator observed that in Rhode Island "every friend of liberty" was "putting on the appearance of Federalism." He was pleased to report that "the conversation of the inhabitants is carried out in a style of Federal purity, and a man may as well expect to make a tour of Europe without any knowledge of the French, as to be distinguished in company without a smattering of the Federal dialect."[2]

In the view of poet, politician, and essayist Joel Barlow, a properly framed constitution "ought to serve not only as a guide to the legislative body, but as a political grammar to all the citizens. The greatest service to be expected from it is, that it should concentrate the maxims, and form the habits of thinking, for the whole community." Although he too viewed the new Federal Constitution as central to the way Americans understood government and law, William Manning, a tavern keeper from Billerica, Massachusetts, cast a more suspicious eye toward the new frame of government, comparing it to "a Fiddle, with but few Strings, but so that the ruling Majority could play any tune upon it they pleased." Manning's musical metaphor differed from Hopkinson's in stressing discord, not harmony. The tavern keeper's description of the Constitution expressed the fears of many who worried that the Constitution had been designed to favor the interests of the few at the expense of the many. It also captured the contingent and open-ended quality of America's new constitutional text.[3]

Barlow was correct to assert that the new Constitution provided a common language. The existence of a common constitutional language did not establish a consensus on how the new document should be interpreted. The Constitution had sketched the basic outlines of American government, but there was much to be worked out before the shape of the nation's legal and political system could be deemed settled. Battles over how to interpret the Constitution began almost immediately. They would prove to be as divisive as the struggle over ratification itself had been.

To understand the era's battles over the meaning of the new Constitution we must unite the traditional court-centered narrative focused on landmark Supreme Court decisions with a constitutional history from the bottom up that includes the voices of artisans, backcountry farmers, women, and slaves. Until quite recently, constitutional history has been written as if judges and politicians were the only actors on the stage. The result has been an essentially Whig and Federalist narrative that details the rise of the courts as the preeminent force in shaping the process of constitutional interpretation and

[2] *United States Chronicle* (Providence), July 17, 1788.

[3] Joel Barlow, "A Letter to the National Convention of France on the Defects in the Constitution of 1791" (New York, 1793), 30; William Manning's "The Key of Libberty," *William and Mary Quarterly* 13 (1956), 234.

the creation of an effective national government. But constitutional debate was not restricted to the new nation's courts or legislative chambers. Americans debated these issues in taverns, staged elaborate protests in the streets, and occasionally took up arms to defend their own vision of constitutionalism. In the case of dramatic events, such as the Whiskey Rebellion, all of these venues were pressed into service by Americans. Nor was the Whiskey Rebellion the only occasion in which constitutional ferment spilled out of doors. Gabriel's Rebellion (1800), a slave uprising in Richmond, Virginia, revealed how constitutional ideas passed easily from masters to their slaves. Finally, the struggles of New Jersey women, who exercised the franchise for a single generation, further complicate efforts to depict constitutional debate in the Early Republic as simply an argument between Jefferson and Madison on the one side and Hamilton and the Federalists on the other.

We must also realize how different the substantive concerns of modern American constitutional law are from those that gripped the Early Republic. Since the 1950s, American constitutional law has been dominated by the rights revolution. Certainly the language of rights was important to the men and women of the Founding generation, but issues of rights were usually bound up in other matters – notably fights over the meaning of federalism and popular sovereignty.

Federalism, the structure of power relations among localities, states, and the new federal government, was not some abstract philosophical principle, but a palpable reality that shaped virtually every political issue of the day. For Joel Barlow, the greatest accomplishment of American constitutionalism lay precisely in linking together the concepts of representative government and federalism. The development of the federal principle was, in his view, one of the greatest achievements that "political experience has yet brought to light." Federalism was "the only resource that nature has offered us at least in the present state of political science for avoiding at once the two dangerous extremes of having the republic too great for any equitable administration within, or too small for security without."[4]

The question of federalism had been hotly contested between Federalists and Anti-Federalists during ratification. Anti-Federalists complained bitterly that their opponents had co-opted the name Federalist. In the view of Elbridge Gerry, a prominent Massachusetts Anti-Federalist, "those who were called antifederalists at the time complained that they had injustice done them by the title, because they were in favor of a Federal Government,

[4] Joel Barlow, "To His Fellow Citizens, of the United States" in Charles S. Hyneman and Donald S. Lutz, eds., *American Political Writing During the Founding Era, 1760–1805*. 2 vols.

and the others were in favor of a national one." Anti-Federalists believed that their opponents, the Federalists, were consolidationists, centralizers bent on reducing state governments to mere ciphers in a powerful new nation-state. The most astute Federalists, including Madison, were forced to admit that the new government was something novel, a system "partly national; partly federal." Such a concept was difficult for many Americans to comprehend. Americans had recognized a functional division in authority between state and federal government since independence, but the issue of divided sovereignty was more complicated. According to traditional constitutional theory sovereignty was indivisible. The notion that the individual states and the new federal government were each sovereign within their own particular sphere of authority was not only difficult to comprehend, but was destined to create conflicts between the states and the new federal government. How would these two boundaries be kept distinct, and who would police disputes in cases where there was a conflict between the states and the new federal government?[5] Virtually every important conflict in the first two decades after adoption of the Constitution was shaped by the struggle to define the nature of the federal system and the battle over whose interpretation of the Constitution would shape law and policy.

The fate of federalism was closely linked to the fight over popular sovereignty. As the staunch Federalist and Massachusetts Supreme Court Chief Justice Theophilus Parsons noted in *Ainslie v. Martin*, the American Revolution had transformed the nature of sovereignty. "The throne was vacant," Parsons declared, "but the people, in their political character, did not look after another family to reign; nor did they establish a new dynasty; but assumed to themselves, as a nation, the sovereign power." Americans might all agree with Parsons in the abstract, but in practice there were serious divisions within American society over how the will of the people would be collected and expressed in matters of constitutional interpretation.[6] Would popular action in the streets retain its status as fully "constitutional" action, perhaps empowering the constitutional agency even of women and African Americans? Or would constitutional meaning rest in the hands of a national elite, only nominally answering to a constricted electorate? In addition to the rifts dividing members of the nation's elite over questions such as federalism, a profound division existed between proponents of a popular constitutionalism and those who sought to restrain the radical potential of unchecked democracy.

[5] Elbridge Gerry, "Speech" in Joseph Gales, ed., *Debates and Proceedings in the First Congress* (Washington, DC., 1834), *Annals of Congress*, August 1789, 731.

[6] *Ainslie* v. *Martin*, 9 Mass. 454 (1813).

I. A BILL OF RIGHTS: LIBERTY, REPUBLICANISM, AND FEDERALISM IN EARLY AMERICAN CONSTITUTIONAL THOUGHT

Ratification of the Constitution did not resolve the basic tensions that had divided Federalists from Anti-Federalists during the ratification debates. Many of the issues simply spilled over into the first federal elections. Federalists defeated their former opponents handily and obtained an impressive majority in the First Congress. Nevertheless, divisions continued to widen, framing the initial conflicts over the meaning of the new Constitution.

The First Federal Congress was faced with a host of questions that required its members to flesh out many features of the new government's structure. Among the questions taken up by Congress were symbolic issues, such as the appropriate form of address for the new president, but also structural matters, such as the removal power of the president. The First Congress also had to complete the design of the federal court system. Most crucial of all Congress had to deal with the question of amendments to the Constitution.

Ironically, the task of drafting amendments fell to James Madison, originally an opponent of the idea of a Bill of Rights. Madison pared the lengthy list of amendments recommended by state ratification conventions to a dozen provisions. The first two amendments dealt with congressional salaries and apportionment, but were not ratified by the states in these years (the salaries amendment finally made it through in 1992). The ten that followed were all adopted by the states and later came to be known as the Bill of Rights. They included protections against the national government's violation of basic individual rights, such as freedom of religion, and provided explicit affirmations of other rights that were more civic in nature, such as the right of the people to form juries, to assemble, and to bear arms in a well-regulated militia. The amendments also addressed structural questions, such as federalism and unenumerated rights retained by the people and the states.

The debate over the language of what would become the Second Amendment demonstrates the contested nature of the original Bill of Rights. It also illustrates the degree to which federalism shaped the language of rights and the structure of constitutional discourse in the First Congress. The Constitution gave to Congress the power to organize, arm, and discipline the militia, but reserved to the states the right to appoint officers and train the militia according to standards set by Congress. The former Anti-Federalist Elbridge Gerry expressed some concern that Madison's original language, particularly the clause allowing conscientious objectors to avoid military service, might be used as a pretext to disarm the militia. Gerry reminded members of Congress of the indispensable role that a militia played in a republican government: "What, sir, is the use of the militia? It is to prevent the establishment of a standing army, the bane of liberty." The importance of this issue was difficult to overstate. "Whenever government[s] mean to invade the rights and liberties of the people," Gerry commented, "they always attempt to destroy the militia, in order to raise an army upon their ruins." The proposal to exempt individuals with religious scruples from having to serve in the militia struck Gerry as a potentially dangerous grant of authority to the federal government that would create "an opportunity to the people in power to destroy the constitution itself." Giving the federal government the power to "declare who are those religiously scrupulous, and prevent them from bearing arms" would allow it to decide who might be excluded from the militia, effectively giving it the capacity to disarm the militia altogether. With the militia rendered ineffective, it would be an easy matter to create a powerful standing army and crush any resistance to federal power.[7]

Although Gerry was alarmed by the prospect that the original language of the Second Amendment would have allowed the militia to be disarmed, he showed no concern that the same power might be used to disarm individuals or challenge the common law right of self-defense. It was the right to bear arms in a well-regulated militia that was at issue. The threat that the new Federal Constitution posed to the militia had been discussed at great length during ratification, but relatively little attention had been paid to an individual right to own guns outside this context. During ratification there had been a few scattered protests that articulated a more expansive right to own guns for hunting and other non-military purposes. The most influential example of this strain of Anti-Federalist thought was the *Dissent of the Pennsylvania Minority*, which singled out a right to hunt for constitutional protection. The right to hunt was one of many in the *Dissent*'s extensive laundry list of rights requiring explicit protection. Federalist Noah Webster confessed that he could barely contain his laughter when he pondered such Anti-Federalist hyperbole. Webster's dismissal of the logic of the Anti-Federalist position was emblematic of a different Federalist approach to protecting liberty. Indeed, he mocked the Anti-Federalist's over-reliance on written bills of rights. If one adhered to the Anti-Federalist approach, he concluded, one would have needed to affirm the following:

> That Congress shall never restrain any inhabitant of America from eating and drinking, at seasonable times, or preventing his lying on his left side, in a long winter's night, or even on his back, when he is fatigued by lying on his right.

[7] Elbridge Gerry, "Speech in Congress," *Annals of Congress*, 17 August 1789, 778.

"You may just as well ask for a clause," Webster added, "giving license for every man to till his own land and milk his own cows."[8]

Webster's rejoinder to the *Dissent* reveals an important but often neglected context for understanding the meaning of rights in the Founding era. While modern Americans have come to view the Bill of Rights and the courts as the primary means of protecting liberty, Americans in the Founding era, most importantly Anti-Federalists, looked to other sources to protect their rights. Many rights were not explicitly protected in bills of rights. The New York constitution did not even have a bill of rights. The common law provided one important source for guarding liberty. Americans also counted more on their legislatures to safeguard liberty. Rather than look to judges as sentinels guarding freedom, Americans were more apt to look to local juries as the proper guardians of rights. Finally, there was broad agreement that federalism was central to the preservation of liberty. The division of power within the federal system was an indispensable mechanism for checking power and protecting liberty.

Faith in the ideal of federalism did not, however, mean there was a consensus on how power ought to be split between the states and the federal government to achieve this goal. Anti-Federalists believed that the greatest threat to liberty came from a distant government; in contrast, Federalists believed that the individual states themselves posed the most serious threats to liberty. But each side at least recognized that the survival of liberty required an effective division of power between these two spheres of authority.

While modern Americans look to the first eight Amendments to the Federal Constitution as the core freedoms protected by the Bill of Rights, Anti-Federalists thought that the Tenth Amendment, which focused on federalism, was the most important of all those proposed. When Congress debated the wording of this key provision of the Bill of Rights Anti-Federalists fought to restrict the powers of the new government to those "expressly delegated" by the Constitution. This effort to limit federal power was resoundingly defeated, and the language of the amendment was distinctly Federalist in spirit: "the powers not delegated to the United States by the Constitution, nor prohibited by it to the States, are reserved to the States respectively, or to the people." The failure to limit federal power to those "expressly delegated" prompted some Anti-Federalists to complain that the Bill of Rights was utterly useless. Without structural changes in the nature of federalism, Anti-Federalists feared that any protections for

[8] [Noah Webster,] "America," in Gary McDowell and Colleen Sheenan, eds., *Friends of the Constitution: Writings of the Other Federalists* (Indianapolis, 1998), 175–76.

liberty embodied in the Bill of Rights would be circumvented easily by the federal courts and Congress.

II. HAMILTONIANISM AND THE REPUBLICAN OPPOSITION

Beginning with the First Congress, the Federalists' program for establishing a nationalist Constitution was shaped by economic policies designed by Alexander Hamilton to place the new national government on a solid financial basis and to bind the wealthy to the new nation by aligning their economic interests with those of the new government. Federalist state-building was not only nationalist in design but self-consciously styled on the British model. The goal was to emulate Britain's fiscal/military state apparatus by creating a national bank, a funded national debt, and an effective military establishment and to surround them with a political culture in which deference, not democracy, was the cornerstone of political life. Although attacked as a crypto-monarchist, Hamilton's vision was not anti-republican. His vision of the power of the federal government was not unbounded. He believed that the powers of the federal government were limited, but within its sphere of authority its powers were considerable.

Opposition to Hamilton's program brought elements of the old Anti-Federalist coalition into league with disaffected Federalists. Together these disparate groups helped form the Republican movement. Given that Hamilton's economic program was partly inspired by the English "court" model of Sir Robert Walpole and his successors, it is not surprising that the opposition to it would draw liberally on the potent oppositional rhetoric of English radical Whig ("Country") ideology. Opponents attacked financial corruption and the threat posed by a powerful and unresponsive government. The critique was not, however, simply a tired rehash of the Old "Country" critique of political corruption. Opponents of Hamilton recast this language and translated it into a distinctly American idiom. The key transformation was the new emphasis on federalism.

One of the most outspoken opponents of Hamilton's program was the Virginian John Taylor, who described the threat posed by the Federalist system in forceful terms: "The funding system was intended to effect, what the bank was contrived to accelerate. 1. Accumulation of great wealth in a few hands. 2. A political moneyed engine. 3. A suppression of the republican state assemblies, by depriving them of political importance, resulting from the imposition and dispensation of taxes."[9] The ultimate goal, according

[9] John Taylor, *An Enquiry into the Principles and Tendency of Certain Public Measures*, (Philadelphia, 1794), 85–87.

to Taylor, was to reduce the state assemblies to mere ciphers in a consolidated system of government. State legislatures, the only truly representative bodies in the new federal system, would be rendered impotent by the machinations and manipulations of the paper banking interest.

William Manning formulated his own democratic critique of Federalist constitutionalism. The tavern keeper was inspired to author his own attack on Federalist economic policy after "reading the Many Altercations proposals & Disputes in the publick papers about funding & the Manner of paying the Continental & State Debts." Manning believed that Hamilton's policies had doubly injured the people. Not only had the Secretary of the Treasury's policies provided a windfall for speculators but new taxes enacted to pay off the speculators bore down hardest on the common people. "It would," he wrote, "Eventually prove the Destruction of our Dear bought Libertyes & of all the State Governments." Manning shared Taylor's concern that Federalist economic policy would undermine federalism and create a consolidated national government dedicated to the interests of the few.[10] This critique was delivered with a more populist slant: "Those that have got the publick Securityes for a trifel their will be a formadale body of powerfull Men" who would easily "Combine in opposition" and work to undermine "the Rights of Mankind." Manning believed that the Federal Constitution had facilitated this process by establishing a government "at Such a Distance from the Influence of the Common people" that the wealthy "think their Interests & Influence will always be the gratest Sway." It was precisely because the state governments were more responsive to the popular will that the wealthy desired to weaken state power.

For the emerging Republican opposition, the various state legislatures would continue to function as deliberative bodies, collecting, refining, and focusing the voice of the people. True federalism could not rest on a system of coercion. Persuasion, not power, was the key to this approach to constitutionalism. In contrast to Federalists, who looked to a strong military/fiscal state capable of using coercion to maintain order, Republicans championed a state-centered vision of federalism that looked to a public sphere of political debate to cement the new nation together. Republican theorists waxed eloquent about the role of public opinion in a republic. The notion of a public sphere, in which citizens debated ideas openly, was essential to this vision of constitutionalism. The creation of Democratic-Republican societies and of an effective network of newspapers was vital to the integrity of the public sphere. This decentralized vision of power fit well with Republican theories of federalism.

[10] William Manning, "'Measures so Glareingly Unjust': A Response to Hamilton's Funding Plan by William Manning," *William and Mary Quarterly* 46 (1989), 320, 322.

Still, there was some division within the ranks of Republicans over how much this public sphere ought to be controlled by elites. John Taylor's vision of a state-centered federal system was shaped by a conservative and essentially elitist vision of republicanism in which the state legislatures would comprise a refined version of the popular will mediated by members of the gentry. Manning, by contrast, espoused a more democratic vision of federalism in which representatives would be drawn from the ranks of the "laboring sort" rather than planter or mercantile elites. Manning also hoped that his proposals for a national Laboring Society (open to all free males over the age of twenty-one who labored for a living) and a reinvigorated democratic press would allow the "laboring sort" to shape public opinion.

Leading Federalists, meanwhile, condemned the Democratic-Republican "Societies" altogether. Washington denounced the clubs as "self-created societies" that corrupted, not revitalized, the political process. For Federalists the opposition exemplified the continuing dangers posed by faction and mobocracy. The opposition, they argued, was merely carrying forward a destructive, Anti-Federalist agenda.

III. THE WHISKEY REBELLION, THE CONSTITUTIONALISM OF THE CROWD, AND THE LIMITS OF RESISTANCE TO FEDERAL POWER

The Hamiltonian economic program included a series of tax increases that prompted protests and armed resistance on the part of farmers in western Pennsylvania and Kentucky. The most violent and sustained popular protest since Independence, the Whiskey Rebellion highlighted the fragility of the new federal system. How could the new nation deal with the powerful and persistent forces of localism? For Federalists the answer was simple: force. Federalists blamed the uprising on the Democratic-Republican societies for fomenting discord. For them, the Whiskey Rebellion demonstrated the dangers of excessive democracy and provided a sobering reminder of the necessity of a strong central government to counteract powerful centripetal forces that threatened to pull the nation apart.

For the most radical voices within the Republican opposition, most notably the Whiskey Rebels themselves, even a state-centered theory of federalism failed to provide adequate local autonomy. For radical localists, the individual state governments were still too far removed from the localities to enjoy legitimacy and could never represent their interests effectively. The people under the new Federal Constitution were hardly better off than under British rule. In contrast to members of the Republican elite, these radicals rejected the authority of both state and federal governments and asserted the right to resort to extra-legal crowd action to preserve the autonomy of localities. Plebeian radicals also continued to embrace the symbols and tactics of the revolutionary tradition, erecting liberty poles, and tarring and feathering excise men. Nor did radicals limit their opposition to symbolic protests; they mustered themselves as local militia units and resisted efforts to collect federal taxes. While the rebels hoped that local militias could serve as a means of checking federal power, the radical potential of the militia was undermined when Washington mobilized the "well regulated" state militias against these local units.

For Republicans, the Washington administration's decision to use force to put down the Whiskey Rebellion confirmed the nefarious designs of Hamilton and his allies. But although united in opposition to Federalist policies, they were divided on what forms of protest were legitimate within the new federal system. Most Republican leaders sympathized with the grievances of the rebels, but few were willing to grant constitutional legitimacy to extra-legal crowd action; the notion that local militia units might act outside the authority of the state would have struck leading Republicans as an exercise in mobocracy, not democracy. Mainstream Republican constitutional theory accepted that public meetings and the press might be used to rally opposition, but fell short of sanctioning crowd action or armed rebellion as an appropriate means to challenge unjust government action.

The militia was only one means by which popular constitutionalism was invoked during the Whiskey Rebellion. Republicans hoped to use local juries as a check on federal authority. Federalists bypassed this potential obstacle by using federal courts to prosecute participants in the western Pennsylvania disturbances. Republicans strenuously opposed this policy. Once again, they argued, Federalists were undermining true federalism and substituting a single national standard dictated by a powerful centralized authority.

IV. THE SEDITION ACT AND THE COMPACT THEORY OF FEDERALISM

No part of the Federalist agenda did more to inflame political passions than did the passage of the Alien and Sedition Acts. Hostilities among European powers during the 1790s threatened to embroil the United States in conflict. Consequent fears about the threat of foreign and domestic subversion led the Federalists to pass legislation making it more difficult to become a citizen and making seditious libel a federal crime. Federalists defended the Alien and Sedition Acts as necessary to prevent foreign agents, radical refugees, and their domestic allies from undermining American republicanism.

They pointed out that the Sedition Act did not limit speech but actually strengthened the protections for speech beyond the common law understanding of seditious libel, which did not allow truth as a defense. Republicans, however, found in these acts – especially the Sedition Act – decisive confirmation of their fears of the Federalists' zeal for centralization and contempt for liberty. Concerned in particular by the Sedition Act's curbs on speech, they objected that it was beyond the national government's limited list of enumerated powers and took a dramatic step toward creating a consolidated government. The most innovative legal thinkers within the ranks of republicanism asserted that the American Revolution had swept away such monarchical notions as seditious libel. At the very minimum, they argued, the limited government created by the Constitution did not incorporate a common law notion of seditious libel.

In their attempts to resist the Federalist offensive, opposition theorists found themselves formulating new meanings for federalism and for the constitutional function of dissent that would irrevocably alter the course of American law. In challenging the constitutionality of the Sedition Act, for example, Republicans inaugurated a new phase of dissenting constitutional theory. Once appeals to the legislature and the courts – the normal political and legal mechanisms for challenging the Alien and Sedition laws – failed, what recourse was left to resist tyranny? Republicans were forced to think of new ways to protect individual liberty and restore the federal government to its proper sphere of authority. They turned to the ideal of federalism. After all, the principles of federalism had been central to opposition thought since ratification. The structure of the federal system had always been seen as the final guarantor of individual liberty.

But although this belief was a cardinal tenet of dissenting constitutionalism, relatively little attention had been devoted to exploring how federalism's checking function would actually operate in practice. Exactly how would the will of the people be collected and invoked? Would the judiciary exercise the final check when a corrupt faction gained control of the federal government and threatened the liberties of the people? The state legislatures? Special conventions of the people of the states? The state militias?

Republican elites favored a states' rights view of federalism. The two most important public expressions of the new approach were Thomas Jefferson's Kentucky Resolutions and James Madison's Virginia Resolutions. Each drew on the anti-consolidationist rhetoric that had defined dissenting constitutional discourse since ratification. In each case, Jefferson and Madison asserted that the protection of individual liberty depended on preserving the balance of power between the states and the federal government. States' rights and individual rights continued to be linked together in oppositional constitutional discourse. The two documents also elaborated a compact theory of federalism. The Kentucky Resolutions affirmed "that the several states composing the United States of America are not united on the principle of unlimited submission to their general government." A corollary of this position was the view that "as in all other cases" involving a "compact among parties having no common judge, *each party has an equal right to judge for itself, as well of infractions as of the mode and measure of redress*." Jefferson's original draft of the Kentucky Resolution had called for state nullification of unconstitutional acts of Congress, but this language was omitted from the final version adopted by the Kentucky legislature. Asserting the right to judge infringements, even without asserting the right to nullify laws, did appear to give individual states a right to determine for themselves the constitutionality of federal laws.[11]

Madison's more temperate response in the Virginia Resolution did not assert an individual state right, but noted that in extraordinary cases, when the Constitution's safeguards had broken down, the states "have a right, and are duty bound to interpose for arresting the progress of the evil." By invoking the right of the states, not individual states, and employing the vague concept of interposition, Madison avoided language that would suggest the right of an individual state to nullify an unconstitutional law. But the Virginia Resolution shared with Jefferson's Kentucky Resolution an emphasis on the compact theory of union. Madison declared that it was the intentions of the states in ratifying the Constitution that controlled the meaning of the text. Madison's theory not only placed a states' rights view of federalism at the heart of Republican constitutional theory, but it gave additional emphasis to the original intent of the ratifiers of the Constitution as the authoritative source of meaning when interpreting it.

The efforts of the Kentucky and Virginia legislatures at redress were rebuffed by the other states' legislatures, which were mostly under Federalist control. A second set of resolutions was drawn up, and in the Kentucky Resolutions of 1799 the term "nullification" was reintroduced. Asserting that the individual states could judge issues of constitutionality, the resolution also affirmed that in extreme circumstances nullification was the rightful remedy. The concept of nullification was tempered by the assertion that Kentucky would "bow to the laws of the Union" while continuing "to oppose, in a constitutional manner," unconstitutional acts." Nevertheless, Jefferson flirted with the notion of secession as the ultimate response to the tyranny of the Alien and Sedition Acts. Once again, Madison counseled

[11] "The Alien and Sedition Laws, and Virginia and Kentucky Resolutions" (Boston, 1798), 2.

Jefferson out of this radical position and helped avert a serious constitutional crisis.[12]

What united the Virginia and Kentucky approaches was the belief that individual state legislatures might serve as a means of collecting and organizing opposition. The most likely mechanisms for such action would be petitions to Congress and the amendment process. In 1788, Federalists reminded their opponents that the states would rally against any potential threat from the federal government. Madison himself had been one of the argument's most forceful proponents. More than ten years later he was restating this gloss on federalism in even more assertive terms: "The appeal was emphatically made," at that time "to the intermediate existence of the state governments between the people and the government." The individual states, Madison observed, "would descry the first symptoms of usurpation" and "sound the alarm to the public." In defending the rights of states, Madison was careful to note that in constitutional matters there was an important distinction between the ordinary acts of the legislature and the acts of the conventions that had ratified the Constitution. Madison, that is, was far more circumspect than Jefferson in asserting the rights of state legislatures to judge constitutional matters.[13]

V. THE NOT SO REVOLUTIONARY REVOLUTION OF 1800: UNDOING THE FEDERALIST LEGACY AND CREATING AN EMPIRE OF LIBERTY

The election of 1800, bitterly contested between Jefferson and Adams, resulted in a tie between Thomas Jefferson and his own running mate, Aaron Burr. Although the Constitution provided a mechanism for handling such disputes, at least two states mobilized their militias as a precautionary measure to guard against the possibility that Federalists might take advantage of the confusion and refuse to turn over the reins of government. After considerable maneuvering by supporters and opponents of Jefferson, a peaceful transfer of power was accomplished. In turn Jefferson's inaugural sounded a conciliatory note, proclaiming that, "We are all Republicans, we are all Federalists." But more than conciliation was at work here. Jefferson's inaugural address stated a set of ideals that would come to define his constitutional politics. He reaffirmed representation and federalism as the twin constitutional pillars of American government, even though the events of

[12] Thomas Jefferson, "The Kentucky Resolutions of 1799," in Jefferson Powell, ed., *Languages of Power: A Sourcebook of Early American Constitutional History* (North Carolina, 1991), 138.

[13] James Madison, "The Report of 1800" in Powell, *Languages of Power*, 146.

the previous decade had revealed profound disagreement over how to implement them and indeed over how to interpret the Constitution to preserve them.

Jefferson's election did not bring the revolutionary transformation that some had hoped for and others feared. Rather than attempt a radical transformation of the state the Federalists had built, Jefferson steered the nation on a path somewhere between Hamilton's federalism and that of the most radical members of his own coalition. Among his own supporters Jefferson was pressed from both sides. Southern conservatives wished to amend the Constitution to stifle federal power. The Old Republicans who dominated the Jeffersonian movement in Virginia wanted a prohibition on the reelection of the president, shorter terms for senators, limits on the government's borrowing power, and Congressional power to remove federal judges. None would occur. For more egalitarian democrats such as William Manning, meanwhile, Jefferson's election brought little of the hoped-for shift in power from the few to the many.

Avoiding both extremes, Jefferson's first Inaugural Address described America as a "chosen country, with room enough for our descendants to the thousandth and thousandth generation." To remain a virtuous yeoman republic and keep alive the ideal of an "empire of liberty," the nation would have to expand westward. Jefferson's yeoman republic had little room for African Americans or Indians. Although Jefferson always viewed Indians in a much more positive light than Africans, he predicted that tribal societies would either assimilate into white culture or face extinction.[14]

At the time Jefferson took office, more than a half-million Americans already lived west of the Appalachian Mountains. For many, access to the Mississippi River had become crucial to their economic prosperity. Pinckney's Treaty (1795) with Spain provided navigation rights to this vital economic corridor, but when the Spanish closed the port of New Orleans to American shipping in 1802, many in Congress were alarmed. In particular, Americans were concerned that Napoleon Bonaparte's effort to regain control of the port was part of a larger plan for reasserting French power in the region. Some Americans even advocated seizing the city. Jefferson preferred a negotiated settlement and sent a delegation to purchase the port from France, only to discover that Napoleon was willing to sell the entire territory of Louisiana to the United States. Jefferson was presented with an opportunity to double the size of the country. His only problem was that the Constitution did not expressly authorize the president to purchase new territory. To fulfill his dream of securing enough land for the

[14] Thomas Jefferson, "First Inaugural Address," in Merrill Peterson, ed., *Thomas Jefferson: Writings* (New York, 1984), 494.

nation to remain a yeoman republic, Jefferson relaxed some of his vaunted constitutional scruples. The purchase was not comparable to Hamilton's efforts to use latitudinarian constructions to expand the power of the federal government at the expense of states' rights, but Jefferson's action nevertheless forced him into a constitutional gray zone. Jefferson contemplated amending the Constitution to make the purchase possible, but feared Napoleon might withdraw the offer before such an amendment could be ratified.

Jefferson was also forced to confront the limits of his own egalitarian vision of the Constitution in providing for governance of the new territory. In the plan he had drafted for the Northwest Territories two decades earlier, Jefferson had been a model republican who sought to include the inhabitants of new territories as equals, not subjects. With respect to Louisiana, however, Jefferson's approach suggested that liberty was not something all men could be expected to exercise with equal discretion. In this regard, Jefferson's treatment of the non-Anglo population of Louisiana was in keeping with his views about African Americans and Native Americans.

Jefferson's goal on assuming the presidency had been to undo the legacy of a decade of Federalist power. Pursuing this goal meant modifying aspects of his own constitutional theory as he energetically used the power of the executive and the federal government to promote his vision of an empire of liberty. Nor would he change these positions during his second term. The Federalist opposition was far weaker than during Jefferson's first term, yet the political challenges he faced were in many respects even more formidable. In response, Jefferson exercised executive power ever more forcefully.

In 1808 Jefferson was poised to resolve the persistent quarrel over direct federal expenditures for internal improvements by backing a constitutional amendment that would have removed any lingering doubts about the constitutionality of such a program. Events in Europe rudely shunted the issue aside. American trade with both Britain and France had prospered hugely during the early phases of the conflict between the two nations. Each, however, had become desperate to exert economic pressure on their enemies and so set out to blockade each other's ports. The United States argued that neutral nations had a right to carry on non-military trade with both sides in the conflict, but neither Britain nor France honored the claim. By 1807 France had seized five hundred U.S. ships and Britain nearly a thousand. The United States also protested the British practice of boarding American ships in search of British nationals to impress (force) into naval service. The dispute reached a crisis in 1807 when the British ship, the *Leopard*, fired at an American Navy ship, the *Chesapeake*. In the skirmish three Americans were killed and eighteen wounded. The British abducted four American sailors who they charged were deserters from the Royal Navy.

Attempting to avoid military conflict with the British and French, Jefferson proposed an economic embargo. By keeping America's ships out of harm's way and depriving Britain and France of the economic benefits of trade, Jefferson hoped to exert pressure on both sides to respect the rights of neutrals. American exports fell from $108 million in 1807 to $22 million in 1808. The constitutionality of Jefferson's "peaceable coercion" was affirmed by a Massachusetts federal judge, the Federalist John Davis, but the embargo was exceedingly unpopular in New England and in seaport cities and was widely flouted by smugglers. To enforce the embargo along the Canadian border Jefferson had to use federal troops, a decision he had decried during the Whiskey Rebellion a decade earlier. Like his Federalist predecessors, Jefferson sought to expand the definition of treason and use it as a means to crush opposition to his administration's policies. The embargo divided Republicans and strengthened the fortunes of the Federalists, who had been in decline in most areas of the nation. In the 1808 presidential election, the Federalist candidate, Charles Pinckney, received three times as many votes as he had in 1804, doing particularly well in New England. Despite the strong showing in the Northeast, however, the Republican candidate James Madison handily defeated Pinckney by 122 to 47 electoral votes.

When war with Britain finally broke out in 1812, some Federalists appeared to outdo their Jeffersonian adversaries in defending the ideal of states' rights. In choosing to invoke the same concept of states' rights that had inspired Jeffersonians less than a decade before, Federalists demonstrated an important reality about the structure of American federalism. During the ratification of the Constitution, Federalists had assured Anti-Federalists that the states would serve as the final check on the power of the federal government. The recycling of these arguments in 1812 did not mean that Federalists had suddenly turned Anti-Federalist. Rather, this strain of states' rights thought was hard-wired into the structure of American federalism. Thus, when faced with the prospect of a draft, Federalist Daniel Webster did not shy away from asserting a right of states to interpose between the federal government and their citizens when individual liberty was threatened. Nor did Webster and other Federalists flinch about asserting the right of states to refuse to muster their militias and march them beyond the borders of their states.

Late in 1814, Federalists in New England met in Hartford to discuss their dissatisfaction with Republican policy. Some flirted with the idea of secession, as they had briefly in 1803, but the Hartford Convention stopped well short of advocating the break-up of the Union. Although New England Federalists had denounced the Virginia and Kentucky Resolutions, they now found themselves echoing many of the same ideas. The convention delegates proposed a series of constitutional amendments that would strengthen New England's influence in the Union. In particular, they wanted majorities of two-thirds to become mandatory for Congressional adoption of commercial regulations and declarations of war, and for the admission of new states. To weaken the South's influence in Congress, the Hartford Convention also called for a repeal of the three-fifths compromise that allowed Southerners to count a percentage of their slaves for the purposes of determining representation in the House. But the Hartford Convention's proposals were publicized at the same time as news of the Treaty of Ghent ending the war (December 1814) and America's impressive victory at the Battle of New Orleans (January 1815) were fueling a new sense of national pride. The Federalists' narrow sectionalism consequently appeared out of step with the public's new patriotic fervor. As a movement Federalists were irreparably damaged even in their stronghold of New England. Both their old consolidationism and their new secessionism were now equally discredited, opening the way for a new moderate Republicanism reconciled to the wise use of national power to preserve the republic.

VI. CONSTITUTIONAL OUTSIDERS AND THE LIMITS OF JEFFERSONIANISM

Notwithstanding heady proclamations of a "second American revolution," Thomas Jefferson's presidency is better cast as a story of caution and compromise, tendencies that grew in part out of domestic and international circumstance, in part out of limitations inherent in Jefferson's own political and constitutional vision. In important ways, those limitations had been evidenced well before Jefferson ever assumed the presidency and tell us much about the kind of republic Jefferson envisioned, the kind of citizenry he thought should influence it, and the kind of people who would endanger it. In 1786, for example, Jefferson had greeted news of Shays' Rebellion calmly; a decade later he had reacted just as mildly to the Whiskey Rebellion. But in 1800, when it came to Gabriel's Rebellion, Jefferson evinced little sympathy for the plight of Virginia's slaves nor much openness to their desires for freedom. Gabriel Prosser, a skilled Richmond artisan, had planned to seize the state arsenal and distribute weapons to all who would join to overthrow the system of slavery. He had planned to march under a banner with the words "death or liberty" emblazoned on it, taking Patrick Henry's Revolutionary credo and transforming it into a rallying cry for an uprising against slavery. Prosser had expected not just slaves but "poor white people" and other "democrats" to rally to his cause. All those whites deemed "Friendly to liberty," notably "Quakers, Methodists, and Frenchmen" were to be spared and the rest killed. Had his original plan not been frustrated by a torrential rain storm, Gabriel's Rebellion might have been the most successful slave uprising in American history. But the delay caused some slaves to waver, the plot was discovered, and its supporters hunted down. Twenty-seven conspirators were executed on the gallows.[15]

The rebellion pushed the Virginia legislature into a confrontation with the problem of slavery. Several proposals were debated, including outright abolition of slavery and the creation of colonies of freed slaves in the western part of the United States. Governor James Monroe broached the idea with the newly elected president. Jefferson rejected the idea. Elaborating the theme articulated in his Inaugural Address, Jefferson outlined America's future expansion in explicitly racist terms. "However our present interests may restrain us with our own limits," Jefferson wrote, it was necessary "to look forward to distant times, when our rapid multiplication will expand itself beyond those limits, & cover the whole northern, if not the southern continent, with a people speaking the same language, governed in similar forms, & by similar laws." Americans could not "contemplate with satisfaction either blot or mixture on that surface." Admittedly, it was not only a belief in the need to preserve his vision of a white yeoman republic that fueled Jefferson's hostility to using western lands to deal with the problem of slavery. Jefferson also shared Madison's view that corruption would be less likely to damage a large republic. "Had our territory been even a third only of what is," Jefferson observed to Nathaniel Niles, the outcome of the Sedition crises might have been radically different. Echoing Madison's argument in *Federalist 10*, Jefferson noted that "while frenzy and delusion like an epidemic, gained certain parts, the residue remained sound and untouched."[16] The West should be saved for virtuous white yeoman and not become a dumping ground for dangerous freedmen.

Gabriel's Rebellion demonstrated the limits of Republican thought. By using the language of American constitutionalism – particularly the potent rights discourse of the revolutionary heritage – as a way to rally support for their insurrection, Gabriel and his followers exposed a profound contradiction in American constitutional thought. The response of the Virginia legislature to the rebellion evinces its reluctant recognition not only of the danger posed by slavery, but of the particularly grave danger posed by slaves living in a society whose political ideology was founded on notions

[15] "Confessions of Ben, Alias Ben Woolfolk, 17 September 1800" in Gordon S. Wood, ed., revised ed., *The Rising Glory of America, 1760–1820* (Boston, 1990), 357–58.

[16] "President Thomas Jefferson to Governor James Monroe, 24 November 1801," in Wood, *Rising Glory*, 365. Jefferson to Nathaniel Niles, March 22, 1801, *The Thomas Jefferson Papers, Series 1. General Correspondence, 1651–1827*. Available online from the Library of Congress at http://memory.loc.gov/ammem/collections/jefferson_papers/index.html.

of liberty and equality. Ironically, the more elitist and deferential views of Federalists allowed them to be more inclusive than their Jeffersonian counterparts. Precisely because all men were not created equally as potential political actors, Federalists could accommodate blacks, Indians, and even propertied women in their vision of an expanding federal Republic.

Just as the principles of universal liberty and equality that animated the Revolution and republican constitution-making inspired Gabriel's rebels – as they had African American attempts to gain freedom in the Northern states after the Revolution – some American women also found in them a basis on which to seek more equitable treatment. Much as blacks in colonial America had experienced occasional, if temporary, opportunities to avoid permanent enslavement, some women in colonial America had enjoyed significant independence from male domination. Both in the ruptures of religious life caused by the Great Awakening and in the developing commercial life of the colonies, women had occasionally found meaningful avenues into public life and a public voice. The disruptions of the Revolution, as well, forced or freed many women to make political choices, including whether to follow their husbands into patriotism or loyalism. One might have expected the Revolution and constitution-making to have directed American society toward further freedom and equality for women. Many women indulged exactly that expectation, only to see it dashed.

Abigail Adams had greeted the Revolution in 1776 by calling on its leaders to "remember the ladies." In the 1790s, American women received with open arms and ready minds the egalitarian arguments of England's Mary Wollstonecraft and her French, post-Revolutionary counterparts. Widely read in the United States, Wollstonecraft and others were joined by a number of (mostly female) American feminists: essayist and playwright Judith Sargent Murray (a Federalist); novelist and journalist Charles Brockden Brown; and less prominent supporters in the newspapers or in the occasional public speech or demonstration. Priscilla Mason captured the fervor in 1793, observing in her salutatory oration to the Young Ladies' Academy of Philadelphia how men had "seized the scepter and the sword . . . [given] laws to society . . . denied women the advantage of a liberal education" and "doom'd the sex to servile or frivolous employments, on purpose to degrade their minds, that they themselves might hold unrivall'd, the power and pre-eminence they had usurped." Other women occasionally seized public space, taking to the streets in support of the French Revolution or attending the Philadelphia productions of feminist plays written by Murray and other women.[17]

[17] "The Salutatory Oration, Delivered by Miss Mason," in *The Rise and progress of the Young-Ladies' Academy of Philadelphia* (Philadelphia, 1794), 92.

Yet the only formal step that elevated the constitutional standing of women in these years was the temporary enfranchisement of women in one state. New Jersey's enfranchisement of women by constitution in 1776 was confirmed by statute in 1790, but was followed nowhere else. Even then, enfranchisement was taken to extend only to single women, not to *femes coverts* – daughters and wives under the legal protection and control of fathers and husbands – and was eliminated altogether in a general reform of the election laws in 1807 (a reform that also rolled back African-American voting rights).

While some women placed their faith in the promise of equality articulated by the Declaration of Independence and other statements of revolutionary ideology, gender inequality remained embedded in law and social practice. The ideology of republicanism adapted itself to this inequality by its celebration of Republican Motherhood. American men (and many women, for that matter) insisted that natural distinctions between the sexes implied a republican role for women legitimately different from that of men. Women were ill equipped to partake of public liberty and equality, according to this view, but they were ideally suited to preserving revolutionary principles in their capacity as mothers and educators of their children in moral and political virtue. Essential to this model of the republican family was the legal notion of the *feme covert*, which preserved the family by unifying ultimate authority and politico-legal personality – not to mention the property that underlay public power – in the husband and father.

The contest between emerging ideologies of gender equality and the traditional legal notion of *feme covert* emerged starkly in the Massachusetts case, *Martin* v. *Commonwealth* (1805), in which the son of a loyalist father sought to reclaim his mother's land that had been forfeited during the Revolution. James Sullivan, the state's Attorney General, rested his arguments on certain assumptions that demonstrate that ideas of gender equality had gained a tentative foothold in American legal thought. Although hardly widespread, the cultural availability of these arguments at this time is one measure of the change wrought by revolutionary ideology. Sullivan insisted that the mother had chosen freely to follow her husband out of Massachusetts and adhere to the British, rightly depriving her (and her heirs) of her land. She could not escape her membership in and obligations to the state by pointing to the authority of her husband, as the younger Martin now argued. Like all women, she bore the privileges and responsibilities of a constitutional actor in her own right. Her choice to withdraw from Massachusetts during the Revolution was hers alone.[18]

[18] *Martin* v. *Commonwealth*, 1 Mass 347 (1805).

But Sullivan lost. The court held that Martin's mother had been a *feme covert*. Her withdrawal from the state had been her husband's doing, not her own. Any attempt on her part to resist that withdrawal – to choose patriotism over her husband's treason – would itself have been wrong. The principle of the *feme covert* was more fundamental than principles of treason or even the principle of equality for which Massachusetts had rebelled.

Although ideas of gender equality did not result in radical changes in the law, women continued to exert their agency as constitutional actors outside the world of courts. The political life of the new nation owed much to the actions of women who functioned as managers of the "private" social life that lubricated policymaking in capital cities – and occasionally in more public roles, as in the agitation for abolition of slavery.

VII. CONSTITUTIONAL POLITICS IN COURT: *MARBURY V. MADISON* AND THE SEPARATION OF POWERS

Judicial review was one of many problems in the nation's early constitutional development, but only one. Traditional constitutional history, however, has misled generations by treating it as *the preeminent* problem. It has done so by putting *Marbury v. Madison* (1803)[19] at center stage in the Early Republic's constitutional growth. Yet as the history of the 1790s attests, constitutionalism was hotly contested by a host of actors in American society who chose to assert themselves outside the world of the courts. American constitutional development in the first decades of the new nation cannot be reduced to Supreme Court cases: neither *Marbury* nor the problem of judicial review, in short, deserves quite the preeminence each has been given.

That said, it would be just as much an error to conclude that *Marbury* has no importance. The case well illustrates the general, political tug of war on questions of federalism and separation of powers that had consumed the Republic and its elite institutions since its creation. Considered as such, *Marbury* allows us to understand the role of the federal judiciary and of the Supreme Court in particular in the era's constitutional development. Rather than function as a grand arbiter, single-handedly settling constitutional conundrums from on high, the Court functioned as a tough and canny player, one of several involved in a tense political-legal game with very high stakes.

In its most immediate sense, the dispute addressed in *Marbury v. Madison* was the product of the Judiciary Act of 1801, itself a major effort to shift power to the center. The Judiciary Act had been passed in the

[19] *Marbury* v. *Madison*, 5 U.S. (1 Cranch) 137 (1803).

immediate wake of the disastrous 1800 election by a lame-duck Federalist Congress. Along with several other statutes, it dramatically expanded the one branch of the federal government – the judiciary – most thoroughly insulated from popular power. President Adams rapidly appointed large numbers of Federalists to the posts created by the new legislation, many of whom were life-tenured. Just weeks before Jefferson's inauguration, Adams also appointed John Marshall to the vacant Chief Justiceship of the United States. And, just hours before the actual ceremony, Adams made a final round of "midnight" appointments. William Marbury, named a justice of the peace for the District of Columbia, was one of them, but never received his commission in the end-of-term bustle. After Jefferson directed his secretary of state, James Madison, not to deliver the appointees' commissions, Marbury sought a writ of mandamus from the Supreme Court compelling delivery. For the Court, Marshall insisted that Marbury had a right to his commission, but held that section 13 of the Judiciary Act of 1789, empowering the Court to issue the necessary writ, violated the Constitution and could not stand.

For generations it has seemed that *Marbury's* importance lay in this allegedly foundational act of judicial review rather than in the dicta that called on Jefferson to do right by one obscure nominee to one minor office. But *Marbury*'s significance did not lie in its exercise of the (already established) power of judicial review to strike down a minor portion of a Federalist statute. It lay in the opinion's intrusion into the general constitutional politics of the day, its judicially gratuitous defense of the lame-duck, consolidationist power grab by the Federalists of 1801.

Few historians would still say that judicial review waited as late as 1803 to be established. During the eighteenth century, under the British regime of Parliamentary sovereignty, significant uncertainty reigned over what tools a court might employ to circumscribe legislative power. In post-Revolutionary America, in contrast, the ascendant notion that only the people were sovereign, never the government, early yielded the implication that courts must implement only that law that was legitimately derived from the people themselves. This was the basic principle of judicial review. In accord with this basic principle, a handful of state courts had already invalidated state laws under their own state constitutions before ratification of the Federal Constitution. James Iredell, a leading North Carolina lawyer and future Justice of the U.S. Supreme Court, clearly articulated the theory behind their action in a newspaper essay of 1786. Precisely anticipating the principles of *Marbury*, Iredell argued for judicial review as a matter of inexorable logic: if all branches of the government, including the judiciary, were bound by a Constitution that represented the sovereign people's will, and if a case presented judges with two ostensible laws, one the act of the legislature and the other the act of the sovereign people, the judiciary must apply the Constitution, which was the act of the people, and disregard the statute, which was merely the act of the legislature. The judges were not reaching out to strike down the acts of the legislature. Rather, the judges were applying appropriate law to the adjudication of a case before them.

As Iredell and others were well aware, constitutions and bills of rights were far more than tools of judicial action. They were written to guide every branch of government and to keep constantly before the people the most fundamental principles of popular government. Indeed, the Constitution might have been held interpretable only by the people and their legislatures in the normal course of politics and not by the judiciary at all. But that possibility did not survive the early years of the Republic. Another possible limitation was that a power of judicial review indeed existed, but extended only to the judiciary's protection of its own institutional and jurisdictional "rights." Sometimes intimated, this approach was never consistently put in effect. Rather, from the very beginning, judicial review protected the individual, constitutional rights of the litigants before the court.

The Framers of the Federal Constitution seem generally to have assumed that the judiciary would exercise a power of review, but also thought it unlikely to prevail in any instance where the concerted political will of a legislative or popular majority opposed its exercise. Throughout the Philadelphia Convention, Madison considered a congressional veto the only practical device for defeating the licentious tendencies of the state legislatures, notwithstanding the availability of judicial review of state legislation by way of the Contracts Clause and other substantive provisions of the Constitution. In *Federalist* 78, Hamilton accepted the Anti-Federalist charge that the Constitution would permit judicial review, but denied this meant judicial supremacy. Like Iredell, he insisted that judicial review reflected the supremacy of the people over legislators and judges alike, not the supremacy of any branch over another. And as a practical matter, the judges could never muster the resources necessary to control the political branches of the government, for judges possessed powers neither of purse nor sword to enforce their decisions. Even with the power of judicial review, Hamilton concluded, the judiciary remained "the least dangerous branch" of the federal government.

Just as a handful of state courts had begun to exercise powers of review before 1789, review powers were generally assumed in the new federal courts after ratification. *Marbury* may have been the first case in which the Supreme Court made a point of invalidating a federal statute, but the previous decade had periodically seen decisions informed by the idea of constitutional review. In 1792, for example, a federal circuit court invalidated a Rhode Island stay law under the Contracts Clause. The same year, federal circuit courts considered the federal Invalid Pensioners Act, some finding it unconstitutional and others using a strained construction to render it valid. In *VanHorne's Lessee v. Dorrance* (1795), Justice Paterson on circuit overrode a Pennsylvania statute as inconsistent with both the Pennsylvania constitution's guarantee of the jury right and its guarantee of fundamental property rights. In *Ware v. Hylton* (1796), the Supreme Court itself invalidated a North Carolina sequestration statute under the Supremacy Clause because the statute conflicted with the Treaty of Paris. The Court also gave full consideration to the constitutionality of the federal carriage tax in *Hylton v. U.S.* (1796), ultimately upholding it on the merits. When *Marbury* invalidated a portion of the Judiciary Act in 1803, then, the Court was exercising a largely uncontroversial power. It was the political context and the political content of the opinion that made *Marbury* explosive, intruding as it did into the ongoing battle between Jefferson and the Federalists, and delivering an extra-judicial lecture to the new ruling party by the new Federalist chief justice.[20]

Perhaps some of *Marbury*'s traditional status as a landmark in the history of judicial review can be preserved, though. Arguably, Marshall's opinion finally rendered the practice routine. Even firm advocates had insisted that, since the Constitution placed initial responsibility for elaborating the Constitution in the legislature – the body closest to and most readily accountable to the sovereign people – the judiciary should overrule statutes on constitutional grounds only in the very clearest cases. *Marbury*, in contrast, can be read to treat judicial review as routine rather than exceptional, opening the door to decisions like *McCulloch* (1819), in which Marshall would indeed intimate a kind of judicial supremacy in constitutional interpretation.

Still, before 1803 and for a good few years thereafter, judicial review was widely embraced as a natural extension of popular, not judicial, supremacy. Acceptance of the premise of popular sovereignty implied that the judiciary was nothing very special or very dangerous, as Hamilton had asserted. Popular sovereignty implied that each branch of government in the American system had equal, coordinate authority to interpret the Constitution and all other applicable laws in the course of its duties.

What complicated matters was that, after Adams' defeat in 1800, the judiciary had become the last redoubt for Federalists at the national level. Driven perhaps equally by devotion to law and hostility to Jeffersonian demagogues, Marshall took advantage of judicial review to lay down law to the Jeffersonian politicians on questions of separation of powers. Seven

[20] *VanHorne's Lessee* v. *Dorrance*, 2 U.S. (2 Dall.) 304 (C.C.D.Pa. 1795); *Ware* v. *Hylton*, 3 US (3 Dall.) 199 (1796); *Hylton* v. *U.S.*, 3 U.S. (3 Dall.) 171 (1796).

years after *Marbury*, in *Fletcher v. Peck* (1810), he would do the same, this time laying down law to the radical "Old Republican" wing of the Jeffersonian movement, the heirs of the Anti-Federalist tradition, on questions of federalism. Judicial review by itself raised little controversy. It was the questions of separation of powers and federalism, with respect to which Marshall exploited the "legal" character of judicial review, that raised hackles.

Questions of separation of powers under the Constitution already had an important history by *Marbury*'s time. The Constitution, of course, had separated the powers of the national government among three branches and defined the powers and duties of each more or less carefully. In theory, this separation ensured that every exercise of power might be checked by other exercises of power. Different governmental institutions could and would check each other because their functions designedly overlapped: the president might veto legislation, the Senate would deliberate on presidential appointments, the courts would review the acts of the other branches. The extent of this overlap, however, could never be defined with precision. What, for example, were the obligations of judges under Article III? Were they free to accept assignments from the executive branch? Most of the early Supreme Court Justices concluded that they were, and repeatedly accepted such assignments. Chief Justices Jay and Ellsworth both undertook diplomatic missions while on the Court. Several Justices accepted the role of federal pension commissioner during their tenure. What about advisory opinions? Would judges overstep their bounds by offering opinions on legal questions before cases raising those questions reached their courts? Or was it in fact an obligation of the judiciary to offer legal opinions when asked, thus participating in the legislative and executive processes? Some of the Justices publicly delivered advisory opinions in 1792 when the constitutionality of the Invalid Pensioners Act was brought into question. And many Justices offered advisory opinions to executive officers and others both formally and informally in a variety of circumstances during the 1790s, apparently with no more qualms than the many state judges who have written formal advisory opinions from that day to this. In 1793, the Justices famously declined to offer an advisory opinion when requested by President Washington (by way of Jefferson), but this was no admission that federal judges lacked constitutional power to render such opinions. The Justices merely exercised a discretion not to grant Washington's request on that occasion, in part to save the Court from involvement in the particular political controversy that that case might have brought.

Marbury's part in separation of powers controversies arose not because the power of judicial review as such was doubted, but because Marshall used the case to lecture Jefferson on the scope of presidential power, exhibiting the Federalists' readiness to make the least dangerous branch as dangerous as possible to the Jeffersonian branches of the government. In the very case in which Marshall launched his supposed campaign to entrench the separation of law from politics and to defend the Court's right to say what the law is, the "great Chief Justice" indulged in a legally irrelevant, political provocation to the executive branch. For, while adjudging the statutory basis for the Court's jurisdiction in the case invalid, Marshall proceeded to advise Jefferson of his obligation to see to the delivery of the commissions of a collection of Federalist judicial appointees. Though the Court acknowledged its lack of authority actually to hand down such a judgment in the case, Marshall implied that the judiciary could give law to the executive on the executive's own obligations in any case. The Court thus stretched the constitutional principle of separation of powers to intervene in the national, politico-constitutional debate that had arisen out of the election of 1800 – a conflict more about federalism than about separation of powers – all the time insisting, as part of that debate, that it was only applying the law.

For the Jeffersonians, *Marbury*'s trespass on executive authority was no isolated provocation, but was of a piece with the long-term campaign of the Federalists. The opinion recalled for them the equally gratuitous lectures on Federalist constitutionalism that Federalist judges had used to bully grand juries throughout the 1790s, especially in the period of the Alien and Sedition Acts. It confirmed, for anyone in need of convincing, that the Federalists were determined to create a judicial stronghold from which to preserve the consolidationist gains of the 1790s in the wake of their crushing electoral defeat in 1800. Just as *Marbury*'s dicta seemed to replicate the Federalist judicial excesses of the 1790s, so its defense of one of Adams's "midnight" appointees seemed an effort to vindicate the Federalist Judiciary Act of 1801 as a step toward judicial supremacy over the popular branches. To the Jeffersonians, *Marbury* perverted the separation of powers to preserve Federalist power in the aftermath of the Federalists' political defeat in 1800.

The Jeffersonian response was, of course, not only to ignore Marshall's extra-judicial endorsement of Marbury's claim but also to repeal the Judiciary Act itself, a move in which the Court acquiesced (possibly over Marshall's objections) in *Stuart v. Laird* (1803).[21] During the original debate over the Bill of Rights, Jefferson had looked to the judiciary as a potential bulwark against tyranny. By the early 1800s, however, expansive federal – and Federalist – judicial power threatened not only a contraction of the power of other branches but an erosion of states' rights and popular sovereignty. Jefferson attacked Federalists for turning the judiciary to

[21] *Stuart* v. *Laird*, 5 U.S. (1 Cranch) 299 (1803).

"party purpose," and he applauded Congress for having "lopped off a parasite limb." Another critic posed the issue as one between those "appointed for life" and the "immediate representatives of the people." Efforts to restrict federal judicial power were understood by Federalists, meanwhile, as both an expansion of the power of the Jeffersonian presidency and as part of a larger agenda to promote the chaos of states' rights at the expense of rightful national power.

The more radical Jeffersonians wanted to go beyond mere repeal of the Judiciary Act. Their goal was to cleanse the judiciary and restore the proper separation of powers by impeaching the worst of the Federalist judges. The first target was John Pickering of New Hampshire, a notorious drunk, probably insane, and certainly not a proper man to have on the federal bench. The use of impeachment as a political tool troubled many, however, including a number of Republicans who doubted that Pickering's deplorable behavior belonged among the "high crimes and misdemeanors" that justified removal from office. The radicals won over enough members of the Senate to convict Pickering, but the case against their second target, Samuel Chase, was far more complicated. Chase had used his position as a judge to denounce Republican ideas, and the most ardent Republicans argued that impeachment was the only tool to check the excesses of unelected judges. But more moderate Republicans and Federalists required that an impeachable offense be a criminal act. Impeachment, they insisted, should not be used as a political tool. The Senate failed to convict Chase, and the episode drove a wedge between the radical and moderate wings of Jefferson's coalition. Still, Chase's impeachment and a rumored threat to impeach Marshall himself chastened the Federalists to a significant degree. The close call showed that Congress would hesitate to intrude too aggressively into the judicial sphere. But it equally established that the judiciary could defend its independence only so long as it plausibly explained its actions as distinctively legal, divorced from politics. This settlement on the question of separation of powers did not truly promise a future of apolitical judging, but, like the language of federalism in politics more generally, it established the fundamental language of constitutional politics in the courts.

VIII. CONSTITUTIONAL POLITICS IN COURT: FEDERALISM

As much as *Marbury* raised separation of powers problems for the Jeffersonians, the chief focus for constitutional conflicts involving the courts was the problem of federalism. The rift that had divided Federalists from Anti-Federalists over the division of authority between the states and the central government only widened in the decade after the Constitution was ratified and the Bill of Rights adopted. At one extreme stood the radical states' rights theories advanced by Jefferson in the Kentucky Resolutions. Federalists rejected this theory and continued to affirm their commitment to a powerful central government.

Although committed to the Federalist vision of a strong central government, including a powerful Supreme Court, Marshall was not a Hamiltonian consolidationist, seeking to build a British-style regime with a powerful standing army to enforce its will. Rather Marshall is better understood as an expositor of a distinctly legalistic style of Federalist ideology. Marshall shared with Hamilton a suspicion of localist democracy, which he believed invariably threatened the fundamental rights of property and contract on which civilization rested. In his view the rule of law required rigid adherence to certain basic principles, particularly the principles of contract and property entrenched in the common law and incorporated into the Federal Constitution's Contracts Clause. On these questions it was manifestly the duty of the judiciary to preserve a uniform federal law without obstruction from individual state governments.

Marshall was not, as his enemies charged, a consolidationist bent on destroying all state authority; in his view state governments would have wide latitude to act within their appropriate spheres of authority demarcated by the Constitution. But the principle of popular sovereignty did not mean that the people could do whatever they wanted, particularly with regard to contract and property rights. The Constitution established legal mechanisms and principles that the people could not change at will but only by the mechanisms of Article V. In practice, then, even the political branches and the states must be controlled by law, and the law's integrity must be preserved by the ultimate authority of a single legal tribunal like the national Supreme Court.

In contrast, the Jeffersonian model of federalism deemphasized the production of a coherent national law and posited instead the indispensable autonomy of the several republics that constituted the nation. For Jefferson, the people were sovereign in a quite active sense, and they normally expressed their sovereign will through the medium of the state governments. Jefferson viewed American government as a pyramid. At the foundation was the mass of politically equal, male, white citizens, each yielding only so much power over his own life as necessary for good government and consistent with the continued political equality of the citizenry. As one moved up the structure of the pyramid, power would be delegated in a limited fashion: local, state, and federal governments enjoyed successively less authority and no more power than was absolutely necessary to execute their political functions. The national government was the most limited of all, entitled only to so much power as it absolutely required to secure a republican peace among the Union's constituent republics and between the Union and the world. While committed to Union, Jeffersonians were not willing to achieve this goal at the expense of the liberty enjoyed by citizens and the states. Jeffersonians were not enemies of a coherent system of law. They did, however, oppose the creation of a powerful central government, since it would inexorably erode liberty. Consistent with that position, they tended to resist the Marshall Court's accumulation of broad authority, notwithstanding the Court's presence at the only spot in the system from which uniform law might be imparted to the nation.

Each of these opposing visions could be gleaned from the text of the Constitution. Jeffersonians could emphasize that the Constitution granted only limited, enumerated powers to the national government and that the document had been ratified by the people of the states, rather than by the people as a single body. In this vision, the federal courts were not superior to, but parallel with, the state courts. Federalists could point out that, although the national government's sphere of action was limited, within that sphere it was supreme and entitled to all the powers necessary to be effective. Moreover, it was entitled to construe its powers generously in pursuit of its legitimate goals and to enforce its laws without regard to the objections of the state governments. Here, the tendency was to elevate the federal courts as an authority that might discipline the unruly states.

The history of federalism in this period can be seen as a history of political negotiation and compromise between these two basic viewpoints. A word of caution, though: in those days, there was no institutionalized two-party system. As described above, political alliances were fluid, politico-constitutional action took many forms, and the idioms of states' rights and national power might be deployed by anyone at the right strategic moment. Still, these two idioms were indeed fundamental, and to the extent that self-identified Republicans and Federalists increasingly came to dominate the public discourse of constitutionalism, they generally drew on these two basic perspectives to distinguish themselves from each other.

The point of departure in negotiating the roles of the courts was the framing and ratification of the Constitution, itself a process of negotiation and compromise among those advocating consolidation and those favoring state autonomy. Born of frustration with the mere league that was the Articles of Confederation, the Constitution itself was a major step toward consolidation. If the Framers had prudently stopped short of full consolidation and even short of granting the new government certain powers that Madison thought essential, they had nevertheless augmented federal power and placed specific limits on the states, even in their regulation of apparently internal matters like contract. The addition of the Bill of Rights – particularly the all-important Tenth Amendment limit on federal power – and the later development of a constitutional theory of strict construction were the two key elements in their continuing struggle against the Federalist vision of a strong national government.

When the original Judiciary Act of 1789 established the federal court system as a national arm intruding into the states, it appeared that another consolidationist step had been taken. The Act, however, fell far short of creating the "imperial" establishment that the Anti-Federalists feared, that the Constitution itself arguably permitted, and that the Judiciary Act of 1801 would more closely approach. It established only a modest number of federal courts, denied federal-question jurisdiction to the federal trial courts except in certain narrow areas, and imposed strict limits on federal diversity jurisdiction and the Supreme Court's appellate jurisdiction. The ability of the federal courts to reach into the lives of most Americans was therefore extremely limited. The Anti-Federalist fear that citizens would be forced to litigate issues in federal courts hostile to liberty and far from the localities in which issues arose would only rarely come to pass.

That said, the Act granted the Supreme Court jurisdiction to review the judgments of the state courts on federal questions and so held out at least some promise of federal judicial control of federal law. The provision caused little controversy at first, but the federal courts did move to bring state law in line with their vision of the Federal Constitution whenever they got hold of the necessary cases. Thus, in *Ware v. Hylton* (1796), the Supreme Court invalidated North Carolina's statutory effort to interfere with the British debt collection that was guaranteed by the Treaty of Paris. Few questioned the Court's power to do so. The federal circuit courts, as well, used the Contracts Clause to invalidate the occasional state law. Two federal courts even granted writs of certiorari to transfer cases involving federal questions from the state courts where they were pending to federal court. The state courts refused to recognize the writs, however, and were sustained by their legislatures. In both cases the federal courts backed off.

A far more violent states' rights reaction to federal court action came when the Supreme Court asserted its jurisdiction over the state of Georgia in another contract case, *Chisholm v. Georgia* (1793). Chisholm was a South Carolina resident and creditor of the state of Georgia suing the state for payment. Georgia claimed immunity as a sovereign state. The Court held that Article III's grant of federal jurisdiction in cases "between a State and Citizens of another State" empowered the federal courts to sit in judgment on the states even when sued by private parties.[22] This claim of judicial power over a sovereign state proved highly controversial. If a mere private person could sue an unwilling state in federal court, some argued, the states

[22] *Chisholm* v. *Georgia* 2 U.S., (2 Dall.) 419 (1793).

would "have relinquished all their Sovereignties, and have become mere corporations." Newspaper essayists predicted that suits against the states would subvert the balance of power within the federal system. The result would be the dreaded consolidation predicted by Anti-Federalists and the destruction of liberty: "the consolidation of the Union for the purpose of arbitrary power . . . the downfall of liberty and the subversion of the rights of the people." Another claimed the grant of federal jurisdiction had been drafted with "craft and subtility" by lawyers and was another example of the conspiratorial designs of "aristocrats to reduce the States to corporations."

The use of Anti-Federalist rhetoric was not surprising. What was more remarkable was the widespread political support for this critique. The Eleventh Amendment, which overturned *Chisholm* and reaffirmed a measure of state sovereign immunity, was adopted by a Congress dominated by Federalists. A full explanation of the Federalist position remains as elusive as the amendment's precise meaning, which the courts have long treated as related only tenuously to its text. But the evidence suggests broad commitment to the idea that the Constitution must have incorporated state sovereign immunity and that *Chisholm*, in other respects a perfectly conventional exposition of Federalist principle, had simply misunderstood that basic commitment. Like the Judiciary Act before it, the Eleventh Amendment suggested a readiness, even among Federalists, to see basic principles of private law go unenforced when the alternative was violation of constitutional (and common law) principles like sovereign immunity. Necessarily, too, the Constitution lived within politics – sometimes politics of the most elevated sort that might vindicate or vitiate sovereign immunity as a matter of principle, sometimes a politics of immediate interest and practical advantage. As it happened, several states at the time faced law suits that the amendment would allow them to avoid.

Following *Chisholm*, the Supreme Court avoided major controversies over federalism until *Fletcher v. Peck* in 1810.[23] Under constant threat from the Jeffersonians after 1801, Marshall and the Court had maintained a fairly low profile. Whether by design or mere circumstance, they afforded the Republicans under Jefferson and Madison the room to drift in a moderately nationalist direction themselves. But in 1810 Marshall seized on a case in which the Court's judgment was not likely to be resisted to establish certain nationalist, legalist, anti-populist principles. *Fletcher v. Peck* in many ways encapsulates the range of possibility open to constitutional actors in the first decades of the Republic. The Federalist viewpoint seemed to win the battle in court and held its own in Congress. But little of Federalism could be salvaged amid the Jacksonian ascendancy of the next generation.

[23] *Fletcher* v. *Peck*, 10 U.S. (6 Cranch) 87 (1810).

Fletcher v. Peck had its origins in the "Yazoo" fraud of 1795, in which apparent wholesale bribery of the Georgia legislature resulted in a mammoth land sale to a group of speculators at a bargain price. The new owners busily resold such title as they had (clouded not just by the bribery but also by continuing Indian claims to much of the land) to purchasers in the Northern states. Meanwhile, in Georgia a political movement arose to invalidate the sale, and in 1796, a newly elected legislature passed a "Repeal Act." That act, however, did not actually repeal the sale, but rather declared it "null and void" from the start as a "usurped act." *Fletcher v. Peck* itself was a feigned (arranged) case, brought years later by a third-party purchaser of Yazoo lands against his seller to determine the validity of the purchased title.

Georgia's "Repeal Act" represented not only an assertion of a legislative right to review the constitutionality of legislation but also a possible challenge to the sanctity of contract. As such it was a direct assault on Federalist constitutionalism (and, indeed, on the constitutionalism of some members of the Jeffersonian elite). Chief Justice Marshall's opinion in *Fletcher* addressed both of these concerns. First, legislative exercise of constitutional review usurped judicial power, according to Marshall, and thus violated basic principles of separation of powers. Although here the limitation was arguably a matter only of Georgia constitutional law, Marshall indicated his belief that it was also a matter of the very nature of legislative power. Second, the "Repeal Act" was a clear violation of property rights, one of the bedrock principles of Marshall's constitutionalism, and an affront to the Federal Constitution's Contracts Clause. To staunch Federalists, the legislature appeared to be replicating the excesses of state legislatures during the Confederation period – the very evil that the Constitution had been designed to eliminate.

Many Republicans, on the other hand, believed Georgia's actions were a legitimate exercise of popular sovereignty and states' rights, an act of popular constitutional review clearly superior to any act of mere judicial review. The Repeal Act did not purport to be the action of one legislature disapproving the act of a previous legislature. Rather, it was the product of a legislature acting in a special constitutional capacity in response to peculiar circumstance. Resolutions of a state constitutional convention, the actions of grand juries throughout the state, and public gatherings of the people (some more peaceful than others) had specially "invest[ed] this Legislature with conventional powers"; that is, with the powers not just of a legislature but of the people themselves assembled in convention. Like their colleagues in other episodes in other states during the 1790s, the people of Georgia had resorted to the entire range of purportedly "constitutional" actions to put their sovereignty into practice. Exercising the powers so conferred, the new legislature had reviewed the passage of the original act, found it marred by fraud and hence an unconstitutional usurpation, and declared it null and void – without effect from the moment of its supposed enactment.

Here was a Jeffersonian expression of active popular constitutional review, superior to judicial review. The affair was hardly uncontroversial, even among Jeffersonians. Who, after all, was to decide when it really was "the people" speaking? Jefferson, Madison, and much of the moderate wing of the Republican party in fact sought a compromise solution rather than stand fully behind the actions of the Georgia legislature. Still, Georgia's assertion that it must be the people – the sovereigns – not their agents who have ultimate power to say what the law is and to interpret the Constitution drew on and perpetuated the constitutionalism of a large swath of the American public before and after 1789.

For Federalists, popular sovereignty could never be taken so far. The supposedly sovereign people of a state were not competent to change the terms of the Constitution except by Article V, nor alter the transcendent rights of contract and property except by forsaking constitutional government itself. Courts, not the people, interpreted and applied the law. This was not judicial supremacy, although some were prepared to go that far; it was simply an argument for leaving adjudicatory functions to adjudicatory institutions, just as legislative functions must be left to legislatures. The people might amend the Constitution and were, in that sense, sovereign. But the Constitution of the United States (and that of Georgia) placed the judicial power in the courts, not in the people or in the legislatures. Otherwise there would be no reliable general law, only guesses about what a legislature or "the people" might do next with individuals' fundamental rights.

This was the perspective that informed Marshall's opinion. After assuming that the sale was a contract within the meaning of the federal Contracts Clause, Marshall offered an empty nod to state sovereignty by refusing to consider the bribery allegations. The Court, he said, must not presume to tell Georgia that an act bearing all the forms of a Georgia law was no law at all. Of course, Georgia's legislature had already decided that matter itself. But therein lay the problem; that the people of Georgia in their sovereign capacity might legitimately declare their own law void could not be permitted. The forms of law must be respected, and if the forms of law appeared to create private, vested rights, then no court could allow an attempt to "devest" those rights in the name of a state. The rule of law required that private rights be governed not by mere sovereign will but by "certain great principles of justice," such as the rule that good faith purchasers never be molested in their title. To assert power to the contrary, Marshall argued, was likely inconsistent with the very idea of legislative power. Even more to the point, it clearly conflicted with the federal Constitution's "bill of rights for the people of each state," by which Marshall did not, of course, mean *the* Bill of Rights, which then limited only national power. Instead, he pointed to those provisions – the Contracts Clause along with the bans on bills of attainder and ex post facto laws – that guaranteed individual rights against unprincipled state majorities and subjected the states to federal discipline.

Fletcher did not settle the rights of the Yazoo claimants in fact, although it certainly strengthened their bargaining position. Nor did it settle the continuing debates about the nature of the Constitution. But the case revealed a series of rifts in the fabric of American constitutionalism. For the most outspoken critics of the Yazoo scandal, heirs of William Manning, the actions of the legislature and the people out of doors vindicated the ideal of popular sovereignty. A more moderate states' rights view, endorsed by many leading Republicans, also persisted. While championing the "principles of '98," which looked to the states as the guardians of popular liberty, it hesitated to endorse the extra-legal authority of the crowd. For moderates, exceptional demonstrations of "popular sovereignty" like the Repeal Act were not the appropriate means of solving constitutional questions.

Among the judiciary, and on the Supreme Court, a decidedly nationalist and Federalist view flourished. The Court was the only practical guarantor of coherence and integrity in national law and of security in those transcendent rights of property and contract that underlay the specific arrangements agreed to by the nation in 1787–88, and civilization in general. In *Fletcher*, Marshall seized a moment when he knew the states' rights versions of the Constitution would not unite in serious opposition (since Jefferson and many other Republicans were looking for a compromise on the Yazoo affair), and he trumpeted Federalist constitutionalism with near impunity. He would expand on this view in later cases, such as *Martin v. Hunter's Lessee* (1816) and *McCulloch v. Maryland* (1819),[24] when the nationalizing trend among Republicans would again clear an opportune space for him to act.

But Marshall, though always a major player in the endless constitutional negotiation, would never manage to vanquish those opposing visions of constitutionalism that looked primarily to the states and even to direct action by the people. In the twilight of his life and career, the resurgence of states' rights in the Nullification Crisis of 1832–3 and the Jacksonian assault on implied-powers constitutionalism and judicial imperialism would leave Marshall despondent.

[24] *Martin* v. *Hunter's Lessee*, 14 U.S. (1 Wheat.) 304 (1816) and *McCulloch* v. *Maryland*, 17 U.S. (4 Wheat.) 316 (1819).

CONCLUSION: MULTIPLE CONSTITUTIONAL TRADITIONS IN THE FOUNDING ERA – A DISCORDANT NARRATIVE

A viable system of federalism was far from secure when America entered the War of 1812. At various moments in the two decades since ratification of the Constitution, powerful centrifugal forces within American constitutional life had threatened to rend the fabric of the new nation asunder. The Whiskey Rebellion and Gabriel's Rebellion both had demonstrated that loyalties remained in flux and highly negotiable. On more than one occasion, state militias had been mobilized to protect the states against potential tyranny of the federal government. The right to bear arms and the well-regulated militia enshrined in the Second Amendment had not functioned quite as Anti-Federalists had hoped. Still, in the fluid world of America's developing constitutional order, the notion that state militias might stand as the final barrier against federal tyranny had come close to being tested.

It is tempting to view Jefferson and the Republicans in cynical terms, abandoning their commitment to states' rights when it suited their political ambitions. Rather than see Jeffersonian constitutional ideology as a thin veil masking their pursuit of power, it makes more sense to recognize that Jefferson and his allies shared with the Federalists a complex amalgam of ideas and goals about constitutional government. When two different constitutional values came into conflict, liberty and federalism, popular sovereignty and the rule of law, or strict construction and republicanism, each side was forced to make difficult choices: which part of its constitutional philosophy should it preserve and which part should it sacrifice to obtain the desired objective?

It is also important to recall that all the various discourses of constitutionalism available to Americans during the Early Republic existed within a set of established structural power relations created by the Constitution. That the states' rights "principles of '98" were used to great effect at different moments of constitutional crisis by both Jefferson and his Federalist opponents does not make such uses unprincipled and opportunistic. The structure of the federal system meant that such arguments were always available for those who wished to formulate a critique of centralizing tendencies within American constitutionalism.

In short, the complex history of constitutional development in the Early Republic does not square easily with the traditional Whiggish narrative of unfolding liberty or with neo-Federalist accounts of rising nationalism. Nor does it square with modern anti-Whig declension narratives, in which civic republicanism simply gives way before the onslaught of liberal capitalism.

The most accurate description of the contested constitutional culture of the Early Republic may well have been William Manning's suggestion that the Constitution was “a Fiddle, with but few strings.” Many actors stepped on the stage of American law hoping to scratch out their own simple tune with this fiddle. Others hoped that this instrument would allow them to create a grand symphonic vision for American law. The contentious history of this period suggests that neither of these visions of law was entirely successful. The early constitutional history of the new nation proved to be more discordant than harmonious.

16

MAGISTRATES, COMMON LAW LAWYERS, LEGISLATORS: THE THREE LEGAL SYSTEMS OF BRITISH AMERICA

JAMES A. HENRETTA

On two occasions in the late 1630s, the magistrates of the Lower Norfolk county court in Virginia imposed extraordinary punishments on white men accused of minor criminal offenses, ordering the sheriff to lay 100 lashes on the bare back. This was arbitrary justice, the summary infliction of severe corporal punishment by a few appointed justices of the peace. Eight decades later, in 1712, the Connecticut Superior Court discovered in the midst of a trial that the laws of colony made no distinction between murder and manslaughter. The court immediately asked for the permission of the Assembly to determine "by the rules of the common law" the seriousness of the crime and the consequent sentence. Legal precedent, the rules of the common law, would decide the defendant's fate. Yet another eight decades later, in 1793, Vermont Chief Justice Nathaniel Chipman declared, "No Court, in this State, ought ever to pronounce the sentence of death upon the authority of a common law precedent, without the authority of a statute."[1] The legitimacy of a major criminal punishment now depended on the sanction of a popularly elected legislature.

Arbitrary seventeenth-century magistrates, rule-conscious eighteenth-century common law courts, statute-enacting nineteenth-century legislatures: in the years between 1600 and 1820, the white residents of British North America lived under three distinct, but overlapping and interrelated, legal systems. Each of these regimes was controlled by different personnel, operated according to different rules and procedures, and embodied a different legal ideology. Although all three systems were present throughout the period, their relative importance changed significantly over time and imparted a definable logic to the course of American law and politics. Over

[1] *The Superior Court Diary of William Samuel Johnson*, ed. John T. Farrell (Washington, DC, 1942), xviii; Nathaniel Chipman, *Reports and Dissertations, in two parts . . . : with an appendix, containing forms of special pleadings in several cases, forms of recognizances, of justices records and of warrants of commitment* (Rutland, VT, 1793), 61.

time, the legal world became more complex and increasingly governed by professional standards and influenced by centralized authorities. Initially, most legal decisions reflected the views of local magistrates and communities. Then, at end of the seventeenth century, common law lawyers and doctrines challenged the supremacy of self-taught magistrates and local customs. Subsequently, after the Revolution, elected republican legislators enacted statewide statutes that altered the substance of the common law and the structure of the courts that administered them. The interaction of three causal factors – an increasingly complex economy and society, English imperial policy and legal principles, and the ideology of revolutionary republicanism – drove this process of legal change forward and shaped its character. Law continued to "occur" at the local level, but larger political and legal doctrines and institutions increasingly shaped its character and content.

I. LOCAL PRIMACY: MAGISTRATES AND ARBITRATORS, 1600–80

In the seventeenth century, the English settlements on the North American mainland were widely scattered. Colony-wide institutions developed slowly. Legal authority was fragile. However, most settlers chose to live in organized communities – villages, townships, and counties – and to reestablish the political and legal institutions of the English communities from which they had come. Consequently, in North America as in England, local legal authority rested in the hands of local oligarchies: influential selectmen, vestrymen, and magistrates who usually lacked formal training in the law but ruled under its authority. Foremost among these local leaders were justices of the peace who, as in England, were men of "ample Fortunes" and social influence. Ideally, they were also "the most able, honest and judicious persons of the county," as a Virginia statute put it.[2] The character of the American magisterial regime differed from that in England, however, and varied markedly from one colony to another.

On their arrival in Massachusetts Bay in 1630, Puritan leaders bestowed the powers of the justice of the peace on six of their company. This action restored at least two men, Richard Bellingham and John Winthrop, to offices they had held in England. As individual magistrates, the Massachusetts Bay justices (and those in other colonies) enforced local bylaws and the statutes enacted by the representative assembly, presided at courts that decided

[2] William Waller Hening, comp. *The Statutes at Large: Being a Collection of All the Laws of Virginia, from the First Session of the Legislature, in the Year 1619*, 13 vols. (Richmond, VA, 1809–23), 2:69.

minor civil cases of debt, and dispensed summary criminal justice to those they found guilty of misdemeanors, such as assault and battery, fornication and bastardy, Sabbath-breaking, and scandal mongering. Many magistrates exerted authority outside the courtroom by upholding the laws and customs of the community. Thus, as Judge (and J.P.) Samuel Sewall traveled from Cambridge to Boston one Saturday evening in 1715, he directed shopkeepers to close up their shops, because the Sabbath had begun at sunset.

As a body of magistrates sitting in the county-based Court of General Sessions, the justices had broad administrative authority and responsibilities. Court officials recorded the patents, sales, and transfers of land, and the justices supervised a variety of local officials: churchwardens and vestrymen, constables, tax collectors, and overseers of the poor. They also enforced laws relating to the militia, roads, fencing, and market regulations and "warned out" from the town or county those individuals who were not entitled to poor relief. Finally, the county court justices awarded franchises: bestowing licenses on ordinaries, ferries, and gristmills; granting permission for new roads; and dispensing contracts for the construction of bridges, jails, and other public works.

The justices' legal powers were equally extensive. Sitting together with a jury as a Court of Common Pleas, magistrates adjudicated civil cases – contested debts, claims to land, contractual disputes – involving substantial amounts of property. Meeting as a Court of General Sessions, they heard cases of serious crimes – rape, robbery, and grievous assaults – and imposed whippings, fines, recognizances (bonds to keep the peace), and other punishments on offenders. Indeed, before 1690 in the colonies of New Haven, Massachusetts Bay, Connecticut, Maine, Maryland, and Virginia magistrates ran jury-less, inquisitorial regimes of criminal justice and summarily decided nearly all non-capital cases. The justices and their courts stood at the center of the community, defining its priorities, setting its taxes, safeguarding its property, and protecting its moral character by relentlessly prosecuting deviant residents.

In fact, conditions in the colonies encouraged magistrates to assume even greater authority than their counterparts in England. Because Virginia (and the other colonies in which the Church of England was legally established) did not create English-style ecclesiastical courts, justices assumed many of the functions of those courts, such as recording wills and probate inventories and regulating marriage and sexual behavior. Twice a year, the justices in Virginia received written reports on the morals of the parish from vestry-appointed churchwardens. However, this justice-run system of moral discipline was mild for the white population, for it punished only the worse offenders and then only sporadically.

In Maryland, justices assumed control over orphans' affairs, also a function of English ecclesiastical courts and, because of high adult mortality in the Chesapeake region, a pressing problem. To protect the property and welfare of orphans, the Maryland assembly enacted a series of acts between 1658 and 1688. This legislation gave county justices the authority to account for the orphans' assets, appoint and dismiss guardians, and bring presentments against guardians who abused the persons or property of their charges. Because these powers derived from a statute and resided in a single court, Maryland justices had greater authority over orphans' affairs than their ecclesiastical counterparts in England.

The character of magisterial rule varied considerably from one colony to another. When the General Court in Massachusetts Bay established a system of county courts in 1635, it placed them in the hands of existing magistrates, all of them elected. The General Court also provided for the appointment of local "assistants" nominated annually by town freemen, that is, by church members. This elective system – and a similar process for choosing town selectmen – gave Massachusetts Bay a stable and respected ruling elite. Year after year, the freemen of the towns reelected or renominated virtually the same slate of magistrates, lay assistants, and selectmen. In Ipswich in Essex County, people usually referred to the selectmen as the "7 men," suggesting their stature. Just sixteen individuals held 62 percent of the selectmen positions in the fifty years after 1636. In Essex County as a whole between 1650 and 1684, only twenty-four men served as justices; four justices sat on the bench until their deaths and averaged twenty-nine years of service.

Throughout most of New England, the magistracy demanded deference, but ruled primarily through consensus. Although residents sometimes resented the summary justice dispensed by the magistracy, there were relatively few instances of the disrespect for authority shown by William Hatton of York County, Virginia. In 1662, authorities hauled Hatton into court "for abuesing severall justices of this County calling them Coopers, hogg trough makers, Peddlars, [and] Cobblers."[3] In Rhode Island and Plymouth Colony, however, anti-authoritarian settlers acted collectively to limit the power of magistrates; in those colonies, juries had great authority and decided virtually all civil and criminal cases.

Consensus of a more complicated sort characterized the religiously and ethnically diverse mid-Atlantic colonies of Pennsylvania, New Jersey, and New York. In 1685, William Penn reported that the Delaware Valley held a "Collection of divers Nations in Europe: As, French, Dutch, Germans, Swedes, Danes, Finns, Scotch, Irish and English." There, Penn boasted,

[3] York County Orders, Oct. 24 1662, Virginia State Library, Richmond (hereafter, VSL).

"they live like People of One Country." In fact, this tranquility reflected the political and legal dominance of the Society of Friends. Between 1680 and 1710, all of the governors and the most of the legislators and Supreme Court judges in the colonies of Pennsylvania and West Jersey were Quakers. Friends also accounted for 79 percent of the magistrates who served during those three decades, nearly twice their proportion in the population. Quakers likewise predominated in the office of sheriff, here as elsewhere a lucrative position, and even in the ranks of the constables, the least desirable court-related office. Likewise, two-thirds of the members of grand and trial juries were members of the Society of Friends, although roughly two-thirds of all civil plaintiffs and civil and criminal defendants were non-Quakers. To ensure that residents fulfilled their public responsibilities, magistrates fined those who missed jury duty and lodged 80 percent of contempt citations for missing jury duty against Quakers.

If Quakers dominated the magistracy and the legal system, they did not corrupt it. The verdicts issued by Quaker-dominated trial juries showed no ethnic or religious bias, whether in the statistical calculations of modern historians or, as far as one can tell, in the minds of the non-Quaker residents. Apparently convinced that they would receive justice in the courts, non-Quakers in the Delaware Valley used the Friends-controlled legal system in numbers proportional to their share of the population. Such usage by minority or maltreated ethnic or religious groups was far from inevitable – or even usual. Following the creation of the Dominion of New England in 1684, for example, many Puritan residents of Essex County, Massachusetts, refused to use the new legal system controlled by the allies of the Anglican governor, Sir Edmund Andros. A similar boycott of the judicial system occurred in New York City after 1673, when many Dutch residents avoided the Mayor's court and other legal institutions taken over by English authorities.

Like the Dutch, English Puritans on Long Island worried that the regime imposed by the Duke of York would endanger the autonomy of their town governments. And with good reason. The Duke's Laws of 1663 restricted the jurisdiction of the local Courts of Constable and Overseers to small causes and directed that the Court of Sessions, which was composed of justices of the peace appointed by the governor, hear all appeals. Indeed, in 1683, a new statute replaced the Long Island town courts with county courts staffed by appointed magistrates. An Act for Establishing Courts of Judicature in 1691 completed this process of centralization (and anglicization) by streamlining the organization of the county courts and providing for review of their decisions by a Supreme Court. Although legal authority in New York remained fragmented because of the resistance of Dutch and Puritan residents and the existence of private manorial courts, centrally appointed magistrates became a powerful force. In 1718 Anglican magistrates in Queens County ignored Presbyterian allegations that taxes levied to support the Anglican minister were contrary to the intent and the letter of the law, and imposed heavy fines on Presbyterians who had forcibly resisted paying them.

This authoritarian potential of magisterial rule, long a conspicuous feature of criminal cases, received its fullest expression in Virginia. During the first decade of settlement, Virginia Company governors and private patent holders ruled the settlers in military-like fashion, trying criminal defendants without juries and ignoring the procedural protections of the common law in civil cases. Then in 1618, at the behest of the Virginia Company, Governor George Yeardley reconstructed the political regime, organizing the disparate settlements into a single "body corporate" and establishing a representative assembly of property owners. The legal regime quickly evolved into a county-based system controlled by members of the local gentry. In a series of laws enacted between 1624 and 1634, the assembly consciously sought to establish a legal order "as neare as may be . . . to the laws of the realm of England." It created eight counties, each administered by a monthly court, and bestowed on local magistrates the authority "to doe and execute, whatever . . . [English] justices of the peace may do."[4] Appeals from the decisions of monthly courts proceeded to the General Court, which was composed of the governor and council, and then to the assembly, which until 1683 sat as a court of final appeal.

Many members of the Virginia assembly and council also served as justices of the peace in the counties, which they ruled with an iron hand. Before 1660, juries were virtually non-existent in both civil and criminal trials, and beginning in the 1680s, the assembly granted single magistrates increasing authority to inflict summary punishments on those of African and Indian descent. By 1700, the justices had also won the right to nominate candidates for vacant positions, thereby wresting control of the courts from the royal governor. The county courts had become self-perpetuating oligarchies of justices who held multiple public offices and shared among themselves the lucrative positions of sheriff, coroner, and public notary. Clearly, they formed local elites: the 215 men who served as magistrates in Lower Norfolk, Lancaster, Northumberland, and York counties between 1634 and 1676 owned 1,000 acres of land on average, at least double the holdings of most planters and considerably more than the average of 200 acres owned by men who served in the minor offices of jurors and appraisers.

The avarice of Virginia's early political elite nearly led to its demise. Living far from the center of imperial authority, the Virginia grandees governed virtually as they wished, especially during the post-Restoration

[4] Hening, *Statutes*, I, 168–69.

regime of Governor William Berkeley (1660–76). Only a strong public outcry in 1673 forced the repeal of an act giving justices of the peace a regular salary in addition to their other emoluments. Two years later, the anger of poor planters against Indians, high taxes, and plundering officials fueled a rebellion led by Nathaniel Bacon. Bacon's "Manifesto and Declaration of the People" asserted, "all the power and sway is got into the hands of the rich" and demanded an end to the rule of wealthy "parasites," many of whom were magistrates. As the pragmatic reforms enacted by a newly elected assembly indicated, Bacon's uprising did not seek to overthrow the magisterial order, but rather to oust a corrupt elite.

The eventual result was a more responsive and responsible system of gentry government that reduced the taxes of ordinary white planters and gradually won their respect, in part by upholding slavery and a repressive system of racial domination. Indeed, with respect to the white population, the political elite of early eighteenth-century Virginia governed in much the same firm but consensual manner perfected by the Puritan and Quaker leaders of the seventeenth-century New England and mid-Atlantic colonies. In each region, transplantation of local legal institutions and local magisterial rule – town and county governments run by justices of the peace – was the great accomplishment of the first century of English settlement in North America.

II. CENTRALIZATION: IMPERIAL AUTHORITY, LEGALISM, AND COMMON LAW, 1680–1720

Surveying the state of early American legal history in 1984, Stanley N. Katz noted that an impressive galaxy of scholars – Roscoe Pound, Perry Miller, and Grant Gilmore – had managed to write histories of American law that largely ignored the colonial period and located the creative period of legal development during or immediately after the Revolution.[5] Two other influential studies, William N. Nelson's *Americanization of the Common Law* (1976) and Morton Horwitz's *Transformation of American Law, 1780–1860* (1976), had likewise taken 1776 as the major dividing line. As Katz explained, Nelson depicted colonial "Massachusetts society as characterized by ethical unity, communitarianism, and stability, all of which were undermined by the socioeconomic effects of the Revolution." Similarly, Horwitz contrasted static eighteenth-century law, "a body of essentially fixed doctrine applied . . . to achieve a fair result between private litigants

[5] Grant Gilmore, *The Death of Contract* (Columbus, OH, 1974); Perry Miller, *The Life of the Mind in America, from the Revolution to the Civil War* (New York, 1965); Roscoe Pound, *The Formative Era of American Law* (Boston, 1938).

in individual cases," with the dynamic world of the nineteenth century, when judges came "to think of the common law as equally responsible with legislation for governing society."[6] Questioning the validity of the dramatic Revolutionary Era transition assumed or posited by these five authors, Katz called on scholars to show the organic development of law between the seventeenth and the nineteenth centuries.

Less than a decade later, Cornelia Dayton confirmed that scholars had begun to revise the traditional chronology and, in the process, challenged the interpretations of Nelson and Horwitz. Surveying recently published books and articles by David Konig, Bruce Mann, John Murrin, and others, Dayton argued that they made "a powerful case for 1680–1720 as a pivotal period, a transition from a communal, informal mode of resolving disputes to a rationalized, lawyerly mode." In Dayton's account, it was the period before 1680 (and not the entire colonial era) that "was radically different from modern legal culture."[7]

There is, in fact, considerable evidence that around 1700 American legal institutions and procedures changed significantly in at least four respects. In America, increasing social complexity meant a decline in resort to communal dispute resolution, notably arbitration. Nearly simultaneously, three interrelated English-influenced developments became manifest: the appearance of centralizing imperial officials, the growing influence of trained lawyers, and the increasing resort to common law procedures.

Like the magistracy, arbitration worked most effectively in a tightly knit community with shared values. During the short life of the New Haven colony (1639–64), its religiously devout members eschewed civil suits and embraced arbitration. Likewise, Puritan migrants to Essex County, Massachusetts, frequently used church tribunals and arbitrators to resolve differences. Informal juries of leading men, either neighbors or fellow church members, met with the disputants, took written statements, and proposed solutions that they believed were fair to the parties and represented community sentiment. Indeed, correspondence with community values was crucial, because collective opinion was the prime means of enforcing the arbitrators' decision. As the communally minded original settlers died off, the weaknesses of this essentially non-coercive enforcement process became apparent. During the 1670s and 1680s, many Essex disputants either refused arbitration or repudiated decisions that were not to their liking – leaving Essex County courts to handle forty-five unresolved disputes.

[6] Quoted in Stanley N. Katz, "The Problem of a Colonial Legal History," in Jack P. Greene and J. R. Pole, eds., *Colonial British America: Essays in the New History of the Early Modern Era* (Baltimore, 1984), 473.

[7] Cornelia Hughes Dayton, "Turning Points and the Relevance of Colonial Legal History," *William and Mary Quarterly*, 3rd ser., 50 (1993), 9, 11.

Arbitration met a similar fate among Quakers in the Delaware Valley. Even more than Puritans, Quakers were suspicious of the legal system, which in England had been used to persecute them. As property holders, Quakers also worried about the many powers of the courts: to take property from one person and award it to another, to seize household goods to pay debts, and to prefer one heir to others. Most Quaker meetings urged their members not to "go to law" but to arbitrate their differences. Many did so. By the early eighteenth century, however, Delaware Valley Quakers were taking the majority of disputes with their co-religionists to the courts. Disputes that still went to arbitration could take months or years to resolve, and the parties often repudiated the results. To deter repudiations, Quaker arbitrators required disputing parties to sign legally enforceable penal bonds. No longer able to rely on the Meeting and the community to enforce their awards, arbitrators turned for sanctions to the very legal system they had hoped to escape.

A similar "formalization of informal law" took place in Connecticut. In 1645, the Connecticut General Assembly had urged residents to avoid unnecessary jury trials and to resolve private disputes through arbitration. As in Essex County and the Delaware Valley, arbitration in Connecticut worked well initially because most disputes were between members of the same community, but by the 1690s declining religious fervor and increasing social complexity made it harder to enforce awards. Many disputants now refused to enter arbitration unless all parties signed conditioned bonds (or, by the 1730s, promissory notes) guaranteeing compliance. Once voluntary, arbitration had become partly coercive and depended for its success on financial instruments enforced by the common law courts. By the 1750s, disputants regularly named justices of the peace as arbitrators, adding to the legalistic tone of the proceedings. Equally significant, in 1753 the Connecticut General Assembly enacted legislation allowing disputants to make their arbitration a "rule of court," which exposed them to contempt of court and a writ of execution if they failed to abide by the terms of the award. By the 1750s, the informal, community-based arbitration of seventeenth-century Connecticut had gradually given way to a formal, court-centered process.[8]

Just as seventeenth-century Puritans and Quakers had urged arbitration in preference to law, they had also discouraged the presence of lawyers in their godly communities. In 1648, the *Laws and Liberties* of Massachusetts Bay prohibited anyone from assisting the parties in a court hearing. Two decades later, the General Court banned any person "who is an usual and

[8] At that precise moment, the first German settlers in backcountry Frederick County, Maryland, were resolving many of their disputes through community arbitration and subsequently would recapitulate the Connecticut experience.

Common Attorney in any Interior Court" from serving in the legislature. Eventually, the colony's leaders softened their stance; in 1673, they enacted legislation allowing lawyers to practice law, but strictly regulating their fees.

The story was much the same in Pennsylvania. There, rumor had it, "They have no lawyers. Everyone is to tell his own case, or some friend for him. . . . Tis a happy country."[9] Believing with George Fox that "blackness" enveloped lawyers and law courts, Quakers promoted arbitration and the resolution of disputes by means of "Gospel order." If resort to the legal system was necessary, William Penn's Laws stipulated that "all Pleadings, Processes and Records in Courts shall be short, and in English, and in an ordinary and plain Character, that they may be understood." Accordingly, Quaker-controlled proprietary courts in Gloucester County, West Jersey, permitted residents to begin all actions with a simple writ of "case" and accepted complaints written in "plain" language. Having simplified legal procedures, the laws of Pennsylvania and West New Jersey allowed litigants to plead their own cause or have friends appear on their behalf. The two Quaker governments allowed lawyers to practice their profession, but, as in Massachusetts Bay, regulated their fees and posted these rates in court.

As these examples suggest, the animus against lawyers and law courts was most acute in colonies controlled by radical dissenters. When Puritan commissioners held sway in Virginia during the English Civil War, the House of Burgesses provided for the licensing of lawyers, required them to take a prescribed oath, and imposed a fine of 5,000 pounds of tobacco on attorneys who accepted pay for pleading a case in court. But the return of Anglican rule in Virginia in 1660 did not bring the repeal of these laws. Having gathered offices and authority into their own hands, Virginia's landed elite firmly resisted the creation of a body of legal professionals. Only in 1680, and then only for ten years, did the assembly allow lawyers to practice freely. From 1690 until the Burgesses approved a new licensing act in 1732, a few English-trained lawyers handled legal matters in the capital at Williamsburg, while a larger group of self-trained "legal literates," mostly gentlemen-planters, performed these functions in the counties. As Robert Beverley II noted in his *History and Present State of Virginia* (1705), "every one that pleases, may plead his own Cause . . . there being no restraint in that case, nor any licensed Practitioners in the law."

Even as Beverley wrote his *History*, a new legal regime staffed by lawyers was coming into existence in British North America. An important cause

[9] Spence's Anecdotes, in "An Essay on Equity in Pennsylvania" (1825), reprinted in *Reports of the Pennsylvania Bar Association*, I (Philadelphia, 1895), 229.

was the program of imperial administrative and legal reform undertaken by English officials in the 1680s. Shortly after his arrival in New York in 1683, Governor Thomas Dongan secured legislation that centralized the court system and instituted English-style legal procedures. Governor-appointed justices of the peace, sitting singly or in Courts of Common Pleas and Courts of Sessions, formed the foundation of the legal regime. The new statute placed these inferior courts under the supervision of a Supreme Court that enjoyed wide appellate and original jurisdiction, which gave it broad authority over local affairs. Equally important, these courts adopted the practices and procedures – the forms of indictment, process, and recordation – used in English common law courts. Following the termination of the corporate charter of the Massachusetts Bay colony in 1684, Governor Edmund Andros introduced a similar set of centralizing institutions and common law procedures in the newly created Dominion of New England. These legal innovations survived the Glorious Revolution because English officials incorporated them into the new charter of 1692 that made Massachusetts a royal colony.

The imperial initiative was multifaceted and affected nearly every colony. Simultaneously with Dongan's arrival in New York in 1683, English authorities stripped the Virginia House of Burgesses of its traditional authority as the final court of appeal and placed that responsibility in the hands of the governor and council, appointed by the king. Imperial officials likewise directed some royal governors to appoint judges at "the pleasure of the crown," rather than on "good behavior," to make it easier to remove them from office. This imperial effort to centralize the judicial system roiled Maryland's politics between 1705 and 1709 and troubled those in Pennsylvania for an entire generation. Between 1701 and 1722, the Pennsylvania assembly passed a series of statutes giving broad jurisdiction to the county courts; each time the Privy Council voided the legislation because imperial officials insisted that the colony's Supreme Provincial Court should have paramount authority.

English officials also increased the number and variety of royal courts, both to address special legal problems and to enhance the power of the royal governors. In 1696, Parliament created a system of colonial vice-admiralty courts to bolster the authority and effectiveness of naval officers and other customs officials. These courts removed many customs violations from the purview of American juries, thereby preventing local courts from dispensing what an imperial administrator termed "summary and domestic justice" that undermined the Acts of Trade and Navigation. In addition, these courts provided royal governors with a new source of patronage. When Governor William Stoughton named William Atwood as judge of the Admiralty Court in Massachusetts in 1701, Samuel Sewall lamented in his diary, "a considerable part of Executive Authority is now gon out of the hands of New England men."

The sudden and systematic creation around 1700 of Chancery Courts in all of the royal colonies (and also in Maryland and, for a time, in Pennsylvania) likewise challenged the power of local legal and political institutions. Chancery was a jury-less prerogative court, presided over by the governor, who sat alone as chancellor in some colonies and acted in concert with his council in others. Members of the representative assemblies feared that governors would use chancery courts, which provided remedies and procedures not available at law, to advance imperial policies and the property interests of their political allies. For their part, landowners worried that proprietors and governors would employ the court's formidable summary powers – of injunction and specific performance – to collect sizable arrears in quitrents. New York governors did just that. Prior to the creation of a Chancery Court, Governor Robert Hunter confided to the Board of Trade in London in 1718, it had been nearly impossible to collect quitrents. Thereafter, "Delinquents were supoeon'd" to the court and the arrears "were immediately brought in and have ever since been regularly paid into the King's Receiver."[10]

The proliferation of courts and of English royal officials after 1680 encouraged the appearance of lawyers and the forms and procedures of the common law. The first settlers had carried with them diverse sorts of legal knowledge – the law and procedure of local borough and manorial courts, which varied significantly from one English region to another, as well as the common law practiced in the king's tribunals. Common law was especially significant with respect to land because it specified the nature of estates, set the procedures for land acquisition and transfer, and prescribed how land would descend by inheritance. Consequently, the wording of the Massachusetts Bay Dower Act of 1647 generally followed that of common law dower. However, Massachusetts judges often interpreted the act in accord with English borough customs. Thus, they sometimes awarded a widow a life-interest in all of her husband's estate, rather than the one-third prescribed by common law. In other cases, they ignored other possible heirs and gave the widow outright ownership (rather than a life-estate) of all or part of the property. As is often the case in isolated communities, judicial decisions reflected local customs or special social circumstances, rather than the outcomes prescribed in the statute.

The early settlers in New England were equally heterodox and inventive in matters of procedure. In seventeenth-century England, rightful owners trying to reclaim land from a trespassing possessor generally used the

[10] Hunter to Board of Trade, n.d.[1717], E. B. O'Callaghan and Berthold Fernow, eds., *Documents Relative to the Colonial History of New York* (Albany, 1856–1887), V, 499.

process of ejectment, a form of action that required a fictitious "John Doe" to have taken possession of the land. However, litigants and courts in Essex County, Massachusetts, devised a form of action, on the "case, for trespass," that was not used in seventeenth-century England. This action (and a somewhat similar Connecticut action "for Surrendry of Seizin and Possession") provided the same remedy as ejectment in a much more straightforward fashion.

The officials of the Dominion of New England checked the evolution of a separate New England common law. Trained to the law in the home country, they insisted on strict adherence to common law precedents and procedures. Thus, in 1686 the fictitious party "John Doe" made his first appearance in an Essex County land possession case, as the plaintiff used the English action of "ejectment" rather than the locally sanctioned "case, for trespass." When disputants did not use the prescribed English forms, their lawsuits often failed; within a few years the percentage of Essex County actions dismissed on technical grounds doubled – from 3.5 to 7 percent. Following the appointment in 1694 of Thomas Rudyard as the attorney general of New York, there was a similar transition to English forms in that colony. Rudyard had practiced law in London and then served as Deputy Governor of East New Jersey, where he also introduced common law forms.

Interestingly, the increasing legalism stemmed in part from the activities of self-taught American litigants, who contested the authority of the magisterial oligarchy. In the 1690s, for example, James Fitch, an ambitious Connecticut land speculator and elected magistrate, taught himself enough law to prosecute trespassers, evict tenants holding leases from other claimants, and defend his own titles. Fitch's skill in land actions raised the standard of pleadings and forced his main adversaries, members of the influential Winthrop clan, to hire attorneys. Charles Story had a similar impact in New Hampshire. An Englishman, Story came to the colony around 1700 as Proprietor Samuel Allen's appointee as judge of Admiralty, a post he never filled, and Secretary of the province. Working as a private lawyer as well as serving as Secretary, Story insisted on technical precision and orthodox procedures and often won cases on technical grounds. Thus, in an appeal of a decision involving a married woman, he successfully argued that "detinue" had been the wrong cause of action because "by the Common Law the wife cannot be a detainer, but {only} the Husband."[11]

The growing legalism of pleadings alarmed sitting judges. Prior to 1720, most magistrates were legal literates, gentlemen who lacked training in the law, but had acquired legal knowledge either from English manuals, such as

[11] *Province and Court Records of Maine*, ed. Neal W. Allen Jr. (Portland: Maine Historical Society, 1928ff), IV, lxiv–lxvi (*Mainwaring and Frost v. Shores*, 1705).

Michael Dalton's *The Country Justice* and Richard Chamberlain's *The Complete Justice*, or from their experience on the bench. "These County Courts having always been held by Country Gentlemen, who had no education in the Law," former Virginia Attorney General Edward Chilton noted in 1697, "it was no Wonder if both the Sense of the Law was mistaken, and the Form and Method of Proceedings was often very irregular."[12] As trained (or self-taught) lawyers introduced the adversary system and the intricacies of pleading, many sitting magistrates grew frustrated and defensive. They were accustomed in criminal cases to act like inquisitors – compiling evidence, questioning witnesses, and passing sentences without challenge – and were loathe to relinquish that power. In addition, they wanted to decide civil cases, as Virginia magistrate Landon Carter put it, by "Good reason and justice" rather than by the "Precedents" of the court or the "Mechanical knowledge" of attorneys.[13]

More nimble magistrates, and litigants, responded in a constructive fashion to the intrusion of the common law and legal experts, gradually becoming fluent in its language and procedures. By the early 1700s in the Delaware Valley, some defendants used the latinate forms "*nihil debet*" or "*non cull*" rather than the simple declarations in English that they "owed nothing" or were "not guilty." Indeed, some jurisdictions prescribed common law pleas. In 1711 a Connecticut statute imposed fines for violating the rules of pleading, and within a decade the court records of some Connecticut justices of the peace – the lowest level of the legal hierarchy – routinely referred to technical pleas: in abatement, in bar, and demurrers.

By this time in Massachusetts, Samuel Sewall and his fellow Superior Court judges expected appeals based on technical issues and handled them with considerable adroitness. The Court non-suited one plaintiff because he "did not sue upon a written covenant"; dismissed the case of another plaintiff for failing to mention time in his demand for a horse, as was required for an action of "trover"; and abated the writ of a third plaintiff "because 'twas for covenants broken and yet did not declare 'twas by Lease under Hand and Seal."[14] By the 1710s, the Maryland Provincial Court likewise regularly decided cases on demurrers and writs of error.

The growing expertise of appellate court judges reflected a higher standard of appointment and professional expertise. Prior to 1701, the chief

[12] Henry Hartwell, James Blair, and Edward Chilton, *The Present State of Virginia and the College* (1727), ed. Hunter Dickerson Farish, (Williamsburg, VA, 1940), 44–45.

[13] *The Diary of Colonel Landon Carter of Sabine Hall, 1752–1778*, ed. Jack P. Greene (Charlottesville, VA, 1965), 75, 93.

[14] Samuel Sewall, "Journal from August 1, 1717 to July 26, 1726," Bb-Ca and 7 (Massachusetts Historical Society, Boston).

justices of the New York Supreme Court were men of prominence rather than of legal ability; thereafter, they were usually skilled lawyers. This process took longer in Pennsylvania, where before 1718 most members of the Supreme Provincial Court were merchants who had no legal training. In Massachusetts in 1692, none of the five judges of the new Superior Court had formal legal training; however, by 1718 the court boasted three lawyers: Benjamin Lynde Sr., Addington Davenport, and Paul Dudley, the last a long-time attorney general. Those members of the appellate bench without a legal education apparently did their best to become knowledgeable. At his death in 1730, Massachusetts Judge Samuel Sewall's personal law library of twenty-six volumes included not only the traditional guides for justices of the peace but also eight volumes of English statutes and ten volumes of treatises on civil and criminal law and procedure.

Nonetheless, the process of legalization was fragmentary and had only a marginal impact on many cases in local courts. Well into the eighteenth century, superior courts did not insist on rigid adherence to prescribed procedure. As attorney Edward Barradall noted in 1735, although "the strict Rules of Law are not very rigidly adhered to either by Judges or Juries" in county courts, the Virginia General Court intervened on appeal "very sparingly . . . where there has been a Verdict & the Merits of the Cause fairly tried."[15]

Still, the four decades between 1680 and 1720 witnessed a significant alteration in the colonial legal system. Social changes brought about the decline of arbitration; English-trained lawyers and increasingly competent colonial attorneys challenged the hegemony of local magistrates. Simultaneously, imperial authorities created a more centralized court system, mandated the use of common law forms and procedures, and appointed trained lawyers as appellate judges. The result was a nascent system of common law courts that, over the next half-century, would emerge as a central institution in the colonies of British North America.

III. COMMON LAW LAWYERS, JUDGES, AND JURIES, 1720–80

Scholars in recent decades have given quite a lot of attention to the relative power of judges, lawyers, and juries in early America. That issue, however, may be less significant than the interrelated decline of magisterial rule and the enhanced importance of the common law court system. As an English commentator put it at mid-century, "The power of a justice of the peace is in restraint of the common law, and . . . is a tacit repeal of that famous clause

[15] *Ludwige v. French*, in *The Reports by Sir John Randolph and Edward Barradall of the Decisions of the General Court of Virginia, 1728–1741*, ed. R. T. Barton (Boston, 1909), B183.

in the great charter, that a man should be tried by his equals."[16] Reflecting this outlook, Maryland began in the early decades of the eighteenth century to use juries in some slave cases. By this time, most white disputants no longer used arbitrators, influential church members, or local magistrates to resolve their differences in an extra-legal or summary fashion. Rather they litigated their complaints in court. In New York, the per capita rate of litigation doubled between 1700 and 1750.

The nature and substantive outcome of that litigation changed as well. The newly active court system was a complex mix of traditional elements – a paternalistic magistracy, custom-minded local juries – and new features, such as trained lawyers, the common law plea system, and specialized legal instruments like conditional bonds and promissory notes. As debt litigation demonstrates, the presence of lawyers and new types of financial agreements meant that disputes that once hinged on arguments over facts now depended on the status of legal contracts. Increasingly judges rather than juries decided such questions of law.

Debt cases were by far the most common form of civil litigation. As farm communities grew in size, they lost the social cohesion that had bolstered the authority of arbitrators and local magistrates. Likewise, as colonial governments introduced paper money to facilitate tax payments and expand trade, they encouraged the creation of a regional market economy. Increasingly farmers dealt not with "neighbors" but with "strangers." They sold goods to distant customers and borrowed money from town-based merchants who insisted on formal contractual agreements. In 1741, Harvard President Edward Holyoke lamented the impact of these new circumstances on peoples' behavior, especially the "want of Brotherly Love evident by their quarrelsome, litigious Disposition and Lawsuits without numbers."[17] Holyoke was not mistaken. In 1700, the Massachusetts Superior Court heard 108 cases; five decades later, the Court annually handled more than 1,000, a ten-fold increase that far surpassed the rate of population growth. As John Adams complained in the 1760s, "dirty and ridiculous Litigations have been multiplied . . . till the very Earth groans and the stones cry out."[18] Ironically, Adams owed his legal career to the rise in debt litigation, which fueled the emergence of an American bar.

[16] Richard Burn, *The Justice of the Peace and Parish Officer*, 3rd ed. (1756), 159.

[17] Edward Holyoke, *The duty of ministers of the Gospel* . . . (Boston: Printed by T. Fleet, 1741), 24–25.

[18] (June 19, 1760) John Adams diary 5, 26 May–25 November 1760 [electronic edition]. *Adams Family Papers: An Electronic Archive*. Massachusetts Historical Society. http://www.masshist.org/digitaladams/.

The process of creating a distinct legal profession was slowest in the Chesapeake region, where legally literate planters resisted the intrusion of trained lawyers. As one wealthy planter put it, "It is a shame for a gentleman to be ignorant of the laws of his country and to be dependent on every dirty pettifogger" for legal advice; like other notables, he wanted to know enough law "to be able to advise his friends, relations, and neighbors of all sorts."[19] When the Virginia House of Burgesses finally provided for the licensing of lawyers in 1732, it rigorously controlled the profession through a centralized examining system and a strict schedule of fees. Given the absence of a professional bar in Virginia, a second group of legal literates – a cadre of county clerks – encouraged uniform procedures and decisions within Virginia's decentralized court system. The clerks were drawn primarily from middling social ranks and owed their appointments to the Secretary of the colony, who provided them with legal training before dispatching them to their posts, where they also handled routine administrative matters relating to probates and wills. After 1750, trained attorneys finally became an integral part of the Virginia court system; their presence was recorded architecturally by the appearance of lawyers' benches inside the bar that separated judges and their clerks from the jury and the spectators.

Before 1700, primarily because of Puritan and Quaker hostility, professional lawyers were not much more in evidence in the Northern colonies. Even in Anglican-dominated New York, until the 1720s, no more than five or six attorneys handled court cases at any one time. New York lawyers profited from this professional monopoly and used their political influence with Governor Montgomerie to maintain it. The Montgomerie Charter for New York City (1731) restricted practice before the Mayor's Court to eight named individuals, a stranglehold that lasted until 1746, when the assembly enacted legislation opening that court to all members of the Supreme Court bar. To protect their monopoly, City lawyers founded a bar association (1748) that regulated admission to the profession and fixed rates for services.

The fledgling legal profession in Massachusetts also fell under political regulation. In 1710, the assembly required lawyers to take an oath of office and instructed inferior and superior courts to examine attorneys who wished to practice before them. This legislation began a decades-long struggle between certified attorneys, most of whom were members of well-established families, and a much larger group of legal literates, many of

[19] Charles Carroll of Doughregan Manor to Charles Carroll of Carrollton, Oct. 16, 1759, *Unpublished Letters of Charles Carroll of Carrollton*, ed. by Thomas M. Field (New York, 1902), 33–34.

whom were rising men who served as minor court officials. "Looking about me in the Country," the young lawyer John Adams noted, "I found the practice of Law was grasped into the hands of Deputy Sheriffs, Pettyfoggers and even Constables, who filed all the Writts upon Bonds, promissory notes and accounts, received the Fees established for Lawyers and stirred up many unnecessary Suits."[20]

To encourage the creation of a professional bar, during the 1720s several Massachusetts courts prohibited individuals not sworn as attorneys from charging legal fees. Then, between 1736 and 1742, the assembly banned sheriffs and other court officials from providing legal advice or filing writs. Helped along by this legislation, a number of capable Massachusetts men, such as Jeremiah Gridley and Edmund Trowbridge, became lawyers, and English-trained lawyers with good political connections – Robert Auchmuty, William Bollan, and the future governor William Shirley – joined them. By the early 1750s a trained bar had taken form not only in Boston (Suffolk County) but also in other Massachusetts jurisdictions. Lawyers organized formal county bar associations that worked with the judges to create a graded profession attractive to men of high social status. Would-be attorneys needed a college education, a three-year apprenticeship in a law office, and the bar association's recommendation to practice before an inferior court. After a few years of practice and a new recommendation, a lawyer could seek admission to the bar of the Superior Court. In 1762, Lieutenant Governor Thomas Hutchinson pushed along this process of professionalization by establishing distinctions between attorneys and barristers that had been common in England since the late seventeenth century. By then, nearly fifty trained lawyers were practicing in Massachusetts, and twenty-five of them won recognition as barristers by the Superior Court. As leading families sent their sons into the profession over the next decade, these numbers nearly doubled. By 1775, there were about forty-five attorneys and forty-seven barristers in Massachusetts.

Professional practice brought prosperity to many Massachusetts lawyers and considerable wealth to a few. However, to earn a decent livelihood, rising attorneys had to undertake petty tasks, such as debt collection, and to pursue clients relentlessly to collect their fees. Outside of Boston, legal literates continued to flourish; in York County (in the Maine district) part-time lawyers handled nearly half of the court cases in the 1760s and an organized bar appeared only in the 1790s. To wipe out these competitors and protect their emergent monopoly, regularly admitted attorneys and

[20] John Adams autobiography, part 1, "John Adams," through 1776, sheet 7 of 53 [electronic edition]. *Adams Family Papers: An Electronic Archive*. Massachusetts Historical Society. http://www.masshist.org/digitaladams/.

barristers refused to counsel clients whose writs had been initially drawn by these self-trained practitioners.

Whatever their degree of expertise, lawyers brought fundamental changes to the civil court system. Traditionally, civil and criminal juries in Massachusetts (and some other colonies) had the authority to decide matters of law as well as matters of fact. Moreover, after 1672 in Massachusetts and after 1700 in Connecticut, a jury verdict was conclusive and a judge could not set it aside, even if the decision was contrary to his instructions. As lawyers began to represent litigants, they began to complicate the dynamics of the courtroom by translating specific disputes between individuals into a confrontation between competing legal doctrines. Thus, attorneys urged jurors to decide a case according to "the custom of the town" whenever strict adherence to common law precedents would undermine their clients' case. Opposing counsel of course told jurors that they should "determine by Law" and ignore local custom and natural equity.[21] "The Laws of Society and Civil Government are not founded upon the strict Rules of natural Justice," Virginia attorney Edward Barradall argued in 1735, in defense of a client who had knowingly sold a terminally ill slave.[22] Pointing out that his client had not explicitly warranted the health of the slave, Barradall invoked the legal principle of *caveat emptor* (let the buyer beware), though without success. Whatever the law of warranties, the local jury preferred a settlement that the community would accept as just. Recognizing the importance of public sentiment, a Massachusetts statute allowed juries that were not "easy" about a case to choose "in open court to advise with any man they all think fit to resolve or direct them, before they give in their verdict."[23]

While technical arguments complicated the deliberations of some juries, lawyers' common law pleas removed many more cases from their purview. Juries had the greatest latitude when defendants in a civil case plead the "general issue." Because this plea denied all the plaintiff's allegations, the jury would hear evidence on all relevant matters. Moreover, because the legal relationships among the various matters were often complicated, the jury had to decide which legal doctrine to apply, giving them effective control of the law. However, trained lawyers knew how to devise pleas "in bar" that

[21] *Colden v. Stockbridge*, in Robert Treat Paine, *Minutes and Trials and Law Cases* (Boston), vol. 1.

[22] R. T. Barton, ed., *Virginia Colonial Decisions: The Reports by Sir John Randolph and by Edward Barradoll of Decisions of the General Court of Virginia, 1728-1741* (Boston, 1909), II: B 48–49.

[23] *The Laws and Liberties of Massachusetts Bay*, intro. by Max Farrand (Cambridge, MA, 1929), 51.

limited the case to a narrow issue, for example, whether or not a defendant who was being sued on a conditional debt bond had in fact performed the condition. Given that plea, the jury only heard evidence that pertained to the performance of the condition (the debt payment) and not the details of the contract that it guaranteed. In such a suit, the "law" was obvious and the jury considered only the "fact" of the payment.

Other pleas offered by defendants might remove the entire case from consideration by a jury. For example, a plea in abatement of a writ asked the judge to dismiss the action because the plaintiff's writ was technically flawed or improperly served. Alternatively, a defendant could demur, which meant admitting the facts alleged by the plaintiff but denying that they constituted a valid cause of action. Whether the defendant's demurrer was good was a legal question decided solely by the judge.

In Connecticut, the percentage of defendants invoking such "technical" legal defenses increased dramatically after 1700. Previously, defendants in contested civil actions nearly always pled the general issue, giving the case after argument to the jury. By the 1720s, only about 15 percent of all civil defendants entered such pleas; instead, they usually pled in abatement, alleging flaws in the plaintiff's writ. If these pleas failed, defendants then pled on the merits. In subsequent decades, between 20 and 30 percent of defendants pled on the merits, while most of the rest filed demurrers. If these demurrers failed, as most of them did, the defendant lost the case without a jury ever hearing it.

Although lawyers (and the broader awareness of common law procedure) facilitated the relative decline of jury trials, they did not cause it. The cause lay in the changing nature of debt cases, which constituted from 75 to 90 percent of all civil cases. In seventeenth-century Connecticut, most farmers, artisans, and merchants dealt with local residents and recorded their credit and debt transactions in ledgers and account books. When disputes arose, plaintiffs filed an action on "book," declaring that the debtors owed a certain sum that they had never paid, "though often requested." The only way to resolve such disputes was for a magistrate (for small sums) or a jury (for larger ones) to examine the accounts and take testimony from the various parties.

By the 1720s, the debt system had changed dramatically. In the new market economy, most farmers and shopkeepers did not record debts in ledgers, and so actions on book constituted only 30 percent of the civil cases heard in Connecticut's county courts. Conversely, actions on written instruments, such as bonds and promissory notes, now represented 70 percent of the cases. Likewise, in Plymouth County, Massachusetts, between 1725 and 1774, only 15 percent of all civil suits were actions of case on book accounts, whereas 59 percent were actions on notes and bonds. The situation in magistrates' courts was similar. Over the course of six months in

1754, a justice of the peace in Windham, Connecticut, heard fifty-six cases: seven minor criminal offenses, four cases on book debts, and forty-seven actions on promissory notes.

Promissory notes were a creditor's dream, because they made payment much more certain. In signing such notes, debtors expressly promised to pay specific sums to creditors, who were often merchants or storekeepers in another town, and that pledge was legally binding. When Nathaniel Collins of Enfield, Connecticut, sued such a debtor, he told his attorney that it was "needless to insist uppon any thing farther, because the bill [the signed note] is the turning point."[24] Recognizing the legal weakness of their position, debtors contested fewer than 10 percent of the cases involving promissory notes and simply defaulted.

In colonies such as Massachusetts, where the local paper money depreciated continually between 1720 and the late 1740s, some debtors may have used non-payment as a financial strategy. By refusing to pay, they forced their creditors to sue and win judgments – which could be paid in cheaper currency. In other cases, non-payment may have been involuntary, the result of periodic scarcities of cash in the economy. For these reasons, and because the currency depreciation cut the real cost of the prescribed legal fees by at least two-thirds between 1700 and 1750, the number of debt cases in Massachusetts increased dramatically. The proportion heard by juries decreased in an equally striking fashion. In the Massachusetts Superior Court, an appellate body that heard criminal as well as civil cases, the proportion of suits that reached a jury decreased from 47 percent in 1722 to 27 percent in 1742.

The declining proportion of jury trials in civil cases was not limited to New England. In New York City, juries heard 17 percent of debt cases in the 1690s, but only 4 percent by the 1750s. In the Quaker colonies of the Delaware Valley between 1680 and 1710, juries heard only 16 percent of all civil cases; most of the rest involved debts or contracts guaranteed by sealed bonds. Use of a sealed bond allowed a creditor to file an action of debt (rather than case) and limited the legal options open to a defendant, who was obligated to pay the penal sum specified in the bond and could not hope for a reduced award from a sympathetic jury. As in Connecticut, most Delaware Valley debtors – some 78 percent – either defaulted on their promissory notes or sealed bonds or confessed judgment against themselves. Of those suits that debtors contested, plaintiffs claimed victories in three-quarters.

Debt litigation took a somewhat different course in Virginia because of the presence there of English creditors. Before 1740, juries heard relatively few cases. Most debtors gave their creditors a power of attorney to confess

[24] Nathaniel Collins to George Denison, 23 May 1711, in *Collins v. Frearman*, New London County Court Records (Connecticut State Library, Hartford), 178.

judgment if the debt was not paid. When creditors presented these claims in an action for debt and asked the court for judgment by petition, defendants frequently pled "for time to imparl." By imparling, debtors signaled their intention to settle the dispute out of court, thereby maintaining both their private credit and their public honor. In many instances, the courts closed their books on these cases with the notation "dismissed, the parties being agreed."[25]

However, after 1740 the number of jury trials increased. Many planters were accruing much larger debts than previously and were reluctant to confess judgment. Moreover, British merchants held most of these obligations and, because of Parliamentary legislation in 1732, could seize land and slaves to satisfy sterling debts. Facing significant financial losses, debtors sought relief from the planter-dominated Virginia assembly and sympathetic local juries. In 1748 and 1749, the assembly enacted two statutes designed to nullify Parliament's intervention. One statute incorporated the common law rule exempting land from seizure unless pledged by mortgage, the other set an artificially low rate of exchange. It allowed residents to pay off their debts in English pounds sterling in Virginia currency at 125 percent of face value at a time when the real exchange rate was higher. Supplementary legislation in 1755 allowed local courts to decide on the proper rate of exchange, so that even the recovery of a debt guaranteed by a sealed instrument was uncertain. As the Virginia agent for the Scottish firm of James Buchanon and Company wrote to his employers, "It would be dangerous to trust Your Claim to the Decision of a jury."[26] The creditor's alternatives were to sue in the Chancery Court, a time-consuming and expensive process, or to accept a lesser sum from the debtor. Virginia planters would pursue a similar strategy after the Revolution. Hauled into court by British creditors over unpaid prewar debts, planters successfully persuaded many Patriot juries to hold them liable only for the principal of the debts and not for the substantial interest charges that had accrued during and after the war.

Suits for debts were ubiquitous in the Revolutionary era. They lay behind the North Carolina Regulator movement in the 1760s, Shays's Rebellion in Massachusetts in the 1780s, and other instances of violence and court closings. Quite apart from their political significance, these uprisings – and the thousands of normally adjudicated debt cases – signaled the increasing involvement of middling farmers in the market economy, the growing influence of trained lawyers, and the shift toward judges in the balance of courtroom power. Given the importance of common law courts and judges

[25] Charles City County Order Book, 1737–57, passim (VSL).
[26] Nov. 24, 1767, William Nelson Letter Book, 1766–75 (VSL).

in the eighteenth-century economic and legal system, it was predictable that they (and not assemblies and governors) would become the prime target of rioters.

IV. THE ANGLICIZATION THESIS AND THE TRIUMPH OF LOCAL LAW

The verdicts rendered by chauvinistic juries in mid-eighteenth century Virginia testify to the importance of local control of legal institutions, a concern of English policymakers since the late seventeenth century. As the political economist and royal official Charles Davenant observed in 1698, "Colonies are a strength to their mother kingdom [only] while they are under good discipline [and] while they are strictly made to observe the fundamental laws of their original country."[27] Even as Davenant wrote, imperial administrators were attempting to impose "good discipline" on various colonial legal institutions. Through grants of chancery jurisdiction, as we have seen, royal governors gained decision-making authority over a host of legal issues. They selected judges of the jury-less vice-admiralty courts and insisted on the crown's "undoubted Right of Appointing Judges."[28] In 1753, the Privy Council made appointment of judges "upon the pleasure of the crown" mandatory for new governors. In 1761 the requirement was extended to all the royal colonies.

These imperial initiatives, along with the increasing importance of English culture, goods, and common law forms and procedures in the colonies, have prompted historian John Murrin to declare that American society and law were increasingly "anglicized" between 1700 and 1775. Murrin's idea has achieved wide currency, but it cannot withstand careful scrutiny. Consider, for example, the changing character of colonial *society*. Because of the influx of tens of thousands of Africans, Germans, Scotch, and Scots-Irish, the mainland colonies were steadily becoming *less* English in composition and in culture. In 1700, those of English birth or ancestry constituted 85 percent of the non-aboriginal residents of British North America; by 1775, that proportion was less than 50 percent. This was no anglicization of colonial *society* and *culture*, but rather just the reverse.

Nor did the imperial initiatives of the late seventeenth century create a legal system dominated by those of English birth or managed in the interest of the English crown. Take the case of religious and legal institutions in Virginia. Although the Church of England was legally established,

[27] *Two Discourses on the Public Revenues and Trade of England* (London, 1698), 17.

[28] Order in Council, 4 March 1735, Colonial Office Papers 5/386, f. 76 (Public Record Office, London).

the colony had no ecclesiastical courts and no ecclesiastical hierarchy. Virginia-born planter-vestrymen controlled the affairs of the parishes and the appointment of their ministers. Likewise in law: of the 151 barristers and attorneys licensed in Virginia between 1716 and 1770, only 27 were English-born and English-trained; the rest were native-born, and most were locally educated. Virtually all eighteenth-century Virginia magistrates and judges were locally born. Relatively few of these legal officials ever visited England, fewer still lived there for any length of time, and virtually none became Loyalists. Most legal patronage remained under the control of well-established local planters and magistrates. When Governor Spotswood created a Court of Oyer and Terminer in 1717, the leading planters who sat on the Council began a long campaign to place their members on the court. Their persistence was rewarded. By mid-century, the Court of Oyer and Terminer was customarily composed only of councilors, nearly all of whom had deep roots in Virginia society.

In Massachusetts, English officials had greater success in anglicizing the legal system – that is, in appointing imperial-minded lawyers, judges, and court officials who would follow the lead of the royal governor. A liberal use of patronage was crucial to this effort. To entice John Adams away from the popular party during the late 1760s, Governor Bernard offered him the position of advocate general of the admiralty court. The rising attorney from Braintree derided the offer as "a first Step in the Ladder of Royal Favour and promotion," but it found a ready taker in Samuel Fitch, a fellow lawyer and future Loyalist.[29] Lawyer Jonathan Sewall, the grandnephew of Superior Court Judge Samuel Sewall, served the crown both as Attorney General of Massachusetts and as the absentee Admiralty Court judge for Nova Scotia and Canada, a post worth £600 annually. Some of the twenty-seven Massachusetts barristers who became avowed Loyalists or Tory sympathizers likewise held patronage positions, while others worked for Loyalist merchants. However, twenty Massachusetts barristers and most of the attorneys gravitated to the patriot side because of ideological inclination, loyalty to their home communities, or a recognition that imperial positions were limited in number and already monopolized by a few intermarried, high-status families. The Hutchinson clan was one such family. It shows what an "anglicized" legal bureaucracy would have looked like. During the 1760s, Thomas Hutchinson served both as Lieutenant Governor of Massachusetts and as Chief Justice of the Superior Court of Judicature. Sitting with him on the five-member court were fellow future Loyalists

[29] (1768) John Adams autobiography, part 1, "John Adams," through 1776, sheet 11 of 53 [electronic edition]. *Adams Family Papers: An Electronic Archive*. Massachusetts Historical Society. http://www.masshist.org/digitaladams/.

Peter Oliver and Benjamin Lynde, each related by marriage to the other and to Hutchinson. Two other members of the Hutchinson family sat on the four-member Court of Common Pleas for Suffolk County. They generally favored imperial interests.

Suffolk County, however, was not Massachusetts. The judges in courts of distant counties showed much greater independence, in part because they held their offices during good behavior. As Governor Bernard complained, the judges could "defy the King, oppose his Laws and insult his Government and [still] be in no danger of losing" their commissions. "It is not unusual," he went on, "for a Person, who has distinguished himself in Political Matters, to get himself recommended to the Governor, as a Man well disposed to Government, and as soon as he has received his Commission to declare for the Party of the Sons of Liberty."[30]

Local legal officials in Massachusetts – magistrates, judges, and juries – were even more autonomous. Although the governor appointed justices of the peace, they derived their authority, and thus their practical capacity to enforce the law, primarily from their standing in the local community. Moreover, the justices were financially independent because they derived their income from fees and county taxes that they levied. Likewise, imperial officials found it difficult to manage Massachusetts juries, partly because local town meetings (and not governor-appointed sheriffs) chose the jury pool. Thus, members of the Scituate Town Meeting inspected a list of eligible residents and then selected those "Such as they Judged most Suitable to Serve as Jurors."[31] Once locally chosen men took their seats in the jury box, Governor Bernard complained, they rendered verdicts "against the express instructions of the judges" and systematically undercut royal authority: "A Custom house officer had no chance with a jury, let his cause be what it will."[32] As the political crisis deepened, Thomas Hutchinson reiterated this point in instructing a Suffolk County grand jury. "We, who are to execute the Law, are not to enquire into the Reason and Policy of it. . . . I mention this, Gentlemen, because, I have found juries taking upon them to judge of the Wholesomeness of the Laws, and thereby subverting the very End of their Institution."[33] To eliminate the problem, Loyalist-minded lawyers

[30] Francis Bernard to Earl of Hillsborough, Nov. 14, 1768, published in the Boston *Evening Post*, April 10, 1769.

[31] Scituate Records: Town Meeting Minutes, 1743–80, 19 (ms. in Scituate Town Hall, Scituate, Massachusetts).

[32] Francis Bernard to Board of Trade, Aug. 2, 1761, in *Reports of cases argued and adjudged in the Superior Court of Judicature of the Province of Massachusetts Bay, between 1761 and 1772. By Josiah Quincy, Junior*, ed. Samuel M. Quincy (Boston, 1865), II, 282 (hereafter Quincy Reports).

[33] Quincy Reports, I, 306–08.

and politicians set about devising doctrines that (according to John Adams) "would render Juries a mere Ostentation and Pageantry, and the Court absolute Judges of Law and fact."[34]

Colonial legal and political institutions, however, remained largely immune from British attempts to control them. Consider, for example, the success of the New York assembly in wresting control of the colony's finances from the Royal Governor and his Council. In a process that began in 1706 and extended over three decades, the assembly gradually channeled most of the colony's tax revenues to its own treasurer and claimed sole authority to spend those funds. In a stunning climax, the assembly asserted its power to act as a court by adjudicating, directly or by delegation, the validity of claims against the public purse. As Archibald Kennedy, an imperial official in New York, complained in 1750, the legislators "take upon themselves to be the sole judges . . . [and insist] that no order for publick money shall issue, untill their judgment has been obtained for it."[35] Other assemblies likewise asserted control over the disbursement of public funds.

If by an "anglicized" colonial legal system we mean one increasingly dominated by imperial officials or sympathizers, then, anglicization does not seem to be the most appropriate term to describe the dynamics of eighteenth-century colonial legal development. This does not mean, however, that the concept has no value. First, anglicization accurately describes the elimination or incorporation within a dominant English legal regime of the pre-1674 system of Dutch law in New York. It also conveys the fate of the inheritance customs brought by German immigrants (and perhaps those from Scotland and Ireland as well), which were gradually adapted to fit within the categories of English law. Second, the term correctly suggests the waning of the critical Puritan and Quaker views of lawyers and legal institutions and the rising importance of a more cosmopolitan Anglican outlook – although, once said, the perspective yields little interpretive insight given that the emergence of the professional bar was more rapid in Puritan New England than in the Anglican Chesapeake. Finally, the concept properly indicates the increasing importance of a *new* system of English rules – the common law – within the American legal system. Of course, one can still ask whether it makes sense to call this "anglicization" when the various legal practices of the seventeenth-century colonies were also of English origin. It is also worth noting that between 1650 and 1800 a similar process was taking place in England, as the forms and procedures of the

[34] (12 February 1771) John Adams diary 16, 10 January 1771–28 [i.e. 27] November 1772 [electronic edition]. *Adams Family Papers: An Electronic Archive*. Massachusetts Historical Society. http://www.masshist.org/digitaladams/.

[35] Archibald Kennedy, *An Essay on the Government of the Colonies* (New York, 1752), 23, 26.

King's common law courts gradually displaced those of borough and manor courts. What Murrin describes as "anglicization" might better be called an attempt at centralization; that is, the subordination to metropolitan control of legal institutions throughout the "provinces" – whether English counties or American colonies.

A crucial step in eighteenth-century legal development was the affirmation in 1720 by British Attorney General Richard West that the American plantations were not conquered territories subject to the rigors of the royal prerogative. Rather they were distant counties, so that "the common law of England is the common Law of the plantations," a declaration that accorded imperial legitimacy to the American assemblies and their court systems.[36] By the 1770s, colonial lawyers had imbibed this understanding and, reflecting their increasing fluency in the common law, were citing cases decided by the King's Courts at Westminster in their legal arguments. Thus, replying to an inquiry from the Board of Trade, New York's last royal governor reported, "The Common Law of England is considered as the Fundamental law of the Province."[37] But the colonists' increasing reliance on the common law did not produce an "anglicized" (and Loyalist) result – another reason for avoiding the term. During the revolutionary crisis, Whig lawyers used the legal institutions of the eighteenth-century common law regime *against* imperial officials. In 1761, Boston lawyer James Otis cited English common law precedents in disputing the legitimacy of a general search warrant. In demanding a jury trial for John Hancock four year later, John Adams argued, "This 29th Chap. of Magna Charta" respecting the right to a jury trial "has for many Centuries been esteemed by Englishmen, as one of the . . . firmest Bulwarks of their Liberties."

Patriot-dominated grand juries likewise used their legal powers to thwart imperial prosecutors by refusing to indict either colonial merchants for smuggling or patriot agitators for seditious libel. As one British administrator lamented, even "the Indians . . . frequently observe that our Governments are weak & impotent [because] . . . whatever these people do their Jurys will acquitt them."[38] Conversely, when patriot lawyers used the liability doctrines of common law to bring civil actions against customs officials for financial losses caused by their enforcement activities, juries awarded substantial sums to injured shopkeepers and merchants. Local Whig law,

[36] George Chalmers, *Opinions of eminent lawyers, on various points of English jurisprudence, chiefly concerning the colonies, fisheries, and commerce of Great Britain* (London, 1814), I, 194–95.

[37] Report of His Excellency William Tryon Esquire, 11 June 1774, *Documentary History of New York*, ed. E. B. O'Callaghan (Albany, 1849–51), I, 754.

[38] Sir William Johnson to the Earl of Dartmouth, O'Callaghan, *New York Colonial Documents*, VIII, 316.

now elaborated in common law courtrooms, checkmated imperial law based on Parliamentary sovereignty, statutes, and supervising officials. The rise of assembly power and Whig law best describe the course of eighteenth-century events.

V. THE SUPREMACY OF THE LEGISLATURE

In his path-breaking monograph, *The Transformation of American Law, 1780–1860*, Morton Horwitz argued that the common law judges of the early nineteenth century played a central role in directing the course of social change. According to Horwitz, the judges adopted an instrumental approach to the common law and fundamentally reinterpreted doctrines that had given a high priority to social stability, prescriptive rights, equitable dealings, and the rights of creditors. By revising these doctrines in dynamic ways, the courts removed traditional burdens on risk-bearing entrepreneurs and encouraged economic development. Indeed, Horwitz maintains that by the 1820s "the process of common law decision making had taken on many of the qualities of legislation" because appellate judges, in deciding specific cases, self-consciously articulated general doctrines. Beyond that, Horwitz intimates that judges were more important than legislatures in shaping the course of nineteenth-century law. He also suggests that they subverted the democratic process by fashioning rules that aided capitalist entrepreneurs at the expense of ordinary citizens.

The truth is somewhat more complex. Nineteenth-century trial court judges did assert greater control over the outcome of civil cases than their predecessors did, and appellate judges did articulate innovative legal doctrines of broad significance. But the republican revolution of 1776 sparked an even more impressive expansion in the authority and activity of the state legislatures. The legislatures quickly asserted their plenary powers, reorganized court systems, and enacted statutes that consciously encouraged economic development and the creation of a more "republican" society. In the Early Republic, we shall see, the legislatures were the leading edge for change. In fact, the increased importance of the nineteenth-century judiciary was related to the ascendancy of the legislatures, for it resulted not only from the judges' growing legal expertise but also from legislatively mandated changes that enhanced the judiciary's powers, and, less directly, from legislative activism.

During most of the colonial era, neither the local magistracy nor the higher judiciary was well trained or distinguished. In 1733, the North Carolina assembly protested the appointment of "so many Evil Magistrates"; in fact, residents accused about one-tenth of the colony's 1,270 justices of the peace of misbehavior and corruption, a pattern of misconduct that sparked the Regulator movement of the 1760s. In New York in 1763, 60 percent of the justices of the peace outside of New York City had no formal legal training. In all of the colonies, plural office holding was common, and justices often used their influence to acquire appointments as sheriffs, coroners, and other fee-charging officials. Moreover, increasing numbers of magistrates evaded their judicial and administrative responsibilities. As the sittings of the Virginia county courts lengthened in duration, from one day in the 1720s to four or five days in the 1760s, many justices only attended on the first day or two. By mid-century in Richmond County, three-fifths of those appointed as justices were dismissed for "Refusing to act" as their commissions required.

Initially, the higher judiciary was almost as unqualified as the magistracy. Before 1740 in Pennsylvania and Massachusetts, most judges appointed to the Superior Court had minimal qualifications: a college degree or a few years of experience as a magistrate. Thereafter, standards improved as governors filled appellate positions with men who came from legal families and had considerable judicial experience. Of the ten men named to the Massachusetts Superior Court between 1746 and 1772, nine had served for at least five years on a lower court and had relatives who were also Superior Court judges. Surprisingly, the Revolution pushed forward the process of professionalization. The statute creating the Massachusetts Supreme Judicial Court in 1782 specified explicitly that justices shall be "learned in the law," and all but two of twenty-six judges named to the Massachusetts Superior Court between 1775 and 1825 were trained lawyers. Similarly, all of the judges named to the post-Revolutionary Pennsylvania Supreme Court were qualified attorneys. Because of their formal training, the appellate judges of the early nineteenth century had the legal knowledge that was a prerequisite for an activist and innovative judiciary.

Favorable legislation was the second factor that enhanced the position of the judiciary. In Massachusetts, Pennsylvania, and several other states, new statutes gave trial judges greater control over their courtrooms. After 1805 in Massachusetts, a single trial judge (rather than a panel of judges) presided at a case and had the authority to throw out verdicts that were "manifestly against the weight of the evidence."[39] In Connecticut, judges took advantage of an eighteenth-century statute that, as Zephaniah Swift explained in 1822, allowed judges to instruct juries "in the opinion of the court, how the case ought to be decided" and to force them twice to reconsider contrary verdicts.[40] If the jury did not follow the court's direction or

[39] *Hammond v. Wadhams*, 5 Mass. 353, 355 (1809).

[40] Henry Dutton, *A Revision of Swift's Digest of the Laws of Connecticut* (New Haven, J. H. Benham 1849), 773.

delivered a verdict that went against the evidence, judges could (and usually did) grant a motion by the losing side for a new trial. Equally important, a Massachusetts statute ended the practice of giving cases appealed from a county court a *de novo* hearing before the Supreme Court. Rather, the appellate court ruled on contested points of law, thereby establishing a coherent substantive body of legal principles. Viewed historically, the termination of de novo retrials signaled the demise of an equitable "culture of appeal"; in its place stood the procedures of common law, which allowed reviews only though writs of legal error.

In Virginia and a few other few states, eighteenth-century practices that limited the powers of the judges continued to command support. Trial court judges in Virginia allowed wide scope to juries and generally refused the demands of plaintiffs to instruct juries that the weight of evidence proved their case. Reinforcing that reluctance, in 1814 the Virginia Supreme Court chastised judges who summed up the evidence at the end of a trial or suggested an appropriate verdict. Nonetheless, like their colleagues in other states, Virginia appellate judges were increasingly active; between 1790 and 1815, newly created District Courts reversed or returned for retrial nearly two-thirds of the county court cases they considered on appeal.

Activism elicited criticism that judges were making law rather than simply applying it. As early as 1767 Daniel Dulany of Maryland warned that if judges "take upon themselves to frame a regulation, in prospect, which is to govern in future . . . they essentially assume a power legislative." Seeking in 1800 to justify such judicial refashioning of legal rules, Massachusetts Chief Justice Isaac Parker suggested that judges had always to interpret the timeless and fundamental "principles of the common law" in the light of present social conditions. Parker's perspective acquired increasing support. Within a few decades, Tapping Reeve and James Gould were advising students at the Litchfield Law School, "theoretical[ly] courts make no law but in point of fact they are legislators."[41]

As this statement hints, the rise of judicial innovation and legal instrumentalism stemmed in part from the legislative activism spurred by revolutionary republicanism. During the colonial era, many Americans believed that their representative assemblies existed primarily to prevent misrule by power-hungry governors and not to devise new legislation. Indeed, colonial assemblies often spent substantial parts of their short annual sessions in thwarting imperial initiatives. In the time that remained, the members – who were primarily local men of high status – focused either on administrative tasks, such as creating governments for new townships, or on

[41] E. Whittlesey, "Reeve & Gould Lectures," I, 1 (1813) (ms 4024) and "Reeve's Lectures," I, 4–5 (ms. 2013), both in Treasure Room, Harvard Law School Library.

legislative patronage, by passing "private" bills that addressed the request of specific communities and individuals. Thus, although the Massachusetts legislature annually enacted several dozen bills during the 1760s, only a few of those statutes altered an existing general law or made a new one. The Virginia House of Burgesses likewise spent much of its time paying claims for services; arbitrating disputes over local boundaries and the location of tobacco inspection warehouses; approving new townships, bridges, and roads; and responding to local demands.

The laws enacted by the New Jersey legislature exemplify the general pattern. Between 1750 and 1775 more than half of the 455 bills enacted into law originated as private petitions submitted by influential men, and 80 percent of them applied only to particular individuals or specific localities – for example, reimbursing expenses, breaking an entail, granting relief to a debtor (or creditor), or constructing a public project at private expense. Indeed, only 7 of the 256 petition-derived laws were of general concern and legally enforceable throughout the colony. Of the remaining laws – an average of only eight per year between 1750 and 1775 – the overwhelming majority were routine: budgetary bills levying taxes or directing expenditures, authorizations creating new towns and other governmental jurisdictions, and statutes reenacting earlier legislation. Instead of legislation, New Jersey and the other colonies relied for their government on "the common law . . . in the English model," one contemporary noted, and on the authority over township and county affairs wielded by local magistrates and county courts. As the activist-minded Governor William Franklin complained in 1772, many representatives believed that any "Measure which must be attended with Expense, and has not a Tendency to benefit every Part of the Province, equally, ought not to be adopted by the legislature."[42]

Given such attitudes, substantive legislation that affected an entire colony was sporadic and crisis-driven. Responding to a severe economic downturn in the early 1720s, the Pennsylvania legislature enacted an array of laws that taxed imports from neighboring colonies; provided incentives for the production of hemp, hops, and flax; and established an inspection system to improve the quality of flour for export. Most important of all, the legislature issued paper money and, to put it into circulation in a fiscally responsible manner, created a system of loan offices that dispensed currency loans in return for mortgages on farmers' lands. Three decades later, the demands of the Seven Years War on Pennsylvania generated a new burst of legislative activity, focused primarily on financing and supplying the provincial militia. Stimulated by the success of this colony-wide effort,

[42] Address of William Franklin to the Assembly, 20 August 1772, *The Votes and Proceedings of the General Assembly of the Province of New Jersey* (Burlington, NJ, 1772).

private entrepreneurs and public officials outlined various schemes of economic development, including the initial proposals for post-Revolutionary ventures, such as the Lancaster Turnpike and the Chesapeake and Delaware Canal.

The war of independence sparked an unprecedented wave of governmental activism. Wartime demands forced the state legislatures to act in dramatically new ways: mobilizing thousands of troops, raising large sums of money, purchasing military supplies, holding down inflation, preserving order, and controlling Loyalists. Equally important, the new republican state constitutions systematically weakened the powers and responsibilities of the governors and increased those of the legislatures. The representative bodies that emerged after the Revolution drew more of their members from the middling ranks than previous legislatures had and saw themselves as the agents of the sovereign people. "In our Governments," a wary James Madison pointed out in 1788, "the real power lies in the majority . . . [and] the government is the mere instrument of the major number of the Constituents."[43]

Whatever Madison's worries about popular power and legislative tyranny, state lawmakers increasingly asserted their plenary powers. During the colonial era, many Massachusetts statutes contained preambles justifying the legislation as a socially necessary extension of existing legal doctrines. Following the adoption of the state constitution of 1780, the use of such justificatory preambles sharply declined and by the end of the decade appeared in only half the enacted statutes. Increasingly, legislators began bills with a "be it enacted" clause, a stark statement of their sovereign power. By 1813, Reeve and Gould had adopted this positivist perspective; they told the prospective lawyers at Litchfield that each statute was "a rule of civil conduct prescribed by the supreme power of the state commanding what is right and prohibiting what is wrong." A few years later, treatise writer John Milton Goodenow extended this maxim of legislative supremacy over the jurisprudential realm. The judge, Goodenow declared, "is governed himself by positive law, and executes and inforces the will of the supreme power, which is the will of the People."[44]

[43] James Madison to Thomas Jefferson, 17 October 1788), in Gaillard Hunt, ed., *James Madison: Writings* (New York, 1904), 5:272.

[44] E. Whittlesey, "Reeve & Gould Lectures," I, 1 (1813) (ms 4024) and "Reeve's Lectures," I, 4–5 (ms. 2013), both in Treasure Room, Harvard Law School Library; John Milton Goodenow, *Historical Sketches of the Principles and Maxims of American Jurisprudence in Contrast with the Doctrines of the English Common Law on the Subject of Crimes and Punishments* (Steubenville, 1819), 33.

State legislatures used their newly consecrated authority to control the legal system. During the Revolutionary War, state legislatures consciously overrode common law property rights to confiscate Loyalist lands. In Massachusetts, the legislature acted as a high court of appeal, granting new trials, reversing decisions, and arbitrarily extending lawsuits. After the war, it continued the colonial practice of regulating the practice of law – setting legal fees, prohibiting minor court officials from drawing up writs and pleas, and allowing individuals to manage their own court suits.

Subsequently, many states revised their laws in accord with "republican" principles. They changed the laws of inheritance to eliminate primogeniture and entail and moderated the criminal code by restricting the use of corporal punishment and the number of capital offenses. Codification of the civil law turned out to be an intractable problem, both because many lawyers preferred the flexibility of the common law and because legal doctrines and protocols had diverse origins – Parliamentary statutes, the enactments of colonial assemblies, and common law decisions – and had been interpreted differently by various juries and judges. However, the failure of Massachusetts, Virginia, and other states to devise the "simplified law code" advocated by Bostonian Benjamin Austin and other reformers is less important for our purposes than the unequivocal assertion of legislative authority over the process of legal revision.

Many state legislatures likewise claimed constitutional authority over the court system. Colonial assemblies had frequently established and regulated courts by statute, defying arguments by the Board of Trade that such actions were the prerogative of the executive. Now they claimed these powers as a right. "Whether courts are erected by a regard to the administration of justice, or with the purpose of rewarding a meritorious faction," declared Virginian John Taylor of Caroline, "the legislature may certainly abolish them."[45] Acting on this premise, the Massachusetts legislature in 1804–05 overhauled the state's judicial system and abolished not only de novo retrials before the Supreme Court but also the criminal jurisdiction of the Courts of Sessions of the Peace. Because of continuing legislative intervention, the General Sessions magistrates gradually devolved into mere administrators, the County Commissioners, elected officials who approved town bylaws and supervised local governments. Legislative supremacy reduced the powerful magisterial oligarchs of the seventeenth century to the status of state bureaucrats.

[45] Taylor to John Breckinridge, Dec. 22, 1801, in John P. Branch, *John P. Branch Historical Papers of Randolph-Macon College*, ed. by W. E. Dodd, 1st ser. (Richmond, 1901–18), I, 284–88.

In New York City, institutional evolution took a similar course. The Montgomerie Charter of 1730 had established the City as a distinct corporate entity with extensive governing powers. With independence, the Corporation of the City of New York occupied the anomalous position of an *imperium in imperio*, an independent lawmaking body within the sovereign state of New York. Recognizing the tension between the City's charter rights and the state's sovereign authority, the City Council dispatched a steady stream of petitions to the state legislature, asking it to reaffirm powers granted by the Montgomerie Charter and to grant new powers of regulation and taxation. Gradually, this restructuring of authority transformed New York City from a privately chartered corporation to a public entity – a municipal corporation – within the legislatively controlled state government. Within the city, the mayor and aldermen forsook their traditional judicial responsibilities; they left law enforcement to the recorder of the Mayor's Court and other legal officials and focused their energies on the tasks of city administration. In 1821, a legislative statute completed the separation of judicial and administrative functions by eliminating the Mayor's Court and creating a judge-run court of common pleas for the City and County of New York. As in Massachusetts, the New York state legislature used its sovereign authority to recast the court system and define counties and cities as subordinate administrative entities.

In Virginia, the post-Revolutionary legislature likewise curbed the powers of the magisterial oligarchies that ran the county courts. For decades, angry residents and reform-minded lawyers had complained about the arbitrary and often controversial decisions of the county justices. Revolutionary era reformers added the charge of anti-republican elitism and exclusivity. "The justices of the County Courts are so far from being the Representatives of the People, or amenable to them," declared a petition submitted by George Mason, "that by a very faulty part of our Constitution, they are a self-contained Body, with the Power of filling their own Vacancies, a power unknown in any other Part of the Constitution."[46] Picking up Mason's theme, Thomas Jefferson contrasted "the vicious constitution of our county court . . . self-appointed, self-contained, holding their authorities for life" with the system of elected selectmen in the townships of New England, "the wisest invention ever devised by the wit of man for the perfect exercise of self-government, and for its preservation."[47]

[46] Robert A. Rutland, ed., *The Papers of George Mason, 1725–1792*, 3 vols. (Chapel Hill, NC, 1970), IIs, 773.

[47] Jefferson to John Taylor, May 28, 1816, *Writings of Thomas Jefferson*, ed. by Paul Leicester Ford (New York, 1904–5), XIs, 527–33. Jefferson held such views as early as 1776.

In 1772 and again in 1779 the Virginia legislature refused to reform the county court system. Roughly half the members of the House of Burgesses sat as justices in their home counties and opposed proposals that would limit their legal authority or replace them with elected aldermen. In addition, Patrick Henry, Spencer Roane, and other influential Anti-Federalists defended the traditional decentralized system of county magistrates and juries as guardians of local liberty. Nonetheless, in 1787 James Madison and other reformers eventually won legislative enactment of a compromise measure that preserved many of the powers of the county judges, but created a system of District Courts, staffed by circuit-riding appellate judges, to review their decisions.

The power of Virginia gentry – in counties, the legislature, and the judiciary – also affected the substantive economic measures enacted by the state legislature. Unlike the legislatures and judges in many Northern states, which encouraged entrepreneurs at the expense of other property owners, Virginia officials undercut many of the development schemes of the state's mercantile and banking leaders. When the legislature granted charters to internal improvement companies, it safeguarded local rights by giving juries control of eminent domain proceedings and compensation. By contrast, when the Western and Northern Inland Lock Navigation Companies complained to the New York legislature in 1790 about the "excessive" eminent domain awards made by local juries and asked that the responsibility be transferred to court-appointed appraisers "whose decisions shall be conclusive," the lawmakers quickly complied.[48] When commercial interests and entrepreneurs in Virginia managed to secure favorable legislation, the state's judges often intervened to protect other property owners. For example, the act incorporating the Slate River Company authorized the destruction of five milldams if the dam owners did not, at their own expense, build and maintain locks for passage of the Company's boats. When the owners refused, arguing that these construction costs – or, alternatively, the destruction of their dams – represented a "taking," they won the backing of the Virginia Supreme Court, which required the payment of fair compensation. The combination of a localist political ideology, a dominant agricultural sector, and a tradition-minded judiciary inhibited economic development in Virginia.

In most Northern states, as Horwitz demonstrated, the courts moved aggressively to encourage entrepreneurial ventures. In doing so, however, they usually walked hand-in-hand with the legislatures. Consider the

[48] "Report of the Directors," in Albert Gallatin, "Report on Roads and Canals," *American State Papers*, Walter Lowrie and William Franklin, eds. (Washington, DC, 1834), Class X, Miscellaneous, I, 772; 1798 N.Y. Stat. ch. 101.

treatment of milldams in Massachusetts. In 1795 and 1798, the legislature amended a colonial-era Mill Act to permit private mill owners to flood neighboring properties without seeking prior court permission (which was required in Virginia) and to pay damages on a yearly basis, even if the land was permanently flooded. More important, the revised act limited injured property owners to specified financial compensation, thereby denying them punitive damages for trespass and the use of traditional common law remedies to abate nuisances. In 1814, the Massachusetts Supreme Court upheld this statutory mode of compensation and thus gave judicial sanction to the legislature's redefinition of traditional property rights. When the legislature again amended the Mill Act in 1825 to facilitate the flooding of adjacent lands, the Supreme Judicial Court accepted the changes and noted, "the encouragement of the mills has always been a favorite object with the legislature."[49] Accepting the legislature's understanding of "offsetting benefits" in another section of the act, the court allowed mill owners to avoid paying any compensation to the landowner by showing that the benefits of irrigation outweighed the injuries caused by the flooding. Such offsets were in fact required by many legislatures and almost always accepted by courts.

Legislatures likewise took the lead with respect to business incorporations. Before 1790, most acts of incorporation were either municipal statutes making towns into "bodies politic" or charters creating religious, educational, and charitable institutions. Thereafter, the number of business-related incorporations soared. In Massachusetts, nearly a third of the charters granted in the 1790s went to internal improvement companies and other businesses, and unexpectedly raised questions about the financial liability of shareholders. In addressing the issue of liability, the Massachusetts Supreme Court initially relied on traditional precepts. Just as municipal corporations could levy taxes on their residents to defray unusual expenses, the court argued by analogy in *Thompson v. Russell* (1800), so business corporations could assess shareholders to cover unanticipated costs. As the negative implications of imposing unlimited liability on investors became apparent, the judges distinguished business corporations from municipal governments. In *Andover and Medford Turnpike Corporation v. Gould* (1809), the Massachusetts Court rejected common law principles and ruled that shareholders were liable for subsequent assessments only if they had explicitly agreed to pay them. As legislatures subsequently mulled over this problem, they followed the lead of the Massachusetts court. By the 1820s, most legislative charters to business corporations provided limited liability to their shareholders; working in tandem, development-minded legislators and judges had resolved the liability issue.

[49] *Wolcott Woollen Mfg. Co. v. Upham*, 22 Mass. (5 Pick.), 292, at 294 (1827).

Northern judges also acted independently to assist public and private developers. In the leading case of *Callendar v. Marsh* (1823), the Massachusetts Supreme Court denied compensation to a property owner when the excavation of an adjoining city street damaged his house.[50] The court's decision was that such "consequential damages" did not constitute a taking, but was *damnum absque injuria* (an injury without a legal remedy). Strikingly, legislatures and constitutional conventions did not override *Callendar* (and similar decisions in other states). Most of their members, like most judges, and most citizens, favored economic improvement at the lowest cost to the public. Developmental policies, that is, reflected the views of a majority of politically active citizenry. Rather than driven by the judiciary in concert with economic elites, they were primarily the product of legislative statutes.

Social issues – religion, temperance, women's rights, and slavery – were more controversial. There was no consensus within the political elite or the populace as whole, so legislatures and courts often disagreed over the proper course of public policy. The contentious issue of the church establishment in Massachusetts is a case in point. The state's constitution of 1780 retained compulsory religious taxation and the territorial parish system. This system favored the numerically dominant Congregational Church, but it did allow members of other sects or denominations to funnel taxes to their churches. Then the judiciary issued a series of contradictory interpretations. Initially, the Massachusetts Supreme Court allowed only incorporated religious societies to receive tax payments; this decision penalized Baptists, who generally refused to subject themselves to state charters. Subsequently, in *Murray v. First Parish Gloucester* (1786), the court eliminated this incorporation stipulation, only to reimpose it in the case of *Barnes v. First Church in Falmouth* (1810). Because this ruling sent the taxes of most Baptists to Congregational ministers, there was a major political backlash. Mustering their forces first at the polls and then in the legislature, Baptists and other religious minorities won passage in 1811 of a Religious Freedom Act. This act overturned *Barnes* and other anti-dissenter court decisions and, equally significant, asserted the authority of the legislature to construe the meaning of the religious clauses in the state constitution.

A generation later, legislatures and judges confronted one another over two other social issues: women's property rights and the restriction of alcoholic beverages. In *Westervelt v. Gregg* (1854), the New York Court of Appeals voided that part of the Married Women's Property Act (1848) that bestowed property rights on women married before its passage; in the process, the court adumbrated the novel legal doctrine of "substantive due process." Two years later, in the prohibition case of *Wynehamer v. People* (1856), the judges

[50] 1 Pick. 418 (Mass. 1823).

fully articulated the due process doctrine and claimed for the courts the broad veto power over legislative actions that shaped constitutional debates for much of the remainder of the nineteenth century.

CONCLUSION

That mid-century enhancement of judicial power is part of another story. In 1820 it was the legislature, not common law judges or powerful magistrates, that stood at the apex of the American legal system. Because of legislative intervention, the powerful oligarchies of county magistrates that in summary fashion had ruled the seventeenth century had become county commissioners lacking jurisdiction over criminal matters and subject to popular election and state supervision. Legislators had also intruded significantly into the eighteenth-century common law system of judges and juries. By enacting laws that diminished the authority of juries and enhanced the power of judges, they continued through statute law the process begun by trained lawyers using common law pleas. Thanks to the new state constitutions, the legislators and their constituents became the prime shapers of the legal system, largely unimpeded by governors and only partially restrained by an emergent judiciary.

For the population of European descent, the first two centuries of English law in North America thus witnessed the successive ascendancy of three legal systems: a seventeenth-century regime of powerful magistrates; an eighteenth-century common law order run by lawyers, judges, and juries; and an early-nineteenth-century republican world of quasi-sovereign state legislatures. Two periods of transition – the first from 1680 to 1720, the second from 1770 to 1810 – witnessed the appearance of new ideologies, procedures, and institutions that changed, sometimes subtly and sometimes dramatically, the ways in which thousands of white Americans conducted their day-to-day lives and legal affairs.

BIBLIOGRAPHIC ESSAYS

CHAPTER 1: LAW, COLONIZATION, LEGITIMATION AND THE EUROPEAN BACKGROUND

ANTHONY PAGDEN

The most recent comparative account of the British and other European colonizing projects in the Americas is J. H. Elliot, *Empires of the Atlantic World Britain and Spain in America 1492–1830* (New Haven, 2006). See also Anthony Pagden, *Lords of all the World. Ideologies of Empire in Britain, France and Spain, 1400–1800* (New Haven, 1995) and "The Struggle for Legitimacy and the Image of Empire in the Atlantic to c. 1700," in Nicholas Canny ed., *The Origins of Empire, The Oxford History of the British Empire* (Oxford, 1998), vol. I, 34–54. David Armitage, *The Ideological Origins of the British Empire* (Cambridge, 2000) provides the most authoritative account of the objectives of the early empire. The articles collected in David Armitage, ed. *Theories of Empire, 1450–1800* (Aldershot, UK, 1998) cover aspects of all the European claims to America. Klaus E. Knorr, *British Colonial Theories 1570–1850* (Toronto, 1944) provides a still useful survey. See also Peter Miller, *Defining the Common Good: Empire, Religion and Philosophy in Eighteenth-Century Britain*. (Cambridge, 1994). For the notion of composite monarchies see J. H. Elliott, "A Europe of Composite Monarchies," *Past and Present* 137 (1992), 48–71.

The rituals of possession employed by European settlers in America are discussed in Patricia Seed, *Ceremonies of Possession in Europe's Conquest of the New World, 1492–1640* (Cambridge, 1995). An earlier, but legally more sophisticated account is also to be found in Friedrich August von der Heydte, "Discovery, Symbolic Annexation and Virtual Effectiveness in International Law," *American Journal of International Law* 29 (1935), 448–71. One of the most extensive accounts of the early English claims to sovereignty in North America is still John Thomas Juricek, *English Claims in North America to 1660: A Study in Legal and Constitutional History*, Ph.D. thesis, University of Chicago, 1970, pp. 512, 669–71, which is unfortunately unpublished and is likely to remain so.

On the legal pluralism of the early modern Atlantic world see the essays in Christopher Tomlins and Bruce H. Mann eds., *The Many Legalities of Early America* (Chapel Hill, NC, 2001), and Christopher Tomlins, "The Legal Cartography of Colonization, the Legal Polyphony of Settlement: English Intrusion on the American Mainland in the Seventeenth Century," *Law and Social Inquiry* 26 (2001), 315–72.

On the question of Parliamentary sovereignty see Ian K. Steele, "The British Parliament and the Atlantic Colonies to 1760: New Approaches to Enduring Questions," in Philip Lawson ed., *Parliament and the Atlantic Empire* (Edinburgh, 1995), 29–46 and Martin S. Flaherty, "The Empire Strikes Back: *Annesely v. Sherlock* and the Triumph of Imperial Parliamentary Supremacy," *Columbia Law Review* 87 (1987), 593–622. For a broader consideration of the relationship between Parliament and the Crown, see David Lieberman, *The Province of Legislation Determined: Legal Theory in Eighteenth-Century Britain* (Cambridge, 1989). David Konig, "Colonization and the Common Law in Ireland and Virginia, 1569–1634," in James A. Henretta, Michael G. Kammen and Stanley N. Katz, eds., *The Transformation of Early American History: Society, Authority and Ideology* (New York, Knopf, 1991) discusses the difficulties involved in extending the common law outside the realm.

Grounds for Possession

Stuart Banner, *How the Indians Lost Their Land: Law and Power on the American Frontier* (Cambridge, MA, 2005) is the most extensive discussion of all the legal debates over the seizure of Indian lands.

A general overview of the status of the American Indians is provided by Robert A. Williams, *The American Indian in Western Legal Thought. The Discourses of Conquest* (New York, 1990). See also Colin G. Calloway, *New Worlds for All: Indians, Europeans and the Remaking of Early America* (Baltimore, 1997). L. C. Green and P. Dickason, *The Law of Nations and the New World* (Edmonton, 1989), provide a context in international law for the occupation of America. See also Patricia Seed, *American Pentimento: The Invention of Indians and the Pursuit of Riches* (Minneapolis, 2001). William Cronon, *Changes in the Land: Indians, Colonists and the Ecology of New England* (New York, 1988) provides a account of the differing views on the land and its possible occupation by the Indians and the Europeans.

Conquest

The most powerful argument for the metropolitan perception of the rights of the Crown in the Americas and for the claim that the colonies were, in effect, lands of conquest is to be found in Craig Yirush, *From the Perspective of Empire: The Common Law, Natural Rights and the Formation of American Political Theory, 1689–1775*, Ph.D. thesis, Johns Hopkins University 2004, which will shortly be published as a book. The still classic account of the relationship between the metropolis and the colonies is Jack P. Greene, *Peripheries and*

Center: Constitutional Development in the Extended Polities of the British Empire and the United States 1607–1788 (Athens, GA, 1986). For the broader political context see Richard Tuck, *The Rights of War and Peace. Political Thought and the International Order from Grotius to Kant* (Oxford, 1999) On feudal tenure and "free and common socage," see A.W.B. Simpson, *An Introduction to the History of the Land Law* (Oxford, 1961).

On the similarities between the Irish and American cases see James Muldoon, "Spiritual Conquests Compared: *Laudabiliter* and the Conquest of the Americas," in Steven B. Bowman and Blanche E. Cody, eds., *Iure Veritas: Studies in Memory of Schafer Williams*, (Cincinnati, 1991), 174–86. The significance of the status of Ireland is discussed in further detail by Martin S. Flaherty, "The Empire Strikes Back: *Annesely v. Sherlock* and the Triumph of Imperial Parliamentary Supremacy," *Columbia Law Review* 87 (1987) 593–622. And see, in general, Nicholas Canny, *Making Ireland British 1580–1650* (Oxford, 2001). The analogous case in Canada is discussed in Bruce Clark, *Native Liberty, Crown Sovereignty. The Existing Aboriginal Right of Self-Government in Canada* (Montreal, 1990).

Discovery

On the question of *terra* or *res nullius* and the seventeenth-century debates over the rights of the American Indians, see James Tully, "Rediscovering America: The *Two Treatises* and Aboriginal Rights," in Quentin Skinner, ed., *An Approach to Political Philosophy: Locke in Context* (Cambridge, 1993), 137–76; "Aboriginal Property and Western Theory: Recovering a Middle Ground," *Social Philosophy and Policy* 11 (1994), 153–80; and "Property, Self-Government and Consent," *Canadian Journal of Political Science*, 27 (1995), 105–32. On the place of America in John Locke's *Two Treatises on Government* see, in general, Barbara Arneil, *John Locke and America: The Defence of English Colonialism* (Oxford, 1996), and for a more detailed discussion, James Tully, "Placing the *Two Treatises*," in Nicholas Philipson and Quentin Skinner, eds., *Political Discourse in Early-Modern Britain* (Cambridge, 1993), 257–58 and *Strange Multiplicity. Constitutionalism in an Age of Diversity* (Cambridge, 1995), 70–81. David Armitage, "John Locke, Carolina and the *Two Treatises on Government*," *Political Theory* 32 (2004), 602–27, assesses the role of Locke's political theory in the foundation of the Carolinas.

For a consideration of the analogous use of the argument from *res* or *terra nullius* in the lands of the Ottoman Empire see Benedict Kingsbury, "Confronting Difference: The Puzzling Durability of Gentili's Combination of Pragmatic Realism and Normative Judgment," *American Journal of International Law* 92 (1998), 713–23. On the discussion of *res nullius* as it applies to Australia see Stuart Banner, "Why *Terra Nullius*? Anthropology and Property Law in Early Australia," *Law and History Review* 23 (2005), 96–132, and Carole Pateman, "The Settler Contract," in Carole Pateman and Charles Mills, eds., *Contract and Domination*, forthcoming. The somewhat different case of New Zealand is discussed by J. G. A. Pocock, "Law, Sovereignty and History in a Divided

Culture: The Case of New Zealand and the *Treaty of Waitangi*," *McGill Law Journal* 43 (1998), 481–506,

On Hugo Grotius, John Selden, and the debate over the freedom of the seas, see especially the introduction by David Armitage to Hugo Grotius, *The Free Sea* (Indiana, 2004), and Anthony Pagden, "Commerce and Conquest. Hugo Grotius and Serafim de Freitas on the Freedom of the Seas," *Mare Liberum* 20 (2000), 33–55.

On Chief Justice John Marshall, see in general Jean Edward Smith, *John Marshall: Definer of a Nation* (New York, 1996). On *Johnson v. M'Intosh* see Lindsay Gordon Robertson, *Johnson v. M'Intosh: Land, Law and the Politics of Federalism, 1773–1842*, Ph.D. thesis, University of Virginia, 1997, and Eric Kades, "History and Interpretation in the Great Case of *Johnson v. M'Intosh*," *Law and History Review* 19 (2001), 67–116. On Marshall's historiography, see Lindsay G. Robertson, "John Marshall as Colonial Historian: Reconsidering the Origins of the Doctrine of Discovery," *Journal of Law and Politics* 13 (1997), 759–77. In *Conquest by Law: How the Discovery of America Dispossessed the Indigenous Peoples of their Lands* (Oxford, 2005), Robertson draws on new documentary evidence to reexamine Marshall's ruling in *Johnson*. For a somewhat different approach see Steven T. Newcomb, "The Evidence of Christian Nationalism in Federal Indian Law: The Doctrine of Discovery, *Johnson v. McIntosh* and Plenary Power," *New York Review of Law and Social Change* 20 (1993), 303–41.

Purchase and Concession

Karen Ordahl Kupperman, *Settling with the Indians. The Meeting of English and Indian Cultures in America, 1580–1640* (Totowa, 1980) provides accounts of the treaty negotiations between Indians the English settlers. See also Dorothy V. Jones, *License for Empire: Colonialism by Treaty in Early America* (Chicago, 1982), on the Proclamation line inter alia.

On differing concepts of property see James Warren Springer, "American Indians and the Law of Real Property in Colonial New England," *American Journal of Legal History* 30 (1986), 25–58. For a detailed account of how one Indian group was paid for its land see Harry Andrew Wright, "The Technique of Seventeenth-Century Indian Land Purchases," *Essex Institute Historical Collections* 77 (1941), 185–976, and John Strong, "Tribal Systems and Land Alienation: A Case Study," in William Cowan, ed., *Papers of the Sixteenth Algonquin Conference* (Ottawa, 1985), 183–200. For a detailed analysis of one particular region see Jean M. O'Brien, *Dispossession by Degrees: Indian Land and Identity in Natick, Massachusetts, 1650–1790* (Cambridge, 1997).

Conclusion

On the aftermath of the Seven Years War see in general and in the broader British context, P.J. Marshall, *The Making and the Unmaking of Empires. Britain, India and America c. 1750–1783* (Oxford, 2005).

On the question of divided sovereignty, see Edward Keene, *Beyond the Anarchical Society: Grotius, Colonialism and Order in World Politics* (Cambridge, 2002) and in the context of the English Atlantic, see J.C.D. Clark, *The Language of Liberty 1660–1832: Political Discourse and Social Dynamics in the Anglo-American World* (Cambridge, 1994).

On the prelude to the Revolution see Barbara Black, "The Constitution of Empire: The Case for the Colonists," *University of Pennsylvania Law Review* 124 (1976), 1157–1211, and Jack P. Greene, "From the Perspective of Law: Context and Legitimacy in the Origins of the American Revolution," in Jack P. Greene, ed., *Interpreting Early America: Historiographical Essays* (Charlottesville, 1996), 467–92.

CHAPTER 2: THE LAW OF NATIVE AMERICANS, TO 1815

KATHERINE A. HERMES

General

Academic scholarship on American Indian legal history has been bifurcated into distinct areas: those who consider the legal history of Native Americans to be a study of first Anglo-European and then U.S. law imposed on the Native Americans, and those who want to know what law meant to Native Americans and what laws they possessed. The earliest scholars fall into the first category, and the most recent group of these wrote in the years prior to and through the 1960s and 1980s as the sole group working on what is called American Indian Law. In the 1970s another group of scholars began the transition from studying the history of case law applicable to Native Americans to studying the effect that Anglo-European and U.S. law had on native communities. This latter group often discussed law only in single chapters of books, although one scholar, Yasuhide Kawashima, made it his field of study. His first book, *Puritan Justice and the Indian: White Man's Law in Massachusetts, 1630–1763* (Middletown, CT, 1986), accepted the dominance of white law on Native Americans and stayed within the parameters of Anglo-American history. Kawashima eventually began to look at the perspective of the Indians themselves, and he has been followed by scholars in legal anthropology and social history. Later books such as *Igniting King Philip's War: The John Sassamon Murder Trial* (Kansas, 2001) include much more of the Indian perspective. The body of historical literature that documents and analyzes the treaties entered into by the European colonial powers and the United States is substantial. The interest in Native American laws and legal practices is much less developed than the historiography surrounding native customs, economics, art, and almost any other subject.

American Indian Law

The classic scholarship on American Indian law that is still of great importance today began with the work of two scholars, Francis Prucha and Wilcomb E.

Washburn. Although these men represent a more traditional form of scholarship, they were not unsympathetic to the Indians. Neither did they focus entirely on the colonial or Early Republican periods. Their works reach into twentieth-century law, and both address the changing historical methods that have affected the study of American Indian legal history. Prucha has sometimes been called an apologist for the United States, but his work on treaties and translated speeches necessarily gave him a perspective that one can either find balanced or tilted toward the United States. In addition to the several bibliographies he compiled for researchers of Native American history, Prucha's significant works include *American Indian Policy in the Formative Years: The Indian Trade and Intercourse Acts, 1780–1834* (Cambridge, MA, 1962), *Documents of United States Indian Policy* (Lincoln, NE, 1975, 1990), *Indian Policy in the United States: Historical Essays* (1981), and *The Great Father: The United States Government and the American Indians* (Lincoln, NE, 1984). Another of his significant works is *Sovereignty, Suppression, and Survival: The Red Man in American History* (1974), which is an overview of the history of American Indians from prehistory to the American Indian Movement and includes chapters on ethnological problems and Indian social structure. Because the book is reflective of a lifetime of study and covers such a vast amount of time, it is less valuable to academics than some of his other works, but it lays out in broad strokes what the U.S. policies regarding Indians have been. It is a good starting point for understanding how the U.S. government has shaped the question of Indian sovereignty because it addresses the question of sovereignty, so central to the 1970s when it was written and a recurring issue.

Washburn was also a narrative historian who sought to lay out clearly the history of the Indians, and especially their dispossession of the land. (He also dealt with anthropology and several Indian topics I have omitted here. He edited several documentary collections.) Although his works are too numerous to list, the best of these specifically on legal matters is Washburn's *Red Man's Land, White Man's Law: A Study of the Past and Present Status of the American Indian* (New York, 1971). His scholarship included complex questions about law and history in such essays as "History Reconsidered: The Supreme Court's Use and Abuse of History," *OAH Newsletter* 11 (1983), 7–9. The persistence of scholarship that accepted the premise that native peoples most often entered the legal arena in the treaty process is evidenced by such books as Jennings C. Wise, *The Red Man in the New World Drama: A Politico-legal Study with a Pageantry of American Indian History*, intro. Vine Deloria, Jr. (New York, 1971).

Scholarship on treaty law has also broadened its scope, though, and now includes works by historians of Indian culture, such as Vine Deloria, Jr. and Raymond J. DeMallie, eds., (with a foreword By Daniel K. Inouye), *Documents of American Indian Diplomacy: Treaties, Agreements and Conventions, 1775–1979* (Norman, OK, 1999). Beyond treaties, there are post-colonial scholars who look broadly at Western law as it applied to Indians, such as Robert A. Williams,

Jr., *The American Indian in Western Legal Thought: The Discourses of Conquest* (New York, 1992). The effects of colonial law on Native Americans have been explored only recently in Eric Cheyfitz, "Native Americans and the Constitution: The Colonial Double-Bind: Sovereignty and Civil Rights in Indian Country," *University of Pennsylvania Journal of Constitutional Law* 5 (2003).

Perhaps the most influential, classic scholar on the history of Indians of early North America was Francis Jennings. His groundbreaking work to a large extent defies exact lines of categorization. He was the editor-in-chief of *The History and Culture of Iroquois Diplomacy: An Interdisciplinary Guide to the Treaties of the Six Nations and their League* (Syracuse, NY, 1985). Jennings wrote his masterful *The Invasion of America: Indians, Colonialism, and the Cant of Conquest* (New York, 1975), which includes a substantial chapter on jurisdiction and how colonial law was applied to Indians. In addition to books on the Iroquois League – including his most famous one, *The Ambiguous Iroquois Empire* (New York, 1984), which continued his work begun in *The Invasion of America* – Jennings offered a compelling but despairing vision of how Indians, through law and through war, were destroyed. His work changed the way in which scholars thought of Indians and of the conquest, and due to his work the word "discovery" disappeared from the historical lexicon when referring to the contact period. Yet Jennings did not include in his work any substance or theory of how to understand Native American law. His most recent book, *The Founders of America* (New York, 1993), showed that Native Americans had not been exterminated but had in fact begun a resurgence.

The Legal History and Study of Indian Law in Law Schools

There are some "cases and materials" books on Indian law. These primarily begin with the Federal Constitution of 1789, but occasionally include such documents as the Northwest Ordinance before the Constitution. Few contain documents written by Indians, such as wills for example, but are instead compilations of federal appellate and Supreme Court opinions on Indians. Most of these contain little before 1815 except the case *Fletcher v. Peck*, but the more important of these works include Robert N. Clinton, Carole E. Goldberg, and Rebecca Tsosie, *American Indian Law: Cases and Materials* (Student ed. 2005).

The Study of Interpreters and Its Importance for Native American Legal History

Although few historians who study the role of interpreters in colonial relations consider themselves legal historians of Native America, their work has tremendous importance for the field. Much of what scholars can discern about Native American law took place at council meetings and treaty negotiations. Among the most important scholarship on negotiation is James Merrell, *Into the Woods: Negotiators on the Pennsylvania Frontier* (New York, 2000) and Nancy L. Hagedorn, "'A Friend to Go Between Them': The Interpreter as Cultural Broker During Anglo-Iroquois Councils, 1740–1770," *Ethnohistory* 35 (1988), 60–80.

The Law of Native America

There exists a great deal of dispute about whether it is possible to write anything about what Native Americans constructed as law. Some authors have tried to use European terms to frame the subject so that one can understand comparatively, at least, what Native Americans said they thought about a given area of law. An example of this is Katherine A. Hermes's "Jurisdiction in the Colonial Northeast: Algonquian, English and French Governance," *American Journal of Legal History* 43 (1999), 52–73. Essays by Katherine Hermes, Ann Marie Plane, and James Brooks in Christopher Tomlins and Bruce Mann, eds., *The Many Legalities of Early America* (Chapel Hill, NC, 2001) approach native history using colonial sources to reveal what can be known of Indian practice and ideas.

There was also a surge during the Law and Literature movement of the 1980s in which people of various disciplines published on law, colonialism, and Indians. Post-colonial studies provided an interdisciplinary avenue for looking at native life, including law, and have been useful both for thinking about methodology and substance. One collection of essays by Native American authors, *Native Voices: American Indian Identity and Resistance*, edited by Richard A. Grounds, George E. Tinker, and David E. Wilkins (Lawrence, KS, 2003), includes, among others, "The Metaphysics of Federal Indian Law and U.S. Colonialism of American Indians" by M. A. Jaimes Guerrero and "Contours of Enlightenment: Reflections on Science, Theology, Law, and the Alternative Vision of Vine Deloria, Jr." by Ward Churchill. Many of the essays deal with current or post-1815 issues, but are valuable to the history of the earlier period. Some scholars have studied law by studying issues of power, such as Claudio Saunt, *A New Order of Things: Property, Power and the Transformation of the Creek Indians, 1733–1816* (Cambridge, 1999), which quickly became a model for other studies.

Recent scholars have greatly enriched our understanding of Native American norms and law, both in indigenous communities and Christianized colonial settlements. Yet many of these scholars still do not confront the question of the law of Native America head on. They examine accommodation strategies, assimilation, and acculturation, touching therefore on what changed in native practices. They often focus on life-cycle events, such as marriage, Ann Marie Plane, *Colonial Intimacies: Indian Marriage in Early New England* (Ithaca, NY, 2002), and work and death, Jean O'Brien, *Dispossession by Degrees: Indian Land and Identity in Natick, Massachusetts, 1650–1790* (Cambridge, 2003). These books use English vital records, probate records, and land deeds to show ways in which Native Americans did or did not use the English law that was increasingly being applied to them.

The praying towns and reserves for Christianized Indians have also yielded information on the law of Native America, but the reader needs to tease it out of the studies. Richard Cogley, *John Eliot's Mission to the Indians Before King Philip's War* (Cambridge, MA, 1999), is not interested per se in law, but shows how Indians develop legal institutions.

With these community studies emerging, some historians have sought to write the broader sweep and have begun to include law as part of their analysis, such as Daniel K. Richter, *Facing East from Indian Country* (Cambridge, MA, 2003), which was influenced to a large degree by Richard White's *The Middle Ground: Indians, Empires, and Republics in the Great Lakes Region, 1650–1815* (New York, 1991). Richter's study often invokes the imagination, but not when he writes about legal matters. White sees trade, not law, as the great mediator of violence between Indians and settlers.

The question of conquest and its legal dimensions has also been reevaluated in Amy Den Ouden, *Beyond Conquest: Native Peoples and the Struggle for History in New England* (Lincoln, NE, 2006).

The Constitutional Controversy

In 1977 a controversial book by Donald A. Grinde, *The Iroquois League and the Founding of the American Nation*, appeared. It was followed by another book by Donald A. Grinde and Bruce E. Johansen, *Exemplar of Liberty: Native Americans and the Evolution of Democracy* (Berkeley, CA, 1991), which further developed the then-nascent thesis that the Iroquois Confederacy had been the model for democracy, the Articles of Confederation, and even the Constitution. Johansen had also published an article, "Native American Societies and the Evolution of Democracy in America, 1600–1800," *Ethnohistory* 37 (1990), with the same thesis. Elizabeth Tooker, "The United States Constitution and the Iroquois League," *Ethnohistory* 35 (1988), had argued against such a thesis on the grounds that only a misunderstanding of Iroquois politics and government could lead to such a conclusion. In 1996 the *William and Mary Quarterly* devoted an issue to the question of Iroquois influence, with Grinde and Johansen arguing their case and Samuel B. Payne, "The Iroquois League, the Articles of Confederation, and the Constitution," *William and Mary Quarterly*, 3rd ser., 53 (1996), arguing against it. The weight of historical opinion remains largely against the thesis advanced by Grinde and Johansen, though aspects of it appear in textbooks and in books for high-school students. It is the one area in the literature, though, in which Native American law is even considered to be of importance to understanding U.S. history. In that way the debate has challenged legal historians to think about how indigenous law might have shaped colonial law, much as Indian trading practices influenced English production for the Indian market.

Books for Non-Specialists or High School Students

In the 1980s, emerging from the civil rights movement, there was an attempt to educate students about American Indian law who had no legal experience or training. *American Indian Legal Studies: An Indian Legal and Social Studies Primer* (1981), now outdated on recent law and scholarship on the early federal period, spoke to a generation concerned with the practical application of Indian law. There are more general books for secondary school students that introduce them to Native American practices. Alvin Josephy, *The Patriot Chiefs: A Chronicle of American Indian Resistance* (New York, 1961), is also somewhat dated, but its complex explanation of conflict touches on legal concerns. Many of these books are regional and therefore have small sections on native customs that enter the legal arena: Nancy Bonvillain, *Hiawatha: Founder of the Iroquois Confederacy* (1992), gives a chronology, whereas Dennis Brindell Fradin, *Hiawatha: Messenger of Peace* (1992), focuses on the Iroquois Confederacy and includes the debate about whether or not the Confederacy had an influence on the U.S. Constitution. Other regional histories include general books, such as Esther K. Braun and David P. Braun, *The First Peoples of the Northeast* (Lincoln, NE, 1994), that touch briefly on law. Local nonfiction books for secondary-school readers such as Keith Egloff and Deborah Woodward, *First People: The Early Indians of Virginia* (Charlottesville, VA, 1992), have sections on Virginia's ethnohistory. Few books on Native Americans written for general audiences or high-school students touch on law, but those that do almost always deal with it only in the modern period.

Methodology

In few fields is methodology as important or diverse as in the study of Native American legal history. Of significant importance to many scholars of Native America is a book in legal anthropology, Sally Engle Merry, *Colonizing Hawai'i: The Cultural Power of Law* (Princeton, NJ, 2000). Indeed, much of Merry's work, including earlier books that had nothing to do with indigenous peoples, has had an influence on the way legal historians of Native America have conducted their research. Nancy Shoemaker, ed., *Clearing a Path: Theorizing the Past in Native American Studies* (New York, 2002), is a substantial addition to how to do Indian history.

Emerging from studies of law and politics are also inquiries into the colonial period's usefulness to understanding the present; for example, Kirsten Matoy Carlson, "Is Hindsight 20–20?: Reconsidering the Importance of Pre-Constitutional Documents," *American Indian Law Review* 30 (2005).

Conclusion

One finds a growing literature on Native American law in the colonial period appearing in journal articles, but books on the subject are still few. No book has considered Native American law in its broad spectrum for the colonial and revolutionary periods. It is therefore necessary to turn to scholarly journals, collections of essays, and collections of primary sources to find materials.

CHAPTER 3: ENGLISH SETTLEMENT AND LOCAL GOVERNANCE

MARY SARAH BILDER

The scholarship addressing the early settlement and governance of the early colonies is very extensive. The following works provide good general discussions or bibliographies of more specific relevant materials or are particularly worthy of attention. Many of the scholars mentioned here have written so widely and prominently that space precludes discussion of more than a fraction of their work. Readers are urged to use this essay as a point of departure for their own more extensive bibliographic research.

The best starting point for colonial institutional history remains Charles M. Andrews, *The Colonial Period of American History*, 4 vols. (New Haven, 1934–1939). Herbert L. Osgood's work – *The American Colonies in the Seventeenth Century*, 3 vols. (1904; Gloucester, 1957) and "England and the American Colonies in the Seventeenth Century," *Political Science Quarterly* 17 (1902), 206–22 – contains useful details. Merrill Jensen's introductions in *American Colonial Documents to 1776* (New York, 1955) deserve wider attention. W. Keith Kavenagh's *Foundations of Colonial America*, 3 vols. (New York, 1973), contains an excellent collection of primary documents and introductions, and Donald S. Lutz's *Colonial Origins of the American Constitution: A Documentary History* (Indianapolis, 1998) offers a nice shorter collection. Good overviews of colonial institutional history appear in T. H. Breen & Timothy Hall, *Colonial America in an Atlantic World* (New York, 2004); Richard Middleton, *Colonial America: A History, 1585–1776* (2d ed., Oxford, 1996); and Alan Taylor, *American Colonies* (New York, 2001). For particular colonies, the volumes of *A History of the American Colonies* (1973–1989) have excellent bibliographies.

Overviews of the historiography can be found in Christopher L. Tomlins, "Introduction," in Christopher L. Tomlins and Bruce H. Mann, eds., *The Many Legalities of Early America* (Chapel Hill, NC, 2001), 1–23; William E. Nelson, "Legal History before the 1960's," in William E. Nelson and John Phillip Reid, eds., *The Literature of American Legal History* (New York, 1985), 1–32; and Stanley N. Katz, "The Problem of a Colonial Legal History," in Jack P. Greene and J. R. Pole, eds., *Colonial British America* (Baltimore, 1984), 457–83. Two region-specific articles are Richard J. Ross, "The Legal Past of Early New England: Notes for the Study of Law, Legal Culture, and Intellectual History," *William and Mary Quarterly*, 3d Ser., 50 (1993), 28–41, and Warren M. Billings, "Seventeenth-Century Virginia Law and its Historians, with an Accompanying Guide to Sources," *Law Library Journal* 87 (1995), 556–75. Good bibliographic essays appear in Peter Charles Hoffer, *Law and People in Colonial America* (rev. ed., Baltimore, 1998) and Kermit L. Hall, *The Magic Mirror: Law in American History* (New York, 1989).

On the trading companies, see Cecil T. Carr, ed., *Select Charters of Trading Companies (1530–1707)* (London, 1913); George Cawston and A. H. Keane, *The Early Chartered Companies (A. D. 1296–1858)* (London, 1896); and Maud Sellers, ed., *The Acts and Ordinances of the Eastland Company* (London, 1906). Vol. I, ch. 8 and Vol. II of William Robert Scott, *The Constitution and Finance of English, Scottish and Irish Joint-Stock Companies to 1720* (1910–1912; New York, 1951) have a fine analysis of the organization of the joint-stock company and the early settlement companies. For background on the forms, see Shelagh Bond and

Norman Evans, "The Process of Granting Charters to English Boroughs, 1547–1649," *English Historical Review* 91 (1976), 102–20; R. E. Latham, "Hints on Interpreting the Public Records II Letters Patent," *The Amateur Historian* 1 (1952–1953), 47–51; Charles Deane, "The Forms in Issuing Letters Patent by the Crown of England," *Proceedings of the Massachusetts Historical Society, 1869–1870*, 11 (1871), 166–96. On corporate governance in England, useful recent discussions include Paul D. Halliday, *Dismembering the Body Politic: Partisan Politics in England's Towns, 1650–1730* (Cambridge, 1998); Catherine F. Patterson, *Urban Patronage in Early Modern England: Corporate Boroughs, The Landed Elite, and the Crown, 1580–1640* (Stanford, 1999); and Patrick Collinson and John Craig, eds., *The Reformation in English Towns, 1500–1640* (New York, 1998).

Most colonial charters are in the seven-volume *The Federal and State Constitutions, Colonial Charters, and Other Organic Laws of the States, Territories, and Colonies Now or Heretofore Forming the United States*, ed. Francis N. Thorpe (Washington, DC, 1909; online version available through Yale University's Avalon site). For an interesting discussion of charters and prerogative powers, see Elizabeth Mancke, "Chartered Enterprises and the Evolution of the British Atlantic World," in Elizabeth Mancke & Carole Shammas, eds., *The Creation of the British Atlantic World* (Baltimore, 2005), 237–62. On specific charters, see Tim Thornton, "The Palatinate of Durham and the Maryland Charter," *American Journal of Legal History* 45 (2001), 235–55, and Albert Carlos Bates, *The Charter of Connecticut: A Study* (Hartford, 1932). On repugnancy, see Mary Sarah Bilder, "The Corporate Origins of Judicial Review," *Yale Law Journal* 116 (2006), 502–66, and Jack P. Greene, *Peripheries and Center: Constitutional Development in the Extended Politics of the British Empire and the United States, 1607–1788* (Athens, GA, 1986), 19–42.

Published official English materials relating to the colonies appear in *Acts of the Privy Council of England, Colonial Series* (1908–1912; Buffalo, 2004), vol. I, 1613–1680; vol. II, 1680–1720; and vol. VI, certain unbound papers; *Calendar of State Papers, Colonial Series* (1860; reprint, Vaduz, 1964; available on CD-ROM), vol. I, 1574–1660; Clarence S. Brigham, ed., *British Royal Proclamations Relating to America, 1603–1783* (Worcester, 1911); Leo Francis Stock, ed., *Proceedings and Debates of the British Parliaments Respecting North America* (Washington, 1924; vols. I–III cover 1542–1727). The *House of Lords Journal* and *House of Commons Journal* are available online. For unpublished materials, Charles M. Andrews, *Guide to the Manuscript Materials for the History of the United States to 1783, in the British Museum, in Minor London Archives, and in the Libraries of Oxford and Cambridge* (Washington, 1908) and Grace Gardner Griffin, *A Guide to Manuscripts Relating to American History in British Depositories Reproduced for the Division of Manuscripts of the Library of Congress* (Washington, 1946) remain invaluable.

On the early settlement period, David Beers Quinn's work remains the standard, in particular, *England and the Discovery of America, 1481–1620* (New

York, 1974); *The Voyages and Colonising Enterprises of Sir Humphrey Gilbert* (1940; Nendeln, 1967); *Set Fair for Roanoke: Voyages and Colonies, 1584–1606* (Chapel Hill, NC, 1985); *The Roanoke Voyages, 1584–1590*, 2 vols. (London, 1955); and, with Alison M. Quinn, *The English New England Voyages, 1602–1608* (London, 1983). The documents in his five-volume *New American World: A Documentary History of North America to 1612* (New York, 1979) are particularly fine. Recent work on the English in Ireland includes the scholarship of Nicholas P. Canny, most recently, *Making Ireland British, 1580–1650* (Oxford, 2001), as well as John McGurk, *The Elizabethan Conquest of Ireland: The 1590s Crisis* (Manchester, 1997). The relationship of the Irish experience to colonial law is elucidated in David Thomas Konig, "Colonization and the Common Law in Ireland and Virginia, 1569–1634," in James A. Henretta et al., eds., *The Transformation of Early American History* (New York, 1991), 70–92.

Of law and governance in the colonies, Virginia and Massachusetts have received the most sustained scholarly attention. For a summary of older work, see George Athan Billias, ed., *Law and Authority in Colonial America: Selected Essays* (1965; New York, 1970). On Virginia, see the scholarship of Warren M. Billings and David T. Konig: Warren M. Billings, "The Transfer of English Law to Virginia 1606–50," in K. R. Andrews et al., eds., *The Westward Enterprise, English Activities in Ireland, the Atlantic, and America, 1480–1650: Essays in Tribute to David Beers Quinn*, (Liverpool, 1978), 215–44, and David T. Konig, "The Virgin and the Virgin's Sister: Virginia, Massachusetts, and the Contested Legacy of Colonial Law," in Russell K. Osgood, ed., *The History of the Law in Massachusetts: The Supreme Judicial Court, 1692–1992* (Boston, 1992), 81–115. On Plymouth, see George L. Haskins, "The Legal Heritage of Plymouth Colony," in David H. Flaherty, ed., *Essays in the History of Early American Law* (Chapel Hill, NC, 1969), 121–6; George D. Langdon, Jr., *Pilgrim Colony: A History of New Plymouth, 1620–1691* (New Haven, 1966), ch. 7; and, for primary sources, see David T. Konig, ed., *The Plymouth Court Records, 1686–1859* and William Bradford's *Of Plymouth Plantation, 1620–1647*, ed. Samuel Eliot Morison (New York, 1952). The materials on the Massachusetts Bay colony are voluminous. On the companies and the vote, see Frances Rose-Troup, *The Massachusetts Bay Company and its Predecessors* (New York, 1930) and Ronald Dale Karr, "The Missing Clause: Myth and the Massachusetts Bay Charter of 1629," *The New England Quarterly* 77 (2004), 89–107. On law and governance, classics include David Thomas Konig, *Law and Society in Puritan Massachusetts: Essex County, 1629–1692* (Chapel Hill, NC, 1979) and George L. Haskins, *Law and Authority in Early Massachusetts: A Study in Tradition and Design* (New York, 1960). The extensive scholarship is discussed well in Daniel R. Coquillette, "Introduction: The 'Countenance of Authoritie,'" in Daniel R. Coquillette, ed., *Law in Colonial Massachusetts, 1630–1800* (Boston, 1984), xxi–lxii. The struggles over power in the 1630s in Massachusetts Bay are analyzed in the works of Francis J. Bremer and Edmund S. Morgan; for example,

Bremer, "The County of Massachusetts: The Governance of John Winthrop's Suffolk and the Shaping of the Massachusetts Bay Colony," in Francis J. Bremer and Lynn A. Botelho, eds., *The World of John Winthrop: Essays on England and New England, 1588–1649* (Charlottesville, VA, 2005), 187–236, and Morgan, *The Puritan Dilemma: The Story of John Winthrop* (Boston, 1958). For a focus on the relationship of covenants to government, see John Witte, Jr., "How to Govern a City on a Hill: The Early Puritan Contribution to American Constitutionalism," *Emory Law Journal* 39 (1990), 41–64.

Other less successful settlements have drawn less attention. On Newfoundland and Nova Scotia, older scholarship should be consulted: D. W. Prowse, *History of Newfoundland from the English, Colonial and Foreign Records* (2d ed., London, 1896); St John Chadwick, *Newfoundland: Island into Province* (Cambridge, 1967); Thomas H. McGrail, *Sir William Alexander, First Earl of Stirling: A Biographical Study* (London, 1940), chapters 5 and 6 on Nova Scotia; George Pratt Insh, *Scottish Colonial Schemes, 1620–1686* (Glasgow, 1922), ch. 2; and George Bourinot, *Builders of Nova Scotia; A Historical Review* (Toronto, 1900; includes the charter). On the Piscataqua settlement, see Genevieve Cora Fraser, "David Thomson: The Scottish Founder of New Hampshire," *The Scottish Genealogist* (June 1999, Sept. 1999, Dec. 2000) and Charles Deane, "Indenture of David Thomson and Others," *Proceedings of the Massachusetts Historical Society, 1875–1876* (1876), 358–85. On Providence Island, see Karen Ordahl Kupperman, *Providence Island, 1630–1641: The Other Puritan Colony* (Cambridge, 1993). On the ubiquitous Ferdinando Gorges, see the fine book by Richard Arthur Preston, *Gorges of Plymouth Fort* (Toronto, 1953); *Sir Ferdinando Gorges and His Province of Maine, comp. James Baxter Phinney*, 3 vols. (Boston, 1890); and Henry S. Burrage, *The Beginnings of Colonial Maine, 1602–1658* (Portland, 1914).

Recent legal histories of individual colonies contain helpful materials. On Connecticut, see Cornelia Hughes Dayton, *Women Before the Bar: Gender, Law, and Society in Connecticut, 1639–1789* (Chapel Hill, NC, 1995) and Bruce H. Mann, *Neighbors and Strangers: Law and Community in Early Connecticut* (Chapel Hill, NC, 1987). On Delaware, see William M. Offutt, Jr., *Of "Good Laws" & "Good Men": Law and Society in the Delaware Valley, 1680–1710* (Urbana, IL, 1995). On Georgia, see Jack P. Greene, "Travails of an Infant Colony: The Search for Viability, Coherence, and Identity in Colonial Georgia" in Jack P. Greene, ed., *Imperatives, Behaviors & Identities: Essays in Early American Cultural History* (Charlottesville, VA, 1992), 113–42. On Maine, see John G. Reid, *Acadia, Maine, and New Scotland: Marginal Colonies in the Seventeenth Century* (Toronto, 1981) and *Maine, Charles II and Massachusetts: Governmental Relationships in Early Northern New England* (Portland, 1977). On New York, see Daniel J. Hulsebosch, *Constituting Empire: New York and the Transformation of Constitutionalism in the Atlantic World, 1664–1830* (Chapel Hill, NC, 2005). On Rhode Island, see Mary Sarah Bilder, *The Transatlantic Constitution: Colonial Legal Culture and the Empire* (Cambridge, MA, 2004), and Sydney V. James, Sheila L. Skemp, and

Bruce C. Daniels, eds., *The Colonial Metamorphoses in Rhode Island: A Study of Institutions in Change* (Hanover, NH, 2000). Wesley Frank Craven's *The Southern Colonies in the Seventeenth Century, 1607–1689* (Baton Rouge, LA, 1949) and *The Colonies in Transition, 1660–1713* (New York, 1968) are indispensable.

The dimensions of the relationship between the colonies and England have been the subject of reinterpretation. Imperial school works such as Oliver Morton Dickerson, *American Colonial Government, 1696–1765* (Cleveland, 1912); George A. Washburne, *Imperial Control of the Administration of Justice in the Thirteen American Colonies, 1684–1776* (New York, 1923); G. H. Guttridge, *The Colonial Policy of William III in America and the West Indies* (Cambridge, 1922); and Lawrence A. Harper, *The English Navigation Laws: A Seventeenth-Century Experiment in Social Engineering* (New York, 1939) remain useful. Books on Anglo-American imperial relations appearing in the 1970s and 1980s, often emphasizing a "center-peripheries" model, include the following: David S. Lovejoy, *The Glorious Revolution in America* (1972; Middletown, CT, 1987); James A. Henretta, *"Salutary Neglect": Colonial Administration Under the Duke of Newcastle* (Princeton, NJ, 1972); Philip S. Haffenden, *New England in the English Nation, 1689–1713* (Oxford, 1974); Richard Johnson, *Adjustment to Empire: The New England Colonies, 1675–1715* (New Brunswick, NJ, 1981); Jack M. Sosin, *English America and the Restoration Monarchy of Charles II: Transatlantic Politics, Commerce, and Kinship* (Lincoln, NE, 1980), *English America and the Revolution of 1688: Royal Administration and the Structure of Provincial Government* (Lincoln, NE, 1982), and *English America and Imperial Inconstancy: The Rise of Provincial Autonomy, 1696–1716* (Lincoln, NE, 1985); Stephen Botein, *Early American Law and Society* (New York, 1983), ch. 4; Stephen Saunders Webb, *1676: The End of American Independence* (New York, 1984); Jack P. Greene, *Peripheries and Center*; Robert M. Bliss, *Revolution and Empire: English Politics and the American Colonies in the Seventeenth Century* (Manchester, 1990); and Alison Gilbert Olson, *Making the Empire Work: London and American Interest Groups, 1690–1790* (Cambridge, MA, 1992). For recent work influenced by Atlantic history, see Bilder, *The Transatlantic Constitution* (2004) and Hulsebosch, *Constituting Empire* (2005).

On the governors, classics are Leonard Woods Labaree, *Royal Government in America: A Study of the British Colonial System Before 1783* (1930; New York, 1958; also contains excellent bibliography for primary sources); Evarts Boutell Greene, *The Provincial Governor in the English Colonies of North America* (1898; Gloucester, 1966); and J. F. Burns, *Controversies Between Royal Governors and Their Assemblies in the Northern American Colonies* (1923; New York, 1969), chapters 1, 4–6. Stephen Saunders Webb, *The Governors-General: The English Army and the Definition of the Empire, 1561–1681* (Chapel Hill, NC, 1979), and Bernard Bailyn, *The Origins of American Politics* (New York, 1968), ch. 2, are also helpful. For instructions, see Leonard Woods Labaree, ed., *Royal Instructions to British Colonial Governors, 1670–1776*, 2 vols. (New York, 1935); Charles M. Andrews,

"List of Commissions, Instructions, and Additional Instructions Issued to the Royal Governors and Others in America," *American Historical Association Annual Report for the Year 1911* I (1913), 393–528. On correspondence, see Gertrude S. Kimball, *The Correspondence of the Colonial Governors of Rhode Island, 1723–1775*, 2 vols. (Boston, 1902–1903); David Cressy, *Coming Over: Migration and Communication Between England and New England in the Seventeenth Century* (Cambridge, 1987), ch. 9. Lists and bibliographies appear in David P. Henige, *Colonial Governors from the Fifteenth Century to the Present* (Madison, 1970), and John W. Raimo, *Biographical Directory of American Colonial and Revolutionary Governors, 1607–1789* (Westport, 1980).

On assemblies, see Michael Kammen, *Deputyes & Libertyes: The Origins of Representative Government in Colonial America* (New York, 1969), and the scholarship of Jack P. Greene, including *The Quest for Power: The Lower Houses of Assembly in the Southern Royal Colonies, 1689–1776* (Chapel Hill, NC, 1963); *Peripheries and Center*; *Negotiated Authorities: Essays in Colonial Political and Constitutional History* (Charlottesville, 1994), particularly chapters 6–8; and *Imperatives, Behaviors & Identities: Essays in Early American Cultural History* (Charlottesville, 1992). Warren M. Billings's *A Little Parliament: The Virginia General Assembly in the Seventeenth Century* (Richmond, 2004) is an outstanding recent contribution. J. M. Sosin, *English America and Imperial Inconstancy* and Mary Patterson Clarke, *Parliamentary Privilege in the American Colonies* (1943; New York, 1971), ch. 1, contain additional useful details and analysis. Additional relevant discussion appears in Bruce C. Daniels, ed., *Power and Status: Officeholding in Colonial America* (Middletown, CT, 1986), and Marchette Chute, *The First Liberty, A History of the Right to Vote in America, 1619–1850* (New York, 1969). On popular sovereignty, see Edmund S. Morgan, *Inventing the People: The Rise of Popular Sovereignty in England and America* (New York, 1988), chapters 2 and 8.

On the Privy Council, invaluable for organization, is Charles M. Andrews, *British Committees, Commissions, and Councils of Trade and Plantations, 1622–1675* (Baltimore, 1908), and for names, John C. Sainty, *Officials of the Board of Trade, 1660–1870* (London, 1974). On the 1660s commissioners, see John G. Reid, *Maine, Charles II and Massachusetts*, 54–123. On Edward Randolph, see Michael G. Hall, *Edward Randolph and the American Colonies, 1676–1703* (Chapel Hill, NC, 1960); Robert Noxon Toppan, ed., *Edward Randolph*, 7 vols. (Boston, 1899–1909). On the review of legislation, Elmer Beecher Russell, *The Review of American Colonial Legislation by the King in Council* (New York, 1915) remains outstanding. On colonial revision, see Erwin C. Surrency, "Revision of Colonial Laws," *American Journal of Legal History* 9 (1965), 189–202. A list of disallowed and confirmed acts is in the appendices of *Acts of the Privy Council, Colonial Series*; additional discussion can be found in Charles M. Andrews, ed., *Reports of the Laws of Connecticut by Francis Fane* (New Haven, 1915). Lists of acts sent to English officials appear in Charles M. Andrews, "Lists of the Journals and Acts of the Councils and Assemblies of the Thirteen Original

Colonies . . . Preserved in the Public Record Office, London," *American Historical Association Annual Report for the Year 1908* 1 (1909), 399–509. Appeals are discussed most recently in Bilder, *The Transatlantic Constitution* (2004) and exhaustively in Joseph H. Smith, *Appeals to the Privy Council from the American Plantations* (1950; New York, 1965) and "Administrative Control of the Courts of the American Plantations," *Columbia Law Review* 61 (1961), 1210–53 (also in *Essays in the History of Early American Law*, 281–335). Two earlier articles remain helpful: Harold D. Hazeltine, "Appeals from Colonial Courts to the King in Council, with Especial Reference to Rhode Island," *American Historical Association Annual Report of the Year 1894* (1896), 299–350, and Arthur Meier Schlesinger, "Colonial Appeals to the Privy Council," *Political Science Quarterly* 28 (1913), 279–97, 433–50. Sharon H. O'Connor is completing a forthcoming publication that will contain the list of all colonial appeals and relevant documentary information.

Attorney and Solicitor General opinions on colonial law appear in George Chalmers, *Opinions of Eminent Lawyers on Various Points of English Jurisprudence Chiefly Concerning the Colonies, Fisheries, and Commerce of Great Britain* (1814; New York, 1971), and R. T. Barton, ed., *Virginia Colonial Decisions: The Reports by Sir John Randolph and by Edward Barradall of Decisions of the General Court of Virginia, 1727–1741* (Boston, 1909), vol. 2, B1-B30 (1681–1726). English decisions usually discussed with reference to early colonial law can be found in multiple locations. *Calvin's Case* (1608) appears in 7 Coke 1a (1608), *English Reports*, vol. 77, 377. *Craw v. Ramsey* (1670) appears in [E. Vaughan], *Reports and Arguments in the Common Pleas* (London, 1677), 274–76, *English Reports*, vol. 124, 1072–85; *The Reports of Sir Peyton Ventris* (London, 1696), vol. 2, 1–8, *English Reports*, vol. 86, 273–7. *Blankard v. Galdy* (1693) appears in *Modern Reports*, vol. 4 (London, 1703), 215–26, *English Reports*, vol. 87, 356–9, 359–62; William Salkeld, *Reports* . . . ([London], 1718), vol. 2, 411–2, *English Reports*, vol. 91, 356–7; [Roger Comberbach], *The Reports of Several Cases* (London, 1724), 228–229, *English Reports*, vol. 90, 445; *Reports of Cases Determined by Holt* (London, 1738), 341, *English Reports*, vol. 90, 1089. *Dutton v. Howell* (1693) appears in Bartholomew Shower, *Cases in Parliament* (1698), 24–34, *English Reports*, vol. 1, 17–24 and *House of Lords Journal* (1771), vol. 15, 353–4. *Smith v. Brown and Cooper* (no date) appears in Salkeld, *Reports*, vol. 2, 666–7, *English Reports*, vol. 91, 566–7; *Reports of Cases determined by Holt*, 495, *English Reports*, vol. 90, 1172. The Memorandum of 9th August 1722 relating to the Privy Council appeal determination was printed in Peere Williams, *Reports*, vol. 2, 75–6 (London, 1740). *An Essay upon the Government of the English Plantations* . . . (1701) (ESTC T033473; reprinted edition edited by Louis B. Wright; San Marino, 1945) contains contemporaneous observations.

Older scholarship struggled with the precise application of Parliamentary statutes and common law in the colonies. For examples, see Paul S. Reinsch, *English Common Law in the Early American Colonies* (Madison, 1899); Julius

Goebel, Jr., "King's Law and Local Custom in Seventeenth Century New England," *Columbia Law Review* 31 (1931), 416–48 (also in *Essays in the History of Early American Law*, 83–120); Richard B. Morris, *Studies in the History of American Law* (New York, 1930), ch. 1; Robert Livingston Schuyler, *Parliament and the British Empire: Some Constitutional Controversies Concerning Imperial Legislative Jurisdiction* (New York, 1929); St. George Leakin Sioussat, "The Extension of English Statutes to the Plantations," *Select Essays in Anglo-American Legal History* (Boston, 1907), vol. 1, 416–30 and *The English Statutes in Maryland* (Baltimore, 1903). Of particular value is Elizabeth Gaspar Brown, *British Statutes in American Law, 1776–1836* (Ann Arbor, 1964), 1–46. Charles M. Andrews, *The Connecticut Intestacy Law* (New Haven, 1933; see also 1894 and 1907 versions) has a fine, clear discussion of various views held by contemporaries regarding the relationship between English law and colonial law. For Jack Greene's excellent work on colonial constitutionalism, see Jack P. Greene, "The Colonial Origins of American Constitutionalism," in *Negotiated Authorities*, 25–42, and *Peripheries and Center*, chapters 1–4. More recent discussions with varied interpretations appear in W. Hamilton Bryson, "The Prerogative of the Sovereign in Virginia: Royal Law in a Republic," *Legal History Review* 73 (2005), 371–84, and "English Common Law in Virginia," *Journal of Legal History*, 6 (1985), 249–56; James Hart and Richard J. Ross, "The Ancient Constitution in the Old World and the New," in Francis J. Bremer and Lynn A. Botelho, eds., *The Worlds of John Winthrop: Essays on England and New England, 1588–1649* (Boston, 2005), 237–89; William M. Offutt, "The Atlantic Rules: The Legalistic Turn in Colonial British America," in Elizabeth Mancke and Carole Shammas, eds., *The Creation of the British Atlantic World* (Baltimore, 2005), 160–81; Bilder, *The Transatlantic Constitution*; Daniel S. Hulsebosch, "The Ancient Constitution and the Expanding Empire: Sir Edward Coke's British Jurisprudence," *Law and History Review* 21 (2003), 439–82, and *Constituting Empire*, chapters 1 and 2; and Ernest G. Mayo, "Rhode Island's Reception of the Common Law," *Suffolk University Law Review* 31 (1998), 609–24. For early American discussion, see Joseph Story, *Commentaries on the Constitution of the United States* (Boston, 1833), Book 1, and James Wilson, *Considerations on the Nature and the Extent of the Legislative Authority of the British Parliament* (Philadelphia, 1774).

Colonial publications of statute law are in John D. Cushing's *The Colony Laws of North America* Series (Wilmington, 1977). For session laws, general assembly records and the numerous nineteenth-century colonial law collections should be consulted. Two useful catalogues are *The Charlemagne Tower Collection of American Colonial Laws* (1890; Littleton, 1990) and Russell Benedict, *Illustrated Catalogue of the Colony and State of New York and of the other Original Colonies and States, Constituting the collection Made by Hon. Russell Benedict* (1922; Union, 1998). The Massachusetts *Body of Liberties* (1641) is in William H. Whitmore, ed., *The Colonial Laws of Massachusetts* (Boston, 1890). For the *Lawes and Libertyes* (1648), see Thomas G. Barnes, ed., *The Book of the General Lawes and Libertyes Concerning the Inhabitants of the Massachusets* (San Marino, 1975) and Max Farrand, ed., *The Laws and Liberties* (Cambridge, MA, 1929). A fascinating contemporary compilation is *An Abridgement of the Laws in Force and Use in Her Majesty's Plantations* (London, 1704) (ESTC T137593).

On the printing of early laws, see David D. Hall, "The Chesapeake in the Seventeenth Century" and "The Atlantic Economy in the Eighteenth Century," in Hugh Amory and David D. Hall, eds., *A History of the Book in America: The Colonial Book in the Atlantic World* (Cambridge, MA, 2000), 55–82, 152–62. Discussions of specific laws have focused on New England, including Daniel R. Coquillette, "Radical Lawmakers in Colonial Massachusetts: The 'Countenance of Authorities' and the *Lawes and Libertyes*," *The New England Quarterly* 67 (1994), 179–206; G. B. Warden, "The Rhode Island Civil Code of 1647," in David D. Hall, John M. Murrin, and Thad W. Tate, eds., *Saints & Revolutionaries: Essays on Early American History* (New York, 1984), 138–51; Richard B. Morris, "Massachusetts and the Common Law: The Declaration of 1646," *American Historical Review* 31 (1926), 443–53 (also in *Essays in the History of Early American Law*, 135–46); Rosezella Canty-Letsome, "John Winthrop's Concept of Law in 17th Century New England, One Notion of Puritan Thinking," *Duquesne Law Review* 16 (1977), 331–57; G. B. Warden, "Law Reform in England and New England, 1620 to 1660," *William & Mary Quarterly*, 3d ser., 35 (1975), 668–90; George T. Haskins, "Codification of the Law in Colonial Massachusetts: A Study in Comparative Law," *Indiana Law Journal* 30 (1954), 1–17; Thorp L. Wolford, "The Laws and Liberties of 1648: The First Code of Laws Enacted and Printed in English America," *Boston University Law Review* 28 (1948), 426–63 (also in *Essays in the History of Early American Law*, 147–85); and Worthington C. Ford, "Cotton's 'Moses his Judicials,'" *Proceedings of the Massachusetts Historical Society*, 2d ser., 16 (1902), 274–84. For laws in other places, see David T. Konig, "'Dale's Laws' and the Non-Common Law Origins of Criminal Justice in Virginia," *American Journal of Legal History* 26 (1982), 354–75, and Caroline Robbins, "Laws and Governments Proposed for West New Jersey and Pennsylvania, 1676–1683, *Pennsylvania Magazine of History and Biography* 105 (1981), 373–92.

For a fine recent discussion of legal literates and the shift toward the common law, see William M. Offutt, "The Atlantic Rules," in *The Creation of the British Atlantic World*, 160–181. General discussions of early legal practitioners appear in Charles Warren, *History of the American Bar* (Boston, 1911) and Anton-Hermann Chroust, *The Rise of the Legal Profession in America*, 2 vols. (Norman, OK, 1965). Definitional problems are discussed in Mary Sarah Bilder, "The Lost Lawyers: Early American Legal Literates and Transatlantic Legal Culture," *Yale Journal of Law and Humanities* 11 (1999), 47–117. The classic article arguing for anglicization of the bar is John M. Murrin, "The Legal Transformation: The Bench and Bar of Eighteenth-Century Massachusetts," in Stanley N. Katz, ed., *Colonial America: Essays in Politics and Social Development* (Boston,

1971), 415–49. For interesting biographies, see Angela Fernandez, "Record-Keeping and Other Troublemaking: Thomas Lechford and Law Reform in Colonial Massachusetts," *Law and History Review* 23 (2005), 235–77; Thomas G. Barnes, "Thomas Lechford and the Earliest Lawyering in Massachusetts, 1638–1641," *Law in Colonial Massachusetts, 1630–1800*, 3–38; and Barbara A. Black, "Nathaniel Byfield, 1653–1733," *Law in Colonial Massachusetts, 1630–1800*, 57–106. Colony-specific accounts include Hoyt P. Canady, *Gentlemen of the Bar: Lawyers in Colonial South Carolina* (New York, 1987); A. G. Roeber, *Faithful Magistrates and Republican Lawyers: Creators of Virginia Legal Culture, 1680–1810* (Chapel Hill, 1981); John E. Douglass, "Between Pettifoggers and Professionals: Pleaders and Practitioners and the Beginnings of The Legal Profession in Colonial Maryland, 1634–1731," *American Journal of Legal History* 39 (1995), 359–84; Alan F. Day, "Lawyers in Colonial Maryland, 1660–1715," *American Journal of Legal History* 17 (1973), 145–65; Paul M. Hamlin, *Legal Education in Colonial New York* (1939; New York, 1970); and Neil W. Allen, Jr., "Law and Authority to the Eastward: Maine Courts, Magistrates, and Lawyers, 1690–1730," in *Law in Colonial Massachusetts*, 273–312. For discussion of female attorneys, see Paul D. Hamlin and Charles E. Baker, *Supreme Court of Judicature of the Province of New York, 1691–1704* (New York, 1952), vol. 1, 108–110; Louise Green Carr, "Margaret Brent: A Brief History" (available online at the Maryland Archives); and Mary E. W. Ramey, *Chronicles of Mistress Margaret Brent* (s.l., 1915). Lists of English-trained colonial lawyers appear in E. Alfred Jones, *American Members of the Inns of Court* (London, 1924). On the comparison with English barristers, see David Lemmings, *Professors of the Law: Barristers and English Legal Culture in the Eighteenth Century* (Oxford, 2000), 225–47. On notaries, see John E. Seth, "Notaries in the American Colonies," *John Marshall Law Review* 32 (1999), 863–86. A contemporary account appears in Robert Beverley, *History and the Present State of Virginia* (London, 1705) (ESTC T071491).

A number of accounts of lawyers' libraries exist, including Alfred Brophy, "'Ingenium est Fateri per quos profeceris:' Francis Daniel Pastorius' *Young Country Clerk's Collection* and Anglo-American Legal Literature, 1682–1716," *University of Chicago Law School Roundtable* 3 (1996), 637–734; Lawrence B. Custer, "William Cummings: A Colonial Lawyer and His Library," *Journal of Southern Legal History* 3 (1994), 221–40; William Hamilton Bryson, *Census of Law Books in Colonial Virginia* (Charlottesville, 1978); Herbert A. Johnson, *Imported Eighteenth-Century Law Treatises in American Libraries, 1700–1799* (Knoxville, 1978); and Edwin Wolf, *The Library of James Logan of Philadelphia, 1674–1751* (Philadelphia, 1971). On the use of libraries, see Michael H. Hoeflich, "The Lawyer as Pragmatic Reader: The History of Legal Common-Placing," *Arkansas Law Review* 55 (2002), 87–122. For a lawyer's notes, see Thomas Lechford, *Note-book Kept by Thomas Lechford, Esq., Lawyer, in Boston, Massachusetts Bay, from June 27, 1638, to July 29, 1641* (Cambridge, 1885). For printed American legal materials, invaluable is Morris L. Cohen's *Bibliography of Early American Law*, 6 vols. (Buffalo, 1998). General discussions appear in Erwin C. Surrency, *A History of American Law Publishing* (New York, 1990) and Morris L. Cohen, "Legal Literature in Colonial Massachusetts," in *Law in Colonial Massachusetts*, 243–272.

On courts, Massachusetts and Virginia again dominate the scholarship. On Massachusetts, see Barbara Aronstein Black, "The Concept of a Supreme Court: Massachusetts Bay, 1630–1686," *The History of the Law in Massachusetts*, 43–79 and *The Judicial Power and the General Court in Early Massachusetts, 1634–1686*, Ph.D. thesis, Yale University, 1975; Mark DeWolfe Howe & Louis F. Eaton, Jr., "The Supreme Judicial Power in the Colony of Massachusetts Bay," *New England Quarterly* 20 (1947), 291–316; and Zechariah Chafee, Jr., "Colonial Courts and the Common Law," *Massachusetts Historical Society Proceedings* 68 (1952), 132–59 (also in *Essays in the History of Early American Law*, 53–82). On Virginia courts, see Philip Alexander Bruce, *Institutional History of Virginia in the Seventeenth Century* (1910; Gloucester, 1964), vol. I, and Warren M. Billings, "Justices, Books, Laws, and Courts in Seventeenth-Century Virginia," *Law Library Journal* 85 (1993), 277–96. In general, see Jack M. Sosin, *The Aristocracy of the Long Robe: The Origins of Judicial Review in America* (New York, 1989), and Erwin C. Surrency, "The Courts in the American Colonies," *American Journal of Legal History* 11 (1967), 253–76. Numerous older institutional accounts exist for most colonies, often in "Bench and Bar" volumes. For an excellent study of late seventeenth-century litigation, see Alfred Brophy, "'For the Preservation of the King's Peace and Justice': Community and English Law in Sussex County, Pennsylvania, 1682–1696," *American Journal of Legal History* 40 (1996), 167–212. For contemporaneous accounts of courts, see Erwin C. Surrency, "Report on Court Procedures in the Colonies—1700," *American Journal of Legal History* 9 (1965), 69–83, 167–78, 234–46. For a discussion of the work of a justice of the peace, see Russell K. Osgood, "John Clark, Esq., Justice of the Peace, 1667–1728," *Law in Colonial Massachusetts*, 107–52.

Court records for almost every level and type of colonial court exist; however, at present, there is no comprehensive guide to published and manuscript colonial court records. Such a bibliography would be of great assistance to the scholarship. One excellent regional example is Diane Rapaport, *New England Court Records: A Research Guide for Genealogists and Historians* (Burlington, MA, 2006), which offers a guide to New England legal materials, including microform and online collections. Another recent work, Michael Chiorazzi and Marguerite Most, eds., *Prestatehood Legal Materials: A Fifty-State Research Guide* (New York, 2006), contains descriptive chapters on legal materials available for each state. Richard B. Morris, *Early American Court Records: A Publication Program* (New York, 1941) provides a helpful, albeit old, overview of unpublished materials. Older works referring to published court records include Richard B. Morris, "Bibliographical Essay," *Studies in the History of Early American Law*,

259–73; William Jeffrey, Jr., *Early New England Court Records: A Bibliography of Published Materials* (Cambridge, MA, 1954); and William Jeffrey, Jr., "Early American Court Records – A Bibliography of Printed Materials: The Middle Colonies," *University of Cincinnati Law Review* 39 (1970), 685–710. For a good explanation of records, see Michael S. Hindus, "A Guide to the Court Records of Early Massachusetts," in *Law in Colonial Massachusetts*, 519–40. There are few known early manuscript reports of colonial courts. For a discussion of early Virginia manuscript court reports, see W. Hamilton Bryson, "Virginia Manuscript Law Reports," *Law Library Journal* 82 (1990), 305–11.

On colonial criminal law in the courts, see Mark D. Cahn, "Punishment, Discretion, and the Codification of Prescribed Penalties in Colonial Massachusetts," *American Journal of Legal History* 33 (1989), 107–36; John M. Murrin, "Magistrates, Sinners, and a Precarious Liberty: Trial by Jury in Seventeenth-Century New England," *Saints & Revolutionaries*, 152–206; Gail Sussman Marcus, "Due Execution of the 'Generall Rules of Righteousness'": Criminal Procedure in New Haven Town and Colony, 1638–1658," *Saints & Revolutionaries*, 99–137; Kathryn Preyer, "Penal Measures in the American Colonies: An Overview," *American Journal of Legal History* 26 (1982), 326–53; Douglas Greenberg, "Crime, Law Enforcement, and Social Control in Colonial America, *American Journal of Legal History* 26 (1982), 293–325; Arthur P. Scott, *Criminal Law in Colonial Virginia* (Chicago, 1930); and Oliver Perry Chitwood, *Justice in Colonial Virginia* (Baltimore, 1905).

On equity, see Peter Charles Hoffer, *The Law's Conscience: Equitable Constitutionalism in America* (Chapel Hill, 1990); Stanley N. Katz, "The Politics of Law in Colonial America: Controversies over Chancery Courts and Equity Law in the Eighteenth Century," *Perspectives in American History* 5 (1971), 257–84; William J. Curran, "The Struggle for Equity Jurisdiction in Massachusetts," *Boston University Law Review* 31 (1951), 269–96; Spencer R. Liverant and Walter H. Hitchler, "A History of Equity in Pennsylvania," *Dickinson Law Review* 37 (1933), 156–84; and Solon Wilson, "Courts of Chancery in America – Colonial Period," *American Law* Review 18 (1884), 226–55 (also in *Select Essays in Anglo-American Legal History*, Boston, 1908, vol. II, p. 779).

CHAPTER 4: LEGAL COMMUNICATIONS AND IMPERIAL GOVERNANCE

RICHARD J. ROSS

Historians of the early modern English, French, and Spanish empires have long discussed how distance and slow, irregular communications affected metropolitan oversight of New World colonies. They commonly treated communications as one factor among many explaining the character of imperial governance and colonial society. In the past fifteen years, some scholars have made communications the primary subject of study. They have traced the routes through which messages passed; asked how the methods and personnel of information exchange influence the creation, framing, and dissemination of knowledge;

studied in what ways empires encouraged or relied on particular communications practices; and explored how trans-Atlantic information systems affected the distribution of power, wealth, and resources. These historians have tended to emphasize the interrelationship of administrative, economic, and social networks in early modern communications. Distinguished work in this vein includes, for English America, David Cressy, *Coming Over: Migration and Communication Between England and New England in the Seventeenth Century* (New York, 1987); Richard D. Brown, *Knowledge is Power: The Diffusion of Information in Early America, 1700–1865* (New York, 1989); Richard D. Brown, *The Strength of a People: The Idea of an Informed Citizenry in America, 1650–1870* (Chapel Hill, 1996); and especially, Ian K. Steele, *The English Atlantic, 1675–1740: An Exploration of Communication and Community* (New York, 1986); for French America, Kenneth J. Banks, *Chasing Empire Across the Sea: Communications and the State in the French Atlantic, 1713–1763* (Montreal, 2002); and for Spanish America, Tamar Herzog, *Ritos de Control, Prácticas de Negociación: Pesquisas, Visitas y Residencias y las Relaciones entre Quito y Madrid (1650–1750)*, in Jose Andres-Gallego, ed., *Nuevas Aportaciones a la Historia Jurídica de Iberoamérica* (Madrid, 2000 [published on CD-ROM]) and *Upholding Justice: Society, State, and the Penal System in Quito (1650–1750)* (Ann Arbor, 2004). For an exploration of these themes in the context of the "second British empire," see C. A. Bayly, *Empire and Information: Intelligence Gathering and Social Communication in India, 1780–1870* (Cambridge, 1996). David Nelken, ed., *Law as Communication* (Brookfield, 1996) offers a list of questions that historians can use as a starting point to investigate the relationship between law and communications in past societies.

Scholarship on communications in the early modern English empire has typically treated law as one of several subjects, but has not focused on it per se. It has also concentrated on providing a rich account of the English empire at the cost of downplaying comparative questions. To reconstruct through comparative inquiry how the strategies and practices of *legal* communications affected England's governance of its North American colonies, one must look for clues in works written for other purposes. Histories of the English empire's administration contain much "raw material." Standard works that put administrative and jurisdictional structures at the center include the following: A. Berriedale Keith, *Constitutional History of the First British Empire* (Oxford, 1930); Leonard W. Labaree, *Royal Government in America* (New Haven, 1930); Herbert L. Osgood, *The American Colonies in the Seventeenth Century*, 3 vols. (New York, 1904–07); Herbert L. Osgood, *The American Colonies in the Eighteenth Century*, 4 vols. (New York, 1924–25); and, especially, Charles M. Andrews, *The Colonial Period of American History*, 4 vols. (New Haven, 1934–38).

Of course, legal communications traveled across the Atlantic through more than the formal institutional and administrative structures of the empire that interested the early imperial historians. From the 1950s onward, scholars have expanded the subject matter of imperial history by broadening their understanding of what ties an empire together and makes it robust. Toward this end, they examined the economic, social, intellectual, and political networks that grew up around the imperial apparatus and that helped integrate the English Atlantic and influence the operation of imperial policies. They also explored how the English empire altered social and religious arrangements, conventions of governing, and identities within colonial society and how it enlisted the cooperation of local elites by promoting their interests and validating their status. The building of the empire came to resemble not so much the imposition of administrative oversight and trade regulation by the metropolis as a multi-sided process of negotiation, recruitment, and cultural adjustment. This reorientation of imperial history broadened our understanding of the channels through which legal communications passed (emphasizing the importance of interest groups, lobbying, trans-Atlantic political alliances, and social networks). And it heightened awareness of the indirect effects of legal communications by demonstrating the value of legal information as a bargaining chip in negotiations, as a marker of elite status, and as a resource in forming political partnerships. Distinguished work that highlights negotiation, network formation, and the social foundation of empire – and that in the process offers glimpses of the multiple, informal pathways of legal communications in the early modern Anglo-American world – includes Bernard Bailyn, *The Origins of American Politics* (New York, 1968); Christine Daniels and Michael V. Kennedy, eds., *Negotiated Empires: Centers and Peripheries in the Americas, 1500–1820* (New York, 2002); Richard R. Johnson, *Adjustment to Empire: The New England Colonies, 1675–1715* (Leicester, 1981); Stanley N. Katz, *Newcastle's New York: Anglo-American Politics, 1732–1753* (Cambridge, MA, 1968); Alison Gilbert Olson, *Anglo-American Politics, 1660–1775: The Relationship Between Parties in England and Colonial America* (New York, 1973); Alison Gilbert Olson, *Making the Empire Work: London and American Interest Groups, 1690–1790* (Cambridge, MA, 1992); Jack P. Greene, *Peripheries and Center: Constitutional Development in the Extended Polities of the British Empire and the United States, 1607–1788* (Athens, GA, 1987); Jack P. Greene, *Negotiated Authorities: Essays in Colonial Political and Constitutional History* (Charlottesville, 1994); and Michael G. Kammen, *A Rope of Sand: The Colonial Agents, British Politics, and the American Revolution* (Ithaca, NY, 1968). The changing orientation of imperial history can be seen by comparing vol. I of J. Holland Rose et al., *The Cambridge History of the British Empire* (Cambridge, 1929) to the recent *Oxford History of the British Empire*, especially vol. I (Nicholas Canny, ed., *The Origins of Empire: British Overseas Enterprise to the Close of the Seventeenth Century* [Oxford, 1998]); vol. II (P. J. Marshall, ed., *The Eighteenth Century* [Oxford, 2001]); and vol. V (Robin W. Winks, ed., *Historiography* [Oxford, 2001]).

Certain channels or clearinghouses were especially important for legal communications in the English empire and deserve particular attention. On the colonial agents, see Beverly W. Bond, Jr., "The Colonial Agent as a Popular

Representative," *Political Science Quarterly* 35 (1920), 372–92; James J. Burns, *The Colonial Agents of New England* (Washington, DC, 1935); Kammen, *Rope of Sand*; and Ella Lonn, *The Colonial Agents of the Southern Colonies* (Chapel Hill, 1945). On the Lords of Trade and Board of Trade, see Arthur Herbert Basye, *The Lords Commissioners of Trade and Plantations, Commonly Known as the Board of Trade: 1748–1782* (New Haven, 1925); Ralph Paul Bieber, *The Lords of Trade and Plantations, 1675–1696* (Allentown, 1919); Oliver Morton Dickerson, *American Colonial Government, 1696–1765: A Study of the British Board of Trade in its Relation to the American Colonies: Political, Industrial, Administrative* (Cleveland, 1912); and Ian K. Steele, *Politics of Colonial Policy: The Board of Trade in Colonial Administration, 1696–1720* (Oxford, 1968). On the customs service, see Thomas C. Barrow, *Trade and Empire: The British Customs Service in Colonial America, 1660–1775* (Cambridge, MA, 1967). On judicial appeals, see Joseph H. Smith, *Appeals to the Privy Council from the American Plantations* (New York, 1950), and Mary Sarah Bilder, *The Transatlantic Constitution: Colonial Legal Culture and the Empire* (Cambridge, MA, 2004). On the review of colonial legislation, see Elmer B. Russell, *The Review of American Colonial Legislation by the King in Council* (New York, 1915), and Joseph H. Smith, "Administrative Control of the Courts of the American Plantations," in David Flaherty, ed., *Essays in the History of Early American Law* (Chapel Hill, 1969), 281–335. On the vice-admiralty courts, see Charles M. Andrews, "Introduction: Vice-Admiralty Courts in the Colonies," in Dorothy S. Towle, ed., *The Records of the Vice-Admiralty Court of Rhode Island, 1716–1752* (Washington, DC, 1936), 1–79, and Carl Ubbelohde, *The Vice-Admiralty Courts and the American Revolution* (Chapel Hill, 1960).

By the 1950s and 1960s, scholarship on the Spanish empire, as on the English empire, was moving beyond its customary focus on the institutions and personnel of imperial and local government. Later work pursued a social history of empire by examining the recruitment and interests of American officeholders, local elites, and Indian leaders and by exploring informal mechanisms for exercising power. Increased attention to the flexibility and negotiated quality of the Spanish empire led, as with the English empire, toward a greater curiosity about how information circulated among the metropolis, administrative institutions in the New World, and colonial society. Though this scholarship was typically not conceptualized as a study of *legal* communications per se, the importance in the Spanish empire of the crown bureaucracy and mixed judicial-administrative tribunals such as the *audiencias* meant that insights about legal communications could be extracted out of work written for other purposes. Useful general studies include the following: Rafael Altamira, *Autonomía y Descentralización Legislativa en el Régimen Colonial Español: Legislación Metropolitana y Legislación Propiamente Indiana (Siglos XVI a XVIII)* (Coimbra, 1945); Peter Bakewell, "Conquest after the Conquest: The Rise of Spanish Domination in America," in Richard L. Kagan and Geoffrey Parker, eds., *Spain, Europe and the*

Atlantic World: Essays in Honour of John H. Elliott (Cambridge, 1995), 296–315; Woodrow W. Borah, "Representative Institutions in the Spanish Empire in the Sixteenth Century: The New World," *The Americans* 12 (1956), 246–57; D. A. Brading, "Bourbon Spain and its American Empire," in Leslie Bethell, ed., *The Cambridge History of Latin America* (Cambridge, 1984), I, 389–439; J. H. Elliott, *Imperial Spain, 1469–1716* (New York, 1990); J. H. Elliott, "Spain and America before 1700," in Leslie Bethell, ed., *Colonial Spanish America* (Cambridge, 1987), 59–111; J. H. Elliott, "Spain and its Empire in the Sixteenth and Seventeenth Century," in *Spain and its World, 1500–1700: Selected Essays* (New Haven, 1989), 7–26; Charles Gibson, *Spain in America* (New York, 1966); Mario Góngora, *Studies in the Colonial History of Spanish America* (Cambridge, 1975); Clarence H. Haring, *The Spanish Empire in America* (New York, 1963); Ricardo Levene, *Introduccion a La Historia del Derecho Indiano*, in *Obras de Ricardo Levene*, vol. III (Buenos Aires, 1962); M. C. Mirow, *Latin American Law: A History of Private Law and Institutions in Spanish America* (Austin, 2004); Frank Jay Moreno, "The Spanish Colonial System: A Functional Approach," *Western Political Quarterly* 20 (1967): 308–20; Jose Maria Ots y Capdequi, *Historia del Derecho Español en America y del Derecho Indiano* (Madrid, 1967); John Leddy Phelan, *The Kingdom of Quito in the Seventeenth Century: Bureaucratic Politics in the Spanish Empire* (Madison, 1967); John Leddy Phelan, "Authority and Flexibility in the Spanish Imperial Bureaucracy," *Administrative Science Quarterly* 5 (1960), 47–65; Horst Pietschmann, "Actores Locales y Poder Central: La Herencia Colonial y el Caso de México," in Hans-Joachim Konig and Marianne Wiesebron, eds., *Nation-Building in Nineteenth-Century Latin America: Dilemmas and Conflicts* (Leiden, 1998), 257–80; and Carmelo Viñas Mey, *El Régimen Jurídico y la Responsabilidad en la América Indiana* (2nd ed., Mexico City, 1993).

The following works examine institutions or practices of particular importance for a history of legal communications: Lauren Benton, "Making Order Out of Trouble: Jurisdictional Politics in the Spanish Colonial Borderlands," *Law and Social Inquiry* 26 (2001), 373–401; Mark A. Burkholder and D. S. Chandler, *From Impotence to Authority: The Spanish Crown and the American Audiencias, 1687–1808* (Columbia, 1977); Tamar Herzog, *Ritos de Control, Prácticas de Negociación* and *Upholding Justice*; John Preston Moore, *The Cabildo in Peru Under the Hapsburgs* (Durham, 1954); J. H. Parry, *The Audiencia of New Galicia in the Sixteenth Century: A Study in Spanish Colonial Government* (Cambridge, 1948); and Victor Tau Anzoátegui, "La Ley 'Se Obedece pero no se Cumple': En Torno a la Suplicación de las Leyes en el Derecho Indiano," in *La Ley en América Hispana. Del Descubrimiento a la Emancipación* (Buenos Aires, 1985), 69–142.

On the legal culture of Spanish America, see Javier Barrientos Grandon, *La Cultura Jurídica en la Nueva España* (Mexico City, 1993); Charles R. Cutter, *The Legal Culture of Northern New Spain, 1700–1810* (Albuquerque, 1995); Tamar Herzog, "Sobre la Cultura Jurídica en la América Colonial (Siglos XVI–XVIII)," *Anuario de Historia del Derecho Español* 65 (1995), 903–11; and Eduardo

Martiré, "La Idea de Justicia y la Organizacion Judicial Indiana," *Lecciones y Ensayos: Facultad de Derecho y Ciencias Sociales* 37 (1968), 45–62.

On the Spanish American legal system's interaction with Indians, the following proved particularly valuable: Woodrow Borah, *Justice by Insurance: The General Indian Court of Colonial Mexico and the Legal Aides of the Half-Real* (Berkeley, 1983); Charles R. Cutter, *The Protector de Indios in Colonial New Mexico, 1659–1821* (Albuquerque, 1986); Susan Kellogg, *Law and the Transformation of Aztec Culture, 1500–1700* (Norman, 1995); and Steve J. Stern, *Peru's Indian Peoples and the Challenge of Spanish Conquest: Huamanga to 1640*, 2nd ed. (Madison, 1993).

Overall, my analysis is indebted to comparative work on the differing colonial states that England and Spain set up in the New World. J. H. Elliott's new and magisterial study, *Empires of the Atlantic World: Britain and Spain in America 1492–1830* (New Haven, 2006), will doubtless become indispensable, but see also his earlier *Britain and Spain in America: Colonists and Colonized* (Reading, 1994) and "Empire and State in British and Spanish America," in Serge Gruzinski and Nathan Wachtel, eds., *Le Nouveau Monde – Mondes Nouveaux: L'Experience Americaine* (Paris, 1996), 365–82. See also James Lang, *Conquest and Commerce: Spain and England in the Americas* (New York, 1975), and Anthony McFarlane, *The British in the Americas, 1480–1815* (London, 1994).

CHAPTER 5: REGIONALISM IN EARLY AMERICAN LAW

DAVID THOMAS KONIG

Regional awareness has been embedded in the writing of early American history, beginning with its first chroniclers. On the extent of the "envy" between the Chesapeake and New England that Captain John Smith lamented in 1624 and that endured as what John Adams called the "damnable Rivalry between Virginia, and Massachusetts" in 1813, see David Thomas Konig, "The Virgin and the Virgin's Sister: Virginia, Massachusetts, and the Contested Legacy of Colonial Law," in Russell Osgood, ed., *The History of the Law in Massachusetts: The Supreme Judicial Court 1692–1992* (Boston, 1992). Awareness of region has informed – indeed, has driven – historical studies of early American law, both normative and descriptive, even if not framed within explicitly declared "regional" or "sectional" interpretive models. It was quite appropriate, therefore, that the legal realist Felix Frankfurter was asked to write a short "Foreward" to Merrill Jensen's collection of essays on *Regionalism in America* (Madison, 1951). Sympathizing with the way the Wisconsin School emphasized the material forces guiding historical development, Frankfurter applied the formula to cite a combination of regionally specific forces that enabled a continental nation to "be governed by organs that fairly represent its disciplined will and at the same time adequately evoke the diverse civilized potentialities of its people." Frankfurter was aware that the relationship of law and regionalism was not always obvious. "To be sure," he wrote, "the social, economic, and cultural influences and needs comprised by regionalism do not appear in litigation with candid impact. But they are there," he insisted, "if only at times in the interstices of legal records."

Frankfurter had identified the powerful influence of regional forces in the narrative of American legal development, but the converse is also true: law has had a powerful impact on the way Americans thought of their societies, as well as on the ways that historians have understood that past. Perhaps because legal records comprise such a significant proportion of archival materials that survive from the colonial period, even those scholars we would not regard as legal historians have relied on legal sources to examine the American past, unavoidably framing their narratives within the parameters of legal institutions. As a result, the teaching of early American history has always applied the regional particularities of institutional legal and constitutional forms as a way to organize a complex narrative embracing many different enterprises undertaken across two centuries, even if scholars did not generate interpretive paradigms involving law or legal institutions. The availability of a master narrative that distinguished among corporate, proprietary, and royal colonies provided an uncomplicated structure of organizational coherence. For better or worse, this model inescapably forced the colonies onto a Procrustean bed made of the three different types of charter forms and defined the nature of the political conflicts of their earliest years, as seen in Herbert L. Osgood's three-volume survey, *The American Colonies in the Seventeenth Century* (New York, 1904). Because these three types of government roughly corresponded to the three general regions of settlement, they produced an implicitly regionalized framework for the earliest studies of early American law, as Osgood devoted separate chapters to legal developments in each of the colonial archetypes.

Osgood's history appeared at the turn of the twentieth century and followed a long interpretive tradition dominated by the rivalry of North and South that culminated in the Civil War, but it coincided with several scholarly trends that combined to regionalize the study of early American law along new and different lines. Even if the schools they produced had little else in common, they left an imprint that has framed a regionally pluralistic paradigm that has dominated the writing of colonial legal history since the turn of the twentieth century. The Wisconsin School of historians was deeply influenced by the work of that state university's most famous historian, Frederick Jackson Turner, and his 1893 paper on "The Significance of the Frontier in American History," published in his book *The Frontier in American History* (New York, 1920). Often overlooked, however, is his less well known and posthumously published collection of essays, *The Significance of Sections in American History* (New York, 1932), in which he acknowledged "the interaction of the various migrating stocks, each in its particular geographic province." Though he left a deep and lasting legacy among legal scholars of the nineteenth century at the

University of Wisconsin Law School, in his lifetime Turner produced few disciples who devoted their work to colonial legal history, though Paul Reinsch was an exception, notable for the boldness of his thesis on *English Common Law in the Early American Colonies* (Madison, 1899). His book presents three chapters – "New England," The Middle Colonies," and "The Southern Colonies" – with a conclusion that reiterated his thesis that the common law in the colonies was "rudimentary and incomplete," shaped by colonial regionally specific codification that exemplified regional impulses. Reinsch's overstated insistence on the frontier-driven simplification of English law in the colonies has been subjected to much revision by other scholars (as has Turner's concept of "frontier" itself). However, his Turnerian environmental determinism that rejected the cultural continuity of English law also helped dissolve the force of a monolithic legal and cultural hegemony over numerous expanding settlements, a process that allowed them to follow their own regional legal course.

Though neither Turnerian nor focused on early America, more recent studies examine the role played by the process of migration in shaping political and legal change and offer their own analytical insights: Andrew Cayton and Peter Onuf, eds., *The Midwest and the Nation: Rethinking the History of an American Region* (Bloomington, 1990) describe the processes at work in migration, whereas John Phillip Reid provides a way of engaging the basics of frontier legal discourses in "The Layers of Western Legal History," in John McLaren, Hamar Foster, and Chet Orloff, eds., *Law of the Elephant, Law of the Beaver: Essays in the Legal History of the North American West* (Regina, 1992), 23–71.

Justice Frankfurter's sympathy for the implications of the Wisconsin School reflected his affinity for the legal realism that supplied additional intellectual support for a regional perspective on law. Legal realism, with its opposition to legal formalism and its skepticism about the existence of commonly honored legal principles, viewed law as socially constructed (and, a fortiori, as judicially constructed). The greater the variety of social forms, the greater would be the variety of legal institutions and principles. Frankfurter spoke for a generation of jurists who saw the connection of law and social policy and who agreed with the observation of Oliver Wendell Holmes, Jr., in *The Common Law* (Boston, 1881), that "the life of the law has not been logic; it has been experience." Holmes's "felt necessities of the time" varied according to social pressures, and legal history would reflect them too.

A third trend among historians in the early twentieth century stands as an unlikely ally of the frontier scholars or the legal realists. As the nineteenth century came to a close, historians were turning their attention to the shared traditions of Britain and America. The imperial school that they represented testified to the centrality of law in the history and identity of both nations. The United States and the United Kingdom drew together diplomatically, and appreciation of their common history of legal and political development – characterized by the rise of powerful national political and economic institutions – reinforced the nationalizing legalism that John Marshall, Tapping Reeve, James Kent, and Joseph Story had tried to spread through opinions, treatises, and law lectures. Efforts to subordinate state law to federal law through constitutional interpretation was one method, but less obvious were efforts to assert and establish a commercial law that would erase the diversity of state law on the subject – Kent was speaking for others when he stated, "I shall not much care what the law is in Vermont or Delaware, or Rhode Island. . . . I shall *assume* what I have to say to be the law of every state." John H. Langbein throws light on Reeve's efforts in "Blackstone, Litchfield, and Yale: The Founding of the Yale Law School," in Anthony T. Kronman, ed., *The History of the Yale Law School: The Tercentenary Lectures* (New Haven, 2004), 17–52. On efforts to achieve a republicanized "American" system of law consistent with the broader aspirations of the Revolution, see David Konig, "Jurisprudence and Social Policy in the New Republic," in Konig, ed., *Devising Liberty: Creating and Preserving the Conditions of Freedom in the New American Republic* (Stanford, 1995).

Even so, politics in the United States had not yet achieved the national, centralized focus that characterized Britain's (nor has it done so yet, for that matter). In yet another of the ironies that characterize American history, the South lost the Civil War, but has managed to keep alive a powerful sectional identity in law. That diversity has been central to Southern identity and is nowhere better expressed than in John C. Calhoun's antebellum taunt that "England is a nation, but the United States are not a nation." Despite efforts of revisionist constitutional historians in the later twentieth century (especially after the New Deal revolution) to show that a nationalizing federal judiciary successfully imposed central authority over regional diversity, the reality of judicial administration after the Civil War still reflected, in no small measure, the contest of Northern political goals and the South's efforts to resist racial desegregation. St. George Tucker had confessed as much in his long examination "Of the Unwritten, or Common Law of England; And Its Introduction into, and Authority Within the United States," which appeared as "Appendix E" to the first volume of his *Blackstone's Commentaries: With Notes of Reference, to the Constitution and Laws, of the Federal Government of the United States; And of the Commonwealth of Virginia*, 5 vols. (Philadelphia, 1803). It is more easily accessible in a modern edition as included with Tucker's *A View of the Constitution of the United States: With Selected Writings*, ed. Clyde N. Wilson (Indianapolis, 1999), 313–70, at 321.

Historians remained acutely aware of the realities of regional variation, especially those embedded in the transplanted cultures of the first two centuries of American history, long before the challenges of the modern nation-state. When Charles McLean Andrews conceptualized his monumental survey of *The Colonial Period of American History* (New Haven, 1934–38), of which he completed only four of a longer, projected multivolume series, he devoted the first three volumes to regional development. This decision is not surprising in view of the fact that Andrews had begun his career as a medieval legal historian studying the most local of legal institutions, the manor. Research into local history by medieval historians had a deep impact on legal scholars. George Lee Haskins, son of the great Yale medievalist Charles Homer Haskins, brought his deep appreciation of the Middle Ages to his writing of early American legal history, which was evident in his many articles on the particularities of New England law; his insights were brought together in his classic, *Law and Authority in Early Massachusetts: A Study in Tradition and Design* (New York, 1960). And at Columbia University, law professor Julius G. Goebel, Jr., wrote his classic and seminal essay, "King's Law and Local Custom in Seventeenth-Century New England, *Columbia Law Review* 31 (1931), 416–48. Forty years later, in the Oliver Wendell Holmes Devise *History of the Supreme Court of the United States*, vol. I: *Antecedents and Beginnings to 1801* (New York, 1971), he demonstrated again the way the "legacy of the Middle Ages" was imprinted on the transmission of law from the Old World to the New, with the "heterogeneous body of local law from the backwaters of the mainstream of the common law."

In planning subsequent volumes in his meditation, "On the Writing of Colonial History," *William and Mary Quarterly*, 3rd ser., 1 (1944), 27–48, Andrews described how his planned (though never written) subsequent volumes would synthesize social and economic factors, but he was forced to return to regional illustrations and comparisons to make sense of the larger picture he sought to paint. Each of the first three completed volumes was subtitled *The Settlements* and set out with lapidary precision the details of political and legal institutions peculiar to the diverse goals of England's overseas expansion. His fourth volume (subtitled *England's Commercial and Colonial Policy*) remains, like the others, unsurpassed in its copious and exact delineation of a patchwork structure of rules and laws whose formulation lacked systematic planning or final consistency, but whose institutions came to serve the economic contributions of each region's role in a commercial empire. The same reversion to regionalism is apparent, too, in Richard B. Morris's *Studies in the History of American Law: With Special Reference to the Seventeenth and Eighteenth Centuries* (New York, 1930). Morris focused his inquiry on doctrinal matters, but his bibliographic essay on primary sources identifies Massachusetts, Connecticut, New York, and Maryland as "representative regions for particular departures from the common law." When he published a new edition of the book in 1959, in fact, Morris called for more regional examination of the subject.

The more closely scholars examined trans-Atlantic legal connections, the more legal differences they discovered. Though not identifying them explicitly or drawing from them any regionally specific patterns of variation, this research revealed powerful localist legal impulses that a later generation of scholars would synthesize within such molds. In *Appeals to the Privy Council from the American Plantations* (New York, 1950), Joseph H. Smith (a student of Julius Goebel) masterfully describes a politically incoherent system of imperial administration that was forced to abandon its attempts to impose legal uniformity across the empire, but nevertheless continued to meddle with regional assertions of legal and judicial autonomy. Britain's colonial policy, that is, sowed the seeds for future regional awareness by arousing locally specific resistance to its heavy-handed attempts at centralization that colonists rejected as "repugnant" to their locally specific legal innovations. Recent work by legal scholars has amply demonstrated the value of such an approach. Examples of this for each region are Mary Sarah Bilder, *The Transatlantic Constitution. Colonial Legal Culture and the Empire* (Cambridge, MA, 2004), which gives its major attention to New England; Daniel J. Hulsebosch, *Constituting Empire. New York and the Transformation of Constitutionalism in the Atlantic World, 1664–1830* (Chapel Hill, 2005); and David Konig, "Virginia and the Imperial State: Law, Enlightenment, and 'the crooked cord of discretion,'" in David Lemmings, ed., *The British and their Laws in the Eighteenth Century* (Woodbridge, Suffolk, 2005).

It was such an irreconcilable difference over the meaning of "law" and "constitution" that had led to the Revolution, as amply demonstrated in John Philip Reid's series of three books on the widening constitutional chasm. Embracing within it a vast territory of legal development, his *Constitutional History of the American Revolution* treats *The Authority of Rights* (Madison, 1986), *The Authority to Tax* (Madison, 1987), and *The Authority to Legislate* (Madison, 1991), all legal questions on which the colonies claimed interpretive sovereignty. Yet embedded within Reid's trans-Atlantic rift were smaller, more localized ones generated by the force of a regional impulse in English law centering on the local jury. Before publishing his *Constitutional History*, Reid examined the jury as the embodiment of the vicinage and local legal definition in two other books, *In a Defiant Stance: The Conditions of Law in Massachusetts Bay, the Irish Comparison, and the Coming of the American Revolution* (University Park, 1977) and *In Defiance of Law: The Standing-Army Controversy, the Two Constitutions, and the Coming of the American Revolution* (Chapel Hill, 1981).

Reid, like other widely read legal scholars, exemplifies the legal scholar's awareness of the work of historians, especially students of England's variegated legal landscape. Unavoidably, this scholarship has pointed them to an appreciation of a common legal dynamic – that of the way the common law has accommodated local norms and assumptions to gain legitimacy in a national history hostile to strong centralizing efforts and wracked by internal conflict. J. G. A. Pocock provides the foundation for examining the searing force of critical "moments" in *The Machiavellian Moment: Florentine Political Thought and the Atlantic Republican Tradition* (Princeton, 1975). More focused on the New World is Jack P. Greene, "Transplanting Moments: Inheritance in the Formation of Early American Culture," *William and Mary Quarterly*, 3rd ser., 48 (1991), 227. Though the "republican paradigm" that Pocock advanced has had great influence, scholars still find enormous influence in the product of another "moment," John Locke's 1690 *Two Treatises of Government*, available in *A Critical*

Edition with an Introduction and Apparatus Criticus, ed. Peter Laslett (New York, 1963). Alan Everitt shows how early modern regional English legal cultures finally became self-consciously so after a long history of unacknowledged variation in "Country, County and Town: Patterns of Regional Evolution in England," *Transactions of the Royal Historical Society*, 5th ser., 29 (1979), 79–81, whereas Richard S. Thompson, *Islands of Law. A Legal History of the British Isles* (New York, 2000), identifies local "battles for survival" in the seventeenth century as a force for entrenching regional distinctiveness. Illustrative of the institutional changes wrought are Norma Landau, *The Justices of the Peace, 1679–1760* (Berkeley, 1984), and Keith Wrightson, "The Politics of the Parish," in Paul Griffiths, Adam Fox, and Steven Hindle, eds., *The Experience of Authority in Early Modern England* (Basingstoke, 1996). Within this model, studies of local English economic patterns gain great relevance for legal inquiry. Most influential in this genre has been Margaret Spufford, *Contrasting Communities. English Villagers in the Sixteenth and Seventeenth Centuries* (Cambridge, 1974). On the persistence of such local patterns in New England, see David Grayson Allen, *In English Ways. The Movement of Societies and the Transferal of English Custom to Massachusetts Bay in the Seventeenth Century* (Chapel Hill, 1981).

The present ascendancy of a regional approach to early American legal history should not obscure the fact the winds of historical fashion have changed direction over the years and will certainly do so again. When Andrews wrote in 1944, he was responding to two powerful trends in the writing of history that would work against the regional paradigm. One was the accelerating emphasis on social science methods, as historians tried to share in the new glow of the rising social sciences, which Andrews, responding to its absence in his own work, would struggle vainly to incorporate. The other, and yet more powerful tide, was that of a post-Progressive reaction that preferred to emphasize common, unifying forces in the history of a nation rising to dominance after World War II. These factors included law and constitutionalism, producing a historiographical "consensus" that searched early America for the values and practices that would later serve as the engine propelling American national triumph, and that, many assumed, would travel with equal success across the globe. Such grand themes thus moved to replace localized and specific material forces.

When scholars look back on the historiography of the middle twentieth century, therefore, they see early America almost segregated off as a distinct period, removed by the great divide of the Revolution, which, by definition, would change the legal landscape so dramatically as to leave it unrecognizable to the Rip Van Winkles of the Early Republic. Michael Zuckerman recognizes this barrier in his illuminating and perceptive essay on "Regionalism" in *The Blackwell Companion to American History* (Malden, MA, 2003), 311–33. In it Zuckerman describes the earlier paradigm of a "real rupture between the study of early America, predicated as it is on the priority of distinctive regions, and of the new nation, devoted as it is to charting the emergence of a new locus of loyalty at the center." The gap that Zuckerman identifies had become especially acute in legal scholarship, where the teaching of law addresses its subject doctrinally, emphasizing appellate decisions that illustrate the articulation of general principles. With the enormous growth of the federal legal system into areas over which it has traditionally had only a limited jurisdiction (crime, for example), this separation of the colonial period only grew throughout much of the second half of the twentieth century. Though Zuckerman gives little attention to law, he quite properly celebrates the contributions and positive interpretive influence of the "regional paradigm" that reappeared and has come to dominate early American scholarship since the 1960s. This trend in scholarship constituted a remarkable historiographical "about-face" that has reversed received conventions of the previous decades asserting a colonial past whose unprofessional bench and bar bequeathed to the new nation a crude system that demanded prompt professionalization and nationalized standards. As law schools have steadily embraced an ever wider academic interdisciplinary focus, moreover, the impact of these changes on legal scholarship has been profound.

In recovering regional identities in an earlier era, Zuckerman observes how historians of early America have drawn on the theoretical and empirical work of many other disciplines, such as Trevor Barnes and James Duncan, eds., *Writing Worlds: Discourse, Text, and Metaphor in the Representation of Landscape* (London, 1992); Stephen Daniels, "Place and the Geographical Imagination," *Geography* 77 (1992), 310–22; J. Nicholas Entrikin, *The Betweenness of Place: Towards a Geography of Modernity* (Baltimore, 1991); Raymond Gastil, *Cultural Regions of the United States* (Seattle, 1975); Henry Glassie, *Patterns in the Material Folk Culture of the Eastern United States* (Philadelphia, 1968); David Lowenthal and Martyn Bowden, eds., *Geographies of the Mind: Essays in Historical Geosophy in Honor of John Kirtland Wright* (New York, 1976); D. W. Meinig, *The Shaping of America: A Geographical Perspective on 500 Years of History*, vol. I, *Atlantic America, 1492–1800* (New Haven, 1986); Edward Soja, *Postmodern Geographies: The Reassertion of Space in Critical Social Theory* (London, 1989); Michael Steiner and Clarence Mondale, eds., *Region and Regionalism in the United States: A Source Book for the Humanities and Social Sciences* (New York, 1988); and Wilbur Zelinsky, *The Cultural Geography of the United States* (Englewood Cliffs, 1973).

The major impact of such work has been to provide theoretical templates for historicizing the foundations of regionalism, a trend made all the more apparent as American scholars have expanded their inquiry to include global and comparative legal perspectives. In the modern world legal regionalism has often appeared in the many strategies of local and traditional resistance to the homogenizing forces of modernity, whether they be political or economic. Because this nation began in an assertion of provincial independence against the encroachments of the modern, centralizing British system, this school of social theory has been especially useful in the analysis of colonial institutions and has informed scholarship with important and direct, if not always explicitly stated, impact on our understanding of colonial law and legal institutions. Among these are Richard D. Brown, "The New Regionalism," in William Robbins et al., eds., *Regionalism in the Pacific Northwest* (Corvallis, 1983), 37–96; Peter S. Onuf and Edward L. Ayers, "Introduction," in Edward L. Ayers, Patricia Nelson Limerick, Stephen Nissenbaum, and Peter S. Onuf, eds., *All over the Map. Rethinking American Regions* (Baltimore, 1996), 1–10; and Onuf's "Federalism, Republicanism, and the Origins of American Sectionalism," in that same volume at 11–37.

The implications of regionalism are clear, too, among many historians whose conclusions and interpretations may differ and who would scarcely be deemed members of a unified interpretive school. Agreeing on the fact – if not the meaning – of political regionalism are John Phillip Reid, whose work has been noted already; Bernard Bailyn, especially in *The Peopling of British North America. An Introduction* (New York, 1986) and his *Voyagers to the West. A Passage in the Peopling of America on the Eve of the Revolution* (New York, 1986), a magisterial analysis of peoples in motion and their transplantation of local cultures in the vast basin of the Atlantic world; and Jack P. Greene, whose *Pursuits of Happiness. The Social Development of Early Modern British Colonies and the Formation of American Culture* (Chapel Hill, 1988) offers five regional models and expands the conceptual framework to include more attention to law in such work as *Peripheries and Center: Constitutional Development in the Extended Politics of the British Empire and the United States, 1607–1788* (Athens, GA, 1986).

Recent scholarship on early American legal history thus rests firmly on the assumption that analysis must begin with or be organized according to the variety of local conditions. This is especially true of studies on the development of the peculiar and unique "law" of slavery. In this one area of law alone, Americans perceived the basis for irreconcilable differences between regions, and many commented on it. One of the more fearful expressions of this divide, made by a Boston lawyer, is described by Daniel R. Coquillette, "Sectionalism, Slavery, and the Threat of War in Josiah Quincy Jr.'s 1773 *Southern Journal*," *New England Quarterly* 79 (2006), 181. Edmund Morgan makes explicit the connection between the enslavement of Africans and the ever increasing enjoyment of freedom by whites in his *American Slavery, American Freedom. The Ordeal of Colonial Virginia* (New York, 1776). Jonathan Bush extends this idea in "Free to Enslave: The Foundations of Colonial American Slave Law," *Yale Journal of Law and the Humanities* 5 (1993), 456, whereas the hypocrisy of white freedom and black enslavement is central to A. Leon Higginbotham, *In the Matter of Color. Race and the American Judicial Process: The Colonial Period* (New York, 1978). Tracing the influence of the Continental civil law tradition is Alan Watson, *Slave Law in the Americas* (Athens, GA, 1989). For a study of its peculiarly West Indian antecedents, see Bradley J. Nicholson, "Legal Borrowing and the Origins of Slave Law in the British Colonies," *American Journal of Legal*

History 38 (1994), 38–54, and Barry David Gaspar, "'Rigid and Inclement': Origins of the Jamaica Slave Laws of the Seventeenth Century," in *Many Legalities*, 78–96.

Gender, as an analytical framework that has been especially prone to cultural construction across the centuries, has attracted insightful scholarship. On the impact of Puritanism in New England, see Cornelia Hughes Dayton, *Women Before the Bar. Gender, Law, and Society in Connecticut, 1639–1789* (Chapel Hill, 1995). As the product of economic and demographic forces, see Lois G. Carr and Lorena S. Walsh, "The Planter's Wife: The Experience of White Women in Seventeenth-Century Maryland," *William & Mary Quarterly*, 3rd ser., 34 (1977), 542–71. Directly concerned with legal matters are Marylynn Salmon, *Women and the Law of Property in Early America* (Chapel Hill, 1986) and Deborah A. Rosen, "Women and Property Across Colonial America: A Comparison of Legal Systems in New Mexico and New York," *William & Mary Quarterly*, 3rd ser., 60 (2003), 364–65 and her *Courts and Commerce. Gender, Law, and the Market Economy in Colonial New York* (Columbus, OH, 1997); see also Linda L. Sturtz, *Within Her Power. Propertied Women in Colonial Virginia* (New York, 2002). Divorce was a legal procedure recognized in New England far in advance of other English-speaking legal communities. See Nancy F. Cott, "Divorce and the Changing Status of Women in Eighteenth-Century Massachusetts," *William & Mary Quarterly*, 3rd ser., 33 (1976), 586–614; Henry S. Cohn, "Connecticut's Divorce Mechanism, 1636–1969," *American Journal of Legal History* 14 (1970), 70–92; and Glenda Riley, *Divorce: An American Tradition* (New York, 1991).

Other topical local legal studies implicitly and explicitly recognize the power of regional impulses and specific regional realities. Herbert A. Johnson's *The Law Merchant and Negotiable Instruments in Colonial New York, 1664 to 1730* (Chicago, 1963) examines one area of law to demonstrate the enduring force of cultural differences existing in the process of conquest. By contrast, the swiftness of legal transformation after political transfer can be seen in Stuart Banner, *Legal Systems in Conflict. Property and Sovereignty in Missouri, 1750–1860* (Norman, 2000). For the Chesapeake, the impact of local economic and demographic forces on the family has been demonstrated by Holly Brewer, "Entailing Aristocracy in Colonial Virginia: 'Ancient Feudel Restraints' and Revolutionary Reform," *William & Mary Quarterly*, 3rd ser., 54 (1997), 307–46, and the same author's more wide-ranging study, *By Birth or Consent. Children, Law, and the Anglo-American Revolution in Authority* (Chapel Hill, 2005), and by Lois Green Carr, "The Development of the Maryland Orphans' Court, 1654–1715," in Aubrey C. Land, Lois Green Carr, and Edward C. Papenfuse, eds., *Law, Society, and Politics in Early Maryland* (Baltimore, 1977), 41–62. On equity and its role, two specialized studies provide insight: Stanley N. Katz, "The Politics of Law: Controversies over Chancery Courts and Equity Law in the Eighteenth Century," *Perspectives in American History* 5 (1971), 257, and Spencer R. Liverant and Walter H. Hitchler, "A History of Equity in Pennsylvania," *Dickinson Law Review* 37 (1933), 156. Crime in New York has been the subject of Douglas Greenberg, *Crime and Law Enforcement in the Colony of New York, 1691–1776* (Ithaca, NY, 1976), and of Julius G. Goebel, Jr., and T. Raymond Naughton, *Law Enforcement in Colonial New York. A Study in Criminal Procedure (1664–1776)* (New York, 1944). Pennsylvania's particular religious heterododoxy and its legal legacy have had the benefit of specialized studies by William M. Offutt, Jr., *Of "Good Laws" and "Good Men." Law and Society in the Delaware Valley, 1680–1710* (Urbana, 1995); G. S. Rowe, *Embattled Bench. The Pennsylvania Supreme Court and the Forging of a Democratic Society, 1684–1809* (Newark, 1994); and A. G. Roeber, *Palatines, Liberty, and Property: German Lutherans in Colonial British America* (Baltimore, 1993).

The historiography of colonial New England has attracted more attention than any region. Studying the special character of law there are George Lee Haskins, "The Beginnings of the Recording System in Massachusetts," *Boston University Law Review* 21 (1941), 281; David H. Flaherty, *Privacy in Colonial New* England (Charlottesville, 1972); William E. Nelson, *Americanization of the Common Law: The Impact of Legal Change on Massachusetts Society, 1760–1830* (Cambridge, MA, 1975) and his "The Utopian Legal Order of the Massachusetts Bay Colony, 1630–1686," *American Journal of Legal History* 47 (2005), 183; David Thomas Konig, *Law and Society in Puritan Massachusetts. Essex County, 1629–1692* (Chapel Hill, 1979); Bruce H. Mann, *Neighbors and Strangers. Law and Community in Early Connecticut* (Chapel Hill, 1987); and Edgar J. McManus, *Law and Liberty in Early New England. Criminal Justice and Due Process 1620–1692* (Amherst. 1993).

The reception of the common law in each colony has been a standard of measuring the legal "sophistication" or backwardness of each, but recent scholars have abandoned such a measurement as misleading. Nonetheless, the extent to which individual colonies adopted identifiable common law principles and procedures serves as a useful comparative tool within a framework of regional analysis. For direct regional inquiries, see Herbert A. Johnson, "The Advent of Common Law in Colonial New York," in George A. Billias, ed., *Law and Authority in Colonial America* (Barre, MA, 1965), 74–91; Mark DeWolfe Howe, "The Source and Nature of Law in Colonial Massachusetts," ibid., 1–16; and Wilcomb E. Washburn, "Law and Authority in Colonial Virginia," ibid., 116–35; David Thomas Konig, "'Dale's Laws' and the Non-Common Law Origins of Criminal Justice in Virginia," *American Journal of Legal History* 26 (1984), 354–56 and the same author's "Colonization and the Common Law in Ireland and Virginia, 1569–1634," in James A. Henretta, Michael Kammen, and Stanley N. Katz, eds., *The Transformation of Early American History. Society, Authority, and Ideology* (New York, 1991). When it appears, the forthcoming multivolume *The Common Law in Colonial America* by William E. Nelson will come as close as is possible to a definitive statement on the subject.

CHAPTER 6: PENALITY AND THE COLONIAL PROJECT

MICHAEL MERANZE

As with the history of early American criminal law so with its historiography: diversity rules. The historiography of the criminal law in early America is marked simultaneously by the presence of a wide-ranging empirical and interpretive base and a surfeit of synthetic and comparative discussions. Scholars – both in law schools and history departments – have conducted careful and imaginative investigations into the penal codes, practices, and rules across early America. They have also produced a wide variety of insightful social histories of the criminal law. But they have been less successful in integrating these studies into the larger history of early America or developing analytical frames that compare to their European and British counterparts. In part, this situation is itself a product of history: the widely decentralized juridical systems make it impossible to generalize in the manner of English historians. But the result is a field in need of new efforts of analytical and comparative synthesis.

There are, to be sure, certain exceptions to these claims. Kathryn Preyer offered a synthesis of the statutory structures of early American criminal law in her "Penal Measures in the American Colonies," *American Journal of Legal History* 26 (1982), 326–53, while Bradley Chapin sought to provide an overview of the situation in the years of conquest and consolidation in his *Criminal Justice in Early America, 1606–1660* (Athens, GA., 1983). David Flaherty in his "Law and the Enforcement of Morals in Early America," *Perspectives in American History* 5 (1971), 203–53, and Douglas Greenberg in "Crime, Law Enforcement, and Social Control in Colonial America," *American Journal of Legal History* 26 (1982), 293–325, sought to provide interpretive arguments about the relationship between law and social order in early America. But these efforts were all limited in scope.

Although no overall synthesis or framework for continuing research exists at present, the production of studies of early American criminal law continues apace – in articles as well as books. As a result scholars are well advised to turn to the leading journals of the early American field, in particular the *William and Mary Quarterly*, as well as the important regional or state-based journals: in particular the *New England Quarterly*, the *Pennsylvania Magazine of History and Biography*, and the *Virginia Magazine of History and Biography*. The more general journals of legal and American history also publish relevant articles, although infrequently. In this essay I have only been able to touch the surface of these ongoing contributions.

In addition, although the vast majority of court records remain only available in manuscript or microfilm form, there are a number of volumes of published collections of court records. For a sampling of records of particular interest to historians of the criminal law, see for example, Joseph Smith ed., *Colonial Justice in Western Massachusetts, 1639–1702; The Pynchon Court Record, an Original Judges'*

Diary of the Administration of Justice in the Springfield Courts in the Massachusetts Bay Colony (Cambridge, MA, 1961); Susie M Ames, ed., *County Court Records of Accomack-Northampton, Virginia, 1640–1645* (Charlottesville, 1973); David Thomas Konig, ed., *Plymouth Court Records, 1686–1859* (Wilmington, DE, 1978–1981) especially vols. 1, 5–16; and Peter Hoffer and William B. Scott, eds., *Criminal Proceedings in Colonial Virginia: (Records of) Fines, Examination of Criminals, Trials of Slaves, etc. from March 1710 (1711) to (1754), (Richmond County, Virginia)* (Athens, GA, 1984). In addition, the *Archives of Maryland*, which includes sizeable holdings of the records of the administration of the criminal law, is now available online.

Any approach to the history of crime and law in early America must begin with the metropolitan context. Here scholars are well served. An eighteenth-century classic, still worth reading for both its perceptions and knowledge, is William Blackstone's *Commentaries on the Laws of England* easily available with an introduction by Thomas A. Green (Chicago, 1979). A more modern classic is Leon Radzinowicz's *A History of English Criminal Law and its Administration from 1750* (London, 1948), especially vol. I, *The Movement for Reform*. Each provides scholars with an analytical overview of the early modern English criminal law, especially its penal components. Beginning in the 1970s, a new wave of revisionist social history of the English criminal law took off. Signal volumes in this wave of writing were E. P. Thompson's *Whigs and Hunters: The Origins of the Black Act* (New York, 1974); Douglas Hay, Peter Linebaugh, and E. P. Thompson, eds., *Albion's Fatal Tree: Crime and Society in Eighteenth-Century England* (New York, 1975); and John Brewer and John Styles eds., *An Ungovernable People: The English and Their Law in the Seventeenth and Eighteenth centuries* (New Brunswick, NJ, 1980). Despite their differences (Brewer and Styles emphasized far greater access to the courts than do Hay et al, who were more concerned with the relationship between class power and law as well as the history of social crime) they shared a turn toward a predominantly social historical approach. Since the 1970s studies that either conform or challenge their particular approaches have been legion. But the two most important figures in recent historiography have been John Beattie (see his *Crime and the Courts in England, 1660–1800* [Princeton, NJ, 1986] and *Policing and Punishment in London 1660–1750: Urban Crime and the Limits of Terror* [New York, 2001]), whose work has charted out in greater depth than ever before the actual practices and complexities of criminal justice, and Randall McGowen – see his "'Making Examples' and the Crisis of Punishment in Mid-Eighteenth-Century England," in David Lemmings, ed., *The British and Their Laws in the Eighteenth Century* (London, 2005); "The Problem of Punishment in Eighteenth-Century England," in S. Devereaux and P. Griffiths, eds., *Penal Practice and Culture, 1500–1900* (London, 2003), 210–31; "'He Beareth Not the Sword in Vain': Religion and the Criminal Law in Eighteenth-Century England," *Eighteenth-Century Studies* 21 (1987–88), 192–211; and "The Body and Punishment in Eighteenth-Century England," *Journal of Modern History* 59 (1987), 651–79 – who, focusing on the death penalty, has reinvented the non-teleological intellectual history of criminal law.

Whereas the metropolitan context is the object of a rich literature, the imperial or colonial context of the criminal law has been less fortunate. For the largest juridical and institutional frames, scholars can still profit from Charles McLean Andrews, *The Colonial Period of American History*, 4 vols. (New Haven, 1934–8), in particular vol. IV, *England's Commercial and Colonial Policy*, and Richard B. Morris, *Studies in the History of American Law: With Special Reference to the Seventeenth and Eighteenth Centuries* (New York, 1930). In addition, the question of to what extent American law diverged from the English has been the theme of numerous writings, including Julius Goebel, Jr., and T. Raymond Naughton, *Law Enforcement in Colonial New York: A Study in Criminal Procedure (1664–1776)* (New York, 1944); George Lee Haskins, *Law and Authority in Early Massachusetts* (New York, 1960); William E. Nelson, *Americanization of the Common Law: The Impact of Legal Change on Massachusetts Society, 1760–1830* (Cambridge, MA, 1975); and G. B. Warden, "Law Reform in England and New England, 1620–1660," *William and Mary Quarterly*, 3rd ser., 39 (1982), 64–86 – all which, in part or in whole, address the criminal law. For an influential caution against seeing the process of change as "Americanization," see John M. Murrin, "The Legal Transformation: The Bench and Bar of Eighteenth-Century Massachusetts," in Stanley N. Katz, ed., *Colonial America: Essays In Politics and Social Development*, (Boston, 1971), 415–49. And for an important argument that historians must recognize the multiplicity of legal traditions in England see David Thomas Konig, "'Dale's Laws' and the Non-Common Law Origins of Criminal Justice in Virginia," *American Journal of Legal History* 26 (1982), 354–75.

In general, the question of the imperial context has not been imagined whole; instead it has been addressed more particularly in the context of Native American relations and in slavery (see below). But for one recent attempt on the bond between colonization and law that, although it does not address the criminal law at any great length, does suggestively reopen the question of the relationship of empire and law, see Christopher L. Tomlins, "The Many Legalities of Colonization: A Manifesto of Destiny for Early American Legal History" in Christopher L. Tomlins and Bruce Mann, eds., *The Many Legalities of Early America* (Chapel Hill, NC, 2000), 1–24. In addition, works that address deep water sailors and pirates also afford insight into the larger imperial context. The literature is large but see in particular Marcus Redikers, *Between the Devil and the Deep Blue Sea: Merchant Seamen, Pirates, and the Anglo-American Maritime World, 1700–1750* (New York, 1987) and *Villians of All Nations: Atlantic Pirates in the Golden Age* (Boston, 2004), as well as Robert C. Ritchie, *Captain Kidd and the War Against the Pirates* (Cambridge, MA, 1986). For an account of maritime punishments that argues for their continuities with labor discipline on shore, see Daniel Vickers with Vince Walsh, *Young Men and the Sea: Yankee Seafarers in the Age of Sail* (New Haven, 2005).

Given its centrality to the colonial world of punishment, the death penalty has attracted a good deal of attention. The standard account now must be Stuart Banner, *The Death Penalty: An American History* (Cambridge, MA, 2002), which surveys developments throughout the colonial and revolutionary periods. Given the difficulty in reconstructing reliable figures for executions, scholars are lucky to have a series of guiding studies: Negley F. Teeters, "Public Executions in Pennsylvania, 1682–1834," *Journal of the Lancaster County Historical Society* 44 (1960), and two works by Daniel Allen Hearn, *Legal Executions in New York, 1639–1963* (Jefferson, NC, 1997) and *Legal Executions in New England, 1623–1960* (Jefferson, NC, 1999), provide access to basic patterns in the North. In addition, Daniel A. Cohen, *Pillars of Salt, Monuments of Grace: New England Crime Literature and the Origins of American Popular Culture, 1674–1860* (New York, 1993) and Karen Halttunen, *Murder Most Foul: The Killer and the American Gothic Imagination* (Cambridge, MA, 1998) each offer extensive treatments of the execution sermon and histories of the changing relationships among popular culture, print, and the criminal law.

For the most part, studies of crime and the law have proceeded along colony and state lines. For helpful investigations, with particular emphasis on social and penal history, see Richard Gaskins, "Changes in the Criminal Law in Eighteenth-Century Connecticut," *American Journal of Legal History* 25 (1981), 309–42; Douglas Greenberg, *Crime and Law Enforcement in the Colony of New York* (Ithaca, NY, 1976); Linda Kealey, "Patterns of Punishment: Massachusetts in the Eighteenth Century," *American Journal of Legal History* 30 (1986), 163–86; Edwin Powers, *Crime and Punishment in Early Massachusetts, 1620–1692: A Documentary History* (Boston, 1966); Arthur P. Scott, *Criminal Law in Colonial Virginia* (Chicago, 1930); Raphael Semmes, *Crime and Punishment in Early Maryland* (Baltimore, 1938); Donna J. Spindel, *Crime and Society in North Carolina 1663–1776* (Baton Rouge, LA, 1989); and Jules Zanger, "Crime and Punishment in Early Massachusetts," *William and Mary Quarterly* 22 (1965), 471–7. For the most systematic treatment of any colony see Jack D. Marietta and G. S. Rowe, *Troubled Experiment: Crime and Justice in Pennsylvania, 1682–1800* (Philadelphia, 2006).

The history of criminal procedure, trials, and magistrates has also proceeded on a colony or regional basis. Not surprisingly, New England has seen some of the richest discussion. For two outstanding analyses of trials and their practices see Gail Sussman Marcus, "'Due Execution of the Generall Rules of Righeousnesse': Criminal Procedure in New Haven Town and Colony, 1638–1658," and John M. Murrin, "Magistrates, Sinners, and a Precarious Liberty: Trial by Jury in Seventeenth-Century New England," both in David D. Hall, John Murrin, and Thad W. Tate, eds., *Saints and Revolutionaries: Essays on Early American History* (New York, 1984), at 99–137 and 152–206 respectively. Carol F. Lee, "Discretionary Justice in Early Massachusetts," *Essex Institute Historical Collections* 112 (1976), 120–39, offers an intriguing analysis of departures from formal codes, whereas Edgar J. McManus, *Law and Liberty in Early New England:*

Criminal Justice and Due Process, 1620–1692 (Amherst, MA, 1993) traces the tensions indicated in his title. Further south, Goebel, and Naughton's classic lawyerly *Law Enforcement in Colonial New York: A Study in Criminal Procedure (1664–1776)* (New York, 1944) offers extensive analysis on practices in New York. For the southern colonies see, among other of his writings, Warren M. Billings, "Pleading, Procedure, and Practice: The Meaning of Due Process of Law in Seventeenth-Century Virginia," *Journal of Southern History* 47 (1981), 569–84; Hugh F. Rankin, *Criminal Trial Proceedings in the General Court of Colonial Virginia* (Charlottesville, 1965); James D. Rice, "The Criminal Trial Before and After the Lawyers: Authority, Law, and Culture in Maryland Jury Trials, 1681–1837," *American Journal of Legal History* 40 (1996), 455–75; and A. G. Roeber, *Faithful Magistrates and Republican Lawyers: Creators of Virginia Legal Culture, 1680–1810* (Chapel Hill, NC, 1981). Martha McNamara examines the evolution of legal spaces in her *From Tavern to Courthouse: Architecture and Ritual in American law, 1658–1860* (Baltimore, 1984). For comparison with England, see the work of John H. Langbein, especially his "The Criminal Trial Before the Lawyers," *University of Chicago Law Review* 45 (1978), 263–316; "Shaping the Eighteenth-Century Criminal Trial: A View from the Ryder Sources," *University of Chicago Law Review* 50 (1983), 1–136; and *The Origins of Adversary Criminal Trial* (New York, 2005).

Beyond these geographically focused studies of crime, law, and its administration there has been growing interest in the relationship of the criminal law to specific social groups, practices, and institutions. Not surprisingly, given the general dynamism of the field, has been a series of works in women's history that have broadened our understanding of early American criminal law. Although not focused on crime and the law Cornelia Hughes Dayton, *Women Before the Bar: Gender, Law, & Society in Connecticut, 1639–1789* (Chapel Hill, NC., 1995); Mary Beth Norton, *Founding Mothers & Fathers: Gendered Power and the Forming of American Society* (New York, 1996); and Terri L. Snyder, *Brabbling Women: Disorderly Speech and the Law in Early Virginia* (Ithaca, NY., 2003) each examine the gendered nature of the criminal law practices in early America. More focused on female criminality are N. E. H. Hull, *Female Felons: Women and Serious Crime in Colonial Massachusetts* (Urbana, IL, 1987); Peter Charles Hoffer and N. E. H. Hull, *Murdering Mothers: Infanticide in England and New England, 1558–1803* (New York, 1981); and two articles by G. S. Rowe, "Women's Crime and Criminal Administration in Pennsylvania, 1763–1790," *Pennsylvania Magazine of History and Biography* 109 (1985), 335–68 and "Infanticide, Its Judicial Resolution, and Criminal Code Revision in Early Pennsylvania," *Proceedings of the American Philosophical Society* 135 (1991), 200–32. Violence against women has also been the subject of a powerful literature. In addition to the above works see the pioneering effort by Barbara S. Lindemann, "'To Ravish and Carnally Know': Rape in Eighteenth-Century Massachusetts," *Signs: Journal of Women in Culture and Society* 10 (1984–85), 63–82. More recent scholarship can be seen in the collections *Over the Threshold: Intimate Violence in Early America*, edited by Christine Daniels and Michael V. Kennedy (New York, 1999), and Merril D. Smith, ed., *Sex Without Consent: Rape and Sexual Coercion in America* (New York, 2002), although the latter extends far beyond the early period.

The historiography on moral regulation is of long standing. Indeed, given the mythical images of Puritans popular in the twentieth century it was central to an understanding of early New England. However, it has increasingly been fused with the growing interest in the history of sexuality. On the latter, in addition to the works discussed regarding women and the law – most of which discuss sexuality and intimacy – see especially Richard Godbeer, *Sexual Revolution in Early America* (Baltimore, 2002), and Clare A. Lyons, *Sex Among the Rabble: An Intimate History of Gender & Power in the Age of Revolution, Philadelphia, 1730–1830* (Chapel Hill, NC, 2006). For questions of the relationship between religion and moral regulation, good places to begin remain David H. Flaherty, "Law and the Enforcement of Morals in Early America," *Perspectives in American History* 5 (1971), 203–53, and Jack D. Marietta, *The Reformation of American Quakerism, 1748–1783* (Philadelphia, 1984). At the intersection of morals, religion, and law – at least in New England – stood witchcraft. This topic has, of course, produced an extensive and complicated literature. But see in particular, Carol F. Karlsen, *The Devil in the Shape of a Woman: Witchcraft in Colonial New England* (New York, 1987), for an innovative linking of the history of gender, moral regulation, and the law.

Not surprisingly, the question of slavery and the penal law has also produced a rich literature. Here the starting points remain Philip J. Schwarz, *Slave Laws in Virginia* (Athens, GA, 1996) and *Twice Condemned: Slaves and the Criminal Laws of Virginia, 1705–1865* (Baton Rouge, LA, 1988). But see as well, Thomas D. Morris, *Southern Slavery and the Law, 1619–1860* (Chapel Hill, NC, 1996), an all but exhaustive treatment. Although not legal histories per se, Edmund Morgan's *American Slavery, American Freedom: The Ordeal of Colonial Virginia* (New York, 1976); Kathleen M. Brown, *Good Wives, Nasty Wenches, and Anxious Patriarchs: Gender, Race and Power in Colonial Virginia* (Chapel Hill, NC, 1996); and Philip D. Morgan, *Slave Counterpoint: Black Culture in the Eighteenth-Century Chesapeake and Lowcountry* (Chapel Hill, NC, 1998) all offer extended discussions of the relationship among the laws of slavery, labor systems, and the evolution of colonial societies. Edward L Ayers, *Vengeance and Justice: Crime and Punishment in the 19th-Century American South* (New York, 1984), takes the story up into the Early Republic. In addition, the growing recognition of the ubiquity of slavery in early America has renewed interest in the New York slave conspiracy of 1741. The standard account is Thomas J. Davis, *Rumor of Revolt: The Great 'Negro Plot' in Colonial New York* (New York, 1975); see as well Peter Charles Hoffer, *The Great New York Conspiracy of 1741: Slavery, Crime, and Colonial law* (Lawrence, Kansas, 2003), and Jill Lepore, *New York Burning: Liberty, Slavery, and Conspiracy in Eighteenth-Century Manhattan* (New York, 2005).

For the reach of colonial law and its relationship with Native American notions of justice, see the work of John Philip Reid, especially his *Patterns of Vengeance: Crosscultural Homicide in the North American Fur Trade* (Pasadena, CA, 1999), and Yasuhide Kawashima, *Puritan Justice and the Indian: White Man's Law in Massachusetts, 1630–1763* (Middletown, CT, 1986) and *Igniting King Philip's War: The John Sassamon Murder Trial* (Lawrence, KS, 2001). But see as well Jill Lepore's treatment of the conflict of criminal laws in her *The Name of War: King Philip's War and the Origins of American Identity* (New York, 1998). For an argument that Native Americans were willing and able to deploy English legal norms see Katherine Hermes, "'Justice Will Be Done Us': Algonquin Demands for Reciprocity in the Courts of European Settlers," in Tomlins and Mann eds., *The Many Legalities of Early America*, 123–49. And for a provocative discussion of the reach of Anglo legal power and criminal punishments, see James H. Merrell, "'The Customes of our Countrey': Indians and Colonists in Early America," in Bernard Bailyn and Philip D. Morgan, eds., *Strangers Within the Realm: Cultural Margins of the First British Empire* (Chapel Hill, NC, 1991).

The transformation of the criminal law and penal practices during and after the American Revolution is an oft-told tale. But see in particular William E. Nelson, "Emerging Notions of Modern Criminal Law in the Revolutionary Era: An Historical Perspective," *NYU Law Review* 42 (1967), 450–82; Kathryn Preyer, "Crime, the Criminal Law and Reform in Post-Revolutionary Virginia," *Law and History Review* 1 (1983), 53–85; Louis P. Masur, *Rites of Execution: Capital Punishment and the Transformation of American Culture, 1776–1865* (New York, 1989); Adam Jay Hirsch, *The Rise of the Penitentiary: Prisons and Punishment in Early America* (New Haven, 1992); and Michael Meranze, *Laboratories of Virtue: Punishment, Revolution and Authority in Philadelphia, 1760–1835* (Chapel Hill, NC, 1996). Unfortunately, Stephen Wilf's fine study of the place of the criminal law in the American Revolution, "Imagining Justice: Politics, story-telling and politics in Revolutionary America," Ph.D. thesis, Yale University, 1995, remains unpublished. But, for questions of the relationship between the vice-admiralty courts and the coming of the Revolution the standard account remains Carl Ubbelohde, *The Vice-Admiralty Courts and the American Revolution* (Chapel Hill, NC, 1961). And for the study that helped trigger new interest in the topic see David J. Rothman, *The Discovery of the Asylum: Social Order and Disorder in the New Republic* (Boston, 1971).

CHAPTER 7: LAW, POPULATION, LABOR

CHRISTOPHER TOMLINS

Historians of early America have given considerable attention to the process of English settlement of mainland North America – the establishment of colonies, migrations of peoples, and formation of labor forces. Law, however, has not until recently figured much in their inquiries, except as a resource (court records) for social historical research and to some extent as an element of studies of local institution-building. Nor have historians of early American law given a great deal of attention to the relationship between law and demography, to law as an instrument for the design of colonies, or to the macrostructural role of law in the recruitment and "management" of population. The purpose of this chapter is to describe and explore these connections. The sources discussed here furnish the essential basis – primary and secondary – for this chapter and collectively constitute the appropriate jumping-off point for additional work. The overarching theme of the chapter is that we miss much of the meaning of English penetration of the mainland if we think of it in the essentially anodyne, self-absorbed terms of "settlement." As conceived here, English penetration of the mainland was a purposeful process of colonization, a taking of possession. Law was one of the most important technologies at its disposal.

Essential Sources on Mainland Colonizing

For extensive exposure to the writings of English colonization's early theorists and propagandists, see E. G. R. Taylor, ed., *The Original Writings and Correspondence of the Two Richard Hakluyts* (London, 1935), which includes among other works the elder Richard Hakluyt's "Notes on Colonisation" (1578) and two iterations of his "Pamphlet for the Virginia Enterprise" (1585); and the younger Hakluyt's "Preface to Diverse Voyages" (1582) and his "Instructions for the Virginia Colony" (1606), as well as his famous "Discourse of Western Planting" (1584). In these works the two Richard Hakluyts outline and develop the political-economic model of colonizing first put into effect in Virginia. For an introduction to other essential writings, see Peter C. Mancall, ed., *Envisioning America: English Plans for the Colonization of North America, 1580–1640* (Boston, 1995). For an exploration of the contemporaneous first stirrings of international law, expressed in legal ideologies of just war and rights of possession, including analysis of the theories of Alberico Gentili and Hugo Grotius, see Richard Tuck, *The Rights of War and Peace: Political Thought and the International Order from Grotius to Kant* (Oxford, 1999). To explore the influence of colonizing ideology and international (and metropolitan) law on the formation of detailed designs for the English colonies themselves, one can do no better than read the colonies' charters. For these, see Francis Newton Thorpe, ed., *The Federal and State Constitutions, Colonial Charters, and Other Organic Laws of the States, Territories and Colonies Now or Heretofore Forming the United States of America*, 7 vols. (Washington, 1909; Buffalo, NY, 1993). For a summary of the legalities of "loco-motion," one can do no better at present than go to Blackstone. See William Blackstone, *Commentaries on the Laws of England: A facsimile of the First Edition of 1765–1769*, 4 vols. (Chicago, 1979). For Massachusetts's *Body of Liberties* of 1641, see *The Colonial Laws of Massachusetts. Reprinted from the Edition of 1660* (Boston, 1889). For the *Lawes and Libertyes*, see John D. Cushing, comp., *The Laws and Liberties of Massachusetts, 1641–1691*, 3 vols. (Wilmington, DE, 1976).

For outstanding summaries and syntheses of the latest research on the imperial context of North American colonizing, see Nicholas Canny, ed., *The Origins of Empire: British Overseas Enterprise to the Close of the Seventeenth Century* and P. J. Marshall, ed., *The Eighteenth Century*, comprising vols. I and II of *The Oxford History of the British Empire*, ed. William R. Louis (Oxford, 1998). For similarly indispensable summaries and syntheses of the general socioeconomic conditions and context of colonizing, see John J. McCusker and Russell R. Menard, *The Economy of British America, 1607–1789* (Chapel Hill, 1989) and Stanley L. Engerman and Robert E. Gallman, eds., *The Cambridge Economic History of the United States. Volume 1: The Colonial Era* (Cambridge, 1996).

Essential Sources on Population and Migration

The literature on the population of and migration to the British mainland colonies is extensive. In its quantitative aspects, particularly where it comes to the presentation of long-term and overall population series, this literature is one of estimation and inference. But over the years methods of estimation have developed in sophistication to the point where magnitudes that were originally wholly conjectural have been refined to ranges of numbers with relatively extensive acceptance. Barring the discovery of wholly new and extensive data sources or the creation of wholly new methods of estimation, one should be able to repose reasonable confidence in the assumptions about population and migration used as the basis for this chapter.

Much more refined "reconstructive" work has been possible in the analysis of specific data sets dealing with particular components of population or particular migrant groups at particular times. The more complete the data, the more reliable the profile of the population in question will be. One must be cautious, of course, in drawing conclusions about overall population characteristics from specific data sets.

(A) THE INDIGENOUS POPULATION

The least certain and hence most conjectural elements of North American population history are those that concern the indigenous population during the sixteenth and seventeenth centuries. For recent syntheses, see Peter C. Mancall, "Native Americans and Europeans in English America, 1500–1700," in Canny, ed., *Origins of Empire*; Daniel K. Richter, "Native Peoples of North America and the Eighteenth-Century British Empire," in Marshall, ed., *The Eighteenth Century*; Neal Salisbury, "The History of Native Americans from Before the Arrival of the Europeans and Africans Until the American Civil War," in Engerman and Gallman, eds., *The Cambridge Economic History of the United States. Vol. 1*; Bruce G. Trigger and William R. Swagerty, "Entertaining Strangers: North America in the Sixteenth Century," and Neal Salisbury, "Native People and European Settlers in Eastern North America, 1600–1783," both in Bruce G. Trigger and Wilcomb E. Washburn, eds., *The Cambridge History of the Native Peoples of the Americas, Vol. 1: North America*, part 1 (Cambridge, 1996);

See also Joyce E. Chaplin, *Subject Matter: Technology, the Body and Science on the Anglo-American Frontier, 1500–1676* (Cambridge, MA, 2001). On the dynamics of contact and consequences for indigenous peoples in particular regions, see Alan Gallay, *The Indian Slave Trade: The Rise of the English Empire in the American South, 1670–1717* (New Haven, 2002); Eric Hinderaker, *Elusive Empires: Constructing Colonialism in the Ohio Valley, 1673–1800* (Cambridge, 1997); Jill Lepore, *The Name of War: King Philip's War and the Origins of American Identity* (New York, 1998); James H. Merrell, *Into the American Woods: Negotiators on the Pennsylvania Frontier* (New York, 1999); and Jean M. O'Brien, *Dispossession by Degrees: Indian Land and Identity in Natick, Massachusetts, 1650–1790* (New York, 1997).

(B) IMMIGRANT POPULATIONS

As to the introduced populations, the existing literature is copious. Fortunately much of it has been summarized, evaluated, and synthesized in several essays: Aaron S. Fogleman, "From Slaves, Convicts and Servants to Free Passengers: The Transformation of Immigration in the Era of the American Revolution," *Journal of American History* 85, 1 (1998); Aaron S. Fogleman "Migrations to the Thirteen British North American Colonies, 1700–1775: New Estimates," *Journal of Interdisciplinary History* 22, 4 (1992); James Horn, "British Diaspora: Emigration from Britain, 1680–1815," in Marshall, ed., *The Eighteenth Century*; Christopher L. Tomlins, "Indentured Servitude in Perspective: European Migration to the North American Mainland and the Composition of the Early American Labor Force, 1600–1775," in Catherine Matson, ed., *The Economy of Early America: New Directions* (University Park, PA, 2005); and Christopher Tomlins, "Reconsidering Indentured Servitude: European Migration and the Early American Labor Force, 1600–1775," *Labor History* 42, 1 (2001).

Particularly useful and influential works, both from the body of literature discussed in these recent essays and beyond it, include the following: Richard Archer, "New England Mosaic: A Demographic Analysis for the Seventeenth Century," *William and Mary Quarterly*, 3rd ser., 47, 4 (1990); Ira Berlin, *Many Thousands Gone: The First Two Centuries of Slavery in North America* (Cambridge, MA, 1998); Virginia Bernhard, "'Men, Women and Children' at Jamestown: Population and Gender in Early Virginia, 1607–1610," *Journal of Southern History* 58, 4 (1992), 599–618; Nicholas Canny, "English Migration into and Across the Atlantic During the Seventeenth and Eighteenth Centuries," in Nicholas Canny, ed., *Europeans on the Move: Studies on European Migration, 1500–1800* (Oxford, 1994); David Cressy, *Coming Over: Migration and Communication Between England and New England in the Seventeenth Century* (Cambridge, 1987); Philip D. Curtin, *The Atlantic Slave Trade: A Census* (Madison, 1969); David Eltis, *The Rise of African Slavery in the Americas* (New York, 2000); Georg Fertig, "Transatlantic Migration from the German-Speaking Parts of Central Europe, 1600–1800: Proportions, Structures, and Explanations," in Nicholas Canny, ed., *Europeans on the Move: Studies on European Migration, 1500–1800* (Oxford,

1994); David Hackett Fischer, *Albion's Seed: Four British Folkways in America* (New York, 1989); Alison Games, *Migration and the Origins of the English Atlantic World* (Cambridge, MA, 1999); Henry Gemery, "Disarray in the Historical Record: Estimates of Immigration to the United States, 1700–1860," *Proceedings of the American Philosophical Society* 133, 2 (1989); Henry Gemery, "Emigration from the British Isles to the New World, 1630–1700: Inferences from Colonial Populations," *Research in Economic History: A Research Annual* 5 (1980); Henry Gemery, "European Emigration to North America, 1700–1820: Numbers and Quasi-Numbers," *Perspectives in American History*, new ser., 1 (1984); Farley Grubb, "German Immigration to Pennsylvania, 1709 to 1820," *Journal of Interdisciplinary History* 20, 3 (1990); James Horn, *Adapting to a New World: English Society in the Seventeenth-Century Chesapeake* (Chapel Hill, 1994); McCusker & Menard, *Economy of British America*; Russell R. Menard, "British Migration to the Chesapeake Colonies in the Seventeenth Century," in Lois Green Carr et al., eds., *Colonial Chesapeake Society* (Chapel Hill, 1988); Jim Potter, "Demographic Development and Family Structure," in Jack P. Greene and J. R. Pole, eds., *Colonial British America: Essays in the New History of the Early Modern Era* (Baltimore, 1984); Thomas L. Purvis, "The European Ancestry of the United States Population, 1790," *William and Mary Quarterly*, 3rd ser., 41, 1 (1984); Roger Thompson, *Mobility and Migration: East Anglican Founders of New England, 1629–1640* (Amherst, MA, 1994), 122–23; William Thorndale, "The Virginia Census of 1619," *Magazine of Virginia Genealogy* 33, 3 (1995); and Marianne Wokeck, *Trade in Strangers: The Beginnings of Mass Migration to North America* (University Park, PA, 1999).

Bernard Bailyn's *Voyagers to the West: A Passage in the Peopling of America on the Eve of the Revolution* (New York, 1986) helped renew general interest in the demography of English colonizing. While conjectural on overall numbers, it offers an extremely comprehensive analysis of specific elements of British migration during the decade prior to the Revolution.

Law, Migration, and Labor Force Formation: Britain

The phenomena of migration and labor force formation that are dealt with here primarily in a trans-Atlantic context have a crucial British backdrop. E. A. Wrigley and R. S. Schofield, *The Population History of England, 1541–1871* (London, 1981), is an indispensable analysis of English demography across the entire period of North American colonizing. Work that is particularly useful in establishing patterns and conditions of migration and labor force formation internal to early modern Britain – social, economic, and political-legal – include A. L. Beier, *Masterless Men: The Vagrancy Problem in England, 1560–1640* (London, 1979); Peter Clark and David Souden, eds., *Migration and Society in Early Modern England* (Totowa, NJ, 1987); Ann Kussmaul, *Servants in Husbandry in Early Modern England* (Cambridge, 1981); Ann Kussmaul, *A General View of the Rural Economy of England, 1538–1840* (Cambridge, 1990); and Michael

Maccarthy-Morrogh, *The Munster Plantation: English Migration to Southern Ireland, 1583–1641* (Oxford, 1986). See also Joan Thirsk, ed., *The Agrarian History of England and Wales, IV, 1500–1640* (Cambridge, 1967). On migration from the provinces to London and eventual trans-Atlantic migration from London, see James P. Horn, "Servant Emigration to the Chesapeake in the Seventeenth Century," in Thad W. Tate and David L. Ammerman, eds., *The Chesapeake in the Seventeenth Century: Essays on Anglo-American Society* (Chapel Hill, 1979). For a fuller exploration of the general relationship between provincial British economies and migration to North America, see Horn, *Adapting to a New World.* On the close identity of youth and servitude in Britain, in addition to the work by Ann Kussmaul already cited, see Ilana Krausman Ben-Amos, *Adolescence and Youth in Early Modern England* (New Haven, 1994); D. C. Coleman, "Labour in the English Economy of the Seventeenth Century," *Economic History Review*, ser. 2, 8, 3 (1956); Paul Griffiths, *Youth and Authority: Formative Experiences in England, 1560–1640* (Oxford, 1996); and Keith Thomas, "Age and Authority in Early Modern England," *Proceedings of the British Academy* 62 (1976).

The police of mobility, particularly labor mobility, became a vital and continuing component of British state action in the fourteenth century. See generally Markus Dirk Dubber, *The Police Power: Patriarchy and the Foundations of American Government* (New York, 2005). For an analysis of the formation of national institutions capable of policing labor mobility on a continuing basis, see Robert C. Palmer, *English Law in the Age of the Black Death, 1348–1381: A Transformation of Governance and Law* (Chapel Hill, 1993). The enforcement (and the long-term effects of enforcement) varied, however, over time and place. Thus, see Bertha Putnam, *The Enforcement of the Statutes of Labourers During the First Decade After the Black Death* (New York, 1908) and L. R. Poos, "The Social Context of Statute of Labourers Enforcement," *Law and History Review* 1, 1 (1983). On the formation of the Statute of Artificers, see Stanley T. Bindoff, "The Making of the Statute of Artificers," in S. T. Bindoff et al., eds., *Elizabethan Government and Society: Essays Presented to Sir John Neale* (London, 1961), 80–3, and F. J. Fisher, "Influenza and Inflation in Tudor England," *Economic History Review*, 2nd ser., 18, 1 (1965). On its enforcement, see Walter E. Minchinton, ed., *Wage Regulation in Pre-Industrial England* (Newton Abbott, Devon, 1972). Perhaps the most thorough study of enforcement is Michael F. Roberts, "Wages and Wage-Earners in England: The Evidence of the Wage Assessments, 1563–1725," unpublished Ph.D. thesis, Oxford University, 1981, although see also Margaret G. Davies, *The Enforcement of English Apprenticeship: A Study in Applied Mercantilism, 1563–1642* (Cambridge, MA, 1956). The most recent study of the general regime of labor regulation and of master and servant law is Douglas Hay and Paul Craven, eds., *Masters, Servants, and Magistrates in Britain and the Empire, 1562–1955* (Chapel Hill, 2004). As their title suggests, this book takes an expansive view of labor force formation across the full panoply of the English colonizing enterprise.

On the general structure of state and society in early modern England, see Steve Hindle, *The State and Social Change in Early Modern England, 1550–1640*. Basingstoke, 2002) and Keith Wrightson, *English Society, 1580–1680* (New Brunswick, NJ, 1982). For extremely suggestive analyses of the civic consequences of state regulatory initiatives, see Margaret Somers, "Citizenship and the Place of the Public Sphere: Law, Community, and Political Culture in the Transition to Democracy," *American Sociological Review* 58, 5 (1993) and Margaret Somers, "Rights, Relationality and Membership: Rethinking the Making and Meaning of Citizenship," *Law & Social Inquiry* 19, 1 (1994).

Migration and Labor Force Formation: Anglophone America

In the early American case, the study of migration, labor force formation, and law, particularly the law of "bound" labor, overlaps considerably. The point is made by the title of the classic and still very useful study of early American labor procurement by Abbot Emerson Smith, *Colonists in Bondage; White Servitude and Convict Labor in America, 1607–1776* (Chapel Hill, 1947), published only a year after the other classic of the literature, Richard B. Morris, *Government and Labor in Early America* (New York, 1946). In the half-century since the time of Morris and Smith, much work has been undertaken, though the focus has largely been on the economic and social history of labor. The revival of legal history in the area dates from the early 1990s (see below).

For an extremely thorough synthesis of migration and labor force formation in the mainland colonies, see David W. Galenson, "The Settlement and Growth of the Colonies: Population, Labor and Economic Development," in Engerman and Gallman, eds., *The Cambridge Economic History of the United States: Vol. 1*. Galenson has also authored *White Servitude in Colonial America: An Economic Analysis* (Cambridge, 1981), itself now something of a classic. See also his "The Rise and Fall of Indentured Servitude in the Americas: An Economic Analysis," *Journal of Economic History* 44, 1 (1984). Other essential works on labor procurement and labor force formation are as follows: Terry L. Anderson and Robert P. Thomas, "The Growth of Population and Labor Force in the 17th-Century Chesapeake," *Explorations in Economic History* 15 (1978); Richard S. Dunn, "Servants and Slaves: The Recruitment and Employment of Labor," in Jack P. Greene and J. R. Pole, eds., *Colonial British America: Essays in the New History of the Early Modern Era* (Baltimore, 1984); A. Roger Ekirch, *Bound for America: The Transportation of British Convicts to the Colonies, 1718–1775* (Oxford, 1987); David Eltis, "Labor and Coercion in the English Atlantic World from the Seventeenth to the Early Twentieth Century," *Slavery And Abolition* 14, 1 (1993), 207–26; David Eltis, "Seventeenth Century Migration and the Slave Trade: The English Case in Comparative Perspective," in Jan Lucassen and Leo Lucassen, eds., *Migration, Migration History, History: Old Paradigms and New Perspectives* (Berne, 1997); Sharon Salinger, *"To Serve Well and Faithfully": Labor and Indentured Servants in Pennsylvania, 1682–1800* (Cambridge, 1987);

Mary Schweitzer, *Custom and Contract: Household, Government and the Economy in Colonial Pennsylvania* (New York, 1987); Robert P. Thomas and Terry L. Anderson, "White Population, Labor Force and Extensive Growth of the New England Economy in the Seventeenth Century," *Journal of Economic History* 33, 3 (1973); and Lawrence W. Towner *A Good Master Well Served: Masters and Servants in Colonial Massachusetts, 1620–1750* (New York, 1998).

Farley Grubb has been a particularly active scholar in this area. The work cited here is but a sampling of his many articles. See Farley Grubb, "The Auction of Redemptioner Servants, Philadelphia, 1771–1804: An Economic Analysis," *Journal of Economic History* 47, 3 (1988), 583–602; Farley Grubb, "The Disappearance of Organized Markets for European Immigrant Servants in the United States: Five Popular Explanations Reexamined," *Social Science History* 18, 1 (1994), 1–30; Farley Grubb, "Fatherless and Friendless: Factors Influencing the Flow of English Emigrant Servants," *Journal of Economic History* 52 (1992), 85–108; Farley Grubb, "Immigrant Servant Labor: Their Occupational and Geographic Distribution in the Late Eighteenth-Century Mid-Atlantic Economy," *Social Science History* 9, 3 (1985), 249–76, at 251–5; Farley W. Grubb, "Immigration and Servitude in the Colony and Commonwealth of Pennsylvania: A Quantitative and Economic Analysis," unpublished Ph.D. thesis, University of Chicago, 1984; Farley Grubb, "The Long-Run Trend in the Value of European Immigrant Servants, 1654–1831: New Measurements and Interpretations," *Research in Economic History* 14 (1992), 167–240; Farley Grubb, "The Transatlantic Market for British Convict Labor," *Journal of Economic History* 60, 1 (2000), 94–122; and Farley Grubb and Tony Stitt, "The Liverpool Emigrant Servant Trade and the Transition to Slave Labor in the Chesapeake, 1697–1707: Market Adjustments to War," *Explorations in Economic History* 20 (1994), 1–31.

On matters of social and economic opportunity, see Lois Green Carr, "Emigration and the Standard of Living: The Seventeenth Century Chesapeake, *Journal of Economic History* 52, 2 (1992); Lois Green Carr and Russell R. Menard, "Immigration and Opportunity: The Freedman in Early Colonial Maryland," in Thad W. Tate and David L. Ammerman, eds., *The Chesapeake in the Seventeenth Century: Essays on Anglo-American Society* (New York, 1979); Lois Green Carr and Lorena S. Walsh, "The Standard of Living in the Colonial Chesapeake," in "Forum: Toward a History of the Standard of Living in British North America," *William and Mary Quarterly*, 3rd ser., 45, 1 (1988), 135–59; Russell R. Menard, "From Servant to Freeholder: Status Mobility and Property Accumulation in Seventeenth Century Maryland," *William and Mary Quarterly*, 3rd ser., 30, 1 (1973), 37–64; Russell R. Menard, "From Servants to Slaves: The Transformation of the Chesapeake Labor System," *Southern Studies* 16 (1977), 355–90; Russell R. Menard, "Immigrants and Their Increase: The Process of Population Growth in Early Colonial Maryland," in Aubrey C. Land et al., eds., *Law, Society and Politics in Early Maryland* (Baltimore, 1977), 88–110; and Lorena Walsh, "Servitude and Opportunity in Charles County, Maryland, 1658–1705," in Land et al., eds., *Law, Society and Politics in Early Maryland.*

For a variety of excellent studies of the social and economic structure of work in early America, see Stephen Innes, ed., *Work and Labor in Early America* (Chapel Hill, 1988). Other, more general studies that are nevertheless of crucial importance to our understanding of migration, population, work, and labor in the mainland colonies are Edmund S. Morgan, *American Slavery, American Freedom: The Ordeal of Colonial Virginia* (New York, 1975); Jeanne M. Boydston, *Home and Work: Housework, Wages, and the Ideology of Labor in the Early Republic* (New York, 1990); Kathleen M. Brown, *Good Wives, Nasty Wenches, and Anxious Patriarchs: Gender, Race and Power in Colonial Virginia* (Chapel Hill, 1996); Stephen Innes, *Creating the Commonwealth: The Economic Culture of Puritan New England* (New York, 1995); Jacqueline Jones, *American Work: Four Centuries of Black and White Labor* (New York, 1998); James T. Lemon, *The Best Poor Man's Country: A Geographical Study of Early Southeastern Pennsylvania* (Baltimore, 1972); Gloria L. Main, *Tobacco Colony: Life in Early Maryland, 1650–1720* (Princeton, 1982); Samuel McKee, *Labor in Colonial New York: 1664–1776* (New York, 1935); Philip D. Morgan, *Slave Counterpoint: Black Culture in the Eighteenth-Century Chesapeake and Lowcountry* (Chapel Hill 1998); Winifred Rothenberg, *From Market-Places to a Market Economy: The Transformation of Rural Massachusetts, 1750–1850* (Chicago, 1992), 181, 182–3; Laurel Thatcher Ulrich, "Martha Ballard and Her Girls: Women's Work in Eighteenth Century Maine," in Innes, ed., *Work and Labor*, 70–105; Laurel Thatcher Ulrich, *Good Wives: Image and Reality in the Lives of Women in Northern New England, 1650–1750* (New York, 1982); Daniel Vickers *Farmers and Fishermen: Two Centuries of Work in Essex County, Massachusetts, 1630–1850* (Chapel Hill, 1994); and Peter H. Wood, *Black Majority: Negroes in Colonial South Carolina from 1670 Through the Stono Rebellion* (New York, 1975).

Finally, on transiency in early America – a subject awaiting sustained treatment – see Ruth Wallis Herndon, *Unwelcome Americans: Living on the Margin in Early New England* (Philadelphia, 2001), which builds on the seminal work of Douglas Lamar Jones, "The Strolling Poor: Transiency in Eighteenth-Century Massachusetts," *Journal of Social History* 8 (1975) and Douglas Lamar Jones, *Village and Seaport, Migration and Society in Eighteenth-Century Massachusetts* (Hanover, NH, 1981). See also Christine Heyrman, *Commerce and Culture: The Maritime Communities of Colonial Massachusetts, 1690–1750* (New York, 1984).

Law, Migration, and Labor Force Formation in Early America

Notwithstanding the publication of Morris's *Government and Labor* in 1946, interest in the law of work and labor in the colonies – indeed, interest in colonial legal history in general – was not marked for some considerable time. The title of Stephen Innes' excellent 1988 collection of essays, *Work and Labor in Early America*, pays homage to Morris's *Government and Labor in Early America* from forty years before, but in omitting governance (a.k.a. "the state") it emphasized the predominance of social history over legal. Still, new interest in early American legal history was beginning to pick up in the 1970s. Research specific to the history of the period's labor law followed on, ten to fifteen years later, often supplemented by or supplementing concentration on the nineteenth century. For general studies, see Jonathan A. Bush, "Free to Enslave: The Foundations of Colonial American Slave Law," *Yale Journal of Law and Humanities* 5 (1993); Marc Linder, *The Employment Relationship in Anglo-American Law: A Historical Perspective* (Westport, CT, 1989); David Montgomery, *Citizen Worker: The Experience of Workers in the United States with Democracy and the Free Market During the Nineteenth Century* (Cambridge, 1993); Thomas D. Morris, *Southern Slavery and the Law, 1619–1860* (Chapel Hill, 1996); Karen Orren, *Belated Feudalism: Labor, the Law, and Liberal Development in the United States* (Cambridge, 1991); Robert J. Steinfeld, *The Invention of Free Labor: The Employment Relation in English and American Law and Culture, 1350–1870* (Chapel Hill, 1991); Christopher L. Tomlins, *Law, Labor and Ideology in the Early American Republic* (Cambridge, 1993); and Christopher Tomlins, "Early British America, 1585–1830," in Craven and Hay, eds., *Masters, Servants, and Magistrates*. Although outside the colonial era, both Amy Dru Stanley, *From Bondage to Contract: Wage Labor, Marriage, and the Market in the Age of Slave Emancipation* (New York, 1998), and Robert J. Steinfeld, *Coercion, Contract and Free Labor in the Nineteenth Century* (New York, 2001), are informative and helpful.

For studies of more specific locales and subjects, see Mary S. Bilder, "The Struggle over Immigration: Indentured Servants, Slaves, and Articles of Commerce," *Missouri Law Review* 61 (1996); Warren M. Billings, "The Law of Servants and Slaves in Seventeenth Century Virginia," *Virginia Magazine of History and Biography* 99, 1 (1991); Alfred L. Brophy, "Law and Indentured Servitude in Mid-Eighteenth Century Pennsylvania," *Willamette Law Review* 28, 1 (1991); Christine Daniels, "'Liberty to Complaine': Servant Petitions in Colonial Anglo-America," in Christopher Tomlins and Bruce H. Mann, eds., *The Many Legalities of Early America* (Chapel Hill, 2001), 219–49; David Barry Gaspar, "'Rigid and Inclement': Origins of the Jamaica Slave Laws of the Seventeenth Century," in Tomlins and Mann, eds., *Many Legalities*, 78–96; and Farley Grubb, "The Statutory Regulation of Colonial Servitude: An Incomplete-Contract Approach," *Explorations in Economic History* 37 (2000), 42–75.

On legal mechanisms specific to the police of mobility, see Sally Hadden, *Slave Patrols: Law and Violence in Virginia and the Carolinas* (Cambridge, MA, 2001); Kunal Parker, "State, Citizenship, and Territory: The Legal Construction of Immigrants in Antebellum Massachusetts," and "Disaggregating Citizenship," both in *Law and History Review* 19, 3 (2001), 583–644, and 655–60; and Robert J. Steinfeld, "Subjectship, Citizenship, and the Long History of Immigration Regulation," *Law and History Review* 19, 3 (2001), 645–54. See also

Bruce H. Mann, *Republic of Debtors: Bankruptcy in the Age of American Independence* (Cambridge, MA, 2002), and Dubber, *The Police Power*.

Finally, for a sampling of work and opinion on the general role of law in the process of colonizing the mainland, see David Grayson Allen, *In English Ways: The Movement of Societies and the Transferal of English Local Law and Custom to Massachusetts Bay in the Seventeenth Century* (Chapel Hill, 1981); Daniel R. Coquillette, "Radical Lawmakers in Colonial Massachusetts: The 'Countenance of Authoritie' and the Lawes and Libertyes," *New England Quarterly* 67, 2 (1994), 179–211; John L. Comaroff, "Colonialism, Culture and the Law: A Foreword," *Law and Social Inquiry* 26, 2 (2001); George L. Haskins, *Law and Authority in Early Massachusetts: A Study in Tradition and Design* (New York, 1968); Daniel J. Hulsebosch, "The Ancient Constitution and the Expanding Empire: Sir Edward Coke's British Jurisprudence," *Law and History Review* 21, 3 (2003); Engin Isin, *Being Political: Genealogies of Citizenship* (Minneapolis, 2002); David Konig, *Law and Society in Puritan Massachusetts: Essex County, 1629–92* (Chapel Hill, 1979); Christopher Tomlins, "The Legal Cartography of Colonization, the Legal Polyphony of Settlement: English Intrusions on the Amèrican Mainland in the Seventeenth Century," *Law and Social Inquiry* 26, 2 (2001); Christopher Tomlins, "The Many Legalities of Colonization: A Manifesto of Destiny for Early American Legal History," and Bruce H. Mann, "The Death and Transfiguration of Early American Legal History," both in Tomlins and Mann, eds., *Many Legalities*.

CHAPTER 8: THE FRAGMENTED LAWS OF SLAVERY

SALLY E. HADDEN

(1) General

The universal quality of slavery in the early modern period has been the subject of many excellent works, including Robin Blackburn, *The Making of New World Slavery: From the Baroque to the Modern, 1492–1800* (London, 1997); David Brion Davis, *The Problem of Slavery in Western Culture* (Ithaca, 1966) and its companion, *The Problem of Slavery in the Age of Revolution, 1770–1823* (2nd ed., New York, 1998); and more recently, David Brion Davis, *Inhuman Bondage: The Rise and Fall of Slavery in the New World* (New York, 2006).

Comparative works about slavery are fairly common, though fewer of them address law beyond a token nod at the outset. One of the first broadly comparative works that addressed legal issues – though at a very simple level – was Frank Tannenbaum's *Slave and Citizen: The Negro in the Americas* (New York, 1963). Later well-known works that followed in this tradition include Carl Degler, *Neither Black nor White: Slavery and Race Relations in Brazil and the United States* (New York, 1971; repr. ed. Madison, 1986), and Herbert S. Klein, *Slavery in the Americas: A Comparative Study of Virginia and Cuba* (Chicago,

1967). The nature of a slave's legal and social death in a multiplicity of societies, ancient to modern, has been explored by Orlando Patterson, *Slavery and Social Death: A Comparative Study* (Cambridge, 1982). Few full-length works, however, have addressed the nature of slave law on a comparative scale, keeping their focus on law and the western hemisphere. Alan Watson, *Slave Law in the Americas* (Athens, GA, 1989) is a rare exception; Lauren Benton, *Law and Colonial Cultures: Legal Regimes in World History, 1400–1900* is another work that, among other topics, considers the law of slavery through a comparison of jurisdictional contexts. Articles by various authors in two special issues of the 1996 *Cardozo Law Review* (May 1996, vol. 17, 6 and November 1996, vol. 18, 2) addressed variations among world slave regimes, with reference to new scholarship and legal historiography. An overview essay soon to be published is Sue Peabody, "Slave Law in the Atlantic World Before 1804," in David Eltis and Stanley Engerman, eds., *World History of Slavery. Vol. 3: 1420–1804* (Cambridge, forthcoming).

The scale and scope of African enslavement have been studied by many scholars since the 1960s, when quantitative methods swept the historical discipline. The original path-breaking work on the size of African slave trade was published by Philip Curtin, *The Atlantic Slave Trade: A Census* (Madison, WI, 1969). Since then, many works have refined his numbers, but none has overturned the basic premises he suggested. See Herbert S. Klein, *The Atlantic Slave Trade* (Cambridge, 1999) and Paul E. Lovejoy, *Transformations in Slavery: A History of Slavery in Africa* (2nd ed., Cambridge, 2000). The most detailed quantitative research can now be done using a database of nearly 30,000 slave trading voyages completed between 1595 and 1866, which contains information on the numbers of slaves transported across the Atlantic, geographic regions visited, owners, captains, ship characteristics, and transatlantic connections made by voyage. Compiled at the W. E. B. DuBois Center of Harvard University, the database was the result of collaboration by David Eltis, Stephen D. Behrendt, David Richardson, and Herbert S. Klein, which produced *The Trans-Atlantic Slave Trade {computer file}: A Database on CD-ROM* (Cambridge, 1999). Analysis of some of the more interesting trends revealed by the database has been published by David Eltis, David Richardson, and Stephen D. Behrendt, "Patterns in the Transatlantic Slave Trade, 1662–1867," in Maria Diedrich, Henry Louis Gates, Jr., and Carl Pedersen, eds., *Black Imagination and the Middle Passage* (New York, 1999). Less quantitative-driven scholarship that still relies on contrasting scales of enslavement can be found in Ira Berlin, *Many Thousands Gone: the First Two Centuries of Slavery in North America* (Cambridge, 1998), which explains the transitions each region experienced depending on whether it was a society with slaves or a slave society (and, thus, fully dependent economically, socially, and culturally on the presence of slaves).

Studies of Native Americans and their enslavement following the arrival of Europeans in the New World have been less plentiful. One general work that includes some discussion of the legal ramifications, including slavery, is Susan Kellogg, *Law and the Transformation of Aztec Culture, 1500–1700* (Norman, OK, 1995). Many more books have focused on land dispossession or have been written about the types of labor performed or the extractive economic quality of slave labor in Central and South America. Very few touch on slave law, and typically they have only approached the issue from a consideration of European legal norms; Native conceptions of slavery are more likely to be discussed as custom rather than law. For extensive treatment of native legal ideas, see Bruce E. Johansen, ed., *The Encyclopedia of Native American Legal Tradition* (Westport, 1998). Rarely are native peoples ascribed any degree of agency when it came to matters of enslavement. More often, they are treated as objects of other cultural, legal, or linguistic systems. See Robert Williams, *The American Indian in Western Legal Thought: The Discourses of Conquest* (Oxford, 1990), and David O'Rourke, *How America's First Settlers Invented Chattel Slavery: Dehumanizing Native Americans and Africans with Language, Laws, Guns, and Religion* (New York, 2004).

Regional studies of the enslavement of Native Americans in North America have begun to appear in recent years. Allan Gallay's *The Indian Slave Trade: The Rise of the English Empire in the American South, 1670–1717* (New Haven, 2002) was one of the first to suggest that the numbers of Native Americans placed into bondage in the northern hemisphere may be much higher than previously suspected. His treatment of intertribal warfare resulting in native bondage and exportation for profit is eminently readable. Margaret Newell is presently examining New England laws and the social effects of Native American slavery in that region (*'The Drove of Adam's Degenerate Seed': Indian Slavery in New England*, forthcoming). James F. Brooks's prize-winning book, *Captives and Cousins: Slavery, Kinship, and Community in the Southwest Borderlands* (Chapel Hill, 2002) provides some suggestions about the contrasting dynamics of Native American slavery among Spanish, Mexican, and American societies prior to the American Civil War, though it has less to say about law specifically. Charles Cutter's *The Legal Culture of Northern New Spain, 1700–1810* (Albuquerque, 1995) addresses the difficult questions arising from conflicts between European and native expectations about law, when clashing legal cultures confronted the subject of slavery, though his work is more narrowly cast than that of Brooks. See also Woodrow Borah, *Justice by Insurance: The General Indian Court of Colonial Mexico and the Legal Aides of the Half-Real* (Berkeley, 1983).

(2) Islamic Slave Law and African, English, and Spanish Legal Traditions

Few studies of slave law and Islam have been translated into English, leaving a narrow band of scholarship in this field open for non-Arabic-speaking researchers who wish to know more. On the relation between slavery and Islam, a good starting point is Humphrey J. Fisher, *Slavery in the History of Muslim Black Africa* (New York, 2001); additionally, see John Hunwick, "Islamic Law and Polemics over Race and Slavery in North and West Africa (16th–19th Century)," *Princeton Papers: Interdisciplinary Journal of Middle Eastern Studies* 7 (1999), 43–68. For more detailed work, one can consult Bernard Barbour and Michelle Jacobs, "The Mi'raj: a Legal Treatise on Slavery by Ahmad Baba," in John R. Willis, ed., *Slaves and Slavery in Muslim Africa, Vol. I: Islam and the Ideology of Enslavement* (London, 1985), which includes a complete Arabic text of the legal treatise under discussion with an English translation. Most works on slavery and Muslim beliefs focus on Northern Africa, not the region of the western coast, from which the majority of slaves were exported to the New World. Among those works about North Africa, Ahmad Alawad Sikainga, "Slavery and Muslim Jurisprudence in Morocco," in Suzanne Miers and Martin Klein, eds., *Slavery and Colonial Rule in Africa* (London, 1998) is well worth consulting (reprinted in *Slavery and Abolition* 19, 2 (1998), 57–72). The most recent statistical data on Christian slaves working in North Africa, with references to their legal status and working conditions, can be found in Robert C. Davis, *Christian Slaves, Muslim Masters: White Slavery in the Mediterranean, the Barbary Coast, and Italy, 1500–1800* (New York, 2003). Islamic law, like English or American common law, is neither immune to the passage of time nor the effects of local custom. Lawrence Rosen, *The Justice of Islam* (Oxford, 2000) gives a fine overview of the effects of local variation on Islamic law as seen through the eyes of a legal anthropologist. Though the examples he uses come from modern-day North Africa, the principles he suggests that underlie Islamic justice could well have application to the variability of Islamic slave law in an earlier period.

On slavery in Western Africa, several new synthetic works have appeared recently, although they have limited references to slave law specifically. Patrick Manning, *Slavery and African Life: Occidental, Oriental, and African Slave Trades* (Cambridge, 1990); Joseph C. Miller, *Way of Death: Merchant Capitalism and the Angolan Slave Trade, 1730–1830* (Madison, WI, 1988); and Paul Lovejoy, *Transformations in Slavery: A History of Slavery in Africa* (2nd ed., Cambridge 2000) are among the best that address West African slavery. Research on specific groups in West African that were heavily represented in the slave trade, like the Igbo, has not slowed since the 1960s, though most has a heavy anthropological bent. See G. T. Basden, *Niger Ibos* (New York, 1966); Victor Uchendu, *The Igbo of Southeast Nigeria* (New York, 1965); and Suzanne Miers and Igor Kopytoff, eds., *Slavery in Africa: Historical and Anthropological Perspectives* (Madison, 1977). On slave law in this region, see Robin Law, "Legal and Illegal Enslavement in West Africa, in the Context of the Trans-Atlantic Slave Trade" in Toyin Falola, ed., *Ghana in Africa and the World: Essays in Honor of Adu Boahen* (Trenton, 2003).

In Europe, there were several competing legal traditions with regard to unfree persons that ultimately saw some degree of transplantation to the New World. For England, no single source exists giving the law of bondage as it related to whites or blacks in the late medieval or early modern periods. A general overview on villeinage and slavery can be found in J. H. Baker, *An Introduction to English Legal History* (4th ed., Bath, 2002), as part of his larger discussion of the status and liberties of persons, and in his essay "Personal Liberty under the Common Law of England, 1200–1600," in R. W. Davis, ed., *The Origins of Modern Freedom in the West* (Stanford, 1995). See also J. Hatcher, "English Serfdom and Villeinage," *Past and Present* 90 (1981), 1–39. A crucial source text on the Spanish law of slavery is Robert Burns, S. J., ed., *Las Siete Partidas*, 5 vols. (Philadelphia, 2001), particularly volume IV, which contains Titles 21 and 22 relating directly to slaves. On the Spanish tradition of *coartacíon*, see Herbert Aimes, "Coartacíon: A Spanish Institution for the Advancement of Slaves and Freedmen," *The Yale Review* 17 (1908–09), 412–31. On the biblical tradition of slavery, as it was received by Christians in Western Europe and then applied to Africans, see David Brion Davis, *Slavery and Human Progress* (New York, 1984) and Winthrop Jordan, *White over Black: American Attitudes Towards the Negro, 1550–1812* (Chapel Hill, 1968).

(3) Slave Law in Caribbean and Central and South American Colonies

Each group that colonized the New World approached the question of slavery from slightly different starting points. A collection of the statutes and case law regarding slavery in the Caribbean, Brazil, England, the United States, and Spanish America is currently in production (Sue Peabody and Keila Grinberg, *Slavery, Freedom and the Law in the Atlantic World* [New York, 2007). Scholarship on slavery and the French colonies has advanced significantly in the past few years, moving the field beyond early texts like Lucien Paytraud, *L'Esclavage aux Antilles Françaises avant 1789 d'après des documents inédits des Archives coloniales* ed. Émile Désormeaux (Paris, 1897; repr. ed. Paris, 1973) or Gaston Martin, *Histoire de l'Esclavage aux Colonies Françaises* (Paris, 1948; repr. ed. Brionne, 1978). A full text of the *Code Noir* (Louis Sala-Molins, *Le Code Noir ou le calvaire de Canaan*, Paris, 1987) appeared in the 1980s with notes and commentary. An in-depth study of its compilers appeared in the 1990s: Vernon Palmer, "The Origins and Authors of the *Code Noir*," in Judith K. Schafer and Warren M. Billings, eds., *An Uncommon Experience: Law and Judicial Institutions in Louisiana, 1803–2003* (Lafayette, 1997). Sue Peabody's *'There are No Slaves in France': The Political Culture of Race and Slavery in the Ancien Regime* (New York, 1996) reexamined the question of slavery as it was known in France during this period.

On the law of slavery among the Portuguese and particularly their Brazilian colony, consult José Joaquim da Cunha de Azeredo Coutinho, *Concordância das leis de Portugal e das bulas pontifícias, das quais umas permitem a escravidão dos pretos da Africa e outras proíbem a escravidão dos indios do Brazil* (reprint, Rio de Janeiro, 1988), and more generally A. J. R. Russell-Wood, *Black Man in Slavery and Freedom in Colonial Brazil* (London, 1982) and Kathleen Higgins, *'Licentious*

Liberty' in a Brazilian Gold-mining Region: Slavery, Gender and Social Control in Eighteenth-Century Sabará (University Park, 1999). On the Dutch, see Cornelis Goslinga, *The Dutch in the Caribbean and in the Guianas, 1680–1791*, ed. Maria J. L. van Yperen (Assen, Netherlands, 1985).

Any examination of slave laws among the English-settled islands of the Caribbean must begin with Elsa Goveia, *The West Indian Slave Laws of the 18th century* (Barbados, 1970). The idea of "legal borrowing" between slaveholding colonies has been explored by Bradley Nicholson, "Legal Borrowing and the Origins of Slave Law in the British Colonies," *American Journal of Legal History* 38, 1 (1994), 38–54; David Barry Gaspar, "With a Rod of Iron: Barbados Slave Laws as a Model for Jamaica, South Carolina, and Antigua, 1661–1697," in Darlene Clark Hine and Jacqueline McLeod, eds., *Crossing Boundaries: Comparative History of Black People in Diaspora* (Bloomington: Indiana University Press, 1999); and more broadly by Alan Watson in *Legal Transplants: An Approach to Comparative Law* (2nd ed., Athens, GA, 1993). On slave law in particular islands, consult Howard Fergus, "The Early Laws of Monserrat (1668–1680): The Legal Schema of a Slave Society," *Caribbean Quarterly* 24, 1–2 (1978), 34–43; Mindie Lazarus Black, *Legitimate Acts and Illegal Encounters: Law and Society in Antigua and Barbuda* (Washington, 1994); David Barry Gaspar, "Rigid and Inclement: Origins of the Jamaican Slave Laws of the Seventeenth Century," in Christopher Tomlins and Bruce Mann, eds., *The Many Legalities of Early America* (Chapel Hill, 2001); and Richard Dunn, *Sugar and Slaves: The Rise of the Planter Class in the English West Indies, 1624–1713* (Chapel Hill, 1972).

Source texts for Barbadian slave laws appear in *Acts and Statutes of the Island of Barbadoes. Made and Enacted since the Reducement of the Same, unto the Authority of the Common-wealth of England* (London, [1654]); William Rawlin, comp., *The Laws of Barbados, Collected in One Volume* (London, 1699); *Acts of Assembly, Passed in the Island of Barbadoes, From 1648, to 1718* (London, 1721); and Richard Hall, comp., *Acts Passed in the Island of Barbados. From 1643 to 1762, inclusive* (London, 1764). As some laws were repealed, allowed to lapse, or replaced, all editions must be consulted to discover the true dimensions of Barbadian slave law in this critical period. No single volume contains a comprehensive list of all Barbadian laws; in addition to these printed volumes, one must also consult the Public Record Office in London for individual laws transmitted back to England that were not included in the various compilations.

Slave law from Spain's Caribbean and mainland colonies was only partially collected in the *Recopilación de las leyes de los reinos de los Indias*, 4 vols. (Madrid, 1841; reprint, Madrid, 1973). Its application in specific colonies has been explored by Manuel Lucena, *Leyes para esclavos: El ordenamiento jurídico sobre la condición, tratamiento, defense y repressión de los esclavos en las colonias de la América española* (Madrid, 2000); Norman Meiklejohn, "The Implementation of Slave Legislation in Eighteenth-Century New Granada," in Robert B. Toplin, ed., *Slavery and Race Relations in Latin America* (Westport, 1974); and Carlos Aguirre,

"Working the System: Slaves and Courts in Lima, Peru," in Darlene Clark Hine and Jacqueline McLeod, eds., *Crossing Boundaries: Comparative History of Black People in Diaspora* (Bloomington, 1999).

(4) Slave Law in the North American Colonies

The transmission of Spanish law to colonial Louisiana, particularly slavery, has been explored by Hans Baade, "The Law of Slavery in Spanish Louisiana, 1769–1803," in Edward W. Haas, ed., *Louisiana's Legal Heritage* (Pensacola, 1983) and Gilbert Din, *Spaniards, Planters, and Slaves: The Spanish Regulation of Slavery in Louisiana, 1763–1803* (College Station, 1999). More contextual studies of the same, incorporating added material on women and free blacks, are Thomas Ingersoll's *Mammon and Manon in Early New Orleans: the First Slave Society in the Deep South, 1718–1819* (Knoxville, 1999) and Jennifer Spear, "Colonial Intimacies: Legislating Sex in French Louisiana," *William and Mary Quarterly*, 3rd ser., 60 (2003), 75–98.

Source texts for the two earliest colonial slave codes can be found in Thomas Cooper and David J. McCord, eds., *The Statutes at Large of South Carolina* (Columbia, 1836–1841), particularly vol. 7, and William W. Hening, ed., *The Statutes at Large; being a collection of all the laws of Virginia, from the first session of the Legislature in 1619* (New York, 1819–1823; reprint Charlottesville, 1969), particularly vols. 1–3. A full list of all mainland colony slave codes can be found in William Wiecek, "The Statutory Law of Slavery and Race in the Thirteen Mainland Colonies of British America," *William and Mary Quarterly*, 3rd ser., 34 (1977), 258–80.

An early effort to analyze slave law in the colonies was A. Leon Higginbotham, *In the Matter of Color: Race and the American Legal Process: The Colonial Period* (New York, 1978), although it has been surpassed by later studies that were more detailed or nuanced. Other early works that scrutinized South Carolina or Virginia slave law, accounting for social and economic context, include Peter Wood, *Black Majority: Negroes in Colonial South Carolina from 1670 Through the Stono Rebellion* (New York, 1974), and Edmund S. Morgan's *American Slavery, American Freedom: The Ordeal of Colonial Virginia* (New York, 1975). These path-breaking books have been augmented by more recent books that have only indirectly addressed the important role of slave statutes and case law. One direct challenge to Morgan's interpretation on the development of slave law in Virginia is Anthony Parent, *Foul Means: The Formation of a Slave Society in Virginia, 1660–1740* (Chapel Hill, 2003). A lengthy work intended to survey all developments in slave law, but that ultimately focuses on case law developments in a broad brush fashion, giving less attention to the early period, is Thomas D. Morris, *Southern Slavery and the Law, 1619–1860* (Chapel Hill, 1996). A document-rich work that attempts to show the interplay between case law and statutes is Warren Billings, ed., *The Old Dominion in the Seventeenth Century: A Documentary History of Virginia, 1606–1689* (Chapel Hill, 1975).

See also his critical article on the Key case: Warren Billings, "The Cases of Fernando and Elizabeth Key: A Note on the Status of Blacks in Seventeenth-century Virginia," *William and Mary Quarterly*, 3rd ser., 30 (1973), 467–74. Philip J. Schwarz, *Twice Condemned: Slaves and the Criminal Laws of Virginia, 1705–1865* (Baton Rouge, LA, 1988), is the best work on slaves who were convicted of crimes and how a colony, or later state, disposed of those slaves through execution or transportation. A briefer work by Schwarz, *Slave Laws in Virginia* (Athens, GA, 1999), is actually less comprehensive than its title implies, but raises important questions about the need for future scholarship to consider the perspective of enslaved persons brought before a European-based justice system for trial.

Slave law in Virginia and South Carolina has attracted the greatest amount of scholarly scrutiny, although other colonies have had research conducted on their slave laws from time to time. Typically, these works have cast their nets more widely than just slave law, like Donna Spindel, *Crime and Society in North Carolina, 1663–1776* (Baton Rouge, LA, 1989), and Gary Nash, *Forging Freedom: The Formation of Philadelphia's Black Community, 1720–1840* (Cambridge, 1988). The most detailed work often highlights comparisons between the criminal law as applied to free and slave persons and can often be found in doctoral or master's theses: see, for example, Glenn McNair, "Justice Bound: Aframericans, Crime, and Criminal Justice in Georgia, 1751–1865," Ph.D. thesis, Emory University, 2001, and James H. Brewer, "An Apocalypse on Slavery: The Story of the Negro Slave in the Lower Cape Fear Region of North Carolina," Ph.D. thesis, University of Pittsburgh, 1949. Traditionally, the majority of these works were about the colonies that later became part of the antebellum South's plantation regime. Since the 1960s, however, more works have begun to address slavery and slave law in the Northeast or mid-Atlantic region. Slave law in New York has attracted numerous scholars, such as Ira Berlin and Leslie M. Harris, eds., *Slavery in New York* (New York, 2005), and Leslie M. Harris, *In the Shadow of Slavery: African Americans in New York City, 1626–1863* (Chicago, 2003). Early classics include Edgar McManus, *A History of Negro Slavery in New York* (Syracuse, 1966), and McManus, *Black Bondage in the North* (Syracuse, 1973). Following a 2004 conference on the subject of New England slavery, the Colonial Society of Massachusetts has a forthcoming volume in its publication series that will include a few articles relating to slave law. The power of narrower historical events to create great change to slave law has been explored by Peter C. Hoffer, *The Great New York Conspiracy of 1741: Slavery, Crime, and Colonial Law* (Lawrence, 2003).

Original source texts of colonial slave law outside the South can be found via the Early State Records microfilm series, but they are scattered among all legislative topics and poorly indexed: Library of Congress, *Microfilm Collection of Early State Records, Prepared by the Library of Congress in Association with the University of North Carolina*, comp. William Sumner Jenkins (Washington,

1950). A paper index, *A guide to the Microfilm Collection of Early State Records*, was published by Lillian Hamrick (Washington, 1950). This same series can be used to track slave laws from the colonial period into the post-Revolutionary era. Print versions of colonial slave laws are frequently inadequate, given space limitations that publishers often impose. See the too-brief Oscar R. Williams, *African Americans and Colonial Legislation in The Middle Colonies* (New York, 1998). For the period following the American Revolution, readers can access the microfilm series, *State Slavery Statutes*, comp. Paul Finkelman (Frederick, 1989), which should still be regarded as an incomplete source on slave control laws, since many important laws regulating slave conduct can only be found in municipal ordinances. A much less thorough print version, though still widely available, is George M. Stroud, *A Sketch of the Laws Relating to Slavery in the Several States of the United States of America* (New York, 1968). Judicial opinions at the state supreme court level relating to slave law have been gathered and excerpted by Helen Tunnicliff Catterall, *Judicial Cases Concerning American Slavery and the Negro*, 5 vols. (Washington, 1926; repr ed, New York, 1968).

Some states have begun to put all their colonial legislation and government papers online in a searchable format, which may improve the ability to locate information on particular states' slave laws. The University of Connecticut has placed online the Public Records of the Colony of Connecticut from 1636–1776 [http://www.colonialct.uconn.edu/]. The Maryland State Archives is likewise digitizing its complete run of colonial documents, previously published in the *Archives of Maryland*, for online users [http://aomol.net/html/index.html]. Another major collection of colonial laws can be found at Yale Law School's Avalon Project [http://www.yale.edu/lawweb/avalon/avalon.htm].

Enforcement of slave laws routinely fell to slave courts and slave patrols. On courts specifically designed to curb slave misbehavior, see James Campbell, *Slavery on Trial* (forthcoming), though like most works that examine slave courts, this study of Richmond magistrate proceedings focuses on the antebellum period. On patrols, see Sally Hadden, *Slave Patrols: Law and Violence in Virginia and the Carolinas* (Cambridge, 2001).

(5) Slave Law in a Revolutionary Age

Wars of the late eighteenth century in France, America, and Haiti were infused with revolutionary ideology that had a direct effect on slave law and the possibility of abolishing slavery. See William Wiecek, *The Sources of Antislavery Constitutionalism in America, 1760–1848* (Ithaca, 1977), and Gary Nash, *Race and Revolution* (Lanham, 1990). More general works have set the impetus for legally changing slave status into detailed contexts of politics, race, and local conditions: Laurent Dubois, *A Colony of Citizens: Revolution and Slave Emancipation in the French Caribbean, 1787–1804* (Chapel Hill, 2004), and Sylvia Frey, *Water from the Rock: Black Resistance in a Revolutionary Age* (Princeton, 1991). Recent studies have maintained a tighter focus on legal changes to slave law in the Revolutionary era by tracking influential individuals, specific courts, or unusual legal developments, such as the "Tyrannicide" affair in Massachusetts: Paul Finkelman, *Slavery and the Founders: Race and Liberty in the Age of Jefferson* (2nd ed., Armonk, 2001), and Emily Blanck, "Revolutionizing Slavery: The Legal Culture of Slavery in Revolutionary Massachusetts and South Carolina," Ph.D. thesis, Emory University, 2003.

The question of slave emancipation has attracted scholarly attention for decades, creating a dense literature on the topic. On emancipation in Northern states, see Arthur Zilversmit, *The First Emancipation: The Abolition of Slavery in the North* (Chicago, 1967). The vexed question of when slavery ended in Massachusetts has received extensive coverage: William O'Brien, "Did the Jennison Case Outlaw Slavery in Massachusetts?" *William and Mary Quarterly*, 3rd ser., 17, 2 (1960), 219–41, and John D. Cushing, "The Cushing Court and the Abolition of Slavery in Massachusetts: More Notes on the 'Quock Walker Case'," *American Journal of Legal History* 5 (1961), 18–144. Broader questions of how emancipation created a more complex understanding of race have been explored by Joanne Pope Melish, *Disowning Slavery: Gradual Emancipation and "Race" in New England, 1780–1860* (Cornell, 1998); Stephen T. Whitman, *The Price of Freedom: Slavery and Manumission in Baltimore and Early National Maryland* (Lexington, 1997); and Shane White, *Somewhat More Independent: The End of Slavery in New York City, 1770–1810* (Athens, GA, 1991). The impact of *Somerset's Case* in England on American judicial thinking is still being evaluated: William Cotter, "The Somerset Case and the Abolition of Slavery in England," *History* [Great Britain] 79 (1994), 31–56; Mark Weiner, "New Biographical Evidence on Somerset's Case," *Slavery and Abolition* 23, 1 (2002), 121–36; James Oldham, *The Mansfield Manuscripts and the Growth of English Law in the Eighteenth Century* (Chapel Hill, 1992), particularly vol. II, ch. 21; Michael Guasco, "Encounters, Identities, and Human Bondage: The Foundations of Racial Slavery in the Anglo-Atlantic World," Ph.D. thesis, College of William and Mary, 2000.

Emancipation beyond the North American mainland has typically been addressed one society at a time, rather than in sweeping fashion: Stuart Schwartz, "The Manumission of Slaves in Colonial Brazil: Bahia, 1684–1745," *Hispanic American Historical Review* 54, 4 (1974), 603–35; Lyman Johnson, "Manumission in Colonial Buenos Aires, 1776–1810," *Hispanic American Historical Review* 59, 2 (1979), 258–79; and Mary Turner, *Slaves and Missionaries: The Disintegration of Jamaican Slave Society, 1787–1834* (Urbana, 1982). More recent studies have addressed the meaning of emancipation in broader strokes: J. R. Ward, *British West Indian Slavery, 1750–1834: The Process of Amelioration* (Oxford, 1988); Laurent Dubois, *A Colony of Citizens: Revolution and Slave Emancipation in the French Caribbean, 1787–1804* (Chapel Hill, 2004); and Rosemary Brana-Shute, "The Manumission of Slaves in Suriname, 1760–1828," Ph.D. thesis, University of Florida, 1985.

(6) Uncovering New Resources About African Slave Law

Until recently, the scholar who sought information on African law in the precolonial period would routinely run into difficulties. For one thing, the major journals devoted to African law – *Recht in Afrika*, the *Journal of African Law*, or the *Revue Juridique Africaine* – rarely touch on the topic of African legal history. Although a major bibliography of African law exists (compiled by Jacques Vanderlinden under the titles *African Law Bibliography/Bibliographie de droit Africain* [Brussels, 1972 and 1980]), its temporal range is limited and it also suffers from the same problem as the journals on African law: it has no categorical treatment of legal history. Presentism is alive and well among scholars of African law, in part because of the adoption of Western legal norms in the nineteenth and twentieth centuries, as African countries decolonized and set about fashioning their own laws: there has been (and in some places continues to be) an incredible disdain for the unwritten law or customary laws that predated the arrival of European colonizers.

However, a book that appeared in 1998 has made it easier to investigate different aspects of African customary law, both present-day custom as well as historical custom. This work provides a 200-page compilation of articles, books, dissertations, and conference papers across a staggering array of disciplines (anthropology, folklore, history, literature, law, and many others) in more than a half-dozen languages. For anyone attempting to know more about what African law may be on a particular topic, the compilation by Effa Okupa will be the starting point for years to come. Okupa's *International Bibliography of African Customary Law* will be invaluable in providing leads to future researchers who wish to know more about ordinary African legal practices in many areas, including slavery: Effa Okupa, *International Bibliography of African Customary Law: Ius non scriptum* (Hamburg, 1998). For instance, his extensive information about the law of sales will eventually inform scholars about typical trading practices that slaves would have known in Africa. The principle of recission (that a contract can be revoked if a fundamental mistake has been made in the bargain – the slave sold as healthy turns out to have a hernia) was well known in several African trading networks. This type of practice, which influenced slave markets in Africa, affected American slave markets in fairly similar ways. The legal philosophies of various tribal groups most affected by the slave trade will naturally demand the closest attention: F. U. Okafor, *Igbo Philosophy of Law* (Enugu, Nigeria, 1992).

In addition to discovering African customary law through Okupa's compilation, we will also need to gain greater familiarity with the writings of persons who explored and traveled through African lands; those writings may provide us with insights about legal customs and practices in various parts of Africa. One starting point will be J. D. Fage, a noted African historian, who compiled *A Guide to Original Sources for Precolonial Africa Published in European Languages* (rev. ed., Madison, 1994). This work, in conjunction with J. F. P. Hopkins and Nehemia Levtzion's compilation of early Arabic sources for West African history (which published side-by-side translations of Arabic source material into English) and other collections of travel literature generally, should be mined by scholars seeking to learn more about African legal practices and laws regarding slavery in various parts of West Africa: *Corpus of Early Arabic Sources for West African History* (Cambridge, 1981). For the Yoruba people found in modern-day Nigeria, an excellent early account of the civil and criminal justice system exists in the work of Osifekunde, a man sold into slavery who eventually told his story to a French ethnographer, D'Avezac-Macaya, in the early nineteenth century: "Osifekunde of Ijebu," in Philip D. Curtin, et al., eds., *Africa Remembered: Narratives by West Africans from the Era of the Slave Trade* (Madison, 1967).

CHAPTER 9: THE TRANSFORMATION OF DOMESTIC LAW

HOLLY BREWER

The historical and legal literature on the many aspects of domestic law is significant. This summary attempts to do justice to the main books in that literature. Of the three areas of domestic law, the most attention has gone to the status of wives and women generally. Significant attention has also been paid to the status of workers and servants. The status of children has been relatively ignored.

On Wives and Women

Of those books concerned primarily with the law, Marylynn Salmon, *Women and the Law of Property in Early America* (Chapel Hill, 1986), and Cornelia Dayton, *Women Before the Bar: Gender, Law, & Society in Connecticut 1639–1789* (Chapel Hill, 1995), stand out. Salmon's densely worked analysis of women and property compares women's legal status in different colonies, particularly as it relates to their control of property. She argues that, from the early stages of colonization, New England gave husbands more control over their wives' estates and earnings than in other colonies, largely due to Puritan religious beliefs, which emphasized the authority of the husband. Southerners, on the other hand, tended to adhere more closely to English tradition. She also attributes women's' greater control over property in the South to the shortage of women along with high death rates, following Lois Carr and Lorena Walsh. Salmon examined premarital contracts in different regions particularly closely. Her astute analysis of the use of such contracts (which shows that they existed much more frequently in the South in the late eighteenth century) is, however, marred by an over-reliance on Blackstone's definition of the common law rules surrounding marriage, which hampers her from seeing some of the ways the common law was changing and the other complex ways in which trusts and entails kept married women's property out of their husband's control. (She does, however, note that women's dower rights were changing in England during the seventeenth and eighteenth centuries.) She also largely ignores questions of status (which she admits). Dayton's analysis of women's interaction in Connecticut courts over two centuries is subtle and fascinating. She found that women had more authority and privileges compared to men in the seventeenth century, but that in the eighteenth century men (as husbands and single) became more privileged and less likely to be punished for wrongs.

Two recent books by Linda Sturtz and Terri Snyder on colonial Virginia (while slightly hampered by an unchanging idea of what the English common law was) likewise point to a much broader legal identity and activity by women in the seventeenth century and a narrowing in the eighteenth century. Sturtz, *Within her Power: Propertied Women in Colonial Virginia* (New York, 2002), in particular, was able to trace the most important ligaments of the common law – the restraints on the wife selling family property without her husband – through two important law cases of the eighteenth century. Likewise, she points to a conceptual framework – that people were mostly identified with families and that it was families that had legal identity (which often restrained the father's/husband's actions as well) during the early modern period. Terry Snyder traces the interconnections between women's legal activities and their political presence, as in the case of Lady Berkeley, and argues that even married women often maintained a legal identity in *Brabbling Women: Disorderly Speech and the Law in Early Virginia* (Ithaca, NY, 2003). These studies follow earlier path-breaking social histories of women's lives in early Maryland by Lorena Walsh, "'Till Death us Do Part': Marriage and Family in Seventeenth Century Maryland," in Thad W. Tate and David L. Ammerman, eds., *The Chesapeake in the Seventeenth Century: Essays in Anglo-American Society* (Chapel Hill, 1979), 126–52 and by Darrett Bruce Rutman and Anita Rutman, *A Place in Time: Middlesex County, Virginia, 1650–1750* (New York, 1984). Julia Cherry Spruill's *Women's Life and Work in the Southern Colonies*, which first appeared in 1938, was groundbreaking in how it used the law to uncover aspects of women's lives.

Still, the disproportionate influence of T.E.'s *Laws Resolutions of Womens Rights* (London, 1632, rpt. Amsterdam, 1979) on historians' interpretations of women's legal status in early America seems to have begun with Spruill, who actually misquoted him in a way that made his arguments seem even stronger (p. 340); this passage has since been widely requoted (e.g., Sturtz, p. 20). On this widely cited text also see Wilfrid Prest, "Law and Women's Rights in Early Modern England," *The Seventeenth Century* 6 (1991), 169–87. Prest recognizes how widely this text is cited by historians, but does not realize how much it differs from other treatises of the period. He speculates that it may have been intended for educating law students and perhaps even to defend women in property disputes in which they were increasingly engaged in the seventeenth century. Yet, it demarcates more restrictive space for women.

While this essay has not dealt extensively with women and crime (since crime is covered in other essays) a brief mention of books that deal with that subject, particularly petty crimes such as slander, is relevant here. Jane Kamensky's *Governing the Tongue: The Politics of Speech in Early New England* (Oxford, 1997) shows how women were often singled out specifically for their speech against public authorities, but that no women were punished for speaking or testifying against their husbands. She speculates that was because women were by and large obedient and modest, but it may well have been because no law specifically forbade it (p. 70).

On witchcraft, Carol Karlsen's *The Devil in the Shape of a Woman: Witchcraft in Colonial New England* (New York, 1989) argues that the differential criminalization of women as witches in Puritan New England derives at least in part from jealousy over their ownership of property.

On domestic law more broadly, see Carole Shammas, *A History of Household Government in America* (Charlottesville, 2002). She points out that Hale and Blackstone borrowed from the Greeks their categorization of master/servant, husband/wife, parent/child under the heading of "relations oeconomical" (p. 3). She argues that most people were dependents on a household head in the colonies, even during the seventeenth century. By her estimation, more than 80 percent of colonists were dependents (p. 31). While her analysis is thoughtful and fascinating – and she may well be right in general about the increased power of the head of household (due to inheritance reform, for example) – she is more interested in social categories than legal constructions. In lumping together these categories and not paying in-depth attention to legal technicalities, she contributes to the perception created by eighteenth-century legal scholars like Blackstone that the categories of dependence and authority had a uniform identity in the earlier period. Also see Cynthia Kierner, *Beyond the Household: Women's Place in the Early South, 1700–1835* (Ithaca, 1998), and Daniel Scott Smith, "Behind and Beyond the Law of the Household," *William and Mary Quarterly* 52 (1995), 145–50.

On the middle colonies, see Joan R. Gunderson and Gwen Victor Gampel, "Married Women's Legal Status in Eighteenth Century New York and Virginia," *William and Mary Quarterly* 39 (1982), 114–33, and Joan M. Jensen, *Loosening the Bonds: Mid-Atlantic Farm Women, 1750–1850* (New Haven, 1986), though this is more of a social history. Karin A. Wulf, *Not All Wives: Women of Colonial Philadelphia* (Ithaca, 2000), explores the legal status of unmarried women.

On the early nineteenth century, see Linda Kerber's probing essay, "The Paradox of Women's Citizenship in the New Republic: The Case of *Martin vs. Massachusetts*, 1805," *American Historical Review* 97 (1992), 349–78, which builds on insights into the conflicts between revolutionary ideology and the common law first offered in her *Women of the Republic: Intellect and Ideology in Revolutionary America* (Chapel Hill, 1980), notably ch. 5; and Rosemarie

Zagarri, "The Rights of Man and Woman in Post-Revolutionary America," *William and Mary Quarterly* 55 (1998), 203–30. Hendrik Hartog, *Man and Wife in America: A History* (Cambridge, MA, 2000) richly traces American legal cases of the nineteenth century as they build on and respond to Blackstone, especially as those develop in the middle of the nineteenth century into a sometimes extreme patriarchal perspective. Also see Nancy Isenberg, *Sex and Citizenship in Antebellum America* (Chapel Hill, 1998) and Mary Beth Sievens, *Stray Wives: Marital Conflict in Early National New England* (New York, 2005).

In the long historiographical picture, some much older (and much harder to find) books have pointed the way toward considering changes in the common law, particularly as it relates to femme covert and the status of women. Probably the most important of these are Charlotte Carmichael Stopes, *British Freewomen: Their Historical Privilege* (London, 1894), an antiquarian work that sifts through the historical evidence to suggest a much richer picture of women's legal involvement in the seventeenth century and before (and the pattern of their exclusion); Stopes fingers Sir Edward Coke as particularly important in pointedly excluding women from the vote. She may well be correct, as he certainly played that role in trying to bar those under 21 from the suffrage (a change he sought by fiat, as it were, in his commentaries). The other important older scholar is Mary R. Beard, *Women as Force in History* (1946), who acknowledges the influence of Blackstone and the common law in the young United States as retrograde in terms of the legal status of women. She does not realize, however, how Blackstone himself was shaping the common law and sees equity courts as crafting an alternative to the common law rather than building on some of its earlier precedents. Also see Richard B. Morris, *Studies in the History of American Law* (New York, 1930), especially ch. 3, "Women's Rights in Early American Law," which though dated, is a rich exploration of cases, including listings of, for example, cases in which wives acted alone (p. 176).

On women and voting, in addition to Stopes, see Hilda L. Smith, "Women as Sextons and Electors: King's Bench and Precedents for Women's Citizenship," in Hilda L. Smith, ed., *Women Writers and the Early Modern British Political Tradition* (Cambridge, 1998), 324–42; Jan Lewis, "Of Every Age Sex & Condition": The Representation of Women in the Constitution," *Journal of the Early Republic* 15 (1995), 359–87; and Alexander Keyssar, *The Right to Vote: The Contested History of Democracy in the United States* (New York, 2001).

In English history, among the most important studies of women's involvement in the civil law are Susan Staves's wonderful *Married Women's Separate Property in England, 1660–1833* (Cambridge, MA, 1990); Eileen Spring, *Law, Land, and Family: Aristocratic Inheritance in England, 1300 to 1800* (Chapel Hill, 1993); and Amy Louise Erickson, *Women and Property in Early Modern England* (New York, 1993). One must be careful about generalizations in these works about women and property and pay close attention to the case law they discuss; the last two, in particular, do not recognize the important role that entails could play in preserving women's property, presuming that entails were always in "tail male" (to bar women) when in fact most were general and sometimes were made specifically to prevent a husband from controlling his wife's estate. All of them tend to assume the post-Blackstone perspective that common law courts did not recognize married women's property, even during the seventeenth century. Even Stretton's rich account of *Women Waging Law in Elizabethan England* (Cambridge, 1998) relies on Blackstone as embodying the common law of the seventeenth century, though it is in other ways a wonderful survey of the many ways women participated in English courts even when married (very often jointly with their husbands, but even suing their husbands in some cases, see ch. 6). Susan Dwyer Amussen's *An Ordered Society: Gender and Class in Early Modern England* (New York, 1994) builds upon this synthesis to argue that gender subordination – especially through the law – was crucial to larger structures of authority. Cynthia B. Herrup's *A House in Gross Disorder: Sex, Law, and the 2nd Earl of Castlehaven* (Oxford, 2004) illuminates the ways in which issues of class and social status helped to shape notions of family order among the elite in England in the early seventeenth century (such that class trumped gender as an issue).

On violence and marriage see especially Elizabeth Foyster, *Marital Violence: An English Family History 1660–1857* (Cambridge, 2005); J. M. Beattie, *Crime and the Courts in England 1660–1800* (Princeton, 1986), esp. 74–112, 135–9; Henry A. Kelly, "Rule of Thumb and the Folklaw of the Husband's Stick" *Journal of Legal Education* 44 (1994), 341–65; J. S. Cockburn, "Patterns of Violence in English Society: Homicide in Kent 1560–1985," *Past and Present* 130 (1991), 70–106; and Peter King, "Punishing Assault: The Transformation of Attitudes in English Courts," *Journal of Interdisciplinary History* 27 (1996), 43–74. The Cockburn and King articles also reveal interesting information about how violence between masters and servants was differentially prosecuted. Another study that tracks violence throughout the household is Christine Daniels and Michael V. Kennedy, eds., *Over the Threshold: Intimate Violence in Early America* (New Brunswick, 1999). On marriage, rape, and sexual violence, see, variously, Kathleen Brown, *Good Wives, Nasty Wenches, and Anxious Patriarchs: Gender, Race, and Power in Colonial Virginia* (Chapel Hill, 1996); Ruth Bloch, "Women and the Law of Courtship in Eighteenth Century America" in her *Gender and Morality in Anglo-American Culture, 1650–1800* (Berkeley, 2003); and Sharon Block, *Rape and Sexual Power in Early America* (Chapel Hill, 2006). Also see Christine Daniels and Michael V. Kennedy, eds., *Over the Threshold: Intimate Violence in Early America* (New York, 1999). On divorces, see Merril D. Smith, *Breaking the Bonds: Marital Discord in Pennsylvania, 1730–1830* (New York, 1991); Richard H. Chused, *Private Acts in Public Places: A Social History of Divorce in the Formative Era of American Family Law* (Philadelphia, 1994); Norma Basch, *Framing American Divorce: From the Revolutionary Generation to the Victorians* (Berkeley, 1999); and Roderick Phillips, *Putting Asunder: A History of Divorce in Western*

Society (New York, 1988). Lawrence Stone, *Road to Divorce: England, 1530–1987* (New York, 1990) is the most important of his several volumes on divorce in England; it provides a vital context for understanding divorce in America as well. On parental custody as it emerged as a legal issue in the wake of divorces becoming more common, see Michael Grossberg, *A Judgment for Solomon: The d'Hauteville Case and Legal Experience in Antebellum America* (Cambridge, 1996).

Many books of social and intellectual history address the subject of women's legal status indirectly, as part of a larger social analysis. Almost by definition, many such books are drawn deeply from legal sources, since those are some of the most important sources we have for the colonial period, for which few other documents about (and especially by) women survive. So Laurel Thatcher Ulrich, *Good Wives: Image and Reality in the Lives of Women in Northern New England 1650–1750* (New York, 1982), relies extensively on legal records, including criminal records and inventories, to make women's lives (especially as wives) come alive; likewise Mary Beth Norton's *Liberty's Daughters: The Revolutionary Experience of American Women, 1750–1800* and her Founding *Mothers and Fathers: Gendered Power and the Forming of American Society* (New York, 1996) draw deeply on legal sources.

On Children

As mentioned above, the literature on the legal status of children is thin. The only broad survey is Holly Brewer, *By Birth or Consent: Children, Law, and the Anglo-American Revolution in Authority* (Chapel Hill, 2005). For the early nineteenth century, see Michael Grossberg, *Governing the Hearth: Law and the Family in Nineteenth Century America* (Chapel Hill, 1985). On the social history of childhood, with some helpful discussion of children's legal status, see John Demos, *A Little Commonwealth: Family Life in Plymouth Colony* (New York, 1970) and Ross W. Beales, Jr., "In Search of the Historical Child: Miniature Adulthood and Youth in Colonial New England," *American Quarterly* 27 (1975), 279–98.

Some helpful primary source collections are Robert H. Bremner, *Children and Youth in America: A Documentary History* (Cambridge, MA, 1970–74), and the older but still useful collection by Grace Abbot *The Child and the State*, 2 vols. (Chicago, 1938).

On children and crime specifically, see Brewer, ch. 6 (above); John R. Sutton, *Stubborn Children: Controlling Delinquency in the United States, 1640–1981* (Berkeley, 1988); and Nancy Hathaway Steenburg, *Children and the Criminal Law in Connecticut, 1635–1855* (New York, 2005). Jane Kamensky, *Governing the Tongue*, also has a chapter on sons' speech and rebellion and punishment (ch. 4), which makes it clear that while New England authorities sought to limit sons' criticism of their parents, they did not effectively do so.

On children and farm labor, see Daniel Vickers, *Farmers & Fishermen: Two Centuries of Work in Essex County, Massachusetts, 1630–1850* (Chapel Hill, 1994).

Vickers sees family labor, and particularly the labor of children, as what the North used instead of the slaves and servants that were more common in the Southern colonies.

On family violence (in addition to the articles mentioned above under the section on wives) see Elizabeth Pleck, *Domestic Tyranny: The Making of American Social Policy Against Family Violence from Colonial Times to the Present* (New York, 1987).

On Labor

There is a broad literature on labor law in England and in early America. On England, see A. L. Beier, *Masterless Men: The Vagrancy Problem in England 1560–1640* (London, 1985); Ann Kussmaul, *Servants and Husbandry in Early Modern England* (Cambridge, 1981); Douglas Hay, "England, 1562–1875: The Law and its Uses" and Christopher Tomlins, "Early British America, 1585–1830: Freedom Bound," both in Douglas Hay and Paul Craven, eds., *Masters, Servants and Magistrates in Britain and the Empire, 1562–1955* (Chapel Hill, 2004); and Peter Laslett, *The World We Have Lost: Further Explored* (New York, 1984), especially chs. 1 & 2, where he lays out an argument that teenage labor of apprentices in others' households was common to all and that early modern England was a "one class" society. Also see E. P. Thompson, *Customs in Common: Studies in Traditional Popular Culture* (New York, 1991).

On apprenticeship particularly, see O. J. Dunlop and Richard Denham, *English Apprenticeship and Child Labor, A History* (New York, 1912); K. D. M. Snell, *Annals of the Labouring Poor: Social Change and Agrarian England, 1660–1900* (Cambridge, 1985); Ilana Krausman Ben-Amos, *Adolescence and Youth in Early Modern England* (New Haven, 1994); and Paul Griffiths, *Youth and Authority: Formative Experiences in England 1560–1640* (New York, 1996).

On the colonial period, see David Galenson, *White Servitude in Colonial America: An Economic Analysis* (Cambridge, 1981); Sharon V. Salinger, *'To Serve Well and Faithfully': Labor and Indentured Servants in Pennsylvania, 1682–1800* (Cambridge, 1987); Lawrence William Towner's dissertation of 1954, which was finally published: *A Good Master Well Served: Masters and Servants in Colonial Massachusetts, 1620–1750* (New York, 1998); Robert Steinfeld, *The Invention of Free Labor: The Employment Relation in English and American Law and Culture, 1350–1870* (Chapel Hill, 1991); Ruth Wallis Herndon, *Unwelcome Americans: Living on the Margin in Early New England* (Philadelphia, 2001), ch. 3 (on apprentices); and Holly Brewer, "Age of Reason?: Children, Testimony and Consent in Early America," in Christopher Tomlins and Bruce Mann, eds., *The Many Legalities of Early America* (Chapel Hill, 2001), 293–332 (on children and forced labor).

On indentured servitude see Peter Wilson Coldham, *Emigrants in Chains: A Social History of Forced Emigration to the Americas of Felons, Destitute Children, Political and Religious Non-Conformists, Vagabonds, Beggars and Other Undesirables, 1607–1776* (Surrey, UK, 1992); Christopher Tomlins, "Indentured Servitude in Perspective: European Migration into North America and the Composition of the Early American Labor Force, 1600–1775," in Cathy Matson, ed., *The Economy of Early America: Historical Perspectives and New Directions* (University Park, PA, 2006), 146–82; and Alison Games, *Migration and the Origins of the English Atlantic World* (Cambridge, MA, 1999). Also see two older books that are rich in cases: Abbot Emerson Smith, *Colonists in Bondage; White Servitude and Convict Labor in America, 1607–1776* (Chapel Hill, 1947), and Richard B. Morris, *Government and Labor in Early America* (New York, 1946). On the Early Republic, see Christopher L. Tomlins, *Law, Labor, and Ideology in the Early American Republic* (Cambridge, 1993); Amy Dru Stanley, *From Bondage to Contract: Wage Labor, Marriage, and the Market in the Age of Slave Emancipation* (New York, 1998); Robert J. Steinfeld, *Coercion, Contract, and Free Labor in the Nineteenth Century* (Cambridge, 2001); Sean Wilentz, *Chants Democratic: New York City & the Rise of the American Working Class, 1788–1850* (New, 1984); and Tomlins, "Subordination, Authority, Law: Subjects in Labor History," *International Labor and Working Class History* 47 (1995), 56–90.

On Blackstone and legal treatises, and the reform of the common law, see Barbara Shapiro, "Law Reform in Seventeenth Century England," *American Journal of Legal History* 19 (1975), 280–312; Shapiro, *Beyond "Reasonable Doubt" and "Probable Cause": Historical Perspectives on the Anglo-American Law of Evidence* (Berkeley, 1991); David Lieberman, *The Province of Legislation Determined: Legal Theory in Eighteenth-Century Britain* (Cambridge, 1989); Herbert A. Johnson, *Imported Eighteenth-Century Law Treatises in American Libraries, 1700–1799* (Knoxville, 1978); and Brewer, *By Birth or Consent*, chs. 5–7 and appendix.

On Blackstone's influence, see Donald S. Lutz, "The Relative Influence of European Writers on Late-Eighteenth-Century American Political Thought," *American Political Science Review* 78 (1984), 189–97; Duncan Kennedy, "The Structure of Blackstone's Commentaries," *Buffalo Law Review*, 28 (1979), 205–382; and Wilfred Prest, *Dictionary of National Biography*, s.v. "William Blackstone." Also see J. R. Pole "Reflections on American Law and the American Revolution," *William and Mary Quarterly*, 3rd ser., 50 (1993), 122–59.

CHAPTER 10: LAW AND RELIGION IN COLONIAL AMERICA

MARK McGARVIE AND ELIZABETH MENSCH

The best general histories on the roles of religion and its establishment in early American society are probably still S. E. Ahlstrom, *A Religious History of the American* People (New Haven, CT, 1972); W. W. Sweet, *The Story of Religion in America* (1930; New York, 1950); R. S. Handy, *A Christian America* (New York, 1971); W. S. Hudson and J. Corrigan, *Religion in America* (New York, 1992); and a collection of essays in honor of Professor Leo Pfeffer edited by J. E. Wood, Jr., *Religion and the State* (Waco, TX, 1985). A recent general history of the colonies by A. Taylor, *American Colonies* (New York, 2001), effectively incorporates the role of religion and also of British colonizing in relation to Indians and African Americans. The decline of colonial religious establishments is best presented in the works of S. E. Mead, most significantly *The Lively Experiment* (1963; New York, 2007).

A growing body of work on Indian missions in the colonial era is highlighted by R. Galgano, *Feast of Souls* (Albuquerque, NM, 2005); K. O. Kupperman, *Indians and English* (Ithaca, NY, 2000); and J. Axtell, *The European and the Indian* (New York, 1981) and *After Columbus* (New York, 1988). Jill Lepore, *The Name of War* (New York,1998), presents insights into the tension within Indian societies precipitated by converted or "praying Indians."

Many authors have emphasized the communitarian aspects of colonial society and the extent to which law and religion worked together to build and sustain a communitarian ethic, including S. Botein, *Early American Law and Society* (New York, 1983), and K. McCarthy, *American Creed* (Chicago, 2003). On communities in the Southern colonies, including Virginia, see D. B. Rutman and A. H. Rutman, *A Place in Time* (New York, 1984); A. Kulikoff, *Tobacco and Slaves* (Chapel Hill, NC, 1986); J. G. Kolb, *Gentlemen and Freeholders* (Baltimore, 1998); and James R. Perry, Jr., *The Formation of a Society on Virginia's Eastern Shore, 1615–1655* (Chapel Hill, NC, 1990). The extent to which deference to a local elite, often reinforced by religious doctrines and institutions, frustrated individualism and democracy throughout colonial America is examined in a series of essays in Michael G. Kammen, ed., *Politics and Society in Colonial America* (Chapel Hill, NC, 1967). The works of Perry Miller establish a strong basis for understanding New England communitarianism in the 1600s, which eroded under the economic and social pressures in the 1700s. Ironically, numerous studies in the 1970s and 1980s tended more to confirm Miller's declension thesis than to fulfill their intention of challenging it: see K. Lockridge, *A New England Town* (New York, 1970); J. R. T. Hughes, *Social Control in the Colonial Economy* (Charlottesville, VA, 1976); L. T. Urich, *Good Wives* (Philadelphia, 1980); E. S. Morgan, *The Puritan Family* (New York, 1966); and B. C. Daniels, *Puritans at Play* (Houndmills, NY,1995). A discussion of New England's Calvinist communitarianism achieved while recognizing the need to separate church and state is presented in T. H. Breen, *The Good Ruler* (New Haven, CT, 1970). A description of the colonial religious establishment and its support of communitarian values appears in an early chapter of a work focusing primarily on the process of disestablishment during and after the Revolution: M. D. McGarvie, *One Nation Under Law* (Dekalb, IL, 2004). *The Many Legalities of Early America*, edited by C. L. Tomlins and B. H. Mann (Chapel Hill, NC, 2001), contains several essays stressing the role of law in negotiating the meaning of "community" in the colonies. The similarity of colonial New Englanders and Virginians in their struggles between pious parochialism and striving cosmopolitanism in the eighteenth century is explored in

K. A. Lockridge, *Settlement and Unsettlement in Early America* (Baton Rouge, LA, 1981). A contrast between colonial Puritan and English Anglican enforcement of Christian ethical prescription can be found in D. Underdown, *Revel, Riot, and Rebellion* (New York, 1987). D. Lovejoy, *The Glorious Revolution in America* (New York, 1972), provides an account of the interplay between religious/political conflict in England and in the colonies. On the growth of religious toleration in the eighteenth century contrasted with the seventeenth-century desires for religious homogeneity achieved through persecution, see Chris Beneke, *Beyond Toleration* (New York, 2006).

Leading works in intellectual history have concentrated on the changing religious beliefs and practices of colonial Americans: see A. E. Heimert, *Religion and the American Mind from the Great Awakening to the Revolution* (Cambridge, MA, 1966); P. Bonomi, *Under the Cope of Heaven* (New York, 1986); J. Butler, *Awash in a Sea of Faith* (Cambridge, MA, 1990); D. Hall, *Worlds of Wonder, Days of Judgment* (New York, 1989); and N. A. Hatch, *The Sacred Cause of Liberty* (New Haven, CT, 1977) and *The Democratization of American Christianity* (New Haven, CT, 1989). Many books have interpreted the intellectual and cultural significance of Jonathan Edwards and his role in the Great Awakening. The classic interpretation is P. Miller, *Jonathan Edwards* (New York, 1949). G. Marsden, *Jonathan Edwards: A Life* (New Haven, CT, 2003), is a recent reinterpretation that questions some of Miller's assertions. These works are easily integrated with complementary works in social and political history that consider changes in American culture as precipitants to revolution. Much of this scholarship has documented the rise of commercial culture and individual freedoms as coterminous with the decline of the communitarian ethic and of religious influence in colonial law and social structure. See R. Godbeer, *Sexual Revolution in Early America* (Baltimore, 2002); B. Bailyn, *The New England Merchants in the Seventeenth Century* (Cambridge, MA, 1955); R. L. Bushman, *From Puritan to Yankee* (Cambridge, MA, 1967); and J. P. Greene, *Pursuits of Happiness* (Chapel Hill, NC, 1988). An excellent general history of poverty in colonial America contains various essays addressing the reliance on religious sentiments and institutions to address this social problem: B. G. Smith, ed., *Down and Out in Early America* (University Park, PA, 2004).

The colonial economy, with its tension between Christian and market norms, is examined in J. Henretta, *The Origins of American Capitalism: Collected Essays* (New York, 1999) and J. McCusker and R. Menard, *The Economy of British America 1607–1789* (Chapel Hill, NC, 1985). A perspective somewhat at odds from that presented herein, asserting that Puritan Massachusetts embodied proto-capitalist values, is presented in S. Innes, *Creating the Commonwealth: The Economic Culture of Puritan New England* (New York, 1995). E. B. Holifield, *Era of Persuasion: American Thought and Culture, 1521–1680* (Boston, 1989), examines the colonists' use of texts and argument in relation to each other and to native cultures.

Probably the leading works on the legal history of early Massachusetts are W. E. Nelson, *Americanization of the Common Law* (Cambridge, MA, 1975) and *Dispute and Conflict Resolution in Plymouth County, Massachusetts 1725–1825* (Chapel Hill, NC, 1981). See also D. T. Konig, *Law and Society in Puritan Massachusetts* (Chapel Hill, NC, 1979); E. Powers, *Crime and Punishment in Early Massachusetts, 1620–1692* (Boston, 1966); and N. E. H. Hull, *Female Felons* (Urbana, IL, 1987). On issues of social and religious conformity, see T. A. Breen, *Transgressing the Bounds* (New York, 2001). On the relation of religion to material culture see C. L. Heyrman, *Commerce and Culture* (Chapel Hill, NC, 1984). See also J. P. Reid, *Rule of Law* (New York, 2004); E. J. McManus, *Law and Liberty in Early New England* (Amherst, MA, 1993); and G. L. Haskins, *Law and Authority in Early Massachusetts* (New York, 1960). On law and religious discipline in early Massachusetts see T. D. Bozeman, *The Precisionist Strain* (Chapel Hill, NC, 2004), and J. F. Cooper, Jr., *Tenacious in Their Liberties* (New York, 1999). Edmund S. Morgan, in *Visible Saints: The History of a Puritan Idea* (Ithaca, NY, 1963), relates the dilemma of inclusion/exclusion in relation to Puritan church membership. A good microhistory case study of law, religion, and cultural values in colonial Massachusetts is J. Pagan, *Anne Orthwood's Bastard* (New York, 2003). The role of dissenters in early Massachusetts is well recorded in W. G. McLoughlin, *New England Dissent, 1630–1833* (Cambridge, MA, 1971). The extent to which law, religious doctrine, and spiritualism were intertwined is developed in D. L. Winiarski, "'Pale Bluish Lights and a Dead Man's Groan': Tales of the Supernatural from Eighteenth-Century Plymouth Massachusetts," *William and Mary Quarterly*, 3rd series, 54 (1998), 497–530.

The era of witchcraft trials has been subject to myriad and various interpretations, among which are P. C. Hoffer, *The Salem Witchcraft Trials* (Lawrence, KS, 1997); C. F. Karlsen, *The Devil in the Shape of a Woman* (Chapel Hill, NC, 1987); C. W. Upham, *Salem Witchcraft* (Boston, 2000); C. Hansen, *Witchcraft at Salem* (New York, 1969); and M. Starkey, *The Devil in Massachusetts* (New York, 1949).

The influence of religion on the laws and institutions of Rhode Island is developed in S. V. James, *Colonial Rhode Island: A History* (New York, 1975); *John Clarke and His Legacies: Religion and the Law in Colonial Rhode Island, 1638–1750* (University Park, PA, 1999); and *The Colonial Metamorphosis in Rhode Island: A Study of Institutions of Change* (Hanover, NH, 2000); as well as in G. S. Kimball, *Providence in Colonial Times* (Boston, 1912). Among the interpretations of Roger Williams' pivotal role are D. Shaggs, *Roger Williams' Dream for America* (New York, 1933); T. Hall, *Separating Church and State: Roger Williams and Religious Liberty* (Champaign, Il, 1998); E. S. Gaustad, *Liberty of Conscience: Roger Williams in America* (Grand Rapids, MI, 1991); and E. Morgan, *Roger Williams: The Church and the State* (New York, 1967).

The complex interaction among law, religion, and cultural change in colonial Pennsylvania is especially accessible through an influential study: B. Levy,

Quakers and the American Family: British Settlement in the Delaware Valley (New York, 1988). Other treatments include F. Tolles, *Meeting House to Counting House: The Quaker Merchants of Colonial Philadelphia, 1682–1763* (New York, 1948); D. Rothermund, *The Layman's Progress: Religious and Political Experience in Colonial Pennsylvania, 1740–1770* (Philadelphia, 1961); S. G. Wolf, *Urban Village: Population, Community, and Family Structure in Germantown, Pennsylvania* (Princeton, 1976); A. S. Fogleman, *Hopeful Journeys: German Immigration, Settlement, and Political Culture in Colonial America 1717–1775* (Philadelphia, 1996); and M. Zuckerman, ed., *Friends and Neighbors: Group Life in America's First Plural Society* (Philadelphia, 1982). A. G. Roeber, *Palatines, Liberty, and Property: German Lutherans and Colonial British America* (Baltimore, 1993), shows the important role of German immigrants in shaping conceptions of public and private. L. Riforgiato, *Missionary of Moderation: Henry Melchoir Muhlenberg and the Lutheran Church in English America* (Lewisburg, PA, 1980), traces the particular career of the influential Lutheran minister. Several authors have described Pennsylvania and the mid-Atlantic states, in contrast to New England, as developing an early emphasis on individualism and a market economy because of heterogeneous populations and a devaluation of religion: G. Nash, "Social Development," in J. P. Greene and J. R. Pole, eds., *Colonial British America: Essays in the New History of the Early Modern Era* (Baltimore, 1984), 233–61, esp. 233–39, and J. T. Lemon, *The Best Poor Man's Country: A Geographical Study of Southeastern Pennsylvania* (Baltimore, 1972).

A number of books provide a general background on the often convoluted politics of colonial New York in relation to its social and economic life. Examples are P. Bonomi, *A Factious People: Politics and Society in Colonial New York* (New York, 1971); M. Kammen, *Colonial New York: A History* (New York, 1975); and M. Klein, ed., *The Politics of Diversity: Essays in the History of Colonial New York* (Port Washington, NY, 1974). G. Smith, *Religion and Trade in New Netherland* (Ithaca, NY, 1973), describes religion in relation to law, politics, and the economy in the early years. For the Glorious Revolution rebellion and its aftermath, see J. Reich, *Leisler's Rebellion: A Study of Democracy in New York 1669–1720* (Chicago, 1953). Both S. Kim, *Landlord and Tenant in Colonial New York: Manorial Society, 1664–1775* (Chapel Hill, NC, 1978), and I. Mark, *Agrarian Conflicts in Colonial New York 1711–1775* (New York, 1940), describe land grant disputes. Those disputes are put in the context of religious conflict in E. Mensch, "The Colonial Origins of Liberal Property Rights," *Buffalo Law Review* 31 (1982), 635, and "Religion, Revival and The Ruling Class: A Critical History of Trinity Church," *Buffalo Law Review* 36 (1987), Part II: 427. Books covering the more immediate pre-Revolutionary period include E. Countryman, *A People in Revolution: The American Revolution and Political Society in New York, 1760–1790* (Baltimore, 1981), and D. Dillon, *The New York Triumvirate: A Study of the Legal and Political Careers of Williams Livingston, John Morin Scott, and William Smith, Jr.* (New York, 1949). A valuable recent study, focusing specifically on the Dutch in relation to Anglican establishment, is R. Balmer, *A Perfect Babel of Confusion: Dutch Religion and English Culture in the Middle Colonies* (New York, 1989).

Any work on the religious and legal culture in colonial Virginia should begin with R. Isaac, *The Transformation of Virginia* (Chapel Hill, NC, 1982), and E. L. Bond, *Damned Souls in a Tobacco Colony* (Macon, GA, 2000). Timothy Breen has written excellent works distinguishing colonial Virginia from colonial Massachusetts: see his books, *Puritans and Adventurers* (New York, 1980) and *Tobacco Culture* (Princeton, 1985). Good summaries of early Virginia legal culture can be gained from A. G. Roeber, *Faithful Magistrates and Republican Lawyers* (Chapel Hill, NC, 1981), and G. L. Chumbly, *Colonial Justice in Virginia* (Richmond, VA, 1938). The extent to which religion and the authority of the church influence criminal prosecutions in colonial Virginia is available in A. P. Scott, *Criminal Law in Colonial Virginia* (Chicago, 1930). Eighteenth-century Virginia ideas on religious freedom are addressed in Daniel L. Dreisbach, "Thomas Jefferson and Bills Number 82–86 of the Revision of the Laws of Virginia, 1776–1786: New Light on the Jefferson Model of Church-State Relations," *North Carolina Law Review* 159 (1990), 69; E. Fleet, "Madison's Detached Memoranda," *William and Mary Quarterly*, 3rd series, 3 (1946): 534–68; F. J. Hood, "Revolution and Religious Liberty: The Conservation of the Theocratic Concept in Virginia," *Church History* 40–2 (1971), 170–81; and T. E. Buckley, *Church and State in Revolutionary Virginia, 1776–1787* (Charlottesville, VA, 1977).

Maryland's colonial legal history and the influences of religious strife and ultimate Anglican establishment on it are available in G. A. Wood, *The French Presence in Maryland, 1524–1800* (Baltimore, 1978); L. G. Carr and D. Jordan, *Maryland's Revolution of Government, 1689–1692* (Ithaca, NY, 1974); M. Graham, "Meetinghouse and Chapel: Religion and Community in 17th Century Maryland," in L. G. Carr, P. D. Morgan, and J. B. Russo, eds., *Colonial Chesapeake* (Chapel Hill, NC, 1988), 242–74; A. E. Matthews, "The Religious Experience of Southern Women," in R. Ruether and R. S. Keller, eds., *Women and Religion in America, Vol. 2: The Colonial and Revolutionary Periods* (New York, 1981), 193–232; J. H. Smith, "The Foundations of Law in Maryland, 1634–1715," in G. A. Billias, ed., *Selected Essays: Law and Authority in Colonial America* (Berkeley, 1965), 92–115; J. D. Krugler, "Lord Baltimore, Roman Catholics, and Toleration: Religious Policy in Maryland During the Early Catholic Years, 1634–1649," *Catholic Historical Review* 65 (1979), 49–75; T. P. Pyne, "A Plea for Maryland Catholics Reconsidered," *Maryland Historical Magazine* 92 (1997), 163–81; B. B. Hardy, "Roman Catholics, Not Papists: Catholic Identity in Maryland, 1689–1776," *Maryland Historical Magazine* 92 (1997), 139–61; E. A. Kessel, "A Mighty Fortress Is Our God: German Religious and Educational Organizations on the Maryland Frontier, 1734–1800," *Maryland Historical Magazine* 77 (1982), 370–87; and J. D. Krugler, "Sir George Calvert's

Resignation as Secretary of State and the Founding of Maryland," *Maryland Historical Magazine* 63 (1973), 239–54.

CHAPTER 11: THE TRANSFORMATION OF LAW AND ECONOMY

BRUCE H. MANN

The rich historiography of law in early America includes little of the sustained discussion of law and the economy that has marked the historiography of the nineteenth century. That is partly because the earlier period does not have its Morton J. Horwitz, whose *The Transformation of American Law, 1780–1860* (Cambridge, MA, 1977) set the terms of debate for the nineteenth century. This is not to say that legal historians of early America have ignored the economy; only that their primary interests have more often lain elsewhere. A few notable exceptions aside, one is most often left to search studies of different elements of the various colonial economies for stray references to law.

One of the notable exceptions is David Thomas Konig, whose *Law and Society in Puritan Massachusetts: Essex County, 1629–1692* (Chapel Hill, NC, 1979) has a fine chapter on the social and economic dimensions of real property litigation. Narrower, but still valuable, discussions of property issues include George L. Haskins, "The Beginnings of the Recording System in Massachusetts," *Boston University Law Review* 21 (1941), 281–304 and the chapter on land distribution and alienation in Richard B. Morris, *Studies in the History of American Law with Special Reference to the Seventeenth and Eighteenth Centuries* (2nd ed., Philadelphia, 1959). The best case study of land tenancy is Stephen Innes, *Labor in a New Land: Economy and Society in Seventeenth-Century Springfield* (Princeton, NJ, 1983).

The essential overview of the economy for the period is John J. McCusker and Russell R. Menard, *The Economy of British America, 1607–1789* (Chapel Hill, NC, 1985). Also valuable is Marc Egnal, *New World Economies: The Growth of the Thirteen Colonies and Early Canada* (New York, 1998). A fine work on the economic culture of New England in the seventeenth century, with particular emphasis on government regulation of the economy, is Stephen Innes, *Creating the Commonwealth: The Economic Culture of Puritan New England* (New York, 1995). For commercial activity in the same period, Bernard Bailyn, *The New England Merchants in the Seventeenth Century* (Cambridge, MA, 1955), remains invaluable. Good discussions of wage regulations are Richard B. Morris and Jonathan Grossman, "The Regulation of Wages in Early Massachusetts," *New England Quarterly* 11 (1938), 470–500 and Richard B. Morris, *Government and Labor in Early America* (New York, 1946).

For law and the economy in Virginia before the rise of tobacco, see David Thomas Konig, "'Dale's Laws' and the Non-Common Law Origins of Criminal Justice in Virginia," *American Journal of Legal History* 26 (1982), 354–75. For the period after tobacco became king, Allan Kulikoff, *Tobacco and Slaves: The Development of Southern Cultures in the Chesapeake, 1680–1800* (Chapel Hill,

NC, 1986), is particularly useful on attempts to regulate tobacco production and quality. For tobacco regulation in Maryland, see Mary McKinney Schweitzer, "Economic Regulation and the Colonial Economy: The Maryland Tobacco Inspection Act of 1747," *Journal of Economic History* 40 (1980), 551–69. A good introduction to bound and unfree labor in Virginia is Warren M. Billings, "The Law of Servants and Slaves in Seventeenth-Century Virginia," *Virginia Magazine of History and Biography* 99 (1991), 45–62. More comprehensive studies of indentured servitude are Abbott Emerson Smith, *Colonists in Bondage: White Servitude and Convict Labor in America, 1607–1776* (Chapel Hill, NC, 1947), and David W. Galenson, *White Servitude in Colonial America: An Economic Analysis* (Cambridge, 1981). Studies of slavery abound. Particularly useful for gleaning insights into the relationship between the law of slavery and the economy are David W. Galenson, "Economic Aspects of the Growth of Slavery in the Seventeenth-Century Chesapeake," in Barbara L. Solow, ed., *Slavery and the Rise of the Atlantic System* (Cambridge, 1991), 265–92, and Jacob M. Price, "Credit in the Slave Trade and Plantation Economies," also in Solow, ed., *Slavery and the Rise of the Atlantic System*, 293–339. Essential discussions of the role of credit in the plantation economies include two studies by Russell R. Menard: "Financing the Lowcountry Export Boom: Capital and Growth in Early South Carolina," *William and Mary Quarterly*, 3rd ser., 51 (1994), 659–76, and "Law, Credit, the Supply of Labour, and the Organization of Sugar Production in the Colonial Greater Caribbean: A Comparison of Brazil and Barbados in the Seventeenth Century," in John J. McCusker and Kenneth Morgan, eds., *The Early Modern Atlantic Economy* (Cambridge, 2000), 154–62; as well as Jacob M. Price, *Capital and Credit in British Overseas Trade: The View from the Chesapeake, 1700–1776* (Cambridge, MA, 1980). Peter Mathias, "Risk, Credit and Kinship in Early Modern Enterprise," in McCusker and Morgan, eds., *The Early Modern Atlantic Economy*, 15–35, provides an even broader perspective.

Bruce H. Mann, *Neighbors and Strangers: Law and Community in Early Connecticut* (Chapel Hill, NC, 1987), offers a sustained discussion of the relationship between law and economy in a Northern colony, with particular reference to different ways of contracting debts. Deborah A. Rosen, *Courts and Commerce: Gender, Law, and the Market Economy in Colonial New York* (Columbus, Ohio, 1997), presents confirming evidence from New York. David Thomas Konig, "The Virgin and the Virgin's Sister: Virginia, Massachusetts, and the Contested Legacy of Colonial Law," in Russell K. Osgood, ed., *The History of the Law in Massachusetts: The Supreme Judicial Court, 1692–1992* (Boston, 1992), 81–115, is an invaluable comparative study. A good technical study of commercial credit instruments is Herbert A. Johnson, *The Law Merchant and Negotiable Instruments in Colonial New York, 1664 to 1730* (Chicago, 1963).

To understand the complex issues of paper money, land banks, and finance, the best place to start is the rich account by Margaret Ellen Newell, *From Dependency to Independence: Economic Revolution in Colonial New England* (Ithaca, NY, 1998). Older, but still valuable, introductions are Roger W. Weiss, "The

Issue of Paper Money in the American Colonies, 1720–1774," *Journal of Economic History* 30 (1970), 770–84, and Theodore Thayer, "The Land Bank System in the American Colonies," *Journal of Economic History* 13 (1953), 145–59. Edwin J. Perkins, *American Public Finance and Financial Services, 1700–1815* (Columbus, OH, 1994), remains an important study, as, of course, does E. James Ferguson, *The Power of the Purse: A History of American Public Finance, 1776–1790* (Chapel Hill, NC, 1961). Peter J. Coleman, *Debtors and Creditors in America: Insolvency, Imprisonment for Debt, and Bankruptcy, 1607–1900* (Madison, WI, 1974), is the standard reference work on colonial and state statutory mechanisms for dealing with failure. A much broader approach to failure is Bruce H. Mann, *Republic of Debtors: Bankruptcy in the Age of American Independence* (Cambridge, MA, 2002). Carl S. Bridenbaugh, *Cities in Revolt: Urban Life in America, 1743–1776* (New York, 1955), remains useful for its descriptions of the impact of war on urban economies.

Recent work on the spread of banks after the Revolution includes Perkins, *American Public Finance and Financial Services* and two works by Robert E. Wright: *The Wealth of Nations Rediscovered: Integration and Expansion in American Financial Markets, 1780–1850* (Cambridge, 2002) and *Origins of Commercial Banking in America, 1750–1800* (Lanham, MD, 2001). Howard Bodenhorn, *State Banking in Early America: A New Economic History* (New York, 2003), despite its title, focuses primarily on the antebellum era, but it touches on the Early Republic. Still useful is Bray Hammond, *Banks and Politics in America, from the Revolution to the Civil War* (Princeton, NJ, 1957). For corporations in the Early Republic, a good place to begin is Pauline Maier, "The Revolutionary Origins of the American Corporation," *William and Mary Quarterly*, 3rd ser., 50 (1993), 51–84. Older works by Joseph Stancliffe Davis, *Essays in the Earlier History of American Corporations*, 2 vols. (Cambridge, MA, 1917), and Shaw Livermore, *Early American Land Companies: Their Influence on Corporate Development* (New York, 1939), remain valuable, but they are reminders of how little has been written on the corporation before its rise to economic and legal preeminence in the nineteenth century.

CHAPTER 12: LAW AND COMMERCE, 1580–1815

CLAIRE PRIEST

(1) Depictions of American Founding Era Policies as Mercantilist

Works describing Founding Era America as "mercantilist" or "neo-mercantilist" or as focused on empire-building include William Appleman Williams, *The Contours of American History* (New York, 1973); James G. Wilson, *The Imperial Republic: A Structural History of American Constitutionalism from the Colonial Era to the Beginning of the Twentieth Century* (Burlington, VT, 2002); Niall Ferguson, *Colossus: The Price of America's Empire* (New York, 2004); Calvin H. Johnson, *Righteous Anger at the Wicked States: The Meaning of the Founders'*

Constitution (New York, 2005); Harry N. Scheiber, "Economic Liberty and the Modern State," in Harry N. Scheiber, ed., *The State and Freedom of Contract* (Stanford, CA, 1998); and John E. Crowley, *The Privileges of Independence: Neomercantilism and the American Revolution* (Baltimore, MD, 1993).

(2) The British Empire Before the American Revolution

LEGAL REGULATION OF COMMERCE: THE NAVIGATION ACTS AND THE COLONIES

Adam Smith's *An Inquiry into the Nature and Causes of the Wealth of Nations* (1776), Book Four, remains an essential account of the legal regulation of the British Empire. Scholarship on the British Empire of the seventeenth and eighteenth centuries is still dominated by older comprehensive accounts, including Lawrence Henry Gipson, *The British Empire before the American Revolution*, 15 vols. (Caldwell, ID, 1936–70); Lawrence Henry Gipson, *The Coming of the Revolution, 1763–1775* (New York, 1954); George Louis Beer, *The Old Colonial System, 1660–1754* (New York, 1912), *The Origins of the British Colonial System, 1578–1660* (New York, 1908), and *British Colonial Policy, 1754 1765* (New York, 1907); Charles M. Andrews, *The Colonial Period of American History*, especially *Vol. 4: England's Commercial and Colonial Policy* (New Haven, CT, 1938); Lawrence A. Harper, *The English Navigation Laws: A Seventeenth-Century Experiment in Social Engineering* (New York, 1939); and Charles Wilson, *Profit and Power: A Study of England and the Dutch Wars* (New York, 1957).

More recent important works are John J. McCusker, "British Mercantilist Policies and the American Colonies," in Stanley L. Engerman and Robert E. Gallman eds., *The Cambridge Economic History of the United States*, vol. 1 (New York, 1996), 337–62; Jack P. Greene, *Peripheries and Center: Constitutional Development in the Extended Polities of the British Empire and the United States, 1607–1788* (Athens, GA, 1986); Michael Kammen, *Empire and Interest: The American Colonies and the Politics of Mercantilism* (Philadelphia, PA, 1970); and Robert Paul Thomas, "A Quantitative Approach to the Study of the Effects of British Imperial Policy upon Colonial Welfare: Some Preliminary Findings," *Journal of Economic History* 25 (1965), 615–38. A more comprehensive list of sources can be found in the notes of John J. McCusker and Russell R. Menard, *The Economy of British America, 1607–1789* (Chapel Hill, NC, 1991), 35–50.

ENGLISH DOMESTIC POLITICS AND POLICIES

Two recent works powerfully demonstrate the links between the emergence of democracy and the English financial revolution of the seventeenth and eighteenth centuries: James Macdonald, *A Free Nation Deep in Debt: The Financial Roots of Democracy* (New York, 2003), and Niall Ferguson, *The Cash Nexus: Money and Power in the Modern World, 1700–2000* (New York, 2001). The connections between the development of the English central state and the English navy are explored in Paul M. Kennedy, *The Rise and Fall of British Naval*

Mastery (Amherst, NY, 1998). For a detailed account of the contested politics underlying the enactment of the Navigation Acts and England's entry into the Anglo-Dutch Wars, see Steven C. A. Pincus, *Protestantism and Patriotism: Ideologies and the Making of English Foreign Policy, 1650–1668* (New York, 1996) and "From Holy Cause to Economic Interest: The Study of Population and the Invention of the State," in Alan Houston and Steve Pincus, eds., *A Nation Transformed: England After the Restoration* (New York, 2001), 272–98.

CUSTOMS ENFORCEMENT AND COLONIAL SMUGGLING

The best accounts of the development of the colonial customs service and the Vice-admiralty courts in colonial America are Thomas C. Barrow, *Trade and Empire: The British Customs Service in Colonial America, 1660–1775* (Cambridge, MA, 1967); Oliver M. Dickerson, *The Navigation Acts and the American Revolution* (Philadelphia, PA, 1951); and Carl Ubbelohde, *The Vice-Admiralty Courts and the American Revolution* (Chapel Hill, NC, 1960). The most important new work on the operation of the vice-admiralty courts is David R. Owen and Michael C. Tolley, *Courts of Admiralty in Colonial America: The Maryland Experience, 1634–1776* (Durham, NC, 1995). On smuggling into North America from the non-English Caribbean and trade with the enemy during the Seven Years War, see Richard Pares, *War and Trade in the West Indies, 1739–1763* (London, 1963); John W. Tyler, "The Long Shadow of Benjamin Barons: The Politics of Illicit Trade at Boston, 1760–1762," *American Neptune* 40 (1980), 245–79; Albert B. Southwick, "The Molasses Act – Source of Precedents," *William and Mary Quarterly*, 3rd ser., 8 (1951), 389–405; and Richard Sheridan, "The Molasses Act and the Market Strategy of the British Sugar Planters," *Journal of Economic History* 17 (1957), 62–83.

(3) Colonial Legal and Economic Development

The section on colonial monetary policy draws from earlier work: Claire Priest, "Currency Policies and Legal Development in Colonial New England," *Yale Law Journal* 110 (2001), 1303–1405; Claire Priest, "Colonial Courts and Secured Credit: Early American Commercial Litigation and Shays' Rebellion," *Yale Law Journal* 108 (1999), 2413–2450; as well as Leslie V. Brock, *The Currency of the American Colonies, 1700–1764: A Study in Colonial Finance and Imperial Relations* (New York, 1975); Curtis P. Nettels, *The Money Supply of the American Colonies Before 1720* (Clifton, NJ, 1973); and James H. Soltow, *The Economic Role of Williamsburg* (Williamsburg, VA, 1965). The section on colonial property policy derives from Claire Priest, "Creating an American Property Law: Alienability and Its Limits in American History," *Harvard Law Review* 120 (2006), 385–459. The section on commercial policy and inspection draws from Albert Anthony Giesecke, *American Commercial Legislation Before 1789* (Union, New Jersey, 2001 [1910]), and Arthur L. Jensen, *The Maritime Commerce of Colonial Philadelphia* (Madison, WI, 1963). The discussion of colonial arbitration draws from Morton J. Horwitz, *The Transformation of American Law, 1780–1860* (Cambridge, MA, 1977), 140–59, and Eben Moglen, "Commercial Arbitration in the Eighteenth Century: Searching for the Transformation of American Law," *Yale Law Journal* 93 (1983), 135–52.

Colonial legislation on economic matters has been studied most extensively by historians and economic historians in local studies. The most useful of these accounts are, for the New England colonies, Bernard Bailyn, *The New England Merchants in the Seventeenth Century* (Cambridge, MA, 1979), and W. T. Baxter, *The House of Hancock: Business in Boston, 1724–1775* (Cambridge, MA, 1945); for the Middle Atlantic colonies, Arthur L. Jensen, *The Maritime Commerce of Colonial Philadelphia* (Madison, WI, 1963); Thomas M. Doerflinger, *A Vigorous Spirit of Enterprise: Merchants and Economic Development in Revolutionary Philadelphia* (Chapel Hill, NC, 1986); Harrold E. Gillingham, *Marine Insurance in Philadelphia, 1721–1800* (Philadelphia, PA, 1933); Herbert Alan Johnson, *The Law Merchant and Negotiable Instruments in Colonial New York, 1664–1730* (Chicago, 1963); and Virginia D. Harrington, *The New York Merchant on the Eve of the Revolution* (New York, 1935); for the Southern continental colonies, James H. Soltow, *The Economic Role of Williamsburg* (Williamsburg, VA, 1965); Jacob M. Price, *Capital and Credit in the British Overseas Trade: The View from the Chesapeake, 1700–1776* (Cambridge, MA, 1980); and S. Max Edelson, *Plantation Enterprise in Colonial South Carolina* (Cambridge, MA, 2006); for the West Indies, Richard B. Sheridan, *Sugar and Slavery, An Economic History of the British West Indies, 1623–1775* (Jamaica, 1994); Russell R. Menard, "Law, Credit, the Supply of Labour, and the Organization of Sugar Production in the Colonial Greater Caribbean: A Comparison of Brazil and Barbados in the Seventeenth Century," in John J. McCusker and Kenneth Morgan, eds., *The Early Modern Atlantic Economy* (New York, 2000), 154–62; Jacob M. Price, "Credit in the Slave Trade and Plantation Economies," in Barbara L. Solow ed., *Slavery and the Rise of the Atlantic System* (New York, 1991), 293–339; Richard Pares, *Yankees and Creoles: The Trade Between North America and the West Indies Before the American Revolution* (Cambridge, MA, 1956) and *Merchants and Planters* (New York, 1960). On indentured servitude, see David W. Galenson, "Labor Market Behavior in colonial America: Servitude, Slavery, and Free Labor," in David W. Galenson, ed., *Markets in History: Economic Studies of the Past* (New York, 1989), 52–96 and David W. Galenson, *White Servitude in Colonial America: An Economic Analysis* (New York, 1981). On slave importation to the colonies, see Darlene Clark Hine, William C. Hine, and Stanley Harrold, *The African-American Odyssey* (Upper Saddle River, NJ, 2006).

The most useful reference surveying the economic history of the four major regions of the continental colonies is John J. McCusker and Russell R. Menard, *The Economy of British America, 1607–1789* (Chapel Hill, NC, 1991). Marc Egnal has synthesized data on colonial economic growth in *New World Economies: The Growth of the Thirteen Colonies and Early Canada* (New York, 1998). Other important general accounts are Edwin J. Perkins, *The Economy of Colonial America* (New York, 1980), and *The Cambridge Economic History of the United States*, Stanley L. Engerman and Robert E. Gallman eds., vol. 1 (New York, 1996). For an examination of cultural differences between colonial regions, see Jack P. Greene, *Pursuits of Happiness, The Social Development of Early Modern British Colonies and the Formation of American Culture* (Chapel Hill, NC, 1988).

(4) Revolutionary War and Founding Era

The section on Founding Era policies draws from reports to Congress in the *American State Papers*; Congressional debates in the *Annals of Congress*; and the sources included in *Early American Imprints, Series I: Evans, 1639–1800* (Readex), *Eighteenth Century Collections Online* (Gale), and *the Making of Modern Law: Legal Treatises, 1800–1926* (Gale).

The following list is a small sample of the tremendous body of scholarship on the legal, political, and economic history of the Founding period. Scholarship on the origins of the American Revolution and the Constitution include T. H. Breen, *The Marketplace of Revolution: How Consumer Politics Shaped American Independence* (New York, 2004); Curtis P. Nettels, *The Emergence of a National Economy, 1775–1815* (White Plains, NY, 1962); Richard Buel, Jr., *In Irons: Britain's Naval Supremacy and the American Revolutionary Economy* (New Haven, CT, 1998); Frederick W. Marks, III, *Independence on Trial: Foreign Affairs and the Making of the Constitution* (Baton Rouge, LA, 1973); Calvin H. Johnson, *Righteous Anger at the Wicked States: The Meaning of the Founders' Constitution* (New York, 2005); James F. Shepherd & Gary M. Walton, *Shipping, Maritime Trade, and the Economic Development of Colonial North America* (Cambridge, UK, 1972); Louis Hartz, *Economic Policy and Democratic Thought: Pennsylvania, 1776–1860* (Cambridge, MA, 1948); Orrin Leslie Elliott, *The Tariff Controversy in the United States, 1789–1833* (Palo Alto, CA, 1892); and Malcolm Rogers Eiselen, *The Rise of Pennsylvania Protectionism* (New York, 1974).

Each of us writing in this field is, of course, indebted to the scholarship of the great colonial and Revolutionary era scholars Edmund S. Morgan, Bernard Bailyn, and Gordon Wood: see Edmund S. Morgan, *American Slavery, American Freedom: The Ordeal of Colonial Virginia* (New York, 1975), *Inventing the People: The Rise of Popular Sovereignty in England and America* (New York, 1988), and *The Birth of the Republic, 1763–89* (Chicago, 1992); Edmund S. Morgan and Helen M. Morgan, *The Stamp Act Crisis: Prologue to Revolution* (Chapel Hill, NC, 1995 [1953]); Gordon S. Wood, *The Radicalism of the American Revolution* (New York, 1993), *The Creation of the American Republic, 1776–1787* (Chapel Hill, 1969), and *The American Revolution: A History* (New York, 2003); and Bernard Bailyn, *The Ideological Origins of the American Revolution* (Cambridge, MA, 1967), *The New England Merchants in the Seventeenth Century* (Cambridge, MA, 1979), *Atlantic History: Concept and Contours* (Cambridge, MA, 2005), and *The Ordeal of Thomas Hutchinson* (Cambridge, MA, 1974).

The best scholarship on Jefferson's economic and political program includes Drew R. McCoy, *The Elusive Republic: Political Economy in Jeffersonian America* (Williamsburg, VA, 1980), and Peter S. Onuf, *Jefferson's Empire: The Language of American Nationhood* (Charlottesville, VA, 2000). Founding Era tensions relating to federalism are explored in Cathy D. Matson and Peter S. Onuf, *A Union of Interests: Political and Economic Thought in Revolutionary America* (Lawrence, KS, 1990) and Max M. Edling, *A Revolution in Favor of Government: Origins of the U.S. Constitution and the Making of the American State* (New York, 2003). Works that have focused on the importance of interstate diversity to Founding Era politics include Merrill Jensen, "The Sovereign States: Their Antagonisms and Rivalries and Some Consequences" and the other essays in Ronald Hoffman and Peter J. Albert, eds., *Sovereign States in an Age of Uncertainty* (Charlottesville, VA, 1981), 226–50, and Jack P. Greene, *Peripheries and Center: Constitutional Development in the Extended Polities of the British Empire and the United States, 1607–1788* (Athens, GA, 1986).

CHAPTER 13: LAW AND THE ORIGINS OF THE AMERICAN REVOLUTION

JACK P. GREENE

The question of the legitimacy of American constitutional pretensions during the pre-Revolutionary debate, the central problem treated in this chapter, has been debated widely in the secondary literature. Indeed, the classic treatments of this problem appeared more than seventy years ago, with Charles H. MacIlwain, *The American Revolution: A Constitutional Interpretation* (New York, 1923), affirming the legitimacy of those pretensions and Robert L. Schuyler, *Parliament and the British Empire: Some Constitutional Controversies Concerning Imperial Legislative Jurisdiction* (New York, 1929), denying them. In the same era, Andrew C. McLaughlin, *The Foundations of American Constitutionalism* (New York, 1932), and *A Constitutional History of the United States* (New York, 1935), suggestively explored early American constitutional development in terms that were more favorable to the interpretation of McIlwain, whereas Randolph G. Adams, *The Political Ideas of the Revolution* (Durham, NC, 1922), and Carl L. Becker, *The Declaration of Independence* (New York, 1922), explored the allegedly shifting grounds of colonial opposition to Parliamentary taxation.

In the quarter-century immediately after World War II, several scholars published important monographs that further illuminated the constitutional and legal issues in dispute in the years before American independence. These include Edmund S. Morgan and Helen M. Morgan, *The Stamp Act Crisis: Prologue to Revolution* (Chapel Hill, NC, 1953); Bernhard Knollenberg, *Origins of the American Revolution, 1759–1766* (New York, 1960); Carl Ubbelohde, *The Vice-Admiralty Courts and the Revolution* (Chapel Hill, NC, 1960); Jack P. Greene, *The Quest for Power: The Lower Houses of Assembly in the Southern Royal Colonies, 1689–1776* (Chapel Hill, NC, 1963); Benjamin Woods Labaree, *The Boston Tea*

Party (New York, 1964); and John Shy, *Toward Lexington: The Role of the British Army in the Coming of the American Revolution* (Princeton, 1965).

At the same time, Bernard Bailyn, *The Ideological Origins of the American Revolution* (Cambridge, MA, 1967) provided an especially penetrating study of the ideological foundations and development of pre-Revolutionary thought, albeit one that slighted the legal dimensions and context of that thought, whereas Pauline S. Maier, "Popular Uprisings and Civil Authority in Eighteenth-Century America," *William and Mary Quarterly*, 3rd ser., 27 (1970), 3–35, sensitively examined the role of the crowd in early American public life, and Hiller B. Zobbel, *The Boston Massacre* (New York, 1970), provided a law-and-order account of mob protests and resistance in Boston.

During the last quarter of the twentieth century, legal historians took up the problem of the coming of the American Revolution in a systematic way. In the process they have produced an impressive body of scholarship that is essential reading for anyone who wishes to understand the legal and constitutional dimensions to the controversy between Britain and the colonies. The most prolific of these historians has been John Phillip Reid. His books dealing with the many aspects of this subject are *In a Defiant Stance: The Conditions of Law in Massachusetts Bay, the Irish Comparison, and the Coming of the American Revolution* (University Park, PA, 1977); *In a Rebellious Spirit: The Argument of Facts, the Liberty Riot, and the Coming of the American Revolution* (University Park, PA, 1979); *In Defiance of the Law: The Standing-Army Controversy, the Two Constitutions, and the Coming of the American Revolution* (Chapel Hill, NC, 1981); *Constitutional History of the American Revolution: The Authority of Rights* (Madison, WI, 1986); *Constitutional History of the American Revolution: The Authority to Tax* (Madison, WI, 1987); *The Concept of Liberty in the Age of the American Revolution* (Chicago, 1988); *The Concept of Representation in the Age of the American Revolution* (Chicago, 1989); *Constitutional History of the American Revolution: The Authority to Legislate* (Madison, WI, 1991); *Constitutional History of the American Revolution: The Authority of Law* (Madison, WI, 1991); and *Constitutional History of the American Revolution: Abridged Edition* (Madison, WI, 1995).

Other important contributions to this new legal history literature on the American Revolution include William E. Nelson, "The Legal Restraint of Power in Pre-Revolutionary America: Massachusetts as a Case Study, 1760–1775," *American Journal of Legal History* 18 (1974), 1–32, and *The Americanization of the Common Law: The Impact of Legal Change on Massachusetts Society, 1750–1830* (Cambridge, MA, 1975); Barbara A. Black, "The Constitution of the Empire: The Case for the Colonists," *University of Pennsylvania Law Review* 124 (1976), 1157–1211; Thomas C. Grey, "Origin of the Unwritten Constitution: Fundamental Law in American Revolutionary Thought," *Stanford Law Review* 30 (1978), 843–93; M. G. Smith, *The Writs of Assistance Case* (Berkeley, 1978); Hendrik B. Hartog, ed., *Law in the American Revolution and the Revolution in the Law* (New York, 1981); and J. R. Pole, "'A Quest of Thoughts': Representation and Moral Agency in the Early Anglo-American Jury," *Proceedings of the 13th British Legal History Conference* (London, 2002), 102–30. Jack P. Greene, "From the Perspective of Law: Context and Legitimacy in the Origins of the American Revolution," *South Atlantic Quarterly* 75 (1986), 56–77 provides an extended discussion of the relevance of many of these works for non-legal historians of the American Revolution.

The most comprehensive study of the constitutional development of the British Empire, which complements the work of legal historians, is Jack P. Greene, *Peripheries and Center: Constitutional Development in the Extended Polities of the British Empire and the United States 1607–1788* (Athens, GA, 1986), from which much of this chapter is adapted.

CHAPTER 14: CONFEDERATION AND CONSTITUTION

JACK N. RAKOVE

There were three main phases in the development of American constitutionalism during the Revolutionary era: the imperial controversy with Britain, 1765–75; the framing of the first state constitutions and the Articles of Confederation, 1775–81; and the reconsideration of these constitutions that began with the final ratification of the Articles in 1781 and culminated in the great debate of 1787–89 over the Federal Constitution. Many scholarly works span two or occasionally all three of these phases, but for reasons of convenience and historical logic alike, it is useful to describe the literature for each phase separately.

Two landmark works dominate the scholarly interpretation of the constitutional origins of the Revolution: Edmund S. Morgan and Helen M. Morgan, *The Stamp Act Crisis: Prologue to Revolution* (Chapel Hill, NC, 1953), and Bernard Bailyn, *The Ideological Origins of the American Revolution* (Cambridge, MA, 1967; enlarged edition, 1992). Together, these two works explained how American and British ideas on essential constitutional ideas, though drawn from common sources, had begun to diverge in critical ways by the 1760s. Also useful in this respect is John Phillip Reid, *Constitutional History of the American Revolution*, 4 vols. (Madison, WI, 1986–93). Jack P. Greene, *Peripheries and Center: Constitutional Development in the Extended Polities of the British Empire and the United States, 1608–1788* (Athens, GA, 1986), examines the divergent conceptions of imperial authority and provincial rights that came to a head after 1765. Other important works on the coming of the Revolution include Merrill Jensen, *The Founding of a Nation: A History of the American Revolution, 1763–1776* (New York, 1968); Ian Christie and Benjamin Woods Labaree, *Empire or Independence, 1760–1776: British-American Dialogue on the Coming of the American Revolution* (New York, 1976); and Pauline Maier, *From Resistance to Revolution: Colonial Radicals and the Development of American Opposition to Britain, 1765–1776* (New York, 1972). Three volumes by Peter D. G. Thomas explain why British leaders found it difficult to acknowledge, much less accommodate, colonial claims: *British Politics and the Stamp Act Crisis: The First Phase of the American Revolution, 1763–1767* (Oxford, 1975); *The Townshend Duties Crisis: The Second Phase of the American Revolution, 1767–1773* (Oxford, 1987); and *Tea Party to Independence: The Third Phase of the American Revolution, 1773–1776* (Oxford, 1991). Benjamin Woods Labaree, *The Boston Tea Party* (New York, 1963), analyzes the episode that prompted the British government to resort to a policy of repression. It should be read in conjunction with two other fine books on the volatile politics of Massachusetts: Bernard Bailyn, *The Ordeal of Thomas Hutchinson* (Cambridge, MA, 1974), and Richard D. Brown, *Revolutionary Politics in Massachusetts: The Boston Committee of Correspondence and the Towns, 1772–1774* (Cambridge, MA, 1970).

The collapse of imperial authority in America is well described in David Ammerman, *In the Common Cause: American Response to the Coercive Acts of 1774* (Charlottesville, VA, 1974); Neil Stout, *The Perfect Crisis: The Beginning of the Revolutionary War* (New York, 1976); and David Hackett Fischer, *Paul Revere's Ride* (New York, 1994). For the origins of the Continental Congress, see Jerrilyn Green Marston, *King and Congress: The Transfer of Political Legitimacy, 1774–1776* (Princeton, NJ, 1987), and Jack N. Rakove, *The Beginnings of National Politics: An Interpretive History of the Continental Congress* (New York, 1979), which also examines the drafting and ratification of the Articles of Confederation while challenging the older Progressive interpretation of Merrill Jensen, *The Articles of Confederation: An Interpretation of the Social-Constitutional History of the American Revolution, 1774–1781* (Madison, WI, 1940). Pauline Maier, *American Scripture: Making the Declaration of Independence* (New York, 1997), offers a brisk account of the final movement toward separation.

The most creative aspects of this phase of revolutionary constitutionalism took place, however, within the individual states. The dominant and paradigmatic study of this process is Gordon S. Wood, *The Creation of the American Republic, 1776–1787* (Chapel Hill, NC, 1969). It can be helpfully complemented by several other works, notably including Willi Paul Adams, *The First American Constitutions: Republican Ideology and the Making of the State Constitutions in the Revolutionary Era*, trans. Rita and Robert Kimber (Chapel Hill, NC, 1980); Marc W. Kruman, *Between Authority and Liberty: State Constitution Making in Revolutionary America* (Chapel Hill, NC, 1997); and Donald Lutz, *Popular Consent and Popular Control: Whig Political Theory in the Early State Constitutions* (Baton Rouge, LA, 1980). Valuable studies of constitution-making within individual states include Jere R. Daniell, *Experiment in Republicanism: New Hampshire Politics and the American Revolution, 1741–1794* (Cambridge, MA, 1970); Ronald Peters, *The Massachusetts Constitution of 1780: A Social Compact* (Amherst, MA, 1978); Ronald Hoffman, *A Spirit of Dissension: Economics, Politics, and the Revolution in Maryland* (Baltimore, 1973); and Edward Countryman, *A People in Revolution: The American Revolution and Political Society in New York, 1760–1790* (Baltimore, 1981). Special mention should be made of the documents collected in Oscar Handlin and Mary F. Handlin, eds., *The Popular Sources of Political Authority: Documents on the Massachusetts Constitution of 1780* (Cambridge, MA, 1966). An exemplary study of the difficulties states faced in meeting the burdens of supporting the war is Richard Buel, *Dear Liberty: Connecticut's Mobilization for the Revolutionary War* (Middletown, CT, 1980). Also useful is John E. Selby, *The Revolution in Virginia, 1775–1783* (Charlottesville, VA, 1988), and the essays collected in Ronald Hoffman and Peter J. Albert, eds., *Sovereign States in an Age of Uncertainty* (Charlottesville, VA, 1981).

The neo-Progressive interpretation of the movement for federal constitutional reform is best represented by Merrill Jensen, *The New Nation: A History of the United States During the Confederation, 1781–1789* (New York, 1950), and E. James Ferguson, *The Power of the Purse: A History of American Public Finance, 1776–1790* (Chapel Hill, NC, 1961). For a different view of Congressional financial policy during the early 1780s, see Clarence Ver Steeg, *Robert Morris: Revolutionary Financier* (Philadelphia, 1954). The central role of questions of taxation in the movement toward constitutional reform after 1783 is analyzed in Roger H. Brown, *Redeeming the Republic: Federalists, Taxation, and the Origins of the Constitution* (Baltimore, 1993), and Calvin H. Johnson, *Righteous Anger at the Wicked States: The Meaning of the Founders' Constitution* (New York, 2005). The relation between ownership of the revolutionary debt and the Constitution was, of course, the subject of Charles A. Beard, *An Economic Interpretation of the Constitution* (New York, 1913), arguably the most influential work ever published on the subject even if its evidentiary shortcomings have long been evident. For more subtle accounts of the relation between economic interests and constitution-making, see Robert McGuire, *To Form a More Perfect Union: A New Economic Interpretation of the United States Constitution* (New York, 2003); Cathy D. Matson and Peter S. Onuf, *A Union of Interests: Political and Economic Thought in Revolutionary America* (Lawrence, KS, 1990); and two works by the ever provocative Forrest McDonald, *We the People: The Economic Origins of the Constitution* (Chicago, 1953) and *E Pluribus Unum: The Formation of the American Republic, 1776–1790* (Boston, 1965). Peter S. Onuf, *Origins of the Federal Republic: Jurisdictional Controversies in the United States, 1775–1787* (Philadelphia, 1983), traces the relation between the competing land claims of individual states and the development of a conception of federalism that would grant each member of the union the territorial security it could not be confident of assuring for itself.

The two best brief introductions to the debates at the Philadelphia Convention are the classic account by Max Farrand, *The Framing of the Constitution of the United States* (New Haven, CT, 1913), and the sprightly recent account by Carol Berkin, *A Brilliant Solution: Inventing the American Constitution* (New York, 2002). For more detailed narratives, see Clinton Rossiter, *1787: The Grand Convention* (New York, 1966); Catherine Drinker Bowen, *Miracle at Philadelphia: The Story of the Constitutional Convention, May to September 1787* (Boston, 1966);

and Christopher Collier and James L. Collier, *Decision at Philadelphia: The Constitutional Convention of 1787* (New York, 1986). More analytical accounts, written from the vantage point of political science, include Calvin Jillson, *Constitution Making: Conflict and Consensus in the Federal Convention of 1787* (New York, 1988), and David Brian Robertson, *The Constitution and America's Destiny* (New York, 2005). Rosemarie Zagarri, *The Politics of Size: Representation in the United States, 1776–1850* (Ithaca, NY, 1987), is helpful on the classic conflict between large and small states. Max Edling, *A Revolution in Favor of Government: Origins of the Constution and the Making of the American State* (New York, 2003), makes a strong case for the primacy of national security concerns in the framing of the Constitution. A similar approach is taken in David C. Hendrickson, *Peace Pact: The Lost World of the American Founding* (Lawrence, KS, 2003).

Numerous studies look beyond the immediate politics of constitution-making to explore the role of ideas and ideologies in the reshaping of American political thinking by the late 1780s. Along with Gordon Wood, *Creation of the American Republic* (cited earlier), leading studies include Forrest McDonald, *Novus Ordo Seclorum: The Intellectual Origins of the Constitution* (Lawrence, KS, 1985), and Jack N. Rakove, *Original Meanings: Politics and Ideas in the Making of the Constitution* (New York, 1996), which takes as its point of departure the modern debate over the theory of constitutional interpretation known as originalism. Cecilia Kenyon, "Men of Little Faith: The Anti-Federalists on the Nature of Representative Government," *William and Mary Quarterly*, 3rd ser., 12 (1955), 3–43, was a seminal essay that influenced scholarly interpretations of the constitutional debate of the late 1780s more generally. Other helpful studies and collections include Ralph Ketcham, *Framed for Posterity: The Enduring Philosophy of the Constitution* (Lawrence, KS, 1993); Samuel F. Beer, *To Make a Nation: The Rediscovery of American Federalism* (Cambridge, MA, 1993); Herman Belz, Ronald Hoffman, and Peter J. Albert, eds., *To Form a More Perfect Union: The Critical Ideas of the Constitution* (Charlottesville, VA, 1992); Michael Lienesch, *New Order of the Ages: Time, the Constitution, and the Making of Modern American Political Thought* (Princeton, NJ, 1988); Jennifer Nedelsky, *Private Property and the Limits of American Constitutionalism: The Madisonian Framework and Its Legacy* (Chicago, 1990); David J. Siemers, *Ratifying the Republic: Antifederalists and Federalists in Constitutional Time* (Stanford, CA, 2002); Richard Beeman, Stephen Botein, and Edward C. Carter II, eds., *Beyond Confederation: Origins of the Constitution and American National Identity* (Chapel Hill, NC, 1987); Terence Ball and J. G. A. Pocock, eds., *Conceptual Change and the Constitution* (Lawrence, KS, 1988); and Leonard W. Levy and Dennis J. Mahoney, eds., *The Framing and Ratification of the Constitution* (New York, 1987). Carl J. Richard, *The Founders and the Classics: Greece, Rome, and the American Enlightenment* (Cambridge, MA, 1994), examines the substantial influence that writings from classical antiquity exerted on American political thinking in the Revolutionary era. The distinguished historian of science, I. Bernard Cohen, does something similar in *Science and the Founding Fathers: Science in the Political Thought of Jefferson, Franklin, Adams, and Madison* (New York, 1995).

A significant portion of scholarly writings on the political ideas expressed in the Constitution has been devoted to James Madison, as both a leading member of the 1787 Convention and one of the two principal authors of *The Federalist*. Leading biographical studies include Ralph Ketcham, *James Madison: A Biography* (Charlottesville, VA, 1971); Lance Banning, *The Sacred Fire of Liberty: James Madison and the Founding of the Federal Republic* (Ithaca, NY, 1995); and Jack N. Rakove, *James Madison and the Creation of the American Republic* (New York, 2006, rev. ed.). Several essays by Douglass Adair were fundamental to the modern understanding of the meaning and significance of Madison's contributions to *The Federalist*, especially in his much-analyzed *Federalist* 10: "The Authorship of the Disputed Federalist Papers," *William and Mary Quarterly*, 3rd ser., 1 (1944), 97–122, 235–64; "The Tenth Federalist Revisited," *William and Mary Quarterly*, 3rd ser., 8 (1951); and "'That Politics May Be Reduced to a Science': David Hume, James Madison, and the Tenth Federalist," *Huntington Library Quarterly* 20 (1957), 343–60. The last essay's emphasis on Hume's "influence" on Madison became an independent source of controversy in itself, perhaps now best approached by beginning with the most recent entry in the scholarly lists: Mark Spencer, "Hume and Madison on Faction," *William and Mary Quarterly*, 3rd ser., 59 (2002), 869–96. Other important interpretive essays include Martin Diamond, "Democracy and *The Federalist*: A Reconsideration of the Framers' Intents," *American Political Science Review* 53 (1959), 52–68; Daniel Walker Howe, "The Political Psychology of *The Federalist*," *American Political Science Review* 44 (1987), 485–509; Charles Hobson, "The Negative on State Laws: James Madison, the Constitution, and the Crisis of Republican Government," *American Political Science Review* 36 (1979), 215–35; and Larry Kramer, "Madison's Audience," *Harvard Law Review* 112 (1999), 611–79. A helpful collection of essays by political scientists is Samuel Kernell, ed., *James Madison: The Theory and Practice of Republican Government* (Stanford, CA, 2003). Leading books on *The Federalist* include Charles R. Kesler, ed., *Saving the Revolution: The Federalist Papers and the American Founding* (New York, 1987); David F. Epstein, *The Political Theory of The Federalist* (Chicago, 1984); Morton White, *Philosophy, The Federalist, and the Constitution* (New York, 1987); Albert Furtwangler, *The Authority of Publius: A Reading of the Federalist Papers* (Ithaca, NY, 1984); and Edward Millican, *One United People: The Federalist Papers and the National Idea* (Lexington, KY, 1990). Alexander Hamilton, Madison's co-author as Publius (and indeed the leading author of the entire work), has received less attention as a constitutional theorist, but two helpful works are Gerald Stourzh, *Alexander Hamilton and the Idea of Republican Government* (Stanford, CA, 1970) and Karl-Friedrich Walling, *Alexander Hamilton on War and Free Government* (Lawrence, KS, 1999). The best life is Forrest McDonald, *Alexander Hamilton: A Biography* (New York, 1979).

Numerous books examine the politics of the ratification of the Constitution. Two good introductions are Robert Rutland, *The Ordeal of the Constitution: The Antifederalists and the Ratification Struggle of 1787–1788* (Norman, OK, 1966), and Jackson Turner Main, *The Antifederalists: Critics of the Constitution, 1781–1788* (Chapel Hill, NC, 1961). Also helpful is Steven R. Boyd, *The Politics of Opposition: Antifederalists and the Acceptance of the Constitution* (Millwood, NY, 1979), and the essays collected in Michael Gillespie and Michael Lienesch, eds., *Ratifying the Constitution* (Lawrence, KS, 1989), and Patrick T. Conley and John P. Kaminski, eds., *The Constitution and the States: The Role of the Original Thirteen in the Framing and Adoption of the Federal Constitution* (Madison, WS, 1988). Saul Cornell, *The Other Founders: Anti-Federalism and the Dissenting Tradition in America, 1788–1828* (Chapel Hill, NC, 1999), examines the political legacy of the Constitution's opponents. Linda Grant De Pauw, *The Eleventh Pillar: New York State and the Federal Constitution* (Ithaca, NY, 1966), is an exemplary study of ratification within a critical state in which Anti-Federalists predominated.

The adoption of the first ten amendments to the Constitution – better known as the Bill of Rights – is often seen as the culmination as well as the sequel to the constitutional debates of 1787–88. Many studies of the subject focus on the historical origins and legal content of the particular rights that finally made their way into the constitutional text. Perhaps the leading scholar in this field has been Leonard Levy, and many of his findings are distilled in his book, *Original Intent and the Framers' Constitution* (New York, 1988). But Levy's approach is better illustrated in two of his monographs: *The Emergence of a Free Press* (New York, 1985) and *Origins of the Fifth Amendment: The Right Against Self-Incrimination* (New York, 1968). For broader surveys, see Patrick T. Conley and John P. Kaminski, eds., *The Bill of Rights and the States: The Colonial and Revolutionary Origins of American Liberties* (Madison, WS, 1992); Jon Kukla, ed., *The Bill of Rights: A Lively Heritage* (Richmond, VA, 1987); and Michael Lacey and Knud Haakonssen, eds., *A Culture of Rights: The Bill of Rights in Philosophy, Politics, and Law: 1791 and 1991* (New York, 1991). Two works that focus on James Madison's special role in the adoption of the amendments are Robert A. Goldwin, *From Parchment to Power: How James Madison Used the Bill of Rights to Save the Constitution* (Washington, D.C., 1997) and Paul Finkelman, "James Madison and the Bill of Rights: A Reluctant Paternity," *Supreme Court Review* (1990), 301–47. For a somewhat idiosyncratic account discounting the significance of Madison's understanding of what he was doing, see Akhil Amar, *The Bill of Rights: Creation and Reconstruction* (New Haven, CT, 1998).

CHAPTER 15: THE CONSOLIDATION OF THE EARLY FEDERAL SYSTEM

SAUL CORNELL AND GERALD LEONARD

Constitutional history encompasses the structures and processes through which the law is made. Of course, it must attend to the specific legal limits imposed on government by or in the name of a written constitution, such as the restrictions enumerated in the Bill of Rights. But it is much broader than that. In the case of the Early Republic – the formative period of American constitutional history – a full analysis must explain how the new Federal Constitution pervasively structured law and politics. Conversely, but just as importantly, it requires understanding how law and politics created constitutional meaning. Writing this history, and understanding the historical dynamics of constitutional government, consequently, requires attention not just to constitutional texts, conventions, and courts but to struggles to reshape the relations of public power in all its forms. With this capacious definition of constitutional history, it is difficult to place any good historical writing categorically beyond the reach of constitutional history. However, this bibliographic essay attempts to offer one definition of the constitutional history of the Early Republic by its selection of those works we think most central.

At the outset, the chapter offers, in effect, a chronological narrative of federalism, the battle in the first generation to bend the Constitution and the Founding in the direction of consolidation, on the one hand, or state autonomy, on the other. The essential background for this story remains, after almost forty years, Gordon S. Wood, *The Creation of the American Republic 1776–1787* (Chapel Hill, NC, 1969). Wood has since followed up with *The Radicalism of the American Revolution* (New York, 1992), which provides a sweeping story of social, political, and constitutional change into the early decades of the nineteenth century.

The foundation of any understanding of the constitutional history of this period is an understanding of the period's political history, which was preoccupied with constitutional issues. See Stanley Elkins and Eric McKitrick, *The Age of Federalism* (New York, 1993); James Roger Sharp, *American Politics in the Early Republic: The New Nation in Crisis* (New Haven, CT, 1993); Saul Cornell, *The Other Founders: Anti-Federalism and the Dissenting Tradition in America, 1788–1828* (Chapel Hill, NC, 1999); Richard E. Ellis, "The Persistence of Antifederalism After 1789," in Richard Beeman, Stephen Botein and Edward C. Carter III, eds., *Beyond Confederation: Origins of the Constitution and American National Identity* (Chapel Hill, NC, 1987); Albrecht Koschnik, "The Democratic Societies of Philadelphia and the Limits of the American Public Sphere, Circa 1793–1795," *William and Mary Quarterly*, 3rd ser., 58 (2001), 615; James A. Smith, *Freedom's Fetters: The Alien and Sedition Laws and American Civil Liberties* (Ithaca, NY, 1956); K. R. Constantine Gutzman, "The Virginia and Kentucky Resolutions Reconsidered: An Appeal to the 'Real Laws' of Our Country," *Journal of Southern History* 66 (2000), 473; Joanne Freeman, *Affairs of Honor: National Politics in the New Republic* (New Haven, CT, 2001); Lance Banning, *The Jeffersonian Persuasion: Evolution of a Party Ideology* (Ithaca, NY, 1978); Peter J. Kastor, *The Nation's Crucible: The Louisiana Purchase and the Creation of America* (New Haven, CT, 2004); J. C. A. Stagg, *Mr. Madison's War: Politics, Diplomacy, and Warfare in the Early American Republic, 1783–1830* (Princeton,

NJ, 1983); Roger H. Brown, *The Republic in Peril: 1812* (New York, 1964); James Banner, *To the Hartford Convention: The Federalists and the Origins of Party Politics in Massachusetts, 1789–1815* (New York, 1970); Forrest McDonald, *States' Rights and the Union: Imperium in Imperio, 1776–1876* (Lawrence, KS, 2000); Andrew C. Lenner, *The Federal Principle in American Politics, 1790–1833* (Lanham, MD, 2001); Mark R. Killenbeck, "Pursuing the Great Experiment: Reserved Powers in a Post-Ratification, Compound Republic," *Supreme Court Review* 81 (1999); R. B. Bernstein, *Thomas Jefferson* (New York, 2003); David N. Mayer, *The Constitutional Thought of Thomas Jefferson* (Charlottesville, VA, 1994); Peter S. Onuf, *Jefferson's Empire: The Language of American Nationhood* (Charlottesville, VA, 2000); Gerald Stourzh, *Alexander Hamilton and the Idea of Republican Government* (Stanford, CA, 1970); Ron Chernow, *Alexander Hamilton* (New York, 2004); and Ralph L. Ketcham, *James Madison: A Biography* (Indianapolis, 1971). Some lawyerly accounts of aspects of this period also make valuable contributions to the constitutional history of the times. See Bruce Ackerman, *The Failure of the Founding Fathers: Jefferson, Marshall, and the Rise of Presidential Democracy* (Cambridge, 2005) and *We the People: Foundations* (Cambridge, 1991); and Akhil Reed Amar, *The Bill of Rights: Creation and Reconstruction* (New Haven, CT, 1998). A recent, brief overview of the period can be found in Paul E. Johnson, *The Early American Republic, 1789–1829* (New York, 2007). A far longer one can be found in the opening chapters of Sean Wilentz, *The Rise of American Democracy: Jefferson to Lincoln* (New York, 2005).

Specifically on the emergence of the new structures of authorities that were political parties, see Richard Hofstadter, *The Idea of a Party System: The Rise of Legitimate Opposition in the United States, 1780–1840* (Berkeley, 1969); but also the corrections offered by Gerald Leonard, *The Invention of Party Politics: Federalism, Popular Sovereignty, and Constitutional Development in Jacksonian Illinois* (Chapel Hill, NC, 2002) and "Party as a 'Political Safeguard of Federalism': Martin Van Buren and the Constitutional Theory of Party Politics," *Rutgers Law Review* 54 (2001), 221. On the same subject, see Ronald P. Formisano, "Deferential-Participant Politics: The Early Republic's Political Culture, 1789–1840," *American Political Science Review* 68 (1974), 473; Ronald P. Formisano, "Federalists and Republicans: Parties, Yes – System, No," in Paul Kleppner, ed., *The Evolution of American Electoral Systems* (Westport, CT, 1981); Ronald P. Formisano, *The Transformation of Political Culture: Massachusetts Parties, 1790s-1840s* (New York, 1983); Donald J. Ratcliffe, *Party Spirit in a Frontier Republic: Democratic Politics in Ohio, 1793–1821* (Columbus, OH, 1998); and Ralph Ketcham, *Presidents Above Party: The First American Presidency, 1789–1829* (Chapel Hill, NC, 1984). Closely related to the rise of parties were the methods of electing presidential electors and the adoption of the Twelfth Amendment. See Tadahisa Kuroda, *The Origins of the Twelfth Amendment: The Electoral College in the Early Republic, 1787–1804* (Westport, CT, 1994).

The literature on "popular constitutionalism" has ballooned in recent years. The purpose of this literature is to demonstrate that actors other than the courts – from mobs to political parties to any number of non-judicial office-holders – controlled the meaning and implementation of constitutions in large degree. In some ways, this writing is just an extension of those political histories that understand their topic as having an important constitutional dimension. But it is also distinguished by its direct engagement with and revision of the history of judicial review, a history that traditionally portrayed the courts as the almost exclusive actors in the elaboration of constitutional meaning. Until recently, the standard citations for the early history of judicial review were Sylvia Snowiss, *Judicial Review and the Law of the Constitution* (New Haven, CT, 1990); Robert Lowry Clinton, *Marbury v. Madison and Judicial Review* (Lawrence, KS, 1989); J. M. Sosin, *The Aristocracy of the Long Robe: The Origins of Judicial Review in America* (Westport, CT, 1989); Christopher Wolfe, *The Rise of Modern Judicial Review: From Constitutional Interpretation to Judge-Made Law* (New York, 1986); and Gordon S. Wood, "The Origins of Judicial Review Revisited, or How the Marshall Court Made More Out of Less," *Washington and Lee Law Review* 56 (1999), 787.

But a raft of more sophisticated work has emerged in very recent years. Snowiss's work, probably the most influential across the 1990s, has been seriously undermined by Dean Alfange, Jr., "*Marbury v. Madison* and Original Understandings of Judicial Review: In Defense of Traditional Wisdom," *Supreme Court Law Review* 329 (1993), and Gerald Leonard, "Iredell Reclaimed: Farewell to Snowiss's History of Judicial Review," *Chicago-Kent Law Review* 81 (2006). More importantly, new and better accounts of the origins of judicial review have appeared in Larry D. Kramer, *The People Themselves: Popular Constitutionalism and Judicial Review* (New York, 2004); Mary Sarah Bilder, *The Transatlantic Constitution: Colonial Legal Culture and the Empire* (Cambridge, MA, 2004); Mary Sarah Bilder, "The Corporate Origins of Judicial Review," *Yale Law Journal* 116 (2006), 502; William Michael Treanor, "Judicial Review before *Marbury*," 58 *Stanford Law Review* 455 (2005); William Michael Treanor, "The Case of the Prisoners and the Origins of Judicial Review," *University of Pennsylvania Law Review* 143 (1994), 491; and Donald F. Melhorn, *"Lest We Be Marshall'd": Judicial Powers and Politics in Ohio, 1806–1812* (Akron, OH, 2003). Many of these offer evidence of extra-judicial control of constitutional meaning, as do Keith Whittington, *Constitutional Construction: Divided Powers and Constitutional Meaning* (Cambridge, MA, 1999); Gary D. Rowe, "Constitutionalism in the Streets," *Southern California Law Review* 78 (2005), 401; and Daniel J. Hulsebosch, *Constituting Empire: New York and the Transformation of Constitutionalism in the Atlantic World, 1664–1830* (Chapel Hill, NC, 2005). The connections among the militia, federalism, and popular constitutionalism are explored in Saul Cornell, *A Well-Regulated Militia: The Founding Fathers and the Origins of Gun Control in America* (New York, 2006).

Many groups, however, had little or only attenuated connections to the levers of power, but still affected constitutional meaning in important ways. These "constitutional outsiders," beginning with William Manning and his world, can be explored further in Samuel Eliot Morison, "William Manning's *The Key of Libberty*," *William and Mary Quarterly*, 3rd ser., 13 (1956), 202; Michael Merrill and Sean Wilentz, *The Key of Liberty: The Life and Writings of William Manning, "A Laborer," 1747–1814* (Cambridge, MA, 1993); Ruth Bogin, "'Measures So Glareingly unjust': A Response to Hamilton's Funding Plan by William Manning," *William and Mary Quarterly*, 3rd ser., 46 (1989), 315; Christopher L. Tomlins, *Law, Labor, and Ideology in the Early American Republic* (Cambridge, 1993); David Waldstreicher, *In the Midst of Perpetual Fetes: The Making of American Nationalism, 1776–1820* (Chapel Hill, NC, 1997); and Simon P. Newman, *Parades and the Politics of the Street: Festive Culture in the Early American Republic* (Philadelphia, 1997). The constitutional status of women and broader questions of gender and public power are discussed in Linda Kerber, *No Constitutional Right to Be Ladies: Women and the Obligations of Citizenship* (New York, 1998); Catherine Allgor, *Parlor Politics: In Which the Ladies of Washington Help Build a City and a Government* (Charlottesville, VA, 2000); Susan Branson, *These Fiery Frenchified Dames: Women and Political Culture in Early National Philadelphia* (Philadelphia, 2001); and Sandra F. Van Burkleo, *"Belonging to the World": Women's Rights and American Constitutional Culture* (New York, 2001). On the pro-slavery character of early constitutionalism, see Paul Finkelman, *Slavery and the Founders: Race and Liberty in the Age of Jefferson* (rev. ed., New York, 2001); on African American resistance, see, e.g., Douglas R. Egerton, *Gabriel's Rebellion: The Virginia Slave Conspiracies of 1800 & 1802* (Chapel Hill, NC, 1993). Related work appears, along with essays treating a great variety of aspects of constitutional politics, in James Horn, Jan Ellen Lewis, and Peter S. Onuf, eds., *The Revolution of 1800: Democracy, Race, and the New Republic* (Charlottesville, VA, 2002). And on the growing but limited scope of voting rights, see Alexander Keyssar, *The Right to Vote: The Contested History of Democracy in the United States* (New York, 2000).

Court-centered and especially Supreme-Court-centered constitutional history focuses much more on the Marshall Court than its predecessors, but the Court in the 1790s gets valuable treatment in William R. Casto, *The Supreme Court in the Early Republic: The Chief Justiceships of John Jay and Oliver Ellsworth* (Columbia, SC, 1995); Scott Douglas Gerber, ed., *Seriatim: The Supreme Court before John Marshall* (New York, 1998); and Stewart Jay, *Most Humble Servants: The Advisory Role of Early Judges* (New Haven, CT, 1997). The famous case of *Chisholm v. Georgia* and the passage, in reaction, of the Eleventh Amendment are described in Clyde E. Jacobs, *The Eleventh Amendment and Sovereign Immunity* (Westport, CT, 1972); John V. Orth, *The Judicial Power of the United States: The Eleventh Amendment in American History* (New York, 1987); William Fletcher, "A Historical Interpretation of the Eleventh Amendment: A Narrow Construction of an Affirmative Grant of Jurisdiction Rather than a Prohibition Against

Jurisdiction," *Stanford Law Review* 35 (1983), 1033; and John J. Gibbons, "The Eleventh Amendment and State Sovereign Immunity: A Reinterpretation," *Columbia Law Review* 83 (1983), 1889.

Works discussing the early years of the Marshall Court itself include R. Kent Newmyer, *John Marshall and the Heroic Age of the Supreme Court* (Baton Rouge, LA, 2001); Charles F. Hobson, *The Great Chief Justice: John Marshall and the Rule of Law* (Lawrence, KS, 1996); William E. Nelson, *Marbury v. Madison and the Origins and Legacy of Judicial Review* (Lawrence, KS, 2000); C. Peter Magrath, *Yazoo: Law and Politics in the New Republic: The Case of Fletcher v. Peck* (Providence, RI, 1967); Robert G. McCloskey, *The American Supreme Court* (Chicago, 1960; 4th ed. 2005); and David P. Currie, *The Constitution in the Supreme Court: The First Hundred Years, 1789–1888* (Chicago, 1985).

Courts less exalted than the Supreme Court have received much less attention, but some useful accounts of their doings, discussing also some of this period's relatively rare litigation of claims of individual constitutional rights, can be found in Steven R. Boyd, "The Contract Clause and the Evolution of American Federalism, 1789–1815," *William and Mary Quarterly*, 3rd ser., 44 (1987), 529; James W. Ely, Jr., *The Guardian of Every Other Right; A Constitutional History of Property Rights* (New York, 1992); James W. Ely, Jr., "The Oxymoron Reconsidered: Myth and Reality in the Origins of Substantive Due Process," *Constitutional Commentary* 16 (1999), 315; F. Thornton Miller, *Juries and Judges Versus the Law: Virginia's Provincial Legal Perspective, 1783–1828* (Charlottesville, VA, 1994); and H. Jefferson Powell, *A Community Built on Words: The Constitution in History and Politics* (Chicago, 2002).

Treatment of the judiciary by the public political process is analyzed in Richard E. Ellis, *The Jeffersonian Crisis: Courts and Politics in the Young Republic* (New York,1971); Wythe Holt and James R. Perry, "Writs and Rights, 'Clashing Animosities': The First Confrontation Between Federal and State Jurisdictions," *Law and History Review* 7 (1989), 89; Peter Charles Hoffer and N. E. H. Hull, *Impeachment in America, 1635–1805* (New Haven, CT, 1984); Brian Carso, *Whom Can We Trust Now?: The Meaning of Treason in the United States, from the Revolution through the Civil War* (Boston, 2006); Maeva Marcus, ed., *Origins of the Federal Judiciary: Essays on the Judiciary Act of 1789* (New York,1992); Kathryn Turner, "Federalist Policy and the Judiciary Act of 1801," *William and Mary Quarterly*, 3rd ser., 22 (1965), 3; and Charles Warren, "Legislative and Judicial Attacks on the Supreme Court of the United States – A History of the Twenty-Fifth Section of the Judiciary Act," *American Law Review* 47 (1913), 1–34, 161–189.

In recent times, it has become easier and easier to get past the secondary literature and go directly to the primary documents, both in printed editions of these documents and increasingly online. A number of sites now have searchable copies (not transcriptions) of primary documents online. See, for example, the huge collection in the Library of Congress's American Memory project:

http://memory.loc.gov/ammem/index.html. Another enormous collection is Readex's Early American Newspapers and other online archives that include hundreds of newspapers from the eighteenth and nineteenth centuries, as well as many books and other primary sources, drawing chiefly on the collections of the American Antiquarian Society: http://www.newsbankonline.com/readex/. For a collection of thousands of law-related books from the period, go to Gale's The Making of Modern Law: http://www.gale.com/ModernLaw/.

From the many printed collections of primary sources for this period, we list here a few of the more broadly focused collections (that is, collections that go well beyond the papers of a single notable person): Charles S. Hyneman and Donald S. Lutz, eds., *American Political Writing During the Founding Era, 1760–1800*, 2 vols. (Indianapolis 1983); Helen Veit et al., eds., *Creating the Bill of Rights* (Baltimore, 1991); Gary McDowell and Colleen Sheenan, eds., *Friends of the Constitution: Writings of the Other Federalists* (Indianapolis, 1998); Philip S. Foner, ed., *The Democratic Republican Societies, 1790–1800: A Documentary Sourcebook of Constitutions, Declarations, Addresses, Resolutions, and Toasts* (Westport, CT, 1976); H. Jefferson Powell, *Languages of Power: A Sourcebook of Early American Constitutional History* (Durham, NC, 1991); Gordon S. Wood, ed., *The Rising Glory of America* (Boston, 1990); Maeva Marcus, ed., *The Documentary History of the Supreme Court of the United States, 1789–1800*, 8 vols. so far (New York, 1985–2007); and Charlene Bangs Bickford et al., *The Documentary History of the First Federal Congress of the United States of America, March 4, 1789-March 3, 1791*, 17 vols. so far (Baltimore, 1972–2004).

CHAPTER 16: MAGISTRATES, COMMON LAWYERS, LEGISLATORS

JAMES A. HENRETTA

I. Local Primacy: Magistrates and Arbitrators, 1600–1680

The best recent legal scholarship on the seventeenth-century Chesapeake is that of David Thomas Konig. See his "Colonization and the Common Law in Ireland and Virginia, 1569–1634," in James A. Henretta, Stanley N. Katz, and Michael Kammen, eds., *The Transformation of Early American History* (New York, 1991), 70–92, and "Country Justice: The Rural Roots of Constitutionalism in Colonial Virginia," in Kermit L. Hall and James W. Ely, Jr., eds., *In An Uncertain Tradition: Constitutionalism and the History of the South* (Athens, GA, 1989), 63–82. Other good studies include Lois Green Carr, "The Development of the Maryland Orphans' Court, 1654–1715," in Aubrey C. Land, Lois Green Carr, and Edward C. Papenfuse, *Law, Society, and Politics in Early Maryland* (Baltimore, 1977), 41–62; James Horn, *Adapting to a New World: English Society in the Seventeenth-Century Chesapeake* (Chapel Hill, 1994); and Christine Daniels, "'Liberty to Complaine': Servant Petitions in Maryland, 1652–1797," in Christopher L. Tomlins and Bruce H. Mann, eds., *The Many Legalities of Early America* (Chapel Hill, NC, 2001), 219–49.

On the magistracy in New England, consult the fine article by John M. Murrin, "Magistrates, Sinners, and a Precarious Liberty: Trial by Jury in Seventeenth-Century New England," in David D. Hall, John M. Murrin, and Thad W. Tate, eds., *Saints and Revolutionaries: Essays on Early American History* (New York, 1984),152–206; David Grayson Allen, *In English Ways: The Movement of Societies and the Transferal of English Local Law and Custom to Massachusetts Bay in the Seventeenth Century* (Chapel Hill, NC, 1981); and two articles by George Haskins, "Reception of the Common Law in Seventeenth-Century Massachusetts: A Case Study," in George Athan Billias, ed., *Law and Authority in Colonial America* (Berkeley, 1965), 17–31 and "Lay Judges: Magistrates and Justices in Early Massachusetts," in Daniel R Coquillette, Catherine S. Menand, and Robert J. Brink, eds., *Law in Colonial Massachusetts, 1630–1800* (Boston, 1984), 39–55.

Informative studies of seventeenth-century New York include Herbert Alan Johnson, *Essays on New York Colonial Legal History* (Westport, CT, 1981) and "The Advent of Common Law in Colonial New York" in Billias, ed., *Law and Authority*, 74–91; Richard B. Morris, "The New York City's Mayor's Court," in Leo Hershkowitz and Milton M. Klein, eds., *Courts and Law in Early New York* (Port Washington, NY,1978); and Douglas Greenberg, *Crime and Law Enforcement in the Colony of New York, 1691–1776* (Ithaca, NY, 1974). On Pennsylvania, consult the interesting scholarship of William M. Offutt, Jr., *Of "Good Laws" and "Good Men:" Law and Society in the Delaware Valley, 1680–1710* (Urbana, IL, 1995), and "The Limits of Authority: Courts, Ethnicity, and Gender in the Middle Colonies, 1670–1710," in Tomlins and Mann, eds., *Many Legalities* 357–87. A nice case study of the power of the magistracy is Jessica Kross and Thomas J. Davis. "Magistrates, the Minister's Rate, and the Question on Authority: The Case of Daniel Bull, the Jamaica Dissenters, and the Tax Collector, 1718–1719," *Journal of Church and State* 32 (1990), 813–30.

II. Centralization: Imperial Authority, Legalism, and Common Law, 1680–1720

The impact of imperial power on the court system is a theme developed in Stanley N. Katz, "The Politics of Law in Colonial America: Controversies over Chancery Courts and Equity Law in the Eighteenth Century," in Donald Fleming and Bernard Bailyn, eds., *Law in American History* (Boston, 1971), 257–86, and L. Kinvin Wroth, "The Massachusetts Vice-Admiralty Court," in Billias, ed., *Law and Authority*. The emergence of lawyers is outlined in the wide-ranging and valuable study by A. G. Roeber, *Faithful Magistrates and Republican Lawyers: Creators of Virginia Legal Culture, 1680–1810* (Chapel Hill, NC, 1981). Other informative works include Stephen Botein, "The Legal Profession in Colonial North America," in Wilfred Prest, ed., *Lawyers in Early Modern Europe and America* (New York, 1981), 129–46; John M. Murrin, "The Legal Transformation: The Bench and Bar of Eighteenth-Century Massachusetts," in Stanley N. Katz and John M. Murrin, eds., *Colonial America: Essays in Politics and*

Social Development (New York, 1983, 3rd ed.), 540–96; and Neal W. Allen, Jr., "Law and Authority to the Eastward: Maine Courts, Magistrates, and Lawyers, 1690–1730," in Coquillette et al., *Law in Colonial Massachusetts*, 273–312. See also the interesting essay by Mary Sarah Bilder, "The Lost Lawyers: Early American Legal Literates and Transatlantic Legal Culture," *Yale Journal of Law & the Humanities* 11 (1999), 47–103.

The decline of arbitration and the increasing importance of the forms and procedures of the common law are the subject of important works by Bruce Mann, *Neighbors and Strangers: Law and Community in Early Connecticut* (Chapel Hill, NC, 1987); David Thomas Konig, *Law and Society in Puritan Massachusetts: Essex County, 1629–1692* (Chapel Hill, NC, 1979); and David H. Flaherty, "Chief Justice Samuel Sewall, 1692–1728," in William Pencak and Wythe W. Holt, Jr., eds., *The Law in America, 1607–1861* (New York, 1989), 114–54.

III. Common Law Lawyers, Judges, and Juries, 1720–1780

The increasing competence of the colonial judiciary emerges in G. S. Rowe, *Embattled Bench: The Pennsylvania Supreme Court and the Forging of a Democratic Society, 1684–1809* (Newark, DE, 1994) and Peter E. Russell, *His Majesty's Judges: Provincial Society and the Superior Court in Massachusetts, 1692–1774* (New York, 1990). Because debt cases constituted most of the business of the civil courts, my account relies heavily on the fine studies of debt and civil procedure by Mann, *Neighbors and Strangers*, and William E. Nelson, *Americanization of the Common Law: The Impact of Legal Change on Massachusetts Society, 1760–1830* (Athens, GA, 1976) and *Dispute and Conflict Resolution in Plymouth County, Massachusetts, 1725–1825* (Chapel Hill, NC, 1981). Other accounts of debt legislation generally confirm the arguments of Mann and Nelson while slightly modifying them. See Claire Priest, "Currency Policies and Legal Development in Colonial New England," *Yale Law Journal* 110 (2001), 1303–1405, and Deborah Rosen, "Courts and Commerce in Colonial New York," *American Journal of Legal History* 36 (1992), 139–63, and *Courts and Commerce; Gender, Law, and the Market Economy in Colonial New York* (Columbus, OH, 1997). See also Richard Lyman Bushman, "Farmers in Court: Orange County, North Carolina, 1750–1776," in Tomlins and Mann, *Many Legalities*, 388–414.

Useful studies of eighteenth-century judges and courts include Gwenda Morgan, *The Hegemony of the Law: Richmond County, Virginia, 1692–1776* (New York, 1989); Donna J. Spindel, *Crime and Society in North Carolina, 1663–1776* (Baton Rouge, LA, 1989); and Deborah Rosen, "The Supreme Court of the Judicature of Colonial New York: Civil Practice in Transition, 1691–1760," *Law and History Review* 5 (1987), 213–47. Broader studies that contain useful legal materials are Mary M. Schweitzer, *Custom and Contract: Household, Government, and the Economy in Colonial Pennsylvania* (New York, 1987), and Rhys Isaac, *The Transformation of Virginia, 1740–1790* (Chapel Hill, NC, 1982). See also David Thomas Konig, "Legal Fictions and the Rule(s) of

Law: The Jeffersonian Critique of Common-Law Adjudication" in Tomlins and Mann, *Many Legalities*, 97–121.

IV. The Anglicization Thesis and the Triumph of Local Law

As Hendrik Hartog explains (in "Losing the World of the Massachusetts Whig," in Hartog, ed., *Law in the American Revolution and the Revolution in the Law* [Cambridge, MA, 1981], 143–66), John Phillip Reid has presented a detailed discussion and a convincing interpretation of the importance of "local" or "Whig" law during the Revolutionary era. See, among Reid's many books, *In a Defiant Stance: The Conditions of Law in Massachusetts Bay, the Irish Comparison; and the Coming of the American Revolution* (University Park, PA, 1977). Important studies of the British constitution and imperial affairs include Barbara A. Black, "The Constitution of Empire: The Case for the Colonists." *University of Pennsylvania Law Review* 124 (1976), 1157–268; Martin Stephen Flaherty, "Note: The Empire Strikes Back: *Annesley v. Sherlock* and The Triumph Of Imperial Parliamentary Supremacy," *Columbia Law Review* 87 (1987), 593–632; and Jack P. Greene, *Peripheries and Center: Constitutional Development in the Extended Polities of the British Empire and the United States, 1607–1788* (Athens, GA, 1986) and "From the Perspective of Law: Context and Legitimacy in the Origins of the American Revolution," *South Atlantic Quarterly* 85 (1986), 56–77. Interesting recent studies are Daniel J. Hulsebosch, "*Imperia in Imperio*: The Multiple Constitutions of Empire in New York, 1750–1777," *Law and History Review* 16 (1998), 319–79, and Christine Desan, "Remaking Constitutional Tradition at the Margin of Empire: The Creation of Legislative Adjudication in Colonial New York," *Law and History Review* 16 (1998), 257–317.

For the impact of politics and ideology on the legal system during the Revolutionary years, see J. R. Pole, "Reflections on American Law and the American Revolution," *William and Mary Quarterly*, 3rd ser., 50 (1993), 123–59; Holly Brewer, "Entailing Aristocracy in Colonial Virginia: 'Ancient Feudal Restraints' and Revolutionary Reform," *William and Mary Quarterly*, 3rd ser., 54 (1997), 307–46; Catherine Menand, "Juries, Judges, and the Politics of Justice in Pre-Revolutionary Boston," in Pencak and Holt, eds., *The Law in America, 1607–1861*, 155–85; and Stanley N. Katz, "Republicanism and the Law of Inheritance in the American Revolutionary Era," *Michigan Law Review* 76 (1977–78), 1–29. Other studies that discuss similar issues include A. G. Roeber, *Palatines, Liberty, and Property: German Lutherans in Colonial British America* (Baltimore, 1998), and Marylynn Salmon, *Women and the Law of Property in Early America* (Chapel Hill, NC, 1986).

V. The Supremacy of the Legislature

The rising importance of the legislature can be traced in Nelson, *Americanization of the Common Law*, and Roeber, *Faithful Magistrates*. In addition, see Jack N. Rakove, "The Origins of Judicial Review: A Plea for New Contexts," *Stanford Law Review* 49 (1997), 1031–64, and Hendrik Hartog, *Public Property and Private Power: The Corporation of the City of New York in American Law, 1730–1870* (Chapel Hill, NC, 1983) and "The Public Law of a County Court; Judicial Government in Eighteenth Century Massachusetts," *American Journal of Legal History* 20 (1976): 282–329. For lawyers, see Gerard W. Gawalt, *The Promise of Power: The Emergence of the Legal Profession in Massachusetts, 1760–1840* (Westport, CT, 1979).

Analysis of the judiciary must begin with the scholarship of Morton Horwitz. See *The Transformation of American Law, 1780–1860* (New York, 1976); "The Emergence of an Instrumental Conception of American Law, 1780–1820," in Fleming and Bailyn, eds., *Law in American History*, 287–328; and "The Historical Foundations of Modern Contract Law," *Harvard Law Review* 87 (1974), 917–56. Studies that criticize or complement Horwitz's interpretation of the judiciary include Jefferson White, "Representing Change in Early American Law: An Alternative to Horwitz's Approach," in Pencak and Holt, eds., *Law in America*, 238–68; F. Thornton Miller, *Juries and Judges Versus the Law: Virginia's Provincial Legal Perspective, 1783–1828* (Charlottesville, VA, 1994); and Dale A. Oesterle, "Formative Contributions to American Corporate Law by the Massachusetts Supreme Judicial Court from 1806 to 1810," in Russell K. Osgood, *The History of the Law in Massachusetts: The Supreme Judicial Court, 1692–1992* (Boston, 1992), 127–52. For the changing importance of juries, see Renee B. Lettow, "New Trial for Verdict Against Law: Judge-Jury Relations in Early Nineteenth-Century America," *Notre Dame Law Review* 71 (1995–96), 505–53, and Mary Sarah Bilder, "The Origin of the Appeal in America," *Hastings Law Journal* 48 (1997), 913–68. Two important studies that focus on the role of the judiciary are Christopher L. Tomlins, *Law, Labor, and Ideology in the Early American Republic* (New York, 1993), and William J. Novak, *The People's Welfare: Law and Regulation in Nineteenth-Century America* (Chapel Hill, NC, 1996).

NOTES ON CONTRIBUTORS (IN ORDER OF APPEARANCE)

ANTHONY PAGDEN is Distinguished Professor of History and Political Science at the University of California, Los Angeles

KATHERINE A. HERMES is Associate Professor of History at Central Connecticut State University

MARY SARAH BILDER is Professor of Law at Boston College Law School

RICHARD J. ROSS is Professor of Law and History at the University of Illinois, Urbana-Champaign

DAVID THOMAS KONIG is Professor of History and Law at Washington University in St. Louis

MICHAEL MERANZE is Professor of History at the University of California, Los Angeles

CHRISTOPHER TOMLINS is a Senior Research Fellow at the American Bar Foundation, Chicago. Research for his chapter was funded by the American Bar Foundation

SALLY E. HADDEN is Associate Professor of History and Law at Florida State University, Tallahassee

HOLLY BREWER is Associate Professor of History at North Carolina State University, Raleigh

MARK MCGARVIE is Visiting Assistant Professor of History and Leadership Studies at the University of Richmond, Virginia

ELIZABETH MENSCH is SUNY Distinguished Teaching Professor at the University at Buffalo Law School, State University of New York

BRUCE H. MANN is Carl F. Schipper, Jr. Professor of Law at Harvard Law School

CLAIRE PRIEST is Associate Professor of Law, Northwestern University School of Law. Research for her chapter was supported by Northwestern's Julius Rosenthal Fund

JACK P. GREENE is Andrew W. Mellon Professor Emeritus in the Humanities, The Johns Hopkins University and Adjunct Professor of History, Brown University

JACK N. RAKOVE is William Robertson Coe Professor of History and American Studies, and Professor of Political Science and (by courtesy) Law, at Stanford University

SAUL CORNELL is Professor of History at The Ohio State University, Columbus

GERALD LEONARD is Professor of Law at Boston University School of Law

JAMES A. HENRETTA is Priscilla Alden Burke Professor of History at the University of Maryland, College Park

INDEX